Social Work Practice in Mental Health

Contemporary Roles, Tasks, and Techniques

Social Work Practice in Mental Health

Contemporary Roles, Tasks, and Techniques

EDITED BY

KIA J. BENTLEY

Virginia Commonwealth University

BROOKS/COLE
CENGAGE Learning™

Australia • Brazil • Japan • Korea • Mexico • Singapore • Spain • United Kingdom • United States

BROOKS/COLE
CENGAGE Learning

Social Work Practice in Mental Health: Contemporary Roles, Tasks, and Techniques
Edited by Kia J. Bentley

Publisher: Edith Beard Brady

Executive Acquisitions Editor: Lisa Gebo

Assistant Editor: Alma Dea Michelena

Marketing Representative: Adrienne Carter

Marketing Team: Carolyn Concilla, Megan Hansen, Tami Strang

Editorial Assistant: Sheila Walsh

Project Editor: Laurel Jackson

Production Service: Buuji, Inc.

Indexer: Marilyn Delson

Manuscript Editor: Heather McElwain

Permissions Editor: Sue Ewing

Cover Design: Denise Davidson

Interior Illustration: Eunah Chang, Buuji, Inc.

Print Buyer: Vena Dyer

Typesetting: Buuji, Inc.

For product information and
technology assistance, contact us at **Cengage Learning Customer & Sales Support, 1-800-354-9706**

For permission to use material from this text or product, submit all requests online at **www.cengage.com/permissions**
Further permissions questions can be emailed to **permissionrequest@cengage.com**

Library of Congress Control Number: 2001035336

ISBN-13: 978-0-534-54920-6

ISBN-10: 0-534-54920-9

Brooks/Cole
20 Davis Drive
Belmont, CA 94002
USA

Cengage Learning is a leading provider of customized learning solutions with office locations around the globe, including Singapore, the United Kingdom, Australia, Mexico, Brazil, and Japan. Locate your local office at **www.cengage.com/global**

Cengage Learning products are represented in Canada by Nelson Education, Ltd.

To learn more about Brooks/Cole, visit
www.cengage.com/brookscole

Purchase any of our products at your local college store or at our preferred online store **www.cengagebrain.com**

Printed in the United States of America
2 3 4 5 6   19 18 17 16 15

This book is dedicated to the very early pioneers in psychiatric social work, especially the women who paved the way for a new field: among them, Mary Brooks Meyer, Julia Lathrop, Edith Burleigh, Edith H. Horton, Mary C. Jarrett, Louisa Lee Schyler, and Alice Chevailler.

About the Editor

KIA J. BENTLEY, PhD, LCSW, is a tenured professor and the director of the PhD program in social work at Virginia Commonwealth University, where she has taught since 1989. Dr. Bentley has all three degrees in social work: a BSW from Auburn University, an MSSW from the University of Tennessee, and a PhD from Florida State University, where she received a "Distinguished Alumni Award" in 1997. A licensed clinical social worker, her current teaching focuses on mental health practice, psychopharmacotherapy and social work, mental health policy, law and ethics, clinical theory, and research. Dr. Bentley is the author of the successful text *The Social Worker & Psychotropic Medication: Toward Effective Collaboration with Mental Health Clients, Families, and Other Providers* (with Joseph Walsh, 2001; Brooks/Cole). She has published numerous other works on mental health including leadership training for consumers, family psychoeducation, the future of community-based care, the evolution of federal mental health legislation, the social worker's role in medication management, the right to refuse medication, prescription-writing privileges for social workers, and psychosocial interventions for people with schizophrenia. She is currently the principal investigator on a project funded by the Ittleson Foundation, which is building a knowledge base on role dilemmas and best practices in medication management for contemporary psychiatric social workers. She has also completed a pilot study and is seeking funding for research that investigates the meaning of medication for mental health consumers.

Dr. Bentley served two terms on the Council on Social Work Education's Women's Commission and has been an active accreditation site visitor for their Commission on Accreditation for seven years. In addition, she is a long-time member of the National Association of Social Workers and was a consulting editor of *Social Work* from 1994–1999. In Virginia, she is the former chair of the statewide Mental Health Planning Council and served six years on the board of Virginia's chapter of the National Alliance for the Mentally Ill. She currently serves as vice-chair of the Human Rights Committee for a state psychiatric facility in Petersburg, Virginia, Central State Hospital. Dr. Bentley is a frequent presenter and speaker at state and national conferences and serves as a clinical supervisor, as well as a consultant and trainer to inpatient, outpatient, and consumer-run mental health programs.

About the Contributors

Beth Angell, MSSW, PhD, is an assistant professor in the School of Social Service Administration and a Junior Faculty Fellow at the Chicago Consortium for Stigma Research (Department of Psychiatry) at the University of Chicago. She received her master's and doctoral degrees from the University of Wisconsin, concentrating on services for persons with serious mental illness. She received training with several model programs in Madison, Wisconsin, including the original Program of Assertive Community Treatment (PACT). Her doctoral research, which was supported by a competitive predoctoral fellowship from the National Institute of Mental Health (NIMH), inquired into the nature and determinants of social relationship problems in persons with serious mental illness. She also completed postdoctoral research training at the Social Work Mental Health Research Center, University of Pennsylvania, where she studied consumer and provider perceptions of involuntary outpatient commitment. Dr. Angell is currently conducting research on consumer–provider interactions in assertive community treatment, seeking to understand how the interplay between supportive and coercive clinical strategies influences both the consumer–provider relationship and adherence to treatment.

Tina Bogart Marshall, MSW, PhD, received her doctoral degree from the University of Pennsylvania, where her dissertation research examined the effects of clarifying confidentiality policies on provider–consumer–family collaboration in the treatment process. Her research interests include collaboration, confidentiality, advanced directives, and the quality of care for persons with severe mental illness. She is the coauthor of a book chapter entitled, "Competencies for Collaborating with Families of Persons with Severe Mental Illness: Improving Client Outcomes," and has published two articles in *Psychiatric Services* on her dissertation topic. Dr. Marshall has worked in a wide variety of positions in the field of mental health over the past 12 years, including social work direct practice, legislative policy, public education, program planning, international social work, and mental health services and policy research. She is currently the director of the DSM program at the American Psychiatric Association.

A. Suzanne Boyd, PhD, received her doctorate in social work from the School of Social Work at Virginia Commonwealth University in Richmond, Virginia, in May 1997. Currently, she is an assistant professor in the School of Social Welfare at the University of Kansas, where she teaches courses at both the undergraduate and graduate levels in research, social policy analysis, and mental health. Her areas of

scholarly interest include consumer-operated services, empowerment, the evaluation and analysis of mental health programs and policies, general social policy analysis, and quality of life. She is currently pursuing research that evaluates
consumer-operated drop-in centers for people with serious mental illness. Prior to
her employment at UK, Dr. Boyd worked as a research assistant for the federally
funded ACCESS Demonstration Project and as a project manager at VCU's Survey
Research Lab, Center for Public Policy. She received a 1998 Excellence in Teaching
Award for her work in the UK undergraduate program.

John S. Brekke, PhD, is a professor of social work at the University of
Southern California. He was a clinical practitioner from 1979–1989 in a range of
community-based settings in Hawaii, Wisconsin, and California. As a clinician, he
specialized in the use of structured intervention methods for aggressive disorders
and in psychosocial rehabilitation for individuals with serious and persistent mental illness. Since 1982, he has devoted his research activity to studying the effectiveness of community-based psychosocial interventions for individuals with
schizophrenia. His current research interest concerns a synthesis of psychobiological and psychosocial approaches to understanding functional outcomes in schizophrenia. He currently is the principal investigator on two research grants from
NIMH that investigate biopsychosocial factors and psychosocial rehabilitation for
individuals with schizophrenia.

Kevin Corcoran, MSW, PhD, JD, is a professor at the Portland State
University Graduate School of Social Work. He holds a BA from Colorado State
University, an MA from the University of Colorado, an MSW and PhD from the
University of Pittsburgh, and a JD from the University of Houston. His practice
experience has included direct practice with individuals, adolescents and families;
conflict resolution; and mediation. His research and teaching interests include
direct human services practice, human behavior, managed mental health care,
empirical evaluation of practice, conflict mediation, and clinical measurement. He
has authored or edited several books, including *Structuring Change: Effective
Practice for Common Client Problems* (1992, Lyceum), *Maneuvering the Maze of
Managed Care: Skills for Mental Health Practitioners* (1996, Free Press), and
Measures for Clinical Practice (2000, 1994, 1987). In addition to teaching and writing, Dr. Corcoran practices commercial and community mediation in Yachats,
Oregon.

Mary Ann Dearborn, MSW, is a research assistant at the Center for the Study
of Mental Health Policy and Services in Portland, Oregon. She teaches at the
Graduate School of Social Work at Portland State University as she finishes her dissertation in the PhD program in social work and social research. Her research focus
is on mental health and aging (for example, what happens to the services of people
with severe and persistent mental illness as they age). Ms. Dearborn has provided
mental health services to adults in a wide range of community-based settings and in
acute care in a state psychiatric hospital, prior to beginning her doctoral studies. She
also maintained a private mediation practice and earned practitioner status in the
Academy of Family Mediators while serving on a statewide task force to modify civil

procedure, encouraging the use of mediation as an alternative to litigation. She supported a community-based victim-offender mediation program that helped juvenile offenders and their victims reach mutually acceptable restitution agreements. Trained by leaders in the mediation field, Ms. Dearborn holds certificates in specialized and advanced mediation and has developed and taught mediation courses for the University of Alaska in Anchorage.

John Farmer is director of the Involved Consumer Action Network (ICAN), a consumer-run project of the Mental Health Association of Southeastern Pennsylvania in Philadelphia. This project encourages people who are consumers of behavioral health services to become more involved in planning and delivering those services and to play a role in developing mental health policy. ICAN provides ongoing technical assistance to mental health consumer groups located throughout Pennsylvania, including more than 80 consumer-run drop-in centers that are in various stages of development. Mr. Farmer received a BS degree and an MEd from Shippensburg University of Pennsylvania. He is a member of the board of directors of the International Association of Psychosocial Rehabilitation, the president of the Pennsylvania Association of Psychosocial Rehabilitation Services, and a member emeritus of the Pennsylvania Mental Health Planning Council. Mr. Farmer is also on the Conference Planning Committee of the Pennsylvania Mental Health Consumers' Association.

Rosemary L. Farmer, PhD, LCSW, received her MSW degree from the Hunter College School of Social Work and her PhD from the School of Social Work, Virginia Commonwealth University. She has been a clinical social work practitioner for 28 years, specializing in work with people who have chronic and serious mental illnesses. Since her employment in a state psychiatric facility, she has maintained a strong interest in public mental health services and for the past several years has served as a consultant to the Outreach Team of the Northern Virginia Mental Health Institute. Dr. Farmer currently is an associate professor at the School of Social Work, Virginia Commonwealth University, where she teaches Human Behavior, Clinical Practice, and a course in Social Work Practice and Psychopharmacology. Her scholarly interests include the incorporation of biological knowledge into social work practice, the evaluation of community programs that provide residential services to people with chronic mental illnesses, and the development of effective practices for social workers related to psychotropic medications.

Susan Gingerich, MSW, received her MSW from Simmons School of Social Work in 1980. She has worked in the mental health field in a variety of positions and locations, including McLean Hospital in Boston, Harborview Trauma Center in Seattle, San Francisco General Hospital, Eastern Pennsylvania Psychiatric Institute, Columbia-Presbyterian Medical Center, Tufts New England Medical Center's spinal cord injury unit, and Long Island Jewish Psychiatric Center. She is currently a psychiatric rehabilitation consultant at the Delaware Psychiatric Center and conducts workshops throughout the United States and Canada. Helping consumers and family members cope with major mental illness is her special interest. She has coauthored two books on this subject, *Coping with Schizophrenia: A Guide for Families*

(1994, New Harbinger) and *Social Skills Training for Schizophrenia: A Step-by-Step Guide* (1997, Guilford), as well as several articles and book chapters. She appears in the video "I'm Still Here: The Truth About Schizophrenia," produced by Wheeler Communications Group in Honeoye, New York.

Debbie Gioia-Hasick, PhD, LCSW, is a recent graduate of the doctoral program at the University of Southern California School of Social Work in Los Angeles. In Fall 2001, she became an assistant professor at the school of social work at the University of Michigan in Ann Arbor. She has worked as a clinician for 17 years at the UCLA Neuropsychiatric Institute on an NIMH longitudinal protocol in schizophrenia research, where she led many skills training groups and helped develop a new skills module on "Friendship and Intimacy" for this population. She received an NIMH predoctoral grant to research her area of interest, *The Meaning of Work for Young Adults with Schizophrenia: A Mixed Method Study.*

Harriette C. Johnson, MSW, PhD, is a professor at the University of Connecticut School of Social Work, where her areas of scholarly interest, publication, and teaching include adult and child mental health, parent and professional collaboration, the impact of professional ideologies on practice behaviors, neurobiological foundations of mental function, and the integration of micro- and macroaspects of mental health. An expanded and updated edition of *Psyche, Synapse, and Substance* will be published in 2001. She also produced an 83-minute documentary video in 1999, "Our Fight: Parents Tell It Like It Is" (Deerfield Valley Publishing, 1-877-758-6877) to educate professionals on parents' perspectives of children and adolescents with mental health issues, their views of professionals, and advice to parents. The video, consisting of seven modules, has been highly acclaimed and is used for classroom teaching, in-service training, and parent support and advocacy.

Wynne S. Korr, PhD, is a professor at the School of Social Work, University of Pittsburgh, and holds a joint appointment in Women's Studies. She received her PhD in psychology from SUNY at Buffalo. She is the former codirector of the Center for Mental Health Services Research and directed the doctoral program at Pittsburgh from 1994–1999. From 1980–1993, she taught at the Jane Addams College of Social Work, University of Illinois at Chicago. Her first professional position was as a Program Evaluator in the Illinois Department of Mental Health. She teaches courses in program evaluation, services research, and mental health policy and has published work on evaluation of mental health services, legal issues in mental health, and other related topics. She is active in the Council on Social Work Education, having served six years on the Women's Commission, and is now on the Commission for Publications and Media. She is currently coprincipal investigator on an NIMH-funded services research study of organizational factors influencing adoption of HIV prevention and education strategies by case managers for adults with severe mental illness.

Ellen P. Lukens, MSW, PhD, is an assistant professor at the Columbia University School of Social Work (CUSSW) and is a research scientist at New York State Psychiatric Institute in New York City. Dr. Lukens has extensive experience in the development and application of educational and psychoeducational interventions designed to improve the course of illness for people with severe mental illness and their family members. She is particularly interested in the use of group interventions in and applying professional and practical knowledge to help leaders and participants work together to enhance treatment, strengthen resiliency and coping skills, and reduce stress. Dr. Lukens has extensive clinical experience working with patients with schizophrenia and their families, as well as teaching and supervising clinicians and students in this arena. At CUSSW, Dr. Lukens is cochair of the Advanced Generalist Practice method in the masters program and teaches advanced clinical practice in the doctoral program, as well as courses in program development, evaluation and grant writing, research methods, and clinical practice with families at the masters level. Her publications include articles and chapters on psychosocial factors in childhood depression, schizophrenia and the family, insight and mental illness, and multiple family group interventions.

Edie Mannion, MFW, has a master's degree in family therapy from Hahnemann University, Graduate School of Mental Health Sciences in Philadelphia. She is the director and cofounder of the Training, Education, and Consultation Family Center (formerly the TEC Network) at the Mental Health Association of Southeastern Pennsylvania, a consultant to the Center for Mental Health Policy and Services Research at the University of Pennsylvania, and an adjunct faculty member of the psychiatric residency program at Thomas Jefferson University. Since 1983, she has been implementing educational interventions for family members of people with mental illness. She has trained clinical staff of public mental health and child welfare facilities since 1985. She has lectured and published extensively on family and spouse education and collaboration in mental illness, including a training manual on family consultation and two training manuals on family and spouse coping skills workshops. Her current areas of scholarly interest include (1) educational interventions based on dialectical behavior therapy for families of people with borderline personality disorder, (2) educational peer support services for children and adolescents who have a family member with mental illness, and (3) the gap between best practices and standard practices for families of adults with mental illness in public behavioral health systems. She has maintained a private practice as a consultant and therapist since 1985.

Jaclyn Miller, PhD, LCSW, BCD, is an associate professor and director of field instruction at Virginia Commonwealth University School of Social Work, where she has taught and held administrative positions for 20 years. She earned her MSSW and PhD at the University of Texas at Austin. In the years prior to returning for her doctorate, Dr. Miller practiced social work in a variety of mental health settings, including five years at the UCLA-Neuropsychiatric Institute in both inpatient and outpatient services. Since 1982, she has maintained a part-time private practice of social work, working primarily with people experiencing depression. From 1996 through 1998, she was a research psychotherapist in a national study that demonstrated the effectiveness of combined medication and a cognitive-behavioral intervention (Dr. James McCullough's model) in the treatment of depression. She is a former president of both the Virginia chapter of the National Association of Social Workers (NASW) and the Virginia Society for Clinical Social Work. She currently serves on the national board of directors of NASW and the National Mental Health Advisory Board for Magellan. Dr. Miller's publications and continuing scholarly work include research on aspects of field education, gatekeeping in the profession, women and AIDS, and constructivist social work practice.

Robert Paulson, PhD, is a professor at the Graduate School of Social Work at Portland State University and an adjunct professor in the Departments of Public Health and Preventive Medicine and Psychiatry at the Oregon Health Sciences University. He received his PhD in social welfare from the University of California at Berkeley. Dr. Paulson is director of the NIMH-funded Center for the Study of Mental Health Policy and Services. He is also principal investigator on several federally funded mental health research projects studying housing, employment, and financing issues for adults and children with major mental illness. He was formerly the director of the Specialized Mental Health Training Program at the School of Social Work, University of Cincinnati, which was funded by NIMH and the Ohio Department of Mental Health to train MSWs to work with people with major mental illness. During the last 15 years, he has served on the boards of community mental health centers, as president of the Ohio Council of Community Mental Health Agencies, and as a board member for the National Self-Help Research Center, the National Community Behavioral Health Care Council (formally the National Council of Community Mental Health Centers), and the Oregon chapter of the National Alliance of the Mentally Ill.

Kimberly Prchal, MSW, is a doctoral candidate at the Columbia University School of Social Work. She worked as a psychiatric social worker for the Los Angeles Department of Mental Health prior to her doctoral studies. She has a master's degree in social work from Tulane University. Her clinical and research experience lies in the area of chronic mental illness and families. She works for the Nathan Kline Institute for Psychiatric Research on a project that examines various housing models for people with chronic mental illness. She has recently taken a position as a program manager on an NIMH-funded grant that examines the effectiveness of trauma-focused interventions targeting risk for violence among adolescents.

Charles A. Rapp, MSW, PhD, is a professor at the University of Kansas School of Social Welfare. He holds a PhD and MSW from the University of Illinois and a bachelor of science from Millikin University. He is the codeveloper of the strengths model of case management and the client-centered performance model of social administration and has extensive related publications. His book, *The Strengths Model: Case Management with People Suffering from Severe and Persistent Mental Illness,* was published by Oxford Press in 1998.

Roberta G. Sands, ACSW, PhD, is an associate professor at the University of Pennsylvania School of Social Work in Philadelphia, where she teaches courses in advanced social work practice, mental health, human behavior, and qualitative research. She began her career as a clinical social worker and practiced in community mental health, health, and child welfare settings. Her clinical experiences and lifelong interest in language sparked her interest in therapeutic discourse and inter-group communication, which she explored in her doctoral work. Recent and ongoing research covers the intersection of mental illness and motherhood, grandparents who are raising their grandchildren, and the impact of religious intensification on mother–daughter relationships. Her ethnographic, sociolinguistic study of interdisciplinary teams is presented in *Interprofessional and Family Discourses: Voices, Knowledge, and Practice* (coauthored with Marleen McClelland; published by Hampton Press, 2001). Dr. Sands is also the author of *Clinical Social Work Practice in Community Mental Health* (1991, Merrill/Macmillan/Allyn & Bacon) and *Clinical Social Work Practice in Behavioral Mental Health: A Postmodern Approach to Practice* (2001, 2nd ed., Allyn & Bacon). In addition to these books, she has written more than 40 articles and book reviews that have been published in social work and other social science journals, and several book chapters.

Shela Silverman, MSW, returned to academia as a nontraditional student for her graduate degree when two of her children entered college. She reports that she found the environment stimulating and had a successful academic career, earning an honors degree and election to Phi Beta Kappa. Her dream of becoming a social worker was accomplished with the loving support of family and friends, although she notes, "it took me five years" to earn a degree. She has been closely involved with the mental health consumer movement in Virginia in the past two decades and has held a number of leadership positions in both statewide and local programs. She initiated the development of the first consumer-operated program in Virginia, called "on our own," located in Charlottesville. She was program director and managed the "on our own" drop-in center, as well as several other programs that were funded through state, local, and federal grants. She is the author of two peer-reviewed journal articles about the drop-in center and of a chapter of *Consumers as Providers in Psychiatric Rehabilitation.* She has presented dozens of workshops at statewide and national conferences on topics as diverse as the consumer movement, PACT, and discharge planning for consumers in state hospitals. Ms. Silverman lives in southwestern Colorado, where she is a social worker with Native American children living on the Ute Mountain Reservation.

Phyllis Solomon, PhD, is a professor in the School of Social Work, University of Pennsylvania, and currently chairs the research sequence in the school. She has a secondary appointment in the Department of Psychiatry, School of Medicine, University of Pennsylvania. She has a master's degree in sociology and a PhD in social welfare, both from Case Western Reserve University. She has more than 25 years of research, planning, and administrative experience. She has worked in the state psychiatric system and in a community research and planning agency, where she conducted research and evaluations and designed service interventions. Dr. Solomon has served on numerous federal research and service review panels and reviews proposals for private foundations. She has extensively published and given presentations on issues concerning adults with serious mental illness and their families. She has co-edited two books on psychiatric rehabilitation, *Psychiatric Rehabilitation in Practice* and *New Developments in Psychiatric Rehabilitation* and coauthored *Community Services to Discharged Psychiatric Patients.* She is the director of an NIMH Social Work Research Development Center that focuses on service interventions for adults with severe mental illness and their families. In 1997, her article with others on the results of a family education intervention, which appeared in *Schizophrenia Bulletin,* received first place by the Society for Social Work and Research. She was the 1999 recipient of the Armin Loeb Award from the International Association of Psychosocial Rehabilitation Services for her research in psychosocial rehabilitation.

William Patrick Sullivan, PhD, is a professor at the Indiana University School of Social Work, where he has taught since 1993. He received his BSW and MSW from the University of Kansas and followed with a PhD from there as well in 1989. Prior to his post at Indiana University, Sullivan taught at Southwest Missouri State University. During his tenure at Indiana University, Dr. Sullivan also served as director of the Indiana Division of Mental Health for three and one-half years and is still an active consultant in Missouri. In addition to extensive clinical experience at mental health centers and clinics, Dr. Sullivan has over 40 professional publications with an emphasis on recovery and strengths-based practice, services for those facing serious and persistent mental illnesses, alcohol and drug treatment, case management across populations, and the role of spirituality in mental illness. Dr. Sullivan teaches in the BSW, MSW, and PhD program in all substantive areas and has received a number of awards for both his scholarship and teaching.

Melissa Floyd Taylor, LCSW, is a PhD candidate at Virginia Commonwealth University. Her undergraduate work in psychology and political science was completed at Miami University in Oxford, Ohio. She received an MSW with a mental health concentration from VCU in 1994. During her MSW, she was a recipient of special grant funding from the Virginia Department of Mental Health, Mental Retardation, and Substance Abuse Services to focus her studies on services to people with serious mental illness, a program that later won an Exemplary Program Award from the National Alliance for the Mentally Ill. She currently works as a licensed clinical social worker in the substance abuse area. Throughout her career, she has worked in direct practice settings, primarily with persons who have serious mental illness, substance abuse issues, or both. She has taught practice and human behavior as an adjunct professor in the MSW and BSW programs at VCU since 1997. Her current research interests include the operationalization of practical social work values with people who have serious mental illness, as well as social work roles in psychopharmacology.

Joseph Walsh, PhD, LCSW, is an associate professor of social work at Virginia Commonwealth University. He received his academic degrees from The Ohio State University. Dr. Walsh has been a direct services practitioner in the field of mental health since 1974, first in a psychiatric hospital and later in community mental health centers. Dr. Walsh has provided services to older adult and general outpatient populations but has specialized in services for persons with serious mental illness and their families. Dr. Walsh has been at VCU since 1993 and currently teaches courses in generalist practice, clinical practice, mental and emotional disorders, and social and behavioral science theory. He continues to provide direct services to clients at the university counseling center and at area shelters, clubhouses, and group homes. Dr. Walsh was the 1998 recipient of the National Mental Health Association's George Goodman Brudney and Ruth P. Brudney Social Work Award, given annually to recognize significant contributions to the care and treatment of persons with mental illness. He is the author of *Clinical Case Management with Persons Having Mental Illness: A Relationship-Based Perspective,* and coauthor with Kia J. Bentley of *The Social Worker and Psychotropic Medication.*

Contents

SOCIAL WORKERS AS THERAPISTS   73

Joseph Walsh

CHAPTER 5

SOCIAL WORKERS AS MEDIATORS   100

Kevin Corcoran and Mary Ann Dearborn

CHAPTER 9

SOCIAL WORKERS AS MEDICATION FACILITATORS   211

Rosemary Farmer and Kia J. Bentley

CHAPTER 10

SOCIAL WORKERS AS CONSUMER AND FAMILY CONSULTANTS   230

Phyllis Solomon, Tina Bogart Marshall, Edie Mannion, and John Farmer

CHAPTER 11

SOCIAL WORKERS AS COLLABORATORS ON INTERAGENCY AND INTERDISCIPLINARY TEAMS   254

Roberta G. Sands and Beth Angell

CHAPTER 12

SOCIAL WORKERS AS ADVOCATES AND COMMUNITY ORGANIZERS   281

Shela Silverman

CHAPTER 13

SOCIAL WORKERS AS PROGRAM EVALUATORS AND RESEARCHERS   297

A. Suzanne Boyd and Wynne S. Korr

CHAPTER 14

SOCIAL WORKERS AS ADMINISTRATORS AND POLICY ANALYSTS IN MENTAL HEALTH SETTINGS: LIVING WITH UNCERTAINTY   322

Robert Paulson

CHAPTER 15

EMERGING KNOWLEDGE AND FUTURE TRENDS IN MENTAL HEALTH: IMPLICATIONS FOR SOCIAL WORK   361

Harriette C. Johnson

Preface

Given the importance of mental health as a field of practice in social work, it is surprising that scholarly resource materials specific to mental health practice in social work are almost nonexistent. Social workers must frequently turn to portions of texts in psychiatry, rehabilitation counseling, education, business, or psychology to piece together the kinds of materials they need to assume their roles in the vast range of mental health settings today.

While this book will not fill every need, it is meant to address the need for approachable, immediately useful, discipline-specific content on the most important social work practice roles in mental health. It may help to redefine and expand the roles social workers fill in mental health settings beyond the more traditional roles of psychotherapist and case manager. It articulates how roles often associated with working with a specific population (for example, those who abuse substances, people with severe mental illness, distressed marital couples) are actually quite relevant to and useful in a much wider range of populations.

This book is consistent with what has been described elsewhere as a partnership model of practice, akin to empowerment or strengths. Social work scholars with special expertise in each area were invited to write a chapter on a different role, aiming at being cutting edge, scholarly, and unambiguously useful and practical. I am pleased to have been able to recruit many of the most well-known scholars and excellent practitioners in our field.

The audience for this book is students in bachelor of social work (BSW) and master of social work (MSW) programs, and to a lesser extent, practitioners working in the field all around the country. Advanced practice courses, whether required or elective, are the specific courses targeted. Approximately two-thirds of all schools of social work offer a mental health concentration and thus provide the specialized content in various areas (such as practice, behavior, or policy) to support it. Virtually every school of social work offers substantial electives in mental health practice, and they are repeatedly the most popular electives.

Each chapter is named for a specific role that social workers play in mental health settings today. Every chapter author (except for Chapters 1 and 15) used the following to guide their description and discussion:

- **The Intellectual Base of Practice** A brief critical review of the specific knowledge base for practice in the designated area, including any relevant research or particularly important theoretical underpinnings. This review includes an explicit discussion of social work and specific social workers' contributions to the knowledge base in this area.

- **Major Tasks and Goals** A review of the major tasks and goals to be accomplished in effectively fulfilling the role with individuals, families, couples, groups, communities, agencies, programs, or organizations (as relevant).

- **Techniques, Strategies, and Skills** A how-to presentation about carrying out the tasks or goals described, across a wide range of client problems and populations (adults and children, oppressed populations, various diagnostic groups, or presenting problems or issues).

- **Exemplar Programs and Models** A detailed description of one or more exemplar programs or of promising new models that are being tried.

- **Unique Challenges for Social Workers** A review of major issues, special challenges and obstacles, or controversies involved in fulfilling the designated role in various mental health settings of contexts in the field.

- **Case Dilemma** For reflection and analysis, one or more case vignettes that capture a real-life dilemma in which social workers attempt to fulfill their roles.

- **Key Terms** A list of key terms discussed in the chapter.

- **Web Resources** A list of relevant Web sites or other resources of particular interest. For a much more complete discussion of the relevance and usefulness of the Internet for social work practice, please see Vernon and Lynch's *Social Work and the Web* (2000; Brooks/Cole).

ACKNOWLEDGMENTS

I would like to thank the following reviewers for their insightful comments and suggestions: Judith Altholz, Florida State University; Bette Burke, Mental Health Mental Retardation Authority of Harris County; Robert Conyne, University of Cincinnati; David Cournoyer, University of Connecticut; Denise Davison, Illinois State University; Patricia Higgins, Western State Hospital; Deborah Padgett, New York University; and Vikki Vandiver, Portland State University.

Deepest heartfelt thanks to my long-time editor, Lisa Gebo, whose seemingly unconditional positive regard, flexibility, talent, and sense of humor make our collaboration a joy in my life. Of course, my thanks to the chapter authors, who are putting it out there and trying to make a difference simply by offering their considerable intellect and insight into topics of import. To my colleagues at VCU, where there is an impressive dual appreciation of excellence in both scholarship and teaching, thank you for helping to make projects like this seem worthwhile. And finally, to Marti for loving me back all these years.

Kia J. Bentley

A Context and Vision for Excellence in Social Work Practice in Contemporary Mental Health Settings

Kia J. Bentley &
Melissa Floyd Taylor

This chapter presents a vision of excellence for social work practice in fulfilling a range of roles across a variety of mental health settings. Mental health is the largest field of practice in social work, and social workers comprise the largest group of professional practitioners in the field. While most social workers in mental health are employed in traditional outpatient settings like community mental health centers, nonprofit counseling agencies, and private clinics (and numbers are actually increasing) (Witkin et al., 1998), social workers are also very well represented in inpatient units, hospitals, and residential programs, as well as in more nontraditional direct and indirect service agencies like clubhouses, consumer-run organizations, rehabilitation centers, advocacy organizations, and state departments of mental health.

Chapter 1 is meant to lay the foundation for the book's core argument that social workers should be doing *more* and *different* things for mental health clients; they should abandon a simplistic and narrow notion of social workers as mere "psychotherapists," or for that matter, case managers. Narrow notions about the role of the social worker are admittedly rarely advocated in social work education, but too often emerge in real world practice. Instead, in order to more comprehensively and effectively respond to clients' needs and wants, individual social workers in mental health settings should aggressively adopt and embrace more diverse roles in their everyday practice. Doing this might be described as making an expanded "jurisdictional claim," a statement of expanded expertise and domain (Vourlekis, Edinburg, & Knee, 1998). Such a process of boundary shifting could be "profession strengthening" (p. 573) and move us away from "defending what is" to "shaping what will be" for social work. The authors of the remaining book chapters each detail what these expanded roles for social workers in mental health should be, some of which are quite familiar and some not; some of which are enacted on a daily basis by social workers, and some of which are thought to be drastically underutilized.

In this chapter, we also want to provide an overview of the contemporary context of social work practice in mental health. What are the scientific, technological, historical, economic, legal, ethical, sociopolitical, and cultural factors that shape contemporary mental health practice? In this way, we are trying to take a relational *"social worker & client*-in-environment" perspective, if you will, which will help us see the complexity of the structure of service delivery today. Using your professional imagination, picture you and your client sitting together in the center of a circle with potentially unseen external and internal forces subtly and not-so-subtly shaping both the direction and pace of your practice (see Figure 1.1).

These forces affect your practice, not just in general or in the abstract, but with a particular client at a particular moment in time. For example, how have biological models of mental illness shaped your practice in general, *and* what you are doing *today* with Juan Doe? How did Tipper Gore's discussion of her own depression influence the willingness of women to seek help in general, *and* your work yesterday with Juanita Doe? How have other cultural help-seeking norms among minorities influenced *who* you see and *what* you do when you see them? What do you think about the public opinion surveys that show continued frustration with managed care? What does that mean for your practice, tomorrow *and* this afternoon? How has the development of sophisticated psychopharmacotherapy algorithms changed your practice? What is the meaning of the murder of two Capitol police officers by a person with a history of severe mental illness? Parity legislation? The introduction of computer-

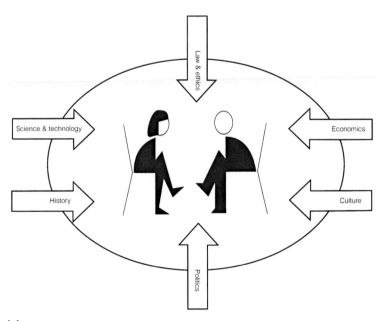

FIGURE 1.1

Social Worker & Client-in-Environment.

based assessment programs? The duty to warn mandate? In summary, understanding the context of service delivery—that is, the scientific, technological, historical, economic, legal, ethical, sociopolitical, and cultural forces that shape the field—helps us to understand the very real challenges to, and supports for, excellent practice. Our contention is that social workers should understand and appreciate the context of service delivery so they can shape it *and* thrive in it.

Following the discussion of factors influencing the context of mental health practice, we will describe how the nature of helping has been, and should be. We will discuss the evolution away from authoritative models that seem to emphasize treatment as a mysterious process, relying most heavily on client introspection, to ones that are alternatively described as "partnership," "strengths," or "empowerment" models of practice, which rely heavily on action. The ultimate role of the social worker in our model is to be an *active resource in the client's recovery and rehabilitation*. Specifically, we can help clients access the information, knowledge, skills, internal and external resources, treatment, and support needed to meet their goals. Of course, our role goes way beyond "mental health treatment" per se, to being concerned with housing, health, employment, education, transportation, recreation, community life, family issues, and significant relationships. When we aid clients in choosing their own goals, we also note that the goals may look very much like those we have chosen for our own lives: a safe and relatively ordered existence, a nice place to live, adequate income, access to quality health care, meaningful work and recreation, and rewarding relationships. The vision of social workers to help clients achieve these goals is characterized by compassion, commitment, collaboration, creativity, and competence, as we will describe.

CONTEMPORARY CONTEXT OF SOCIAL WORK PRACTICE IN MENTAL HEALTH

Scientific and Technological Factors

The biological revolution in psychiatry continues as we write this chapter. While the official "decade of the brain" may have passed, mainstream psychiatry, psychology, and nursing still look to research on genetics, neurotransmission, and brain function to understand the mysteries of cognitive, mental, and emotional functioning, in general, and mental illness in particular. Indeed, we also hold to the stress-diathesis model of mental illness, which says that while the cause of many mental disorders is likely to be related to genetics, brain function, and brain structure, an individual's unique course is in part related to environmental stresses and the impact of life events. The nature-nurture controversy seems bound to stay with us longer, however, as more scholars question the extent to which we seemed to have "blamed the brain" in Valenstein's language (1998). Have we ignored data that suggests that psychosocial events and interventions *cause* changes in brain chemistry? And if we have ignored such data, how come? Who wins and who loses? (Taylor & Bentley, 2000).

"Evidence-based practice" is the relatively new language being used to capture the idea that those of us in the helping professions should be relying most heavily on interventive techniques that have actually been shown to help. This is somewhat akin to earlier terms, such as *empirical practice* or being a *scientific practitioner.* There is much discussion in social work about the desire to use rigorous practice and program evaluation studies as the basis for action. Answers to many of the precise practice questions that emerge in the real world continue to remain unanswered. Therefore, in the absence of controlled clinical trials, and certainly in addition to existing ones, new respected forms of "evidence" may be emerging, such as compilations of expert opinions or professional consensus surveys drawn from the experiences of practitioners. Their dissemination in the form of practice guidelines, algorithms, or treatment protocols is increasingly found in traditional journal review articles, published workbooks, organizational newsletters, and even on the Internet.

Finally, the technological context of mental health care is important to consider. Farrell (1997) comprehensively reviews the impact of computer technology on practice and suggests a solid future. Computers now help practitioners keep notes, interview clients, do behavioral assessments, assign diagnoses, and actually provide interventions. In addition, clients can be taught to self-administer and score clinical assessments and tests. Clients as regular citizens and consumers have already widely searched the Internet for information about mental health topics. While there are issues to face (namely, practitioner and client attitudes, ethics, and the need for standards and training), evidence suggests that both practitioners and clients can use computers as part, or even in whole, for delivering or receiving mental health services. Importantly, as Farrell reports, the experience is usually favorable.

Historical Factors

The history of mental health treatment reflects a swinging pendulum of conceptualizations about mental health and mental illness. Those who have examined the history of our treatment system have noted that a tension has always existed between "doing the right thing" and "doing the thing right," of balancing "conscience and convenience," hope and despair (Rothman, 1971; Morrissey, Goldman, & Klerman, 1980). For example, the era of institutionalization was associated with tremendous excitement about the asylum's potential to cure the "mad." This gave way under the weight of institutional overcrowding and the reality of limited successes.

Deinstitutionalization, the term used to describe the gradual reduction of state hospital populations in the 1950s, 1960s, and 1970s, was in part spurred by legislation that supported community-based care. In addition, discoveries in psychopharmacology, philosophical shifts in society, and several important legal cases also supported the movement away from institutions. Now this well-intentioned social movement is noted for being oversold and for its failure. Others say true deinstitutionalization has never been tested because adequate allocation of resources never materialized to support community-based care. The question remains: Have we, in the words of Brown (1985), merely "transinstitutionalized" people with mental illness to nursing homes, group homes, or the streets? It has been suggested that deinstitutionalization was really not a well-intentioned movement with a goal to move inpatients closer to their families to live a more "normalized" community life. Rather, it was a thinly veiled plot to reduce the financial burden on states (who ran asylums) and increase the money-making potential of private sector players such as nursing home administrators, group home operators, physicians, and others. Were humanitarian motives the major factor, or should we more closely analyze professional factors such as the medical profession's desire to remain dominant, the state's desire to shift financial responsibility, the private sector's interest in getting a piece of the pie? This leads us to the next contextual issue influencing the structure of mental health services today: economics.

Economic Factors

Many of the questions above clearly suggest that some historians (e.g., Scull, 1977) explain the evolution of mental health care primarily through an economic lens. Others would say that is "economic reductionism." Nevertheless there can be little doubt that economic forces are one of the powerful "structural forces" that influence mental health practice. These forces include the profit motive, reimbursement mechanisms, and government *in*action (Brown, 1985). Of course, in a capitalist system, the exchange of goods and services, including the provision of mental health services, relates to money and maximizing income. American society seems at once appalled by the idea of health care as a commodity like clothes, cigarettes, or cable TV, and yet strangely resistant to having it any other way. The fact that there is no national health care plan is recognized by many to be related most powerfully to the gigantically powerful private health care industry's fears of loss of control and economic power.

The issue of profit is complicated when human lives and human suffering are involved. How much "profit" will the American public tolerate in this sector? While capitalists applaud the billions that manufacturers like the makers of Windows software earn, we recoil at the thought of those in the human service industry, like our local mental health center's executive director, making millions. We are even suspicious and a bit dismayed when drug companies post record earnings. Doesn't this mean they could lower the price and thereby increase accessibility, and still have their executives make a living?

Certainly an examination of reimbursement mechanisms gives us another perspective for understanding the economic context of service delivery. What is reimbursed and what is not may tell us the societal value we place on certain activities, and give us more hints into power and decision-making processes in contemporary mental health practice. For example, only diagnosable conditions, which to many implies "medical conditions, are reimbursed. Those in need of marital counseling, help in dealing with grief, or adjusting to a new community rarely have their psychological services reimbursed *unless* they first are given a so-called medical diagnosis. This clearly gives domain and sanction, and thus the financial advantage, to physicians and others in medicine. The increasing reliance on psychiatric medication, and expansion of conditions under which it is thought to be useful, cannot be divorced from speculation about the profit motive of the drug companies, nor can it be separated from their hope that it will slow the encroachment of nonmedical providers into the traditional foray of psychiatry and medicine (Bentley & Walsh, 2001). It may also explain the very slow and spotty dissemination of information on effective psychosocial interventions, for which the medical field has no corner on the market.

The growth of the number of forms of managed mental health care in recent years also focuses us on the economic factors associated with contemporary practice (Ross & Croze, 1997). Described as a shift from a simple "fee-for-service" transaction, managed care infuses a new level of involvement by the insurance companies in the oversight of mental health practice in the name of cost containment. Two major issues seem to exist in managed mental health care. First, limitations on access to care are set, including the restriction of medications to certain generics or to conventional medications, and the requirement of a prescreening mechanism to restrict access to care up front. The second, perhaps even a larger issue for social workers, is the introduction of so-called quality assurance, where a third party from the insurance company makes decisions about the allowable lengths of treatment and its nature. It has yet to be determined whether managed care is a "fact of life" for the foreseeable future as is so often stated. Continuing disillusionment by many providers and clients with the inattention to *quality* of care may lead to the demise of, or radical shifts in, the nature of managed care.

Sociopolitical and Cultural Factors

Regrettably, as Brown's (1985) analysis details, too many examples demonstrate how those in the mental health field, including social workers, have served to reinforce and replicate the existing class, gender, and race stratification—essentially perpetuating the status quo. Medical concepts have been used in history to defend everything from slavery to preference for women's submissiveness to demoralization of gays and lesbians. Professionals of all kinds have searched for professional dominance by, among other things, controlling and expanding the definitions of mental health problems. Important in this regard has been the growth of the American Psychiatric Association's *Diagnostic and Statistical Manual of Mental Disorders (DSM)*. Since its introduction in 1952, it has grown from a few pages to almost 900 pages in the current fourth edition, listing hundreds of possible disorders and a sophisticated multi-axial system (Williams, 1998). With various specifiers and modifiers for each disorder, thousands of unique diagnoses covering a vast domain of human experience are now possible.

The development of a large and powerful mental health "lobby" or political voice by physicians and insurance companies has meant that many people are highly invested in maintaining the core of the service delivery system as it is (Brown, 1985). Even defining emotional problems and "mental health issues" largely as an individually based phenomenon, rather than being related to the social order or to social conditions like poverty and discrimination, serves to keep individual practitioners in the driver's seat in terms of providing service to individuals. Social reform is not a reimbursable activity. Interestingly, one of the most powerful mental health "lobbies" now is family and consumer groups who often are the most vocal critics of existing services and professionals. At the same time, they have been an influential force in supporting the new "status quo" in mental health: the emphasis on biological factors in etiology and their implications. While rarely advocating for massive changes to the structure of service delivery, these family and consumer groups have served as an important influence in destigmatizing mental illness and in advocating for more responsive systems of care.

Thankfully, the literature on the influence of culture on defining mental illness and its treatment has attracted a great deal of study and discussion. For example, there is new knowledge about the added stressors that people from different cultures experience in everyday life, including oppression, poverty, racism, gender bias, cultural conflict, and language barriers. In addition, more attention is paid to how differing perceptions of "health," "illness," and "mental disorder" affect help-seeking behaviors (Sands, 2000). A response to an inaccessible or unresponsive system has been a call for culturally competent practice, or practice which transcends traditional approaches and incorporates culturally sensitive techniques that reflect familiarity with the culture and congruence with its values.

Legal and Ethical Factors

To understand the legal context of contemporary mental health care, social workers should appreciate the influence of both legislation and case law on their practice. The evolution of federal legislation, and particularly the role of presidential politics, is fascinating and may provide hints to changes in the near future. Interestingly, President Franklin Pierce had slammed the door on federal involvement in mental health care when he vetoed legislation in 1854 that would have allowed for the use of federal money to build a system of asylums. Dorothea Dix had successfully rallied passage of the legislation as part of her well-known crusade. President Pierce, however, rejected it, fearing the "whole field of public beneficence" would be "thrown open to the care of culture of the Federal government" (cited in Foley & Sharfstein, 1983, p. 2). After a century of such resistance, the federal government passed legislation in 1946 establishing the National Institute of Mental Health (NIMH) and, for the first time, provided monies for training and research related to mental health. The first comprehensive piece of federal legislation was the 1963 Community Mental Health Centers Act, which passed in spite of vigorous initial opposition by the American Medical Association. This bill supported the creation of hundreds of local community mental health centers across America, which are some of the largest and most consequential employers of social workers in the country. Significantly, the bill was passed with the visible support and leadership of President Kennedy, a close relative of a person with mental disabilities, highlighting the fact that the importance of the personal experiences of our leaders cannot be underestimated. Other legislation refined this initial bill, and President Carter's later attempt to re-energize and improve the system was made moot by Ronald Reagan's election. The most recent legislative activity at the federal level relates to specific areas of concern, as opposed to broad sweeping legislation: protection and advocacy, state planning for people with serious mental illness, employment rights of persons with mental disabilities, and insurance parity.

Case law, especially those few mental health-related Supreme Court cases, has also served as a powerful tool for shaping mental health service delivery and reflects any given era's politics. Concepts like "duty to warn," "least restrictive alternative," and "right to treatment" have all emerged out of the resolution of specific suits. Whereas the 1970s are known as a time of expanded rights of consumers, the 1980s with President Reagan were known for the rise of conservatism, and retrenchment from human rights. (See Table 1.1.)

Social workers in mental health must constantly examine where we stand in trying to balance "patient rights" (now generally referred to as "human rights") or the liberty interests of the individual with safety rights of society. Table 1.2 summarizes key rights issues in the mental health arena, many of which interface with case law and legislation addressed previously. Recently, a great deal of attention has been focused on an individual's access to health care. We know that in spite of the Domenici-Wellstone Parity Act of 1996, treatment limits and low capitation rates still exist, which many describe as discriminatory. Former President Clinton was a major proponent of the "Consumer Bill of Rights and Responsibilities," which would have provided for advanced treatment directives and allow for greater input from families and consumers. Possibly due to the power of the family movement and in spite of opposition by consumers, today we see a trend to expand commitment standards to include the "gravely disabled."

A VISION FOR THE NATURE OF HELPING

Excellent social work practitioners in mental health will not only appreciate the contextual forces that shape their daily encounters with clients, but embrace contemporary philosophies and models of practice. The following is an overview of key ideas.

Empowerment

Most will recognize empowerment as a concept with broad relevance and application that has been popular in social work over the past two decades. Gutiérrez and colleagues (1998) describe practice that derives from an empowerment perspective as simply being about clients gaining power. For example, clients may increase their personal sense of control or they may take action to change larger social systems. An analysis of power blocks, individual or systemic, and education and skills development are seen as key aspects of achieving change. The topic of empowerment is

TABLE

1.1

KEY MENTAL HEALTH COURT CASES

Cases	Results
Olmstead v. L.C. (1999), U.S. Supreme Court	The Supreme Court ruled that states be required to place persons in community settings rather than institutions, provided that treating professionals have determined it appropriate, the individual is not opposed, and state resources and needed placement accommodations are considered.
Jaffee v. Redmond (1996), U.S. Supreme Court	The Supreme Court extended the "psychotherapist privilege" to licensed clinical social workers.
Washington v. Harper (1990), U.S. Supreme Court	The Supreme Court overruled a lower court determination that greater procedural protections were needed in cases where an incarcerated person determined to be a danger to self or others refuses to take psychiatric medication.
Osheroff v. Chestnut Lodge (1985), Maryland Health Care Arbitration	A former patient sued an inpatient facility for failing to use medications to treat his depression and using psychoanalysis alone. This case settled out of court.
Youngberg v. Romeo (1982), U.S. Supreme Court	The Supreme Court stopped short of saying institutionalized patients have a right to treatment but said they do have a right to be ensured safe conditions, freedom from bodily restraints, and minimally adequate "training."
Addington v. Texas (1979), U.S. Supreme Court	The Supreme Court established that "beyond a reasonable doubt" was too strict a standard to be used in commitment hearings, but mere preponderance of the evidence is too lenient. Thus, "clear, unequivocal, and convincing evidence" was established as an appropriate standard.
Parham v. J. R. (1979), U.S. Supreme Court	The Supreme Court found that a full-blown adversarial hearing was not needed when determining whether or not to commit children to psychiatric care; rather, merely some sort of "inquiry" by a "neutral factfinder" was all that was needed.
Tarasoff v. Regents of Univ. of CA (1976), CA Supreme Court	Court found that privileged communication rights must be weighed with public interests in safety, and thus therapists have a duty to warn certain third parties when a specific threat to physical safety is made and harm is foreseeable.
O'Connor v. Donaldson (1975), U.S. Supreme Court	Defendant claimed he was confined against his will in spite of no evidence of dangerousness and had never in 15 years received treatment. The Supreme Court found that the mere presence of mental illness is not a sufficient basis for involuntary commitment.
Wyatt v. Stickney (1972), Middle District, AL	In the first major class-action suit addressing the rights of institutionalized patients, court found the state needs to provide a humane psychological and physical environment, individualized treatment plans, and qualified staff in adequate numbers.
Lake v. Cameron (1966), U.S. Court of Appeals (DC)	Noting that deprivation of liberty should not exceed what is absolutely necessary, the Court found that people have a right to be treated in the least restrictive alternative available and that the courts have some responsibility in exploring the alternatives.

TABLE 1.2	KEY HUMAN RIGHTS ISSUES IN MENTAL HEALTH

1. Access to Health Care	• Insurance parity and access to health insurance
	• Right to receive mental health treatment
	• Access to newer medications in public mental health programs
	• Access to general medical care in psychiatric facilities
2. Due Process Rights	• Commitment standards
	• Commitment and detention procedures for adults versus children
	• Nature and frequency of periodic reviews
	• Voluntary admissions and release
	• Standards of proof in differing circumstances
	• Protection and advocacy mechanisms
3. Institutional Rights	• Distinguishing commitment status from incompetence
	• Right to be free from physical restraints
	• Right to be paid for work
	• Right to communicate with persons outside the institution
	• Right to be treated with dignity and respect
4. Treatment Rights	• Right to refuse medication
	• Least restrictive alternative
	• Outpatient commitment
	• Right to effective treatment
	• Informed consent for treatment and research
	• Prior consent and substituted judgment/guardianship
	• Confidentiality and privileged communication
	• Disclosure and duty to warn
	• Access to mental health records
5. Civil Liberties of Special Concern	• Right to bear arms
	• Right to reasonable accommodation in employment
	• Access to safe and affordable housing

actually found in the human services literature across disciplines, fields of practice, and populations of interest. Even a cursory review of the literature reveals similarities. First, empowerment implies that clients should be seen as capable and resourceful. Because of discrimination and bias, however, clients may experience powerlessness or oppression. In mental health practice, this may be true for most clients, including women, gay and lesbian clients, homeless people, people with serious mental illness, those who are economically disadvantaged, and people with disabilities. In fact, empowerment practice is in stark contrast to the so-called "medical model," which stresses mental disability as "disease" and clients as rather passive recipients of professionals' "expertise" in diagnosing the problem and then prescribing the treatment (Manning, 1998).

Empowerment practice is consistently described as helping clients to

- Be self-determining
- Participate actively in their own life changes
- Develop a sense of "mastery" of their environment
- Develop a consciousness about their situation and power
- Influence decision makers

Empowerment, considered by some to be the professional catch term of the 1990s, has come under some criticism of late, perhaps some undeserved. Critics suggest that if we say our role is to *empower* clients, aren't we claiming that we really hold the power—that it is ours to give or withhold? The question reflects an important ability critically to analyze and question the language we use in the field (Taylor & Bentley, 2000) and to speculate on underlying assumptions or implications. Nevertheless, in a partnership model as described, social workers and clients alike share power and expertise.

Strengths

In recent years, there has also been a great deal of rhetoric about the need to focus on client strengths, *not* client problems. Specifically, strengths are unique aspirations, positive characteristics, gifts, capacities, contributions, and assets. In addition, the strengths perspective says the client's environment should be viewed as an "oasis of resources," rather than be blamed or scapegoated (Rapp, 1998). Practice should be about building strengths, and using them to help clients reach their goals. Again, this perspective is billed as a radical departure from the "medical model," which some would say forces clinicians to spend most of their time asking about a client's pathology, symptoms, failures, or weaknesses (after all, we are reimbursed by insurance companies for fixing problems, not for building attributes). There has been substantial acknowledgment that most social workers are intuitively comfortable with the strengths perspective, but difficulties emerge when social workers try to adopt the perspective without adequate training or practice and in the face of significant organizational and societal barriers (Weick, Rapp, Sullivan, & Kisthardt, 1989).

TABLE

TABLE 1.3   PARTNERSHIP PRINCIPLES: HOW HELPING HAPPENS

- **Helping happens** when mental health clients are seen as normal, competent adults who, although they happen to be experiencing emotional distress or have a mental disorder, are capable of making informed decisions about their needs and desires, and when clients' perspectives are not only seen as valid and authentic, but become the centerpiece of helping.

- **Helping happens** when there is a relationship between peers based on honesty and trust, mutual respect, equal power, and an appreciation of respective strengths and limits of participants. Participants are constantly seeking greater empathy and clearer communication.

- **Helping happens** in all sorts of ways: through relaxed, caring dialogue and sharing between peers, through structured problem solving, and through active hands-on interventions and collaboration. At the center of helping is shared knowledge and expertise.

- **Helping happens** in clinics, hospitals, neighborhoods, homes, parks, restaurants, drop-in centers, and jails. Over the long haul, it is important to be with another person in need in nonjudgmental, nonthreatening ways.

- **Helping happens** when participants (clients and social workers) believe change and growth can and does happen, that improved quality of life is not only possible but also probable with a little planning, support, and utilization of coping skills and resources.

Partnership

The "partnership model" refers to a new way of conceptualizing the relationship between client and social worker, one that is very consistent with empowerment practice and the strengths perspective. The focus is the essential difference in discussions of partnership. While empowerment and strengths focus more on the purpose of intervention and vehicles for achieving change, discussions of partnership tend to emphasize the nature of relationship and the interaction between and roles of the social worker and client. Specifically, the ideal relationship is one of genuine collaboration and shared power, or as some put it, "power *with* and *among*, not power *over*." While "mutuality" and "genuineness" have historically been reflected in the lexicon of social work, clearly the reality has not always matched. In a partnership model, clients are seen as having significant "expertise," centered in their own lived experiences of learning, growing, adapting, and coping. Likewise, social workers have knowledge about human behavior and human behavior change, both individually, and in communities and organizations. Thus, shared expertise calls for active participation from the client, shared leadership, and negotiated decision making—not in the abstract, but in the real moment-to-moment encounters between a client and social worker (see Table 1.3).

Recovery and Rehabilitation

The goal of contemporary mental health practice is the client's own recovery and rehabilitation. The language reflects ideas of "a process of restoration" and a "return to normalcy" rather than those of old models that stressed "reducing psy-chopathology" or "achieving treatment compliance." Too often in mental health systems, "a person's energy is devoted, not to creating a better life, but to con-forming to the dictates of professional staff" (Rapp, 1998, p. 11). Rapp's review of the personal accounts of people recovering from mental illness yielded a number of themes about recovery: the importance of separating oneself from one's illness, increasing personal control, finding a sense of purpose, cultivating hope, and build-ing significant relationships. These new emphases usually place the thrust of help-ing on information sharing, skills building, and the development of meaningful activities aimed at improving the client's quality of life. This requires a shift in focus, away from the social worker's or the agency's preconceived notions of where clients should be headed. While the agency or referral source might suggest some parameters of care, they cannot dictate client goals or circumscribe roles of the social worker. Most importantly, a social worker must discover what "recovery" and a "better life" are to the client. *That discovery* should then define the direction and pace of practice.

CHARACTERISTICS OF THE EXCELLENT SOCIAL WORKER

Excellent mental health social workers are effective and have the knowledge, values, and skills to help generate meaningful change in their clients' lives and in the ser-vice delivery system. These changes could be in behavior, thoughts, emotions, atti-tudes, beliefs, programs, policies, or priorities. We suspect effectiveness is not the technical mastery of a few techniques, but a more complex combination or synthe-ses of qualities. Our framework for excellent social work consists of the 5 Cs. Specifically, the following are characteristics an excellent mental health social work-er must possess.

Compassionate

To be compassionate means to have an emotional understanding and empathetic appreciation of the experiences of clients and families. The social worker strives to understand the client's unique history and circumstances, past problems, strengths, and dilemmas. Social work emphasizes a holistic biopsychosocial-spiritual under-standing of human behavior informs practice, because we are taught to understand the interplay of factors that influence behavior, thoughts, and feelings. We can avoid blaming the victim, which seems to derive from simplistic notions of causality. Social workers need to hear stories, both from reading personal accounts literature and from listening to people with whom they are working. By remaining immersed in their sto-ries, social workers maintain a high level of compassion for clients and their families, and avoid the opposite fate of depersonalization. Allowing themselves to be inspired and moved, infuriated and exasperated, social workers will find that few stories are benign; most are enlightening and revealing. Practitioners also learn that, though

TABLE 1.4	STRATEGIES TO DEAL WITH BURNOUT AND PROMOTE PROFESSIONAL SATISFACTION

Organizational Level: Allow flexible work structure; create mechanisms to honor and reward staff work that reflects commitment to clients; assign reasonable caseloads; ensure adequate administrative resources; increase training and professional development opportunities; and attend to environmental conditions in the workplace.

Professional Life: Set realistic and clear goals for yourself; focus on successes; reflect on job expectations and concerns; clarify beliefs, attitudes, and roles; identify and acknowledge daily hassles; build peer support either through formal groups or informal consultation; break the cycle of negativism with peers and instead take pride in your own and their achievements; and use strategies and techniques that have been shown to be effective.

Personal Life: Do relaxation exercises; exercise; use meditation or prayer regularly; nurture your significant relationship; listen to music; journal; develop interesting hobbies or collections; and build a friendship network.

clients face a similar stigma and struggle, they are men, women, and children; young and old; gay, straight, and bisexual; rich, poor, and in-between; Christian, Jewish, Muslim, Hindi, and agnostic; African American, white, Latino, Native American, and multiracial. The challenge for mental health social workers is to take the compassion and the appreciation of diversity and make it a visible part of their professional selves.

Committed

Excellent mental health social workers are personally invested in their work at the micro, mezzo, and macro levels. This may be reflected in energy and determination, in the extent to which they advocate for issues of importance to clients and families, and in the degree to which they take professional development and lifelong learning seriously.

Much has been written about the realities of burnout in mental health practice. It is often described as having three components: emotional exhaustion, depersonalization, and feelings of low personal achievement. This is seen in mental health social workers when they speak about clients as if they are diagnostic labels, not people, or express hopelessness about client progress, or are easily angered or frustrated when clients "don't act right." Preventing burnout and remaining committed to mental health practice requires attention to the work environment and to one's personal and professional life (see Table 1.4). It is important to ensure that those in your mental health agency or organization do not subtly reinforce or model burnout behaviors (like apathy and negativism) or extinguish more positive behaviors (like celebrating client progress, rewarding collegial achievements) by ignoring them or labeling them as pathology (e.g., overinvolved, without boundaries, or competitive). Committed social workers not only think about their own professional development and growth, but plan for it.

Collaborative

Being collaborative means having the ability to relate to mental health clients, families, and other providers in a way that conveys respect and appreciation for their legitimacy and their perspective. Their views are considered valid and valuable. For example, how does the unique training of psychiatric nurses in group and family work help the team more fully understand the client? How does a psychologist's training in behavioral assessment and psychological testing extend our knowledge of the client? What specialized knowledge does a psychiatrist bring about the connection between the immune system and stress? Avoiding professional arrogance (such as when social workers suggest they are the only ones with a "holistic" perspective, or the only ones who value a biopsychosocial understanding of behavior) is key to being collaborative.

We have already stressed collaboration with clients and families in the previous section on the nature of helping. One more point may add to the discussion: In terms of collaboration with families, DeChillo (1993) notes that explicitly recognizing the family as a key resource in the care of clients, including involving the family in goal formulation, is a crucial component of family collaboration. His research found that the most significant factor associated with the level of collaboration between families and social workers was the social workers' attitudes toward family involvement in treatment. Positive attitude toward family involvement meant increased collaboration, suggesting again that our attitudes are essential in creating a cooperative climate for work with others.

Creative

Being creative means using your professional imagination and clinical judgment to apply all or any piece of knowledge or skill to a unique and different situation. Effective social workers are familiar with the experience of "trying on" different interventions to meet the needs of individual clients. Ingenuity in practice may involve such things as asking a client to write a poem, create a sculpture, or somehow integrate art or ritual into the helping process. Practitioners might use favorite rock lyrics in working with teenagers, set up a fish tank at the office to help relax clients who may be anxious, or encourage children to draw pictures of themselves or their families. This ability to be flexible and ingenious in social work practice has inspired some scholars to describe social work as an art and speak to the value of "practice wisdom" (Goldstein, 1990).

Competent

Competency means having the power to perform and the internal and external resources to act. Social workers in mental health must have current knowledge about mental, emotional, and behavioral disorders, up-to-date information on psychopharmacology, an intimate familiarity with mental health policies and the context of service delivery, technical skills in using effective interventions, professional confidence to direct the helping process with clients and families, and political savvy and assertiveness to work toward improvements in the service delivery system. Mental health social workers should know what they are doing and why they are doing it.

SUMMARY

Chapter 1 suggests that to be an excellent social worker in contemporary mental health practice, one should appreciate the context of practice, that is understand the scientific, technological, historical, economic, legal, ethical, sociopolitical, and cultural forces that influence service delivery. We summarize key ideas that form a foundation for practice including "partnership," "strengths" or "empowerment," and "recovery and rehabilitation." We emphasize the meta-role of the social worker as that of resource for goal achievement, which is fulfilled by embracing the range of roles presented in this book, including crisis counselor, diagnostician, educator, mediator, advocate, community organizer, therapist, skills trainer, case manager, medication facilitator, policy analyst, administrator, consumer and family consultant, interdisciplinary and interagency team member, researcher, and program evaluator.

The vision we have of social workers who want to help clients achieve these goals is characterized by the 5 Cs: compassion, commitment, collaboration, creativity, and competence. There are other Cs that students and practitioners have offered over the years as additional characteristics of excellent social workers. According to them, social workers in mental health should, at least at times, be combat-ready, capable, considerate, courageous, cautious, concerned, consistent, candid, colorful, clear, credible, crafty, courteous, conversant, connected, concise, confident, circumspect, conscientious, cunning, companionable, credible, communicative, classy, connected, confident, curious, and sometimes even captivating.

REFERENCES

Bentley, K. J., & Walsh, J. (2001). *The social worker and psychotropic medication: Toward effective collaboration with mental health clients, families, and providers* (2nd ed.). Belmont, CA: Wadsworth.

Brown, P. (1985). *The transfer of care: Psychiatric deinstitutionalization and its aftermath.* London: Routledge and Kegan Paul.

DeChillo, N. (1993). Collaboration between social workers and the families of the mentally ill. *Families in Society, 74,* 104–115.

Farrell, A. D. (1997). The influence of technology on mental health services. In T. R. Watkins & J. W. Callicut (Eds.), *Mental health policy and practice today.* Thousand Oaks, CA: Sage.

Foley, H. A., & Sharfstein, S. S. (1983). *Madness and government: Who cares for the mentally ill?* Washington, DC: American Psychiatric Press.

Goldstein, H. (1990). The knowledge base of social work practice: Theory, wisdom, analogue, or art? *Families in Society, 71,* 32–43.

Gutiérrez, L. M., Parsons, R. J., & Cox, E. O. (1998). *Empowerment in social work practice: A sourcebook.* Pacific Grove, CA: Brooks/Cole.

Manning, S. (1998). Empowerment in mental health programs: Listening to the voices. In L. M Gutiérrez, R. J. Parsons, & E. O. Cox (1998). *Empowerment in social work practice: A sourcebook* (pp. 89–109). Pacific Grove, CA: Brooks/Cole.

Morrissey, J, P., Goldman H. H., & Klerman, L. V. (1980). *The enduring asylum: Cycles of reform at Worcester State Hospital.* New York: Grune & Stratton.

Rapp, C. A. (1998). *The strengths model: Case management with people suffering from severe and persistent mental illness.* New York: Oxford University Press.

Ross, E. C., & Croze, C. (1997). Mental health service delivery in the age of managed care. In T. R. Watkins & J. W. Callicut (Eds.), *Mental health policy and practice today.* Thousand Oaks, CA: Sage.

Rothman, D. (1971). *Conscience and convenience: The asylum and its alternatives in progressive America.* New York: Little, Brown.

Sands, R. G. (2000). *Clinical social work practice in behavioral mental health: A postmodern approach to practice with adults.* Needham Heights, MA: Allyn & Bacon.

Scull, A. T. (1977). Madness and segregative control: The rise of the asylum. *Social Problems, 24,* 337–351.

Taylor, M. F., & Bentley, K. J. (2000, February). *Changing conceptualizations of mental health and mental illness: Implications for social work education in the 21st century.* Paper presented at the 46th Annual Program Meeting of the Council on Social Work Education, New York City.

Valenstein, E. S. (1998). *Blaming the brain: The truth about drugs and mental health.* New York: Free Press.

Vourlekis, B. S., Edinburg, G., & Knee, R. (1998). The rise of social work in public mental health through aftercare of people with serious mental illness. *Social Work, 43,* 567–575.

Weick, A., Rapp, C., Sullivan, W. P., & Kisthardt, W. (1989). A strengths perspective for social work practice. *Social Work, 34,* 350–354.

Williams, J. B. W. (1998). Classification and diagnostic assessment. In J. B. W. Williams & K. Ell (Eds.), *Advances in mental health research: Implications for practice* (pp. 25–48). Washington, DC: NASW Press.

SOCIAL WORKERS AS CRISIS COUNSELORS

Susan Gingerich

Social workers employed at agencies that specialize in crisis situations, such as suicide hotlines, sexual assault centers, women's shelters, children's protective services, emergency rooms, and crisis clinics, expect to deal with crises, psychiatric emergencies, or both on a regular basis. In every mental health setting, however, it is almost inevitable that social workers will sooner or later encounter a crisis with at least one of their clients.

The following statistics (Roberts, 1996, pp. 24–25) give an idea of the scope of crises that social workers might encounter. Each day of the year,

- 254,820 persons visit emergency rooms.
- 357 individuals are victims of rape.
- between 685 and 1,645 individuals attempt suicide.
- 41,488 adults are diagnosed with affective disorder.
- 54,887 adults are diagnosed with anxiety disorder.
- 41,244 adults are diagnosed with substance abuse disorders.

Given the millions of people encountering situations that are highly linked with crisis, the need for crisis intervention and brief treatment is vital, and "an enormous number of social workers and psychologists will be needed to help people to cope with and resolve social impairments" (Roberts, 1996, p. 26).

This chapter will provide information and guidelines for responding to mental health clients who are experiencing crises and for responding to those whose crises are better described as "emergencies," because there is an imminent danger of harm to themselves or to others (Callahan, 1998, p. 22). Particular attention will be given to crisis situations involving risk of suicide or violence. The reader is cautioned, however, that all crises and emergencies are unique and that there are no foolproof formulas for dealing with them. Reading specific literature, knowing risk factors, following a model, and adhering to a set of guidelines are helpful. Social workers must guard against overconfidence, however, and never hesitate to seek additional help in responding to a crisis.

must help decide which problem to pursue first and explore alternatives that are available to address that problem. At the same time, the social worker must consider the other problems and how to keep them from spiraling out of control. In this example, the social worker decided to first assess the level of danger to the client's child, and then to evaluate the alcohol abuse and possibility of referral to treatment.

Although social workers must keep in mind clients' strengths and coping abilities, they should also be aware that clients who are a danger to self or others frequently experience chaotic emotional states and impaired judgment. Therefore, social workers may need to take a more active role than usual, and may need to adopt "more of an evaluative than a therapeutic approach" (Kleespies, Deleppo, Mori, & Niles, 1998). Developing rapport and establishing a working alliance remain important, but the social worker must not lose track of the importance of focusing on accurate assessment and disposition of very complex situations, and the extremely short time frame available.

Understanding relevant statistics is becoming increasingly important. The National Institute of Mental Health provides the following information about suicide in the US (http://www.nimh.nih.gov/research/suifact.htm):

- Suicide is the 9th leading cause of death (30,903 in 1996).
- One out of every 1,000 deaths is caused by suicide.
- Suicide by firearms is the most common method.
- More men than women die by suicide.

Dale McNiel (1998, pp. 95–104) reports the following statistics about violence:

- Violence is most common among younger people.
- Among psychiatric patients, males and females have comparable rates of violence.
- People who were victims of child abuse are more likely to commit violence later in life.
- Substance abuse disorders are associated with higher risk of violence.
- Rates of violence among psychiatric patients fluctuate depending on whether they are taking medication and whether they are in an acute episode.

Statistical studies are helpful in terms of identifying which clients are more at risk for specific types of emergencies. However, a word of warning is in order. When predicting suicide and violence, social workers must always keep in mind that the presence of certain risk factors does not guarantee that an individual will manifest such behavior, and the absence of risk factors does not guarantee that the client will *not* manifest the behavior. Social workers must never be overconfident when it comes to assessing for suicide or violence; they should be ever alert to the possibility that someone may be a danger to self or others. The signs may be subtle, misleading, or unique to the individual, so the social workers must bring all of their training, experience, and intuition to each assessment.

MAJOR GOALS

Crisis Intervention

People who come for help during a crisis often have a host of long-standing problems, a variety of current problems, or both. Although the social worker may be tempted to address these, it is essential to focus on the presenting problem or crisis. The other problems deserve attention and intervention, but given the urgency of a crisis situation, priorities must be set and followed. Crisis intervention is by definition time-limited, often one to six sessions, and the techniques of long-term therapy cannot be applied. However, the social worker is advised to become familiar with referring clients to appropriate agencies for assistance with more ambitious goals. In fact, getting help in a crisis may be an important first step for some clients who may have been reluctant in the past to seek assistance with problems.

Several authors have described the importance of setting realistic goals for crisis counseling (Aguilera, 1994; Gilliland & James, 1997; Roberts, 1996; Stroul, 1993), which are summarized as follows:

- Ensure the safety of the clients and others who may be at risk of harm.
- Assist clients to return to their precrisis level of functioning.
- Assist clients to resolve situations that may have precipitated or contributed to the current crisis.
- Link clients with services and supports in the community.

Social workers can pursue two additional goals if they have the opportunity to meet with clients after the immediate crisis is resolved. They can help clients avoid similar crises in the future and help clients respond more effectively if the same crisis recurs (Mueser & Gingerich, 1994, pp. 279–282).

Emergency Intervention

The goals of emergency intervention are essentially the same as those of crisis intervention. However, in many emergency situations, social workers may have to spend all their available time on the first goal, that of ensuring safety for clients and any others who may be at risk.

TECHNIQUES, STRATEGIES, AND SKILLS

Most crisis-focused agencies have their own extensive training programs, involving lectures, written materials, videotapes, role plays, discussion, observation, and supervised performance of tasks, with an emphasis on experiential learning. If an agency is not crisis focused, however, there is still a need for social workers to prepare for the eventuality of a crisis. This applies even if the likelihood of encountering a crisis is small. For example, even social work students in training who are making initial phone calls to referrals have unexpectedly encountered clients who were suicidal or experiencing violent impulses. Every mental health agency benefits from having a crisis policy or protocol, and every social worker should be aware of the steps to follow and whom they should contact.

Crisis Intervention

The crisis intervention literature contains several lists of 10 to 15 necessary skills for responding to crises. Most sources describe the following skills: showing regard for client safety, listening, problem solving, assessing, communicating, counseling, decision making, tolerating stress, handling conflict, negotiating several tasks at once, establishing rapport with many types of clients, interacting effectively with multiple persons and systems, and working as part of a team. Although these skills are certainly all relevant, it appears that only a combination of Superman and Mother Theresa could manage to have them all! It may be helpful, however, to describe some of the major categories of skills needed in crisis situations: knowledge of mental illness, familiarity with resources, knowledge of commitment laws, assessment, communication, and problem solving.

Knowledge of Mental Illness

Social workers benefit from learning as much as possible about mental illnesses, which often contribute to crises or make clients more vulnerable to them. It is especially helpful to be knowledgeable about depression, bipolar disorder, schizophrenia, borderline personality disorder, and substance abuse. Several user-friendly resources are available for social workers to learn about depression (Copeland, 1992; Papolos & Papolos, 1992), bipolar disorder (Miklowitz & Goldstein, 1997; Mondimore, 1999), schizophrenia (Keefe & Harvey, 1994; Mueser & Gingerich, 1994; Torrey, 1995; Weiden, Scheifler, Diamond, & Ross, 1999), borderline personality disorder (Kreisman & Straus, 1989; Linehan, 1993; Mason & Kreger, 1998), and substance abuse (Marlatt & Gordon, 1985). Other books contain information about a variety of mental illnesses (Kaplan & Sadock, 1993, 1995; Mueser & Glynn, 1999; Woolis, 1992).

First-person accounts by people with mental illness or by their family members can be extremely helpful in understanding their experiences and the kinds of crises they have endured (Jamison, 1995; Sheehan, 1982). Videotapes of clients and their family members can also further social workers' understanding and help them see clients' points of view (Wheeler, 1996).

It is important to note that in many mental health settings, crises often occur, at least in part, because clients take their medication inconsistently or stop taking it altogether. This is a complex problem, given that psychotropic medications can cause one or more side effects that are unpleasant, such as drowsiness, dry mouth, weight gain, and lethargy. Helping clients identify side effects and develop strategies to decrease them can be extremely helpful (Mueser & Gingerich, 1994). In addition, it is important to note that in many instances, failures of the mental health system contribute to clients' crises. For example, clients who are referred to outpatient counseling may find themselves waiting months to see a counselor, during which time their situation worsens considerably. Therefore, social workers should never assume that clients are receiving services just because of a referral.

Familiarity with Available Resources and Referrals

Each city and state has a different set of agencies available to assist in crisis situations. Social workers should know the services that agencies provide, their hours, whom they serve, how to contact them, and how to make a referral. Many communities publish directories of human services that are useful; however, it is usually preferable to develop an easy-to-use, easy-to-access, up-to-date list or Rolodex of resources and referrals that are most commonly used in a specific setting. For example, social workers in emergency rooms may want to include referral information about emergency food and housing, mobile outreach teams, case management services, drop-in centers, legal assistance agencies, substance abuse treatment centers, women's shelters, sexual assault counseling centers, children's protective services, police, ambulance, fire departments, inpatient psychiatric units, and outpatient clinics, to name a few.

In today's managed care environment, it is also important to know about coverage for services at each agency. For example, knowing which inpatient units accept clients with medical assistance can be vital. When possible, it is helpful to develop positive relationships with staff members at other agencies, by introducing oneself by phone or in person and visiting their facility. When working with another agency on a case, it is important to stay in good communication, to let the other agency know what is transpiring, how soon the client might be using their services, or if the client has decided not to follow through with the referral.

Social workers must be cautioned to call for assistance as soon as possible when they find themselves in situations that are becoming difficult to control or becoming dangerous in a way that they are not prepared to handle. Emergency resources such as mobile outreach teams, police, and ambulances, are excellent resources in such cases. New social workers often feel that they "should" be able to handle any situation that arises with their clients, and are embarrassed to call for help, sometimes worrying that they might be "calling wolf" or further upsetting the client. However, experienced social workers recognize that knowing when to ask for help is a sign of strength, that calling for assistance is critical for ensuring safety for clients and those around them (*including* the social worker).

Knowledge of Commitment Laws and Other Legal Issues

Most social workers in crisis-focused agencies have experienced working with clients who need to be evaluated for admission to a psychiatric hospital because they present a danger to themselves or others because of a psychiatric illness. It is preferable to convince clients that a voluntary evaluation is in their best interest, but in the event they cannot be persuaded, the social worker must seek an involuntary evaluation. Even if social workers do not anticipate being in such a situation, they should become familiar with their own state's laws and procedures for involuntary commitment. In most states, the criteria for involuntary psychiatric hospitalization are that the person has symptoms of mental illness and is dangerous to himself or herself, or dangerous to other people, or is gravely disabled and unable to care for himself or herself. Many states require a petition to be completed by someone who has *directly observed* the person behave in a way that presents an immediate threat or injury to self or others. The specific commitment laws of each state, however, are quite different and can be very complicated. Social workers benefit from having a clear plan for whom to call first, and perhaps second, if a client refuses a psychiatric evaluation.

In addition to commitment laws, there are other legal issues of concern to social workers, such as "duty to protect" statutes, which have been adopted by a majority of the states. These statutes require mental health professionals to evaluate their clients' potential for dangerous actions toward others and to warn intended victims of danger. Each state varies as to the specific terms of their statutes, although in most states the duty to warn is only triggered by a specific threat, and warning a potential victim is one of several possible actions. In Massachusetts, for example, mental health professionals must take at least one action from the following list: communicate the threat directly to the identified person, notify the appropriate law enforcement agency, arrange for voluntary hospitalization for the client, or take steps to initiate involuntary admission (if the client refuses hospitalization) (Kleespies, 1998). Social workers are advised to learn the specific requirements in their own states.

Assessment

Assessment involves two evaluations. The first evaluation is to determine whether there is a life-threatening situation and whether there is a need for "immediate control and stabilization" (Kaplan & Sadock, 1995, p. 1753). It would be fruitless to attempt a thorough evaluation of the presenting problem if the client is currently a danger to self or others or is too agitated or unstable to communicate clearly. During the first evaluation, both the social worker and the client benefit when the social worker is able to establish initial rapport and show interest in the well-being of the client. At some point early in the first evaluation, however, social workers must ask directly about current thoughts of suicide or violence and any history of suicidal or violent behavior. If the client expresses such thoughts, the social worker would conduct a more thorough evaluation for suicide or violence, as described later under "Emergency Intervention." If the client denies having thoughts of suicide or violence, the social worker may still have made observations that give rise to suspicion, because many clients who have thoughts of suicide or violence are wary of admitting them. If the social worker remains concerned about the risk of violence or suicide, additional information might be sought to conduct a further evaluation.

The second evaluation, focusing on the presenting problem, can be conducted once it has been determined that there is no immediate danger to self or others. In the second evaluation, social workers must also consider the limited time frame. As social workers find out more about the problem, they begin to gauge how much time they have for helping the client. Social workers often ask themselves, "What are the parameters within which I have to work? What is my hypothesis about the problem and the solution now? What are the resources available now? What resources will be available in the near future?"

In the second evaluation, social workers attempt to determine as much as possible about the presenting problem, to determine the thoughts and feelings of clients, to contact relevant third parties (such as family members and treatment providers), to evaluate clients' strengths and resources, to determine past coping strategies, to inventory the available community resources, and to check out clients' responses to possible courses of action. During the assessment, it is often necessary for social workers to periodically reevaluate their definition of the problem and to revise their thinking about possible solutions.

Communication Skills

The communication skills used in crisis intervention are very similar to those commonly used by social workers conducting brief therapy (see "Social Workers as Therapists," in Chapter 5 of this book), although social workers in crisis situations need to consider some specific skills: active listening, being clear and specific, avoiding blaming, and instilling a sense of hope.

Listening is perhaps one of the most important skills in dealing with crises. Clients are frequently upset, confused, and agitated, and social workers must listen very closely to make sense of what they are saying. It is important for social workers to attend carefully to what is being said, to ask questions when something is unclear, and to ensure they understood correctly. One way social workers can check their understanding is to paraphrase what they heard and to ask the client if that was what was meant. It is often necessary to ask questions and to check for understanding frequently, especially during the assessment of the crisis.

Because clients in crisis often have difficulty focusing and handling their emotions, it is helpful for social workers to be as clear and specific as possible. Clients find it easier to understand when social workers avoid long wordy sentences and roundabout introductions to topics. This is especially relevant in crises that involve the symptoms of major mental illness, where it is preferable to use direct, everyday language, to concentrate on one topic at a time, and to pause frequently to review and make sure the client understands. Even in situations where concentration is a significant problem, however, social workers should avoid talking down to clients or treating them like children.

Clients who experience crises often feel that they will be blamed for their situation. Even in cases where the client is partially responsible, it is usually not helpful for either the client or the social worker to dwell on who is to blame. Rather, it is more useful for the social worker to abbreviate discussions of guilt and blame, and to focus on finding solutions to the problem situation. When clients feel criticized or judged, they become either more distressed or defensive, neither of which lends to resolving a crisis.

Instilling a sense of hope is a complex skill, but one that is worth developing. When clients feel optimistic, they are more likely to feel calm and to participate actively in problem solving. Social workers can instill hope by speaking in a calm, respectful way, by helping clients identify their strengths and assets, and by pointing out previous instances where the clients either resolved or survived a crisis. Social workers can also encourage clients to think about possible alternatives to the current situation and to look forward to a time when things will be better.

Problem-solving Skills

The major steps of problem-solving involve the following: clearly defining the problem, generating several solutions, evaluating the pros and cons of each solution, choosing the most effective and viable solution, making an action plan to implement the solution, and planning for follow up (Mueser & Gingerich, 1994, pp. 136–153). In crisis situations, social workers often benefit from spending the most time on clearly defining the problem, which involves getting as much information as possible from as many points of view as possible. Once the problem has been defined, social workers who maintain a clear focus usually help clients come up with the best solutions.

Emergency Intervention

The skills described previously are also relevant in situations that involve a danger to self or others. Some additional skills in emergency assessment and management should also be noted, including knowledge of the Mental Status Exam, assessment of suicide risk, managing suicidal clients, assessment of risk for violence, and managing violent clients.

Mental Status Exam

Social workers can learn a great deal from their observations of clients and from responses to questions about the chief complaint, precipitating factors, current functioning, mental health, and substance use history. However, it may be necessary to conduct a Mental Status Exam (MSE), which is a systematic series of questions and objective observations that give a comprehensive view of the client's mental state. In some settings, the social worker conducts the formal MSE; in others, a psychologist or psychiatrist must conduct the MSE. There is some variability in the MSE, but most professionals conducting such an exam cover similar general areas (Kleespies, Deleppo, Mori, & Niles, 1998, pp. 54–62). Many agencies have standardized forms to be used for a mental status exam. Examples of such forms can be found in *Practical Psychiatric Practice: Forms and Protocols for Clinical Use* (Wyatt, 1994).

The following is an example of an MSE containing the most common subject areas, completed by a social worker employed in the emergency room of a general medical hospital. He was asked to evaluate a young man who had appeared in the emergency room several times in extreme distress, saying, "I think I'm having a heart attack." The examination and tests conducted by the emergency room revealed no physical signs of a heart attack or any cardiac irregularities. A physician also completed an exhaustive evaluation of the client, finding no medical reasons for the client's complaints. At his most recent emergency room visit, he clutched the doctor's hand, saying, "I can't get rid of this feeling that I'm going to die." The emergency room physician asked for the MSE when he became concerned about the possibility of a mental health problem.

Appearance: Client is a well-groomed, slender 25-year-old male. He is dressed appropriate to the season and current weather. His clothing is clean and pressed.

Behavior: Client is restless while seated, frequently standing up, walking to the window, and glancing at the scene outdoors. His voice has a breathless quality and trembles slightly while describing his symptoms. He pauses occasionally to take a few deep breaths. He sits forward in the chair, with an air of vigilance, keeping his back very straight.

Attitude toward Examiner: Client stares intently at the examiner, both while speaking and listening. He describes his cardiac symptoms in considerable detail and appears unsettled when the examiner asks about other things that are occurring in his life.

Orientation: Client is oriented to person, place, time, date, and situation.

Attention/concentration: Client is able to spell "world" backwards but is only able to do two serial subtraction of 7s from 100. "My mind is just somewhere else," he says, "I'm too worried about my heart."

Memory: Client displays no impairment in memory. He is able to describe a major news event from the past 6 months. He is able to recall three items ("baby," "pen," and "tree") after 5 minutes.

Mood and Affect: Client reports feeling worried and anxious. When asked for examples beyond his cardiac symptoms, he admits that he worries constantly at work, and "my friend keeps telling me I should 'chill out.'" His brow is furrowed, and his affect is anxious. He reports having trouble falling asleep ("I have too much on my mind") but denies vegetative symptoms and suicidal ideation. He reports that he feels edgy when he has to meet new people and worries that they won't like him or will look down on him. In fact, he frequently avoids situations, such as office parties, where he will have to be around people he doesn't know. He says he often feels panicked at the idea of social events and business meetings. "I feel like I might die if I go to one of those meetings. Seriously." He reports that sometimes his strong anxious feelings are not connected to any situation, but seem "to come out of the blue."

Intelligence: Client appears to be of at least normal intelligence. He has a college education and works full-time as a computer specialist at a local university.

Speech and Thought: Client speaks in a hesitant manner, but there is no evidence of a thought disorder. The content of his speech, however, tends to focus on fears and worries. He frequently repeats, "I feel like I'm losing control; something really bad is going to happen."

Perceptual Disturbance: Client reports no hallucinations or delusions.

Judgment and Insight: Client responds appropriately to questions about social judgment ("What would you do if you were the first person in a theater to see smoke?"). His insight into his situation is difficult to ascertain. He is understandably concerned about symptoms that appear to be cardiac in nature, and it is difficult for him to respond to questions that do not relate to his physical concerns.

The social worker reported back to the emergency room physician, recommending a thorough evaluation for an anxiety disorder. He noted that many symptoms that occur during an anxiety attack or a panic attack overlap with symptoms that occur during a heart attack or other cardiovascular events (Kleespies, 1998).

Assessing Risk for Suicide

There is no foolproof way to assess the seriousness of suicidal intentions. Because clients often do not make direct statements of suicidal intent, the social worker must listen closely to clients' words and how they are spoken, look for behavioral clues, and make direct inquiries. Social workers should also keep in mind that thoughts and intentions of suicide are often fluctuating; that is, sometimes clients feel better for a short period, but they are still in danger of dipping back into a suicidal frame of mind.

In looking for clues, the symptoms of severe depression are important warning signs, including feelings of worthlessness, guilt, and hopelessness about the future. Some clients also become preoccupied with death or topics related to death (such as funerals or whether there is an afterlife). Some clients make veiled threats, such as, "I'm so tired, I just want to sleep and be at peace," "Maybe people would be better off if I wasn't around," or "I don't have anything to live for." On the other hand, some clients who were initially very conflicted about suicide might show an improved mood when they have decided firmly to end their lives. To some clients, it feels like a relief to "finally decide" and to be free of the indecision that has been tormenting them. Therefore, when family members report that the client has suddenly been in a cheerful mood, it can be a clue to investigate further.

When suspicions have been aroused, direct questions must be asked. New social workers sometimes shy away from direct questions for fear that it will plant ideas or make the situation worse. On the contrary, many clients are relieved at the direct questions, as it gives them an opening to talk about thoughts and feelings with which they have been struggling. Questions are usually asked in an order that indicates progressively more danger of a suicide attempt. For example, the danger is very high if clients feel hopeless about the future, have made a plan for carrying out their intentions, have already taken steps toward this plan, and feel that there is nothing to hold them back. Mueser and Gingerich (1994, pp. 288–289) provide some examples of such questions:

- Have you been feeling sad or unhappy?
- Does it ever seem like things will never get better?

- Have you ever felt so badly that you had thoughts about hurting yourself?
- Do you have any thoughts of ending your life?
- Have you had thoughts of how you might kill yourself?
- Have you made plans to do so?
- What are your plans?
- What have you done to prepare for your plan?
- When do you intend to do it?
- Are there any things that might hold you back, such as people you care about, religious beliefs, responsibilities to others, or something you wanted to live to do or see?

Given the answers to these questions, social workers will proceed to assess the psychological intent (What does the client intend to accomplish by killing himself or herself?), the lethality of the plan (If the plan were carried out, how likely would it be to result in death?), previous history of suicidal ideation or attempts, and the presence of the most common risk factors associated with suicide.

The NIMH reports risk factors associated with suicide as the following:

- One or more diagnosable mental or substance abuse disorder
- Impulsivity
- Adverse life events
- Family history of mental or substance abuse disorder
- Family history of suicide
- Family violence, including physical or sexual abuse
- Prior suicide attempt
- Firearm in the home
- Incarceration
- Exposure to the suicidal behavior of others, including family, peers, or in the news or fiction stories (http://www.drkoop.com/wellness/mental_health/suicide, 1999)

It is important to remember, however, that assessing for suicide is an inexact science. The literature gives many examples of clients who showed no common warning signs, answered all direct questions with negative answers, and who demonstrated no risk factors, and then proceeded, to everyone's horror, to commit suicide. Conversely, the suicide literature also gives several examples of clients who seemed to fit all the criteria, and yet did not commit suicide. Social workers need to keep a very open mind when evaluating for suicide.

Management of Suicidal Clients

When clients are assessed to have significant suicidal risk, social workers must decide on a course of action that reflects the urgency of the situation. Often social workers must take steps to protect clients in the immediate situation. In settings such as inpatient psychiatric facilities, emergency rooms, and crisis centers, which are designed for emergency cases, there will be a safe room without any access to potential weapons. In other settings, such as outpatient clinics, vocational programs, and psychosocial clubhouses, social workers may have to remove any potentially lethal objects from the area, including scissors, medicines, keys, silverware, and penknives. The social worker should ensure that the client is not left alone; someone should be sitting close by at all times. In extreme cases, clients may have to be physically restrained from hurting themselves.

If the immediate danger decreases, social workers can then evaluate clients' willingness to avoid hurting themselves for a specific period of time. Social workers must be warned, however. Although clients may sound convincing when making "no-suicide contracts," they are often not able to follow through when the fluctuating suicidal feelings return later in force. One writer compared the strong pull of the suicide option to a "siren song," the tempting mermaids' song that lured sailors to their death on hidden rocks in *The Aeneid* (Clark, 1998, p. 89). Clients can be susceptible to this siren song in spite of their best intentions.

If clients are able to shift to thinking about living and to concentrate on problem solving, social workers can turn their attention from the immediate situation to managing the suicidal impulses in the near future. It is helpful to talk about decreasing stress in the clients' lives and to work on solving some of the problems that have contributed to suicidal ideation. If clients are considered to be a low risk and to have sufficient supports to go home, plans are often made for someone to stay with them and to keep an active watch. Follow-up appointments are scheduled as soon as possible to work on understanding the current episode of suicidality, and developing strategies for preventing or managing future episodes.

In some cases, clients are not able to shift to thinking about living; their risk of suicide remains high and unrelenting. The safety of such clients may only be possible in the hospital. Some clients will agree to hospitalization, while others will need to be involuntarily committed (see the previous section on "Knowledge of Commitment Laws"). Social workers are often reluctant to pursue involuntary commitment, but it may be the only safe disposition.

Assessing Risk for Violence

Social workers should avoid dealing with potentially violent clients alone. If physical intervention becomes necessary, it is extremely difficult for one social worker to accomplish this safely, even if the social worker is large and strong. As in assessing for suicidal risk, there is no foolproof way to predict the seriousness of a client's threatening violent behavior. Social workers must observe clients closely, listen to their words, look for behavioral clues, and ask direct questions relating to violent thoughts and actions.

Some clients make direct statements concerning their own recent violent behavior, which should be taken seriously. Social workers may need to follow up on such self-reports, investigating whether the object of violence was hurt and whether care is being provided. Some clients may make direct statements threatening violence to someone, which should also be taken seriously. As noted earlier, social workers have a duty to protect the intended victim of a client, which may involve communicating the threat to the identified person, notifying the appropriate law enforcement agency, or arranging for voluntary or involuntary hospitalization (McNiel, 1998, pp. 97–98). The legal issues in such a situation are complicated; social workers would be wise to learn the laws in their state and about the policy of their agencies. Some hospitals have legal counsel for consultation on such matters.

In looking for clues about risk for violence, social workers must be alert to interview behavior. Are the clients tense, menacing, irritable, looking at others in a hostile manner? Do they make the social worker uneasy or apprehensive? Social workers should also note vague statements, such as, "Somebody should teach her a lesson." Such statements should be followed up with questions:

- Who do you think should teach her a lesson?
- How would she be taught a lesson?
- Do you really want to hurt her?
- How would you go about it?
- What have you done to prepare for it?
- What would you do first?
- What would keep you from following through?
- Have you done that kind of thing before?

As with suicide risk, social workers will need to consider the risk factors associated with violent behavior. Eddy and Harris (1998, p. 222) report the following factors that have been shown to correlate with violence:

- Past history of violence
- White male, 30–50 years old
- History of poor interpersonal relationships, usually a loner
- Difficulty with authority
- Poor job performance
- History of substance abuse
- History as victim of abuse
- Interest in weapons

The data is mixed regarding the presence of mental illness as a risk factor, and depends on whether the client is currently being treated and whether the client is currently symptomatic. In the absence of psychotic symptoms, the risk of violence for mentally ill individuals was found to be "no higher than for demographically similar members of the same community who were never treated" (Link, Cullen, & Andrews, 1992). Other research indicates that the presence of a mental disorder "may be a consistent, albeit modest, risk factor for the occurrence of violence" (Eddy & Harris, 1998). Clients who feel threatened by the content of their psychotic perceptions or beliefs, however, or who experience command hallucinations, may be at a higher risk of violence. If clients have a history of violence while experiencing paranoid delusions or hallucinations, and are currently psychotic, social workers would be wise to investigate further.

As with suicide risk factors, relying on a profile of the common factors associated with violence would be foolhardy. Some clients who commit violence may have none of the risk factors, whereas others may have several risk factors and do not commit violence.

Management of Violent Clients

When clients are assessed to have significant risk for violence, social workers may need to take steps to protect others in the immediate environment. Clients with extreme risk of violence should not be treated by a lone social worker in an outpatient setting. Social workers may need to call for assistance from 911 to transport the client to a more secure evaluation setting, such as the emergency room.

Early intervention to prevent violence is much preferred, as it has the highest likelihood of avoiding injury both to the client and to others. Interventions are often conceptualized as progressing from the least restrictive alternatives, to the most restrictive alternatives or progressing from verbal interactions to physical interactions. The following are examples of possible alternatives:

- One-on-one verbal interaction
- Separating the client from the area or from specific stimulation
- Redirecting the client
- Setting limits
- Voluntary administration of medications
- Quiet room or time out
- Involuntary administration of medications
- Seclusion
- Restraint (Delaware Psychiatric Center P.E.A.C.E. Manual, 1998, p.19)

Verbal interactions are most effective in a safe environment with no potential weapons, including such items as heavy ashtrays, staplers, and scissors, and with the social worker removing necklaces, dangling earrings, and neckties. In speaking to the potentially violent client, social workers are advised to present a calm appearance and speak in a moderate, firm tone. It is helpful to be as neutral and nonprovocative as possible, and to avoid making intense eye contact.

Most settings that serve potentially violent clients have a structured training program that teaches verbal and physical interventions. These programs teach self-defense moves and safe seclusion and restraint techniques; the most effective programs demonstrate specific moves and require the participants to practice them. Follow-up of such programs is encouraged, where social workers can review and practice the moves on a regular basis (Kleespies, 1998). There are specific laws and regulations regarding the use of seclusion and restraints; most settings have developed specific policies to comply with them.

If potentially violent clients are able to be calmed and the risk of violence is sufficiently reduced, social workers can then focus on the presenting problem and how to resolve it. If the risk remains dangerously high, hospitalization should be considered.

EXEMPLARY PROGRAM

Following an extensive survey of 69 communities, Stroul (1993, pp. 2–3) concluded that the most effective crisis response systems include the following: telephone services, walk-in crisis services, mobile crisis teams, crisis residential services, and acute psychiatric inpatient services. Montgomery County Emergency Service (MCES), an example of such a comprehensive facility, is considered a model program by the U.S. Department of Justice, the Law Enforcement Assistance Agency, and the Public Citizens Health Research Group. (The author is extremely grateful to John Stachowski, Bob Bond, and Eva Schwartz for providing helpful information about this exemplary program.)

MCES is a not-for-profit, freestanding psychiatric hospital and crisis intervention agency in Norristown, Pennsylvania, which focuses on providing a full range of services to the residents of Montgomery County who experience crises. Their crisis hotline is staffed by trained professionals 24 hours per day and provides information, referral, and support for callers. Walk-in service and emergency evaluations are provided in the Crisis Intervention Department, the emergency room of MCES, which is also the sole designated facility in the county to handle involuntary commitments. In the Crisis Intervention Department, clients meet with a crisis worker and a psychiatrist for a comprehensive assessment. If there are physical problems, these will be assessed by a physician assistant or the psychiatrist; clients may be referred to a local hospital for further evaluation or treatment of physical problems. Psychiatric problems may be referred to an MCES program or to outside services.

The Mobile Crisis Intervention Service provides outreach. Their staff members visit clients in crisis in the community who are at risk of hospitalization, and also provide follow-up to some clients who need assistance with medication, treatment, and navigating the system. Their own ambulance service provides transportation for behavioral emergencies, including both voluntary and involuntary clients. The ambulance staff is licensed and trained to handle both medical and behavioral emergencies. If clients need hospitalization, MCES has a 61-bed inpatient program, which provides the usual inpatient services, such as assessment, medication management, and group therapy. It also provides valuable programs that are not available in other facilities, such as patient education, family and marital therapy, family education and support groups, placement service, individual psychotherapy, drug and alcohol detoxification services, and dual diagnosis (substance abuse and mental illness) programs.

Their newly opened Crisis Residential Program is a short-term, voluntary treatment facility in a homelike setting for adults who are experiencing a psychiatric crisis. This program helps prevent hospitalization by temporarily separating clients from a stressful environment or situation and assisting them in achieving psychiatric stability. The Outpatient Program provides evaluation, consultation, counseling, psychotherapy, drug and alcohol counseling, medication follow-up, and referral for psychiatric and developmentally disabled clients. Individuals who have special language needs, including Spanish, Italian, French, Portuguese, Tagalog, Hindi, Yiddish, and Hungarian, can receive therapy there. MCES Forensic Services provides therapeutic services to clients involved in the criminal justice system, including on-site services at Montgomery County Correctional facility, and diversion from the Criminal Justice System into appropriate treatment. The staff also provides training for police officers, probation officers, parole officers, and correction staff, as well as consultation to the courts regarding issues of criminal responsibility and competency.

As would be expected, MCES employs a large staff of approximately 200 and serves a large number of clients. For example, in the month of December 1998, there were over 160 clients admitted for inpatient services, with an average length of stay of under 8 days. Staff members of the Crisis Intervention Department are provided with comprehensive training that combines 20 to 30 hours of didactic training with another 30 to 40 hours of experiential learning. Training consists of a wide range of information, from recognizing the signs and symptoms of increased agitation to specific Pennsylvania commitment laws. Staff members receive ongoing education and training during their employment.

MCES is an unusually comprehensive crisis response service, which encourages continuity of care and helps clients avoid "falling through the cracks." It should also be noted that MCES does not refuse service based on the ability to pay, an exceptional situation in today's financial climate.

UNIQUE CHALLENGES FOR CRISIS COUNSELORS

Crisis intervention is a challenging field in mental health. It requires all the clinical skills of assessment and counseling, combined with the ability to work under extraordinary time pressure. Life and death issues are often at stake, and there are no reliable formulas for determining such crucial factors as risk for suicide or risk for physical violence. In addition, there are legal issues, such as confidentiality and the duty to warn and protect, which must be balanced with the needs of the clients. The clients are often in great need of referrals and services, which are becoming more scarce every day. Professionals from any discipline would find crisis work challenging, and there is increasing evidence of burnout for many disciplines (Gilliland & James, 1997, pp. 553–598). Until recently, classroom training and field experiences for social workers did not prepare them for dealing with serious mental illness and for responding to suicidal or violent clients. In the past, social work training was also often psychodynamically oriented, with an emphasis on long-term counseling. That model is not particularly helpful in crisis work. However, there has been recent progress in training social workers in the techniques of brief treatment and in educating them to recognize and respond to symptoms of serious mental illness.

Social workers are also challenged in the crisis field with their inability to prescribe medications. When dealing with clients with major mental illness, it is often necessary to use quick-acting medications to help calm them, or to prescribe medications that will help prevent symptoms when taken on a regular basis. This challenge is shared by other professionals, of course, including counselors and psychologists (as of this writing), and makes it necessary to have access to a psychiatrist when working with certain crisis clients.

One of the main advantages that social workers bring to the field is that their traditional training has emphasized the need to "begin where the client is," which is a very useful orientation to crisis work. One of the main tasks of the social worker is to determine what the client is experiencing and what stresses and possible risks may exist. Another advantage is that many social workers have experience with referring clients to multiple community agencies for the variety of help they might need, which is often part of the problem solving that occurs in crises. Finally, social workers often have training and experience in working with families. In a crisis, families are often a significant source of helpful information and of support for clients. Being comfortable approaching families and having respect for their strengths is extremely useful in a crisis situation.

CASE EXAMPLE

Michele Jones is a 33-year-old woman who is the single parent of a 6-year-old son, Raymond. She works in the food service department of the local elementary school, where she has a strong record of reliability and good performance. She does not enjoy the work but feels that she needs the income and the health benefits offered by the job. She has received therapy from a social worker, Elaine Warren, for eight sessions at the community mental health center. Her presenting complaint was depression, and after a psychiatric evaluation, she was placed on a moderate dose of an antidepressant medication. In her weekly therapy sessions with Ms. Warren, she has been talking about her feelings of loneliness and about the frustrations and pressures of having sole responsibility for her son. She has few social supports, although her mother helps by babysitting for Raymond, and one friend, Iris, is described as a good listener. In the past two sessions, Ms. Jones reported that it was very helpful to have Ms. Warren to talk to and that her mood was improving.

At her ninth session, Ms. Jones focuses on financial problems, saying that her salary is barely adequate to meet her regular bills. She is particularly concerned because Christmas is approaching, and she has not been able to buy Raymond the video game he has been asking for. She is also upset that a recent boyfriend, Al, has just terminated their relationship. Ms. Warren helps Ms. Jones to do some problem solving about saving money for Christmas and explores her feelings about the loss of her relationship with Al. At the beginning of the session, Ms. Warren notices nothing unusual. However, as the session proceeds, she notices that Ms. Jones is less animated than usual, with a slightly flat expression, and she is sitting slightly hunched over in her chair. When her handbag drops on the floor, she takes an unusually long amount of time to pick it up. However, when asked about her mood, Ms. Jones denies that she has been feeling sad or depressed.

With 10 minutes left in the session, Ms. Jones says, "No wonder Al left me. I think everyone would be better off without me." Ms. Warren is concerned and pursues this statement, saying, "Tell me more about that, Ms. Jones." Ms. Jones at first laughs and says that she was "just kidding." Her laughter is not matched by any change in her flat expression. Ms. Warren continues by asking, "What did you mean when you said that everyone would be better off without you?" Ms. Jones replies that she thinks she's a bad parent to Raymond, that she's unattractive as a woman, and that her mother is very disappointed in her. At this point, Ms. Warren decides that she needs more time with Ms. Jones and makes arrangements for her next appointment, an intake interview, to be seen by another therapist.

Ms. Warren then asks, "Have you felt so bad about yourself that you thought about ending your life?" Ms. Jones hesitates, then says, "Not exactly." When Ms. Warren asks, "If 'not exactly,' how exactly?" Ms. Jones replies, "I have thought it would be better if I didn't wake up some morning." Ms. Warren then asks, "How strong are those thoughts?" She continues to ask questions that reveal that Ms. Jones has a plan for killing herself (taking an overdose of her antidepressant medication at bedtime after leaving her son at her mother's for an overnight visit). Ms. Jones also has the means for doing so (25 pills, stored in a container in the back of her spice cabinet), and she started to follow through with the plan last weekend but lost her resolve after she took two pills. As Ms. Warren is assessing the seriousness of Ms. Jones's risk of suicide, she is also thinking about what possible recommendations she might make and what time frame with which she has to deal.

After extensive discussion, Ms. Warren asks, "Do you think that you're going to follow through with your plan today?" Ms. Jones replies that she does not plan to take an overdose today. However, Ms. Warren continues by asking, "Would you be safe at home?" Although Ms. Jones says, "Yes," her tone is tentative and her expression remains bleak. In spite of Ms. Warren's efforts to help her identify her own positive attributes, Ms. Jones remains convinced that she is a bad parent, girlfriend, and daughter. She states that her son would be better off if his grandmother raised him. Ms. Warren then asks, "Do you think you would be safer in a hospital?" Ms. Jones hesitates, then says, "Maybe so. But who would take care of Raymond?"

At this point Ms. Warren helps Ms. Jones think of options regarding her responsibilities for Raymond. She assists Ms. Jones in calling her mother about child care. Her mother is upset and expresses strong concern about Ms. Jones's depression. She agrees to pick up Raymond from day care and to have him stay with her for the next several days. Ms. Jones prefers to wait to call her employer regarding a possible short-term absence.

With permission, Ms. Warren then calls Ms. Jones's insurance company, and she and Ms. Jones wait for a return call regarding approval for psychiatric evaluation. After half an hour, the insurance company representative calls back with approval but stipulates that Ms. Jones must be seen in the emergency room of one of two general hospitals with psychiatric wards that are approved providers for the company. Ms. Warren suggests the hospital that is closer to Ms. Jones's mother's home.

The next problem to be solved is transportation. Ms. Warren explores whether Ms. Jones can take the two buses required to get to the emergency room. Noting how confused Ms. Jones becomes with the directions, Ms. Warren suggests that they call her friend, Iris. Although Ms. Jones is at first reluctant to explain her situation to Iris, she eventually makes the phone call from Ms. Warren's office. Iris agrees to pick her up from the community mental health center and drive her to the emergency room.

As they wait for Iris, Ms. Warren asks for permission to call ahead to the emergency room. Ms. Jones agrees and listens while Ms. Warren briefly explains when Ms. Jones will be arriving and the reason for the evaluation. As they continue to wait for Iris, Ms. Warren praises Ms. Jones for her decision and talks in a very optimistic manner about the benefit of hospitalization. She also talks about looking forward to working with her again as soon as possible and making more progress on some of the stressors in her life. When Iris arrives, Ms. Warren thanks her for her help and asks Ms. Jones to call as soon as she has been evaluated for hospitalization.

At the emergency room, Iris waits with Ms. Jones. After a few minutes, they see a triage nurse who has been informed of Ms. Warren's phone call. They then wait for 30 minutes for a designated staff member from the psychiatric unit to come to the emergency room to evaluate Ms. Jones. After Ms. Jones describes her feelings and her suicidal plans, the staff member recommends admission and calls the doctor on the psychiatric ward to begin the procedure for admission. Ms. Jones calls Ms. Warren from the psychiatric unit. Ms. Warren expresses encouragement and tells her she will call daily during her hospitalization.

Ms. Jones is hospitalized for five days and receives group and individual therapy and an adjustment of her medication. Her group is conducted by a social worker, and she sees another social worker to make aftercare plans, which include discussion on how to access emergency services if her suicidal feelings return and plans for outpatient follow-up with Ms. Warren. Ms. Warren is contacted regarding the discharge and follow-up recommendations.

Ms. Jones does not call Ms. Warren to schedule a follow-up visit as planned. Ms. Warren therefore calls her and suggests setting up an appointment after work the next day. Ms. Jones states, "I'm fine now; I don't need any more help." With encouragement, however, she agrees to "just one visit." At the session, Ms. Warren begins to work with Ms. Jones on building a wider support network, including membership in Parents Without Partners and a parenting class at the YMCA. She also talks about agencies that donate toys for children at Christmas, which Ms. Jones might use for Raymond. Furthermore, she tells Ms. Jones of plans for future sessions focusing on stress management, particularly how to recognize she is under stress and how to maintain her mood when she is stressed. Ms. Jones agrees to one more visit.

SUMMARY

Crisis counseling is a fast-paced and stressful field that challenges social workers to use a wide range of skills with a wide range of clients. However, it is also an exciting and rewarding field. In the words of an experienced crisis worker, "In crisis intervention, you are directly helping people when they need it most. You're always aware that the work you are doing is important and meaningful. And it's different every day, never dull. It's not predictable, but that means it's always interesting and fresh" (E. Schwartz, personal communication, 1999).

KEY TERMS

Crisis: The perception of an event or situation as a difficulty that exceeds the individual's resources, coping abilities, or both.

Emergency: A crisis that includes an imminent risk of harm to the individual or to someone else, including suicidal or violent behavior.

Mental Status Exam (MSE): A systematic series of questions and objective observations that give a comprehensive view of someone's mental state.

Risk factors: Characteristics that are associated with a higher probability of a specific event occurring.

Suicide: The act of intentionally killing oneself.

Trauma: An emotional shock that creates damage to the psychological development or psychological health of the individual.

Violence: Physical force exerted for the purpose of hurting other people or stopping them from their course of action.

WEB RESOURCES

American Association of Suicidology (http://www.suicidology.org/). AAS provides relevant research and statistics concerning suicide and the risk factors associated with suicidal ideation and behavior.

International Critical Incident Stress Foundation, Inc. (http://www.icisf.org/). OCISF addresses the problems of persons who have experienced a traumatic event.

U.S. Department of Justice, Violence Against Women (http://www.ojp.usdoj.gov/vawo/). The U.S. Department of Justice offers a range of information concerning the widespread problem of violence against women.

National Institute of Mental Health (http://www.nimh.nih.gov/home.cfm). NIMH provides extensive information about the

symptoms of mental illness, recommended treatment, and current research.
Centers for Disease Control and Prevention Site (http://www.cdc.gov). This site provides up-to-date information about the numbers of persons diagnosed with physical and mental illnesses and includes statistics about suicide and violence.

REFERENCES

Aguilera, D. (1994). *Crisis intervention: Theory and methodology* (7th ed.). St. Louis: Mosby.

Callahan, J. (1998). Crisis theory and crisis intervention. In P. Kleespies (Ed.), *Emergencies in mental health practice: Evaluation and management* (pp. 22–40). New York: Guilford.

Clark, D. (1998). The evaluation and management of the suicidal patient. In P. Kleespies (Ed.), *Emergencies in mental health practice: Evaluation and management* (pp. 75–94). New York: Guilford.

Copeland, M. (1992). *The depression workbook: A guide to living with depression and manic-depression.* Oakland, CA: New Harbinger.

Delaware Psychiatric Center's PEACE manual (1998). New Castle, DE: Training Department of Delaware Psychiatric Center.

Eddy, S., & Harris, E. (1998). Risk management with the violent patient. In P. Kleespies (Ed.), *Emergencies in mental health practice: Evaluation and management* (pp. 217–231). New York: Guilford.

Ell, K. (1995). Crisis intervention: Research needs. In R. Edwards & J. Hopps (Eds.), *Encyclopedia of social work* (19th ed., Vol. 1). Washington, DC: NASW Press.

Gilliland, B., & James, R. (1993). *Crisis intervention strategies* (2nd ed.). Pacific Grove, CA: Brooks/Cole.

Gilliland, B., & James, R. (1997). *Crisis intervention strategies* (3rd ed.). Pacific Grove, CA: Brooks/Cole.

Golan, N. (1978). *Treatment in crisis situations.* New York: Free Press.

Jamison, K. R. (1995). *An unquiet mind: A memoir of moods and madness.* New York: Knopf.

Janosik, E. (1994). *Crisis counseling: A contemporary approach* (2nd ed.). Boston: Jones & Bartlett.

Kaplan, H., & Sadock, B. (1993). *Pocket handbook of emergency psychiatric medicine.* Baltimore: Williams & Wilkins.

Kaplan, H., & Sadock, B. (1995). *Comprehensive textbook of psychiatry* (6th ed.). Baltimore: Williams & Wilkins.

Keefe, R., & Harvey, P. (1994). *Understanding schizophrenia: A guide to the new research on causes and treatment.* New York: Free Press.

Kleespies, P. (Ed.). (1998a). *Emergencies in mental health practice: Evaluation and management.* New York: Guilford.

Kleespies, P. (1998b). The domain of psychological emergencies: An overview. In P. Kleespies (Ed.), *Emergencies in mental health practice: Evaluation and management* (pp. 9–21). New York: Guilford.

Kleespies, P., Deleppo, J., Mori, D., & Niles, B. (1998). The emergency interview. In P. Kleespies (Ed.), *Emergencies in mental health practice: Evaluation and management* (pp. 41–72). New York: Guilford.

Kreisman, J., & Straus, H. (1989). *I hate you: Don't leave me.* New York: Avon.

Linehan, M. (1993). *Cognitive-behavioral treatment of borderline personality disorder.* New York: Guilford.

Link, B., Cullen, F., & Andrews, H. (1992). The violent and illegal behavior of mental patients reconsidered. *American Sociological Review, 57,* 275–292.

Marlatt, G., & Gordon, J. (Eds.). *Relapse prevention: Maintenance strategies in the treatment of addictive behaviors.* New York: Guilford.

Mason, P., & Kreger, R. (1998). *Stop walking on eggshells: Taking your life back when someone you care about has borderline personality disorder.* Oakland, CA: New Harbinger.

McNiel, D. (1998). Empirically based clinical evaluation and management of the potentially violent patient. In P. Kleespies (Ed.), *Emergencies in mental health practice: Evaluation and management* (pp. 95–116). New York: Guilford.

Miklowitz, D., & Goldstein, M. (1997). *Bipolar disorder: A family-focused treatment approach.* New York: Guilford.

Mondimore, F. (1999). *Bipolar disorder: A guide for patients and families.* Baltimore: Johns Hopkins University Press.

Mueser, K., & Gingerich, S. (1994). *Coping with schizophrenia: A guide for families.* Oakland, CA: New Harbinger.

Mueser, K., & Glynn, S. M. (1999). *Behavioral family therapy for psychiatric disorders.* Oakland, CA: New Harbinger.

Papolos, D., & Papolos, J. (1992). *Overcoming depression* (Rev. ed.). New York: Harper Collins.

Puryear, D. (1979). *Helping people in crisis.* San Francisco: Jossey-Bass.

Roberts, A. (Ed.). (1996). *Crisis management and brief treatment: Theory, technique, and applications.* Chicago: Nelson-Hall.

Sheehan, S. (1982). *Is there no place on earth for me?* New York: Vintage Books.

Slaikeu, K. (1990). *Crisis intervention: A handbook for practice and research* (2nd ed.). Boston: Allyn & Bacon.

Social workers outnumber other mental health professionals. (1999). *NAMI Advocate 21*(2), 1.

Stroul, B. (1993). *Psychiatric crisis response systems: A descriptive study.* Rockville, MD: Center for Mental Health Services/Substance Abuse and Mental Health Services Administration.

Torrey, F. (1995). *Surviving schizophrenia: A manual for families, consumers, and providers.* New York: Harper Perennial.

Weiden, P., Scheifler, P., Diamond, R., & Ross, R. (1999). *Breakthroughs in antipsychotic medications: A guide for consumers, families, and clinicians.* New York: W.W. Norton.

Wheeler, W. (Producer). (1996). *I'm still here: The truth about schizophrenia* (Film). Honeoye, NY: Wheeler Communications Group.

Woolis, R. (1992). *When someone you love has a mental illness: A handbook for family, friends, and caregivers.* New York: Jeremy P. Tarcher/Perigee Books.

Wyatt, R. (1992). *Practical psychiatric practice: Forms and protocols for clinical use.* Washington, DC: American Psychiatric Press.

SOCIAL WORKERS AS DIAGNOSTICIANS

Jaclyn Miller

In preparing to write Chapter 3, I asked a number of students and former students in mental health practice settings what would be helpful to them in a chapter on social work diagnosis. The answers were deceptively simple, which mirrors the subject itself. First, they said it was important to be explicit about the fact that diagnosis is not a simplistic process. It is not just "filling in the blanks," and it does not follow a linear pattern of "if this . . . then that." Second, and related, was a plea for inclusion of sociocultural factors and how they might influence diagnosis. Third, they requested case examples that do not easily fit into a single diagnostic category. Their impression was that case material in most textbooks present full-blown examples of mental illnesses, whereas the clients these social workers see present complex qualities and traits of more than one diagnosis. It is this complexity that often becomes the real work in case management, therapy, and crisis interventions, all of which focus specifically on behaviors related to overall social functioning and maintenance in the community.

In the material that follows, I consider these comments as I focus specifically on the role of social worker as diagnostician. The main purpose of this book is to prepare social workers to work with persons, families, and others in their social surroundings who are experiencing the multiple sequelae of mental illness. Therefore, I will be writing about diagnosis per se, as it is delineated in the American Psychiatric Association's *Diagnostic and Statistical Manual of Mental Disorders (DSM)*, of which the most recent revision is the *DSM-IV-TR* (APA, 2000). I assert that these diagnoses, defined by the *DSM* (particularly on Axis I), for good or ill at this time in our society, define the threshold for entry into the public and private mental health service delivery systems. Such diagnoses are the keys to accessing resources, such as community mental health center programs, clubhouses, psychotropic medications, public disability benefits, and rehabilitation programs, as

---

I am appreciative of the continued dialogue with my colleague Dr. Mary Katherine O'Connor, that deepens and clarifies every project, including this chapter.

well as coverage under public and private insurance programs and significant public policies such as the Americans with Disabilities Act. In addition, the *DSM* is the language spoken by professionals when the problem at hand is an experience with a mental illness. The outside world requires that we be conversant in the language of behavioral health, or as Kutchins and Kirk (1988) call it, the "business of diagnosis" while attending to the experience of our clients. As social work diagnosticians, we must be Janus-like, with one face toward the outside world and one toward the inner and interpersonal world of the person with whom we are working.

The word *diagnosis* is from the Greek, meaning "to distinguish, discern, to learn to know, perceive" (*Oxford Dictionary*, p. 596). However, more commonly assumed meanings come from the term's use in medicine, the "determination of the nature of a diseased condition; identification of a disease by careful investigation of its symptoms and history," or its use in biology, "distinctive characterization in precise terms" (*Oxford Dictionary*, p. 596). Barker, writing in the *National Association of Social Workers (NASW) Dictionary* (1999), defines diagnosis as the "process of identifying a problem (social and mental, as well as medical) and its underlying causes and formulating a solution" (p. 127). He notes the strong medical implications of the word *diagnosis* and recognizes that because of this association, many social workers prefer the term *assessment*.

One expression of the profession's continuing ambivalence about the appropriateness and usefulness of diagnosis in our practice can be found in our attempts to distinguish diagnosis from assessment and to stake out a unique position for social work's approach to assessment. Kirk and Kutchins's (1988) statement is an example of this, "[S]ocial work distinguishes itself as a profession in part through its approach to the assessment of clients and their problems" (p. 295). This approach is usually described as being multifaceted, client-in-situation centered, focused on problems in living, and as nonpathologizing. Historically, this diagnosis-assessment differentiation debate emerged from the very bedrock of social work's struggle to develop into a full-fledged profession and to be recognized as such (Rodwell, 1987). There is probably no document more frequently cited than Abraham Flexner's (1915) speech, in which he is reputed to have arrived at the conclusion that social work was not a profession. The gauntlet consisted of defining characteristics of a profession, and being "scientific" was one of those hallmarks to which social work aspired. One element of a scientific approach to professional practice was the medical model of solving patient's problems: study, diagnosis, and treatment. That social work wanted to emulate this rigor can be seen in Mary Richmond's (1917) introduction of the term *social diagnosis*. Her goal was to distinguish social work diagnosis, with our focus on the social and psychological aspects of human experience, while providing a recognizable framework for scientific rigor.

Assessment, then, is seen as an ongoing process, using different tools at different points in our work and based on the different professional roles in which we operate. *Assessment* and *diagnosis* are not interchangeable terms, even though they often have been used interchangeably in the social work literature (Goldstein, 1995;

Hepworth, Rooney, & Larson, 1997; Kirk, Siporin, & Kutchins, 1989; Rauch, 1993; Turner, 1994; Woods & Hollis, 2000). Although there are overlaps in the dictionary definitions of these terms and commonalities in many of the skills required for each of these tasks (e.g., professional judgment, information-processing ability, and critical thinking), *assessment* is the term that describes a broader process. Specifically, in social work practice in mental health, the process of assessment surrounds the diagnosis and informs it. Assessment is ongoing and provides both continuous feedback about the accuracy, usefulness, and relevance of the diagnosis, as well as continuous data and feedback to guide the goal-directed work of the helping partnership.

For present purposes, because our focus is on understanding the category of human experience called mental illness, arriving at and fully understanding the meaning of a *DSM* diagnosis per se is a pivotal step in our professional work. As we shall see in the next section of this chapter, a holistic and interactional, biopsychosocial framework for understanding the etiology and management of mental illness is currently endorsed by most research and most mental health care professionals. This framework, so familiar to social work, appears in the conceptualization of the social work diagnostic process in Figure 3.1. The top of the hourglass represents the current biopsychosocial multicausal perspective of mental illnesses. These categories of causal and explanatory biospsychosocial variables become the data sources for the material of a diagnostic study. This part of the process is variously referred to in the social work literature as biopsychosocial history taking, biopsychosocial assessment, or the diagnostic study process (Goldstein, 1995; Jordan & Franklin, 1995; Rauch, 1993). In mental health practice, this part of the process provides the information for making a diagnosis using the *DSM*—the funnel part of the hourglass. Following the determination of the diagnosis, the hourglass widens again and becomes the ongoing biopsychosocial, multifactorial assessment process, which in turn becomes the information source for our work with our clients. The ongoing assessment, using the diagnosis as an information organizer, provides direction for our collaborative work with our clients (e.g., what our target goals and desired outcomes are, what our interventions may be), and aids in determining the accuracy and usefulness of the diagnosis itself.

A critical question regarding diagnosis in social work practice is, diagnosis for what? The role of diagnosis may be different for the various social work roles discussed in this book. For example, a crisis counselor, therapist, and supervisor will, at times, use diagnosis as a first step in planning appropriate interventions, based on the research available regarding differential effectiveness of such strategies. A case manager, interdisciplinary team member, skills trainer, and medication manager will need to be extremely knowledgeable about diagnostic categories as a way of attending to clients' symptoms, intended and unintended medication effects, and adaptive challenges.

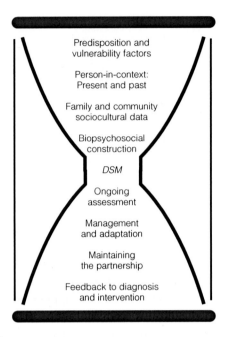

Predisposition and
vulnerability factors

Person-in-context:
Present and past

Family and community
sociocultural data

Biopsychosocial
construction

DSM

Ongoing
assessment

Management
and adaptation

Maintaining
the partnership

Feedback to diagnosis
and intervention

FIGURE **3.1**

The practice of diagnosis.

THE INTELLECTUAL BASE OF THE DIAGNOSIS AND THE DIAGNOSTIC PROCESS

What knowledge do we need to complete a diagnosis as previously described? In general, the knowledge base of social work practice has to be large enough to be inclusive of the range of roles in which we engage with our clients. Therefore, we must draw from many social and behavioral sciences, from practice experience, and from the research of many disciplines, including our own. For the social work diagnostician, the intellectual base in the diagnostic process proposed in this chapter is composed of four elements. The first element is the biopsychosocial, person-in-environment holistic, an interactive perspective that informs our increasing appreciation of the complexity of the etiology of mental illness. The *DSM* is the second element. It provides a mechanism, a model for processing information, through which we funnel this biopsychosocial data. It is a useful tool for capturing the complexity of the entity or phenomenon we are describing and collapsing the multifaceted nature of the relevant variables into descriptive categories called diagnoses. The third and fourth elements emerge from research on clinical judgment/human decision making and from cross-cultural studies on psychopathology and illness, respectively. From these elements of our intellectual base, we discover some unique challenges to our ability to manage the data from the first two elements in meaningful and useful ways in our practice.

The First Element: The Biopsychosocial Perspective

The strength of an interactive, biopsychosocial approach to understanding mental illness, etiologically as well as conceptually, has ascended and has been supported in the very recent literature of a number of mental health disciplines (Kiesler, 1999; Ross & Pam, 1995; Valenstein, 1998). This, however, is not the first time such a perspective has been advanced as the most effective way of understanding and treating mental illnesses.

In the 1950s, the psychiatrist Adolph Meyer (1957) proposed a psychobiological life history approach to mental disorder, in which psychosocial stressors were seen as important in understanding each individual patient's mental illness. Meyer also felt that individuals could not be fitted into simple classifications, nor could they be treated except as whole human beings. In the late 1970s, Engel (1978, 1980), a physician practicing in both medicine and psychiatry, proposed an interactive systems model for medical education that encouraged the study of the natural interactions of biological, psychological, and social factors that determine a physical disorder in each person. Further critiques of simple biomedical explanations of mental illness, particularly schizophrenia, also came in the 1960s and 1970s in the form of diathesis-stress (Meehl, 1962) and vulnerability-stress models (Neuchterlein & Dawson, 1984; Zubin & Spring, 1977). Diathesis refers to an inherited or constitutional predisposition to a mental illness. It is proposed that this predisposition can lower an individual's reactive threshold to life stressors that can then trigger a mental illness such as schizophrenia. Extending this model further results in the position that what is chronic about mental illness is not the illness itself, but the predispositional vulnerability to such an illness.

If the vulnerability to psychosocial/environmental stressors is biological, what do we know about what constitutes the significant psychosocial stressors? This aspect of the biopsychosocial knowledge base of mental illness has been expanded through research as well, and the actual concept of the interactive nature of vulnerability and protective factors has continued to help researchers shed light on mental illness. In 1995, the National Advisory Mental Health Council reported to the U.S. Congress that empirical research had identified a number of risk factors for mental illness, all of which are related to socioeconomic status, minority race and ethnicity, and other psychosocial factors such as chronic and acute stress, lack of social supports, hopelessness and alienation, or instability in the social-interpersonal environment. While hereditary influence continues to be included in the category of vulnerabilities, others include lower socioeconomic status, family instability, and gender and ethnicity (American Psychological Society Task Force, 1996; Belle, 1990; Dohrenwend, 1990; Kiesler, 1999; Valenstein, 1998). Through research on "stress-resistant" children, we understand protective factors to include such psychological and social factors as family cohesion, support from extended family members, higher socioeconomic status, higher general intelligence and self-esteem, and individual and systemic external supports that encourage the child's efforts to cope and function (Shapiro, Friedman, Meyer, & Loftus, 1996).

In a groundbreaking book, the interpersonal psychologist, Donald J. Kiesler (1999), makes an important contribution to the development of this line of thinking through a rigorous, comprehensive, and critical review of the extant research and writing on the biomedical model of mental disorder. The main thesis of his book is that reliance on a model of "monocausation needs desperately to be abandoned . . . available evidence makes it clear that most of the major psychiatric disorders are etiologically heterogeneous" (p. 11). Kiesler summarizes the relevant scientific findings into a list of "unavoidable conclusions for the twenty-first century" (p. 83). These conclusions have direct implications for our work as social work diagnosticians: (1) there is no single biomedical starting point for any mental disorder—in fact, the extant scientific genetic evidence overwhelmingly contradicts any monocausal theory of psychopathology; (2) mental disorders do not meet the defining conditions to be classified as a biological disease; (3) people do not inherit mental disorders, however, when genetic factors are present, they create a likely predisposition; (4) in virtually all cases of mental disorder, both genes and environment contribute substantially; (5) for the majority of mental disorders, multiple genes (in the form of predisposition) interact with multiple environmental events to shape particular disorder experienced; (6) common-shared family environment is minimally associated with subsequent onset of a specific mental disorder; (7) unique-unshared environments experienced by individuals in the same family are more likely to be significant causal influences for mental disorders (pp. 83–84).

The paradigm shift from models of monocausation-monoexplanation to more complex, dynamic approaches of understanding human health phenomena is not limited to the realm of mental illness or to these professions. Beginning as early as 1917, with Mary Richmond's work explicating social diagnosis, the social work profession has espoused a number of theoretical perspectives and models of intervention. They each have as their common denominator this same complex, inclusive, and interactive approach to understanding and intervening in human problems, usually written about as the biopsychosocial perspective (Germain & Gitterman, 1980; Goldstein, 1995; Hepworth, Rooney, & Larsen, 1997; Turner, 1996; Woods & Hollis, 2000).

Following a similar line of thought, Kleinman (1995), a physician and anthropologist who has done extensive writing on cross-cultural medicine, has critiqued the simple biomedical model of any illness for "leaving the experience of suffering out of assessment of the disease" (p. 100). The individually lived human experience of suffering is yet another aspect of the biopsychosocial perspective. What is particularly interesting about Kleinman's critique is that he applies it to any imbalanced explanation of disorder or disease. He criticizes the medicalization, as well as the anthropolization of these experiences of distress: "[W]hat is lost in biomedical renditions—the complexity, uncertainty, and ordinariness of some man or woman's world of experience—is also missing when illness is reinterpreted as social role, social strategy, or social symbol . . . as anything but human experience" (p. 96).

In summary, social workers must use a biopsychosocial knowledge base and perspective to continually formulate, check, and reformulate interpretations and explanations of an experience of mental illness. Whether or not a diagnosed mental illness even presents a problem for an individual, the degree to which it is a problem, and the exact expressions of the problem in terms of social functioning, are variable enough for us to consider them social constructions. What this means is that an individual's experience of distress or dysfunction and her or his explanation of that distress must be viewed, at a minimum, with bicultural sensitivity, with that of the dominant American culture and that of the individual or family within their unique culture. The *DSM*, however, is a definitional funnel for experiences of human distress known as mental illness, and as such, provides a common language, a starting-point, and a tool for the differential access to services and resources.

The Second Element: The DSM

The current *DSM*'s lineage reaches back to 1952, when the American Psychiatric Association Committee on Nomenclature and Statistics produced the *DSM-I*, primarily in response to a need for a uniform framework within which to collect statistical information on mental disorders in the United States. *DSM-I* was designed to be useful primarily as a clinical tool. Adolph Meyer's psychobiological understanding of mental disorders, particularly his view that "mental disorders represented reactions of the personality to psychological, social, and biological factors" (*DSM-IV*, APA, 1994, p. xvii), provided a conceptual base. As a result of his work, the term *reaction* can be found in the definitions and descriptions of disorders throughout the first classification system. A reaction implies an interactive process that recognizes that variables external to the individual, such as those in the sociocultural environment, are as important in understanding and treating mental illness as are those internal to the individual. This Meyer-inspired view of mental disorders was eliminated in the *DSM-II*, as was the use of the term *reaction*. The significant changes made in the *DSM-III* included more explicit diagnostic criteria, a multiaxial system of classification, and a descriptive approach to symptom clusters and diagnoses that were designed to be theory-free. Further revisions were made in specific diagnosis work groups to further clarify diagnostic criteria in the *DSM-III*. This work produced the *DSM-III-R*.

The revisions in the *DSM-IV* were made through a process that relied more on empirical literature and data from field trials using the *DSM-III*. It is fully compatible with the ninth revision of the *International Classification of Diseases (ICD-9)*, published by the World Health Organization (Kaplan & Sadock, 1998). The *DSM-IV* is atheoretical, does not attempt to explain causation, and focuses specifically on how each disorder is manifested, descriptively, through its unique composite of clinical features. These descriptive clinical features translate into specific diagnostic criteria, many of which are behaviorally specific, that must be present for the diagnosis to be made. The *DSM-IV* delineates additional relevant information on each diagnostic category to further assist the clinician in the diagnostic process. Such background information can include what is known about the relationship of variables to each diagnostic category (e.g., age, culture- or gender-related features, predisposing factors and familial patterns, and differential risk, as well as common differential diagnoses to be considered). The following is the specific definition of a mental disorder framing the entire work of the *DSM-IV* (APA, 1994):

> A significant psychological syndrome or behavioral pattern that occurs within a person and that is accompanied by (a) distress, as reported by the person, (b) disability in an important area of functioning, or (c) considerable risk of death, pain, disability, or loss of freedom . . . and may be considered an expression of a behavioral, psychological, or biological dysfunction "in the person." (p. 5)

The *DSM-IV* (APA, 1994) recognizes the use of the term *mental disorder* is problematic and that, among other things, it implies a continued adherence to a false dichotomization of mind and body. The writers of the document also warrant that "no definition adequately specifies precise boundaries for the concept of 'mental disorder,'" and that, while many indicators for each disorder have been identified, no single one is "equivalent to the concept" (p. xxi). In addition, syndromes or behavioral patterns should not be considered disorders if they are expectable and culturally sanctioned responses to a particular event, such as the death of a loved one. Whatever the original source, the configuration of descriptors must be considered the manifestation of a behavioral, psychological, and/or biological dysfunction in the individual. The manual also contains the following statements about how the classification system is intended to be used and not used: deviant behavior and conflicts between individuals and society per se are not to be classified as dysfunctions in the *DSM-IV;* the system does not classify people, but disorders, and avoids such labeling language in the text (e.g., not "a schizophrenic," rather, "an individual with schizophrenia"). *DSM-IV* categories are like the average size suit one finds on the a rack: they fit no one exactly, and no one should be made to fit them (*DSM-IV,* APA, 1994, p. 1). This is where experience and the art involved in diagnosis and clinical judgment contribute to the process. Although these caveats may not obviate other criticisms of the *DSM-IV* (related to increasing numbers and kinds of human behaviors being included as disorders), they do caution us to attend carefully to whether it is the text itself that is biased and stigmatizing or its implementation and interpretation by those who use it.

In all our professional partnerships, we must work to combine clinical astuteness and interpersonal sensitivity with our awareness of human diversity and cultural variability. This is a useful strategy for decreasing the likelihood we will use powerful professional tools, such as the *DSM*, in biased ways. This more complex approach to the diagnostic process can also counteract the potential for using diagnoses as stigmatizing, dehumanizing labels. To accomplish this, we need to incorporate the findings from research on cross-cultural understanding of psychopathology (Draguns, 1995).

The Third Element: Different Ways of Knowing

How do we know what to call psychopathology? What behaviors do we refer to as a mental illness? There are two diametrically opposed approaches to learning about and explaining what groups of behaviors are called mental illnesses. These two approaches are different ways of knowing about phenomena: universalist or relativist. Universalist approaches look at and for those aspects or elements of illnesses that are objective and comparable across cultures, also taking the position that basic syndromes of mental disorders are essentially the same from one period of time, geographic location, or culture, to another. This is referred to as an *etic* approach to learning about and knowing phenomena. The relativist approach is quite the opposite, taking the position that there is "complete cultural plasticity of abnormal manifestations, expressions and experiences" (Draguns, 1995, p. 80) of human behavior. This is the *emic* approach to knowing, which investigates what is culturally indigenous, personally unique, and not universal. Rodwell (1998) defines emic approaches to data gathering as those that provide an insider's view of a phenomenon. The insider's view is the window to understanding the world and/or specific phenomena from the perspective of those who are involved in the situation, while the etic approaches provide "an outsider's perspective"(p. 256). In the study domain of cross-cultural mental illness and psychopathology, there is very little empirical support for either of these extreme positions; however, each contribute unique insights to understanding the phenomena of mental illness, and thus to the diagnostic process.

Kleinman's (1988) cross-cultural study of medicine and illness is congruent with the findings on psychopathology. Kleinman's work leads him to the position that, "[I]f there is no purely 'natural' cause of a disease, there also can be no purely 'cultural symptomatology'" (p. 101). Pure, unidimensional explanations do not hold for physical or for mental illness. Kleinman strongly suggests we make the most of the enlightening information available to us as helping professionals. He suggests we move our focus back and forth constantly between what we learn from abstract universalizing processes (our etic knowledge, such as our classification schemes and diagnostic categories), and what he calls the "particularizing content of ethnopsychological meanings" (p. 99), or our emic knowledge.

Draguns's (1995) summary of cross-cultural research on mental illnesses demonstrates that, while no disorder is free of some degree of "cultural shaping," none of the major mental illnesses that have been studied across cultures can be entirely explained by cultural or social variables. Research has demonstrated that schizophrenia and other such severe mental disorders are shaped less by cultural factors than disorders that are less socially and psychologically disabling. Similarly, cross-cultural studies have demonstrated that the differential expression of major depression is more shaped by cultural features than is schizophrenia (Biafora, 1995; Egeland et al., 1983; Good, 1993). Such differences can also be seen in the varying patterns, by gender, of the behavioral expression of depression in our western culture (e.g., more acting-out types of behaviors in males and more sadness, crying, and slowed motor activity in females). Overall, cultural differences appear more in the expression of signs and symptoms than in syndromes. Signs are what we, as clinicians, objectively observe in our clients; symptoms are those subjective experiences our clients describe to us when telling us what is bothering them; and syndromes are known conditions, made up of a number and configuration of signs and symptoms (Kaplan & Sadock, 1998, p. 275). As Draguns (1995) notes, symptoms reflect the "social, technological, religious and other features of their societies" (p. 87). This same process of social shaping also affects diagnosticians' perceptions and thus their judgments about the signs and symptoms that are presented to them.

As one way of recognizing the interplay of culture, behavior, and the determination of what is mental disorder, a number of culturally bound psychotic syndromes have been delineated in frequently referenced psychiatric texts (APA, 1994; Kaplan & Sadock, 1998).[1] The affects and behaviors exhibited in each of these syndromes are diagnostic clinical features that can be found in the *DSM* as evidence of a mental disorder, but these same behaviors are elsewhere described as culturally syntonic, and as expected and accepted expressions of human distress in different cultural contexts.

The work of Javier et al. (1995) points to this same phenomenon in a somewhat different way. They demonstrated that particular behaviors, or symptoms, are given a diagnosis (rendered understandable through categorization) or not, depending on the framework used by the person who is trying to make sense of the presented problem. Human beings are pattern seekers and meaning-makers. We search for patterns and regularities through our own observations and experiences as one way to understand our world. Patterns and regularities imply predictability and stability. Predictability and stability reduce the anxiety we might otherwise experience in the face of uncertainty about a phenomenon that we feel we need to understand. Sometimes, naming these patterns makes people feel understood and safer (Wetzel, 1991). For example, our reference points for health and illness, for normal and abnormal, often are not explicitly in our awareness, and yet we use them as tacit measures in making sense of clinical information we observe or have elicited from our clients. By understanding these implicit cognitive tools, we can unravel why African Americans and other people of color, often referred to as minority groups, are diagnosed with more severe mental illnesses in comparison with Caucasians, and how they also come to be an overrepresented population in mental health institutions (Dawson, 1986). Perhaps these tools will also help us understand why gender has been found to predict significant differences in types of diagnoses given to men and to women. We may also understand the differential success of various interventions when no gender difference has been found in the likelihood of experiencing a mental illness (Kessler et al., 1994).

Maintaining a professionally skeptical attitude about our diagnostic tools and toward the diagnostic process, even as we engage in it, is thus essential in our professional work. Indeed, there is extant practice literature on cross-cultural, diversity-sensitive, and culturally competent mental health practice (cf. Devore &

---

[1]*Amok:* Found in Southeast Asia and Malaysia. Occurs in males. Consists of sudden violent homicidal or suicidal rampage that ends in exhaustion and amnesia; *Hi-Wa itck:* Mohave American Indian. Unwanted separation from loved one can trigger anorexia, insomnia, depression, and even suicide (Kaplan and Sadock, 1998, p. 499).

Schlesinger, 1994; Green, 1995; Jayasuriya, 1992; Lum, 1996). These various practice models, approaches, and techniques are all based on at least tacit acceptance of the validity and reliability of both etic and emic ways of knowing and the recognition that information-processing biases do operate. Although it may not be comforting to those on the receiving end of such biases, "prejudiced people stereotype, but people who stereotype are not necessarily prejudiced" (Ridley, 1989, p. 95). As we have seen, bias can result from information-processing errors as well as lack of knowledge or prejudice. Empathy counteracts stereotyping, and empathy increases as social distance between different groups (e.g., ethnic, age, gender, ability, sexual orientation) decreases. What we need to know more about is how to recognize our biases and how to promote more effective and realistic modes of processing the vast array of information we must integrate to arrive at a mental health diagnosis.

The Fourth Element: Clinical Judgment and Decision Making

The social work profession defines its mission in terms of solving complex social problems. Certainly, the experience of mental illness can be placed in this category: a complex social and personal problem. By definition, complex problem-solving situations are characterized by high levels of uncertainty. As we have seen, the diagnosis of a mental disorder involves a vast number of variables that are not related in a formulaic pattern and are not easily predicted to co-occur, nor do they submit to simple post hoc modeling once they do emerge. Such a situation of uncertainty and complexity directly mirrors the vast complexity of information that surrounds the phenomena. We, as professional social workers, are required to use our clinical judgment and make critical decisions as we access the information we need in making a diagnosis.

What do we know about how effective our clinical judgment and decision making are during the specific task of making a diagnosis? We do know that the validity and reliability of clinical diagnosis as an information-processing task has been of longstanding concern in the helping professions (Bieri et al., 1966). To develop counter strategies for increasing professionals' judgment abilities, research has been applied in a number of disciplines concerned with human judgment and decision making to try to uncover specific weaknesses. For example, little, if any, evidence exists that experienced, so-called "expert," professionals do better on clinical judgment tasks than do beginning professionals (Dawes, Faust, & Meehl, 1989; Faust, 1986).

Data integration is arguably the most critical functional element of the clinical diagnostic process, yet research undertaken to maximize accuracy in diagnosis has found data integration to be the weakest element in the overall process. Because effective treatment is said to follow from an accurate diagnosis, even in social work (Turner, 1994), knowing the skills and processes that contribute to better clinical judgment is highly salient for our profession. Faust's (1986) work focused on the application of human judgment to clinical practice, a professional decision-making domain he recognized as having an almost limitless universe of potentially available and useful information about its subjects (p. 423). He described the process for managing such a vast data source in the following way: first, decide which information is most relevant; next, decide how to access it; then, think carefully about how to integrate what you elicit and collect; and finally, decide how it all relates to "what are often nebulous and ill-defined categories" (p. 423), such as diagnoses. Other approaches to studying data integration emerged with similar results. For example, in studies that have been conducted, mechanical models of data integration, such as assessment tools, always outperformed clinical methods (i.e., engaging the individual clinician directly in assessing information and making a judgment). In other studies, practitioners who were given only client demographic data performed as well in making a diagnosis as did those who based their diagnosis on a complete psychosocial history and a series of diagnostic tests (Dawes, Faust, & Meehl, 1989; Faust, 1986). Why is this so? And if we know why this is so, are there implications for the development of strategies to enhance our performance as social work diagnosticians?

Tversky and Kahneman (1974), psychologists who have studied human judgment and decision making under conditions of uncertainty, have found that people engage in a number of unconscious cognitive strategies, called *heuristics*, as they make judgments or decisions using available information. Their major position in undertaking this research was that people's decisions in situations of uncertainty or risk did not mirror the then prevalent rational theory of decision making. In fact, they thought the departure from these logical decision models was significant and in some ways systematic. Their work demonstrated that "people rely on a limited number of heuristic principles which reduce complex tasks of assessing probabilities and predicting values to simpler judgmental operations" (p. 1124). These are unconscious information-processing strategies that result in a simplification of the integrative task by reducing the complexity of the information actually processed. These heuristics operate ubiquitously across decision venues, from the most experienced researcher's activities, to the expert clinician's work, to the common person's need to make everyday decisions. The term *heuristic* may have more meaning for you if you think of it as a strategy for simplifying an array of data or information (Gambrill, 1997). Faust (1986), however, calls them "bad habits" or "cognitive limitations." In fact, while the use of cognitive strategies to simplify incoming information is common to all of us, heuristics are not benign in their effects. These information-processing strategies can result in cognitive biases that we must become aware of, particularly as they affect the diagnostic process. The following are a number of heuristics that have been identified in the literature that are likely to have significant implications for the diagnostic process (Kahneman, Slovic, & Tversky, 1982).

Representativeness
This cognitive bias occurs in situations when we must determine how likely it is that an entity/event A is an example of a category of entities/events B or in determining the probability that an entity/event A is caused by B. Both of these judgment tasks are highly relevant to the diagnostic process (e.g., if the person before you is experiencing category A symptoms, how likely is it that the person's experience is a B diagnosis?). According to research, people will respond based on the degree to

which *A* resembles *B*. They generally do not base their response on any concrete information they might have or be given regarding the statistical probability of its occurrence (such as the base rates of the entity/event in the population or subgroup of which the person is a member). As we can see, representativeness can be based on some valid knowledge of the entity/event, but it can also be based on stereotyped and biased formulations.

Availability

When asked to classify a new entity/event, people are more likely to think of well-known or larger classes of entities/events than less well-known or smaller ones. They are also more likely to recall those entities or events they have actually experienced than those less familiar or less likely to occur to them. For example, in the process of diagnosis, we are more likely to think of a diagnostic category that has been discussed frequently in our clinic, at conferences, or in the contemporary literature than one that is less current or one we have never experienced in our own practice. In many instances, behaviors and symptoms presented by our clients may conform to elements of the criteria for these mental illness diagnoses. In fact, some of our clients are well aware, through the popular media, of these characteristic behaviors and feelings and may use this language as they tell us what their experience has been. This heuristic bias may help us understand the phenomena of "designer diagnoses" (Bentley et al., 1993) and the over-use of popular psychological constructs, such as "codependency."

Confirmatory Bias

People draw on the most frequently co-occurring events/entities when asked to make a decision about the level of association of two or more new events/entities, rather than look for a less frequently co-occurring explanation or for actual exceptions. Social workers may look for evidence to support a diagnosis and will ignore or explain away evidence that does not fit (Kahneman, Slovic, & Tversky, 1982). On a very discrete, individual basis, this can occur when we too quickly diagnosis a major depression (based on appropriately fitting behavioral criteria) without fully evaluating the total biopsychosocial picture. Therefore, we miss an underlying organic cause because we did not explore physical well-being and recommend a physical checkup.

Historically, social work educators, and practicing social workers, have explicitly attended to the information-processing biases that can result from students' personal values, personality variables, and the affective elements of the professional self, through an emphasis on self-awareness in professional education. Now, there is a growing emphasis on the importance of attending to cognitive, information-processing biases such as those discussed above (Gambrill, 1997; Gibbs & Gambrill, 1999; Mumm & Kersting, 1997). It is essential that we explicitly include these aspects of self-awareness into social work education, especially because the profession has implicitly assumed it is possible to enhance students' capacity in these skills (clinical judgment and decision making) through the educational process.

While we may work to increase social workers' skills in critical thinking to enhance clinical judgment and decision making, it is also possible to increase their abilities through the use of specific information-processing tools. Some of the research on clinical judgment indicates that mathematically determined linear models of judgment may be superior methods to use when the goal is to arrive at diagnoses that are reliable and replicable. According to Benbenishty (1992), such an approach "may produce a treelike model that outlines a process of consecutive steps for using information about a case in order to reach a decision"(p. 607). Just such a decision tree, to be used as a guide for clinicians in making differential diagnoses of psychotic disorders, can be found in the *DSM-IV* (APA, 1994, pp. 694–95). Most social work practitioners and educators tend to reject dependence on such machine-like mechanical models in favor of using the human instrument in relationship and partnership with our clients, relying on critical thinking skills to enhance our clinical judgment in the diagnostic process. However, assessment tools that standardize our information collection and reduce total reliance on human judgment have fervent support in the profession (Corcoran & Fischer, 1987; Hudson, 1982). The use of such instruments can control many of the heuristic biases that were discussed previously. For example, they control for bias by reducing our ability to focus on only a few salient pieces of information that can overinfluence the collection and analysis of subsequent information. Without such a correction, we may be engaging in an information gathering process that has a "confirmatory bias," in that we find what we are looking for.

Given what we have learned about clinical judgment, emic and etic ways of knowing, the *DSM,* and the biopsychosocial model of mental disorder, it would appear that Kurfiss's definition of critical thinking is a perfect fit for the practice of diagnosis: "[T]he process of figuring out what to believe or not about a situation, phenomenon, problem or controversy for which no single definitive answer or solution exists . . . implies a diligent, open-minded search for understanding, rather than for discovery of a necessary conclusion" (Mumm & Kersting, 1997, p. 75).

MAJOR TASKS AND GOALS IN THE PRACTICE OF DIAGNOSIS

How then do we engage in this "diligent, open-minded search for understanding" in the practice of diagnosis? The four intellectual bases of social work diagnosis, described in the previous section, define the major tasks and goals of diagnosis, as seen in Table 3.1. Table 3.1 addresses Figure 3.1, the hourglass-shaped diagnostic process, and presents an outline of techniques, strategies, and skills. The outline is generic enough for social work practitioners to use as they engage in the diagnostic process with children, adolescents, adults and older adults, as well as in a range of practice settings. There are, of course, special issues regarding the diagnosis of mental illnesses specific to children and adolescents (Johnson, 1993; Jordan & Franklin, 1995; Kaplan & Sadock, 1998; Ollendick & Hersen, 1993), and older adults (Kane & Kane, 1981; Morrow-Howell, 1993) that practitioners should pursue in depth as needed in their practices.

TABLE 3.1	TECHNIQUES, STRATEGIES, AND SKILLS IN THE PRACTICE OF DIAGNOSIS

The Context: Principles of Social Work Practice

- Operate from a base in social work values and ethics.
- Respect partnership and mutuality.
- Establish effective professional relationships with all stakeholders.
- Promote active self-awareness and the use of professional self.
- Remain empathic and open-minded.
- Include emic and etic sources of knowledge.

The Top of the Hourglass: Biopsychosocial Construction

- Exercise skills in critical thinking.
- Learn the individual's psychosocial history, including the following elements:
    1. Developmental history
    2. Personality characteristics
    3. Temperament
    4. Intellectual/cognitive functioning
- Learn the individual's genetic and physical/biological history.
- Research the individual's family history and current context.
- Explore socioeconomic and community contexts.
- Define the problem.

Entering the Funnel: Establishing a DSM Diagnosis

- Integrate the individualized biopsychosocial construction.
- Determine what is salient for this specific person-situation.
- Use the *DSM* Multiaxial system:

    Axis I = clinical disorders

    Axis II = personality disorders and mental retardation

    Axis III = physical disorder or medical conditions

    Axis IV = psychosocial and environmental problems

    Axis V = global assessment of functioning (GAF)
- Name the diagnosis.
- Share the diagnosis.
- Clarify the meaning of the diagnosis with the client or clients.

The Bottom of the Hourglass: Ongoing Assessment

- Establish a working partnership.
- Implement and evaluate interventions.
- Engage in interdisciplinary collaboration.
- Keep dialogue with all stakeholders open, and use a feedback loop.

Embodying the Principles of Social Work Practice

The entire diagnostic process occurs within the context of a professional social work relationship. This relationship is marked by an appreciation of the centrality of clients' experiences in context (person-in-situation), as well as respect for the part-nership and mutuality of the professional endeavor, and it is embedded in the values and skills that are the foundation of the profession. Belief in the intrinsic worth and dignity of all people, in their uniqueness and individuality, in their right to equal access to resources, and in their capacity for growth and change in a self-determined process, reflect the profession's basic values (Hepworth, Rooney, & Larsen, 1997). These values translate into an abiding respect for human diversity as well as com-monality, a deep concern for social justice, and a commitment to developing and maintaining a professional level of self-awareness.

Interpersonal relationship skills, including sensitivity to and skill in verbal and nonverbal communication techniques, are essential in creating, maintaining, and using the professional relationship purposefully to address clients' goals. These skills are the building blocks of effective professional relationships. Many social work prac-tice texts, such as Hepworth, Rooney, and Larsen's *Direct Social Work Practice* (1997), provide exercises to increase these and other communication skills, including the ability to perceive and address clients' feelings, to convey empathy and authen-ticity, to engage in verbal following skills, and to decrease "counterproductive com-munication patterns"(p. ix). Being empathic, however, requires more than mastering the techniques of empathic communication. True empathy rests on the assumption that we are open to hearing and/or experiencing clients' inner reality—hearing and experiencing it and then communicating back to them what we have understood. As we have seen in the section on different ways of knowing, "being where the client is" involves being aware of and sensitive to diverse ways of knowing. To be open to emic knowledge, Kleinman (1988) believes we must listen carefully to the client's unique-ly human and socially constructed experience of a problem or disorder. He proposes we do this by asking the following simple yet specific questions designed to elicit a client's personal understanding of an illness experience:

1. What do you call the problem?
2. What do you think has caused the problem?
3. Why do you think it started when it did?
4. What do you think the sickness does? How does it work?
5. How severe is the sickness?
6. Will it have a short or long course?
7. What are the chief problems the sickness has caused?
8. What do you fear most about the sickness? (pp. 260–261)

Understanding the personal and culturally embedded meaning given to such an experience is as important as the facts of the disorder itself, but understanding our-selves as we engage these meanings and facts is equally important. Self-awareness has almost achieved the status of a mantra in social work practice, and yet it is diffi-cult to define. It involves more than knowing about oneself and one's values, pref-erences, biases, and blind spots. Self-awareness is both a product and a process.

Social workers must consciously and purposefully use what they learn about themselves to recognize and manage realistic and unrealistic attitudes and responses to clients and their situations, to address barriers to effective communication with clients, and to avoid projecting our feelings and beliefs onto others (Woods & Hollis, 2000). A lifelong commitment to self-awareness and respect for different ways of knowing contribute greatly to our ability to avoid becoming professionally myopic and confusing difference with deviance (Sweitzer & King, 1999).

Creating the Biopsychosocial Construction

Bloom et al. (1991) have proposed that the profession of social work itself has six languages, or sources of information, for all practitioners to master for effective practice. Mastery of all of them is of particular importance in the phases of practice that rely on the collection and synthesis of data. The languages they identify are the lay language of the client, the abstract language of theory, the researcher's empirical language, categorical language, jargon or technical language, and the language of values (p. 530). These languages also identify major sources of information for the task of creating a biopsychosocial construction of a mental disorder. Although this task will be a process of co-creation with our client, we must be aware that these multiple languages, these sources of information, are as vulnerable to misuse and distortion as they are to making positive contributions to our understanding. As a result, we need to be conscious of potential information-processing biases as we access these languages and use the information they provide. Skills in critical thinking will assist us in managing such biases. The following questions, paraphrased from Gibbs and Gambrill (1999), are presented as a way of approaching the task of biopsychosocial construction critically:

1. What is the purpose of my information collecting?
2. What is the precise problem I am trying to understand?
3. What *point of view* am I taking as I gather and think about this information?
4. What *concepts* or ideas are central to my thinking about this client?
5. What am I taking for granted, what *assumptions* am I making?
6. What *information* (emic/etic, empirical, abstract) am I using?
7. How am I *interpreting* the information?
8. What *conclusions* am I coming to?
9. If I accept these conclusions, and arrive at a biopsychosocial construction, what are the implications? (p. 4)

Asking these questions constitutes only a part of the biopsychosocial process, but their orientation can frame any collaborative inquiry process with our clients. For example, taking a good history begins with the presenting problem, no matter the specific format one uses to collect and analyze the relevant biopsychosocial information. Given the multidimensionality of mental disorders, the biopsychosocial construction must be arrived at through a multidimensional approach to understanding the problem (Franklin & Jordan, 1992; Mattaini & Kirk, 1991). The history and course of the present complaint needs to be considered along with pertinent medical history, including previous physical and psychiatric disorders and treatment. The client's personal, family, social, school and/or occupational history and current situations contribute to the biopsychosocial construction as well. Genograms and family-tree strategies can be used to access relevant information regarding family pattern disorders that may inform us about a client's predisposition or vulnerabilities to mental illnesses, such as depression and bipolar disorder. Knowing the nature of predispositional and development issues that are part of a client's reality and experience, as well as the current stressors that might exacerbate them, contributes significantly to the biopsychosocial construction.

Establishing the Diagnosis

A *DSM* diagnosis, located at the funnel of our diagnostic process in Figure 3.1, can be described as a tentative resting place that is revisited with regularity, incorporating information and understanding that emerges while we engage in intervention activities with our client. By diagnosing, we are trying to translate a problem, distress, or dysfunction into language that can be communicated and can guide the development of a plan of intervention. We begin with the integrated biopsychosocial construction we have developed with the client. One way of organizing and communicating this complex construction is to use a format, such as the schema proposed by Sperry et al. (1992), which is based on a biopsychosocial model of mental disorder. The following seven components are suggested in this schema, the first five of which would be used at this stage of our work: (1) presentation, (2) predispositions, (3) precipitants, (4) pattern and level of functioning, (5) perpetuants. The remaining two components are (6) plan and (7) prognosis, both of which can be completed after the diagnosis is determined. Using such an organizing format, we can see what is salient for this specific client-situation to take forward into the *DSM* diagnostic process.

Although the *DSM-IV* is not to be applied mechanically, it is organized specifically around behavioral criteria that can be assessed and evaluated without a full biopsychosocial construction. A Mental Status Examination (MSE) is one tool often used to assess the presence or absence of major signs and symptoms that are considered positive findings of specific mental disorders. (See also Chapter 2.) The MSE assesses such factors as the client's orientation (time, place, person), attention and concentration, memory, reasoning and abstract thinking, social maturity, reality testing, and insight (Hays, 1984).

Education about, training in the use of, and experience with the *DSM* are all required to maximize reliability in our use of the *DSM*. Courses are taught and books have been written that provide specific strategies for learning and applying the *DSM* (Kaplan & Sadock, 1998; Munson, 2000). The *DSM* multiaxial system is so named because it has five axes (see Figure 3.1). Major mental illnesses, considered clinical syndromes and disorders, are coded on Axis I, and personality disorders and specific developmental disorders in children are coded on Axis II. Other information from our biopsychosocial construction can be coded on Axis III (physical disorders or medical conditions), Axis IV (psychosocial and environmental problems), and Axis V (global assessment of functioning). Determining what is clinically significant impairment or distress and determining that a client's experience meets the threshold for a particular diagnosis both require skills beyond the use of the *DSM;* arriving at a diagnosis requires well-honed clinical judgment.

The process of naming, sharing, and clarifying the meaning of the diagnosis in partnership with our clients calls on the same basic social work practice skills we use in all other phases of our professional relationship with them (e.g., communication skills, authenticity and empathy, and openness). McWilliams's (1999) observation is absolutely correct: mystification has no place in our work with clients, including the process of diagnosis. She recommends sharing the diagnosis, explaining the basis for it, and discussing how it can guide referrals, interventions, and activities. In line with this, she suggests giving the *DSM* to the client, showing them one or two categories, asking if the labels seem to them to accurately describe their complaints, and which might be most accurate (p. 39). The collaborative process of keeping our inferences tentative and checking things out with our client contributes to establishing and maintaining the working partnership. This facilitates our ability to move forward with clients, to keep the dialogue open, and to engage in ongoing assessment and feedback into the diagnostic process.

Keeping the Dialogue Open through Ongoing Assessment

"The key task in human living . . . involves acquiring the capacity to protect the self through learning to cope with the stressful events in a way that avoids their potentially destructive impacts" (Kiesler, 1999, p. 151). A key task in living with mental illness is to develop the capacity to cope with aspects of the illness itself and with the additional stressors that occur in everyday life. Life stresses can exacerbate mental disorders and compromise clients' functioning. Psychoeducational groups that focus on coping skills and general life management skills, as well as on education, are often effective in helping clients maintain and enhance social functioning while experiencing a mental illness. Making referrals and implementing these interventions and assessing their effectiveness are some of the practice concerns and activities in the bottom half of the hourglass in Figure 3.1. It is here that the ongoing social work assessment occurs, which provides data for feedback, evaluation and monitoring of the diagnosis and of the related interventions. There are many formats that can be used during this ongoing assessment process (Rauch, 1993). Structured assessment tools become useful in this phase of the work, not only to monitor significant symptoms and complaints (e.g., depression inventories, symptom-targeted behavioral measures), but also to provide information regarding the effectiveness of medication and the appropriateness of the diagnosis.

In this phase of the work, a client may be working collaboratively with a case manager to establish goals. These goals must be things that are important to the client. It is most helpful if the goals are behavioral and specific, realistic and achievable, focusing on the presence of something rather than on its absence.

Being realistic in our work with clients also means assessing what cannot be changed and translating it into coping and managing that which will not change.

EXEMPLAR PROGRAMS AND MODELS: ALTERNATIVE APPROACHES TO DIAGNOSIS

The diagnostic model proposed in this chapter incorporates the diagnosis of a mental disorder with the surrounding process of assessment. In various places in the social work literature, the terms *diagnosis* and *assessment* have been used interchangeably; they have been framed in opposition to one another, or they have been combined (Goldstein, 1995; Hepworth, Rooney, & Larsen, 1997; Jordan & Franklin, 1995; Mattaini & Kirk, 1991; Woods & Hollis, 2000). Examples abound of the various positions taken on diagnosis in social work practice: Rauch (1993), writing on assessment in social work, dismissed the term *diagnosis* as "passé"; Kirk et al. (1989) argued the term is simply unacceptable in social work because of its medical lineage and its conceptual and methodological flaws, while Turner (1994) characterized the profession's move away from using the term *diagnosis*, an example of political correctness in action. Historical (Rodwell, 1987), conceptual (Turner, 1994), and political (Kirk et al., 1989) analyses have been applied to the controversy, but no clear, universally agreed-on distinction between diagnosis and assessment has emerged in the social work literature. However, a great deal of thoughtful and practical work on assessment in social work practice has emerged (Franklin & Jordan, 1992; Goldstein, 1995; Jordan & Franklin, 1995; Mattaini & Kirk, 1991; Rauch, 1993; Rodwell, 1987; Turner, 1994; Woods & Hollis, 2000), including one structured system for the classification of problems in social functioning called the Person In Environment (PIE) system (Karls & Wandrei, 1994a, b).

In 1981, the California chapter of National Association of Social Workers (NASW) received funding from the national NASW's Program Advancement Fund to develop a system of problem classification that would be useful to social workers in all realms of practice. The system was to be a tool for describing, classifying, and recording problems in social functioning. Although the authors stated that PIE was intended "as a complement to the existing manual that describes mental illnesses" (Karls & Wandrei, 1994a, p. xiv), in the material that accompanied the 1996 PIE training tape, the system was described as being a social work alternative to the *DSM*.

The PIE system was developed and field-tested from 1981 to 1984. Although NIMH funding was sought to conduct national reliability trials, no major external funding was garnered. As a result, the Task Force involved in these efforts was not able to complete the modifications of the PIE system that were needed, and NASW, the original supporter, has not endorsed further work on the document either. The purpose of the PIE system was to provide a uniform system for social workers all over the world to use in assessing the social functioning of adult clients (18 years or older). It was also viewed as a way of clarifying the profession's domain of activity and expertise without framing it in any one theory of human behavior. The system was to be as atheoretical as possible, primarily descriptive, and cognizant of client strengths and would use the client's community as the definition of environment. Although atheoretical in terms of cause, effect, and intervention, the PIE system is grounded in sociology and social psychology's role theory. Kirk, Siporin, and Kutchins (1989) reviewed and critiqued the PIE system and found no clear articulation of the conceptual framework, even though the language of role theory is clearly used for classifying and delineating clients' problems in social functioning.

The PIE classification system is composed of four factors. The first two encompass the core social work framework of person-in-environment: Factor I, which embodies Social Functioning Problems (problem type, severity, duration, and client's coping ability) and Factor II, which includes Environmental Problems (problem severity and duration). The remaining two factors (mental and physical health problems) use the standard classification systems developed by other professions (i.e., *DSM* and *ICD-9-CM*). The *DSM* (Karls & Wandrei, 1994b) provides explicit guidance on how to use the system. The structure of Factor I is presented with a brief sample of how it can be used (Karls & Wandrei, 1994a):

Factor I: *Social Functioning Problems*

A. Social role in which each problem is identified:

   Family roles: parent, spouse, child, sibling

   Other interpersonal roles: lover, friend, etc.

   Occupational roles: worker-paid economy, student

   Special life situation roles: consumer, inpatient, prisoner

B. Type of problem in social role (nine types): e.g., power, ambivalence, responsibility, dependency, loss, isolation

C. Severity of problem (6-point indicator)

D. Duration of problem (6-point indicator)

E. Ability of client to cope with problem (pp. 24–28)

Case Study

Diane, a 35-year-old single woman, has been employed for 4 years in a government agency as a mid-level professional. She has been seeing a social worker at the local community mental health center for a year, ever since her second psychiatric hospitalization for what was diagnosed as an episode of bipolar disorder with psychotic features. Although managing well in her everyday living, she has been experiencing episodes of anger at work and feels her supervisor is "out to get her." Diane's supervisor has called her in to talk about her performance on the job. Diane reports she is unable and unwilling to present her side of the story during these meetings. She also resents having to defend herself or ask questions about what she could do differently to correct the situation. Using the PIE system, we can assess her problem or situation as follows:

Factor I: 3170.345
Worker-Paid Economy Problem: victimization type, moderate severity, 1–6 months' duration, inadequate coping skills.

This is only one element of what would be a complex PIE classification of Diane's current challenges. If we were to classify each area of Diane's social functioning, and had completed all four factors on each, it would be quite a lengthy statement. In many situations, a thorough PIE assessment ends up being a more complex statement than a good narrative description of the person-in-situation being assessed.

There have been other attempts to create systems of classification that are neither framed in terms of a medical model of disease processes nor in terms of a linear model of cause and effect. For example, the American Orthopsychiatric Association developed a psychosocial functioning classification system in 1964; a similar system for social work client's was developed in England in 1978; in 1985, health care social workers, developed a list of psychosocial codes for use in primary care settings; and, as recently as the mid-1990s, a multidisciplinary task force of professional groups identified with family theory and therapy met to develop and advocate for the inclusion of diagnostic categories in the *DSM-IV*, which dealt with multi-person, interactive dysfunction. All of these endeavors support the notion that the helping professions continue to search for relevant and useful ways of codifying patterns of meaning in human experiences and problems.

UNIQUE CHALLENGES FOR SOCIAL WORKERS AS DIAGNOSTICIANS

The central challenge for all social workers in mental health services is to bring the social justice mission of the profession into their daily work with clients who experience mental illnesses. To effectively problem solve and advocate in professional partnership with our clients who experience mental illness, we must be knowledgeable about and participate critically in the "dominant discourse" of our profession and of our field of practice (Foucault, 1980; see also Chapter 8). Because the *DSM* is a pivotal element of the dominant discourse today in the domain of mental illness and mental health practice, it behooves us to be cognizant of the controversies and criticisms that surround it and to engage in the critical dialogue with our colleagues.

In 1994, Turner did a useful summary of reasons social work avoids the term diagnosis. While recognizing that the term *assessment*, as an alternative to diagnosis, represents a broader approach to understanding the complex biopsychosocial realities of clients and their environments, Turner maintained that ultimately the "critical step is to synthesize our assessments into accurate diagnoses" (p. 169). So, it became important to him to critically analyze the challenges surrounding the use of diagnosis in the profession. The first challenge Turner identified was in the intellectual and practical potential for diagnostic terminology to be misused and abused to the detriment of clients and society. *Labeling, pathologizing, stigmatization,* and *reification* are terms used to define what many consider to be these unavoidable and abusive negative effects of *DSM* diagnoses. For example, reification is defined as the "process of converting an abstraction into a supposed real thing" (Bentley et al.,

1993, p. 464). Reification can be understood as the dark side of classification: taking a "real thing" and converting it into a symbol or an abstraction that is no longer connected to the experience or the person. In this way, diagnostic labels often develop a life of their own in the popular culture and in professional jargon. These same concerns, however, can be expressed about other classification tools or methods the profession employs to aggregate and codify information. Public and agency policies and procedures, as well as statistically determined standards for services, can also be misused and can misrepresent the unique characteristics and needs of individual clients or whole client populations. It is our responsibility to be vigilant about the potential for such misuse and be assertive in counteracting harmful generalization no matter what professional tool is being used.

Turner addressed a second challenge for diagnosis, in that the term implied a level of precision and expertise that was not supported and that, if assumed, distanced social workers from their clients in a judgmental way. Turner found the last concern a false argument and a retreat from accepting professional responsibility. Most of social work practice requires the active engagement of our professional judgment, while holding us to the standard of being nonjudgmental. Dealing more directly with the issue of precision, in terms of validity and reliability of the *DSM*, are studies in which few, if any, of *DSM*'s disorders conclusively appear to be discrete, independently existing diagnostic entities (Kiesler, 1999; Kutchins & Kirk, 1997; Valenstein, 1998). In addition, many studies of the reliability of the *DSM* have demonstrated weaknesses as well: "[T]wenty years after the reliability problem became the central scientific focus of *DSM*, there is still not a single major study showing that *DSM* (any version) is routinely used with high reliability by regular mental health clinicians" (Kutchins & Kirk, 1997, p. 53). A more recent study, however, by Simoneaux, Warren, Thyer, and Myers (2000) resulted in a 71% interrater agreement between clinical social workers and psychiatrists on Axis I diagnoses, using the *DSM-III-R*. Indirect support for the reliability of mental health diagnoses appears in a statement found in the 1999 Summary of the Surgeon General's Report on Mental Health, which notes that "[D]iagnoses of mental disorders made using specific criteria are as reliable as those for general medical disorders" (p. xiii).

Reliability can also be applied to the discreteness of boundaries in the domain being classified. Kutchins and Kirk (1997), among others, believe the *DSM* has lost its boundaries, and thus its meaningfulness, by pathologizing an ever-increasing range of everyday behaviors, thus slipping from a system classifying real disorders, to a seemingly endless process of medicalizing human problems. The *DSM* and the mental health empire have simply transformed "what used to be considered volitional behaviors, requiring self-control and personal responsibility, into emotional disorders or illnesses ripe for treatment" (Gomory, 1997, p. 168). Many of these same critics believe the infusion of *DSM*-diagnosis professional jargon into social work is the vehicle by which the medical model has once again inappropriately reshaped our traditional social work mission (Bentley et al., 1993; Karls & Wandrei, 1994a; Kirk & Kutchins, 1988; Kirk, Siporin, & Kutchins, 1989; Kutchins & Kirk, 1997; Specht & Courtney, 1994).

The *DSM's* usefulness in clinical work has also been challenged. For example, McWilliams (1999) critiques the *DSM's* total reliance on observable behaviors in classifying disorders using antisocial personality disorder as an exemplar. She notes that sociologist Lee Robins's work on antisocial phenomena was used to formulate the *DSM-IV* diagnostic criteria for this disorder and that Robins's work focused only on behavioral deviations from the norm. A "lack of remorse" is the only non-behavioral criterion that was included in *DSM*. As McWilliams notes, clinicians often see people who do not meet the behavioral criteria for antisocial personality disorder but who nonetheless have a manipulative, unempathic, and power-oriented approach to life and other people. These individuals are usually law-abiding middle class people. By focusing solely on behavioral criteria, and not internal dynamics, *DSM-IV* allows for the over-diagnosis of socially marginalized groups such as adolescent gangs and inner city kids, while under-diagnosing those in society who are more successful, such as those in politics and business (McWilliams, 1999, pp. 88–89). McWilliams proposes that "understanding the internal subjective world of the psychopathically inclined person is much more useful therapeutically than locating him or her in an 'antisocial' role"(p. 89).

Finally, the dilemma of precision and expertise as a measure of our work has been questioned by others as a misplaced and uncritical acceptance of the scientific model of knowing and doing, which puts all knowledge and expertise in the hands and person of the professional and not the client. It becomes the job of the social worker to determine what the problem is, discern the diagnosis, establish the plan of intervention, while the client remains a passive recipient of our expertise (Weick, 1993). The critical question is, whose meaning is given primacy?

As pointed out throughout this book, social work is the dominant profession staffing mental health services in the United States (O'Neill, 1999). A significant number of our profession have taken the position that mental illness, as an "illness," is deserving of parity with physical illnesses in insurance coverage and service availability. This is a strong advocacy position for social justice for persons with mental illness and for societal destigmatizing of mental illnesses. The profession also has successfully lobbied in nearly every state for clinical licensing laws that sanction social workers to diagnose and treat mental and emotional disorders (see In re Adoption/Guardianship No. CCJ14746 in the Court of Appeals of Maryland). However, these two positions result in an interesting dilemma for the profession. The sanction of our skills and knowledge in the diagnosis and treatment of mental and emotional disorders, and support for the "brain disease" model of these disorders places mental illness right back into the very medical model some in our profession and the current multidisciplinary research reject.

Case Dilemma: A Person and a Mental Illness

Ms. Y, a 35-year-old, single Asian American woman, began to work with a social worker in private practice after her third psychiatric hospitalization, all of which had taken place over a period of 4 years in three different hospitals. With the initial referral to the social worker came a summary from each hospitalization as well as the *DSM* diagnosis that had been the basis for treatment during each. The discharge summaries from the first two hospitalizations indicated a diagnosis of major depression with psychotic features (*DSM-IV* = 296.34). The third discharge diagnosis was bipolar disorder, mixed, with psychotic features (*DSM-IV* = 296.65). Ms. Y was prescribed imipramine and Navane with the first diagnosis, then lithium and Navane with the diagnosis of bipolar disorder. She has continued taking the lithium, but the antipsychotic medication was recently changed to Loxitane. Between her second and third hospitalizations, she saw a psychiatrist every 4 to 6 weeks for medication management. Since the third hospitalization, these visits have taken place every 3 to 6 months.

After working for several years with this same social worker, Ms. Y's insurance company denied continuation of services. A quarterly treatment plan submitted to the reviewing case manager was turned down, although the problems, goals, and interventions were behaviorally specific and the diagnosis would be interpreted by almost anyone as one meeting the criterion of "medical necessity." Ms. Y's managed care insurance company refused further visits and two levels of appeal were denied. Continued medication management with a psychiatrist was approved. However, individual sessions with the social worker that focused on Ms. Y's adaptation to her illness and her social and occupational functioning, which had been effective in maintaining her outside of the hospital, were not approved. The social worker and Ms. Y agreed to continue their work together and made arrangements for a reduced fee. The social worker and the psychiatrist each have "release of information" forms signed by Ms. Y, authorizing them to consult, share observations, and collaborate as necessary. Although she has not needed to be hospitalized, Ms. Y's social and occupational functioning has declined in the past 2 years. She is no longer working, and although she is doing some volunteer work and managing her daily life, she applied for social security disability benefits, and it was recently determined that she was eligible to receive them.

Ms. Y is the eldest of five children, raised by both parents in a rural community in California. Her mother was highly educated and worked as a nurse during all the years of Ms. Y's childhood. Her father worked at home on the family land and in the community doing odd jobs. Everyone describes the family as very close. This family is large, extremely inclusive, with extended members like grandparents, aunts and uncles, and cousins who have played an active role in Ms. Y's life. Openness and inclusiveness, however, does not extend to feelings or emotional issues. Family members are also part of a very tight church community and "everyone knows everyone." Ms. Y and her brothers and sisters have all gone away from home to college. The college experience was Ms. Y's first time out of the protected family environment and she has described this as a confusing time, although she did very well academically. One brother returned to the family home several years after completing college and is also on disability for an emotional disorder. Other members of the extended family have been described as being "odd," "difficult," and "moody," and one grandmother was in an institution until she died. Ms. Y describes her own temperament and interpersonal style as "accommodating." She says she was taught to be a "good girl," to do what people asked of her, but to be wary of non-Asians. This last message was covert rather than overt, and Ms. Y claims she approaches all new people with the assumption that they will like her and even that they will "take care of her." When situations do not conform to this expectation, she experiences feelings of anger, often rage, but she attributes them to her illness because she interprets her religious teachings as saying such strong feelings are evidence of moral weakness . . . illness is more acceptable than moral failing.

Discussion

We know there is a more significant genetic component in bipolar I disorder than there is with other affective disorders such as major depression. About 50% of all clients who experience bipolar I disorder also have at least one parent with a mood disorder, although most often, their diagnosis is major depressive disorder (Kaplan & Sadock, 1998, p. 543). Family studies have also shown that first-degree relatives of a person with bipolar I disorder are 8 to 18 times more likely to have bipolar I disorder than a control group of clients (p. 543). Significant clinical observation has recognized that psychosocial factors such as stressful life events often precede the first, but not subsequent, episodes of bipolar disorder.

Ms. Y's biopsychosocial construction matches elements of what we know about bipolar I disorder in terms of a likely family predisposition or vulnerability. Certainly, affective disorder-type words and behaviors have been used to describe the actions of many members of her family (e.g., a father who is quiet and withdrawn, a brother who is on disability for an emotional problem). In addition, Ms. Y has responded very well to lithium, a medication used quite specifically for bipolar disorder, and has experienced no side effects from its use.

But it is equally important to recognize and try to understand Ms. Y's unique personality, psychological adaptation, and lived experience of her illness (she describes herself as having an illness). Ms. Y's personality style can be described as extremely dependent and nonassertive. She struggles with guilt over past events and uses this as a rationale for decision-making difficulties in the present. She either expresses very low self-esteem or grandiose assessments of her status compared to others. It is difficult to assess the impact of racism on her development, either directly, or through her parents' experiences in California during World War II. And, it does seem that movements toward independence on the part of children in this family are associated with negative mental and emotional experiences. These psychosocial and sociocultural elements of Ms. Y's experience with bipolar I disorder actually define her adaptation more substantively than does the *DSM* diagnosis alone.

KEY TERMS

Diagnosis: To distinguish, discern, to learn to know, perceive; determination of the nature of a diseased condition; identification of a disease by careful investigation of its symptoms and history (Webster's *New World Dictionary*, 1964, p. 403).

Assessment: Process occurring between practitioner and client in which information is gathered, analyzed, and synthesized into a multidimensional formulation (Hepworth, Rooney, & Larsen, 1997, p. 194).

DSM: *Diagnostic and Statistical Manual of Mental Disorders,* published by the American Psychiatric Association; a classification system of mental disorders originally developed as a uniform framework for collecting statistical information on mental disorders in the United States; DSM-IV, the current manual, labels each disorder and provides a numerical code and systematic behavioral criteria for distinguishing it from other mental disorders.

Biopsychosocial Construction: A conceptual framework applicable to diagnosis, intervention, and ongoing assessment that operationalizes our current understanding of the multidimensional nature of human experience, problems, and disorders.

Critical Thinking: Involves the critical appraisal of beliefs, arguments, and claims in order to arrive at well-reasoned judgments; involves open-mindedness, flexibility, and self-awareness, as well as specific cognitive skills (Gibbs & Gambrill, 1999, p. xiii).

Universalistic: Investigating mental disorders by looking for those aspects or elements of disorders that are objective and comparable across culture; takes the position that basic syndromes of mental disorders are essentially the same across time and culture; uses etic approaches to knowing.

Particularistic: A more relativistic approach to learning about mental disorders that takes the position there is total cultural plasticity in the experience and determination of mental disorders; uses emic approaches to knowing.

Pathologizing: Attributing the characteristics of a disease process or of an abnormal condition to an entity, a person, or a behavior.

Stigmatization: To characterize or mark with disgrace; detract from someone's character or reputation; indicate something is not normal (Webster's *New World Dictionary*, 1964, p. 1433).

WEB RESOURCES

Mental Health Information (http://www.athealth.com). This web site has a consumer and a practitioner homepage. Information on diagnoses includes the American and European descriptions of the disorders, research information, and articles. Useful links to other internet mental health resources. A weekly, topical e-mail, called Friday's Progress Notes, is available to practitioners.

Online Dictionary of Mental Health (http://www.human-nature.com/odmh/). This is a global information resource and research tool covering all disciplines that contribute to understanding mental health. The site accomplishes its purpose through links to many other sites that offer different viewpoints on mental health and mental illness.

National Institute of Mental Health (http://www.nimh.nih.gov/). NIMH provides information on specific mental disorders, their diagnosis, and their treatment, as well as up-to-date research and information on where and how to find help for various disorders.

REFERENCES

Abate, F. R. (Ed.). (1998). *The Oxford American desk dictionary.* New York: Oxford University Press.

Adoption/guardianship, In re: No. CCJ19746, Circuit Court for Washington County (Md. 2000).

American Psychological Society. (1996, February). Human Capital Initiative (HCI) (Report No. 3). *APS Observer* (special issue). Washington, DC: Author.

American Psychiatric Association. (1994). *Diagnostic and statistical manual of mental disorders* (4th ed.). Washington, DC: Author.

American Psychiatric Association. (2000). *Diagnostic and statistical manual of mental disorders* (4th ed. rev.). Washington, DC: Author.

Belle, D. (1990). Poverty and women's mental health. *American Psychologist, 45*(3), 385–389.

Benbenishty, R. (1992). An overview of methods to elicit and model expert clinical judgment and decision making. *Social Service Review, 66*(4), 598–616.

Bentley, K. J., Harrison, D. F., & Hudson, W. W. (1993). The impending demise of "designer diagnoses": Implications for the use of concepts in practice. *Research on Social Work Practice, 3*(4), 462–470.

Biafora, F. (1995). Cross-cultural perspectives on illness and wellness: Implications for depression. *Journal of Social Distress and the Homeless, 4*(2), 105–129.

Bieri, J., Atkins, A. L., Briar, S., Leaman, P. L., Miller, H., & Tripodi, T. (1966). *Clinical and social judgment: The discrimination of behavioral information.* New York: John Wiley & Sons.

Bloom, M., Wood, K., & Chambon, A. (1991). The six languages of social work. *Social Work, 36*(6), 530–534.

Corcoran, K., & Fischer, J. (1987). *Measures for clinical practice.* New York: Free Press.

Dawes, R. M., Faust, D., & Meehl, P. E. (1989). Clinical versus actuarial judgment. *Science, 243*, 1668–1673.

Dawson, W. B. (1986). Racial and ethnic factors in psychiatric research. *Hospital and Community Psychiatry, 37,* 50–54.

Devore, W., & Schlesinger, E. G. (1994). *Ethnic-sensitive social work practice.* (3rd ed.). Columbus, OH: Charles E. Merrill.

Dohrenwend, B. P. (1990). Socioeconomic status (SES) and psychiatric disorders. *Social Psychiatry and Psychiatric Epidemiology, 25,* 41–47.

Draguns, J. G. (1995). Cultural influences upon psychopathology: Clinical and practical implications. *Journal of Social Distress and the Homeless, 4*(2), 79–103.

Egeland, J. A., Hofstetter, A. M., & Eshleman, S. K. (1983). Amish study III: The impact of cultural factors on diagnosis of bipolar illness. *American Journal of Psychiatry, 140,* 67–71.

Engel, G. L. (1978). The biopsychosocial model and the education of health professionals. *Annals of the New York Academy of Science, 310,* 169–181.

Engel, G. L. (1980). The clinical application of the biopsychosocial model. *American Journal of Psychiatry, 137,* 535–544.

Faust, D. (1986). Research on human judgment and its application to clinical practice. *Professional Psychology: Research and Practice, 17*(5), 420–430.

Flexner, A. (1915). Is social work a profession? In *Proceedings of the 42nd National Conference of Charities and Corrections* (pp. 576–590). Fort Wayne, IN: Fort Wayne Printing.

Foucault, M. (1980). *Power/knowledge: Selected interviews and other writings, 1972–1977.* (C. Gordon, Ed. and Trans.). New York: Pantheon.

Franklin, C., & Jordan, C. (1992). Teaching students to perform assessments. *Journal of Social Work Education, 28*(2), 222–241.

Gambrill, E. (1997). *Social work practice: A critical thinker's guide.* New York: Oxford University Press.

Germain, C., & Gitterman, A. (1980). *The life model of social work practice.* New York: Columbia University Press.

Gibbs, L., & Gambrill, E. (1999). *Critical thinking for social workers: Exercises for the helping professions* (Rev. ed.). Thousand Oaks, CA: Pine Forge Press.

Goldstein, E. (1995). *Ego psychology and social work practice* (2nd ed.). New York: Free Press.

Gomory, T. (1997). Mental Health Services. In M. Reisch & E. Gambrill (Eds.), *Social Work in the 21st Century* (pp. 163–174). Thousand Oaks, CA: Pine Forge Press.

Good, B. J. (1993). Culture, diagnosis, and comorbidity. *Culture, Medicine, and Psychiatry, 16,* 427–446.

Green, J. W. (1995). *Cultural awareness in the human services: A multi-ethnic approach* (2nd ed.). Boston: Allyn & Bacon.

Hays, A. (1984). The set test to screen mental status quickly. *Geriatric Nursing, 5*(2), 96–97.

Hepworth, D. H., Rooney, R. H., & Larsen, J. (1997). *Direct social work practice: Theory and skills* (5th ed.). Pacific Grove, CA: Brooks/Cole.

Hudson, W. W. (1982). *Clinical measurement package.* Chicago: Dorsey.

Javier, R. A., Herron, W. G., & Bergman, A. (1995). A psychosocial view of mental illness: An introduction. *Journal of Social Distress and the Homeless, 4*(2), 73–78.

Jayasuriya, L. (1992). The problematic of culture and identity in social functioning. *Journal of Multicultural Social Work, 2*(4), 37–58.

Johnson, H. (1993). The disruptive child: Problems of definition. In J. B. Rauch, (Ed.), *Assessment: A sourcebook for social work practice.* Milwaukee, WI: Families International.

Jordan, C., & Franklin, C. (1995). *Clinical assessment for social workers.* Chicago, IL: Lyceum Books.

Kahneman, D., Slovic, P., & Tversky, A. (Eds.). (1982). *Judgment under uncertainty: Heuristics and biases.* Cambridge: Cambridge University Press.

Kane, R., & Kane, R. (1981). *Assessing the elderly: A practical guide to measurement.* Lexington, MA: Lexington Books.

Kaplan, H. I., & Sadock, B. J. (1998). *Synopsis of psychiatry* (8th ed.). Baltimore, MD: Williams & Wilkins.

Karls, J. M., & Wandrei, K. E. (Eds.). (1994a). *Person-in-environment system.* Washington, DC: NASW Press.

Karls, J. M., & Wandrei, K. E. (1994b). *PIE manual.* Washington, DC: NASW Press.

Kessler, R. C., McGonagle, K. A., Khao, S., Nelson, C. B., Hughes, M., Eshleman, S., Wittchen, H.-U., & Kendler, K. S. (1994). Lifetime and 12-month prevalence of *DSM-III-R* psychiatric disorders in the United States: Results from the National Comorbidity Survey. *Archives of General Psychiatry, 51,* 8–19.

Kiesler, D. J. (1999). *Beyond the disease model of mental disorders.* Westport, CT: Praeger.

Kirk, S. A., & Kutchins, H. (1988). Deliberate misdiagnosis in mental health practice. *Social Service Review, 62,* 225–237.

Kirk, S. A., Siporin, M., & Kutchins, H. (1989). The prognosis for social work diagnosis. *Social Casework, 70,* 295–307.

Kleinman, A. (1988). *The illness narratives: Suffering, healing and the human condition.* New York: Basic Books.

Kleinman, A. (1995). *Writing at the margin: Discourse between anthropology and medicine.* Berkeley, CA: University of California Press.

Kutchins, H., & Kirk, S. A. (1988). The business of diagnosis: *DSM-III* and clinical social work. *Social Work, 33*(3), 215–220.

Kutchins, H., & Kirk, S. A. (1997). *Making us crazy.* New York: Free Press.

Lum, D. (1996). *Social work practice and people of color: A process stage approach* (3rd ed.). Pacific Grove, CA: Brooks/Cole.

Mattaini, M. A., & Kirk, S. A. (1991). Assessing assessment in social work. *Social Work, 36*(3), 260–266.

McWilliams, N. (1999). *Psychoanalytic case formulation.* New York: Guilford Press.

Meehl, P. E. (1962). Schizotaxia, schizotypy, schizophrenia. *American Psychologist, 17,* 827–838.

Meyer, A. (1957). *Psychobiology: A science of man.* Springfield, IL: Charles C. Thomas.

Morrow-Howell, N. (1993). Multidimensional assessment of the elderly client (pp. 123–139). In J. B. Rauch, (Ed.), *Assessment: A sourcebook for social work practice.* Milwaukee, WI: Families International.

Mumm, A. M., & Kersting, R. C. (1997). Teaching critical thinking in social work practice courses. *Journal of Social Work Education, 33*(1), 75–84.

Munson, C. E. (2000). *The mental health diagnostic desk reference.* New York: Haworth Press.

National Advisory Mental Health Council Report. (1995). *Basic behavioral science research for mental health: A national statement.* Washington, DC: US Government Printing Office.

National Association of Social Workers. (1999). *Code of Ethics.* Washington DC: Author.

Nuechterlein, K. H., & Dawson, M. E. (1984). A heuristic vulnerability/stress model of schizophrenic episodes. *Schizophrenia Bulletin, 10,* 300–312.

Ollendick, T. H., & Hersen, M. (Eds.). (1993). *Handbook of child and adolescent assessment.* Boston: Allyn & Bacon.

O'Neill, J. V. (1999, June). Profession dominates in mental health. *NASW News,* p. 1.

Rauch, J. B. (Ed.). (1993). *Assessment: A sourcebook for social work practice.* Milwaukee, WI: Families International.

Richmond, M. E. (1917). *Social diagnosis.* New York: Russell Sage Foundation.

Ridley, C. R. (1989). Racism in counseling as an adversive behavioral process. In P. B. Pedersen, J. G. Draguns, W. L. Lanner, and J. E. Trimble (Eds.), *Counseling across cultures* (3rd ed., pp. 55–78). Honolulu, HI: University of Hawaii Press.

Rodwell, M. K. (1987). Naturalistic inquiry: An alternative model for social work assessment. *Social Service Review, 61*(2), 231–246.

Rodwell, M. K. (1998). *Social work constructivist research.* New York: Garland Publishing.

Ross, C. A., & Pam, A. (Eds.). (1995). *Pseudoscience in biological psychiatry: Blaming the body.* New York: Wiley.

Schwartz, R. J., & Perkins, D. N. (1990). *Teaching thinking: Issues and approaches.* Pacific Grove, CA: Critical Thinking Press & Software.

Simoneaux, R., Warren, K., Thyer, B., & Myers, L. (2000). Diagnostic agreement between clinical social workers and board-certified psychiatrists: A field evaluation of the *Diagnostic and Statistical Manual. Journal of Applied Social Sciences, 25*(1), 21–29.

Shapiro, J. P., Friedman, D., Meyer, M., & Loftus, M. (1996, November 11). Invincible kids. *U.S. News & World Report, 121*, 62–71.

Specht, H., & Courtney, M. (1994). *Unfaithful angels: How social work has abandoned its mission.* New York: Free Press.

Sperry, L., Gudeman, J. E., Blackwell, B., & Faulkner, L. R. (1992). *Psychiatric case formulations.* Washington, DC: American Psychiatric Press.

Sweitzer, H. F., & King, M. A. (1999). *The successful internship.* Pacific Grove, CA: Brooks/Cole.

Turner, F. J. (1994). Reconsidering diagnosis. *Families in Society, 75*(3), 168–171.

Turner, F. J. (1996). *Social work treatment: Interlocking theoretical approaches* (4th ed.). New York: Free Press.

Tversky, A., & Kahneman, D. (1974). Judgment under uncertainty: Heuristics and biases. *Science, 185*, 1124–1131.

U.S. Department of Health and Human Services. (1999). *Mental health: A report of the Surgeon General-Executive Summary.* Rockville, MD: U.S. Department of Health and Human Services, Substance Abuse and Mental Health Services Administration, Center for Mental Health Services, National Institutes of Health, National Institute of Mental Health.

Valenstein, E. S. (1998). *Blaming the brain.* New York: Free Press.

Weick, A. (1993). Reconstructing social work education. *Journal of Teaching in Social Work, 8*(1/2), 11–30.

Wetzel, J. W. (1991). Universal mental health classification systems: Reclaiming women's experiences. *Affilia, 6*(3), 8–31.

Woods, M. E., & Hollis, F. (2000). *Casework: A psychosocial therapy* (5th ed.). Boston: McGraw Hill.

Zubin, J., & Spring, B. J. (1977). Vulnerability: A new view of schizophrenia. *Journal of Abnormal Psychology, 86*, 103–126.

SOCIAL WORKERS AS THERAPISTS

Joseph Walsh

Given that social workers are the primary providers of mental health therapy services in the United States, it is important to consider *what* they do in practice and *how well* they do it. Is there anything *unique* about the therapies provided by social workers, compared to the practices of other professionals such as nurses and psychologists? Have they been able to adapt to the changing health care environment, with its focus on symptom relief, without compromising their value of client self-determination? With therapy, are social workers *effective* and *efficient* in helping clients achieve their desired outcomes? In this chapter, we will attempt to answer these questions by considering the intellectual base of social work therapy; the major tasks and goals of social workers as therapists with individuals, families, and groups; the techniques, strategies, and skills utilized for carrying out these tasks; several exemplar therapy programs; and some major challenges facing social workers as therapists. This chapter concludes with a case vignette, which illustrates the dilemmas faced by social workers as they attempt to fulfill the therapist role.

THE INTELLECTUAL BASE OF THERAPY

The provision of therapy by social workers has long been a controversial professional issue. From the 1920s through the 1960s, psychoanalysis and ego psychology that focused on individuals, families, and small groups, dominated the casework arena. Some social workers who were more involved in community development practices believed that therapy was not true to the goals of the profession. They alleged that social workers as therapists overemphasized the psychological person and underemphasized social and environmental factors (Specht & Courtney, 1994). The *Code of Ethics* (1996), compiled by the National Association of Social Workers (NASW), attempts to bridge the micro- and macroperspectives, stating that, "The primary mission of social work is to enhance human well-being and help meet the basic human needs of *all* people, with *particular attention* to the needs and empowerment of people who are vulnerable, oppressed, and living in poverty" [italics added] (p. 1).

DEFINING THERAPY

We will first consider some general definitions of *therapy* (or *psychotherapy*), and then we'll examine social work's perspectives on the concept. Dorfman (1996) defines psychotherapy as "a process of treating emotional or mental disorders psychologically, especially through verbal communication" (p. 41). Campbell (1996) defines it as "any form of treatment for mental illness, behavioral maladaptations, and/or other problems that are assumed to be of an emotional nature, in which a trained person deliberately establishes a professional relationship with a patient for the purpose of removing, modifying, or retarding existing symptoms, of attenuating or reversing disturbed patterns of behavior, and of promoting positive personality growth and development" (p. 519). Corsini and Wedding (2000) characterize the concept tentatively (by their own admission) as a process of interaction between a worker and client for the purpose of ameliorating the client's disability or malfunction regarding cognitive, affective, or behavioral functions. They assert that the worker should always utilize a theory of personality and change, and a treatment modality logically related to those theories.

Frank and Frank (1993) provide a detailed definition of therapy that can be summarized as a systematic application of the scientific understanding of human nature to the treatment of people with a mental, emotional, or behavioral disturbance. These authors, who have conducted cross-cultural studies on the topic, summarize that all effective therapies include the following: an emotionally charged, confiding *relationship* between a client and a helping person; a healing *setting*, which provides the client with a sense of safety, and strengthens the client's expectation of help by symbolizing the therapist's prestige as a healer; a rational, *conceptual scheme* that provides a plausible explanation for the client's symptoms and prescribes procedures for resolving them; and a *procedure* that requires the active participation of both the client and therapist, and is believed by both to be a means for restoring the client's health. The common functions of the role of the therapist are to combat the client's sense of alienation, inspire and maintain the client's expectation of help, provide the client with new learning experiences, arouse emotions (which is essential for promoting motivation, facilitating attitude change and sensitivity to the environment, and breaking up personality and behavioral patterns), enhance the client's sense of mastery and self-efficacy, and provide opportunities for the practice of new behaviors.

The previous definitions focus on the *psychological* rather than the *social* person. Social workers have defined psychotherapy in ways that maintain a focus on psychological issues, but also attend more to the client's social and environmental needs. For example, Goldstein (1995a) writes that all social work practice (including therapy) embodies a *psychosocial* or person-in-situation perspective, with an assessment and treatment of individuals in transaction with their social environments. Its goals are "to restore, maintain, and enhance the social functioning of individuals by mobilizing strengths, supporting coping capacities, modifying dysfunctional patterns for relating and acting, linking people to necessary resources, and alleviating environmental stressors" (p. 1948). Hollis (1972), referring to this holistic focus, characterized clinical social work as psychotherapy *plus*.

Lieberman (1982) writes, "social work psychotherapy has the objective of bringing about that change in behaviors that will improve individual functioning and the relationship between individuals and their social environment. To achieve this objective people are understood and treated differentially in relation to social problems as well as to intrapsychic problems, which are perceived as interrelated" (p. 17). Saari (1986) defines the goal of clinical social work as "the improvement of social functioning through the enhancement of the meaningfulness of life experiences and an expansion of the range of choices for individual behavior in an environment capable of supporting a variety of adaptive patterns...effectiveness of the interventions is presumed to rely upon the strengthening and reordering of the organizational structures in the client's life, including those structures that have traditionally been seen as intrapsychic, interpersonal, institutional, and/or societal" (pp. 11–12). Barker (1988) defines psychotherapy as a "specialized, formal interaction between a social worker or other mental health professional and a client (an individual, couple, family, or group) in which a therapeutic relationship is established to help resolve symptoms of mental disorder, psychosocial stress, relationship problems, and difficulties in coping with the social environment" (p. 131).

Swenson (1995) prefers the term *therapeutic conversations* to psychotherapy, as this conveys a notion of healing change but is compatible with a strengths perspective and reduces the power differential between the client and social worker. It also conveys that the social worker, as well as the client, may be positively changed through the process. Mattaini (1997) promotes an *ecobehavioral* approach to clinical intervention, which attends to the behavior of the individual and also the behavior of members of the multiple cultures in which the client is embedded. He prefers the term *personal consultation* to therapy, as it emphasizes collaboration and suggests a process in which the social worker outlines options, assists the client to understand factors that are relevant to personal goals, and guides and encourages the client to make effective decisions. Of course, in many settings, third-party payers have great influence over the range of services and the time frames that can be provided to clients. It is far from clear whether their values are compatible with environmental approaches.

While not specific to the practice of *therapy* (although certainly incorporating it), NASW defines clinical social work practice as "the application of social work theory and methods to the treatment and prevention of psychosocial dysfunction, disability, or impairment, including emotional and mental disorders, in individuals, families, and groups. It is based on an application of human development theories within a psychosocial context" (NASW, 1994).

Because it is so difficult to determine what social workers in the role of therapist actually *do* in their practice, as opposed to what they *say* they do, it is unclear if the therapy they provide is unique from that of other professions. Cooper (1994) argues that professions such as psychology and nursing have become more psychosocial in focus in recent years, and that when providing psychotherapy, all professions basically engage in the same practices. Meyer (1994) disagrees, stating that social workers are driven by a unique value base and provide the only therapy that truly assumes a person-in-environment perspective. Later we will consider how we might resolve this issue.

THERAPY CREDENTIALS

Social workers who practice as therapists must acquire credentials that reflect a considerable level of education and experience. These credentials are typically greater than those required of social workers who practice as case managers, or who are employed in *people-processing* rather than *people-changing* agencies (Netting, Kettner, & McMurtry, 1998). The acquisition of licensure and other certifications does not always distinguish the practice of therapy from other direct services by social workers, but they bolster the credentials of those who wish to practice as therapists.

Social workers who provide therapy usually have a master's degree from a program accredited by the Council on Social Work Education. They may have specialized in a clinical concentration that includes a field placement and supervision. Often social workers who provide therapy choose to be *licensed* in many states. This is a standard intended to regulate the practice of the profession, including who can practice independently, what services they can provide, and the titles they can present to the public (Biggerstaff, 1994). Licensing requirements for clinical social workers, now in existence in every state, usually require a specified length of practice experience under the supervision of another qualified social worker, passing an examination, and in some states, ongoing, continuing education.

NASW (1999) provides additional, optional credentials for social workers who wish to enhance their credentials as therapists. The Academy of Certified Social Workers (ACSW) requires a master's degree from an accredited program, 2 years of full-time practice, the submission of professional references, and the passing of an examination. The Diplomate in Clinical Social Work, the highest clinical certification offered by NASW, requires the same educational and experience requirements of the ACSW, but also 3 additional years of clinical experience, the highest level of licensure in the state, professional references, and the passing of an examination. Societies for Clinical Social Work have been established in 31 states (Clinical Social Work Federation, 1999). These are voluntary associations that promote high standards of professional education and clinical practice. These societies, coordinated by a national Clinical Social Work Federation, seek to keep clinical social work visible, to generate clinical research, and to promote professional training and publications.

THERAPY THEORIES

Most social workers in the role of therapist intervene with clients from the perspective of one or more practice theories. A *practice theory* may be defined as a coherent set of ideas about human nature, including concepts of health, illness, normalcy, and deviance, which provide verifiable or established explanations for behavior and ratio-nales for intervention (Turner, 1996). There is no *single* theory that guides the activ-ities of all or even most social workers. Psychosocial theory may come closest to doing so, but it is a broad systems theory and must be incorporated as a guiding perspective into other practice theories. *Any* theory with which the practitioner is comfortable and experienced will provide a means for organizing the universal therapeutic prac-tices of assessment, planning, and intervention. As we will see later, no theory has been found generally superior in effectiveness to others across practice settings.

Individual Therapy

Following are some practice theories commonly used by social workers in the role of therapist:

Ego psychology focuses on the activities of the ego, a mental structure of the personality that negotiates between one's internal needs and the demands of the environment (Goldstein, 1995a). Interventions may be *ego-supportive* (building on existing ego strengths) or *ego-modifying* (attempting to repair major deficits in ego functioning). Ego psychology, like object relations theory, assumes the significance of *unconscious thought* on behavior, and therapists are attentive to the client's uti-lization of adaptive and maladaptive *defense mechanisms.*

Object relations theory, another psychodynamic perspective, views the client's ability to form lasting attachments with others, based on early experiences of separa-tion and individuation, as a primary determinant of personality and quality of social functioning (St. Clair, 1999). Interventions based on this theory tend to be ego-mod-ifying and focus on enhancing the client's ability to form stable relationships, to trust others, and to persist with positive relationships during times of conflict.

Self-psychology focuses on the client's development of a cohesive sense of self. The self, which includes the functions of *action* and *reflection,* consists of three parts which, when integrated, can optimize need fulfillment (Flanagan, 1996). The cohe-sive self includes the *grandiose self* (in which self-esteem, ambitions and enthusiasm are forged), the *idealized parent image* (in which ideals, self-direction, and goal set-ting arise), and the *twinship self* (in which the behaviors of others are modeled, and talents and skills are developed). The social worker helps the client to make better connections with *self-objects*—people, things, or interests that can provide emo-tional stability, energy, and the sense of cohesion. Self-psychology is said to be con-sistent with the person-in-environment perspective in its assertion that objects need not always be people. A social reformer, for example, may be considered to have a particular cause as a primary object.

Cognitive theory assumes that the organization of one's conscious thinking activities *(schema)* are the basis for most emotional experiences and behaviors (Granvold, 1994). Many problems are the result of *cognitive distortions,* or habits of thought that perhaps were once functional for a person, but now sustain beliefs and perceptions that are not supported by objective evidence. The social worker helps the client identify distortions and replace them with perceptions that are more consistent with environmental evidence, and thus are more conducive to problem solving and goal attainment.

Behavior theory (of which social learning theory is a derivation) asserts that the quality of one's social functioning is the result of certain *reinforcement patterns* and *observational learning*, and that change is realized by adjustments in these patterns (Granvold, 1994). The social worker as therapist is concerned about the client's reports of internal conflict, but does not emphasize the process of reflection. The focus of intervention is on mutually devising structured environmental tasks that will produce new and more functional reinforcements for the client.

Solution-focused therapy de-emphasizes issues of human development in assessment and may be conceptualized as a theory of change (O'Connell, 1998). The social worker as therapist acts as a collaborative guide in helping the client identify and amplify behaviors that are associated with *exceptions* to problems, rather than focusing on the problems themselves. There is a focus on the client's interpersonal and environmental systems, and an emphasis that change in any one element of a system (however small), will reverberate throughout the system.

Constructivist (or *narrative*) *therapies* assume that one's perception of reality is a social construction, that meaning is created out of personal experience (Rodwell, 1998). The stories people tell about themselves, rather than the objective facts of their lives, serve to make sense of their experiences and define who they are. Change occurs through a process of re-interpreting situations, filling information gaps with new knowledge and experiences, or better articulating personal goals. The social worker helps the client experience problem resolution or personal growth through a process of constructing new narratives that enhance mastery and self-esteem. Cognitions are considered neither accurate nor distorted, but as representing a person's unique view of the world.

Family Therapy

When providing therapy for family systems, social workers may utilize the theories previously described or utilize others that have been developed more specifically for family work. Following are some examples.

Structural theory assumes that satisfactory family functioning is maximized when there is appropriate executive authority and a clear structure (set of functional demands that organize how members interact) that includes proper limits on behavior (Minuchin, Lee, & Simon, 1996). Intervention is focused on making adjustments to the family structure, such as placing power with appropriate adult members, developing appropriate rights, roles, and responsibilities among members and subsystems (spouses, siblings, etc.), and articulating member and subsystem boundaries (barriers regulating amounts of contact).

Family emotional systems theory assumes that one's patterns of emotional behavior are established in the family of origin (Kerr & Bowen, 1988). Optimal social functioning is characterized by one's differentiation of self from others, which means achieving a balance between needs for attachment and self-efficacy.

Emotional problems are said to result from experiences of emotional cutoff and fusion that begin in the family of origin. The goals of intervention are to promote the differentiation of self with each member, to increase the reflective capacity of all members, and to ensure that members do not become negatively *triangled,* that is, drawn in by two others as a means of stabilizing an unstable relationship.

Strategic theory, like solution-focused theory, is more attentive to change strategies than to explaining and categorizing human behavior (Nichols & Schwartz, 2001). It views families as systems that may become rigid in responding to new challenges. The social worker helps devise new, creative ways to solve family problems, and many of these strategies are designed to overcome anticipated family resistance to doing things differently. Because the social worker as therapist is viewed more as an expert than a collaborator, and interventions sometimes rely on deception, this approach has fallen out of favor with many social workers. More recently, its proponents have embraced more collaborative values. This is a viable therapy alternative for family situations in which strong resistance must be addressed.

Group Therapy

Therapy groups may be the intervention of choice for people with mental health problems who are assessed as potentially benefiting from an interpersonal process. Any of the theories previously described may be adapted for group use. Therapy groups may focus on *support* (to develop or enhance coping skills), *education* (to learn about themselves and their social environments), *growth* (providing opportunities for members to become aware of or change their thoughts, feelings, and behaviors regarding themselves and others), *rehabilitation* (to make positive adjustments or rehabilitate after a social or health trauma), or *social issues* (to develop social skills and new behavior patterns) (Toseland & Rivas, 1998).

Social workers as group therapists need to titrate and focus their activities depending on the stage of the group. While there is no standard outline of group stages, one model includes five stages: (1) *pre-affiliation* (characterized by approach and avoidance behavior); (2) *power and control* (a transitional stage in which members work out issues of status and role); (3) *intimacy* (in which a productive familial frame of reference develops); (4) *differentiation* (characterized by a group identity and internal frame of reference); and (5) *separation* (breaking away) (Hepworth, Rooney, & Larsen, 1997). Each of these stages features a different set of *processes* (patterns of interaction among members) and *dynamics* (properties that result from the group process, such as norms and roles). Because therapy groups emphasize the growth-enhancing potential of interaction, the leader must be highly active in the beginning two stages, less active during stages three and four (which are considered to be the working stages), and more active during termination, to ensure appropriate closure.

MAJOR TASKS AND GOALS

The purpose of mental health services provided by social workers in the role of therapist is to promote the mental well-being, and alleviate the mental disorders of individuals, families, and groups (Lin, 1994). NASW (1994) states that such services should be provided in the least restrictive environment, on a continuum that includes community-based services, prevention services, full and partial hospital care, outpatient therapy, outreach and emergency services, and support services to significant others. In this broad context, the major goal of therapy is to bring about social and psychological change for clients, and increase their access to social and economic resources (Swenson, 1995). Social workers as therapists help their clients make particular changes through a variety of tasks, many of which are described later. NASW (1994) further states that all providers, including therapists, should participate in political action to further the interests of their clients.

TECHNIQUES, STRATEGIES, AND SKILLS

We will consider here the major activities of the social worker as therapist when implementing the theoretical perspectives noted earlier. First, with any theoretical perspective, a constructive therapist-client relationship provides a context for positive outcomes (Sexton & Whiston, 1994). This working alliance consists of a positive emotional bond between the parties, mutual comfort in their interactions, and an agreement on goals and tasks. Horvath (1994a) found that the quality of the working alliance, represented by a mutual sense of collaboration, was more predictive of positive final outcomes in therapy than any other variable. Toward this end the social worker must possess the interpersonal skills to present a safe, accepting, and encouraging presence. In this atmosphere, clients can more easily share their thoughts and feelings, feel less alone, try out new ways of thinking, feeling, and behaving, and get support in times of disappointment (Goldstein & Noonan, 1999). To facilitate an appropriate relationship, social workers need skills of *empathy* (the ability to perceive accurately and sensitively the inner feelings of a client, and to communicate understanding of those feelings to the client) and *authenticity* (relating in a natural, sincere, spontaneous, genuine manner) (Hepworth, Rooney, & Larsen, 1997).

Individual Therapy

In ego psychology and object relations theory, the social worker utilizes six major techniques (Woods & Hollis, 2000). Ego-sustaining techniques focus on helping the client understand their motivations and behaviors more clearly, and mobilize the client to resolve present difficulties. These techniques include *sustainment* (developing and maintaining the positive relationship), *education-description-ventilation* (encouraging the client's emotional expression for stress relief and to gain better objectivity about problems), and *person-situation reflection* (facilitating self-exploration so that the client can arrive at solutions to present difficulties). The social worker also provides *education* to the client, often about environmental resources, and to a lesser degree *direct influence*, particularly when the client is in crisis and temporarily unable to exercise good judgment about self-care issues.

The major ego-modification technique, which is *developmental reflection*, is used when clients experience severe deficits in interpersonal functioning that require an exploration of unconscious processes (as in, for example, personality disorders). The social worker facilitates the client's self-exploration and understanding by providing new interpretations of the client's relationship patterns, interpreting the client's reactions to the therapist (transference), confronting maladaptive defenses, and providing a corrective relationship and other corrective interpersonal experiences. This technique is utilized more commonly in object relations therapy, with that theory's focus on helping the client resolve early interpersonal conflicts.

The social worker's major strategies in self-psychology are to provide the client with a corrective interpersonal experience and to teach the client that close relationships can survive conflicts and other disappointments. To help the client develop a cohesive sense of self, the social worker utilizes empathy as a primary technique. The social worker encourages a positive transference and demonstrates empathic understanding by affirming the client's strengths and efforts to develop. However, the client may eventually discover the social worker's fallibility, so disruptions in the relationship may be anticipated. The social worker acknowledges this fallibility, interprets the results of relationship disruption for the client, and again helps the client repair the damaged relationship. If the outcome of the relationship is positive, the client will be better able to cope with future self-object failures.

The techniques of cognitive theory are focused on altering the client's cognitive patterns (Lantz, 1996). The social worker helps the client learn to analyze problems more clearly through the modeling process of Socratic questioning, and through reframing, the client is encouraged to think about problems more flexibly. There are two major therapy strategies within this theory. *Cognitive restructuring* is the process of challenging clients to experiment with new ways of thinking so that they can develop patterns that are more productive for goal attainment. Such techniques as self-instruction training, the triple column technique, attribution training, cost-benefit analysis, and education (particularly for children and adolescents) are used toward this end. Secondly, *problem-solving* techniques involve teaching the client systematic ways to break problems down into manageable parts and then considering a range of creative solutions.

All techniques in behavior theory follow a structured pattern (Thomlison & Thomlison, 1996). The client and social worker collaborate in the process of stating problems in behavioral terms, establishing measurable objectives, gathering baseline data, specifying steps toward problem resolution, specifying personal and environmental resources, identifying relevant others for participation, identifying possible obstacles to problem resolution, applying the intervention, documenting changes, and then evaluating outcomes. The specific interventions from which the social worker and client may choose include modeling, vicarious learning, behavioral rehearsal, reinforcement and stimulus control, exposure, systematic desensitization, shaping, and overcorrection. Behavior therapy techniques are widely used to help clients develop social, stress management, and relaxation skills.

The cognitive and behavior theories are frequently combined into strategies in which the client uses tasks as a means of testing out and reinforcing new thinking patterns. The best known of these is *task-centered practice*, a concrete, structured, and goal-directed process of articulating and addressing specific client concerns through corrective tasks (Reid, 1997). This approach is based on the processes of systematic problem solving previously described and the assumption that change is more likely to persist if the client is an active participant in that process. Meetings between the therapist and client involve the specification of target behaviors (which may involve cognitive and emotional experiences), development of task assignments, evaluation of the outcome of tasks assigned earlier, and the formulation of new tasks.

Constructivist (and solution-focused) therapies focus on solutions and exceptions, and helping the client develop cohesive meaning out of life experiences (O'Connell, 1998). The social worker tends to divert focus away from the presenting problem after the assessment. Social workers may use various strategies from this perspective including normalizing problems, affirming the uniqueness of the client's experience, providing compliments when the client demonstrates competence, externalizing problems (placing them outside rather than within the client), encouraging motivation, collaborative goal setting, developing task interventions that tend to enhance the client's positive behaviors, using scales to measure progress, and presenting any setbacks as normal. The social worker can be creative in developing unique techniques for each therapy situation.

Family Therapy

With its emphasis on strengthening executive authority within families and developing appropriate roles for subsystem members, all strategies in structural family therapy focus on building, strengthening, weakening, or dissembling *alliances* among members (Cleveland, 1999). This is done in a number of ways, all of which are concrete and activity-based. There is a major focus on the social worker's teaching of communication skills (clear speaking, listening skills, redirecting the processing of stress, and training family members to stop when communication is breaking down). The social worker is very active in this therapy, manipulating space in the room to either facilitate or impede certain interactions. The family's goals are achieved by enactments (role plays and rehearsals), rather than extended discussions. The social worker directs new family transactions, facilitates spontaneous behavior sequences, reverses family member roles, adjusts boundaries (opening areas of interaction to some members but not others), and even joins an alliance at times to help strengthen it. The social worker as therapist teaches relaxation and stress management skills to defuse family member anxieties that tend to persist through part of the therapy process. The social worker also frequently assigns tasks for implementation in the family's natural environment, so that they can rehearse what has been learned in therapy.

In family emotional systems therapy, the social worker acts to reduce the anxiety within the family system and then to promote differentiation of the members (Pippin & Callaway, 1999). Techniques include first the *multigenerational genogram*, which helps all members to understand their functions within the family, as well as sources of triangulation and fusion. The client or family is then guided into new *functional attachments* with nuclear *and* extended family members through a process that is both reflective and active. The social worker provides didactic teaching about family systems, and then facilitates person-situation and developmental reflection so that all members can observe themselves within the central triangles. Family member behavior is examined in terms of multigenerational family themes. Members are instructed to seek out other members of the family with whom they may not have strong relationships, toward the goal of securing new sources of attachment and to disentangle problematic triangles.

Group Therapy

Leader intervention strategies vary depending on the type of therapy group. The social worker always faces challenges that are different than those inherent in individual and family therapy, however (Hepworth, Rooney, & Larsen, 1997). First, the social worker must be a good therapist. They must also possess skills for (1) promoting good communication (by monitoring the cues and reinforcements that members receive, developing emotional bonds, and ensuring equal power and status among members); (2) developing group cohesion (by attending to members' needs for affiliation and promoting member expectations about the consequences of the group); (3) enforcing controls (establishing rules and boundaries, a task orientation, a sense of shared responsibility, positive attitudes, and acceptable ranges of emotional expression); (4) attending to issues of group culture (shared values and traditions which are influenced by member characteristics); (5) developing productive roles for members; (6) managing subgroups (neutralizing negative subgroups, drawing out less involved members); and (7) developing a shared leadership structure (encouraging member-to-member exchanges, soliciting member input into all decisions, and supporting the development of indigenous leadership).

Social workers can identify key leadership strategies and skills by considering common tasks across the stages of therapy groups. In the pre-affiliation stage, the therapist must establish guidelines and objectives, clarify goals and expectations, provide structure, model desired behavior, assure all members the opportunity for participation, encourage discussion of member anxieties and ambivalence, and encourage trust. In the power and control stage, the social worker must minimize changes in membership, encourage balanced feedback, increase communication through feedback, and create and model norms for group behavior. During the intimacy and differentiation stages, the therapist needs to focus on the universality of group themes, support member differentiation, balance time allotments to members, keep the focus on goals and tasks, and become a less dominant presence. Finally, during termination, the therapist must generalize group themes, help members practice new skills, plan with members for setbacks, reinforce the gains of group, facilitate member review of learning, facilitate the resolution of unfinished business, and identify areas for continued work for each member.

THE INCREASED PREVALENCE OF SHORT-TERM THERAPIES

Beutler and Baker (1998) assert that a therapist's theoretical base is often not directly related to subsequent intervention activities. This is not to say that having a theoretical base is unimportant, however, as an organizing framework helps the social worker structure the process of therapy. To put this issue into a context, the authors identify three levels of the therapy process. These include the worker's guiding theoretical perspective, a general intervention strategy that is related to the presenting characteristics of specific clients, and subsequent intervention techniques that are selected in response to a client's unique presentation. They suggest that in comparing practice outcomes, *strategy* is a more appropriate variable to study than theory.

Regardless of the social worker's theoretical orientation, therapies have become more short-term in many settings. Some social workers provide short-term therapy only because it is a requirement of their insurance companies or agencies; others do so because they believe it is the most appropriate clinical approach. There are shared characteristics of short-term approaches across practice theories (Dziegielewski, Shields, & Thyer, 1998). The client's strengths are highlighted during assessment and are then mobilized by the social worker in the process of problem solving. The therapist also taps into the client's areas of motivation for treatment to facilitate the process, even when the client is involuntary or uncooperative. Social workers do not impose the goals of therapy, but they do openly negotiate them with the client. These goals tend to be concretely defined and emphasize the resolution of current problems in living, rather than the development of insight through lengthy exploration of the client's past. The practitioner tends to be active in the process and assumes a collaborative role with the client. Plans for termination are discussed early in therapy; time limits and ending criteria may be elaborated during the first session. While some therapies are considered by nature to be long-term (e. g., object relations) or short-term (e.g., task-centered practice), most can be adapted to short-term use. Practice theories are quite different in how they guide the assessment process, but intervention strategies and tasks may be similar among them.

EXEMPLAR PROGRAMS AND MODELS

In this section, we will review three examples of social workers as therapists. All of them demonstrate how the professional's knowledge and value base can be incorporated into the therapy process.

Individual Therapy

Lackstrom (1999) describes a structured social work approach for working with clients who have the eating disorders, anorexia or bulimia. The comprehensive approach may involve some family and group work, but the focus is on individual therapy. This therapy is conceptualized as a *two-track* intervention with a stepped approach. Track one addresses the client's eating behaviors and track two, implemented later, addresses the core conflicts in the client's life that have resulted in the problematic eating behaviors. The stepped strategy involves monitoring the client's oscillating motivation to change during the difficult work of therapy, and increasing or decreasing the intensity of the interventions in an effort to preserve motivation. Clients with eating disorders are often motivated to change their eating symptoms, but may be less motivated to face underlying psychological causes of those behaviors and make fundamental changes in their lifestyles and relationships.

During assessment, the social worker focuses on the circumstances of the onset of the disorder and the client's weight history, daily calorie intake, and bingeing and purging behaviors. The social worker should possess the necessary knowledge to assess evidence of medical complications including dermatologic, cardiovascular, gastrointestinal, endocrine, musculoskeletal, and cognitive changes. Of course, a medical consultation is required to fully evaluate these complications. The client's family history is important in identifying any developmental issues that have contributed to the onset of the eating disorder, as well as the family's potential to assist in the client's recovery.

Track one begins with a consultation with a registered dietician who develops a meal plan with the client. The social worker, beginning with the least intrusive intervention and moving to more intrusive interventions only if necessary for the client's physical health, provides formal psychoeducation to the client. This approach, with its cognitive-behavioral theoretical perspective, has been found effective with clients who have eating disorders (Fairburn et al., 1991; Olmstead, Davis, Rockert, Eagle, & Garner, 1991). Most clients make significant improvements in their eating behaviors within six sessions. Topics include causes of the disorder, the meaning of the diagnosis, the role of dieting as a coping mechanism, the dangers of medical complications, normal eating behavior, and strategies for changing eating behaviors and preventing relapse. Social workers use the cognitive behavioral strategies in this process. They encourage clients to identify healthy and unhealthy eating patterns by keeping a food journal, challenge distorted beliefs about the role of food and nutrition in their lives, separate thoughts and feelings from eating behaviors, and develop self-soothing strategies to counteract the intense feelings and racing thoughts that often accompany improved eating practices.

Medications may or may not be used as a part of this intervention. Drugs have not been found helpful in reducing obsessions associated with the recovery process or in restoring weight (Garfinkel & Walsh, 1997). Antidepressants are helpful in reducing bingeing behaviors in some clients, and anti-anxiety drugs may be helpful as short-term interventions for the anxiety associated with changing eating behaviors.

Track two intervention begins when the client's eating habits have normalized and he or she is otherwise symptom-free. At this time the social worker shifts from a focus on symptom control to an exploration and resolution of the traumatic or upsetting life events that have contributed to the presence of the disorder. While there is no research to support the use of specific techniques in this process, there is agreement in the literature that this shift in emphasis is necessary to ensure a client's full recovery (Kaplan & Sadock, 1998). The social worker continues to monitor eating behaviors and weight, and in fact the client's physical status helps the worker to pace the intensity of the track two interventions.

The social worker may be described as utilizing an ego psychological perspective for intervention in track two. Through exploration, person-situation reflection, and developmental reflection, the social worker and client consider problematic coping and defensive patterns that might initially be outside the client's awareness. The client's new skills at behavior management will be tested by stress associated with this focus on psychological issues that have been masked by the eating disorder. Any relapse behaviors mandate that the social worker return to the cognitive-behavioral strategies discussed earlier. It is always important for the therapist to temporarily stop or reduce the intensity of insight-oriented work during a relapse and normalize the client's eating behaviors by returning to a more supportive approach.

Although difficult to predict its duration, the length of track-two intervention may be determined by third-party payers. Ideally, the therapy ends when both parties have decided that the client has achieved and can maintain a satisfactory level of social functioning and personal growth. Behavioral indicators related to the client's level of social and occupational functioning can be used as a guide in this process.

Family Therapy

One community mental health center has implemented a family therapy program featuring a two-tiered, home-based intervention with ecological and structural components (Aponte, Zarski, Bixenstine, & Cibik, 1991). Home-based therapy provides a viable means of intervention for those families that are not receptive to office-based counseling, either for cultural reasons or because they do not have the necessary resources to regularly travel to an office. This model is based on structural family theory and is particularly effective in reaching high-risk families experiencing intergenerational conflicts. The families that are suited to this model of intervention tend to be poor and underorganized, meaning that member roles are ill-defined and parental authority is diffuse or overbearing. These families often become involved with numerous social agencies and thus lose some control over their own destiny. With a two-tiered approach, social workers as therapists help families resolve their internal problems, and then help them address community problems that they share with other families. The intervention persists for 12 to 16 weeks.

The first and primary focus in this therapy is the provision of structural family intervention, so that all family members can develop a clearer awareness of, and agreement on, their roles and responsibilities as a unit. The adults are helped to develop and enforce appropriate controls over the younger family members. The social workers attempt to provide practical solutions to the family's concrete problems, which tend to be initially centered on one child's problem behavior but are eventually accepted as systems problems. Intervention strategies include redirecting the family processing of stress (communications interventions), developing new patterns of family transaction via enactments, exploring behavior patterns with directed discussions, role playing (including role reversals), manipulating physical space for acting out new role behaviors, adjusting personal and subsystem boundaries, and assigning tasks between family sessions that reinforce therapy themes.

If the structural interventions are successful, the second tier of intervention is introduced, and the family is invited to participate in a multiple-family support group composed of other families who have received the structural therapy from the agency. This open-ended group is conducted in a public community setting by different agency staff members. The goals of the ongoing group are for the members to increase their awareness of community factors that influence their lives, and to empower themselves to take action toward enhancing their community supports. While attending to community issues, this second-tier process continues to strengthen the family units.

Group Therapy

Saulnier (1997) provides an interesting example of a constructivist approach to group therapy with a special population. She developed the 12-session group, sponsored by a university counseling center, for lesbians with mild to moderate alcohol abuse problems. The group aimed for individual and social change, based on literature that suggested lesbians used alcohol as a coping mechanism for social marginalization. Twelve women responded to advertisements for group participation.

The group therapist drew upon an empowerment and self-determination intervention model that focused on increasing members' sense of control over their lives. In keeping with the leader's commitment to social work values, the group did not observe a disease model of alcohol abuse but one that focused on *choices*. Consistent with constructivist theory, the women were encouraged to set individual goals about drinking. They were then encouraged to consider what personal limitations hindered their progress toward goals, to define their needs, to consider what social changes would support their goals and strengths, and to take steps to change themselves and their social environments. The leader's roles during the open-ended discussion process included teaching, skill building, facilitation, and interpretation of the group process for the members. The leader evaluated the group using a pre-experimental pre-test, post-test design, using standardized measures of alcohol consumption (quantitative) and semi-structured interviews (qualitative).

Of the eight women on whom post-test data was collected, both alcohol consumption and episodes of drunkenness decreased significantly. The qualitative results indicated processes by which the women increased their ability to set personal goals, decreased their alcohol consumption, worked well together despite having different goals, and maintained a focus on personal and social goals. From each other, members learned various ways to control aspects of their environments that contributed to their desire to drink, such as conflicted relationships with significant others, family stress, the coming-out process, loneliness, the loss of a partner, a desire to overcome shyness, the centrality of bars as social centers in lesbian communities, and the need to drink to be sexual. The group leader admitted that she failed to engage the group in planned social change process, but concluded that the members had simply chosen to continue their struggles on a more personal level.

UNIQUE CHALLENGES FOR SOCIAL WORKERS AS THERAPISTS

Social work practitioners engaging in therapist roles must be alert to several critical issues that have emerged in the field of mental health during the past 35 years. They need to increase their capacity to serve clients with multiple needs, to integrate early intervention and natural support system interventions, and increase the amount and quality of research for understanding the kinds of therapies and programs that serve clients most effectively (Lin, 1994).

The most striking related development in the psychotherapy field during the past decade was the growth of the *managed care industry* (Wineburgh, 1998). In 1992, approximately 44% of Americans with health insurance had their mental health benefits managed by a specialty program; in 1997, this had risen to 75% (or 223.7 million) of Americans with health insurance. At the same time, the consolidation of managed behavioral health care entities has concentrated benefit plans in the hands of fewer organizations. The economic interests of the industrialized health care sector and its core constituencies are linked to progress in the development of scientifically based practice guidelines (Hayes, 1998). Managed care corporations have come to understand that the best means of cutting costs and ensuring competitive success is not to delay or deny treatment, but to promote empirically demonstrated efficient and effective practices. This involves efforts to *triage* clients, funneling those with lesser needs into less-expensive but effective treatment alternatives, and placing high-utilization clients with serious but treatable conditions into more time-intensive programs that also demonstrate efficacy. Government efforts to impose effectiveness criteria have been slow and politically troublesome. A better alternative may be one that pulls together professional organizations, consumer groups, health care associations, and other stakeholders into cooperative efforts.

OUTCOME RESEARCH

The methods by which social work therapies, as well as therapies offered by other professionals, are tested for effectiveness have evolved greatly in the past 50 years (Conte, 1997). During the 1950s and 1960s, nonspecific theories and strategies were applied to heterogenous client populations and examined for evidence of any impact. Case studies were common in the social work literature. While informative, they were not usually based on structured single-subject or pre-experimental designs. Today, research questions are often (but not always) more specific. What theoretical perspectives (and related interventions) work for what types of clients or problems in what situations? Are certain therapies preferable to others with certain types of clients? Related to outcome research, it is also important to determine what treatments are found to be efficacious in research settings, and which are feasible and cost-effective in natural settings.

Myers and Thyer (1997) assert that clients have a right to effective treatment, and that the profession's code of ethics should be amended to emphasize one's responsibility to use only empirically validated treatments. This positive move toward evidence-based therapy is due to social work's increased emphasis on accountability to clients and to third-party payers, and its desire to further the knowledge base of the profession. Still, the results of outcome research activities to date have been mixed and quite controversial. Meta-analytic research (that which combines the results of many individual research projects) in social work and related disciplines sometimes does, and sometimes does not, identify particular therapies, or therapy in general, as helpful to clients. The state of the science of outcome evaluation is still developing. We will consider some existing findings relative to social work practice, and then consider the larger issue of outcome evaluation.

While all social workers strive to be effective in the therapist role, there has been surprisingly little effectiveness research published on their work. Rosen, Proctor, & Staudt (1999) reviewed the research contents of 13 major social work journals between 1993 and 1997 and found that, proportionately, only one of every six research articles, and one of every 14 articles in general, addressed any relationship between intervention and outcome. Further, fewer than half of those interventions were articulated clearly enough to permit replication. Still, the amount of evaluation research in the social work profession is growing. Fischer (1976) was only able to locate 17 empirical studies for his well-known casework effectiveness study, but Gorey (1996) reported that 88 such studies were conducted between 1990–1994.

So what is known about effective social work therapy? Almost 30 years ago, two literature reviews by Fischer (1973, 1976) created a stir within social work by concluding that there was no evidence for the effectiveness of casework. Later, Reid and Hanrahan (1982) analyzed 44 studies and stated that conclusions about effectiveness were difficult to reach because of a lack of rigor in clinical research. They recommended that social workers increase the structure of their interventions so that well-constructed effectiveness studies might be developed.

Thomlison (1984) made a positive contribution to this issue with a meta-analysis of social work literature (focused on psychotherapy, marital therapy, family therapy, and behavior therapy). He did not set out to determine whether general interventions were effective, but to identify particular components of effective practice. His analysis found that effective social workers were able to adjust their practice to the problem at hand, prepare the client for intervention, specify the purposes of interventions, and attend to time limits (not necessarily short-term). He further identified elements of effective practice in working with people having serious mental illnesses (orientation to the process, concreteness, time limits, advocacy activities, limit setting, between-session contacts to provide information, outreach, supportive attitudes, and the communication of expectations for change), and child abusers (structured sessions, the provision of stress management, parenting and social skills training, and the cultivation of informal support systems).

Corcoran and Videka-Sherman (1992) further noted that in outpatient mental health settings, effective social workers tended to provide *active* interventions focused on exploration, modeling, advice, reinforcement, and task assignments. They concluded that adherence to a particular theory did not seem to be related to effectiveness—what mattered was what the social worker did, not the theory behind the action. They admitted that much remained to be learned about effectiveness with various types of clients, and called for more studies using comparison groups, unbiased samples, and long-term clients.

Gorey, Thyer, and Pawluck (1998) conducted the most recent meta-analysis of outcome research in social work, examining 45 studies conducted between 1990 and 1994. They attempted to compare the effectiveness of practice by social workers' theoretical orientations. The researchers found no overall differences in outcomes by theoretical orientation (which were primarily cognitive behavioral, but also included psychosocial, psychoanalytic, problem solving, task centered, systems, and radical-structural approaches). However, they did find that theoretical frameworks focused on individual client change were most effective at changing client behaviors, and that systems and structural frameworks were most effective at changing target systems beyond the individual client. In essence, therapies intended to produce particular types of outcomes were more effective at producing those outcomes than other therapies. The authors concluded by echoing sentiments voiced by many practice researchers, that greater specificity in social workers' therapy procedures is needed to facilitate useful future studies of outcome effectiveness.

The field of psychology has specified more rigorous effectiveness criteria. A task force of the American Psychological Association put forth a list of recommendations for evaluating clinical practice, which could also be used by social workers (Crits-Cristoph, 1998). The goal of this project was not to endorse certain interventions, but to facilitate the education of practitioners by identifying those treatments with a scientific basis. The criteria for "well-established" treatments include: (1) at least two group comparison experiments that demonstrated efficacy in terms of superiority to pill, placebo, or other treatment, or which were experimentally equivalent to another established treatment; or (2) a series of at least nine single-subject experimental designs demonstrating efficacy in comparison with a pill, placebo, or other treatment. Additional criteria include (3) the use of treatment manuals to maximize treatment specificity, (4) clearly described sample characteristics, and (5) the demonstration of effects by at least two different investigators or investigative teams. A somewhat less rigorous set of criteria for determining best practices includes two experiments showing a treatment to be more effective than waiting-list control group outcomes, one or more experiments meeting all of the previous criteria except for that of replication, and at least three single subject designs using manuals and clear sampling procedures.

These recommendations have been controversial among psychologists, for a number of reasons, as noted in the following list (Beutler & Baker, 1998; Chambless, 1998; Elkin, 1999; Goldfried & Wolfe, 1998).

- The methodologies are not able to examine relationship factors in therapy. These are fundamental to such theories as ego and self-psychology, among others.
- Therapist characteristics are often overlooked, such as their experience with particular problem areas and overall competence in carrying out particular interventions.
- There seems to be a methodological bias toward cognitive and behavioral strategies. Chambless (1998) agrees that a majority of the demonstrably effective therapies to date are cognitive or behavioral, but she asserts that this is due to the under-representation of other theories in research studies, rather than an inherent superiority of the featured therapies.
- Using manuals (highly structured protocols that direct the therapist's course of intervention and duration) may unduly limit the natural responsiveness of therapists to clinical situations. In fact, they may not be carefully adhered to in practice, as therapists may respond quite differentially to challenges that emerge in the course of therapy. There are multiple approaches to addressing a single theory.
- Diagnostic categories are rarely precise in capturing the essence of a clinical condition. That is, researchers tend not to be sensitive to differences in client characteristics, such as possible co-morbid (dual diagnosis) conditions. Clients are not passive recipients of therapy. Variables such as social support, socioeconomic status, distress level, motivation, and intelligence may be more important predictors of response than diagnosis.
- If clients are randomly assigned to an intervention that they would not choose, or are not compatible with, outcomes may be negatively affected.

There are, however, practical ways in which research regarding therapy effectiveness can be enhanced, and social workers in the role of therapist can be at the forefront of these developments. Most of these derive from a basic principle of collaboration between researchers and social work therapists, and the development of the therapist/researcher model of practice for enhancement of the use of small systems designs (Bloom, Fischer, & Orme, 1995). Such strategies might include:

- Matching therapists to clients by client preference for a particular type of therapy, to minimize client dissatisfaction or drop-out.
- Developing university/agency relationships in which social workers are given control of the therapy being provided and the researcher functions as the design expert.
- Disentangling the therapist vs. therapy confound by assessing the personal characteristics of the therapist. Monitoring the therapist/client relationship might be a productive way to better take this variable into account. Horvath's (1994) *Working Alliance Inventory* is one example of a means for doing so. The client and social worker complete the 36-item instrument at various intervals to provide comparison data on their perceptions of bonding, goal-orientation, and task focus.
- Studying theoretically integrated therapies.
- Make greater use of the methodology of replicated case studies.
- As noted earlier, Beutler and Baker (1998) assert that in evaluation research, *strategy* may be a more relevant variable to study than theory. Characteristics dictating therapeutic strategy include such factors as the client's defensive style, coping style,

levels of social support, and problem severity. These variables might be important to include in large-scale research when client homogeneity is sought.

- Instead of comparing the value of two or more therapies for one diagnostic group, the characteristics held by clients who respond differentially to the therapies might be determined.

In summary, it must be emphasized that the practice of evaluating one's own therapy interventions through the application of *single-systems* (comparing baseline and treatment measures) or *pre-experimental* designs (comparing pre-treatment with post-treatment measures) can be implemented in most agency settings. All that is required is a social worker with a background in basic research methods, and these are taught in all graduate programs. Any theoretical perspective, strategy, or intervention can be translated into observable indicators for use in this process, and doing so will help the social worker go a long way toward establishing the quality of his or her therapy practice with supervisors, funders, and administrators.

A Case Dilemma

Heidi was a 29-year-old, married, working mother (of a 12-year-old son) who came to the mental health center requesting individual therapy because of stresses associated with her job and troubled marriage. Heidi, an assistant manager at a grocery store in charge of bookkeeping, wanted to better manage stress so she could function effectively at work and qualify for a promotion during the coming year. During his assessment, the social worker took note of Heidi's reported history of sexual acting out prior to her marriage, and her patterns of obsessive-compulsive behavior at work. Trained primarily in ego psychology, he further noted Heidi's tendencies to intellectualize problems and avoid affective experience. He was also impressed with her strengths of intelligence, motivation, and resilience.

Early Intervention
In keeping with the client's stated preferences for working on her problems, the social worker initiated a cognitive/behavioral intervention strategy toward coping skill development. He concentrated more on behavioral techniques, however, as he did not want to support Heidi's tendencies to intellectualize. They contracted that Heidi would develop and practice new coping strategies including finding a comfortable, secluded space for reviewing her day's work once she returned home; developing a daily pattern of communication with her husband (who was reportedly reluctant to come to the center) about their moods, mutual plans, and parenting responsibilities; and implementing a set of relaxation activities. The social worker also helped Heidi devise a regular exercise regimen (walking) to reduce her overall tension, and he encouraged her to contact several friends more regularly as a social outlet (Heidi was reluctant to reach out to others).

The social worker estimated that Heidi would achieve significant improvement in six sessions (the agency permitted a maximum of 16 sessions, unless special permission was granted), and they agreed to review their work at that time. The social worker noted quick progress in Heidi's ability to manage her job responsibilities, as evidenced by her self-reports. The interactions with her husband were less successful, even though the social worker spent much time helping her rehearse strategies for better connecting with him. The worker noted that Heidi became more relaxed in their sessions over time and shared personal information more freely, which was evidence of their positive working alliance. It appeared that this would indeed be a short-term intervention.

After their fourth session, however, Heidi's depression and anxiety increased. The worker observed that the more personal content she shared, the more negative feelings she experienced. Heidi eventually admitted that she was, in fact, a survivor of long-term sexual abuse by her father and brothers, beginning at the age of 5 and extending into her high school years. She added insightfully that she had learned as a young girl to suppress her emotions as a means of coping with that trauma. Heidi had been in therapy once before to attempt to resolve her abuse issues but terminated that work prematurely, she said, because she became more depressed and feared becoming suicidal. The present therapy experience had reawakened her range of emotions and she had not been able to control them. Heidi was experiencing insomnia, nightmares, and poor concentration. Most disturbingly, she began to experience additional memories of abuse. She became more aware of her father's and brothers' actions and was overwhelmed with anger, despair, shame, guilt, and depression. She admitted to occasional suicidal wishes.

Later Intervention

The social worker felt that their work together was at a turning point. Heidi had sought help to deal with one set of problems, but another set of serious problems had emerged. He recognized that for Heidi to manage the effects of her abuse history, she would need to explore her emotions rather than avoid them. In doing so, she would likely become more distressed before developing new self-control. The social worker suggested, and Heidi agreed, that they expand their work together and utilize the ego psychology techniques of exploration and reflection in addition to the behavioral interventions, to gradually work through the negative emotions stemming from her abuse. He suggested occasional marital therapy sessions and offered to refer Heidi at a later date to an abuse survivor's group led by a social worker at another agency.

Heidi's new goals included increasing her external social supports, abuse history awareness, feelings of self-control, anger management skills, ability to manage negative emotions, self-esteem, and clarity of communication with her husband. The social worker first helped Heidi solidify her friendships and positive family supports as resources to draw upon when she became overwhelmed with distress. He referred Heidi to the agency physician for a medication evaluation when she requested medications, and an antidepressant was prescribed. The social worker also presented this case to the agency's peer review team for extended care, as it seemed likely that their work would require more than 16 sessions. He was granted up to 16 additional sessions with her.

Together, Heidi and the social worker balanced her needs for nurturing and support with her needs to face the facts of her abuse history and family trauma, and to learn to positively cope with it. From his ego psychology framework, the social worker encouraged a graduated process of reflection, providing Heidi with guidance and suggesting limits to the pacing of her self-exploration. He helped her to give up some defenses and to strengthen others, recognize and build on her personal strengths, and continue to develop stress-coping skills. Recognizing the agency's limits on service delivery, they met three times monthly, for 6 months. It was agreed that Heidi could phone the social worker twice weekly when in distress to ask what she might do to help herself calm down.

The social worker needed to establish linkages with the agency psychiatrist, the staff at a local crisis facility (which Heidi attended three times), and staff at a psychiatric hospital, where she was admitted once for suicidal ideation. The social worker monitored Heidi's progress by charting the frequency of her self-reported anxiety attacks, feelings of self-harm, phone calls and visits with friends, conversations with her spouse, and productive work days. The therapy contributed to Heidi's greater awareness of her needs, conflicts, and assets. It added to her stress at times; Heidi's psychological growth was erratic but continuous. She was able to make better decisions about her life goals and relationships with family and friends.

The social worker integrated family and group work into her therapy. Three months into their clinical relationship, Heidi agreed to the social worker's suggestion that her husband come for several marital therapy sessions. The social worker had observed that Heidi increasingly avoided sharing her feelings with her husband. Also, she and her husband seemed to focus attention on their son rather intrusively at times, largely to avoid a relationship with each other. Their son was experiencing normal adolescent drives to separate from his parents, and he was frustrated with their resistance to his changes. The social worker used a family systems approach over the course of four sessions with the couple, and learned that they had developed avoidance patterns of dealing with intimacy in their families of origin. These patterns were now creating tensions in their own household. Heidi's relationship with her husband improved in that they could talk more openly in the supportive atmosphere of the clinic about their mutual needs and feelings. Heidi found her husband to be more supportive than she had expected. Still, she made a decision near the end of her therapy to separate from him, allegedly as a means of testing her ability to take care of herself but also indicating that she was questioning her commitment to him.

Near the end of Heidi's individual therapy, she joined the group therapy program for survivors of sexual abuse. Designed for women who had been receiving individual therapy, it was an open-ended group that met every 2 weeks. The social worker-leader organized the group as a mutual support rather than an insight-development experience for the 10 members. The social worker provided educational material for the members about the prevalence of sexual abuse and the normalcy of their reactions to the trauma. Heidi still struggled with her need to face the reality and consequences of her abuse history, but stated that the group experience made her feel much less like an outsider. She developed additional supportive relationships there.

All of the interventions ended when Heidi made the decision to take a break from therapy, after 24 total individual sessions. She had been confronting her abuse history for 6 months and learned that she could integrate those facts into her sense of self without suppressing all of her emotions, losing herself in her work, or looking for others to rescue her. She was not completely at ease with herself and her past, but she had learned much and now wanted to focus her energies on other life pursuits, including her adjustment to living alone. The social worker agreed that her desire to end was indicative of Heidi's growth. She seemed to be communicating that she felt ready to get on with her life without the support of a therapist. She had been following the leads of older men all her life, and now was ready to take control of herself.

SUMMARY

Social workers have acted as therapists in mental health settings throughout the history of the profession. Trends within the profession, as well as the field of mental health, indicate that they will continue to thrive in that role. There are a variety of theoretical perspectives available to social workers, all of which have utility in particular settings. It is a hallmark of the profession's person-environment perspective that, as indicated in several of the earlier examples, the activities of the therapist usually involve linkage, medication, and advocacy activities. One challenge of social work therapists includes the attempt to preserve their professional values as they confront potentially negative external pressures, such as service limits imposed by funding bodies and administrations. Their need for social workers as therapists to provide more efficient and effective services is a positive challenge, and there is no reason that they cannot rise to this challenge through the application of single-system and macroresearch projects. Finally, although not emphasized in this chapter, interprofessional practice skills and leadership will continue to be crucial in the therapist role, as social workers combine their skills with those of physicians, nurses, psychologists, and others in the field of mental health to meet the holistic goals of clients.

KEY TERMS

Behavior Therapy: A therapy that asserts that the majority of one's thoughts, feelings, and behaviors are the result of reinforcement patterns and observational learning.

Cognitive Therapy: A therapy that asserts that people comprehend reality and problem solve in accordance with their individual schema, or habits of thought, that may or may not be functional toward their goal attainment.

Constructivist (Narrative) Therapy: A therapy that asserts that perceptions of reality are based on stories people tell themselves, and that change occurs through a process of reinterpreting situations, filing information gaps with new knowledge and experiences, or clarifying life goals.

Ego Psychology: A therapy that, while assuming the mental functions of id, ego, and superego, focuses on supporting or modifying the ego, the mental structure of personality that mediates between internal needs and the demands of the environment.

Family Emotional Systems Therapy: A therapy that focuses on the emotional lives of family members, and assumes that one's patterns of emotional behavior throughout life are largely established in the family of origin through processes of differentiation and fusion.

Group Therapy: The practice of treating mental, emotional, or behavioral disorders through a collective process of sharing experiences and emotions that help members move toward greater self-understanding and adjustment.

Object Relations Theory: A theory that emphasizes the client's capacity to form lasting attachments with others, based on early experiences of separation and individuation within the family of origin. The social worker as therapist relies on an exploration and adjustment of the client's relationship patterns as primary strategies for enhancing social functioning.

Psychosocial Theory: A systems theory that considers social functioning as a transactional process between people and their environments. It is a perspective that may be incorporated into a variety of therapy theories.

Relationship: The emotional bond between a social worker and client system that, when positive, facilitates the therapy process.

Self-psychology: A theory that emphasizes the importance of a client's development of a cohesive sense of self. The self includes the functions of action and reflection, and consists of the grandiose self, idealized parent image, and twinship self.

Solution-focused Therapy: A therapy that emphasizes that change is facilitated by amplifying exceptions to a client's problems, rather than focusing on problems themselves. It assumes that change in any element of a system will reverberate throughout the system.

Strategic Therapy: A therapy which, in the context of this chapter, is sometimes effective in overcoming anticipated family resistances to change by utilizing deception and paradoxical intervention strategies.

Structural Family Therapy: A therapy that conceptualizes quality of family functioning as determined by the presence of executive authority and clear structure, or sets of functional demands that organize how members and subsystems interact.

WEB RESOURCES

American Association of Marriage and Family Therapists (http://www.aamft. org/). This site is sponsored by the AAMFT professional association. It includes some resources for practitioners, and useful links, but is primarily a policy site.

American Association of State Social Worker Boards (Licensing) (http://www. aasswb.org). This association develops and monitors the social work licensing examination and is a central resource for information on the legal regulation of social work practice.

Association for the Advancement of Social Work with Groups (http://www. aaswg.org/). This site includes teaching resources, many useful links, discussion groups, articles, and conference information regarding group therapy.

Mental Health Net (http://www.mental help.net/). Sponsored by an organization known as CMHC Systems, this site provides information on many issues of concern to mental health practitioners, including assessment and intervention with a wide variety of client populations.

NASW Online (http://www.naswdc.org/). NASW includes recent materials gathered by the professional organization on a variety of broadly defined practice issues. These tend to reflect policy developments on practice.

World Wide Web Resources for Social Workers (http://www.nyu.edu/socialwork/wwwrsw/). This site provides descriptive information about many mental, emotional, and behavioral disorders, along with methods of assessment and intervention.

REFERENCES

Aponte, H. J., Zarski, J. J., Bixenstine, C., & Cibik, P. (1991). Home/community-based services: A two-tier approach. *American Journal of Orthopsychiatry, 61*(3), 403–408.

Barker, R. L. (1988). *The social work dictionary.* Silver Spring, MD: National Association of Social Workers.

Beutler, L. E., & Baker, M. (1998). The movement toward empirical validation: At what level should we analyze, and who are the consumers? In K. S. Dobson & K. D. Craig (Eds.), *Empirically supported therapies: Best practice in professional psychology* (pp. 43–65). Thousand Oaks, CA: Sage.

Biggerstaff, M. A. (1994). Licensing, regulation, and certification. In *Encyclopedia of Social Work* (pp. 1616–1624). Silver Spring, MD: National Association of Social Workers.

Bloom, M., Fischer, J., & Orme, J. G. (1995). *Evaluating practice: Guidelines for the accountable professional* (2nd ed.). Needham Heights, MA: Allyn & Bacon.

Campbell, R. J. (1996). *Psychiatric dictionary* (7th ed.). New York: Oxford University Press.

Chambless, D. L. (1998). Empirically validated treatments. In G. P. Koocher, J. C. Norcross, & S. S. Hill (Eds.), *Psychologists' Desk Reference* (pp. 209–219). New York: Oxford.

Cleveland, P. (1999). Structural family interventions. In A. C. Kilpatrick & T. P. Holland (Eds.), *Working with families: An integrative model by level of need* (2nd ed., pp. 103–121). Boston: Allyn & Bacon.

Clinical Social Work Federation (2001). "What is CSWF?" http://www.cswf.org/info.html.

Conte, H. R. (1997). The evolving nature of psychotherapy outcome research. *American Journal of Psychotherapy, 51*(3), 445–448.

Cooper, S. (1994). Do mental health professionals basically offer clients the same services? Yes. In S. A. Kirk & S. D. Einbinder (Eds.), *Controversial issues in mental health* (pp. 203–208). Boston: Allyn and Bacon.

Corcoran, K., & Videka-Sherman, L. (1992). Some things we know about effective social work. In K. Corcoran (Ed.), *Effective practice for common client problems* (pp. 15–27). Chicago: Lyceum.

Corsini, R. J., & Wedding, D. (Eds.). (2000). *Current psychotherapies* (6th ed.). Itasca, IL: F. E. Peacock.

Crits-Cristoph, P. (1998). Training in empirically validated treatments: The division 12 APA task force recommendations. In K. S. Dobson & K. D. Craig (Eds.), *Empirically supported therapies: Best practice in professional psychology* (pp. 3–25). Thousand Oaks, CA: Sage.

Dorfman, R. A. (1996). *Clinical social work: Definition, practice, and vision.* New York: Brunner/Mazel.

Dziegielewski, S. F., Shields, J. P., & Thyer, B. A. (1998). Short-term treatment: Models, methods, and research. In J. B. W. Williams & K. Ell (Eds.), *Advances in mental health research: Implications for practice* (pp. 287–308). Washington, DC: NASW Press.

Elkin, I. (1999). A major dilemma in psychotherapy outcome research: Disentangling therapists from therapies. *Clinical Psychology Science and Practice, 6*(1), 10–32.

Fairburn, C., Jones, R., Peveler, R., Carr, S., Solomon, R., O'Connor, M., Burton, J., & Hope, R. (1991). Three psychological treatments for bulimia nervosa: A comparison trial. *Archives of General Psychiatry, 48*, 463–469.

Fischer, J. (1976). *The effectiveness of social casework.* Springfield, IL: Charles C. Thomas.

Fischer, J. (1973). Is casework effective? A review. *Social Work, 18*, 5–20.

Flanagan, L. M. (1996). The theory of self psychology. In J. Berzoff (Ed.), *Inside out and outside in: Psychodynamic clinical theory and practice in contemporary multicultural contexts* (pp. 173–198). Northvale, NJ: Jason Aronson.

Frank, J. D., & Frank, J. B. (1993). *Persuasion and healing: A comparative study of psychotherapy* (3rd ed.). Baltimore: Johns Hopkins University Press.

Garfinkel, P., & Walsh, P. (1997). Drug therapies. In D. Garner & P. Garfinkel (Eds.), *Handbook of treatment for eating disorders* (2nd ed., pp. 372–380). New York: Guilford.

Goldfried, M. R., & Wolfe, B. E. (1998). Toward a more clinically valid approach to therapy research. *Journal of Consulting and Clinical Psychology, 66*(1), 143–150.

Goldstein, E. G. (1995a). *Ego psychology and social work practice* (2nd ed.). New York: Free Press.

Goldstein, E. G. (1995b). Psychosocial approach. In *Encyclopedia of Social Work* (19th ed., Vol. 3, pp. 1948–1954). Silver Spring, MD: National Association of Social Workers.

Goldstein, E. G., & Noonan, M. (1999). *Short-term treatment and social work practice: An integrative perspective.* New York: Free Press.

Gorey, K. (1996). Effectiveness of social work intervention research: Internal versus external evaluations. *Social Work Research, 20*, 119–128.

Gorey, K., Thyer, B. A., Pawluck, D. (1998). The differential effectiveness of social work interventions: A meta-analysis. *Social Work, 43*, 269–278.

Granvold, D. K. (Ed.). (1994). *Cognitive and behavioral treatment: Methods and applications.* Pacific Grove, CA: Brooks/Cole.

Hayes, S. C. (1998). Scientific practice guidelines in a political, economic, and professional context. In K. S. Dobson & K. D. Craig (Eds.), *Empirically supported therapies: Best practice in professional psychology* (pp. 26–42). Thousand Oaks, CA: Sage.

Hepworth, D., Rooney, R., & Larsen, J. (1997). *Direct social work practice: Theory and skills* (5th ed.). Belmont, CA: Brooks/Cole.

Hollis, F. (1972). *Casework: A psychosocial therapy* (2nd ed.). New York: Random House.

Horvath, A. O. (1994a). Research on the alliance. In A. O. Horvath & L. S. Greenberg (Eds.), *The working alliance: Theory, research, and practice* (pp. 259–286). New York: Wiley.

Horvath, A. O. (1994b). Empirical validation of Bordin's pantheoretical model of the alliance: The *Working Alliance Inventory* perspective. In A. O. Horvath & L. S. Greenberg (Eds.), *The working alliance: Theory, research, and practice* (pp. 109–128). New York: Wiley.

Kaplan, H. I., & Sadock, B. J. (1998). *Synopsis of psychiatry: Behavioral sciences/clinical psychiatry* (8th ed.). Philadelphia: Lippincott Williams & Wilkins.

Kerr, M. E., & Bowen, M. (1988). *Family evaluation: An approach based on Bowen theory.* New York: W. W. Norton.

Lackstrom, J. (1999). Eating disorders and social work. In F. J. Turner (Ed.), *Adult psychopathology: A social work perspective* (2nd ed., pp. 530–554). New York: Free Press.

Lantz, J. (1996). Cognitive theory and social work treatment. In F. J. Turner (Ed.), *Social work treatment: Interlocking theoretical approaches* (4th ed., pp. 94–115). New York: Free Press.

Lieberman, F. (1982). Psychotherapy and social work. In F. Lieberman (Ed.), *Clinical social workers as psychotherapists* (pp. 3–20). New York: Gardner Press.

Lin, A. M. P. (1994). Mental health overview. In *Encyclopedia of Social Work* (19th ed., Vol. 3, pp. 1705–1711). Silver Spring, MD: National Association of Social Workers.

Mattaini, M. A. (1997). *Clinical practice with individuals.* Washington, DC: NASW Press.

Meyer, C. (1994). Do mental health professionals basically offer clients the same services? No. In S. A. Kirk & S. D. Einbinder (Eds.), *Controversial issues in mental health* (pp. 209–213). Boston: Allyn & Bacon.

Minuchin, S., Lee, W., & Simon, G. M. (1996). *Mastering family therapy: Journeys of growth and transformation.* New York: Wiley.

Myers, L. L., & Thyer, B. A. (1997). Should social work clients have the right to effective treatment? *Social Work, 42*(3), 288–298.

National Association of Social Workers. (1999). *About NASW.* [On-line]. Available: http://www.naswdc.org/

National Association of Social Workers. (1996). *Code of ethics.* Washington, DC: Author.

National Association of Social Workers. (1994). *Social work speaks: NASW policy statements* (3rd ed.). Washington, DC: NASW Press.

Netting, F. E., Kettner, P. M., & McMurtry, S. L. (1998). *Social work macro practice* (3rd ed.). New York: Longman.

Nichols, M. P., & Schwartz, R. C. (2001). *Family therapy: Concepts and methods* (5th ed.). Boston: Allyn & Bacon.

O'Connell, B. (1998). *Solution-focused therapy.* Thousand Oaks, CA: Sage.

Olmstead, M., Davis, R., Rockert, W., Eagle, M., & Garner, D. (1991). Efficacy of brief group psychoeducational intervention for bulimia nervosa. *Behavioral Research and Therapy, 29,* 71–83.

Pippin, J, A., & Callaway, J. T. (1999). Family systems interventions. In A. C. Kilpatrick & T. P. Holland (Eds.), *Working with families: An integrative model by level of need* (2nd ed., pp. 155–168). Boston: Allyn & Bacon.

Reid, W. J. (1997). Research on task-centered practice. *Social Work Research, 21*(3), 132–137.

Reid, W. J., & Hanrahan, P. (1982). Recent evaluations of social work: Grounds for optimism. *Social Work, 27*(4), 328–340.

Rodwell, M. K. (1998). *Social work constructivist research.* New York: Garland.

Rosen, A., Proctor, E. K., & Staudt, M. A. (1999). Social work research and the quest for effective practice. *Social Work Research, 23*(1), 4–14.

Saari, C. (1986). *Clinical social work treatment: How does it work?* New York: Gardner.

Saulnier, C. F. (1997). Alcohol problems and marginalization: Social group work with lesbians. *Social Work with Groups, 20*(3), 37–59.

Sexton, T. L., & Whiston, S. C. (1994). The status of the counseling relationship: An empirical review, theoretical implications, and research directions. *The Counseling Psychologist, 22*(1), 6–78.

Specht, H., & Courtney, M. (1995). *Unfaithful angels: How social work has abandoned its mission.* New York: Free Press.

St. Clair, M. (1999). *Object relations and self psychology* (3rd ed.). Pacific Grove, CA: Brooks/Cole.

Swenson, C. R. (1995). Clinical social work. In *Encyclopedia of Social Work* (19th ed., Vol. 1, pp. 502–511). Silver Spring, MD: National Association of Social Workers.

Thomlison, R. J. (1984). Something works: Evidence from practice effectiveness studies. *Social Work, 29,* 51–57.

Thomlison, B., & Thomlison, R. J. (1996). Behavior theory and social work treatment. In F. J. Turner (Ed.), *Social work treatment: Interlocking theoretical approaches* (4th ed., pp. 39–68). New York: Free Press.

Toseland, R. W., & Rivas, R. F. (1998). *An introduction to group work practice* (3rd ed.). Boston: Allyn & Bacon.

Turner, F. J. (1996). An interlocking perspective for treatment. In F. J. Turner (Ed.), *Social work treatment: Interlocking theoretical approaches* (pp. 699–711). New York: Free Press.

Wineburgh, M. (1998). Ethics, managed care, and outpatient psychotherapy. *Clinical Social Work Journal, 26*(4), 433–443.

Woods, M. E., & Hollis, F. (2000). *Casework: A psychosocial therapy* (5th ed.). Boston: McGraw Hill.

SOCIAL WORKERS AS MEDIATORS

Kevin Corcoran
& Mary Ann Dearborn

An emerging role for social workers has been that of mediator. Social workers often serve as a mediator, regardless of the field of practice, client populations, or practice settings. As a mediator, the social worker is a neutral and impartial third party who helps facilitate a mutually agreeable resolution to a dispute by following the structured process of mediation. Similarly, the National Association of Social Workers (NASW) defines mediation as "an approach to conflict resolution in which a mutually acceptable, impartial third party helps the participants negotiate a consensual and informed settlement" (NASW, 1991, p. 1). It is often an alternative to litigation (Goldberg, Sander, & Rogers, 1992).

Social workers use mediation as an intervention in a number of settings and with a variety of client troubles. This chapter will review mediation, illustrate some of its uses in mental health, and provide an intervention protocol for mediation in mental health or other settings. Admittedly, mediating in mental health in general, and with people with serious mental illness in particular, is relatively new (Clement & Schwebel, 1997), although mediation of health care conflicts (e.g., malpractice claims) has been practiced for some time (Mazade, Blanch, & Petrila, 1994).

THE INTELLECTUAL BASE OF MEDIATION

Mediation as Social Work Practice

Mediation is about as eclectic as any intervention imaginable. It is based on theories from several different social sciences, such as sociology, law, communications, human relations, and just about every other field where people are people. That is, wherever people have conflicts (and that is just about everywhere), mediation is needed.

While there is no generally agreed-on theory of mediation—and in fact there are many theories—certain common elements of mediation are generally recognized. Conflicts, disputes, quarrels, "7s & 6s" (i.e., a vernacular phrase from the

1930s used to refer to being "at odds" with one other), or whatever term you use for disagreements, are an inevitable consequence of the human condition and the social world. Disagreements by any name are the results of differences between people. For social workers using mediation, these differences are often the results of "perceived" incompatible goals or expectations between at least two people. We say perceived incompatibility because one of the social worker's roles as a mediator is to help people with diverse views to see their similarities and to find common ground for resolution that meets all parties' needs.

Mediation is clearly a domain for social workers, because their roles place them in so many different settings. Not only do social workers often serve as mediators, but also as administrators of mediation programs. Social workers as mediators are found in child welfare, with such creative programs using mediation for open adoption or the relinquishment of parent rights. Social work mediation is also found in community-based social service settings, family treatment mental health clinics, and especially in criminal and juvenile justice. Social workers in juvenile and adult justice use mediation with victims and offenders for reconciliation, the establishment of restitution, and in some circumstances, even retribution.

Mediation fits well in the social work domain because it is designed to promote social justice. Mediation does this in a number of ways. First of all, mediation assumes equity between the disputing parties and strives to create a climate where both parties have equal power. For mediation to work, the parties must be empowered to obtain a *mutually* beneficial resolution to the dispute. Thus, mediation underscores and advances at least two of social work's major principles: equality and self-determination.

Mediation also advances social justice as it creates more affordable access to a more responsive court system (Goldberg, Sander, & Rogers, 1992), and allows for the representation of disenfranchised groups. An example of this concerns cultural conflicts and Native Peoples' rights for repatriation of ancestral remains (Thom, Myers, & Klugman, 1993). Consumers in a residential setting who are at odds with the neighborhood association provide an example of needed mediation that affects mental health. This type of dispute is not uncommon between the "chronic mentally ill" and the "chronic normal world," and may be readily addressed when the social worker uses mediation to reach an agreement. In both of these cases, the voice of the oppressed is amplified by mediation.

The role of mediation in the advancement of social justice is probably best illustrated with its most established use: labor negotiations and the procurement of livable wages and a safer environment for workers. Proof positive of how mediation has advanced social justice is a simple contrast between conditions for the average American worker today and a worker during the 1930 labor struggles, or those with very few rights at the beginning of the 20th century (Ellis, 1970, 1975). Social justice for many—although not all—workers in America has been advanced by mediation.

Additionally, Harry Specht (1990) asserted that mediation is developmental socialization, a core element in social work. Unlike resocialization and restoration, which Specht considered the primary purpose of clinical social work, mediation as developmental socialization helps "people perform in the appropriate social roles by providing information and knowledge, social support, social skills and social opportunities" (Specht, 1988, pp. 354–355).

This developmental role of mediation in social work is nothing new, even though mediation as a formalized intervention with specific procedures emerged in the mid-1970s. For example, William Schwartz (1961) identified the function of social workers as the mediation between the individual and society. There are conflicts in the promotion of well-being—"blockages," as Schwartz called them. Examples include maintaining communications in a family relationship, threats of violence, adequate housing, employment, discrimination, and access to affordable health and social services. When a social worker mediates these conflicts, the individual's developmental socialization includes a mutually beneficial solution to a problem.

Another strong nexus between mediation and social work is the role of problem solving in mediation. According to the widely read Compton and Galaway (1994) and most good introductory textbooks, problem-solving processes are central to social work practice. In their opinion, the problem-solving process is a way social workers put Schwartz's concept of mediation into action. Social work mediators use problem solving to resolve conflicts (illustrated in Figure 5.1). Problem solving is an essential element of all mediations.

Mediation in Multicultural Social Work

The mediation process can be adapted for use with a wide range of people and across a wide range of settings. These features of mediation give rise to an intervention that is particularly useful in cross-cultural circumstances, the field where social workers have a professional preeminence. In part, this is because mediation facilitates communication and understanding from the view of the commonality of human experience while concomitantly respecting the diversity of groups and the uniqueness of individuals. The theory and practice of mediation in the multicultural context strives to separate the behaviors of individuals in the dispute from their culturally imposed expectations of disputatious behavior. For example, the belief in the need to defend one's honor, whether as a gentleman of the south (the origin of much of this, Fischer, 1989) or a young street-wise teenager who will not be "*diss*-ed"(the contemporary manifestation of defending honor, Butterfield, 1995).

In addition, mediation in multicultural settings strives to minimize the role of inaccurate attributions of a group of people to the individuals in the conflict. Finally, mediation, as a flexible process, may be adapted to differences between cultures, such as being sensitive to eye contact when meeting with Native Americans (Haberfeld & Townsend, 1993). As is apparent, skills in mediation are particularly useful to social workers who work with diverse and oppressed populations.

An excellent example of adapting mediation with diverse cultures is described in Huber's (1993) *Mediation Around the Medicine Wheel*. With the guidance of a

Text continues on page 108

INTRO ⟹ OPENING ⟹ VENTILATE & CLARIFY ⟹
PROBLEM SOLVING ⟹ AGREE

Phase 1: Introduction

STEP 1: Introduce yourself and both of the parties.

↓

STEP 2: Define mediation:
- A negotiation process of settling a dispute with the help of a neutral third party.
- If a settlement is reached, it is because the parties of the dispute agreed.

IT IS THEIR DISPUTE AND THEIR SETTLEMENT.

↓

STEP 3: Define your role:
- To help the parties understand each other.
- To help them problem solve.
- To help them reach an agreement.

↓

STEP 4: Explain how you are impartial or neutral:
- Ask: "Is there any reason, _____, you think I may be

Party 1
  biased for or against you?"
- Ask the other party: "Is there any reason, _____, you

Party 2
  think I may be biased for or against you?"

↓

STEP 5: Explain confidentiality:
- The agreement to keep the content of the mediation private between each other.
- The agreement that topics discussed in mediation will not be discussed elsewhere.

↓

STEP 6: Explain ground rules:
- No name calling.
- No interruptions—therefore, each has a pen and paper.
- No criticizing the other persons.

↓

STEP 7: Explain caucusing/private session:
- A time for a mediator to meet privately with each party for additional information.
- The mediator or either party may call for a private session.
- Private sessions are confidential: The information will not be brought back to the table without the permission of the party.

↓

STEP 8: Agreement to mediation:
- Determine if both parties are willing to try mediation. Ask: "Are you both willing to give mediation a try?"

↓

STEP 9: Sign an agreement to mediate and give to both parties.

FIGURE **5.1**

Manual Developed for Mental Health Consumers

INTRO ⟹ OPENING ⟹ VENTILATE & CLARIFY ⟹
PROBLEM SOLVING ⟹ AGREE

Phase 2: Opening Statements

STEP 1A: "I need to understand what the dispute is all about. So who wants to go first and give their view of the problem?"
ANSWER: _____

↓

STEP 1B: If both agree, congratulate them for their first agreement.

↓

STEP 1C: If there is no agreement on who goes first, flip a coin.

↓

STEP 2: Ask for a brief explanation of the conflict: "Okay, _____, briefly tell me what the conflict is all about."

↓

STEP 3: After a brief explanation, paraphrase the party's view: "In summary, then, your position is _____."

↓

STEP 4: Ask the other party, "Okay, _____, what is your view of the problem?"

↓

STEP 5: Paraphrase the second party's view of the problem: "In summary, then, your position is _____."

↓

SUMMARY NOTES

Party One: _____   Party Two: _____

Record Your Notes Here

Phase 3: Ventilation and Clarification

STEP 1: Ask: "How do you feel about, or what are your opinions of, this problem?" (Encourage communication between the parties and give plenty of time for this.)

PARTY ONE: _____   PARTY TWO: _____

Record Notes Here

STEP 2: Be certain the parties understand each other. Ask: "_____, what do you think _____ is saying about this issue?"

STEP 3: Repeat the question to the other party. Ask: "_____, what do you think the other person is saying?"

PARTY ONE: _____   PARTY TWO: _____

Record Notes Here

STEP 4: Separate "must have" from "need." Ask: "What do you each *need* to settle this conflict?"

PARTY ONE: _____   PARTY TWO: _____

Record Notes Here

STEP 5: Ask: "What is most important about what you want?"

STEP 6: Ask: "What other ways can you get what you need to settle?"

PARTY ONE: _____   PARTY TWO: _____

Record Notes Here

Phase 4: Problem Solving

STEP 1: What does each need to settle? Summarize Step 6 from previous page.

PARTY ONE: _____   PARTY TWO: _____

_____   _____
                    Record Notes Here
_____   _____

_____   _____

STEP 2: Ask each how else they can get what is needed. Give your opinion as well.

PARTY ONE: _____   PARTY TWO: _____

Altern. 1 _____   _____
Altern. 2 _____   _____
Altern. 3 _____   _____

STEP 3: What is the *best* outcome if there is no settlement? Ask: "What is the best outcome if you don't settle today?"

PARTY ONE: _____   PARTY TWO: _____

_____   _____
                    Record Notes Here
_____   _____

_____   _____

STEP 4: What is the *worst* outcome if there is no settlement? Ask: "What is the worst outcome if you don't settle today?"

PARTY ONE: _____   PARTY TWO: _____

_____   _____
                    Record Notes Here
_____   _____

_____   _____

STEP 5: Compare the "best" and "worst" outcomes and ask: "Does this comparison help you reach an agreement?"
(Remember to consider **who** will do **what, how well, when,** and **where.**)

STEP 6: What will each party do to settle the conflict?
Party 1 will do _____

if Party 2 does _____

Party 2 will do _____

if Party 1 does _____

Phase 5: Agreement Contract

⇌ STEP 1: Summarize Step 6 from the previous page.
"Okay, it is my understanding that, _____, you will do...,
                                 Party 1
and _____, you will do...."
                Party 2

↓

⇌ STEP 2: Reality checking.

Ask: " _____, are you actually capable of doing what you say?"
            Party 1
Ask: "And _____, are you actually capable of doing what you say?"
               Party 2

↓

⇌ STEP 3: Writing the contract.
- Write the contract using each party's first name.
- Be concrete and use terms others can observe.
- Write in positive terms: what will be done, not what someone won't do.
- Balance the agreement.
  (e.g., Party One will do and Party Two will do, then Party Two will do and Party One will do. Do not include anybody in the agreement if they were not part of the mediation.)

↓

⇌ STEP 4: Read the contract to the parties and ask if this is a correct reflection of their agreement.
        REMIND THEM IT IS THEIR AGREEMENT, NOT YOURS.

↓

⇌ STEP 5: Have both sign the contract and give each a copy.

↓

⇌ STEP 6: Thank both for coming to mediation and for working so hard.

↓

⇌ STEP 7: Remind them that you will call them in a couple of weeks to see if they complied with the mediated agreement.

↓

⇌ STEP 8: Invite them back to mediation if they continue to have problems.

GOOD JOB!

work group, Huber developed a model of mediation for use with Native American communities. The model incorporates widely held aboriginal values. For example, primary ideals for dealing with conflicts include equality among people, cooperation, sharing, harmony, consensus, privacy, patience, and modesty. Huber also enumerated other indigenous values relevant to mediation, including respect for elders, holistic approach to life including spirituality, relativity of time, cultural heritage, and the value of family and community. These traits, along with communication styles, were incorporated into four general procedures, which are based on the four directions of the medicine wheel: (1) the East, which sets the climate; (2) the South, which is the telling of the story; (3) the West and the discovery of what is important; and (4) the North and the creation of solutions. Huber recommends displaying this in visual form at the mediation to facilitate an understanding of the dispute resolution process. The goal of the model of mediation with Native Peoples is to provide for growth and healing from the conflict, and the restoration of the harmonious relationships between the disputants and their community.

The foundation of Huber's model is that resolution is grounded in aboriginal spirituality and healing through understanding, dignity, and respect. In the view of Zumeta (1993), Native Peoples' spirituality is generally based on the connectedness of all things. Mediation can utilize this to facilitate a resolution of a dispute. The connectedness of all things brings the disputes to some form of commonality. This is very similar to one of the techniques used in mediation with European Americans, which is to get the parties to see their similarities, that is, how they have much in common. In both incidences, the connectedness of the individuals helps bring the disputants to a common ground.

Social Work's Contribution to Mediation

Social work's contribution to the development of mediation has encompassed family social work, including improving child-parent relations, family mediation (Lemmon, 1985), and divorce mediation, which received some of its initial development by social workers (e.g., Haynes, 1981). Social work's contribution to mediation has been particularly important in the justice system, for both juveniles and adults. This includes restorative justice, such as victim-offender reconciliation and restitution. The primary social work contributions are the works of Galaway, Umbriet, and Nugent.

Social work's most significant contribution to mediation is probably in juvenile and criminal justice, particularly the former. Social work researchers have illustrated the value of mediation when used with crime victims and juvenile offenders, essentially applying mediation with delinquent and antisocial behaviors (Galaway, 1988; Umbreit, 1993, 1995). The role of mediation with these problems is especially valuable, because so few effective interventions are available (Kazdin, 1995). The goals of a victim-offender mediation are to provide a safe environment for sincere dialogue, to meet emotional and informational needs, and for the offender to "make things right" (i.e., restorative justice, Galaway, 1988).

One indicator of success in victim and offender mediations is the sheer prolif-eration of programs, which have grown from just a few in 1978 to more than 300 by 1998 (Umbriet & Greenwood, 1998). Additionally, and more importantly, five stud-ies of mediation—most having been done by social workers—have evaluated medi-ation and generally report a reduction in the rate of re-offending (Nugent, Umbreit, Wiinamaki & Paddock, 2001).

In summary, it is difficult to aver the exact contribution of social work to media-tion. In part, as we mentioned earlier, mediation is very eclectic, and no profession can lay claim to this intervention. It is, indeed, "meat and potato" social work. It is also applied sociology, intergroup psychology, and good lawyering, and encompasses just about every other professional and intellectual discipline. For example, at various academic institutions, the mediation program is housed in the departments of phi-losophy and speech communication. In general, though, mediation has had important contributions by social workers in the area of family relations and juvenile justice.

Mediation in Mental Health

There are many uses of mediation in mental health. Clement and Schwebel (1997) argue that mediation in mental health has been influenced by two forces, managed care and the recovery movement. The former affords opportunities for resolving disputes when mental health care is denied or payment reduced. The recovery movement, in contrast, has played a role in guiding the development of communi-ty-based mediation programs for people with severe and persistent mental health conditions (Anthony, Cohen, & Farkus, 1990).

A venue for this type of mediation in mental health care is the small claims court. A small claim may range from a few dollars to several thousand dollars. The claim in mental health care may be against a third party insurance company, a state mental health association, or a fourth party in the form of a managed care organization, and there are numerous legal redresses in managed care (see, e.g., Corcoran & Winslade, 1994). One particularly appealing aspect of mediation in managed care is that in most state jurisdictions, some form of alternative to litigation is mandated—mediation or otherwise (e.g., arbitration; see *Osheroff v. Chestnut Lodge*, 1985).

In these situations, social workers using mediation may overwhelm persons with severe and persistent mental illness, and they run the risk of exacerbating the symptoms of the person with mental illness. This risk factor is furthered by the fact that the courtroom has a high level of stimulation, which is counterindicated for people with some mental health conditions, schizophrenia in particular (Kaplan & Sadock, 1998). Mediations, in contrast, may be heard in a smaller, more intimate setting, with lights turned down low, and the cognitive and environmental stimuli restricted. We have found that this is critical to mediating with people who have a mental health condition.

One of the critical roles of the social worker in this situation is as an advocate or agent of the person with a mental illness, versus the managed care organization, men-tal health agency, or whatever other adversary confronts your client. When social workers are using this type of mediation, we suggest taking frequent breaks during the mediation, and spending a little extra time explaining the process in concrete terms. Additionally, in many jurisdictions, lawyers are not allowed, which is especially helpful when the mediation is with a person with a mental health condition.

There are various other uses of mediation with people who have the challenges of mental health conditions, including mediating disputes between members of a social club or a supportive housing unit. Mediation is also useful when addressing issues between mental health consumers and family care providers. For example, mediation could help a family determine how long a recently discharged family member may stay in the house and under what conditions.

A rather unique use of mediation in mental health concerns civil commitments, involuntary as well as those determined by the relatively new "advanced directive." An advanced mental health directive is essentially a "living will," which is executed should a person with a mental illness become incapacitated. The negotiation of a living will or advanced directive is a great use of mediation. Oftentimes the social worker will work with a mental health consumer in a position of trust for what is in the best interest of the client. This client trust must be balanced against social costs (Sabin, 1994). For example, in the event of mental incompetence, the consumer may want to live in his or her parents' basement, but the parents may not have the same desires. If the wishes of the consumer and the parents are to be squared, then a variety of terms and conditions are subject to a mediated agreement.

In summary, the literature has addressed the viability and mediation services for mental health clients, as a tool in the arsenal of intensive case management (Banyan & Antes, 1992), and as a procedure in mental health consumer-run services. It appears, however, that there has been little systematic effort to integrate mediation in case management. There is also little empirical evidence about mediation with mental health consumers, though training does have a noted impact on consumers and family members (Mayer, 1995). Empirical evidence of the efficacy of mediation with mental health consumers is not available at this time.

MAJOR TASKS AND GOALS

So far, we have considered mediation in general and its use in various settings, including mental health. However, we have not discussed mediation techniques. This section will delineate the major tasks and goals of mediation. Because mediation is itself a fairly structured intervention, many of the tasks are actual procedures, or steps followed in the mediation process. The major task or goal of mediation is to empower two parties with divergent and disagreeable views to problem solve for the purpose of reaching a mutually agreeable resolution to their conflict. As is apparent from this definition, the goal of mediation is to agree to settle a dispute, which is frequently a written settlement.

The mediated agreement is best obtained by adhering to a structured process, a specified procedure, if you will. Most views of mediation agree that it is a structured process that follows a specified set of steps, procedures, or phases (Nugent, 2001). As we discussed earlier, some models have only a few phases; others have many. Huber's model for Native Peoples has four phases. Moore, in contrast, identifies 12 stages, of which five occur prior to the actual mediation. Therefore, the actual mediation itself has seven stages.

There is, in fact, no agreement on the actual phases or steps in mediation. As is apparent from Huber's examples and the model at the top of Figure 5.1, most of the phases overlap. Moreover, our experiences have shown that most mediators are trained in a systematic mediation procedure, but they soon adapt the process to their own style and the circumstances of the conflict. For example, there may be times when the number of steps are 10, as illustrated in Table 5.1, a 10-step approach to school-based mediation. A 10-step approach may be operationalized as 10 questions and made useful by reproducing them on pocket-sized laminated cards. Students trained in school-based mediation carry cards with the 10 questions as they patrol the recess yard, much like the crosswalk guard helps at the intersection. Even with this very standardized approach, the 10 steps are often modified. An 8th grader suggested modification of these cards when he indicated that step 3 was not useful, "because guys lie."

As you learn to conduct mediations, we suggest that you stick with a more structured set of procedures and follow them closely. With time, your own style will emerge. We will present a set of procedures in the next section that has been developed for use with and by people with mental health conditions, and has been used in disputes of up to $175,000. The procedures are particularly useful for mental health consumers, because each phase has a number of delineated steps and prompts to facilitate the mediation, should the mediators become stuck.

TECHNIQUES, STRATEGIES, AND SKILLS

When working with people who have a mental health condition, social workers may find it necessary to limit the number of stages of mediation. This is important, in part, because of the need to restrict environmental and cognitive stimuli for people with severe mental illness. It also allows for better comprehension for people on psychotropic medication or when symptomatology impedes the mediation process, such as anxiety or psychomotor agitation.

Regardless of the various delineations of the proper number of phases or steps, suffice it to say that mediation will almost always be accompanied by a specified set of procedures. Most importantly, because the process is a fairly well-enumerated procedure, mediation is easily operationalized in a manual format.

Figure 5.1 presents a manual developed for mental health consumers. The manual was based on input from a group in dispute resolution. The group consisted of 13 mental health consumers and 12 professionals who were also familiar with mental health (including, e.g., a judge from the civil commitment court). Each phase encompasses the general steps to reaching a resolution to the dispute, and

TABLE

5.1

PROMOTING PEACE ON THE PLAYGROUND

Ten-Question Approach for School-based Mediation

1. Do you want help solving the conflict?

2. Do you think I will be fair to each of you?

3. Do you promise to be honest and tell the truth?

4. Do you promise not to interrupt or call each other names?

5. Do you promise to keep everything confidential, you know, just between you guys?

6. All right, what happened? (Remember to give parties equal time to talk it out.)

7. What do you want as a fair resolution to this disagreement?

8. What are you willing to do to help resolve it?

9. Okay, Party 1, you agree to _____, and Party 2, you agree to _____. Is that correct?

10. Will you agree to come for mediation if this agreement does not work?

many of the steps include prompts to help guide the mediator. One useful and permissible way to use this manual is to enlarge it and reproduce it for use as a working document during the mediation.[1]

The first phase of mediation is the Introduction, which has nine steps. The purpose of the introduction is to provide an overview and understanding of what mediation is, the role of the mediator, and the expectations of the parties. This phase is critical because it establishes the cooperative and voluntary basis of any mediation. One of the reasons the introduction is so crucial is because the clients are entering into an arrangement that is likely unfamiliar to them. First of all, there is the fact that there is a dispute of some sort; and secondly, the process is largely legal and unknown to the parties. The clients will need an explanation of what to expect from the process and what is expected of them.

Oftentimes mediation requires two written agreements: an agreement to actually mediate and the mediated settlement. An example of an agreement to mediate is displayed in Figure 5.2. We recommend enlarging this form and reproducing it on noncarbon reproduction paper for use at the actual time of the mediation.

The second agreement is the one obtained from participating in the mediation. Both agreements have common elements of a binding contract, a legal agreement, if you will. A contract is simply an offer by one person and the acceptance of that offer by another "with consideration," which means the exchange of something, like money. A handshake may even be sufficient consideration to make a binding contract.

---

[1] The mediation manual was developed by the senior author with a grant from the Center for the Study of Mental Health Policy and Services, a NIMH Research Development Center at Portland State University. The manual is in the public domain and may be copied ad libitum with authorship properly credited.

AGREEMENT TO MEDIATE

We agree to mediation on _____, 200__. We agree to the following:

1. We agree to enter mediation voluntarily.

2. We agree to bargain in good faith.

3. We agree to the following three rules of mediation:

      a. to use common courtesy (e.g., no name calling or interruptions),

      b. not to criticize the other person(s),

      c. to keep the content of the mediation confidential between us.

4. Either party or the mediator may end the mediation at any time.

5. Each party agrees that the mediator will not be held liable for any act or omission resulting from the mediation.

_____   _____
Party 1's Name   Party 2's Name

_____
Mediator

_____
Date

FIGURE **5.2**

Sample "Agreement to Mediate" Form

The Agreement to Mediate is important because it establishes the parameters of the procedures. Common elements of almost all mediation include both parties participating voluntarily and in good faith. As suggested by the 10-question approach in Table 5.1, this means they agree to tell the truth. The ground rules of the procedures are also delineated and discussed. Additional ground rules may be added, if necessary. For example, a mental health consumer in a mediation may ask the other person not to roll her eyes because it makes him suspicious; the parties could agree to this out of a mutual understanding of mental health conditions and respect for the other person. This idea, or "rule," could be added to the agreement to mediate.

The second phase of mediation is the Opening Statements by each party. The purpose of the opening statement is to get an understanding of each party's view on the dispute. You will notice in Figure 5.1 that, at this phase, it must be determined who will speak first (Step 1a), and the next step points out to the parties that they have, in fact, agreed upon something already. This illustrates a powerful tool of mediation: reinforcing the parties for each and every agreement between the disputing parties. Steps 2 and 4 are designed to facilitate each party's brief overview of the dispute, and Steps 3 and 5 provide prompts for paraphrasing the parties' views. By paraphrasing, mediators show the parties that they understand, and this leads directly to the next phase in the mediation.

The third phase in the mediation process is generally two stages. We have combined these phases in the mediation process to appear more manageable to mental health consumers and because the two seem to occur concomitantly. Ventilation is the process of having both parties fully express their views, and to do so with communication directed between the two of them. The role of the mediator is to facilitate this expression and understanding. More often than not, the ventilation will include the expression of feelings as well as circumstances of the dispute. Steps 1 and 3 are presented to facilitate the expression of affect and content.

This is important for both parties, because it helps uncover hidden agendas in the disputes or other hidden disputes. For example, a dispute between two elderly men over a $25.00 battery cable—where weapons were actually drawn by both!—was fueled by the scurrilous language used by one man's wife toward the other man. Movement toward a resolution began when the husband dropped his head, shook it from side to side, sighed, and said, "Man, she talks to me like that, too." It was, in fact, the assault against honor that was of issue more than the pecuniary predicament.

The second part of this phase allows for clarification by the disputants. As the preceding example illustrates, the ventilation of affect allowed for a clarification of the actual dispute. Steps 4 through 6 facilitate the clarification. The understanding of the assault of honor made it relatively easy to resolve the issue of the $25.00 battery cable. Like the earlier phases of mediation, the Ventilation and Clarification phase leads directly to the Problem-Solving Phase. You will note that Step 1 of this phase is, in fact, a summary of the last step of the previous phase, suggesting that the phases are distinguishable but that mediation is a continuous process.

Much of the problem-solving phase is an effort to help each party differentiate their positions from their interests. This is based on the work of Fischer and Ury

time. Sally agreed to take her medication regularly, assisted by Sue, who would keep track of the doses for Sally, in writing, on a calendar.

All three, spontaneously, agreed that talking about these issues in this way was new (they'd not done this before) and important (much of what was said in the meeting had not been communicated previously). The mediator suggested that they could continue to hold family meetings like this one in their own home, without a mediator. They discussed holding weekly meetings in a quiet, private setting, each taking turns telling their stories, learning what is important, and working together to explore options and come up with solutions for making things better, not worse.

Sally was confident that the agreement they had reached would work out ("everything will be fine"), and wanted to go home right away. Sue and Sam seemed less sure. The mediator suggested a test of the terms of the agreement. Sue and Sam agreed that Sally could come home for a day, then an overnight, and finally for a weekend to see how things worked out. It was agreed that each would help the others to keep the agreement ("gentle reminders"), and that if there were no problems, Sally could come home from the hospital, to stay. Pat's role in the mediation process was to help the family arrange the passes from the hospital for the day, overnight, and weekend home visits.

One week after the mediation, Sally had her discharge, Pat had one less name on her discharge planning list, and the hospital had an open bed to offer on the acute care unit. What had started out as a dilemma had become a win-win situation, not uncommon when mediation is employed.

About 15 months after the mediation, Pat was thinking about Sally and checked her hospital case file. Pat was surprised to see that Sally had no readmissions. This was a positive change from her pre-mediation hospital admission pattern (three admissions in 2 years). Could the mediation have had a positive impact beyond the resolution of the out-of-home placement dispute?

KEY TERMS

Developmental Socialization: What mediation encourages; when people perform in appropriate social roles through the provision of resources, such as information and knowledge, social support, social skills, and opportunities.

Mediation: An approach to conflict resolution, based on principles of equality and self-determination—most often voluntary and often an alternative to litigation—in which a mutually acceptable, neutral, impartial third party helps participants in the structured process of mediation negotiate a consensual and informed settlement.

Mediator: A neutral, impartial third party who facilitates a mutually agreeable resolution to a dispute by following the structured process of mediation learned through specialized training.

Mediation Agreement: An agreement to use mediation to try to resolve a disagreement; the people involved in a disagreement (sometimes called the parties) become participants in a process facilitated by a mediator.

Mediated Agreement: A practical guide of what each person expects of the other to resolve a disagreement. A written form is recommended, with each item of what is to be done by each person set out separately (called a clause) and alternated throughout the agreement, not everything one person will do and then everything the other person will do. It is common for a mediated agreement to include a clause that, should there be a problem with the agreement, the people will come back to mediation to try, again, to reach an agreement.

Mediation Use: A wide range, including settling disagreements related to adoption, relinquishment of parental rights, reconciliation and restitution between victims and offenders, neighborhood problems, school yard conflicts among children, labor and employment issues, family matters, living arrangements between nonfamily members, benefits, health care, business, cultural misunderstandings, and more.

WEB RESOURCES

Like so many other topics found on the Web, resources related to mediation are nothing less than overwhelming. A simple search of the key term *dispute resolution* produces 814 sites, which is nothing compared to a search of the key word *mediation*, resulting in 2,315 sites.

By the time you read this chapter, however, many of these thousands of sites will perhaps be replaced with many others. Consequently, we believe it is most beneficial to list just a few seminal sites that we know will be around for a while. These are essentially the sites of professional organizations in mediation and the National Association of Social Workers Web site, where the *Standards of Practice for Social Work Mediators* is posted. Information about the following organizations is posted on each of their Web sites.

If you are looking for more Web sites on mediation, try placing your key word search through a Web site that links a number of large search engines. We have found http://www.meta crawler.com/ particularly helpful.

Academy of Family Mediators (AFM) (http://www.mediators.org/). E-mail: afmoffice @mediators.org.

American Bar Association Section on Dispute Resolution (ABA-SDR (http://www. abanet. org/dispute/). E-mail: dispute @abanet. org.

National Association for Community Mediation (NAFCM) (http://www.nafcm. org). E-mail: nafcm@nafcm.org.

Society for Professionals in Dispute Resolution (SPIDR) (http://www.spidr. org/). E-mail: spidr@spidr.org.

National Association of Social Workers (http://www.naswdc.org/). E-mail: info@nas wdc.org (see "Practice Standards" under "Publications").

REFERENCES

Anthony, W., Cohen, M., Farkas, M. (1990). *Psychiatric rehabilitation.* Boston, MA: Boston University.

Banyan, C. D., & Antes, J. R. (1992). Therapeutic benefits of interest-based mediation. *Hospital and Community Psychiatry, 43*(7), 738–739.

Butterfield, F. (1995). *All God's Children: The Bosket family and the American tradition of violence.* New York: Avon.

Clement, J. A., & Schwebel, A. I. (1997). Mental health: Mediation: An intervention to facilitate the empowerment of mental health consumers. In E. Kruk (Ed.), *Mediation and conflict resolution in social work and the human services* (pp. 195–210). Chicago: Nelson-Hall.

Compton, B. R., & Galaway, B. (1994). *Social work processes.* Pacific Grove, CA: Brooks/Cole.

Corcoran, K., & Winslade, W. J. (1994). Eavesdropping on the 50-minute hour: Confidentiality and managed mental health care. *Behavioral Sciences and the Law, 12,* 351–365.

Dearborn, M. A., & Parkes, J. (April 2, 1998). Healthcare mediation: A case study of an out-of-home placement dispute mediated at a state psychiatric hospital. Paper presented at the Alaska Dispute Settlement Association Conference, Anchorage, AK.

Ellis, E. R. (1970). *A nation in torment: The Great American Depression, 1929–1939.* New York: Kodansha.

Ellis, E. R. (1975). *Echoes of a distant thunder: Life in the United States, 1914–1918.* New York: Kodansha.

Fischer, D. H. (1989). *Albion's seed: Four British folkways in America.* New York: Oxford.

Fischer, R., & Ury, W. (1981). *Getting to yes: Negotiating agreement without giving in.* New York: Houghton Mifflin.

Galaway, B. (1988). Crime victim and offender mediation as a social work strategy. *Social Service Review, 62,* 668–683.

Goldberg, S. B., Sander, F. E. A., & Rogers, N. H. (1992). *Dispute resolution: Negotiation, mediation, and other processes.* Boston: Little Brown.

Haberfeld, S., & Townsend, J. (1993). Power and dispute resolution in Indian Country. *Mediation Quarterly, 10,* 405–422.

Haynes, J. (1981). *Divorce mediation: A practical guide for therapists and counselors.* New York: Springer.

Huber, M. (1993). Mediation around the medicine wheel. *Mediation Quarterly, 10*(4), 355–365.

Kaplan, H. I., & Sadock, B. J. (1998). *Synopsis of psychiatry: Behavioral sciences clinical psychiatry* (8th ed.). Baltimore: Williams & Wilkins.

Kazdin, A. E. (1995). *Conduct disorders in childhood and adolescence* (2nd ed.). Thousand Oaks, CA: Sage.

Lemmon, J. A. (1985). The mediation method throughout the life cycle. *Mediation Quarterly, 7,* 5–22.

Mayer, B. S. (1995). Conflict resolution. In R. L. Edwards et al. (Eds.), *Encyclopedia of social work* (11th ed., pp. 613–622). Silver Spring, MD: NASW Press.

Mazade, N., Blanch, A., & Petrila, J. (1994). Mediation as a new technique for resolving disputes in the mental health system. *Administration and Policy in Mental Health, 21*(5), 431–445.

Moore, C. W. *The mediation process: Practical strategies for resolving conflict.* San Francisco: Jossey-Bass.

NASW. (1991). *Standards of practice for social work mediators.* Washington, DC: National Association of Social Workers Press.

Nugent, W. R. (2001). Mediation techniques for persons involved in disputes. In H. Briggs & K. Corcoran (Eds.), *Social work practice: Treating common client problems* (2nd ed.). Chicago: Lyceum.

Nugent, W. R., Umbreit, M. S., Wiinamaki, L., & Paddock, J. (2001). Participation in victim-offender mediation and re-offense: Successful replications. *Research on Social Work Practice, 11,* 5–23.

Osheroff v. Chestnut Lodge (1985). 490 A2d. 720.

Sabin, J. E. (1994). Caring about patients and caring about money: The American Psychiatric Association Code of Ethics meets managed care. *Behavioral Sciences and the Law, 12,* 317–330.

Schwartz, W. (1961). Social worker in the group. In National Conference on Social Welfare (Ed.), *Social welfare forum.* New York: Columbia University Press.

Specht, H. (1988). *New directions for social work practice* (pp. 49–56). Englewood Cliffs, NJ: Prentice-Hall.

Specht, H. (1990). Social work and the popular psychotherapies. *Social Service Review, 64,* 345–358.

Thom, S. N., Myers, L., & Klugman, J. (1993). Mediation and Native American repatriation of human remains. *Mediation Quarterly, 10,* 397–404.

Umbreit, M. (1993). Crime victims and offenders in mediation: An emerging area of social work practice. *Social Work, 38,* 69–73.

Umbreit, M. (1995). The development and impact of victim-offender mediation in the United States. *Mediation Quarterly, 21,* 263–276.

Umbreit, M., & Greenwood, J. (1998). *National survey of victim offender mediation programs in the United States.* Washington, DC: Office of Victims of Crime, U.S. Department of Justice.

Zumeta, Z. (1993). Spirituality and mediation. *Mediation Quarterly, 11,* 25–38.

SOCIAL WORKERS AS EDUCATORS

Ellen P. Lukens
& Kimberly Prchal

THE INTELLECTUAL BASIS OF EDUCATION AS PRACTICE

A Bit of History

The role of educator in social work practice has a rich history, starting as the profession emerged in the late 1800s (Simkovitch, 1939). At this time, two similar yet different movements were formed to address the needs of underprivileged populations: the Charity Organization Society (COS) and the Settlement House Movement (Addams, 1897; Watson, 1922). The two movements were similar in the underlying commitment to education as fundamental to change, and the assumption that an adequate understanding of social problems emerges through firsthand contact with people within their own communities (Simkovitch, 1939). But their approach to carrying this out differed somewhat.

The COS movement used education as a means of "teaching economical cooking or buying and enforcing habits of thrift and helpful recreation" (Richmond, 1910, p. 32). However, the Settlement House Movement found this predominantly charitable approach to be lacking and condescending. The "settlers" believed no permanent improvements would occur if one class addressed social problems on behalf of another. Rather, participation and collaboration among all concerned would be necessary for real change to occur (Simkovitch, 1939). This approach attracted the support of social scientists, who began to live and work in the settlements around the country to gain hands-on experience and knowledge, collect social data concerning community and neighborhood problems, and in turn, conduct classes for community residents. Hence, the settlement houses served as information centers for people in the community, places where residents could introduce the value of good nutrition to local families or teach the "arts of homemaking to children and adults" (Simkovitch, 1939, p. 270). Residents provided specific services for the neighborhoods and encouraged community members to voice their own concerns, address what were now shared problems, and develop their own leadership.

This both contributed to improved living conditions and promoted mutual understanding (Addams, 1897; Simkovitch, 1939).

Throughout the early years of the profession, education continued to serve as a fundamental method for the social service worker, who was involved in all aspects of health care. Given poor housing conditions, unsanitary working environments, and a lack of understanding regarding personal hygiene and disease susceptibility, workers developed techniques of teaching community members about public health measures to prevent the spread of diseases. Specifically, social workers exhibited photographs, statistical tables, charts, and slides showing comparative death rates, symptoms of disease, unsanitary dwellings, and preventative measures to the general public. For example, they stressed the importance of sputum analysis in an attempt to detect tuberculosis, and the disinfection and renovation of apartments occupied or vacated by those infected (Cannon, 1913; Charity Organization Society, 1903).

Education emerged as a primary clinical modality in the mental health field as well. In 1905, the first hospital social service department was organized at Massachusetts General Hospital in Boston. Members of the social work department routinely made home visits to investigate social conditions that might contribute to illness. Much of the service provided by these social workers was educational and preventive in nature, designed to foster early detection, prevention, and enhance knowledge as to how to best treat "abnormality." Specific educational content included explanations of psychological concerns in the context of mental health. Hospitals, private mental hospitals, and universities established their own psychiatric care units to promote mental health by providing education and advice in the community. Parents were provided with information based on newer scientific data concerning the impact of family conflict, verbal and physical abuse, and neglect on the developing personality (Heely, 1917; Lee & Kenworthy, 1931). Clinics began to offer training on child-rearing practices, and to work with parents in conjunction with schools and courts, to prevent or decrease delinquency. Such clinics gave a tremendous impetus to the social work profession by stressing the need for trained caseworkers, ones who could both set standards for child care based on new mental health knowledge, and provide effective educational interventions (Day, 1989).

In 1909, Clifford Beers founded the National Committee on Mental Hygiene. This committee was primarily concerned with improving treatment by teaching people to recognize healthy behaviors and advocate for mental health concerns within their communities. Much later, by 1950, this organization merged with other groups to form the National Association for Mental Health. This group also contributed to the development of parenting education programs designed to promote mental health, and served as the foundation for many of the educational interventions used today (Brim, 1959). During the 1950s, leading social work organizations used their publications to recognize parent education as a significant aspect of social work practice. For example, in 1957, the *Social Work Year Book* described family life education as a primary function for the profession. Social workers were described as familiar with the psychodynamic approach to human behavior, with specialized training in child development and family relations, and the recognition of pathology in the individual and family behavior. Furthermore, they were seen as sensitive to wide variations in cultural values, especially regarding children. Methods used for parent education included mass media, family counseling, and because of time and cost restraints, an emphasis on group discussion (Brim, 1959).

This brief overview outlines some of the early emphasis on education as a significant aspect of social work practice, which helps to frame a discussion regarding the current theoretical basis of practice. As the profession has evolved over time, it has drawn on a number of theories about learning, human change, and development, which have contributed substantially to how education is understood as an important role for social workers. Among others, these include social learning theory, cognitive-behavioral theory, and group theory, as well as the stress and coping models described in Chapter 1.

Theories that Support the Role of Educator

Social learning theory emphasizes learning through observation, practice, and interaction among the person (i.e., client) and others in the environment, who could include other mental health clients as well as the social worker. Focus is on creating support for learning and building on the social context in which the learning takes place, such as within a group of individuals or families. It rests on the belief that desirable behavior will increase with the use of positive consequences and that a supportive social context contributes to motivation, retaining information, and transfer of knowledge across situations (Turner, 1986).

Cognitive-behavioral theory draws on the perspective that learning occurs by identifying and changing both internal mental processes or cognitions (i.e., insight, memory, and perceptions) and external behaviors. Attention is placed on teaching people how to learn, and to develop and refine skills by rethinking goals and priorities through cognitive restructuring and relearning. Goal-setting, problem definition, and problem-solving techniques are the focal aspects of this process (Zacks, 1980).

Drawing on both cognitive-behavioral and social learning theory, group approaches provide opportunity for socialization, exchange of experience and information through narrative and education, externalization of thoughts and feelings, and the infusion of hope and power through interpersonal learning, increased self-understanding, and expanded social network and community. Creating an atmosphere conducive to exchange and reflection is particularly important. Group leaders use techniques such as identification of both positive and negative behaviors and thoughts, modeling and role playing how to handle challenging situations or behaviors, positive feedback or communication skills, and teaching and rehearsing problem-solving skills. As group members become more knowledgeable and comfortable with the techniques, they can begin to serve as co-facilitators, which has the potential to enrich and reinforce the process and the work.

MAJOR GOALS

The focus of this chapter is on the role of social workers as educators in mental health settings. As mental health practitioners, social workers are called upon to educate clients about mental health issues and topics in different situations and settings. In this context, *client* is broadly defined from a generalist perspective and across systems, as an individual or family case, or as a group, community, institution, or even country. At the most fundamental level, education involves the dissemination and exchange of information between social worker and client, and ongoing professional development and self-education for the social worker.

Both professionals and mental health clients make important contributions to such educational work. For social workers, the role of educator brings the opportunity to introduce a body of professional knowledge to a client, a set of ideas gained through breadth of experience based on formal training, and experience with people challenged with different problems in many situations (Borkman, 1976; Geertz, 1983). Social workers understand common patterns of health and illness through their work with many mental health consumers over time and in different circumstances. They bring external perspective and distance, as well as knowledge of different kinds of coping skills and how these can be applied in different situations. They can decide to teach clients about any range of topics, including diagnoses, normal response, crisis and stress management, or parenting, and they can model or demonstrate related skills for their clients. Meanwhile, helping individual clients appreciate the value of their own contributions is an important part of the work.

The social worker strives to juggle the role of teacher and student, simultaneously drawing on professional knowledge and life experience, and the expert practical knowledge that the client brings to the situation (Freire, 1970/1999). To fully appreciate the client's contribution, the social worker must develop both empathic skills and humility (Gutiérrez, Alvarez, Nemon, & Lewis, 1996). Because social workers hold professional titles, they must be ever aware of the power differentials that occur naturally between worker and client, and which may be further complicated by the mental health concerns or status of the consumer, by gender, and by cultural differences. Such discrepancy in power must be considered and addressed if the educational exchange is to be fully collaborative (Mack, 1994).

The unique, everyday information that clients bring to a situation can be described as experiential knowledge (Borkman, 1976; Geertz, 1983). Although clients are not always aware of their own strengths and fund of knowledge, they bring a tremendous fund of information based on their own experiences with mental health and related issues, and their own formal and informal education. They often notice situational changes and internal patterns either individually or within a family or community that can help explain factors that contribute to or inhibit growth and change. They have an immediate and long-standing personal investment in outcome, which is profoundly different than professional investment. If the social worker and client can establish a truly collaborative model in which knowledge is exchanged, and power differences are recognized and confronted, a kind of synergy evolves, in which the stage is set for growth and the generation of new ideas.

This has multifaceted benefits. For the mental health client, educational interventions can

- Provide concrete information regarding established or state-of-the-art knowledge on a particular area of health or mental health (i.e., diagnoses, medications and side-effects, effective treatment).
- Introduce language for understanding and describing a problem or set of problems in the context of mental health.
- Dismantle myths regarding normal or abnormal response, diagnoses, outcomes associated with health and mental health.
- Create a frame of reference or set of boundaries for a particular problem.
- Increase the repertoire of skills associated with problem solving, stress management, conflict resolution, enhanced communication, illness management, and coping.
- Reduce barriers to change and broaden perspectives through awareness of resources or alternatives.
- Suggest strategies for change and how to transfer skills across situations.
- Increase options and solutions.
- Encourage people to share information with others (e.g., family members, community members), which in itself is an empowering experience.
- Increase self-sufficiency and self-esteem.
- Decrease stigma, fear, and shame.
- Generate hope.

For social workers, educational interventions can

- Serve as an important bridge between themselves and the mental health consumer.
- Serve as a tool that can be effectively used alone or in combination with other techniques, both to prevent illness and to promote health and mental health.
- Promote ongoing self-education and professional growth.
- Serve as a focal point for coordinating services across agencies.
- Be utilized as a tool with other professionals regarding social work models and values.
- Be adapted for use with a range of client groups confronting different mental health concerns and challenges.
- Serve as an important tool in community development, outreach, and consumer advocacy.

Social workers are often challenged to educate colleagues and the broader community regarding programmatic interventions and also regarding the nature of the work that they carry out. As such, they utilize assessment and intervention skills not only at the case level and within the community, but also within the professional setting. Implementing and evaluating programs requires a careful blending of outreach, internal and external community building, timing, assessment, education, and flexibility (Hatch, Moss, & Saran, 1993; Runyan & Faria, 1992).

The overarching goal for educating mental health clients is to generate knowledge, on the assumption that knowledge promotes empowerment, opportunity, and potential for change. In support of this primary goal, social workers are called upon to align themselves with their clients in a manner that identifies strengths, recognizes cultural values, and builds on these strengths and values to create an environment in which learning about mental health can flourish.

TECHNIQUES, STRATEGIES, AND SKILLS

Medical professionals have traditionally used knowledge as a means of separating themselves from their clients or patients and maintaining a power differential (Gliedman & Roth, 1980). When social workers use the medical model as their platform, they too easily become paternalistic as well (Lukens, Thorning, & Herman, 1999; Marsh et al., 1996; Volland, 1996). Moving away from this position requires a shift in thinking from an illness-based medical model to a strengths-based model, where sharing of knowledge (i.e., education) is central to the process of intervention and prevention (Poole, 1997, p. 287). The illness-based model assumes pathology on the part of the client, whether defined as individual, group, or community, and emphasis is placed on diagnosis and the expert-based intervention of the professional. In contrast, the strengths-based model builds on mental health and competence, and emphasis is placed on ongoing assessment, collaboration, and sharing of information between professional and client as a means of moving towards empowerment for the client (Gutiérrez et al., 1996; Marsh et al., 1996; Poole, 1997; Saleebey, 1996).

The strengths-based approach, with its emphasis on solutions and resiliency, provides the foundation for the strategies and techniques involved in defining and implementing educational interventions, regardless of the nature of the mental health concern, or the population served. This section will focus on these strategies and techniques, which include (1) initial and ongoing assessment, (2) individual and group, including both educational and psychoeducational approaches, and (3) community and organizational assessments. A description of several exemplary programs will follow, as a means of illustrating the practice techniques.

Assessment: Determining Context, Audience, Rationale, and Content

The first step in implementing an educational intervention designed to maximize mental health is to simultaneously complete several tasks. These include identifying strengths, defining the problem or set of problems (while assessing the need for intervention and how educational techniques might be used to address that need), and moving toward solutions through problem solving.

From this perspective, assessment includes several steps that may happen simultaneously or sequentially but that must inform each other. The context and audience (or target) of the assessment must be determined, which also sets the parameters for the kind and content of educational intervention that the social worker intends to make. For example, in a community devastated by a major hurricane, the target for mental health services may be the individual or family client, a group of individuals or families within the agency, the greater community in which the individual or family resides, or a change in public policy that provides emergency or ongoing mental health services that may help these clients both immediately and over time. Depending on this target, the problem definition and solution, and the development of the rationale for the intervention, strategy will vary, although there are important parallels in approach.

To prepare a strategy for service requires assessment of need. Mental health assessment at any system level typically includes a clear description of strengths and challenges. This means collecting data from various sources, including people and records, the use of critical thinking to interpret material and determine patterns of service need and utilization, an evaluation of available strengths and resources, and an overriding sensitivity to social, cultural, and demographic variables that complicate both access to and use of mental health services. The intervention plan follows, including a broad-based goal and more specific objectives, time frame, focus of attention/point of intervention, choice of modality (i.e., educational), and expected outcome. The plan should be continually refined as additional information is gathered.

Assessment and intervention at the case level are guided by an in-depth analysis of individual or family circumstances, drawing on information provided by the individual or family and formal and informal supports with whom they interact (Gambrill, 1992; Meyer, 1993). The assessment strategy should cover a range of variables, including the mental health client's readiness and openness for work, particular strengths and coping skills, life-cycle variables, stage and duration of the problem situation, social supports and other resources, access to and involvement with self-help groups, and evaluation of existing knowledge and understanding among family members regarding mental health concerns. Cross-cultural and sociodemographic variables are also critically important to consider, because they reflect differences in help-seeking behavior, attribution (i.e., how the particular mental health challenge is understood), social support, and religious values.

Case assessment can, in turn, serve as the point of reference for community based assessment. Looking across a group of clients who face similar mental health problems or challenges, the social worker can begin to describe strengths and define problems at the community (or other systems) level, and then target the neighborhood, agency, community, or other political or social unit as the arena for analysis and change (Gutiérrez et al., 1996; Hoechstetter, 1996).

Such community-based needs assessment draws on information gathered from and in collaboration with community and religious leaders and groups, the agency itself, opinion and survey data, social indicators and normative data at the local and national level, and expert knowledge drawn from the literature (Gutiérrez et al., 1996; Hatch et al., 1993). Regardless of whether the social worker plans to intervene at the individual, family, or community level, clear problem definition is critical, as well as ongoing collaboration, sensitivity, and openness to the mental health concerns of the client or community.

Once the initial assessment of need is completed, the next task is to determine when and how to initiate an educational intervention. Timing is critical, regardless of point of intervention. Returning to our discussion of social learning theory, it is important to determine readiness and openness to learning, as well as availability of supports to encourage this process (Merriam & Caffarella, 1991). A simple case vignette illustrates this point:

> Two social workers who worked in a community-based mental health agency had combined forces to develop and provide a simple curriculum regarding the symptoms and diagnosis of depression among children and adolescents. They were quite enthusiastic about the information they had compiled, and initiated their program by scheduling brief, weekly educational sessions for parents who were new enrollees in the clinic. Unfortunately, the families met the sessions with resistance and hostility, to the point that they complained bitterly to agency administrators that they "weren't getting anything" from the social workers. After rethinking their approach, the social workers realized that the families were typically in crisis at the point of admission to the clinic and were emotionally unready to hear and assimilate more than the most basic information. The introduction of more complex information proved to be much more successful after the social workers had taken some initial time to talk individually with the families, hear their stories, and attend to the presenting crisis, before trying to provide a more formal educational intervention.

Educational Interventions

Across system levels, educational interventions focus on information sharing or the imparting of information and concepts that are unknown, unfamiliar, or unclear to the mental health client. Depending on funding and available resources and personnel, such interventions can range from a very brief informal approach, in which a social worker reviews the mental health concerns related to a situation or illness, to a well-developed curriculum presented in a 1- or 2-day workshop or in modules over time (McDonald, Stetz, & Compton, 1996; McFarlane et al., 1995). Standard intake procedure for an acute hospitalization for either a medical or psychiatric illness might include a brief educational session using tools such as informational brochures covering diagnostic information, specific mental health concerns, medications and side effects, informational Web sites, and suggested readings. For example, a social worker meeting a new client confronting an acute episode of a serious medical illness such as cancer or diabetes might provide basic information and resources about both the illness and related mental health concerns, such as anxiety and depression, and associated treatment options. In an outpatient setting, the social work staff might offer a series of groups with well-defined curriculum that provides information on the characteristics and symptoms associated with a particular form of mental illness, such as an eating disorder, borderline personality disorder, or childhood depression. Such groups are based on the premise that the more people know about how to cope with their situation, the greater their chances of achieving their maximum level of well-being. When thoughtfully implemented, they convey respect for the ability of clients to take responsibility for their own care. Such groups provide a forum for those who want to learn more but are not ready to talk about their feelings. They also provide an excellent springboard and structure for self-help models of support and education (Solomon, et al., 1996). With individuals who have encountered severe trauma, such as family abuse or the loss of a family member through terminal illness, educational group leaders may employ cognitive-behavioral interventions to assist mental health clients in gaining the skill needed to learn how to manage and reduce stress, alter thoughts that increase depression, and develop adaptive behavioral coping strategies (Fobair, 1998).

In working with individual clients or small client groups, several practical steps are involved (Murphy & Dillon, 1998). Placed in the context of mental health concerns, these steps include the following:

- Helping clients find information regarding the impact of any form of life challenge or illness on mental health.
- Providing or creating concrete resources and information such as books, brochures, Web resources, audio and videotapes, or newsletters regarding mental health as it relates to a particular problem or set of problems.
- Directly providing information through lectures, discussion, and other formal or informal curriculum that examine the relationships among illness, stress, resources, supports, and mental health.
- Teaching clients how to gather information for themselves regarding the relationship between their particular concerns and mental health issues.
- Accompanying mental health clients when they gather information for themselves as a means of providing support and encouragement, and modeling techniques for self-advocacy.

Curriculum content will vary depending on the circumstances, the particular presenting situation, the audience, and the overall goals of the intervention. For example, the descriptive content of a curriculum for the parents of adolescents who have threatened suicide will be significantly different than for caregivers of people diagnosed with Alzheimer's disease. However, both might include content on stress management, coping skills, and anger management. Workers may also try to discern what method, or combination of methods, their mental health clients use to learn most effectively. Some people learn best by doing, others through visual and organizational techniques, and still others through abstract and conceptual means (Brunner, 1966; Gitterman, 1995).

In reflecting on teaching about social work, which can as aptly be applied to teaching clients and learning with and from them, Gitterman differentiates between two levels of knowledge. *Knowing that* refers to having facts and information; *knowing how* refers to actually using and applying the facts and information (Gitterman, 1995).

Other authors refer to this difference in terms of kind of learning. *Instrumental learning* involves actually acquiring concrete knowledge and skills such as facts about a particular illness, or information delineating the steps involved in how to handle a crisis or mediate a conflict (Lightburn & Kemp, 1994; Whittaker & Tracy, 1989). This provides the foundation for *transformative learning,* which involves moving to a higher and more integrated level of knowledge. Helping clients make this transition is a critical part of enabling them to fully use new information regarding the role of mental health in their lives. For example, people who begin to recognize the warning signs of relapse of illnesses (such as depression or bipolar disorder) can begin to think proactively in preventing relapse. Once people understand how to integrate knowledge in a manner that is useful to them, they can begin to apply it in a range of situations. This in turn contributes to a sense of competence and comfort in using information to problem solve and make decisions about their own health and care.

To facilitate this process involves interpreting information, translating it into language that the mental health client can understand and use. This in turn can serve as the foundation for more broad-based educational programs. For example, health and mental health care providers may work in interdisciplinary teams that include physicians, social workers, nurses, and other non-physicians, such as occupational or recreational therapists. Together they may work directly with individuals, groups, or communities to help translate and synthesize complex medical or psychiatric information so that the clients can understand and make informed decisions regarding treatment choices or other aspects of care (McDonald et al., 1996). This may involve a range of possible outreach approaches, including media-based efforts, community-based educational or informational sessions, or meetings designed to inform and promote mental health.

For any form of educational intervention, underlying beliefs or understanding regarding a particular situation or set of situations may need to be adjusted or discarded, either on the part of the social worker or the mental health client. This provides a particular challenge from the perspective of culturally sensitive practice, in which the social worker and client inevitably bring different sets of values and beliefs to the table (Gould, 1991; Hart, 1991; Lightburn & Kemp, 1994). This is exemplified by the following vignette, in which a social worker and a group of colleagues began to educate themselves about the needs of a particular community.

A social worker in a large city hospital serving persons with different forms of severe mental illness, including bipolar disorder, schizophrenia, depression, and obsessive-compulsive disorder, began to notice a pattern among a group of individuals with illness who were members of the Hasidic community. This particular group of patients and their families seemed relatively unwilling to comply with treatment protocols and more likely than others to resist efforts to encourage participation in regular treatment and educational meetings offered to families. Because the social worker was not Jewish, he began to educate himself about this particular group, both by talking with colleagues, friends, and some of the patients, and by exploring culturally relevant literature. After some brainstorming, discussion, and efforts to focus on the problem, the social worker and a small group of colleagues identified a community-based clinic serving the mental health needs of the Hasidic community. Through an initial series of outreach and planning meetings, the social workers from the hospital and the clinic worked with a small group of community representatives, including a rabbi and several family members who were particularly invested in the clinic. Together they devised a series of community-based sessions designed to educate families and patients at the clinic, regarding the value of early intervention, medication and treatment compliance, and ongoing symptom recognition and monitoring. The link among hospital, community clinic, families, and clients was mutually respectful, and based on responsiveness to the particular strengths and challenges inherent in this closely knit but isolated community. By obtaining funding from a small foundation serving the Jewish community, a project was initiated that included a series of regular educational meetings co-led by a social worker from the hospital and a social worker of orthodox background from the clinic. The program design was strictly didactic in nature; findings from both individual family assessments and the community-based needs assessment suggested that initially, families would find any program that involved therapeutic dimensions too threatening.

Psychoeducational Interventions

The psychoeducational interventions are a particular form of educational intervention that are increasingly common, particularly in mental health settings. Although definitions vary, these interventions generally include models that focus on education in combination with some form of psychotherapeutic intervention, the therapeutic use of education, or education regarding mental health issues (Hatfield, 1997; Lukens et al., 1999; Solomon et al., 1996). These approaches are especially applicable for social workers, because they encourage the combining of educational interventions with other practice roles valued and promoted by the profession, including therapist, mediator, crisis counselor, consultant, community organizer, and advocate.

As with the more purely educational models, the psychoeducational models are strengths based, and encourage the social worker to serve as collaborator or learner in parallel with the mental health consumer. As such, they are receiving increasing attention in the literature, and have been successfully adapted for a range of disorders, including schizophrenia, bipolar illness, eating disorders, AIDS, and HIV (Cunningham, Edmonds, & Williams, 1999; Gunderson, Berkowitz, & Ruiz-Sancho, 1997; Pomeroy, Rubin, & Walker, 1996). They can be effectively used with adults or with adults and children together (Fristad, Gavazzi, & Soldano, 1998; Rhodes, 1995). Recently, various models have been adapted and evaluated in other countries, particularly China, with attention to cultural differences and needs (Xiong et al., 1994; Zhang, Wang, Li, & Phillips, 1994).

Ideally, the therapeutic aspect in psychoeducation enhances and facilitates the educational process by providing emotional support, removing barriers to learning, and helping people use the educational component to increase understanding and extend coping skills. The components of psychoeducation, including education, social support, development of coping and stress management skills, and identification of mental health services and rehabilitation programs contribute to an improved sense of equilibrium within the family and help to serve a protective function. Typically, mental health clients struggle with some aspect of mourning or loss related to their situation or illness, and the profound impact that a particular health- or mental health-related challenge has had on their lives (Brave Heart, 1998; Lukens & Thorning, 1998). The literature suggests that in group or family sessions, participants enhance both the educational and therapeutic process by contributing to the knowledge base, and supporting and providing feedback for each other in a setting that is monitored and safe (McFarlane et al., 1995; Wolff, Pathare, Craig, & Leff, 1996).

One approach to psychoeducation that has been successfully included in various models described in the literature is teaching problem-solving skills. Although not a universal component of psychoeducation, it is a frequently used tool in this modality, and in more strictly educational interventions as well (Anderson, Hogarty, & Reiss, 1986; Falloon & Liberman, 1983). It has its basis in cognitive-behavioral techniques, with an emphasis on breaking down both thoughts and tasks into simple components. Although it appears to be a quite simple technique, to the point that its usefulness is sometimes downplayed, it requires attention and practice to begin to master. Once understood, the results are satisfying and can be used quite successfully and creatively in educational or psychoeducational sessions with individual clients or a group of clients, or in professional (i.e., within or across agencies) or community development. Teaching mental health clients or professionals how to problem solve enables them to transfer the skills to other situations, a critical step in helping them to apply and integrate knowledge (Gitterman, 1995; Lightburn & Kemp, 1994). The work is best done with some kind of paper recording tool (i.e., flip chart, etc.) to facilitate and record the process, and to provide a written record of the plan. The following are steps for integrating problem-solving skills:

- Identify a concrete problem. The challenge is to select a problem that can be realistically addressed so that the individual or group experiences success and some level of empowerment. Typically, this is the most difficult aspect of both learning and teaching the technique. Students, professionals, and clients alike will initially tend to select a problem that is vague, unwieldy, or impossible to address either because of circumstances, resources, or timing. This then becomes a setup for failure and frustration because it is unlikely that a positive solution can be easily defined. For example, a client with severe mental illness may state that his problem is that he only wants to work as a lawyer, when he has not yet completed a college degree and has been out of school and out of work for more than 5 years. Or a professional in consultation with a client suffering from depression may identify one problem as a rigid work environment with an overbearing supervisor, when in reality the client has been arriving later and later for work each day, and on occasion has not shown up at all. What may be surprising to the client and the trainee alike is that once a more realistic description of the problem is achieved, possibilities for solutions seem more readily available, and the situation seems less ominous and hopeless (Duckworth, Nair, Patel, & Goldfinger, 1997). In the case of the worker with depression, the supervisor may well be rigid, but the client response probably complicated the situation.
- Lay out alternative solutions. Once a specific problem is identified, the second critical step in problem solving is to focus on identifying solutions through active brainstorming on the part of all involved. This can be successfully done one on one, but is particularly effective in a group setting, where people can serve as resources for each other. The idea is to encourage creativity with some attention to boundaries and time. People are first asked to identify solutions regardless of whether these seem immediately realistic or feasible. Until they understand the approach, people will frequently try to refute the suggestions of others, making statements such as "that's ridiculous," or "that won't work at all!" It is a challenge to the trainer or leader to remind participants that the solutions are not judged at this point, which increases the positive nature of the approach. This provides opportunity for humor, which if used sensitively, can create insight and can be both directly and indirectly supportive and empowering for all involved. For example, in brainstorming about how to comply with a complex medication regimen for someone with both major depression and a heart condition, one group member suggested a relatively simple approach that required a marked pillbox and setting the timer on a watch. As she laid out her idea, she laughed ironically and said, "I guess this plan would help me a lot too."
- Identify the positive and negative aspects of each. After a number of solutions are laid out, the next step is to briefly identify the pros and then the cons of all solutions. This provides another opportunity to encourage input from all participants, and for people to really think about why one approach will work or not work, given a particular set of

circumstances or resources. Again, an important challenge to the leader or facilitator is to make sure that the cons are not used to put down the ideas of other participants, and that the discussion does not turn to debate or argument.

- Lay out an acceptable plan for tackling the problem. As people discuss the alternatives, the realistic possibilities for approaching the problem become increasingly clear. It is at this point that a plan is devised in a simple and stepwise fashion. If more than one person is involved in the plan, particular tasks or responsibilities are determined and a timetable is laid out. It is most effective if this is recorded, so that both facilitator and participants have a concrete point of reference for the plan.
- Follow-up and review. After a predetermined period of time has passed, the next step is to review the plan with the client or group of clients. Particularly as people are learning the technique, some aspect of the plan will have failed or partially failed, and will require attention and revamping. Here the challenge is to maintain interest, highlight the aspects of the work that have been successful, and encourage participants to learn from the difficulties and rethink the process.

As both worker and client become increasingly adept with the skills involved in these steps, they can be successfully and creatively transferred to other settings and situations. Such mutual learning is empowering for both the client and worker as they extend the benefits of the learning process and apply the skills in other aspects of their daily life or work.

Community Practice

Another important aspect of educational or psychoeducational practices, which sets them apart from more purely psychotherapeutic approaches, is the value placed on community outreach and team building, and how the work that is done with mental health clients is mirrored in either the immediate or larger community (McFarlane et al., 1993). A critical function for both education and psychoeducation is to develop cross-disciplinary professional teams that collaborate with families or community members to build liaisons, both within and across agencies, assuming that a successful program cannot be realized in isolation. This promotes continuity and coordination of care by facilitating communication among formal support systems, family, and informal social and community supports (Lundwall, 1996; Pescosolido, Wright, & Sullivan, 1995). This cohesion also requires significant openness and flexibility, both within and across disciplines, while maintaining ethical standards and attending to issues of confidentiality (Edlefsen & Baird, 1994). It builds on the problem-solving model, broadly defined, as exemplified by the following vignette.

A staff social worker and student intern co-led a regularly scheduled Wednesday evening psychoeducational group meeting for families and patients on an inpatient unit for persons suffering from depression and bipolar disorder. The educational topic for the evening was medication and medication compliance, and the plan was to problem solve around compliance issues. As usual the social worker opened the meeting with announcements, and without having thought it through, casually stated that a formal nonsmoking policy would be initiated on the inpatient unit the following Monday. The change in policy had been initiated by senior hospital administrators and her mandate from the treatment team was to pass this on to the families and inpatients. To her initial surprise, the announcement was met with outrage and concern among group members. Although family members noted that they didn't value smoking per se, they felt that it was one of the few pleasures afforded the inpatients, and to implement a nonsmoking policy so abruptly seemed to be physically and emotionally taxing and cruel.

After regrouping, the social worker realized that the educational module scheduled for the evening was irrelevant to the issue at hand. Instead, she took the opportunity to listen to and work with the group to first air their feelings and discuss the situation, and then to problem solve and identify a plan of action. With her support, the group was able to describe their position and request a delay in a brief petition, which they all signed. They also submitted a formal request for a group meeting to air their views with the interdisciplinary treatment team on the inpatient unit.

The social worker realized she still had work to do in order to successfully implement the group's request when the petition was met by initial hostility by the treatment team. They wanted her to meet again and alone with the families, and essentially restate and reinforce the administrative position. After some negotiation and discussion with the staff, they acknowledged the negative impact this would have on the psychoeducational group and their investment and support of the inpatient unit, and on her legitimacy as well. As a result, an interdisciplinary group (including the social worker, a psychiatrist, nurse, and occupational therapist) agreed to meet with the families and patients. In fact, the meeting was quite successful. The staff agreed to negotiate with the hospital administrators for a step-down approach to the policy change. The families felt empowered, and the team recognized the value of a more inclusive approach to decision making that would have an impact on both the professional and patient community.

This example occurred within a hospital setting and reflected the role the social worker played in promoting communication among that particular group of professionals and families. However, the approach the social worker took could also be effectively used in promoting communication and mutual openness and education between agencies, or between agency and community (i.e., self-help groups or other community-based organizations).

EXEMPLARY PROGRAMS AND MODELS

In this section, three programs are briefly described that illustrate important aspects of the role of education in social work and mental health. All are collaborative models, in that they have evolved and changed as a result of the value placed on mutual respect and openness to learning between mental health professionals and community, or among mental health and other professionals from a range of disciplines.

Child Development—Community Policing Program in New Haven, Connecticut

This program has provided the structure and impetus for an ongoing relationship among very different professional disciplines, and includes involvement from a range of institutions, including schools, police, mental health professionals, child welfare and juvenile justice agencies, and churches. Over time, the program has been highly effective in identifying and assisting children and families in need of assistance, decreasing violence, and increasing a sense of safety, among children, adolescents, and the greater community. It has been increasingly replicated across the country.

Although not a social work program per se, it includes important elements that can be applied in the development of community-based programs that emphasize education, prevention, and community development. This program is particularly noteworthy for the cross-disciplinary education and exchange (i.e., professional to professional), which has served as its foundation. In describing the relationship between the police and the mental health professionals, Marans and his colleagues state, "Learning from each other, these unlikely partners have established close working relationships that improve and expand the range of interventions they are able to provide while preserving the areas of expertise and responsibilities of each professional group" (Marans, Berkowitz, & Cohen, 1998).

The Family Psychoeducation in Schizophrenia Project in New York State

The Family Psychoeducation in Schizophrenia Project was a demonstration project initially conducted in public hospitals across the State of New York during the late 1980s (McFarlane et al., 1993, 1995). It included both individuals with schizophrenia and their families who were randomly assigned to one of two psychoeducational treatments at the point the person with illness was admitted to hospital. One intervention consisted of a series of multiple family group meetings co-led by two mental health professionals, usually social workers. The second followed the same format, but the structure was that of traditional single-family therapy, with one family and a therapist. The work began during the hospitalization and continued for 2 years, and practitioners were on call 24 hours per day. The person with illness joined the sessions upon discharge and the intervention continued for 2 years. Practitioners were extensively trained and supervised, following a comprehensive treatment manual.

The goals for treatment were to educate, support, and empower the families through the formation of a collaborative relationship with the practitioners, who served as family advocate and liaison to the mental health system. Two hypotheses were tested: first, multiple-family, group psychoeducation would lead to lower relapse rates over the course of treatment, as compared to single-family psychoeducation; and second, regardless of treatment, the people with schizophrenia would be less likely to need psychiatric hospitalization than prior to entering the program. The assumption was that the multiple-family group would enhance the psychoeducational process through opportunity for cross-family communication and learning, group problem solving, and expanded support system. In these models, both the clinical and educational aspects of the intervention were well-defined, with clearly outlined treatment principles, treatment manuals, and delineated educational curriculum.

The interventions were highly successful and both hypotheses were supported. Among the final group of about 170 families who completed treatment, there were fewer relapses for people with illness in the multiple-family groups (16%) compared to single-family treatments (27%). This is particularly important, given that national relapse rates after 2 years for people treated only with medication range from

50% to 65% (Anthony, Cohen, & Farkas, 1990; Liberman, 1994). Regardless of treatment, there were no differences between number of hospitalizations for the people with illness during the 2 years prior to entering the project and during the first 18 months after entering the project. However, when hospitalization rates during the last 6 months of treatment were compared to rates during the 2 years prior to treatment, the differences were significant.

These findings indicate that psychoeducational models can be highly effective using either individual or multiple-family group formats, and that time in treatment may provide an important added support. This provides the mental health practitioner and family some leeway in determining which model or combination of models best fits their particular educational and emotional needs.

The SAFE Project in Garfield County, Oklahoma

The SAFE Project is a citizen-driven partnership that was initiated in Oklahoma in the late 1980s, designed to prevent early school failure through partnership and mutual education among families, educators, health and mental health providers, and public officials (Poole, 1997). Initially based on a community needs assessment conducted by a social worker skilled in community development, early school failure was designated as a major problem in the rural county of Garfield. The county includes about 50,000 residents, of whom about one-tenth are African American, Native American, or other ethnic and racial minorities.

The services provided by the social work-led team include a series of major support functions such as early identification and assessment, counseling, consultation (i.e., information, advice) for parents and teachers both in the school and in the home, advocacy, referral and service coordination, and performance monitoring. The SAFE Project model extended earlier school-based helper models in two critical ways. First, the model focused on prevention rather than crisis. The team worked proactively with families and educators using a strengths-based collaborative model, rather than the more traditional medical- or illness-based model. Second, resource development was a central component of the approach, with emphasis on identifying gaps and developing support programs, such as tutoring or art programs to enhance the work and to further build parental and educational supports. Importantly, the program was monitored by the SAFE Project Local Advisory Council, an arm of a larger community action structure that includes community leaders, teachers, parents, school administrators, and agency professionals (Poole, 1997).

UNIQUE CHALLENGES FOR SOCIAL WORKERS

This chapter has focused on the history and application of educational interventions as an important aspect of social work practice in mental health. The literature, case examples, vignettes, and techniques all speak to the possibilities in this rich approach to practice.

As we have observed through our earlier discussion, individual and community outreach, development, and education have clearly been a central focus of social work practice since the profession first evolved at the end of the 19th century. Across system levels, the strategy involved in such practice requires client/community involvement and initiative, accompanied by flexibility, openness, and optimism. In turn, this provides a platform for mutual education, empowerment, and change (Hatch et al., 1993; Runyan & Faria, 1992). Social work practitioners are uniquely prepared to contribute to this process through their ability to function in many roles, as presented in this book, and to use these roles in an integrated and flexible manner.

Developing human resources, attending to and fostering the talents and skills of people in a community or organization, and building on these resources is an important means of promoting health and mental health, well-being, social justice, and functioning at both the individual and group or community level (Hoechstetter, 1996; Kawachi, Kennedy, & Glass, 1999). Creating opportunities for such potential is critical to the social work mission. The profession stresses the importance of recognizing and confronting power differentials among people, which is particularly critical to this process.

Over time, community education has also become an important aspect of public health and plays a large part in health and mental health prevention at both the local and national level. Clearly, social work as a profession has much to offer in this arena and has historically been integrally involved in such practice. To build on this, it is important to emphasize evaluation- and efficacy-based practice so that effective educational and psychoeducational models can be accurately described, replicated, and disseminated effectively, both locally and nationally. As such, the potential for this important role within the profession will be more fully realized at both the practice and policy level.

KEY TERMS

Experiential Knowledge: Everyday knowledge gained through life experience.

Instrumental Learning: Acquisition of information and skill development.

Medical Model: A model based on illness and diagnosis as central to treatment.

Prevention: Social, economic, legal, or educational interventions designed to promote health and prevent illness.

Professional Knowledge: Knowledge gained through formal training, education, and experience in the field.

Psychoeducation: Broadly described as some form of psychotherapeutic intervention in combination with an educational intervention.

Solution-based Treatment: A brief treatment model designed to focus on strengths and solutions.

Strengths-based Model: A model emphasizing strengths, potential, resiliency, and ongoing assessment as fundamental to treatment.

Transformative Learning: A developmental process in which experience, knowledge, and beliefs influence changes in understanding.

WEB RESOURCES

Center for Independent Living (http://www.cilberkeley.org/). This organization is a leader in helping people with disabilities live independently and become productive, fully participating members of society. This is an excellent Web site for mental health consumers or practitioners.

Family Caregiver Alliance (http://www.caregiver.org/). Particularly relevant for individuals who are primary caretakers of mentally ill children or adults, this site provides caregiver tips, statistics and research, and information about educational programs, conferences, and publications.

Family Peace Project (http://www.family.mcw.edu/ahec/ec/ dom_vi_h.html) Providing education, training, and consultation to citizens, health care professionals, organizations, and communities, Family Peace Project works to help citizens use the power of individual responsibility, civic action, and the democratic process to engage the community, problem solve, and find solutions. This Web site adheres to a social work philosophy of self-determination and empowerment.

Institute for Mental Health Initiatives (http://www.imhi.org). This organization provides summaries of current mental health research for the media and the general public, and strives to build bridges among mental health practitioners and researchers in the field of mental health, the general public, and the members of the media.

Mental Health Net (http://www.mentalhealth.net/). This site provides information on disorders such as depression, anxiety, panic attacks, chronic fatigue syndrome, and substance abuse, as well as professional resources in psychology, psychiatry, and social work journals.

National Alliance for the Mentally Ill (http://www.nami.org/). With an award-winning Web site dedicated to the needs of people confronting mental illness and their families, this organization's site includes a broad range of resources, including educational materials and references, policy papers, press releases, and perspectives on current concerns regarding ethics, research, treatment, stigma, and legal issues.

REFERENCES

Addams, J. (1897). *Social Settlements.* Paper presented at the National Conference on Charities and Corrections.

Anderson, C., Hogarty, G., & Reiss, D. (1986). *Schizophrenia and the family.* New York: Guilford Press.

Anthony, W., Cohen, M., & Farkas, M. (1990). *Psychiatric Rehabilitation.* Boston: Center for Psychiatric Rehabilitation.

Borkman, T. (1976). Experiential knowledge: A new concept for the analysis of self-help groups. *Social Service Review, 50,* 445–456.

Brave Heart, M. Y. H. (1998). The return to the sacred path: Healing the historical trauma and historical unresolved grief response among the Lakota through a psychoeducational group intervention. *Smith College Studies in Social Work, 68*(3), 287–305.

Brim, O. G. (1959). Education for child rearing. New York: Russell Sage Foundation.

Brunner, J. (1966). *Toward a theory of instruction.* Cambridge: Harvard University Press.

Cannon, I. (1913). *Social work in hospitals: A contribution to progressive medicine.* New York: Russell Sage.

Charity Organization Society. (1903). *Handbook on the prevention of tuberculosis.* New York: Author.

Cunningham, A. J., Edmonds, C. V. I., & Williams, D. (1999). Delivering a very brief psychoeducational program to cancer patients and family members in a large group format. *Psycho-oncology, 8,* 177–182.

Day, P. J. (1989). *American history of social welfare.* Englewood, NJ: Prentice-Hall.

Duckworth, K., Nair, V., Patel, J. K., & Goldfinger, S. M. (1997). Lost time, found hope and sorrow: The search for self, connection and purpose during "awakenings" on the new antipsychotics. *Harvard Review of Psychiatry, 5*(4), 227–233.

Edlefsen, M., & Baird, M. (1994). Making it work: Preventive mental health care for disadvantage preschoolers. *Social Work, 39*(5), 566–573.

Falloon, I., & Liberman, R. (1983). Behavioral family interventions in the management of chronic schizophrenia. In W. McFarlane (Ed.), *Family therapy in schizophrenia* (pp. 117–137). New York: Guilford.

Fobair, P. (1998). Cancer support groups and group therapies. In J. B. W. Williams & K. Ell (Eds.), *Advances in mental health research: Implications for practice.* Washington, DC: NASW Press.

Freire, P. (1970/1999). *Pedagogy of the oppressed.* New York: Continuum Publishing Company.

Fristad, M. A., Gavazzi, S. M., & Soldano, K. W. (1998). Multi-family psychoeducation groups for childhood mood disorders: A program description and preliminary efficacy data. *Contemporary Family Therapy, 20*(3), 385–403.

Gambrill, E. (1992). *Critical thinking in clinical practice: Improving the accuracy of judgments and decisions about clients.* San Francisco: Jossey-Bass.

Geertz, C. (1983). *Local knowledge: Further essays in interpretive anthropology.* New York: Basic Books, Inc.

Gitterman, A. (1995). Reflections about teaching and learning. *Reflections, 1*(2), 9–18.

Gliedman, J., & Roth, W. (1980). *The unexpected minority.* New York: Harcourt Brace Jovanovich.

Gould, R. W. (1991). The therapeutic learning program. In J. Mezirow (Ed.), *Fostering critical reflections in adulthood* (pp. 134–156). San Francisco: Jossey-Bass.

Gunderson, J. G., Berkowitz, C., & Ruiz-Sancho, A. (1997). Families of borderline patients: A psychoeducational approach. *Bulletin of the Menninger Clinic, 61*(4), 447–457.

Gutiérrez, L., Alvarez, A. R., Nemon, H., & Lewis, E. A. (1996). Multicultural community organizing: A strategy for change. *Social Work, 41,* 501–519.

Hart, M. (1991). Liberation through consciousness raising. In J. Mezirow (Ed.), *Fostering critical reflection in adulthood* (pp. 47–73). San Francisco: Jossey-Bass.

Hatch, J., Moss, N., & Saran, A. (1993). Community research: Partnership in black communities. *American Journal of Preventive Medicine, 9* (Suppl. 6), 27–31.

Hatfield, A. B. (1997). Family education: Theory and practice. *American Journal of Orthopsychiatry, 67*(2), 2–11.

Heely, W. (1917). *The bearings of psychology on social case work.* Paper presented at the National Conference on Social Work, Chicago.

Hoechstetter, S. (1996). Taking new directions to improve public policy. *Social Work, 41*(4), 343–346.

Kawachi, I., Kennedy, B. P., & Glass, R. (1999). Social capital and self-rated health: A contextual analysis. *American Journal of Public Health, 89*(8), 1187–1193.

Lee, P., & Kenworthy, M. (1931). *Mental hygiene and social work.* New York: Commonwealth Fund.

Liberman, R. P. (1994). Psychosocial treatments for schizophrenia. *Psychiatry, 57,* 104–114.

Lightburn, A., & Kemp, S. P. (1994). Family-support programs: Opportunities for community-based practice. *Families in Society, 75*(1), 16–26.

Lukens, E. P., & Thorning, H. (1998). *Psychoeducation and severe mental illness: Implications for social work practice and research, Advances in mental health research: Implications for practice.* Washington, DC: NASW.

Lukens, E. P., Thorning, H., & Herman, D. B. (1999). Family psychoeducation in schizophrenia: Emerging themes and challenges. *Journal of Practical Psychiatry and Behavioral Health, 5,* 314–325.

Lundwall, R. A. (1996). How psychoeducational support groups can provide multidiscipline services to families of people with mental illness. *Psychiatric Rehabilitation Journal, 20*(2), 64–71.

Mack, J. E. (1994). Power, powerlessness, and empowerment in psychotherapy. *Psychiatry, 57,* 178–198.

Marans, S., Berkowitz, S. J., & Cohen, D. J. (1998). Police and mental health professionals. Collaborative responses to the impact of violence on children and families. *Child and Adolescent Psychiatry Clinics of North America, 7*(3), 635–671.

Marsh, D. T., Lefley, H. P., Evans-Rhodes, D., Ansell, V. I., Doerzbacher, B. M., LaBarbera, L., & Paluzzi, J. E. (1996). The family experience of mental illness: Evidence for resilience. *Psychiatric Rehabilitation Journal, 20*(2), 3–12.

McDonald, J. C., Stetz, K. M., & Compton, K. (1996). Educational interventions for family caregivers during marrow transplantation. *Oncology Nursing Forum, 23*(9), 1432–1439.

McFarlane, W., Lukens, E., Link, B., Dushay, R., Deakins, S., Newmark, M., Dunne, E., Horen, B., & Toran, J. (1995). Multiple family groups and psychoeducation in the treatment of schizophrenia. *Archives of General Psychiatry, 52,* 679–687.

McFarlane, W. R., Dunne, E., Lukens, E., Newmark, M., McLaughlin-Toran, J., Deakins, S., & Horen, B. (1993). From research to clinical practice: Dissemination of New York State's family psychoeducation project. *Hospital and Community Psychiatry, 44*(3), 265–270.

Merriam, S. B., & Caffarella, R. S. (1991). Key theories of learning. In A. B. Knox (Ed.), *Learning in adulthood* (pp. 123–139). San Francisco: Jossey-Bass.

Meyer, C. H. (1993). *Assessment in social work practice.* New York: Columbia University Press.

Murphy, B. C., & Dillon, C. (1998). *Interviewing in action. Process and practice.* Pacific Grove, CA: Brooks/Cole.

Pescosolido, B., Wright, E., & Sullivan, W. (1995). Communities of care: A theoretical perspective on case management models in mental health. *Advances in Medical Sociology, 6,* 37–79.

Pomeroy, E. C., Rubin, A., & Walker, R. J. (1996). A psychoeducational group intervention for family members of persons with HIV/AIDS. *Family Process, 35,* 299–312.

Poole, D. J. (1997). The SAFE Project: Community-driven partnerships in health, mental health, and education to prevent early school failure. *Health and Social Work, 22*(4), 282–289.

Rhodes, R. (1995). A group intervention for young children in addictive families. *Social Work with Groups, 18*(2/3), 123–133.

Richmond, M. E. (1910). *The friendly visitor.* New York: Macmillan.

Runyan, C. L., & Faria, G. (1992). Community support for the long-term mentally ill. *Social Work in Health Care, 16*(4), 37–53.

Saleebey, D. (1996). The strengths perspective in social work practice: Extensions and cautions. *Social Work, 41*(3), 296–305.

Simkovitch, M. (1939). *Neighborhoods.* New York: W. W. Norton.

Solomon, P., Draine, J., Mannion, E., & Meisel, M. (1996). Impact of brief family psychoeducation on self-efficacy. *Schizophrenia Bulletin, 22*(1), 41–50.

Turner, F. J. (1986). *Social work treatment. Interlocking theoretical approaches.* New York: Free Press.

Volland, P. J. (1996). Social work practice in health care: Looking to the future with a different lens. *Social Work in Health Care, 24*(1/2), 35–51.

Watson, F. D. (1922). *The charity organization movement in the United States*. New York: Macmillan.

Whittaker, J., & Tracy, E. (1989). *Social treatment* (2nd ed.). New York: Aldine de Gruyter.

Wolff, G., Pathare, S., Craig, T., & Leff, J. (1996). Public education for community care: A new approach. *British Journal of Psychiatry, 168*, 441–447.

Xiong, W., Phillips, M. R., Hu, X., Wang, R., Dai, Q., Kleinman, J., & Kleinman, A. (1994). Family-based intervention for schizophrenic patients in China (A randomized controlled trial). *British Journal of Psychiatry, 165*, 239–247.

Zacks, H. (1980). Self-actualization: a midlife problem. *Social Casework, 6*(4).

Zhang, M., Wang, M., Li, J., & Phillips, M. R. (1994). Randomized-control trial of family intervention for 78 first-episode male schizophrenic patients (an 18-month study in Suzhou, Jiangsu). *British Journal of Psychiatry, 165*(24), 96–102.

SOCIAL WORKERS AS SKILLS TRAINERS

Deborah Gioia-Hasick
& John S. Brekke

Jeff is a 22-year-old male diagnosed with schizophrenia. He had his first psychotic episode at age 20, when he was a sophomore in college. He had always been shy but had some close friends and a few girlfriends before his illness struck. He now takes medication and still has some residual symptoms, but he has been able to enroll in one college course. He complains that he has lost his confidence in interacting with people but wants to start dating again. He has begun spending more and more time alone because of his fear of interacting with others. He is beginning to show some signs of mild depression. He now lives with his parents.

James and Marty have been married for 15 years. They have a 14-year-old daughter named Sarah. Recently, James and Marty have begun to feel that they are becoming estranged from her. They complain that it has become increasingly difficult to talk with their daughter, and that while she is doing fine in school, they get into arguments with Sarah that no one in the family seems to be able to understand or resolve. They are feeling more and more confused, and scared that they might lose the close relationship they have had with Sarah. She wants to start going on group dates, and they are very unsure about what to do. Sarah gets extremely angry with them if they express their concerns about her new activities.

Both of these situations involve individuals who are struggling with changes and transitions in their lives. In one instance, Jeff is trying to recover from a mental illness that has derailed his psychosocial development. In Sarah's family, everyone is confused by a normal developmental transition that is played out in families all over the world. In both instances, these individuals are faced with situations where their usual methods of dealing with life's challenges are not working. In this chapter, we will present a perspective on social work practice, and a set of skills and techniques, that can be used to assist these individuals to achieve greater emotional and mental balance, and to realize new behavioral competence in their lives. The focus of this chapter is on social workers as skills trainers in direct practice.

In this chapter, we will provide the intellectual foundations of skills training. We will then discuss the overall rationale, goals, and empirical findings on the skills training packages presented. Next, we will provide a specific guide to the tasks and techniques of a variety of skills training approaches. Finally, we will present exemplar skills training programs, and discuss several unique challenges for social workers in implementing skills training in practice settings.

INTELLECTUAL FOUNDATIONS OF SKILLS TRAINING

The intellectual base of skills training is not complicated, but an introduction to it is essential for understanding the techniques and applications of skills training. There are three intellectual themes that underlie skills training. First, skills training uses a here-and-now focus to behavior change. This does not mean that behavior is caused by only here-and-now forces or contingencies. Many behavior theorists acknowledge that a variety of biological, psychological, and social factors are responsible for the occurrence of behavior (Craighead, Craighead, Kazdin, & Mahoney, 1994; Schwartz, 1982). But the focus of skills training is on altering existing behavior, or learning new behavior in the here and now of an individual's life (Emmelkamp, 1994; Hollon & Beck, 1994).

Second, learning theory and its application in behavioral treatment methods undergird skills training (O'Donohue, 1998). The behavioral methods encompass behavioral, cognitive, and cognitive-behavioral techniques (Emmelkamp, 1994; Hollon & Beck, 1994; Thorpe & Olson, 1997; Bedell, 1997). While we will not spend much time making conceptual distinctions among these three traditions in psychology and social work, we will make an important distinction in this chapter between socially interactive and self-regulatory skills. Interactive skills concern social behavior such as communication, assertiveness, and problem solving. Self-regulatory skills concern noninteractive techniques such as relaxation, self-talk, and cognitive restructuring, which are used in a variety of skills training packages. We will use this distinction throughout the chapter.

Third, skills training also emerges from a tradition that analyzes behavior and teaches behavioral skills from the perspective of cognitive problem solving, coping, and strategies for skill mastery and competence within an environmental context (McFall, 1982; McFall, Treat, & Viken, 1998). Therefore, the skills training approach will use a person-in-environment model that is congruent with the tradition of social work.

OVERVIEW OF RATIONALE, GOALS, AND APPLICATION OF SKILLS TRAINING

We begin this section by introducing the framework by which we will conceptualize skills training. There are two overarching domains to skills training that we will refer to as (1) global skills, and (2) population-specific skills. First, the global skills of communication, problem solving, and assertiveness are key areas for skills trainers.

These global skills provide a foundation for many skills training packages, and are applicable to a wide range of challenges in life. We will provide goals, applications, and empirical evidence for each global skill covered in this section. Second, the population-specific skills target a specific problem or a specific clinical population. Population-specific skills might relate to sexual dysfunction, to eating disorders, or to individuals with specific social phobias.

Within these two domains, the skills will be further broken down into two distinct types. First, skills can be taught with the desired outcome of more positive social interaction. For example, individuals with anxiety disorders who have been socially avoidant for years may find that a new medication provides relief from debilitating symptoms, but then discover that their skills of engaging in any type of social situation are impaired. These people would clearly benefit from social skills training. Second, skills can be taught with the desired outcome of a greater degree of self-regulation. An example here would be an individual with an eating disorder who desires change but finds that when alone they lose their resolve and thus could benefit from skills that would help them achieve their goals when their support system is not present. This person would benefit from relaxation training or a personal reward system for recognized behavior change. The terms *socially interactive* and *self-regulation* will be used throughout the chapter to conceptualize the global and the population-specific skills.

One final goal of this section will be to overlay a broad framework of adult development onto the skill areas. The rationale for this is that, despite the fact that the basic tenets of the behavioral model remain constant, skills training may need adaptation when developmental stage is taken into account. In this chapter, we will look at the delivery of skills in three broad developmental areas: (1) adolescence/early adulthood, (2) mid-adulthood, and (3) older adulthood. There is a rich and extensive body of literature that provides overviews of the use and outcomes of skills training with children. Skills training for young children has been delivered primarily within the school setting and it does require a population-specific level of training and competence to administer these skills. Yet the basic skills taught to children do mirror the same learning theory principles as those used with adult populations. In fact, children may be more adept at behavior changes than adults because their brains have a greater degree of flexibility to incorporate new information. While we do touch on some examples of adolescent skills training, we do not explore a full range of skills packages for children in this chapter. We will, however, cite a few examples in the resources section of the chapter.

It should be noted that later in the chapter we will place the skills in the context of here and now or everyday clinical applications. In addition, we will address the population-specific skills. You will also note that some skills are easily mastered, can provide some immediate benefit, and can be taught in a time-limited manner. Therefore, skills training should not be dismissed in treatment settings where short-term interventions are mandated (e.g., managed care). While in-person follow-up (often referred to as booster shots) is very helpful in the model, this follow-up can be achieved with some additional phone contact after the sessions are complete.

Global Skills Introduction

Each new developmental stage or life challenge demands a unique set of skills. Within these transitional states, there is often an immediate need to demonstrate some new skill competencies. For many of us, this skill acquisition is a reflexive venture and we fulfill the roles and learn new skills without too many obstacles. For others, feeling stuck may involve a breakdown in the ability to acquire the necessary skills.

Skills training has a generic component that is a very active, directive, here-and-now focus. The issues to be worked on in treatment are the ones that the client is currently involved with on a daily basis. The social work practitioner also needs skills to provide the energy, structure, and direction required by this model. Regardless of the problem, a repertoire of empirically tested behavioral skills can be introduced into individual, group, or family sessions, to facilitate desired outcomes.

Repetition is required for all new skill learning; therefore, we will briefly summarize the skill area distinctions (global and specific) before providing expanded descriptions. Global skills are comprised of normative behaviors and actions that may be governed by some social rules, are learned by experience or observation, and are organized and retained in one's memory for retrieval and use in particular situations (Trower, 1982). For example, shaking a prospective employer's hand when one is on a job interview would be an example of a global socially interactive skill.

Global skills can also go hand-in-hand with the development of behaviors that are more self-regulatory. The adoption and integration of global self-regulatory skills, like anger management, relaxation training, biofeedback, and other stress management techniques, will facilitate the discussion of population-specific skills. These self-regulatory skills can also be utilized in combination with the global socially interactive skills. To continue the job interview example, taking some deep, relaxing breaths in the waiting room, prior to shaking the hand of the prospective employer, would be an example of a global self-regulatory skill. We will begin with the global socially interactive skills.

Global Socially Interactive Skills

Because skills training is based on a cognitive-behavioral model, it is important to use part of this chapter to describe the global skills in behavioral terms. All social behavior is complex, but basic elements can be taught through linear steps, modeling, and imitation (Kopelowicz & Liberman, 1999; Liberman, DeRisi, & Mueser, 1989). In fact, that is how most of us learned the basic global social skills that are ingrained into our daily functioning. We also use more intuitive and creative modes when we learn these behaviors in our daily lives (Brammer, 1990). This first section introduces three global socially interactive skills: (1) communication skills, (2) problem-solving skills, and (3) assertiveness skills.

Communication/Conversation Skills   Language is a core component of human social interactions and we are constantly being affected by communication. Communication skills appear basic, but are often the most difficult to master.

Conversations can be broken down into an array of component behaviors such as (1) the amount of speech, (2) rate of speech, (3) voice volume, (4) voice inflection, and (5) intelligibility of speech. There are also a wide range of nonverbal behaviors, such as eye contact, body language, and use of personal space. In terms of communication, affect and verbal expression are inseparable. As mental health practitioners, we are very concerned about this interplay and the window it provides to an emotional state or disorder (Guerrero, Andersen, & Trost, 1998).

Social workers who utilize skills training can teach people to have congruent verbal and nonverbal communication in dyads and small groups, and will provide the client with a toolbox of basic behavioral skills to practice. Just as you need to practice an instrument to become proficient, you need to repeatedly practice the behaviors to become proficient in the global skill. Joining public speaking groups, asking someone on a date, enrolling in a class at the local junior college, or attending a city council meeting and presenting an issue could all be excellent practice sites. All in vivo experiences, positive and negative, would be brought back to the next individual group or family session for discussion and feedback. Later in the chapter, the steps of training in conversational skills will be provided.

It is clearly not your goal as skills trainer to become an expert linguist or speech pathologist. However, numerous studies have dealt with methods for improving the communication skills of various populations, such as adolescents and their parents (Tripp & Cockett, 1998), employees (Bolman & Deal, 1991), senior adults (Jeste et al., 1999), and people with schizophrenia (Leff & Vaughn, 1985; Mueser, Bellack, Douglas, & Wade, 1991). Theoretical perspectives on communication and emotion are discussed in Guerrero, Andersen, & Trost (1998).

Problem-Solving Skills, Mediation Skills, and Conflict Resolution

Problem solving in real-life situations is a comprehensive skill area, closely tied to the core philosophy of the social learning approach (see Table 7.1). The term *problem solving* refers to the cognitive-affective-behavioral process in which a person attempts to identify, discover, or invent effective coping responses for specific problematic situations encountered in everyday living (D'Zurilla, 1990).

In the past decade, studies have analyzed problem solving in relation to gender (Radecki & Jacard, 1996), differences across the adult life span (Blanchard-Fields, Chen, & Norris, 1997), the efficacy of different approaches (Bradshaw, 1993), diagnostic categories (Bedell & Archer, 1980; Nezu, 1985; Nezu, Nezu, & Perri, 1990), individual problem-solving styles (Brammer, 1990), and the appraisal of problem-solving skills (Neal & Heppner, 1986). Other variables, such as ethnic differences, need to be addressed in future research to understand the problem-solving model more fully.

Mediational and conflict-resolution skills can be regarded as a subset of problem-solving skills. Mediational skills precede problem solving and can be thought of as the subvocal self-talk we engage in when confronted with a challenging issue (Jensen, 1971). Most often the problem is solved at this level. People without this capacity must learn to problem solve out loud or with a worksheet. For example,

TABLE

7.1   STEPS IN PROBLEM SOLVING

---

1. Establish the basic rationale for wanting to solve the problem.

2. Define the problem in behavioral terms.

3. Brainstorm all the possible solutions for the problem without judgment or evaluation from anyone.

4. Evaluate every suggestion in a pro-and-con fashion; use a flip chart or board to do this in a group. A pad of paper is fine for individual sessions.

5. Choose the optimal solution, given the evaluation process.

6. Plan to implement this solution, tconsidering the resources needed and anticipated obstacles.

7. Rehearse the planned interaction. Praise frequently for all attempts.

8. Provide feedback as utilized in the communication skills training.

9. As homework, set a timetable to try out the planned solution and report what happened to the group and skills trainer at the next session.

(Adapted from Mueser & Glynn, 1999)

---

young adults with anger control issues may overlook the simple steps they could take to solve their problem. They receive a grade they think is unfair, they storm out of the class, and may get involved in an altercation that would have been unnecessary if they had been able to mediate their concern internally. In your social work office, the teen would write down all the possible ways of handling the situation, including what they actually did following the incident. After brainstorming the alternatives together, and evaluating the pros and cons, a solution could be selected for a trial run in a future situation.

The steps for this process are discussed above, and although it may seem similar to what you are already doing intuitively in your sessions with clients, the steps will be delineated because behavioral changes are based on learning theory that is compatible with specific developmental stages. Older adults can benefit from this set of communication/problem-solving skills as well (Worrall, Hickson, Barnett, & Yiu, 1998). The difference for this group is that brain functioning has changed for many seniors, so increased repetition or other cues may need to be added to achieve success. With sufficient practice, these mediational skills can enable a person to become more adept and confident in handling situations that have greater degrees of tension and emotional complexity.

Despite the fact that the problem-solving model lands in the global, socially interactive skill area, it is comprised of self-regulatory coping skills, such as stress management and the ability to appraise a situation. Appraisal denotes the ability of a person to evaluate the significance of a possible solution to a complex situation (Lazarus & Folkman, 1984). Lazarus (1999) now views the appraisal process from a systems perspective and creates a holistic way to integrate the emotional and reasoning components of problem solving within the appraisal process. In essence, each problem is comprised of what you think about it, what you feel about it, and how it stacks up with other issues in your life. For example, young adults with schizophrenia may have a greater inability to handle the stress of their favorite cashier leaving their job at the local market, than they experience when a more significant person in their lives moves away. You really need to utilize the subjective appraisal component of the model, so as not to make premature assessments about the importance of potential problems.

The sequential steps of the problem-solving model are presented in detail elsewhere in the volume, but essentially are as follows: (1) definition of the problem, (2) generation of alternative solutions, (3) decision making, and (4) implementation of the solution. These steps will be made more explicit in the next section, and will be coupled with a case example to highlight the mechanics of the process.

Recently, there has been a theoretical shift away from the term *problem solving* and toward terms like *solution-focused models* (Berg & Reuss, 1998). Problem-solving theorists have already made the distinction between the definition of the problem and the implementation of the solution, and view both skills as necessary components of their model (D'Zurilla, 1990). In fact, they view the solution as the particular coping response that is generated by the problem-solving method, and the ability to be successful at the problem-solving phase does not necessarily ensure success at the implementation phase. We will now turn to the last global socially interactive skill, assertiveness training.

Assertiveness Training   The term *assertiveness* was coined by Wolpe (1958) to describe an approach to help people overcome their social fears, by acquiring skills for expressing both positive and negative feelings clearly (Lewinsohn, Munoz, Youngren, & Zeiss, 1992; Liberman et al., 1989). Key aspects of the skill include communication, problem solving, and cognitive restructuring. Additionally, the skill of "standing up for your rights" is taught and practiced (McDonald, 1982). Women's growth in advocating for their own rights led to an increase in the use of assertiveness skills for women (Linehan & Egan, 1979). Alberti and Emmons (1995) developed an approach to teaching assertiveness skills, individually, within groups, and across the lifespan, as a tool for self-esteem and relationship building that became popular in both the personal and professional worlds.

More recently, assertiveness training (AT) has been a skill area in many multi-faceted intervention packages for a variety of problems and populations. For example, verbal refusal skills taught in teen drug and alcohol avoidance programs, HIV/AIDS and pregnancy prevention programs, and in methadone treatment centers, is one component of assertive behavior that has been combined with other treatments (Roberts, Shaner, & Eckman, 1999; Schilling, El-Bassel, Hadden, & Gilbert, 1995). In a study, self-esteem improvements were seen during a program of AT and continued at follow-up (Temple & Robson 1991). A second study showed that visually impaired older adults seemed less depressed following AT (Donohue, Acierno, Hersen, & Van Hassalt, 1995). A third study demonstrated that psychiatric patients were less anxious than matched controls after AT (Aschen, 1997). Assertive skill deficits are particularly amenable to the structured format of AT and the real-life practice that leads to positive demonstrations of assertive behavior (see Table 7.2). Implementation of this skill area will be demonstrated in the strategies and techniques section below.

Global Self-Regulatory Skills

In this section, we introduce the second desired global goal of a skills training approach, self-regulation. Self-regulatory skills are especially critical when applied to specific behavioral changes, such as weight loss and smoking cessation. They are equally essential with specific populations or in distinct diagnostic categories (i.e., male-batterers, panic disorders) as an important adjunctive facet of an overall treatment program. As an introduction to self-regulatory skills, three global areas, anger management, stress management, and relaxation training will be briefly explored. These three skills fall into the global domain because the basic self-regulatory principles can be applied solely or in combination to a range of problem areas, and they are thought to be good generic skills for most people to possess.

Anger Management   Anger is a strong and often misunderstood human emotion that can have far-reaching and often devastating consequences in our society. The expressive component of anger has been a part of this world since the beginning of recorded history, but we are still in the early stages of understanding anger. Understanding may come from exploring the contextual conditions from which the anger arises (Novaco, 1993), or anger may be assessed according to unique client characteristics (Deffenbacher, 1999). Anger can be a normative response to some of life's difficulties, or it may be related to a pattern of aggressive and violent behavior. Anger treatment research for aggressive disorders is complicated and sparse (Novaco, 1997); therefore, we will address the generic skills required to deal productively with angry feelings.

Anger self-regulation is a skills training approach that can be systematically applied to many situations with the desired outcome of managing emotional issues so that they don't culminate in uncontrollable anger. Ellis and Tafrate (1997), in their self-help text, *How to Control Your Anger Before it Controls You*, apply Rational Emotive Behavior Therapy (REBT) to assist in some of these global self-regulatory skills. In their ABC method, (a) they first assist the client in identifying the activating event; (b) they help the individual to explore their belief system; and (c) they help people to define the emotional or behavioral consequence. The basic steps and self-help forms are included in the Ellis and Tafrate (1997) text.

Beck and Fernandez (1998) analyzed outcome data from 50 studies to evaluate the effectiveness of various treatments aimed at anger reduction. The vast majority of these studies utilized cognitive-behavioral therapy (CBT), meaning some form of cognitive reappraisal of the anger-producing situation, coupled with some form of relaxation technique. The meta-analysis study subjects ($n = 1640$) spanned a broad

TABLE 7.2	STEPS IN ASSERTIVENESS TRAINING

1. Identify an area in your life that is causing you some problems interpersonally.

2. Determine whether assertive skills would be helpful in that situation.

3. Design a chart to keep a daily record of your assertive attempts.

4. Self-monitor your assertiveness for one week, noting the situation, your level of comfort (from 0 to 10), and your skill in assertion (from 0 to 10). (Note that 0 represents an unsatisfactory comfort or performance level.)

5. Practice assertive imagery by imagining the interaction and then substituting an assertive statement that is satisfying to you, and which creates a positive response in the other person.

6. Rehearse the assertive situation with another person, in a group setting or in front of the mirror.

7. Try out the situation in real life.

8. Evaluate your progress and continue to practice daily.

9. Always use imagery before proceeding to the natural situation and continue utilizing the rating form.

(Adapted from Mueser & Glynn, 1999).

spectrum from school children to prison inmates. The major finding from this meta-analysis was that CBT recipients fared much better than their untreated cohorts in their ability to manage their anger more effectively. Another area of current research concerns adolescent anger, substance abuse, and the active use or avoidance of skills (Catalano, Wells, Jensen, & Hawkins, 1989). For social work clinicians, this rich research on the treatment of anger provides a significant rationale to incorporate and teach anger management skills to appropriate clients.

Relaxation Training   In the mid-1970s, two books, *The Relaxation Response* (Benson, 1975) and *The Relaxation Book* (Rosen, 1977) were published. Both of these best-sellers introduced the notion that relaxation was a skill that was simple to learn, could be done in most settings, and was necessary due to the increasing pace of life. People realized that they could tune into their bodies and have some effect on the body's autonomic responses (e.g., blood pressure) and arousal states (e.g., anxiety). Relaxation techniques were the focus of the second stage of Meichenbaum's Stress Inoculation Therapy (SIT) (Meichenbaum & Cameron, 1973). SIT, a form of exposure therapy, was particularly helpful in a variety of disorders, including panic, anxiety, anger, and pain. Biofeedback also emerged as a technique to identify some of the corollary physiological processes that accompany stress responses, and it provided training in regulating the response (Cotton, 1990).

The premise of relaxation training is to take the body quickly to a physical state of relaxation, which presumably will bring about a parallel mental state of reduced thought production (Brammer, 1990). Tuning into various parts of the body and focusing on isolating these parts in a systematic way by tensing and then releasing muscles has become the most well-known method of systematic relaxation, also known as progressive muscle relaxation (Bernstein & Borkovec, 1973). One needs to teach these skills first, but the true benefit will come from encouraging the client to practice regularly on their own. Because of its contribution to physiologic change (i.e., heart rate, respiration), relaxation training has become a well-represented treatment in studies of psychiatric problems such as panic disorder (Beck, Gayle, Stanley, Baldwin, & Edwin, 1994; Michelson, Marchione, Greenwald, Testa, & Marchione, 1996), generalized anxiety (Rickard et al., 1994), and anger control (Deffenbacher, Thwaites, Wallace, & Oetting, 1994). In the area of panic disorder, a review of long-term outcome data from 31 medication and cognitive-behavior therapy (CBT) studies (some of which included relaxation techniques) found that gains achieved from the therapies were maintained after therapy was completed (Milrod & Busch, 1996).

The importance of relaxation training as an adjunctive treatment in the following physical disorders is also well-represented in studies such as pain management (Subramanian, 1994; Subramanian & Rose, 1988), hypertension (Godaert, 1982), irritable bowel syndrome (Blanchard-Fields et al., 1997) and asthma (Lehrer, 1998). It is becoming increasingly difficult to locate studies in the last decade where relaxation training was not paired with some form of CBT to measure its efficacy (Davis, Eshelman, & McKay, 1995). Meditation needs to be mentioned as an additional means of teaching relaxation technique. More study is needed, but the effect of meditation on overall reports of relaxation is promising, and most people are receptive to learning something that offers immediate benefit and can be used in many settings (Janowiak & Hackman, 1994; Murphy, 1996). We will next turn to a final, albeit more inclusive, skill—stress management.

Stress Management   Stressful life events expose our bodies to all sorts of activating responses and may lead to physical and mental malfunctions if left unmanaged over time (Dohrenwend & Dohrenwend, 1974; Falloon, Morosini, & Roncone et al., 1998; Pearlin, 1985). In the late 1990s, we have heard about stress-related diseases at an increasingly alarming rate. Cardiovascular disease, allergic responses, and irritable bowel syndrome have components of stress vulnerability and overreactivity to stress. Psychiatric disorders can be triggered by stress or have stress as a coexisting feature of the illness. Unremitting stress can lead to chronic depression for the individual and involved caregivers (Coyne et al., 1987).

Not all stress is harmful because it contributes to the basic "fight or flight" reaction, which helps in basic human preservation. Mild stress may enhance our memories in the short run, like during a final exam; but extreme stress can shut down the brain's ability to create a memory of an event (i.e., crime victim) (LeDoux, 1996). Coping with stress represents a large body of literature that is too vast for this brief section. In their research on coping with stress, Lazarus & Folkman (1984) include four interactive dimensions related to skills training: (1) the functions of coping, including problem solving and the regulation of emotions; (2) the determinants of coping, including personal factors (i.e., skills) and situational factors (i.e., availability of resources); (3) the appraisal of coping, including primary and secondary use of one's cognitive assessments; and (4) the actual coping modes, including skills of direct action and information seeking.

As one can see, stress management uses many cognitive-behavioral skills that have already been introduced in both the socially interactive and self-regulatory domains. Learning these skills (communication, problem solving, assertiveness training, anger management, and relaxation training) will make significant contributions to lowering stress. To illustrate this point, an innovative yet simply designed study was conducted. The employees of a bank were mailed behavioral modules every 3 weeks over the course of 6 months on strategies to reduce workplace stress. Half of the randomized group received additional phone prompts, as well as the mailed module materials. The findings showed that all of the study participants reduced their levels of stress, as recorded by self-report measures, strengthening the value of learning new skills to reduce job strain and increase personal efficacy in coping strategies (Pelletier et al., 1999). A meta-analysis of stress management techniques in the workplace showed that the interventions that were self-regulatory (i.e., relaxation, meditation, and cognitive strategies) had their greatest effect on psychological stress (Kelley, 1996). We now turn our attention to specific case examples of skills training sessions with families, groups, and individuals.

TECHNIQUES, STRATEGIES, SKILLS, AND APPLICATIONS

In this section, we will focus on the three global areas of socially interactive skills, namely communication skills, problem-solving skills, and assertive skills. For each of these areas, we will provide steps for training, as well as a case example with trainer prompts. We will begin with an overview of worker skills needed for each area.

The social work skills trainer needs to operate within the treatment sessions in a very proactive manner, whether or not specific training materials or modules are being utilized. Within each individual, family, or group session, there are three consistent skills that you want to maintain. First, you need to provide relevant education and establish new behaviors through the steps and tasks that have been created to help the learning activities of the client (they will be illustrated below). Second, to ensure success, the client needs to receive consistent praise from the trainer for all approximations of the desired goal. Third, the trainer needs to use a lot of energy in administering all the training steps, because it is likely that the client has chosen a difficult area to work on and will require both structure and encouragement from you to attain their goal.

The steps of the training are very explicit and what is transmitted to the client by the trainer in the session is highly behavioral and based on principles of social learning theory (see Table 7.3). Training in these skills represents an intervention strategy that should mesh with the social worker's basic beliefs about how a person can accomplish change. However, if the steps are followed in the skills training, one can remain a skeptic and try on the model to experience its potential value before deciding to wholeheartedly embrace it. There are many comprehensive training materials, books, and articles that will be instructional to you as you begin to develop this role for yourself. Resources can be found in the reference section of this chapter.

Many of these skills procedures or packages are manualized and available in print versions and in other formats. It is very important to note that careful assessment of the presenting problem remains a critical step in implementing these skills. Clients must be assessed for the presence and absence of needed skills so that their appropriateness for a particular skills training regimen can be carefully established. In addition to being manualized, many skills training packages include assessment tools that measure the skill performance of clients before the intervention begins, during their progress, and at the end of the skills training.

Skills training procedures are most effective when viewed in the sequential steps utilized by most skills trainers. The three global socially interactive skill areas that were chosen for this chapter (communication, problem solving, and assertiveness) will be presented as a sequence of steps. In addition to the basic steps, each skill area will be demonstrated in a case example utilizing a different unit of service delivery. First, communication skills will be delivered in a family setting; second, problem-solving skills will be viewed in a group format; and last, assertiveness skills will be seen from an individual treatment perspective.

In the three global skill areas, we will provide a trainer's prompt for each step of the model, rather than a full dialogue with the client. A brief introduction to the specific dilemmas and skill deficits will be provided in the case examples to establish a context for the treatment.

Communication Skills

In a family case example, Sarah, age 14, and her parents arrive at the clinical social worker's office late one afternoon. It is evident from their body language that this is a family in conflict. Sarah is trudging a great distance behind her parents, wearing work boots, layers of black clothing, darkly outlined eyes, and black nails. She seemed to be towed in by an invisible string by her straightforward, socially adept parents. Sarah is an only child, born as a late surprise to James and Marty, who thought that they could not conceive children. Sarah's mother, Marty, explained the problem to the therapist as the erosion of communication. Marty stated that there has been almost no communication since the last big argument, in which Sarah requested to go out with a group of friends to a horror movie. They refused to let her go. James has felt a growing distance between the bright, affable girl of a couple years ago and the transformed Sarah sitting with them now. He couldn't say exactly when Sarah stopped talking to them, but her lack of responsiveness, change in appearance, and new requests for independent activities, all seemed to come at once. All of Marty's and James's friends had grown children and both sets of grandparents were deceased, so they felt that they needed professional help. In the session, the family agreed that they could benefit from initial communication skills.

TABLE

7.3   STEPS IN SKILLS TRAINING

1. Establish a rationale for learning the skill. Present the component steps of the skill and the importance of each step.

2. Engage an individual, family, or group member in a role play to simulate a problematic communication scenario in daily life.

3. Provide positive feedback about the role play. Include your suggestions, as well as those from other people who participated.

4. Use creative or constructive criticism to establish what could have been done differently to enhance or strengthen the communication.

5. Do the role play again. This time, incorporate the suggestions of the skills trainer and the group.

6. Repeat Steps 4 and 5 at the completion of the second role play.

7. At this point, the skills trainer can provide some modeling of the communication with another member of the group or family so that the person seeking change can observe. Elicit feedback from the participants about what they saw in the modeled role play.

8. Assign homework to practice the new skill prior to the next session.

(Adapted from Mueser & Glynn, 1999)

The skills trainer prompts the family in the following way:

Establishing Rationale   *Skills trainer:* I would like to start by asking each of you how you think talking to each other more would help the family.

Presenting the Steps of the Skill   *Skills trainer:* It seems that one of the communication skills with which we could begin, if everyone agrees, would be expressing positive and negative feelings to one another. This is a skill that a lot of people have difficulty doing, and that is why we are going to practice this many times in our family sessions. You may want to express feelings in a conversation to facilitate some understanding or common ground between yourself and another family member. (*At this point, the trainer can provide education about the skill utilizing a flip chart.*)

Establishing a Role Play   *Skills trainer:* Sarah, would you choose one of your parents and recreate the scenario of the evening you asked to go to the movies with your friends? I want you to end with what you said or didn't say to them after they refused your request. Your remaining parent and myself will be the audience and provide feedback when you are finished.

Providing Positive Feedback   *Skills trainer:* James, can you tell Sarah what she did well in her role play? What can you tell Sarah about her eye contact, voice volume, etc.? (James says one thing and then seems finished.) James, can you tell Marty some things that she did well in her role play?

Utilize Constructive Criticism to Provide Additional Feedback   *Skills trainer:* Sarah and Marty, I want to compliment both of you on your abilities to make this situation come alive in the role play. You both did a great job. Sarah in particular, I really liked how you made a very concise, clear, request to your Mom about wanting to go to the movies. Marty, you really were a good listener at that point and did not interrupt Sarah at all. It is not an easy job to recreate difficult situations in our lives, but when we do it well, we can really learn something. Now, to make this role play even better, I'm going to make a few suggestions. Marty, it seemed like you had a lot of fears about Sarah going with this group. I want you to use more "I" statements with regard to these feelings. Sarah, instead of muttering under your breath and averting your eyes when your Mom says no to you, I want you to maintain eye contact and tell her how disappointed you are that you can't go to this event. I will coach each of you if you get stuck, and James, I still need you to pay close attention to what each of them is doing and saying.

Repeat of Role Play   *Skills trainer:* Let's stop right here. (*The trainer stops the scene after Sarah says, "You never let me go anywhere I want to go."*) Sarah, I want you to try this instead. (*She whispers to Sarah, "I am disappointed when you tell me that I can't go. I really don't understand what makes you so scared. Can't you tell me more about your fears so that I can understand?"*)

Providing Additional Feedback   *Skills trainer:* James, did you notice anything different about the role play this time? What did they do well and what else could they still improve?

Modeling of Role Play by Trainer   *Skills trainer:* James, let us do the role play one last time so that Sarah and Marty can get a chance to observe. Because one area of feedback came up again in the second role play, Marty's expression of her fears, I would like to demonstrate that skill for you. (*They reposition and begin.*) So, I will be Marty for a few moments. "Sarah, when you are in the car with a group of other young people, my biggest fear is that you will get into an accident and be seriously hurt or killed.

Homework   *Skills trainer:* Remember that new skills need to be practiced quite often before they become an established part of the way you respond to situations. So each of you needs to begin to practice the direct expression of feelings to someone else several times over the next week. Although at least one of the practice times should be with each other, you should be mindful of times when you can express feelings, both positive and negative, to a friend, co-worker, or neighbor in real-life situations. Record these incidents on the homework sheets by briefly recording the interaction where you used the skill, and add an appraisal of how you think you did. Bring the homework sheets to the next session.

Problem-Solving Skills

In this group case example, six young adults, recently diagnosed with schizophrenia, are meeting in a biweekly group with two skills trainers to work on Skill Area 3, "Coping with Persistent Symptoms," in the *Symptom Management Module of the Social and Independent Living Skills* series (Liberman, 1988). In this module, individuals learn how to identify early warning signs of relapse, how to intervene early to prevent relapse once these signs appear, how to cope with the persistent psychotic symptoms that continue despite medication, and how to avoid alcohol and other drugs of abuse (Kopelowicz & Liberman, 1999). A brief overview will be given of this manualized curriculum in the section on program exemplars.

Two of the six patients in the group hear voices daily, despite following their medication regimen. As a group, they have viewed the sections of the tape and answered questions related to what they have seen. The worksheet for this skill area requires each person to write down their persistent symptoms and rank them according to severity so they can begin to monitor them daily. In the course of this exercise, one of the group members, Gary, who has persistent symptoms, requested help to develop some coping strategies for his auditory hallucinations when they interfere with his job as a bagger in a supermarket. The skills trainers took this opportunity to employ the global skill of problem solving to this individual issue.

The skills trainer prompts the group:

Rationale   *Skills trainer:* Who can tell us why it might be important for Gary to address this problem? What would his goal be in solving this problem?

Defining the Problem Behaviorally   *Skills trainer:* To determine what is causing Gary the most concern, we need to ask him to tell us what typically occurs when he hears voices while working. Of all the problem areas you mentioned, Gary, can you pick one of those for us to work on as a group? (*Gary chooses the issue of how to ask his boss for short cigarette breaks when things get too intense.*)

Brainstorm Solutions   *Skills trainer:* We would like everyone to think of at least one solution to Gary's problem and we will write them on the board. There are no right or wrong answers, we just want to generate as many of our own creative ideas as we can in order to help Gary solve this problem.

Evaluate Each Solution   *Skills trainer:* We will weigh each solution by a pros-and-cons method. Let's take the first suggestion and walk through this process. The first solution offered was to pre-arrange with the boss to be able to step outside anytime there is a lull in the checkout line and have a cigarette. Why do people think that might be good solution? (*Write these down on the board.*) Why might it not be helpful to step outside at every lull?

Choose a Solution to Implement   *Skills trainer:* After weighing the pros and cons of each idea, is there one that stands out as an idea that you would want to try and implement? Gary, what do you think?

Make a Plan to Implement the Solution   *Skills trainer:* What does Gary need to make this plan work? Can we break that down into smaller steps?

Role Play the Proposed Solution   *Skills trainer:* Who would like to play Gary? Who will play the boss? Here's the scene we want you to do. (*Give directions to the role play participants.*) Gary, you will go to your boss's office first thing in the morning and explain the difficulties you are having at work during the day, but you will tell him that you have already come up with a solution and you will describe that to him. Mr. Taylor (boss), you will start telling Gary why his request would be difficult to honor. Gary, you will finish by asking him if he is willing to let you try the plan today and then see how it goes. Both of the skills trainers will provide you with some coaching during the scene. Okay, let's give it a try.

Provide Feedback   *Skills trainer:* That was great! You both did a terrific job! Who can tell them what they did well? Was there anything that could be improved when we do this again? What about voice volume, body position . . . ?

Homework   *Skills trainer:* Gary, do you feel comfortable trying this solution with your boss before we meet again? Do you want to rehearse again? We would like you to record what happens in the meeting with your boss and how you think you did in that meeting, and let us know at the next group. Good luck!

Assertiveness Training

In an individual case example, Marco, a 15-year-old Latin American, had emigrated 18 months ago with his family from his native home of Chile. He mastered the language within the first few months, and was doing well in school, but he continued to struggle with social relationships at school. He had few friends and frequently endured teasing and humiliation from the older, larger boys, because he was having a lot of difficulty standing up for himself. Recently, he had become more withdrawn, depressed, and avoided most school activities. He confided in his parents, after much prompting, that he was aware of a big cheating scheme going on at his private school. Because he consistently received good grades, some of the boys were pressuring him to forge homework assignments and papers for them. Marco wanted to fit in socially, but was uncomfortable with these requests. He did not understand how to assertively refuse their requests and stand up for his own beliefs. Marco's parents received a referral to a private psychologist who sees many teenagers in his practice and who has adapted the learning activities from the social skills modules for psychiatric patients to fit the needs of adolescents who were in the process of learning these skills for the first time. Although this could have been a family referral, it was more important that Marco develop confidence around the practice of these skills at an individual level.

Following are the skills trainer's prompts to the individual:

Identify the Problem   *Skills trainer:* Marco, can you tell me, in your own words, a detailed description of the school problem that has been of concern to your parents and to yourself?

Rationale for Assertive Skills   *Skills trainer:* It is not possible to always do what other people ask us to do. It is okay to refuse a request, and in your situation, where the consequence could be school suspension or expulsion, it is advisable not to do what these other students are asking you to do. I can help teach you this assertive skill, and help you practice so that you can be clear and firm when you talk to the other students.

Keeping a Daily Log   *Skills trainer:* Every day, we utilize assertive skills without clearly defining them. We ask for directions, make a complaint or a request, or refuse an extra piece of cake because we are too full. I want you to write down detailed examples over the next week, of when you recognize assertive behavior in your life.

Appraisal of Skills   *Skills trainer:* An additional item that I would like you to add to your chart is a score from 1 to 10, on your level of comfort when you were assertive, and also your assessment of your skill level from 1 to 10 when you were assertive. Remember to be honest in your accounts, because this is how we will learn together what assertive skills you will need to practice. Bring the chart next week to our session.

Practice Assertive Imagery   *Skills trainer:* One of the powerful ways that we shape our behavior toward something new is to imagine ourselves doing it first. This technique is called imagery. Lots of people use it to help them succeed: athletes, students, and job interviewees. I would like you to take one of the situations from your chart, where you thought you needed improvement, and imagine how you would have liked it to go. Take your time, and then we will talk about what you see for yourself.

Rehearse   *Skills trainer:* Now that you've visualized this scenario, you and I will rehearse it as a role play.

Practice in Real Life   *Skills trainer:* Marco, because my office is located in a large building with a coffee shop, and one of your areas of difficulty was ordering a soda when the shop was busy, we are going to use our session to practice this skill. Here are some suggestions for ordering assertively in a busy restaurant.

Praise, Evaluate, and Offer Feedback   *Skills trainer:* Marco, you did a really great job of catching the waitress's attention and placing your order. You made good eye contact, spoke up a bit more than usual because it was so noisy, and did it in a way that was very direct and you got your soda! Next time, I want you to say, "Excuse me, miss, but I need to order my soda right away because I'm late for my appointment." This will be much stronger than saying, "I'm sorry to bother you, but could I trouble you for a soda when you get a chance?"

Use All of the Previous Steps When Transitioning to the More Difficult Problem. *Skills trainer:* Marco, we can start to think about how you can refuse to complete someone's homework when you are feeling pressured. Tell me what usually happens first.

In summary, the skills, techniques, and strategies of a skills trainer are founded on solid, clinical social work principles and ethics of client change. The difference lies in the proactive, sequential, and systematic delivery of this cognitive-behavioral model. Social workers who utilize skills training in their practice understand that this approach encompasses the following three features: (1) it utilizes generalist social work assessment and intervention skills; (2) it requires establishing proficiency in rationale and training steps to deliver the model effectively; and (3) specific knowledge of population needs and developmental stages are critical to the model. The next section highlights skills training in three specific psychiatric disorders.

Population-Specific Skills

Population-Specific Skills and Psychiatric Disorders

One of the strengths of the skills training approach is that it has applications across developmental stages and across population groups. We will look at the application of skills training in two distinct categories. The first category deals with populations where the disorder has been so disruptive to one's life that the individual may have lost the skills necessary for basic daily functioning. In this section, we have chosen major depression, schizophrenia, and borderline personality disorder. In the second category, the emphasis will be on acquiring skills across the life cycle that can enhance normal functioning and create a better quality of life for the participants. In this second section, we will describe three groups: (1) adolescents, learning refusal skills; (2) adult workers, reducing their occupational stress; and (3) senior adults, relearning communication and assertiveness skills.

   We will begin with a look at a common and debilitating condition—depression—which can erode life skills.

Depression   Clinical depression is the most common, serious, and disabling psychiatric disorder in the United States today, affecting between 5 and 10% of adults each year (Hyman, 1998). It is most prevalent in women, and the estimate is that between 2 and 25% of women will experience depression in their lifetimes (Pfizer, 1996). It is also a pervasive and recurrent problem in adolescence (Harrington, Whittaker, & Shoebridge, 1998). Although medications play a big part in the alleviation of symptoms in this mood disorder, successful recovery requires a variety of psychosocial interventions, including changing cognitive patterns (i.e., faulty information processing) to protect the client from future episodes.

   Because social workers are very likely to see clients with clinical depression in their practice, it is important to become familiar with the outcomes of studies utilizing cognitive behavioral approaches. Two meta-analyses of CBT for depression (Dobson, McDougall, Busheikin, Aldous, & Tasman, 1989; Gaffan, Tsaousis, & Kemp-Wheeler, 1995) found that there was a superior outcome for those patients given CBT versus those given other forms of psychotherapy or pharmacotherapy alone. For adolescents, it has also been demonstrated that those teens who were depressed and received CBT showed a significant improvement by the end of their treatment and also stability in these therapeutic gains (Harrington et al., 1998; Lewinsohn & Clarke, 1999).

   The basic premise of the CBT models is that certain ways of thinking may cause, exacerbate, or maintain specific symptoms of depression (Hartlage & Clements, 1996). Aaron T. Beck was prolific in his research, writing, and theorizing about the cognitive processes in depression. His notion is that cognitive restructuring is a major skill area to be taught and practiced to achieve progressive recovery from depression. Practicing occurs with planned homework that includes scheduling and recording activities, especially those that increase pleasure (Beck, Rush, & Shaw, 1979). Homework completion seemed to be positively correlated with patient improvement in several studies, especially in those subjects who started out more severely depressed (Persons, Burns, & Perloff, 1989).

Changing negative thought patterns, distortions, and views of self are some of the challenges the skills trainer needs to address for this specific population. Intervention may include a combination of self-regulatory and socially interactive skills. We now turn to another major mental illness that is amenable to a skills approach.

Schizophrenia   Schizophrenia is a thought disorder that manifests itself very differently from individual to individual, and has a wide range of functional outcomes. The core features of the illness are classified in three ways: (1) positive symptoms (i.e., delusions, hallucinations), (2) negative symptoms (i.e., withdrawal, blunted affect), and (3) disorganized symptoms (i.e., inability to concentrate, incoherent speech). The stress-vulnerabilty-coping-competence model attempts to explain the onset, course, and outcome of the symptoms of schizophrenia as they interact with biological, environmental, and behavioral factors (Neuchterlein & Dawson, 1984; Neuchterlein et al., 1992). Based on psychosocial models like this, the field was able to understand the role of recovery beyond medication, and develop and incorporate a broader range of psychosocial interventions to improve a person's life.

Aside from the initial teaching of social and other skills to children, there has not been a more substantial body of skills training programs in the field of psychiatric rehabilitation than for people with schizophrenic disorders. Medications alone do not adequately prevent relapse and re-hospitalization for these individuals (Dixon, Lehman, & Levine, 1995; Hogarty et al., 1991; Hogarty, Anderson, & Reiss, 1986). Many of the social and cognitive deficits, as well as the negative symptoms of the disorder (i.e., decreased motivation, dampening of feelings), have not shown marked improvement with medication. These negative symptoms might contribute to a poorer outcome in skill acquisition (Fenton & McGlashan, 1994; Kopelowicz, Liberman, Mintz, & Zarate, 1997), but few would deny that medications and skills training have an additive effect when used together (Smith, Bellack, & Liberman, 1996).

Social skills training (SST) with this population has been studied in great depth, and three meta-analyses (Benton & Schroeder, 1990; Corrigan, 1991; Dilk & Bond, 1996) have given empirical support to the positive effects of this form of structured training on skill acquisition and skill maintenance for people with schizophrenia. It is not surprising that a highly structured model would work so well, because the identified cognitive deficits are in the areas of memory, attention, concentration, and overall information processing. Skills training is currently considered one of the optimal treatments in schizophrenia. It should be noted, however, that there is very little research to suggest that the effects of skills training generalize to the noninstitutional lives of schizophrenic individuals in the community (Dilk & Bond, 1996).

Manualized treatment modules can be effective bridges in enabling a patient to move from the hospital to the community (Kopelowicz, Wallace, & Zarate, 1998). Once settled in the community, a self-esteem module, which emphasizes empowerment skills, could be helpful in keeping people in their community environment (LeComte et al., 1999). Parallel populations, experiencing cognitive deficits, such as people with developmental disabilities and those recovering from head injuries, may also find that SST is an effective path to relearn and recover this basic functioning.

Borderline Personality Disorder   Borderline personality disorder (BPD) is a personality diagnosis that has varied and difficult diagnostic features, including affective instability, anger, chronic feelings of emptiness, and frantic efforts to avoid real or imagined abandonment (*DSM–IV*, APA, 1994). These individuals are often engaged in a very intense and often chaotic response to their environment. People with BPD are often very difficult to engage in treatment and very few treatment strategies have been effective. Linehan (1993) originally developed a behavioral therapy, known as Dialectical Behavioral Therapy (DBT), to treat suicidal behavior, but discovered the model's effectiveness for people with BPD over usual community care. People with BPD often appear to observers to be fairly competent and possess good social skills; however, their learning does not appear to generalize well from one mood state to another, or from one situation to another (Linehan & Schmidt, 1995).

In an excellent empirical review of DBT, Scheel (2000) describes an eclectic treatment that is a combination of client-centered techniques and strategies, psychodynamic orientation, and Zen beliefs. It utilizes cognitive-behavioral procedures of skills training, behavioral analysis, contingency management, and exposure to difficult stimuli as the tools of treatment. It is a manualized treatment (Linehan, 1990) that incorporates skills coaching, lots of feedback and client validation, establishing target goals, and prescriptive phone use. Treatment is intense and expensive, and therapists do need specialized training. The jury is still out on its overall effectiveness because of its limited empirical base, and it provides the most effective breakthroughs for individuals when used according to the model, which makes managed care settings and community mental health centers unlikely service settings.

Despite the severity of the symptoms of schizophrenia, depression, or BPD, the application of skills training has been an avenue of continued, successful intervention in both the social and self-regulatory areas. Depression can occur at any point in the life course; schizophrenia has its onset in young adulthood but continues as the person ages; and BPD is most often diagnosed in late adolescence or young adulthood, and can be severe and chronic for many years. These population-specific and disorder-specific areas can often overlap other developmental issues; therefore, social workers can benefit greatly from skills training.

Population-Specific Skills and Normal Developmental Stages

Adolescent Refusal or Resistance Skills   Coming of age in the United States is recognized as one of the more difficult developmental hurdles to navigate. A successful transition to adulthood often depends on resisting very difficult social influences to use drugs, alcohol, or engage in risky sexual behavior without becoming socially isolated along the way. An adolescent's decision to participate in or refrain from destructive behaviors is often dependent on the ability to resist the situational social pressures by learning to recognize these pressures and learning to cope by developing social skills. From a social learning theory perspective, adolescents are at a greater risk for developing addictive or destructive behaviors if these have been modeled for them by family, peer groups, and society at large (Howard, 1992).

In a large-scale study of 11,995 public and private middle-school students in the Los Angeles and San Diego areas, students received one of four treatment conditions (Donaldson, Graham, Piccinin, & Hansen, 1997). The main hypothesis stated the following: normative education consisting of four lessons about consequences of drug and alcohol use, five lessons that corrected myths about peer substance use at their school (cognitive approach), plus three lessons on resistance training (how to refuse drugs and alcohol), would reduce future drug use. The findings supported the use of this program in delaying the onset of substance use. Although there have been other large-scale efforts to teach resistance skills, like the nationwide law-enforcement–based Drug Abuse Resistance Education (DARE) Program, the average age of initiation to alcohol is now 12 years old, which greatly increases the continued likelihood to abuse substances over one's lifetime (Werner & Adger, 1995).

If adolescent substance abuse is co-morbid with other psychological disorders (i.e., depression), then both issues have to be addressed with the introduction of new skills. It is especially difficult to address the substance use if it positively counteracts the depressive symptoms, because the substance has reinforcing properties for the individual. Skills training can also be viewed as either a remedial treatment after the substance abuse has been identified, or as a prevention intervention (Hall, 1995). Once a significant problem has emerged, there are many routes in the complex path of adolescent recovery, and research is just starting to scrape the surface. Listening to adolescents tell their stories of recovery makes one cognizant of interventions, in addition to skills training (relationship rebuilding, AA, religious beliefs), which must coexist for change to occur (Vaughn & Long, 1999).

A second beneficial area for skills training is in enhancing the ability of female teens to refuse unwanted sexual activity. There are four components of refusal skills that can be taught and practiced in role play scenarios: making eye contact, making an audible refusal, specifying the unacceptability of sexual behavior, and leaving the situation (Warzak, Grow, Poler, & Walburn, 1995). It is difficult, however, to predict whether the practiced behavior will occur in the actual context. This requires attention after the training is complete.

We now turn to a brief discussion of skills that can be helpful in alleviating aspects of stress in the workplace.

Adult Workers and Occupational Stress   In our fast-paced world, we often dismiss occupational stress. The success of television programs like "ER" and "Law and Order" and movies like *Jerry Maguire* gives the public a dose of the stressful complexities of the workplace. Clients might feel like they do not measure up to societal work expectations if they cannot meet their job demands. Some stress is beneficial to work function, but an overload of workplace stress is often laden with a strong component of social anxiety (SA). SA emerges when individuals believe themselves unable to cope with the demands of their job; it may also occur in individuals who believe that they are underestimated or overestimated by their supervisor or colleagues (Agathon, 1994).

In addition, the social and economic costs of depression in the workplace are an increasing individual and national burden (Croghan, Melfi, Dobrez, & Kneisner, 1999). There is an understandable interplay between depression, absenteeism, and diminished productivity (Claxton, Chawla, & Kennedy, 1999). If employee assistance programs (EAP) were able to educate and evaluate their employees using standardized measures for assessing depression and anxiety, individuals might prevent measures of devastating consequence, like unemployment (Mintz, Mintz, Robertson, Liberman, & Glynn, 1996). A social worker within an EAP would have the perfect opportunity to teach global and self-regulatory skills to intervene with an employee's generalized anxiety and depression. Work-based groups would provide the right balance of imparting education about self-regulatory skills, and would provide the opportunity for a new worker to decrease social anxiety in becoming a group member.

With incidents of extreme workplace violence in the news, it is important to consider the occupational stress, coping resources, and positive and negative affect of individuals when they are at work (Fogarty et al., 1999). Workplace stress has definite health outcomes, both psychological and physiological (Murphy, 1996). Studies have documented the influence of job strain on numerous medical conditions, including high blood pressure and hypertension risk (Carels, Sherwood, & Blumenthal, 1998; Curtis, James, Raghunathanm, & Alcser, 1997), alcohol and drug abuse (Cooper, Russell, & Frone, 1990; Crum, Muntaner, Eaton, & Anthony, 1995), and chronic back problems and other work-related injuries (Greenberg, Stiglin, Finkelstein, & Berndt, 1993). A review of recent research on stress-management techniques used at the worksite concluded that these methods can be effective, but the choice of stress management techniques (i.e., cognitive-behavioral versus self-regulatory) needs to match the desired health outcome to be most effective (Murphy, 1996).

Studies have demonstrated a very strong relationship between high job stress and low job satisfaction (Decker & Borgen, 1993). Continual dissatisfaction with jobs could actually lead to a pattern of stress and job mobility that could have fatal consequences (Pavalko, Elder, & Clipp, 1993). Unresolved issues within the workplace can magnify stress. Life issues outside of the workplace (i.e., financial strain and family or care-giver burdens) also add to the burden of occupational stress. On a positive note, many companies recognize the importance of global socially interactive skills, including assertiveness, communication, and relaxation. To facilitate the health and effectiveness of the organization, such companies incorporate these skills into training programs as more attention is paid to the needs and skill requirements of employees (Bolman & Deal, 1991).

Senior Adults Relearning Communication and Assertiveness Skills The nature and perception of stressful experiences changes during one's life. Unlike younger adults, most senior adults are retiring competely or slowing down in their work. They may be experiencing more profound health-related concerns, and there will undoubtedly be more issues of grief and loss as one ages (Aldwin, 1992). In terms of coping strategies and retention of life skills, most seniors were found to be just as effective in their ability to cope with stressful life events as their younger counterparts (Lazarus & Cohen, 1987; Segrin & Abramson, 1994). Older adults have a maturity and wisdom when dealing with problems because most situations are not novel. Appraisals of particularly stressful events may change due to the vulnerability and the shift in control that older people may experience as a result of aging and becoming more dependent. Seniors have been found to have more dysphoria, suicidal ideation, and lower self-esteem than was evident during earlier periods of life, but it may go unrecognized (Duberstein et al., 1999; Lewinsohn et al., 1992; Segrin & Abramson, 1994). Most importantly, stress and depression, if untreated in this age group, are more likely to contribute to physical and psychological decline. Social workers need to assess for co-morbid issues to avoid missing the higher rates of anxiety and depression in older adults.

Arean, Perri, Nezu, and Schein (1993) randomized 75 clinically depressed seniors into three groups: (1) problem-solving therapy (PST), (2) reminiscence therapy (RT), and (3) a wait-list control group. Although both PST and RT showed significant effects on the depressive symptoms, only those participants in the problem-solving group showed enough progress to be considered as improved or in remission after the 12-week session. This is an important justification for including training or retraining on global social skills for seniors.

Skill interventions for seniors encompass the same basic steps covered in problem solving, assertiveness training, and communication skills. The change occurs in the scenarios of role plays, with increasing sensitivity to issues of pride and its role in help-seeking behavior (Donohue et al., 1995). Issues of pride surface especially when a disability (i.e., visual impairment) necessitates daily requests of help from family, friends, and strangers. Learning how to make direct requests for social involvement will cut down on isolation and the likelihood of depression. Donohue et al. (1995) provides a treatment manual, with examples and trainer prompts, which should prove helpful in your practice with seniors.

In summary, this section provided a chance to recognize the potential of skills training within a life-long developmental process. We omitted specific medically based populations where training and skills application would be a critical and necessary part of the rehabilitation process (i.e., brain injuries, hearing impairment, cardiac recovery, aphasia, mental retardation). There is a wealth of literature in these areas.

EXEMPLAR PROGRAMS AND MODELS

There are numerous skills training programs currently in use, and some will be listed in the resource section. We have chosen to highlight two skills approaches that have been led by the chapter authors. As you will see, the practitioner uses the principles and practices of the behavioral model, regardless of population group. To transmit this effectively to the individual client or group, trainers are expected to be well-versed in the rationale for this particular intervention. Trainers need to know as much as possible about the developmental phase of the client and be prepared to offer relevant teaching about the disorder or significant life event that the client is experiencing. The two models chosen as exemplars are the UCLA Series of Social and Independent Living Skills (SILS) and Alternatives to Aggression (ATA).

The UCLA Series of Social and Independent Living Skills (SILS) Modules for People with Serious Mental Disorders

This program was developed in the mid-1980s as a means for clinicians, working in both inpatient and outpatient settings, to strengthen the social and psychiatric skills and to improve the independent community living of people with schizophrenia and other major psychiatric disorders (Wallace & Liberman, 1985; Liberman, 1992). Each module is highly structured as a complete package of materials. These materials include a trainer's manual, a patient workbook, a videocassette, and a user's guide for each skill area. There are currently six skills training modules available, with more in development. They cover symptom management, medication management, recreation-for-leisure, basic conversation skills, community re-entry, and family involvement in services. These modules are used in hospitals, community mental health centers, private practice, and residential programs. They have also been adapted for use in other countries. There is a separate in-service training program available for mental health professionals wanting to learn the modules.

Each skill area consists of seven learning activities: (1) introduction to the skill area, (2) videotape with questions and answers, (3) role play exercises, (4) resource management, (5) outcome problem solving, (6) in vivo exercises, and (7) homework assignments (Kopelowicz & Liberman, 1999). Clients can meet within groups on a daily, biweekly, or weekly schedule. Groups are led individually or co-led by professional or paraprofessional staff, who have received training in the method of behavioral learning (rehearsal, coaching, shaping and fading, modeling, and positive reinforcement). Each session begins with a review of the homework and questions from the prior skill area.

A unique component of the SILS training program is the use of the videotape to demonstrate socially appropriate and assertive behaviors to learn within the skill area. The tapes provide informational scenarios, followed by questions for the group. The trainer's manual details the steps of the module. Patient worksheets for the skill areas are in the workbooks and are usually to be completed after the tape has been viewed. The group's pace is up to the trainer(s) and very dependent on the functional level of the group. When the group is mixed with high- and low-functioning patients, the higher-functioning patients can be engaged as "co-trainers." Trainers will want to involve all participants to assess whether they understood the video presentation.

The effectiveness of this model has been well-documented. Skills seem to be readily learned and retained by patient groups (Eckman, Wirshing, Marder, & Liberman, 1992). They also seem to be relatively elastic in applying the skills to other areas of life, although this is difficult to fully assess (Bellack, Mueser, Gingerich, & Agresta, 1997). Once patients learn the behavioral model, they tend to use techniques like problem solving, with increasing frequency due to positive results. Lastly, skills training modules have been translated into Spanish and used in mental health centers in Los Angeles, where native Spanish-speakers comprise a dominant cultural group (Kopelowicz, 1997). Although adjustments were required, this learning approach appears suited for diverse ethnic groups, but more study is needed.

Alternatives to Aggression

Alternatives to Aggression (ATA) is a program for male batterers that was started in the Midwest (Saunders, 1996; Saunders & Hanusa, 1986). It is a fully manualized cognitive-behavioral intervention that can be delivered in group or individual formats. Three major intervention components are delivered in the context of a feminist perspective.

The first component is relaxation training. In this model, relaxation is a self-regulatory skill that is based on the assumption that anger is partially an autonomic arousal state. Clearly, one cannot be angry and relaxed at the same time, and this skill can be used to de-escalate one's autonomic state at any time. The second component is assertiveness training. Assertiveness is a set of behavioral skills that focus on negotiating and having needs met without resorting to aggression. The third component is cognitive restructuring. A major goal of the intervention is the nature of self-talk and how to use it to promote self-control and assertiveness.

The ATA group format is a 12-week intervention. The individual format is a 20-week intervention. Each of the sessions is highly structured, and homework is to be completed between sessions. Each session begins with a review of homework and any difficulties encountered in the application of the learned skills. Next, trainers begin guided relaxation. Third, participants engage in a role-play rehearsal, using specific behavioral or cognitive strategies, and based on incidents from a client's life. Fourth, specific behavioral or cognitive skills are then taught and rehearsed. Each session ends with a discussion of a specific behavioral issue related to domestic violence. This is a carefully constructed cognitive-behavioral intervention that is sequenced within and across the sessions. Finally, because domestic violence is seen within a sociocultural context of patriarchy and socialized aggression, the intervention is feminist in its perspective. It is meant to raise consciousness in this regard, with guided discussions introduced throughout the sessions.

Two studies attest to the effectiveness of ATA with male batterers (Saunders, 1996; Saunders & Hanusa, 1986). Saunders (1996) found that it was most effective with individuals who had antisocial personality traits. There are also more unstructured process-oriented group models (Browne, Saunders, & Staecker, 1997). Saunders (1996) found that men with dependent personalities did better in the process groups than in the structured skills groups. This suggests that future research could be helpful in determining which kinds of groups are better for which kinds of clients.

UNIQUE CHALLENGES FOR SOCIAL WORKERS

One of the greatest assets of a professional social work degree is the versatility and flexibility it provides to engage in work with diverse populations, and to choose from a broad repertoire of interventions best suited to serve that population. This broad base can also be its downfall, because it is impossible to be cognizant of all that is available for assisting clients. The familiar adage, "Jack of all trades, master of none," is reflective of the struggle that social workers sometimes feel when their population base is multifaceted. The boundaries of social work practice are a construction of a variety of different elements. The school where you receive your social work degree, the years of training in field placements, and your field of practice have all been instrumental in shaping the kind of social work practitioner you have become. The benefit of utilizing a skills training approach is that its core features allow it to bridge many different population bases. There is practical utility to a skills approach for social work clinicians in a majority of practice settings, especially in mental health settings. It is a solution-focused model (Berg & Reuss, 1998), and in the truest adherence to the model, we have given you the positives first. We will briefly discuss controversies in the field that may challenge your ability to fulfill the skills trainer role.

First among these challenges is the natural inclination by most social workers not to be directive. Social work training has trained professionals in a role that is client-centered and respectful of "starting where the client is at." Skills training does not override this basic premise, but it does offer a model where motivation and readiness are not always precursors to learning skills. Skills training is a continuous learning model, and there are multiple opportunities for the client to learn the skill, in a "no fail" approach. In this approach, we enhance the skills that clients bring to the session by encouraging them for all their efforts, and we are not reticent to make concrete suggestions for improvement in their next effort.

A second challenge of this approach is the effort involved in obtaining skills training. In general, adequate training can vary from the intense and expensive learning involved in DBT, to a much quicker understanding and translation of basic communication skills. Assertiveness training and anger management skills can be gleaned from manuals or learned if one co-leads group or family therapy with a skilled trainer. Trainers need to engage in the learning activities to demonstrate them to clients, and this takes time. A skills package may cost $300.00, if it includes tapes, manuals, and workbooks. These costs may be prohibitive for some agencies and private practitioners.

Third, becoming a skills trainer does not require a professional degree or any state licensing requirements. Because paraprofessionals can be taught to conduct relaxation therapy and other groups, social work professionals could feel devalued in this role. To overcome this possible bias, we need to promote a collaborative relationship between social work and other mental health disciplines. For social workers who provide training and supervision to other professionals and paraprofessionals, it is also very important to become skills trainers and train those who might want to learn these interventions.

Fourth, in our experience, it is best to co-lead a group. While one social worker provides the skills training, the other can follow the process of the group or family, make appropriate comments, and actively coach and facilitate role plays. In this way, clinical and didactic processes can proceed together. Unfortunately, this can place demands on agency resources that will need to be negotiated.

Fifth, there can be frustration when the intervention does not work. Certain population-specific issues may interfere with the outcome of the training. Although skills training is helpful in many situations, there will always be some rate of failure. For example, people with schizophrenia who receive skills training may not fully benefit from the training due to cognitive factors such as impaired memory functioning. People with depression may have substantial problems with social withdrawal and be unable to complete any exercises using socially interactive skills. Skills acquisition needs to be a positive experience, so if significant obstacles are present, the adaptation or postponement of the training may be necessary.

Sixth, how does one integrate behavioral skills into other practice models to avoid working exclusively in a behavioral mode? Social workers are generally eclectic in the interventions used with clients. Because a biopsychosocial perspective is used most often for assessment and intervention, with particular attention on the person within their broader environment, it is incumbent to tailor the intervention based on individual strengths. Every treatment assessment needs to include a "what works well, for whom" approach. Skills training is particularly well-suited for concrete behavioral change. Other therapeutic interventions can precede or follow the skills work.

It is also important for us to briefly examine some dilemmas in using skills training, from the perspectives of the agency, the clinician, and the client. We will follow this with an in-depth case example of the use and outcome of skills training.

The challenges for social workers utilizing skills training would appear to be threefold, because there are at least three levels of "buying in" to this model. This acceptance relates to the first skill step, establishing a rationale. If all the participants, including the client, do not believe that developing new skills will provide benefit, then the motivation is too low to justify the training and work required to integrate a skills training approach. The trainer will need to ask specific questions of all participants (agency, clinician, and client) to assess their desire and ability to proceed.

The first level of acceptance or "buy in" would need to come from the mental health agency, hospital, or organization responsible for the delivery of services. Although simple to explain in behavioral terms, and capable of eliciting measurable client change, there is a possibility that the skills approach may not mesh with care plans and session limits. Clinicians might need to request extended payment for treatment sessions to identify and target the skills necessary for the production of clinical change; to teach and train the client in new behaviors (modeling, rehearsal, practice, and feedback); and to provide the necessary support to ensure the durability of the change.

Provided training fits into the allotted number of sessions, most skills training modules or programs encourage using a booster session (often conducted a number of months after the training is completed) to check on the application of the skills in real-life situations. Again, this may be difficult to justify in certain agency or hospital settings. Similarly, in an agency context, clinicians need time and resources to learn the skills training approach. These resources need to be explicitly negotiated before initiating a client program.

The second acceptance level necessary for this particular model involves the clinician "buy-in." With a generalist or eclectic approach to practice, mastery of a particular model is difficult given time and practice limitations. The skills trainer role could be enhanced with a prior social work role that included team member participation on a behavioral research protocol. Many clinicians already possess rigorous training in the following: (1) assessment of client deficits and strengths, (2) the teaching of the skills, and (3) the measurement of behavioral change in research design conditions. Interrater reliability and monitoring of behavioral change would be areas to address. These issues must all be addressed before skills training is adopted.

Clinicians may also deliver a condensed or incomplete version of a training package that may not achieve the desired outcome. Clinicians may end up with a different outcome than anticipated if the manual is not followed or skills training is not completed. Also, because the client will provide most of the feedback regarding behavior change in self-reports, some of the richness of witnessing the change process as it occurs will be lost and confidence in the model may suffer (Deffenbacher et al., 1994). These constraints may lead the social worker to choose a model that provides more flexibility and is easier to deliver within the context of the session or agency, despite awareness that behavioral skills training might be the most effective intervention.

The third level of "buy-in" acceptance in utilizing skills training involves the client. The following case vignette will highlight some of the issues that a client with schizophrenia (paranoid-type) wrestled to recognize the benefits of skills training in her life. The senior author developed this account as a result of a 15-year case manager and therapist association with the client in a longitudinal research project. She acknowledges that the preferred way of obtaining this narrative would have been in a semistructured in-depth interview. This would have elicited the personal meaning that this client attributed to the role of skills training in her life and its effect on her ability to cope with her schizophrenia (Davidson & Strauss, 1992; Estroff, 1989; Kleinman, 1988). In this instance, however, the client was asked to review and validate the history and impact of this specific-skills training in her life.

Case Vignette

Annie is a Japanese American woman in her late 30s, diagnosed with schizophrenia in 1982. Her family experienced more than their share of mentally ill members. Her mother and brother also had schizophrenia, making the disorder even more frightening in its familiarity. Annie had severe episodes over the years, multiple hospitalizations, and one very serious suicide attempt. Her suicidal ideation stabilized dramatically over the last 5 years, and now she rarely thinks about hurting herself.

With the guidance and collaboration of her psychiatrist, she has tried almost every available neuroleptic medication, as she attempted to gain control over her persistent delusional symptoms. She has been fully compliant with her medication regimen, with the exception of a brief period of acupuncture and herbal remedies. Co-morbid with her psychotic symptoms are affective symptoms of anxiety and depression that interfere with her daily functioning. These have also been treated with medications, plus supportive individual and group therapy.

Annie has a large family, but she does not live with any family members. She has lived independently and in large group facilities. Currently, she resides in an apartment with one roommate who also has a mental illness. Annie has a good social network, attends classes at a junior college, and is a clubhouse member of a community mental health services agency. After her initial episode, she was able to work competitively, but she has not worked in many years because a number of relapses were related to workplace stresses. She currently works for family, cleaning their homes weekly.

Annie has been a participant in a comprehensive, longitudinal research protocol at UCLA, starting in 1989. She has had the benefit of most of the skills training modules, developed as part of the UCLA SILS Program (1990). The same skills training package was also taught at the clubhouse program she attended.

The training format uses a video and workbook approach, as explained earlier. The content covers conversation skills, symptom and medication management, and use of leisure time for patients with psychiatric disorders. They are easy to use, cover basic skill areas in a routine manner, utilize the same seven stepwise learning objectives, and provide additional homework exercises to practice the skills (Wallace & Liberman, 1985).

Because of her long tenure in both programs, Annie had the benefit of participating in the group training of these modules with more frequency than most clients. Overlearning the skills can often benefit patients with severe deficits. On many occasions, she served as co-facilitator of the group because she knows the curriculum so well. She is a great example of someone who has truly integrated the skills training and consistently utilizes the approach to combat her persistent symptoms and avoid rehospitalization.

So how did she do it? Because Annie is medication compliant, has good social and communication skills, and knows how to fill her free time, the module that best suited her needs was symptom management. In this module, there is a worksheet that serves as a decision tree. The client, skills trainer, and family member, if possible, select and weigh three symptoms that have caused difficulty, currently or in the past. They list the symptoms, with examples, and rank them as mild, moderate, or severe. This process can be completed individually or as a quiet group exercise with the trainer checking each person and providing coaching and prompts to facilitate the process.

The client transfers these three symptoms to a monthly tracking sheet. A checkmark next to mild, moderate, or severe indicates the daily degree of interference of that symptom. As with all behavioral models, the trainer must provide a certain amount of habit training, baseline tracking, support, and encouragement prior to advancing to the next level. The next step is to get ideas for managing persistent symptoms by reviewing the workbook page with suggested coping mechanisms. This can be part of a group exercise, enhancing the opportunity to trade coping secrets. It can also occur in an individual or family session. A formal problem-solving method can be used if the person is unable to figure out a plausible coping response.

Because Annie has a quasi-delusional response to the word *relax*, examples were limited to solutions other than relaxation training. She chose some self-regulatory skills (thought stopping, distraction, self-talk) and some global socially interactive skills (call a friend, go to her clubhouse program). These skills were practiced in the group and as homework.

There were two innovative components to Annie's success with her symptom management skills. First, she used her checklists daily. She posted them on her refrigerator and set a time each day to complete them. She brought them with her to her sessions so that we could note changes on a particular day and over the month. Second, Annie and her trainer developed "coping cards." These were 3-inch by 5-inch cards kept in her purse and at home as reminders for selected coping methods. These reminders are important in a thought disorder because simple cognitive tasks and concentration are affected by symptoms. Annie's symptom exacerbation was often accompanied by anxiety and depression, which further complicated her ability to remember how to cope. Coping cards have been effective tools for serving Annie's needs. The accumulation of skills has changed her hospitalization pattern, raised her confidence and self-esteem, preserved her social networks, and enhanced her daily functioning.

SUMMARY

Social workers have several opportunities to become skills trainers, if they choose. First, skills trainers use an intervention model that meshes well with basic social work knowledge, practice, and ethical issues. Second, skills trainers can meet the needs of a wide range of populations and problems. Third, they can use the intervention with individuals, families, and groups. Last, skills trainers can empower the client with skills they can use outside of the treatment session.

Skills training has had a long and active history in the treatment of profound mental health problems and daily struggles. Social workers should educate themselves and not let this model slip from their treatment repertoire, because the effectiveness of teaching skills in correcting deficits is well-documented, and its broad use across populations will continue to be a focus of research and practice for many years. As the providers of most of the mental health services in this country, social workers owe to their clients and to themselves an opportunity to offer a treatment approach known to improve the quality of life.

WEB RESOURCES

Internet access has been steadily gaining ground with all of the groups mentioned in this chapter who could benefit from skills training. Senior citizens and those with severe mental illness are discovering the potential for connections and information through the Internet that were previously inaccessible to them because of features of their disability (e.g., social withdrawal, limited mobility). While there are drawbacks to the exclusive use of a Web site for skills training (i.e., the lack of human interaction necessary to really learn the skill), we feel that there is valuable information about the various disorders on these sites. In addition, we have provided sources for ordering social skills module packages.

The site found at http://www.mhsource.com/ provides excellent overviews of schizophrenia, bipolar disorder, and depression. It also offers self-screening tools and an interactive "Ask the Expert" section. The following are helpful links to other mental health sites.

National Institute on Mental Health (http://www.nimh.nih.gov/). This site is incredibly rich with information, press releases, protocol opportunities, grant information, and national meetings. It now has a great fact sheet on anxiety disorders, highlighting social phobias. It provides a basic understanding of cognitive behavioral therapy and links to resources.

Metanoia (http://www.metanoia.org/). Metanoia.org, a consumer-oriented site, has some very basic cognitive steps in helping people to reduce their pain and increase their coping abilities.

Training Institute for Suicide Assessment and Clinical Interviewing (http://www. suicideassessment.com/). This site seems to be geared more toward the professional. Because the disorders mentioned in this chapter all have a greater risk of suicide, this is an important resource.

The Eating Disorders Awareness Program (http://www.edap.org/). Home of the Eating Disorders Awareness Program, this site boasts some very good statistics and links. We were most interested in the Body Wise program, which is a downloadable information packet for Middle School Students, developed by the Department of Health and Human Services. (http://www.imt.net/~randolfi/StressLinks. html). This is a Web directory of multiple sites on stress management, anger management, and relaxation techniques. It provides an entire section on stress and college students, with links to universities that have their own mental health site for their students.

UCLA Center for Research on Treatment and Rehabilitation (http:// www.mental-health.ucla.edu/) This site provides information on the UCLA Center for Research on Treatment and Rehabilitation (medication trials and psychosocial interventions).

ADDITIONAL RESOURCES

To order a catalog of Products and Services for Biobehavioral Rehabilitation of Persons with Disabling Mental Disorders, call the UCLA Psychiatric Rehabilitation Program at (310) 794-1060 or order through http://www.mentalhealth.ucla.edu/.

Linehan, Marsha. (1993). *Skills Training Manual for Treating Borderline Personality Disorders.* Available at http://www.amazon.com/.

Wexler, David. (1999). *Domestic Violence 2000: An Integrated Skills Program for Men* (Group Leader's Manual; includes audiocassette). Wexler incorporates many of the features of the Alternatives to Aggression (ATA) model. For skill workshops, contact: Relationship Training Institute, 4036 3rd Ave., San Diego, CA, 92103, or call (619) 296-8104.

REFERENCES

Agathon, M. (1994). Social anxiety: Occupational and life stressors. *Homeostasis in Health and Disease, 35*(1–2), 94–97.

Alberti, R. F., & Emmons, M. L. (1995). *Your perfect right* (7th ed.). San Luis Obispo, CA: Impact.

Aldwin, C. M. (1992). Aging, coping and efficacy: Theoretical framework for examining coping in life-span developmental context. In Wykle, M. L., Kahana, E., & Kowal, J. (Eds.), *Stress and health among the elderly.* New York: Springer.

American Psychiatric Association. (1994). *Diagnostic and statistical manual of mental disorders* (4th ed.). Washington, DC: Author.

Arean, P. A., Perri, M. G., Nezu, A. M., & Schein, R. L. (1993). Comparative effectiveness of social problem-solving therapy and reminiscence therapy as treatments for depression in older adults. *Journal of Consulting and Clinical Psychology, 61*(6), 1003–1010.

Aschen, S. R. (1997). Assertion training in psychiatric milieus. *Archives of Psychiatric Nursing, 11*(1), 46–51.

Beck, A. T., Rush, A. J., & Shaw, B. F. (1979). *Cognitive therapy of depression.* New York: Guilford Press.

Beck, J., Gayle, S., Stanley, M. A., Baldwin, L. E., & Edwin, A. (1994). Comparison of cognitive therapy and relaxation for panic disorder. *Journal of Consulting and Clinical Psychology, 62*(4), 818–826.

°Beck, R. & Fernandez, E. (1998). Cognitive-behavioral therapy in the treatment of anger: A meta-analysis. *Cognitive Therapy and Research, 22*(1), 63–74.

°Bedell, J. R. (1997). *Handbook for communication and problem-solving skills training: A cognitive behavioral approach.* New York: Wiley.

Bedell, J. R., & Archer, R. P. (1980). Peer managed token economies: Evaluation and description. *Journal of Clinical Psychology, 36*(3), 716–722.

°°Bellack, A. S., Mueser, K. T., Gingerich, S., & Agresta, J. (1997). *Social skills training for schizophrenia: A step-by-step guide.* New York: Guilford Press.

Benson, H. (1975). *The relaxation response.* New York: William Morrow.

°Benton, M. K., & Schroeder, H. E. (1990). Social skills training with schizophrenics: A meta-analytic evaluation. *Journal of Consulting and Clinical Psychology, 58*, 741–747.

°°Berg I. K., & Reuss, N. H. (1998a). *Solutions step by step: A substance abuse treatment manual.* New York: W. W. Norton.

°°Berg I. K., & Reuss, N. H. (1998b). *Solutions step by step videotape.*[Videotape recording]. Dunsmore, PA: W. W. Norton.

°°Bernstein, D. A., & Borkovec, T. D. (1973). *Progressive relaxation training.* Champaign, IL: Research Press.

Blanchard-Fields, F., Chen, Y., & Norris, L. (1997). Everyday problem-solving across the adult life span: Influence of domain specificity and cognitive appraisal. *Psychology and Aging, 12*(4), 684–693.

Bolman, L. G., & Deal, T. E. (1991). *Reframing organizations: Artistry, choice, & leadership.* San Francisco, CA: Jossey-Bass.

Bradshaw, W. H. (1993). Coping skills training versus a problem-solving approach with schizophrenic patients. *Hospital and Community Psychiatry, 44*(11), 1102–1104.

°Brammer, L. (1990). Teaching personal problem solving to adults. *Journal of Cognitive Psychotherapy: An International Quarterly, 4*(3), 267–279.

Browne, K. O., Saunders, D. G., & Staecker, K. M. (1997). Process-psychodynamic groups for men who batter: A brief treatment model. *Families in Society, 78*(3), 265–271.

Carels, R. A., Sherwood, A., & Blumenthal, J.A. (1998). Psychosocial influences on blood pressure during daily life. *International Journal of Psychophysiology, 28*(2), 117–129.

Catalano, R. F., Wells, E. A., Jenson, J. M., & Hawkins, J. D. (1989). Aftercare services for drug-using institutionalized delinquents. *Social Service Review, 63*(4), 553–577.

Claxton, A. J., Chawla, A. J., & Kennedy, S. (1999). Absenteeism among employees being treated for depression. *Journal of Occupational & Environmental Medicine, 41*(7), 605–611.

Cooper, M. L., Russell, M., & Frone, M. R. (1990). Work stress and alcohol effects: A test of stress-induced drinking. *Journal of Health and Social Behavior, 31*(3), 260–276.

Corrigan, P. W. (1991). Social skills training in adult psychiatric populations: A meta-analysis. *Journal of Behavior Therapy and Experimental Psychiatry, 22*(3), 203–210.

Cotton, D. H. G. (1990). *Stress management: An integrated approach to therapy.* New York: Brunner/Mazel.

Coyne, J. C., Kessler, R. C., Tal, M., Turnbull, J., Wortman, C. B., & Greden, J. F. (1987). Living with a depressed person. *Journal of Consulting and Clinical Psychology, 55,* 347–352.

°Craighead, L. W., Craighead, W. E., Kazdin, A. E., & Mahoney, M. J. (Eds.). (1994). *Cognitive and behavioral interventions: An empirical approach to mental health problems.* Boston: Allyn & Bacon.

Croghan, T. W., Melfi, C. A., Dobrez, D. G., Kneisner, T. J. (1999). Effect of mental health specialty care on antidepressant length of therapy. *Medical Care, 37*(4), AS20–AS23.

Crum, R. M., Muntaner, C., Eaton, W. W., & Anthony, J. C. (1995). Occupational stress and the risk of alcohol abuse and dependence. *Alcoholism: Clinical and Experimental Research, 19*(3), 647–655.

Curtis, A. B., James, S. A., Raghunathanm, T. E., & Alcser, K. H. (1997). Job strain and blood pressure in African Americans: The Pitt County study. *American Journal of Public Health, 87*(8), 1297–1302.

Davidson, L., & Strauss, J. S. (1992). Sense of self in recovery from severe mental illness. *British Journal of Medical Psychology, 65,* 131–145.

°°Davis, M., Eshelman, E., & McKay, M. (1995). *The relaxation and stress reduction workbook* (4th ed.). Oakland, CA: New Harbinger.

Decker, P. J., & Borgen, F. H. (1993). Dimensions of work appraisal: Stress, coping, job satisfaction, and negative affectivity. *Journal of Counseling Psychology, 40*(4), 470–478.

°Deffenbacher, J. L. (1999). Cognitive-behavioral conceptualization and treatment of anger. *Journal of Clinical Psychology, 55*(3), 295–309.

Deffenbacher, J. L., Thwaites, G. A., Wallace, T. L., & Oetting, E. R. (1994). Social skills and cognitive-relaxation approaches to general anger reduction. *Journal of Counseling Psychology, 41*(3), 386–396.

Dickstein, C., & Jefferson, J. W. (1996). *Depression in women: Why it occurs, what can be done.* Pfizer U.S. Pharmaceutical (Rockville, MD: available from NIMH Information Line, 1-800-421-4211).

°Dilk, M. N., & Bond, G. R. (1996). Meta-analytic evaluation of skills training research for individuals with severe mental illness. *Journal of Consulting and Clinical Psychology, 64*(6), 1337–1346.

Dixon, L. B., Lehman, A. F., & Levine, J. (1995). Conventional antipsychotic medications for schizophrenia. *Schizophrenia Bulletin, 21*(4), 567–577.

Dobson, D. J. G., McDougall, G., Busheikin, J., Aldous, J., & Tasman, A. (1996). Effects of social skills training and social milieu treatment on symptoms of schizophrenia. *Yearbook of Psychiatry and Applied Mental Health, 4,* 118–119.

Dohrenwend, B. S., & Dohrenwend, B. P. (1974). *Stressful life events: Their nature and effects.* New York: Wiley.

Donaldson, S. I., Graham, J. W., Piccinin, A. M., & Hansen, W. B. (1997). Resistance-skills training and onset of alcohol use: Evidence for beneficial and potentially harmful effects in public schools and in private Catholic schools. In G. A. Marlatt & G. R. VandenBos *Addictive behaviors: Readings on etiology, prevention and treatment.* Washington, DC: American Psychological Association.

°Donohue, B., Acierno, R., Hersen, M., & Van Hassalt, V. B. (1995). Social skills training for depressed, visually impaired older adults: A treatment manual. *Behavior Modification, 19*(4), 379–424.

Duberstein, P. R., Conwell, Y., Seidlitz, L., Lyness, J. M., Cox, C., & Caine, E. R. (1999). Age and suicidal ideation in older depressed patients. *American Journal of Geriatric Psychiatry,* 7(4), 289–296.

D'Zurilla, T. J. (1990). Problem-solving training for effective stress management and prevention. *Journal of Cognitive Psychotherapy: An International Quarterly,* 4(4), 327–354.

Eckman, T. A., Wirshing, W. C., Marder, S. R., & Liberman, R. P. (1992). Techniques for training schizophrenic patients in illness self-management: A controlled trial. *American Journal of Psychiatry,* 149(11), 1549–1555.

°°Ellis, A., & Tafrate, R. C. (1997). *How to control your anger before it controls you.* New Jersey: Carol.

°Emmelkamp, P. M. G. (1994). Behavior therapy with adults. In A. E. Bergin & S. L. Garfield (Eds.), *Handbook of psychotherapy and behavior change.* New York: Wiley and Sons.

Estroff, S. E. (1989). Self, identity, and subjective experiences in schizophrenia: In search of subject. *Schizophrenia Bulletin,* 15(2), 189–196.

Falloon, I. R. H., Coverdale, J. H., Laidlaw, T. M., Merry, S., Kydd, R. R., & Morosini, P. (1998). Early intervention for schizophrenic disorders: Implementing optimal treatment strategies in routine clinical services. *The British Journal of Psychiatry,* 172(33), 33–38.

Falloon, I. R. H., Morosini, P., Roncone, R., Casacchia, M., Coverdale, J., Economon, M., Erickson, D., Grawe, R., Harangozo, J., Held, T., Ivarsson, B., Malm, U., Lussetti, M., Mizuno, M., Murakami, M., & Ventura, J. (1998). Cognitive-behavioral strategies for the treatment of schizophrenic disorders. In E. Sanavio (Ed.), *Behavior and cognitive therapy today: Essays in honor of Hans J. Eysenck.* Oxford, England: Elsevier Science.

Fenton, W. S., & McGlashan, T. H. (1994). Antecedents, symptom progression, and long-term outcome of the deficit syndrome in schizophrenia. *American Journal of Psychiatry,* 151, 351–356.

Fogarty, G. S., Machin, M., A., Albion, M. J., Sutherland, L. F., Lalor, G. I., & Revitt, S. (1999). Predicting occupational strain and job satisfaction: The role of stress, coping, personality, and affectivity variables. *Journal of Vocational Behavior,* 54(3), 429–452.

Gaffan, E. A., Tsaousis, J., & Kemp-Wheeler, S. M. (1995). The case of cognitive therapy for depression. *Journal of Consulting and Clinical Psychology,* 63(6), 966–980.

Godaert, L. R. R. (1982). Relaxation treatment for hypertension. In R. S. Surwit, R. B. Williams, A. Steptoe, & R. Biersner (Eds.), *Behavioral treatment of disease.* New York: Plenum.

Greenberg, P., Stiglin, L. E., Finkelstein, S., & Berndt, E. (1993). Depression: a neglected major illness. *Journal of Clinical Psychiatry,* 54, 419–424.

Guerrero, L. K., Andersen, P. A., & Trost, M. R. (1998). Communication and emotion: Basic concepts and approaches. In P. A. Andersen & L. K. Guerrero (Eds.), *Handbook of communication and emotion: Research, theory, applications, and context.* San Diego, CA: Academic Press.

Hall, J. A. (1995). Skills training for pregnant and parenting adolescents. In E. Rahdert & D. Czechowicz (Eds.), *Adolescent drug abuse: Clinical assessment and therapeutic interventions.* Rockville, MD: NIDA. NIH Publication No. 95–3908.

Harrington, R., Whittaker, J., & Shoebridge, P. (1998). Psychological treatment of depression in children and adolescents. A review of treatment research. *The British Journal of Psychiatry,* 173(10), 291–298.

Hartlage, S., & Clements, C. (1996). Cognitive deficits in depression. In P. W. Corrigan & S. C. Yudofsky (Eds.), *Cognitive rehabilitation for psychiatric disorders.* Washington DC: American Psychiatric Press.

Hogarty, G. E., Anderson, C., & Reiss, D. (1986). Family psychoeducation, social skills training, and maintenance chemotherapy in the after-care treatment of schizophrenia. *Archives of General Psychiatry,* 43, 633–642.

Hogarty, G. E., Anderson, C. M., Reiss, D. J., Kornblith, S. J., Greenwald, D. P., Ulrich, R. F., & Carter, M. (1991). Family psychoeducation, social skills training, and maintenance chemotherapy in the aftercare treatment of schizophrenia. Two year effects of a controlled study on relapse and adjustment. *Archives of General Psychiatry, 48*(4), 340–347.

°Hollon, S. D., & Beck, A. T. (1994). Cognitive and cognitive behavioral therapies. In A. E. Bergin & S. L. Garfield (Eds.), *Handbook of psychotherapy and behavior change.* New York: Wiley and Sons.

Howard, M. C. (1992). Adolescent substance abuse: A social learning theory perspective. In G. W. Lawson & A. W. Lawson (Eds.), *Adolescent substance abuse: Etiology, treatment, and prevention.* Gaithersburg, MD: Aspen.

Hyman, S. E. (1998). A new image of fear and emotion. *Nature, 393*(6684), 417–418.

Janowiak, J. J., & Hackman, R. (1994). Meditation and college students' self-actualization and related stress. *Psychological Reports, 75*(2), 1007–1010.

Jensen, A. (1971). The role of verbal mediation in mental development. *Journal of Genetic Psychology, 118*, 39–70.

°Jeste, D. V., Alexopoulos, G. S., Bartels, S. J., Cummings, J. L., Gallo, J. J., Gottlieb, G. L., Halpain, M. C., Palmer, B. W., Patterson, T. L., Reynolds, C. F., & Lebowitz, B. D. (1999). Consensus statement on the upcoming crisis in geriatric mental health: Research agenda for the next 2 decades. *Archives of General Psychiaty, 56*(9), 848–853.

°Kelley, P. L. (1996). Stress management techniques in the workplace: A meta-analysis of stress intervention techniques. *Dissertation Abstracts International, 56*(9-B): 5207.

°Kleinman, A. (1988). *The illness narratives: Suffering, healing & the human condition.* New York: Basic Books.

Kopelowicz, A. (1997). Social skills training: The moderating influence of culture in the treatment of Latinos with schizophrenia. *Journal of Psychopathology and Behavioral Assessment, 19*(2), 101–108.

Kopelowicz, A., & Liberman, R. P. (1998). Psychosocial treatments for schizophrenia. In P. E. Nathan & J. M. Gorman (Eds.), *Treatments that work.* London: Oxford University Press.

°Kopelowicz, A., & Liberman, R. P. (1999). Biobehavioral treatment and rehabilitation of people with serious mental illness. In J. R. Scotti & L. H. Meyer (Eds.), *Behavioral intervention: Principles, models, & practices.* Baltimore, MD: Paul H. Brookes.

Kopelwicz, A., Wallace, C. J., & Zarate, R. (1998). Teaching psychiatric inpatients to re-enter the community: A brief method of improving continuity of care. *Psychiatric Services, 49*, 1313–1316.

°Kopelowicz, A., Corrigan, P. W., Schade, M., & Liberman, R. P. (1998). Social skills training. In K. T. Mueser & N. Tarrier (Eds.), *Handbook of social functioning in schizophrenia.* Boston, MA: Allyn & Bacon.

Kopelowicz, A., Liberman, R. P., Mintz, J., & Zarate, R. (1997). Comparison of efficacy of social skills training for deficit and nondeficit negative symptoms in schizophrenia. *American Journal of Psychiatry, 154*(3), 424–425.

Lazarus, R. S. (1999). *Stress and emotion: A new synthesis.* New York: Springer.

Lazarus, R. S., & Cohen, J. B. (1987). Theory and method in the study of stress and coping in aging individuals. In L. Lennart (Ed.), *Society, stress and disease* (Vol. 5). Oxford, England: Oxford University Press.

°Lazarus, R. S., & Folkman, S. (1984). *Stress, appraisal, and coping.* New York: Springer.

°°LeComte, T., Cyr, M., Lesage, A. D., Wilde, J., Leclerc, C., & Ricard, N. (1999). Efficacy of a self-esteem module in the empowerment of individuals with schizophrenia. *Journal of Nervous and Mental Disease, 187*(7), 406–413.

LeDoux, J. (1996). *The emotional brain: The mysterious underpinnings of emotional life.* New York: Touchstone.

Leff, J. P., & Vaughn, C. E. (1985). *Expressed emotion in families.* New York: Guilford Press.

Lehrer, P. M. (1998). Emotionally triggered asthma: A review of research literature and some hypothesis for self-regulation therapies. *Applied Psychophysiology and Biofeedback, 23*(1), 13–41.

Lewinsohn, P. M., & Clarke, G. N. (1999). Psychosocial treatments for adolescent depression. *Clinical psychology review, 19*(3), 329–342.

°°Lewinsohn, P. M., Munoz, R. F., Youngren, M. A., & Zeiss, A. M. (1992). *Control your depression.* New York: Simon & Schuster.

°°Liberman, R. P. (1988). *Social and independent living skills (SILS) modules.* (Trainers manuals, patient workbooks, video package.) Camarillo, CA: UCLA Research Center.

°Liberman, R. P. (Ed.). (1992). *Handbook of psychiatric rehabilitation.* New York: Macmillan.

°Liberman, R. P., DeRisi, W. J., & Mueser, K. T. (1989). *Social skills training for psychiatric patients.* New York: Pergamon Press.

Linehan, M. M. (1990). *Individual and skills training treatment manuals for DBT.* Seattle: University of Washington.

Linehan, M. M. (1993). *Skills training manual for treating borderline personality disorder.* New York: Guilford Press.

°Linehan, M., & Egan, J. (1979). Assertion training for women. In A. S. Bellack & M. Hersen (Eds.), *Research and practice in social skills training.* New York: Plenum.

Linehan, M., & Schmidt, H. (1995). The dialectics of effective treatment of borderline personality disorder. In W. O'Donahue & L. Krasner (Eds.), *Theories of behavior therapy: Exploring behavior change.* Washington, DC: APA.

°Marlatt, G. A., & VandenBos, G. R. (Eds.). (1997). *Addictive behaviors: Readings on etiology, prevention, and treatment.* Washington, DC: APA.

McDonald, M. L. (1982). Assertion training for women. In J. Curran & P. Monti (Eds.), *Social skills training: A practical handbook for assessment and treatment.* New York: Guilford.

°McFall, R. M. (1982). A review and reformulation of the concept of social skills. *Behavioral Assessment, 4,* 1–33.

McFall, R. M., Treat, T. A., Viken, R. J. (1998). Contemporary cognitive approaches to studying clinical problems. In D. K. Routh & R. J. DeRubeis (Eds.), *The science of clinical psychology: Accomplishments and future directions.* Washington, DC: APA.

Meichenbaum, D., & Cameron, R. (1973). Training schizophrenics to talk to themselves: A means of developing self controls. *Behavior Therapy, 4,* 515–534.

Michelson, L. K., Marchione, K. E., Greenwald, M., Testa, S., & Marchione, N. J. (1996). A comparative outcome and follow-up investigation of panic disorder with agoraphobia: The relative and combined efficacy of cognitive therapy, relaxation training, and therapist assisted exposure. *Journal of Anxiety Disorders, 10*(5), 297–330.

°Milrod, B., & Busch, F. (1996). Long-term outcome of panic disorder treatment: A review of the literature. *The Journal of Nervous and Mental Disease, 184*(12), 723–730.

Mintz, J., Mintz, L. I., Robertson, M. J., Liberman, R. P., & Glynn, S. M. (1996). Treatment of depression and the restoration of work capacity. In J. Lonsdale (Ed.), *The Hatherleigh guide to managing depression.* New York: Hatherleigh Press.

Mueser, K. T., Bellack, A. S., Douglas, M. S., & Wade, J. H. (1991). Predictions of social skill acquisition in schizophrenic and major affective disorder patients from memory and symptomatology. *Psychiatry Research, 37,* 281–296.

°°Mueser, K. T., & Glynn, S. M. (1999). *Behavioral family therapy for psychiatric disorders* (2nd ed.) Oakland, CA: New Harbinger.

°Murphy, L. R. (1996). Stress management in work settings: A critical review of health effects. *American Journal of Health Promotion, 11*(2), 112–134.

Neal, G. W., & Heppner, P. P. (1986). Problem solving self-appraisal, awareness, and utilization of campus helping resources. *Journal of Counseling Ppsychology, 33,* 39–44.

Neuchterlein, K., & Dawson, M. (1984). A heuristic vulnerability/stress model of schizophrenic episodes. *Schizophrenia Bulletin, 10,* 300–312.

Neuchterlein, K. H., Dawson, M. E., Gitlin, M., Ventura, J., Goldstein, M. J., Snyder, K. S., Yee, C. M., & Mintz, J. (1992). Developmental processes in schizophrenic disorders: Longitudinal studies of vulnerability and stress. *Schizophrenia Bulletin, 18,* 387–425.

Nezu, A. M. (1985). Differences in psychological distress between effective and ineffective problem solvers. *Journal of Counseling Psychology, 32,* 135–138.

Nezu, A. M., Nezu, C. M., & Perri, M. G. (1990). Psychotherapy for adults within a problem-solving framework: Focus on depression. *Journal of Cognitive Psychotherapy, 4*(3), 247–256.

Novaco, R. W. (1993). Clinicians ought to view anger contextually. *Behaviour Change, 10*(4), 208–218.

Novaco, R. W. (1997). Remediating anger and aggression with violent offenders. *Legal and Criminal Psychology, 2*(Pt. 1), 77–88.

O'Donohue, W. (Ed.). (1998). *Learning and behavior therapy.* Boston: Allyn & Bacon.

Pavalko, E. K., Elder, G. H., & Clipp, E. C. (1993). Worklives and longevity: Insights from a lifecourse perspective. *Journal of Health and Social Behavior, 34*(4), 363–380.

Pearlin, L. I. (1985). Life strains and psychological distress among adults. In A. Monat & R. S. Lazarus (Eds.), *Stress and coping: An anthology* (2nd ed.). New York: Columbia University Press.

Pelletier, K. R., Rodenburg, A., Vinther, A., Chikamoto, Y., King, A., & Farquhar, J. W. (1999). Managing job strain: A randomized, controlled trial of an intervention conducted by mail and telephone. *Journal of Occupational & Environmental Medicine, 41*(4), 216–223.

Persons, J. B., Burns, D. D., & Perloff, J. M. (1989). Predictors of dropout and outcome in cognitive therapy for depression in a private practice setting. *Cognitive Therapy and Research, 12,* 557–575.

Radecki, C. M., & Jacard, J. (1996). Gender role differences in decision-making skills. *Journal of Applied Social Psychology, 26*(1), 76–94.

Rikard, H. C., Scogin, F., & Keith, S. (1994). A one-year follow-up of relaxation training for elders with subjective anxiety. *The Gerontologist, 34*(1), 121–122.

°°Roberts, L. J., Shaner, A., & Eckman, T. (1999). *Overcoming addictions: Skills training for people with schizophrenia.* New York: Norton Professional Books.

Rosen, G. (1977). *The relaxation book.* Englewood Cliffs, NJ: Prentice-Hall.

Saunders, D. G. (1996). Feminist-cognitive-behavioral and process-psychodynamic treatments for men who batter: Interaction of abuser traits and treatment models. *Violence and Victims, 11,* 393–414.

Saunders, D. G., & Hanusa, D. (1986). Cognitive-behavioral treatment of men who batter: The short term effects of group therapy. *Journal of Family Violence, 11,* 357–372.

Scheel, K. R. (2000). The empirical basis of dialectical behavior therapy: Summary, critique and implications. *Clinical Psychology: Science and Practice, 7*(1), 68–86.

Schilling, R. F., El-Bassel, N., Hadden, B., & Gilbert, L. (1995). Skills training groups to reduce HIV transmission and drug use among methadone patients. *Social Work, 40*(1), 91–101.

Schwartz, A. (1982). *The behavior therapies.* New York: Free Press.

Segrin, C., & Abramson, L. Y. (1994). Negative reactions to depressive behaviors: A communications theories analysis. *Journal of Abnormal Psychology, 103*(4), 655–668.

°Smith, T. E., Bellack, A. S., & Liberman, R. P. (1996). Social skills training for schizophrenia: Review and future directions. *Clinical Psychology Review, 16*(7), 599–617.

Subramanian, K. (1994). Long-term follow-up of a structured group treatment for the management of chronic pain. *Research on Social Work Practice, 4*(2), 208–223.

Subramanian, K., & Rose, S. D. (1988). Social work and the treatment of chronic pain. *Health & Social Work, 13*(1), 49–60.

Temple, S., & Robson, P. (1991). The effect of assertiveness training on self-esteem. *British Journal of Occupational Therapy, 54*(9), 329–332.

Thorpe, G. L., & Olson, S. L. (1997). *Behavior therapy: Concepts, procedures and applications.* Boston: Allyn & Bacon.

Tripp, J. H., & Cockett, M. (1998). Parent, parenting, and family breakdown. *Archives of Disease in Childhood, 78*(2), 104–108.

Trower, P. (1982). Towards a generative model of social skills: A critique and synthesis. In J. Curran & P. Monti (Eds.), *Social skills training: A practical handbook for assessment and treatment.* New York: Guilford.

Vaughn, C., & Long, W. (1999). Surrender to win: How adolescent drug and alcohol users change their lives. *Adolescence, 34*(133), 9–24.

Wallace, C. J., & Liberman, R. P. (1985). Social skills training for patients with schizophrenia: A controlled clinical study. *Psychiatry Research, 15,* 239–247.

Warzak, W. J., Grow, C. R., Poler, M. M., & Walburn, J. N. (1995). Enhancing refusal skills: Identifying contexts that place adolescents at risk for unwanted sexual activity. *Developmental and Behavioral Pediatrics, 16*(2), 98–100.

Werner, M. J., & Adger, H. (1995). Early identification, screening, and brief intervention for adolescent alcohol use [Commentary]. *Archives of Pediatric and Adolescent Medicine, 149*(11), 1241–1248.

Williams, J. B. W., & Ell, K. (Eds.). (1998). *Advances in mental health research: Implications for practice.* Washington, DC: NASW Press.

Wolpe, J. (1958). *Psychotherapy by reciprocal inhibition.* Stanford, CA: Stanford University Press.

Worrall, L., Hickson, L., Barnett, H., & Yiu, E. (1998). An evaluation of the keep on talking program for maintaining communication skills into old age. *Educational Gerontology, 24*(2), 129–140.

° Denotes meta-analyses, articles of particular interest, or edited textbooks not referenced in the chapter.

°° Denotes handbooks and skills training packages.

SOCIAL WORKERS AS CASE MANAGERS

William Patrick Sullivan
& Charles A. Rapp

Over the past two decades, case management has become a ubiquitous service in public mental health and in the diverse arenas where social workers perform. From today's perspective, it seems unfathomable that there was ever a time when this practice method struggled for legitimacy and acceptance. However, the growing popularity of case management signified that important changes in the organization, focus, and mission of public mental health were under way.

Any discussion of the successes and failures of community mental health produces a lively debate (Bentley & Belcher, 1994). Indeed, when considering a wide range of social problems, from homelessness to violence, the perceived inadequacies of public mental health, particularly community care, are commonly noted. In reality, most social problems are highly complex, the result of a wide range of converging forces, and this complexity renders them invulnerable to simplistic solutions. These issues are germane to any exploration of the role of, and subsequent impact, of case management in mental health.

The landscape of mental health services has been transformed dramatically in the post-World War II era. Previously, state-operated psychiatric hospitals anchored the public mental health system. These inpatient facilities provided extensive treatment and rehabilitative services for people facing the most severe forms of mental illness—and treatment commonly extended over a period of several years. The predominance of this model would end, and by the late 1970s, the census of state hospitals began a precipitous decline, placing greater demands on a fledgling system of community treatment services.

As the roles of state psychiatric hospitals began to decline, the country was introduced to a new public utility, the community mental health center. These centers now brought mental health treatment and expertise closer to home. Soon, the populace was sensitized to issues of mental health and illness, and as a result, the demand for services was increased. Saddled with a heterogeneous mission and hampered by the limited technology available at that time, community mental health centers were ill-equipped to address the needs of former psychiatric inpatients and those just facing serious and persistent mental illnesses.

Clearly, the mental health system was stretched to capacity. In many respects, the families of those affected by serious mental illness were the first to recognize the crisis at hand (Hatfield & Lefley, 1987). Many former inpatients landed in other institutional settings (notably nursing homes) in the first wave of deinstitutionalization; however, significant numbers of consumers also returned to the care of parents and family (Mechanic and Rochefort, 1992; Timko, Nguyen, Williford, & Moos, 1993). Consider the difficulties faced by these family members, particularly in the early days of community mental health. While developments in psychopharmacology are commonly cited as a major force in the movement to community care, initially there was little sophistication in the use of medication and scant few options. Furthermore, community programming, except perhaps in a few major metropolitan areas, was nonexistent (Joint Commission on Mental Illness and Health, 1961). To add to the frustration, these family members contended with professionals trained in models that blamed them, either individually, or as a unit, for the illness of loved ones. The picture was certainly bleak.

Yet, the needs of these former inpatients, and others that would soon face the challenge of mental illness, extended far beyond basic psychiatric treatment. Hospital life, even in the most barren setting, provided some activities, structure, and a degree of protection. Some facilities went well beyond offering admirable basic care, as well as educational and work opportunities. However, a state hospital, regardless of the amenities and relative comforts that may be available, is not a home. Not surprisingly, consumers who are hospitalized overwhelmingly long for discharge and prefer community life to the hospital (Okin & Pearsall, 1993).

As their first task, families and interested professionals needed to ensure that the basic necessities of life were arranged for consumers exiting the hospital or already on their own. It soon became painfully obvious that there were few professionals available to assist these families and consumers. For families, the task of organizing necessary supports and navigating a fragmented social service system is an emotional and financial burden. Without the help of families, many former consumers began a revolving-door pattern that involved the emergency room, occasionally a return to the state hospital, and in the worst case scenario, jail or the streets (Lamb & Weinberger, 1998).

The unforeseen plight of people facing serious mental illness alarmed consumer advocates, professionals, and family members. It became increasingly clear that mid-stream corrections were desperately needed in community mental health as costs, in both financial and human terms, continued to rise. By the late 1970s, community mental health centers across the nation embarked on an ongoing process to respond to the needs of the most severely ill. Case management has been a cornerstone in the evolving task of re-engineering the system of community-based mental health services. It is hoped that this revamped service system can realize a generation-old goal of integrating those most in need, and help consumers recover from serious mental illness (Anthony, 1993).

The Emergence of Case Management

It is easy to see why case management has become such a popular service modality in mental health and other human service endeavors. The issues faced by consumers suffering from mental illnesses are complex and far-reaching, affecting all aspects of life. The phrase *serious and persistent mental illness* is certainly descriptive. The phrase not only indicates the presence of a major form of mental illness (such as schizophrenia or major depression), but also underscores that the condition has been enduring. Like other major disorders, mental illness affects a consumer's overall quality of life and their ability to function effectively in society. The illness often hinders social functioning directly and emphatically. Schizophrenia, for example, can impact the ability to distill information and deal with the intricacies of social discourse and interaction. When a person is most profoundly ill, they may find it difficult to sort out feelings and emotions, and find the presence of hallucinations and delusions to be particularly troubling. While the nature of these illnesses presents obvious challenges, many of the social difficulties experienced by consumers are related to the forces of discrimination and the stigma associated with mental illness. Mental illness is still poorly understood, and popular culture only perpetuates myths that cause many to fear those who face emotional and biophysical challenges.

Left to survive by their wits, or with only the help of beleaguered families, many mental health consumers had little chance at a quality life in the community. Some consumers, in contrast, have shown amazing resilience, and many have succeeded without the help of (and perhaps in spite of) mental health professionals. We can learn much from these consumers. Nonetheless, the plight of those termed *the chronically mentally ill* began to grab the attention of policymakers, program developers, and the general public (Talbott, 1981). Traditional outpatient treatment was simply insufficient to address the breadth of needs faced by these consumers. In conjunction, few community-based professionals had been specifically trained to care for the most seriously ill or commited to do so. The field of mental health needed a new cadre of professionals, and in time, these people were known as case managers.

The Intellectual Base of Case Management Practice

The title of this new role in community mental health made perfect sense and drew from the classic roots of medical practice. First you begin with a person. In medical parlance, this is a "case." A review of the person's presenting problems usually revealed serious illness, many social disabilities, and often an inability to organize his or her life. This suggested a need for outside help—a manager. In fact, when you consider the origin of this term, it is easy to see why some consumers and professionals find the term *case manager* distasteful, and antithetical to empowerment and strengths models of practice (Everett & Nelson, 1992). Objections to the title notwithstanding, strengths and empowerment principles are at the core of many models of case management (Rapp, 1998; Rose, 1992).

Nonetheless, the basic template previously detailed guided the development of many early models of case management. One of the first case-management models to emerge was the broker model. This model emphasized the role of case managers as the links between consumers and the range of services they required. As previously discussed, state psychiatric hospitals provided important services, and consumers and families struggle to recreate a network of care and services. As a broker, the case manager serves as linchpin and central point of contact, upon which consumers rely as they access needed resources. In theory, this seems simple enough. Certainly, good case managers do understand the formal and informal rules of other important organizations and sources of support vital to consumer welfare, and they also develop relationships with those key personnel who serve as gatekeepers to these needed resources. In reality, even with inside knowledge, it is difficult and time-consuming to skillfully maneuver through the human service system and other bureaucracies, including those systems that provide necessary basic services. The daily hassles that can drive the calmest person to the brink can paralyze those facing serious mental illness, and for many consumers, trips to license bureaus or benefits offices can invoke great anxiety (Segal & VanderVoort, 1993). To succeed in case management, professionals should provide labor-intensive, face-to-face consultations. The broker model has little chance of success if configured as an information and referral service, and when caseloads continue to expand. In the latter situation, professionals will find themselves simply responding to crisis situations, even when the direct service function of case management is emphasized. Thus, there is little time to work proactively with consumers on the goals that are important to them.

As case management gained a foothold in mental health services, debates began to rage on the professional status of these new colleagues. In part, this debate centered on the nature of the relationship between consumers and case managers. It was soon apparent that the impersonal broker model was conceptually and practically flawed, and incongruent with the actual experience of case managers and consumers in the field. As case managers and consumers worked side by side in the community, it became obvious that the nature of the relationship between the parties was central to the overall success of the intervention. Even when explicit distinctions were made between case-management practice and individual therapy, the roles were often blurred. Case managers, through necessity alone, deal with the thoughts and feelings of consumers, intervene when aspects of illness impede community functioning and goal attainment, address issues raised by families and loved ones, and are first in the line of defense in true crisis situations.

Opposite the broker approach is the therapist–case management model (Lamb, 1980). It is here argued that competent therapists should perform many of the duties commonly ascribed to case management, as a routine part of their job. It is difficult to argue with the conceptual foundations of this model. Therapists often have well-established relationships with those facing serious and persistent mental illness, and are specifically trained to deal with the range of emotional issues that consumers confront. In contrast to those identified as case managers, therapists are unequivocally granted professional status and usually hold advanced degrees. This creates an advantage, because those with the most training are working with those challenged by the most severe illnesses.

While the therapist–case manager model makes sense conceptually, it falls short in practice. In reality, few therapists have the time or proclivity to engage in classic case-management activities. Certainly, it can be argued that case management has emerged as a specialty role precisely because existing professionals are reluctant and/or unable to assimilate these duties in daily practice. This issue has become more salient given current trends in behavioral health care. Managed care, brief therapy, capitation, prior authorization, and concurrent review are relatively recent additions to the lexicon of community mental health. The new language of health care is more than cosmetic. In essence, it reflects notable changes in the delivery of mental health services and, concomitantly, significant alterations in organizational structure. The deployment of staff resources and the titration of services, to use the mantra of managed care, stipulates that consumers receive the right treatment, at the appropriate intensity, for the proper duration. Practice behavior and fiscal policy are no longer separate.

The broker and therapist–case management models previously described were the primary models that set the stage for future developments and innovation in the field. Embodied in these approaches were the two basic thrusts of case management, resource acquisition and coordination, and individual support and guidance. Over time, a host of case management models have evolved. Some have placed greater emphasis on classic therapeutic functions, others highlight resource acquisition activities, and comprehensive models attempt to synthesize the fundamental functions of case management in one overall approach (see Pescosolido, Wright, & Sullivan, 1995; Raiff & Shore, 1993).

Some structural variations in case management utilize programs configured as a team responsibility, while others rely on an independent practitioner model. The Assertive Community Treatment (ACT) model and its sire, Program of Assertive Community Treatment (PACT), from Wisconsin have demonstrated effectiveness across many replications (see Dixon, 2000). The strengths model has similarly been shown to produce superior client outcomes. We will use the strengths model as an exemplar primarily because it was developed, tested, and disseminated by social workers, and reflects most closely the values and legacy of social work. The strengths model is consistent with the major tenants and values of social work practice and reflects the person-in-environment framework so basic to the field (Rapp, 1998; Sullivan & Rapp, 1994; Weick, Rapp, Sullivan, & Kisthardt, 1989). However, in a unique twist, this model, while recognizing the tremendous challenges presented by mental illness, suggests that accenting and capitalizing on the inherent strengths in people and the social environment can activate the process of recovery. Given these assumptions, case management in the strengths model is an active process focused on enriching personal strengths and consumer self-identity through created and existing environmental transactions. It is defined as a form of personalized helping, directed at connecting individuals to resources for improving their quality of community life.

It has been noted that case management is an example of limited reform (Moxley, 1997). Case managers alone cannot fix the gaps in the existing service network, redefine fiscal policy, make entire communities more compassionate, or compensate for the disparities between needs and resources (Moore, 1992). There have been times, however, when far too much has been expected of this modest intervention. Moxley (1997) argues that "we should recognize and value case management for what it is: a somewhat limited but nonetheless important way of trying to make human service delivery work better" (p. 4). Regardless of the degree of integration of any system of mental health services, case managers provide an important and distinct function (Anthony, Cohen, Farkas, & Cohen, 2000). When case managers move from the office to the streets and develop authentic relationships with consumers, they become important agents in the recovery effort. These unique people provide a unique service that, in spite of perceptions to the contrary, requires a multiskilled practitioner.

All human service interventions are predicated on a set of assumptions about the etiology and remedies for the problems presented by consumers. Fallot (1993) has suggested that each model of case management makes claims about the "nature of psychological difficulties and strengths, about the processes of human development and change, about the dynamics of the interpersonal world, and about the goals and purposes which animate human life" (p. 258). It is widely agreed that biophysical conditions and functions largely account for those behaviors that lead to the diagnosis of a serious mental disorder. That being said, what precisely has gone awry in the body and mind is the subject of intense research and ongoing debate. The inability to discern the cause of mental illnesses with certainty and precision naturally obstructs the ability to design effective treatments and cures. Over time, the knowledge gleaned from research has aided the development of efficacious medications and treatment protocols. A similar method of trial, error, and research has guided the design and implementation of nonsomatic interventions.

There is a key difference, however, in the quest for effective somatic therapies and those efforts referred to as psychosocial rehabilitation. Medications are employed to directly impact the cause of the pathology or those mechanisms that lead to the expression of the pathological conditions. Here, medications may help one organize thoughts, feelings, and moods and hopefully lead to more productive and healthy behavior. Psychosocial interventions, including case management, attempt to deal directly with those aspects of daily life and social functioning that have been negatively impacted by the presence of illness. Case management, it follows, is not designed nor currently thought to directly influence the basic and primary forces that cause mental illness.

Given the current state of our knowledge, serious mental illnesses in particular must be considered intractable conditions if the only acceptable outcome is cure. On the other hand, the field of psychosocial rehabilitation has adopted *recovery* as a concept that best captures the experience of a significant number of individuals who face mental illnesses. This powerful term affirms the ability of consumers to live satisfying and meaningful lives, despite the challenges and limitations imposed by serious mental illnesses (Anthony, 1993). Accordingly, recovery presents an inspiring vision and attainable goal for both consumers and practitioners. Additionally, the concept of recovery fits well with those ecological principles that have been widely adapted in social work practice. In practical terms, recovery can be understood as the effort to regain or reclaim something lost, and/or compensate for a deficit or limitation. In social work practice, the ecological metaphors of equilibrium and homeostasis are similarly used when describing interventions gauged to restore order in the life of an individual, family, or group. In our example, mental illness is a threat to personal stability and growth that must be surmounted, ameliorated, or embraced. Interventions are designed to aid individuals in regaining lost skills, or re-establishing a usual development trajectory.

Case management and, more specifically, case managers can play important roles in the recovery process (Sullivan, 1994). We must consider, however, that recovery involves those activities that are central to the development of all people. While the trauma of mental illness may be extraordinary, most people have experienced personal setbacks, and face limitations in some areas that influence the course of their lives. Understanding how others get back on track and become proficient in daily life guides our understanding of recovery from mental illness.

The term *competence* also provides an important construct for understanding the functions of case management in mental health (White, 1959). Human development, regardless of whether in physical, social, emotional, or moral realms, occurs in context. A range of variables, from genetics to the quality of the neighborhood a person calls home, affects this development. There are people who appear to maximize their inherent potential and exploit opportunities in the world around them, while others with similar opportunities appear to falter. Even more intriguing are those who live productive and successful lives in spite of limited opportunities and the presence of an impinging environment that most would experience as toxic. Ultimately, there are a host of internal and external inputs, with both positive and negative valence, that shape human behavior. Competence refers to the facility and success of the individual in dealing with the social environment. This includes the ability to adapt to the demands of the external world and the capacity to actively influence those interactions (White, 1959). Case managers, as is true in social work practice generally, strive to help consumers enhance the quality of those transactions vital to their success and survival.

In most helping endeavors, including social work practice, the power and importance of the professional/client relationship is underscored. Indeed, a fundamental principle of strengths-based case management affirms the centrality of consumer/professional relationships to the ultimate success of the intervention (Rapp, 1998). Simply put, consumers tend to value case management when they enjoy their relationship with a case manager (Sullivan, 1994). In fact, how case managers relate to consumers as people may be far more important than the specifics of the model they employ. However, it is argued here that case management models that embrace strengths and empowerment principles provide the optimum context for a positive relationship to develop in the act of helping.

A cardinal value of social work practice implores professionals to treat all people with respect and dignity. Like most principles, this common standard provides broad direction but little in the way of specifics. Empowerment and strengths models of case management unabashedly run counter to decades of practice with those most seriously mentally ill. Rose (1992), argues that case management "should express a commitment to supporting client's change from objects, known and acted upon, to subjects who know and act" (p. 273). Unfortunately, many consumers have been diagnosed, segregated, and ignored—in short, objectified. In combination, the force of mental illness, social rejection, and deficits-based treatment models can produce an attitude of resignation among consumers. These experiences may sap motivation and energy, and recovery itself is a difficult and potentially painful process that can cause one to retreat. Moreover, for many, the socially embraced temporal benchmarks that reflect the attainment of adulthood have come and gone; with the passing of time, perhaps the key ingredient for recovery, hope, fades (Deegan, 1996).

Case managers can help renew hope by bringing passion and energy to their work, and by demonstrating unwavering respect for consumers. This respect is conveyed in both attitude and action. Unlike other models of helping that are predicated on emotional distance, most consumers need case managers to work in close partnership with them as they strive to recover (Sullivan, 1994). Two decades ago, Deitchman (1980) recognized the utility of this style of helping and posited that consumers need travel companions, not travel agents. Like a good companion, case managers may offer suggestions and present the range of available options, but ultimately consumer choice and preference prevails. In essence, respect is actualized when professionals acknowledge consumers as the experts on their own lives. To great excess, the consumers' thoughts, feelings, and behaviors have been probed, analyzed, and interpreted. The demoralizing impact of having basic rights and freedoms stripped cannot be overstated.

Sharing power with consumers is an easy sentiment for professionals to express, but far more difficult to exercise. As the consumer movement has progressed, and strengths and empowerment models gained in popularity, some cursory changes have been made in mental health services. For example, it is now commonplace to ask consumers to sign treatment plans and even participate in planning meetings. However, to fully implement the strengths model requires fundamental change in the delivery of service. Thus, operationalizing the strengths model requires more than securing permission on a plan of action; it includes accepting the consumer as the final arbitrator in determining the direction of the work.

Using the principles of strengths-based helping to guide social work practice is not easy—a subject that will be explored in greater depth later in the chapter. Any seasoned clinician can quickly recognize a number of practical and ethical dilemmas that will be confronted daily. Such dilemmas are pronounced when serving those facing severe and persistent mental illnesses. These individuals can be overwhelmed by endogenous and exogenous stimulation, ranging from overall hypersensitivity to the sights, sounds, and smells in the surrounding world, to racing thoughts and hallucinations. At such times, consumers can easily become immobilized and withdraw socially and emotionally, or panic and engage in behavior that is distressing to others. In both cases, a downward spiral can be activated that, if unimpeded, may lead to prolong hospitalization.

Clinical models emphasize the case manager's role in counterbalancing the chaos and confusion caused by mental disorders (Roach, 1993). To neutralize these forces, particularly in the early stages of the relationship, case managers may be tempted to assert more control to protect the consumer from undue stress, and to assure that basic needs are met. Clearly, case managers, much like the family, can be a stabilizing and reassuring presence in the life of a consumer. Thus, taking charge may be a commonsense approach to an immediate situation. Over the term of the relationship, however, the failure to hand responsibility over to consumers will place an artificial ceiling on their potential.

While mutual respect sets the stage, the relationship can flourish when consumers and case managers are jointly engaged in such mundane matters as looking for an apartment, shopping, cleaning, and cooking. At these moments, case managers have the opportunity to model an organized and proactive style of life. By teaching problem-solving skills, incremental goals setting, and self-monitoring techniques in the field, case managers underscore that consumers are competent, or in Rose's (1992) terms, subjects who know and act. Therefore, a positive relationship with a case manager can prove to be the anchor upon which consumers depend when they endeavor to tackle those goals that ultimately lead to greater independence. Of course, consumer narratives indicate that many people, including family members, psychiatric attendants, teachers, janitors, and others in similar circumstances, can provide the spark needed to move toward recovery (Sullivan, 1994).

Social work practice in mental health settings and beyond is grounded in awareness that human behavior is best understood from a person-in-environment framework. More often, this framework is employed to comprehend the troubling situations individuals and families face, but this same perspective can also be used to understand how people succeed. From a deficit viewpoint, individual or environmental maladies, separately or in combination, are implicated in the analysis of a presenting problem. From this model, mental illness may be understood primarily as a biophysical problem that results in the inability of the individual to adapt to community pressures and demands. This paradigm has traditionally held sway in mental health policy and practice. As a result, mental health professionals have expended great effort to creating specialized environments that are designed to serve as a social prosthesis for consumers.

The strengths model offers a different perspective. A central premise of strengths/empowerment case management is that all people, including those who are labeled seriously and persistently mentally ill, can recover and develop to their full potential if they are provided the necessary supports, both material and emotional, and are afforded equal opportunity (Rapp, 1998; Rose, 1992). Emotional support, as noted previously, serves as an important foundation for recovery to begin. Unfortunately, over time the social support networks of those facing serious mental illness tend to shrink (Sullivan & Portner, 1989). This often leaves the consumer with few close associates beyond the family. Not surprisingly, family members can only provide so much material and emotional support before they face exhaustion. Sadly, loneliness can be a constant companion in the life of a person suffering from mental illness, and ultimately this isolation can lead to further deterioration and self-neglect.

It can be argued that an essential component of all case management models lies in "the reconstruction and management of social support and networks that may have been damaged, altered due to illness, or simply inadequate to deal with the challenges which chronic illness present" (Pescosolido et al., 1995, p. 39). To advance recovery, a reconstructed support network should not be saturated with professional helpers but instead tie the consumer with a wide range of social resources. This precept is a natural extension of the classic broker model and underscores, as suggested earlier, that recovery is influenced by social context. Bebout (1993) agrees with this position and hypothesizes that contextual factors *are* more powerful predictors of long-term outcomes than individual variables, such as personality traits or diagnostic features, or treatment parameters (pp. 77–78).

From its infancy, strengths-based case management has been guided by the premise that human behavior is largely a function of the resources available to people and that, as citizens, mental health consumers deserve equal access to social resources (Rapp & Chamberlain, 1985). This assumption directs case managers to view the panoply of community resources as available and useful to consumers, and further confirms that advocacy is often necessary to ensure that the rights of consumers as citizens are honored. The assumption that behavior is a function of the resources available to people has important ramifications for both understanding and treating mental illness, particularly the psychosocial consequences that follow. Bebout (1993), in contrast with the premise of many therapeutic models, argues that change occurs from the outside in. From this perspective, behavioral change occurs within the context of a system so, "if you change the system, you change the individual" (p. 62). In this case, changing the system may entail simply securing the resources that consumers need, but it also involves altering environments and developing necessary support structures that enhance consumer strengths while minimizing challenges.

Taylor (1997) observes that exceptional conditions like extreme poverty can result in niche entrapment. When entrapped, the ability to escape, or more simply put, to improve one's lot in life, is restricted by the lack of available resources, role models, and support. Note that these are the same variables that have been identified as vital for individual growth and development. In such cases, mutual support, either formally or informally constituted, can serve as a springboard for success. When groups of people converge due to common interests and beliefs, the resolve of individuals is enhanced. To describe this phenomenon, Taylor (1997) has coined the term *support pods*, and while the label is both conceptual and speculative, understanding it may provide important clues in ascertaining the recovery process.

For some consumers, the ability to have a positive and consistent relationship with one person is often an important first step in recovery. Like all people, consumers vary in their desire for contact and relationships with others. Yet, as consumers consolidate their gains, a supportive network often provides an important factor in their willingness to move to a new phase in recovery. As America has become more mobile, individuals have lost many natural supports that were once found in families and communities. As a result, a wide range of support and affiliation groups has developed. In recent years, virtual support networks have emerged via the Internet, and consumer-run support groups and programs have also become an important addition to the range of resources available to people suffering from mental illnesses. Consumer-centered programs succeed by virtue of the common bond that exists among participants. Sharing common experiences is reassuring, and people who are struggling find role models when learning from those who have persevered through difficult times.

Case managers primarily focus on the psychosocial challenges presented by serious and persistent mental illness. The impact of these illnesses extends from the personal level of thoughts, feelings, and emotions, to the social rejection experienced in community life. Recovery is also multidimensional, although researchers tend to focus more on the observable manifestations of recovery (Sullivan, 1998). Consumers exercise strong will as they learn how mental illness affects them and how they can counteract the impress of these illnesses through their attitudes and action. Case managers must also be prepared to help consumers at multiple levels, as neither traditional individual therapy or brokering social services alone is sufficient to advance recovery.

In spite of all efforts to understand and dissect the phenomenon called "recovery," it must be noted that this is an inherently personal journey. Longitudinal research indicates that recovery is marked by a series of starts and stops and, as a result, is rarely a linear course (Strauss, Hafez, Lieberman, & Harding, 1985). In essence, progress, as marked by observable behavior, may be followed by a moratorium period where consumers may regroup before taking the next step (Strauss et al., 1985). Recovery is a process that may extend for years or a lifetime. Even the declaration of recovery as a status, given the ambiguity of the term conceptually, is also individually determined. While there is still much to learn about recovery, longitudinal research and the life stories of consumers verify that diagnosis does not constitute a life sentence.

MAJOR TASKS AND GOALS IN CASE MANAGEMENT PRACTICE

The previous sections have discussed the historical context that accounts for the proliferation of case management and a preliminary look at the theoretical foundation that informs practice behavior. In this section, the major tasks and goals of case management will be described. The key tasks of case management mirror the standard features of social work practice. This fact alone leads many to observe, albeit simplistically, that case management is akin to classic social casework (Austin, 1990). Once again, exemplars will be drawn from the major tenets and activities consanguine with strengths-based case management.

Engagement and Relationship Building

Given the primacy of the relationship to effective case management, this ongoing aspect of helping deserves special attention. The establishment of a positive working relationship is so engrained in the fabric of social work practice that it is easy to simply accept this as a given. After all, skillful social workers tend to be empathic, nonjudgmental, and good listeners. Forming productive relationships is generally viewed as second nature for veteran practitioners. In reality, the nature of serious and persistent mental illness, coupled with the life history of consumers, can make the engagement phase a vexing task even for the most experienced social worker.

In the throes of illness, many consumers are described as suffering from blunted affect, suggesting that there is little expression of emotion and, at times, little communication with others. Some medications only exacerbate the problem. Other aspects of the illness present additional challenges. At the worst moments, hallucinations make concentration difficult, and delusional thought process and content can be difficult to penetrate.

The personal histories of consumers can also create a general reluctance to trust professionals. For some consumers, contacts with professionals have ultimately led to incarceration in hospitals, and as noted earlier, many families have had equally unsatisfying experiences. Other consumers have years of treatment, many transitions, and with this, many different social workers with varying ranges of competence. More serious issues, often undetected, can also hamper the engagement process. Extensive abuse and victimization histories, including sexual assault, are not uncommon (Rose, 1992). Matters are complicated further when these traumatic events occur while the consumer resides in a treatment facility.

If a productive relationship is to form between the consumer and case manager, each of the issues described singularly and in combination must be surmounted. We'll examine engagement and relationship building in greater detail later. Suffice it to say, case managers must demonstrate patience, persistence, and devote significant time and effort to this phase of helping.

Assessment

Assessment and diagnosis are common activities in formal mental health services, and have traditionally been designed to decipher the precise nature of an individual or family problem. Over time, specialized language and nomenclature has been developed to describe various mental illnesses and allow professionals to communicate with each other. Yet, even staunch advocates of diagnostic schematas, particularly in mental health, recognize that these labels are simply tools that, used singularly, fail to capture the inherent complexity of the human experience.

The nature of the assessment process is logically connected with the model used to both understand and address the issues faced by consumers. To illustrate, the pervasiveness of the medical model in mental health care is reflected in the language used in the workplace. Hence, those who present for services are considered patients, and the assistance offered is referred to as treatment. From this perspective, the effort to define or diagnose the problem makes perfect sense. Because the focus of case management is on the social functioning of consumers and not the illnesses, the assessment process should take a different turn.

Differences between standard diagnostic procedures and psychosocial assessments are further accented when the practitioner adopts the strengths model (Cowger, 1997; McQuaide & Ehrenreich, 1997; Rapp, 1998). Regardless of whether a case manager completes a standard psychosocial assessment or one that is informed by the strengths model, there is interest in consumer performance, past and present, and current aspirations in primary life domains such as education, work, and use of leisure time. The difference in the two approaches is one of emphasis. Standard psychosocial assessments can be used to decipher deficits in consumer performance and skills with the intent to target interventions in these specific areas. While the work of case managers can be directly tied to the products of such assessments, it has been more common to develop day programs and skills training curriculum to address these consumer needs.

Strengths-based assessments are designed to capture a different set of information. While focused on the key life domains offered earlier, there is a greater emphasis on consumer success, past and present, and a keen interest in the life goals of consumers. Where day programming is, by necessity, organized on the basis of commonly held problems and deficits, strengths-based case management thrives on consumer uniqueness. Therefore, the outcome of this assessment process is rarely the development of a curriculum, but rather an individually tailored work plan.

The exploration of past involvement in areas such as employment is certainly important. Here the case manager and consumer can use the past to help clarify the kinds of jobs that are preferred and the characteristics of work environments that seemed to provide a good match. Yet, for the most part, attention is focused squarely on the present. Mosher and Burti (1992) have offered two key questions that are pivotal to this exploration. The first question for case managers to ask consumers is straightforward—what do you want? This is obviously a simple and basic question, but it is one that has been rarely asked of people facing mental illness, especially when it comes to life goals. In fact, it has been so rarely asked that consumers often have a difficult time answering it. When struggling daily to cope with the total impress of mental illnesses, consumers have difficulty maintaining an orientation toward the future, particularly when they have not been encouraged to do so. The potential power of strength assessments, beyond the quality of information that can be gathered, lies in the opportunity to reactivate the dormant goals and desires of consumers.

If the case manager can successfully engage the consumer in a discussion of personal goals and desires, no matter how outlandish they may seem, the second key question should be immediately asked—how can I help you get it? Another simple question to be sure, but one that is important on multiple levels. First, all of the activity previously described, beginning with a formal assessment, establishes the groundwork for the development of initial care plan. When taking consumers' desires seriously, case managers can help pique consumer interest in the services offered. This discussion can also point to the range of activities, behaviors, and resources needed to accomplish even simple goals and guide the creation of a set of initial action steps. Secondly, a fundamental precept of the strengths model values consumers as the director of the helping process. Much like the effort required to uncover the goals of consumers, gaining this initial input is often more difficult than it appears. The medical model, nearly by definition, adopts an expert/consumer approach to helping, and passivity is rewarded in some treatment settings. Helping consumers take charge of their own care, even if it begins with small decisions, is an important step in recovery.

Goal and Case Planning

Social programs or policies are well-designed when they mirror the best available model of the causes and consequences of a target problem or issue. We determine success by the effective impact the programs and policies have on these same variables. It has been noted on several occasions that, at present, little can be done to alter the root cause of serious mental illnesses. Even medications are designed to deal with the consequences of primary biophysical operations. Consumers can learn about the illnesses that affect them, however, and take preventative measures that forestall relapse or minimize the impact these conditions have on their daily lives. Consistent with the basic premise of recovery, consumers can also live satisfying and contributing lives when afforded opportunity and support, thus reducing the potential consequences of serious and persistent mental illnesses.

Goal setting may appear to be a mundane and rather mechanical feature of case management. To the contrary, this is an essential component of the strengths-based approach. We argue that goal setting, as an activity, is inherently therapeutic and deals directly with one problematic consequence of many serious mental illnesses. The chaos engendered by serious and persistent mental illness manifests itself in the thought process and subsequent behavior of consumers. When troubled by illness, many consumers report feeling overwhelmed and, at times, out of control. Even simple tasks can stymie consumers at this moment. When feeling overwhelmed, consumers are unable to simply ponder actions that can reduce anxiety. Herein are the roots of total despair and the feelings of powerlessness over one's destiny.

When overwhelmed by life tasks, many people learn that it is best to tackle one item at a time in a systematic fashion. By breaking larger tasks into smaller steps, the world suddenly becomes more manageable and rational. When people succeed at such times, confidence expands, which increases the odds of future accomplishment. In essence, the more experience people have in mastering life challenges, the more risks they are willing to take in the future. Working toward goals provides meaningful structure and counters the personal turmoil that can be omnipresent when ill.

Consumer goals are the centerpiece of the case management care plan and should flow naturally from the psychosocial assessment and consumer preferences. The ability to translate consumer goals into a series of attainable action steps is one measure of exceptional case management. Not only does the goal-setting method provide a blueprint for significant life accomplishments, it also establishes a model consumers can use to tackle other life tasks in a proactive and thoughtful manner. The use of specific goal-setting standards is also an important component of the strengths model (DeJong & Miller, 1995; Rapp, 1998). These standards, described later, increase the odds of successful completion in part by stipulating that the goals are clear and concrete. As always, the case manager must work collaboratively in establishing overall goals and the incremental action steps. The necessity of consumer involvement in all phases of helping is a bedrock principle of the strengths model. The downfall of many treatment endeavors is rooted in the failure to include consumers in the planning, thereby severely limiting any ownership they feel in the execution of the final plan.

Good goals are concrete, specific, and behavioral; they are written in a style that consumers understand, and they are easy to measure. These goals are devoid of jargon and set clear standards for success. Writing goals in this style is beneficial for multiple parties in the organization, including quality assurance teams, supervisors, and case managers. When goals are concrete and clearly written, it is easy to assess the number of goals established for a specific individual or in the aggregate, the life domains affected, and the percentage of overall goal attainment. This scorecard provides a ready reference for the case manager and consumer to highlight areas of success, to decipher patterns in the recovery, and to provide needed encouragement that progress has been made.

Goals should also be written positively. Outcomes tend to improve when consumers work toward a desired end, rather than strive to eliminate something negative in their lives (DeJong & Miller, 1995). This simple proposition is another subtle feature that distinguishes the strengths approach from deficit-based helping. Consider the notion of improving one's personal appearance and hygiene, a common goal found in treatment plans. The goal itself is uninspiring for many consumers, in part because there is no inherent reward for accomplishment. In contrast, when consumers are motivated to join the workforce, they can realize that their appearance must improve if they are to succeed. The motivation is now changed and the consumer can now choose to behave differently on their volition.

The final key standard suggests that goals should be realistic. This is a guideline that can be easily misunderstood and abused. Too often, professionals discourage the dreams of consumers. As a result, this standard can be seen as permission to supersede consumers' judgments. In this case, realism means ensuring that necessary supports and resources are aligned, and that the steps detailed to reach the goal are consistent with the needs of the individual consumer. In some cases, consumers need help breaking a larger goal into minute detail, while others possess the skills and confidence to take longer strides. Finding the right balance while working closely with the consumer is another aspect of the art of good case management. Rapp (1998) notes that "breaking a goal down is a principle mechanism for building realism" (p. 106).

Resource Acquisition and Advocacy

Throughout this chapter, we posit that both illness and health must be understood in context. Thus, the quality and nature of the person/environment interaction is a key factor in the maintenance of illness and the promotion of health. If behavior functions as a resource available to people, a key role of case management is to help consumers procure and organize such resources. It is important to understand that the term *resource* is broadly conceived in the strengths model. In deficit-based models, what constitutes helping resources is often too narrowly conceived. The first clue is in the language. When conversations about opportunities for consumers are dotted with discussion of programs or bed availability, it is a sure bet that individual and environmental strengths are not being exploited.

Earlier, we noted that case goals should flow naturally from the strengths assessment. The next step is to acquire those resources needed to help consumers attain their goals. Some specialized strengths assessment instruments focus on an initial compilation of potential resources (Rapp, 1998). Resources here may be a friend, a job coach, a house, or a bicycle. Hence, resources are more than group homes, support groups, and sheltered workshops. In the traditional model, resources are scarce and limited. From the strengths perspective, resources are a function of hard work and creativity.

Kisthardt and Rapp (1992) suggest that the acquisition of naturally occurring resources focuses on four dimensions: availability, accessibility, accommodation, and adequacy. To assess the availability of needed resources, case managers and consumers must engage in an environmental scan to determine the level of opportunities. Success can be achieved by creativity and by focusing on precise consumer needs. If a consumer wants to learn to cook, it may matter little if they learn by attending a formal class in a public school or home extension class, by watching television, or alongside a relative.

Accessibility is of critical importance to people facing serious mental illness, given the number of obstacles they often face gaining entry to needed resources. Sometimes these obstacles involve important ancillary items, such as a lack of transportation. A far more serious matter arises when consumers are actively discriminated against due to their challenge. In the former situation, case managers should serve as brokers as they help consumers overcome immediate barriers. When discrimination is present, advocacy is necessary. However, being an advocate does not mean that the case manager must intervene directly. When possible, case managers can help consumers confront discrimination on their own. At all times, case managers should teach and model skills that consumers can use long after the professional is no longer involved. As a key principle of the strengths model, case managers must encourage consumers to do as much work for themselves as possible. At times when discrimination is rooted in policy and procedures, a more active and public advocacy may be necessary. Simply educating people can accomplish much, as misinformation and myths have made many fearful of people struggling with mental illness.

Accommodation is a vital aspect of recovery and signals important changes in paradigm that shape mental health services. For so long, the prevailing model that guided formal and informal policy and practice underscored a belief that those with serious challenges and disabilities simply could not meet the demands of community life. As a result, people who were different lived, learned, worked, and played in special environments. In the past two decades, new models of helping have offered the view that environments can be changed or restructured in a fashion that can accommodate the needs of others. The monolithic model of normalcy was contested, creating liberating opportunities for many with special needs. Case managers are often in the position of translating the accommodation needs of consumers to employers, landlords, program directors, and policymakers.

A final issue of extreme importance to consumers is the issue of adequacy. Does the resource meet the needs of consumers? Is there an alternative that may be a better match? These are key questions that require an ongoing assessment and dialogue between the consumer and case manager. The ability of many consumers to enjoy greater freedoms is cause for much celebration. On the flip side, many consumers live in environments that fail to meet minimum standards of decency. In such environments, consumers can be exploited in a wide variety of ways. For example, some congregate living facilities feature impoverished environments that can be best described as squalid. This state of affairs is unacceptable, and case managers strive to help consumers secure safe, stimulating environments and activities that promote, rather than obstruct, recovery.

This review of the tasks and goals of case management is hardly exhaustive. A variety of texts have been devoted to case management, and the interested reader can learn about the role and existing models in greater detail (see Moxley, 1997; Raiff & Shore, 1993; Rapp, 1998; Rose, 1992). The primary functions offered provide the basic framework that underpins most case management models and, in general, classic social work practice. The following sections will flesh out the art of practice in greater detail along with the difficult decisions and dilemmas that are a constant companion in the field.

TECHNIQUES, STRATEGIES, AND SKILLS IN STRENGTHS-BASED CASE MANAGEMENT

With the basic framework established, this section highlights key features of the practice of strengths-based case management. Throughout the section, a case vignette will illustrate this, with emphasis placed on assessment, goal setting, and resource acquisition activities.

John R. is a 27-year-old man who is diagnosed with schizophrenia (paranoid-type). In the absence of a group home or transitional apartment in the community, he was discharged to his parents' care, following a 3-month stay at a state hospital. The mental health center staff noted that John displayed the following that needed attention: (1) lack of motivation to participate in social activities; (2) poor money management skills; (3) poor communication skills; (4) noncompliance with treatment, including a history of alcohol abuse; and (5) an inability to individuate from his family of origin. It was also noted that John enjoyed sports, was in good physical health, and was assertive in expressing his wants and needs.

An experienced practitioner has seen hundreds of assessments that resemble this one, as the issues presented in John's case are nearly synonymous with, and are in fact diagnostic indicators of, serious and persistent mental illness. Often, medication clinic and partial hospitalization programming are offered to consumers like John.

During the subsequent weeks, John's behavior began to concern the staff. His parents reported that he was staying up late watching television and that he was drinking despite their protests. He had also stopped attending the partial hospital program, and it was feared that he had discontinued his medication. Discussions ensued on the advisability of rehospitalization. It was agreed that a case manager should make a home visit to assess the situation.

The first contact with a consumer can set the stage for the work to follow. The case manager may need to be persistent to establish the initial contact but must not come on so strong that consumers retreat. First, the case manager must begin the strengths assessment, but this must proceed in a way to facilitate, not hinder, the engagement process. Consequently, the case manager should employ an easy conversational style, marked by a great deal of encouragement and praise for consumer accomplishments. Given the nature of this assessment, case managers may naturally spend more time discussing things that have gone well, and dreams that consumers still hold dear as opposed to failures and disappointment. Consumers should be given preference on the initial meeting place, often a neutral site, such as a park or restaurant. When family is directly involved, they should be consulted as well, with the consumer's permission. These individuals possess a wealth of information, and more often remain deeply concerned about their loved ones. The family must feel comfortable and included in the process, and a vigilant case manager should detect their support and information needs as well.

After arriving at John's home, the case manager spent a few minutes chatting with the family before John reluctantly came downstairs. John quickly announced that he had no intention of returning to the day program and spending time with all those crazy people. Quickly, the case manager indicated that the intent of the visit was to learn how she could be of assistance. John expressed a desire to remain with his parents at this time, but noted that he did want to get his driver's license and earn enough money to purchase a car. The stage was now set to begin the strengths assessment.

In discussing brief therapy, de Shazer (1988) remarks that one task incumbent on the therapist is to note the sorts of things clients do that are good, useful, and effective. This is an important guideline for case managers as they begin the strengths assessment. Using Rapp's (1998) model, consumer and environmental assets should be assessed in six life domains: daily living situation, financial, social and spiritual supports, leisure and recreation, vocational and educational, and health status. Furthermore, the case manager strives to assess the consumer's current status, past history, and current desires and aspirations in each of these discrete domains.

These domains correspond to the life areas that consumers are appropriately most concerned about, given they comprise the major niches of social life. Thus, case managers focus on actual daily activities that indicate the current community functioning of the person and the resources, individual and environmental, required for success. Each individual's behavior is influenced by the confluence of personal history, social context, and individual goals (Kisthardt & Rapp, 1992). Tied to theory of strengths, the case manager seeks information reflective of the person's talents, aspirations, and confidence, as well as the opportunities and resources available in their proximal social environment. Case managers should follow several important guidelines when completing the strengths assessment. The following guidelines are included:

- Information is gathered at the consumer's pace.
- Information is collected in each life domain.
- The information collected is recorded in the consumer's language.
- The strengths assessment is a dynamic document. No time limit is specified for completion, and it should be regularly updated.
- All consumer interests and aspirations (past, present, and future) are explored in depth.

As the case manager explored John's interest in obtaining a driver's license, she discovered that he had a great interest in cars. For the first time in their conversation, John appeared animated. He asked the case manager to come upstairs, where he proudly showed her many model cars that he had constructed. Here, the case manager also learned that auto mechanics was his favorite class in high school, and that he harbored a wish to become a mechanic some day.

This brief interlude underscores several key features of the process of assessing consumer strengths. Note that the information gathered is consistent with the overall mission of case management. Case managers usually work within an interdisciplinary team, operating from a different framework, providing different services, and thus needing information specific to the function they perform. Where traditional deficits-based assessments explore problems and pathology, strengths-based assessments assess possibilities. In standard assessments, case managers rarely capture this kind of specific and individualized information, like John's interest in automobiles. It is also significant that John's affect changed during the interview, in part due to the opportunity to speak of his interests. Finally, a subtle but important aspect of strengths is their portability. John's interest in automobiles is an asset that can contribute to positive changes in many life domains, from his use of leisure time, vocational and educational opportunities, and to overall financial stability. In short, this interest can be a cornerstone in his recovery process.

In the strengths model, personal planning establishes the mutual agenda of work between the consumer and case manager at any one point in time. Personal planning requires the dyad to discuss, negotiate, and agree upon long-term goals, short-term goals and tasks, areas of individual responsibility, and target dates for accomplishment. Goals are inherent to hope and indispensable precursors to achievement. As Lock, Shaw, Saari, and Latham (1981) state, the beneficial effect of goal setting on task performance is one of the most robust and replicable findings in the psychological literature (p. 145).

Personal planning and goal setting are considered normal and routine aspects of case management practice in the strengths model. Goal setting should be woven in the daily routine with clients. Case managers should always have goal sheets handy, refer to them often, work with consumers to establish goals on a regular basis, and always begin each meeting with a review of progress. Like the assessment process, goals should be deciphered and created in a conversational style. For neophyte case managers, goal writing often seems unnatural and mechanical, but over time, the task can be completed with great ease.

At first, John was surprised that the case manager took his interest in auto mechanics seriously, and seemed reluctant to move forward. The case manager assured John that they could move into this slowly and asked him to consider how he might begin to work toward his goal. John noted that it had been some time since his high school course, but he did not wish to pursue his education at present. The idea of working in the field did interest him, in part because he still wanted to save money to purchase a car. After a few meetings where various options were explored, John and the case manager agreed on a course of action. John agreed to check the newspaper on a daily basis for any job openings and also agreed to generate a list of possible job-related activities for the next meeting. The case manager and John agreed to these two goals, which were recorded and signed by the participants.

It is not unusual for consumers to experience some apprehension when embarking on a defined course of action, even when this involves cherished goals. Many have experienced a host of disappointments and rejections in life, and some are fearful that the stress involved in pursuing a goal may provoke a relapse. Breaking goals into incremental, achievable steps can help assuage anxiety and create a pattern of success. Additionally, there are times when accomplishing a single step is noteworthy and worthwhile. In the face of inactivity and growing apathy, taking a simple step, like reading the paper or generating a list of ideas, is a noteworthy achievement. Consumers who have been in a dependent position for some time, where their preferences have not mattered and where they have lost sight of their own preferences, are often seen as unmotivated and reluctant to make decisions. The case manager's task here is to continually encourage choices, no matter how small, and then successively support more important life choices (Carling, 1995, p. 288).

In a previous section, the guidelines for good goal writing were presented. In addition to these instructions, the following guidelines are suggested when developing the personal plan:

- Long-term goals are developed from consumers' stated aspirations, as noted in the strengths assessment.
- During every contact, case managers and consumers update the personal plan, acknowledging accomplishments.
- Write tasks so they may be accomplished by the next contact.
- Set specific target dates for each task.
- Write goals and tasks in the consumer's language.
- As noted in the strengths assessment, prepare tasks and steps using the consumer's abilities and interests.
- For the personal plan, use naturally occurring community supports (e.g., family, community members, friends, parks, clubs, recreation facilities, etc).

At the next meeting, John presented a list of possible ideas, based on his suggestions and review of the newspaper. One of his ideas involved observing and perhaps volunteering at a place where he could learn more about automobiles. The case manager suddenly thought of a local gas station she frequented and pondered the possibility of a volunteer position there. Fortuitously, the station was also on the bus line near John's home. He readily agreed to set up an interview with the proprietor, but asked the case manager to accompany him at any subsequent meeting.

While some communities can be a source of stress, most are a source of health and opportunities. Resource acquisition should emphasize normal or natural resources, not exclusively mental health services. Counterintuitive as it seems, an abundance of mental health services can act as an obstacle to community integration (Sullivan, 1997; Syx, 1995). Based on our experiences, there are a sufficient number of caring and potentially helpful people to assist and support consumers in any given population. When completing a review of resources available to assist consumers, consider that each community boasts a unique combination of assets upon which to build (Kretzman & McKnight, 1993, p. 6–7). Natural resources foster true community integration and recovery. Therefore, an important principle in strengths-based case management holds that the identification and use of community strengths and resources are as critical as the identification and use of individual strengths.

In the case vignette offered earlier, the ability to secure a volunteer position in a service station likely holds more promise that attending a vocational skills group or toiling in a sheltered workshop. The competent case manager or case-management team becomes adept at finding these commonplace community resources, and strives to find the right match of consumer needs and talents and community opportunities. From the beginning of the relationship, the consumer and case manager must begin generating an expansive list of possible helping resources for each goal and aspiration recorded in the strengths assessment.

Identifying resources is often a matter of pure creativity; accessing these resources, however, often proves more difficult. At all possible moments, consumers must be encouraged to deal directly with those key people who control the resources they need. Yet, there are moments when consumers face blatant discrimination and when important policy and legal standards are violated. Stakeholders often need simple reassurance and information about mental illness, and with consumer permission, case managers can intervene on their behalf.

The following are a few guidelines that can help shape the resource-acquisition activities of case managers and consumers:

- Goals and activities should increase consumer contact with naturally occurring community resources.
- Case managers and consumers should anticipate obstacles to acquiring valued resources and plan specific strategies to remove such obstacles.
- Community services, case managers, and consumers should formally recognize the support of key community stakeholders, programs, and businesses.
- Case managers must assure resource holders that they will provide ongoing support, and will intervene if problems arise.
- The denial of resources must be countered by advocacy efforts on the part of consumers and case managers.
- Case managers will work to alter policies and procedures that discriminate against consumers.

When the day arrived for the meeting with the service station manager, John took great pains to look his best. The case manager met with John before the meeting and, after providing some needed reassurance, discussed some possible questions that might arise during the interview. The service station manager was favorably impressed and agreed to allow John to volunteer for 2 hours each day, doing odd jobs around the shop. He even suggested that John do errands in town provided he secured his driver's license. During the next few weeks, John began to take his medication regularly, and he even began attending the partial hospital program, particularly those modules dealing with work skills. His parents also reported marked improvement, noting that he was no longer staying up late watching television and that he had stopped drinking. After 3 months, John began considering moving out of his parents' home and joining a mechanic he had met at the station. The owner of the shop was also considering hiring John as a part-time employee.

It is certainly true that things do not always go this smoothly. Recovery, it has been observed, rarely follows a linear course. Nonetheless, this simple vignette, drawn from an actual practice situation, illustrates several key aspects of strengths-based practice. Of particular importance, many items of concern prior to John's enrollment in the case-management program rectified themselves without direct intervention. Until the consumer deems them important, many items commonly expressed as points of concern in standard mental health services are never addressed. For example, consumers become far more concerned with matters of personal appearance when it is vital to their ability to gain something they want. If a person finds a job, companion, or a nice place to live, taking medication may seem more beneficial. Motivation is equally complex. Certainly, some medication and the impress of illness can result in consumer inertia. But context and interaction also influence motivation, as we are all more motivated to do the things we like and enjoy. Going to a concert is generally more pleasing than a trip to the dentist. The enduring lesson in cases like John's is that most people succeed when they can identify their talents and are given the opportunity to exercise this talent in a supportive environment. This is the essence of strengths-based case management.

EXEMPLAR PROGRAMS: THE RESEARCH ON THE STRENGTHS MODEL

The strengths model of case management is widely popular and has been introduced across the United States and internationally. Like many mental health programs, the model is often modified to match the needs, norms, and structure of host settings. This section will review the empirical research on the strengths model to date. It is hoped that more studies will be conducted and that future program and policy efforts will be shaped by what is learned.

Eight studies have been conducted, testing the efficacy of the strengths model as delivered to people with severe and persistent mental illnesses. Five of the studies employed experimental or quasi-experimental designs, and three used nonexperimental methods (see Table 8.1 for a summary). The research conducted on the strengths model thus far is suggestive of its efficacy. On the downside, the research is limited to two experimental and three nonempirical studies. Comparability of these studies poses some problems, including variation in the measures used (Chamberlain & Rapp, 1991).

On the plus side, the strengths model research results have been remarkably resilient. The research conducted to date has occurred in multiple sites involving many case managers and supervisors. In most sites, attention has been devoted to assessing how services are delivered, thus the fidelity to the principles and values of the strengths approach appears to be high. This increases confidence in the results obtained thus far.

Research offers credence to the centrality of goal setting in the strengths method. In the areas of independent living, educational and vocational functioning, and leisure time use, goal attainment rates have been found to consistently exceed 75% (Kisthardt, 1993; Rapp & Wintersteen, 1989). In experimental studies, Macias, Kinney, Farley, Jackson, and Vos (1994) and Modrcin, Rapp, and Poertner (1998) report that consumers in strengths-model case management demonstrate improved community living skills and competence, in comparison with control groups. The results also appear to hold in the area of vocational and educational endeavors, where Modrcin et al. (1988) found statistically significant differences in the area of vocational training. Stannard (1999) similarly reports differences in educational and vocational status for consumers served in the strengths model. All three nonexperimental studies also report high rates of goal attainment in the area of leisure time and social support, with controlled studies finding statistical differences that favored the strengths model in this domain (Macias, Farley, Jackson, & Kinney, 1997; Modrcin et al., 1988).

Case management services have been primarily geared to impact the life domains noted earlier, but in the general mental health arena, a host of important outcomes must be considered. One common dependent measure in mental health outcome studies is hospitalization. Five of the eight studies reviewed include hospitalization as a dependent measure. In the three nonexperimental studies, the

TABLE
8.1

SUMMARY OF STRENGTHS-MODEL CASE-MANAGEMENT RESEARCH

Study	Sample Size	Character of Sample	Design	Outcomes
Modrcin et al. (1988), Kansas	N = 44	Mostly persons with psychotic disorders (schizophrenia or depressive) referred to a community mental health center	Experimental	After 4 months, no differences appeared in the number of hospitalizations; quality of life, social functioning, and income increased.
Ryan, Sherman, & Judd (1994), Colorado	N = 382	People with psychotic diagnosis in multiple hospitals	Three group post hoc, Correlational, CSS, strengths, traditional	Social functioning increased.
Macias et al. (1994), Logan, Utah	N = 37	Seriously mentally ill	Experimental	In experimental group the number of hospitalizations decreased; social and occupational/vocational functioning increased; no differences appeared in family burden; and the amount of service contracts increased.
Macias et al. (1997), Utah	N = 97	Seriously mentally ill	Pre-post, quasi-experimental	Independence of residential living showed no changes; behavior symptomatology showed reductions; social support and networks improved; there were no differences in the amount of service contracts; and physical health and income increased.
Stannard (1999), Ohio	N = 44	Seriously mentally ill	Pre-post, quasi-experimental	The number of hospitalizations showed no change; quality of life, occupational/vocational functioning, and independence of residential living increased or improved; and behavior symptomatology showed no differences.
Rapp & Chamberlain (1985), Lawrence, Kansas	N = 19	Seriously mentally ill	Nonexperimental	The number of hospitalizations and family burden decreased.
Rapp & Wintersteen (1989), Kansas	N = 235	Seriously mentally ill	Nonexperimental	The number of hospitalizations were decreased.
Kisthardt (1994), Kansas	N = 66	Seriously mentally ill	Nonexperimental	Social functioning increased, and social isolation decreased.

incidence of hospitalization was 50% lower than the usual rate for the locale. In the Modrcin et al. (1988) experimental study, the 50% reduction was not statistically significant, owing perhaps to small sample size. Macias et al. (1994) did find a statistically significant reduction in hospitalization incidents for a group receiving strengths-model case management. In addition, they found that the frequency of crisis center contacts was dramatically reduced over time, while control subjects showed an increase in such contacts. Ryan, Sherman, and Judd (1994) report similar findings, as consumers receiving strengths-model case management experienced fewer hospitalization and emergency room visits than those in control group. A more recent study by Stannard (1999) failed to detect differences in this domain.

Another interesting area of concern to most key stakeholders is symptomatology. Not only do the expression and experience of symptoms interfere with the life performance of consumers, they are confusing and at times frightening to others in the community. On the surface, nothing inherent in case management practice should impact the expression of symptoms. Yet, as was noted in the previous case example, the indirect impact of holding meaningful goals and engaging in worthwhile activities can result in behaviors and attitudes that may influence symptoms. Two studies by Macias et al. (1994, 1997) support the important role of strengths-model case management in reducing symptoms and maintaining physical health. It is also interesting to note that strengths-model case management has been reported to reduce family burden (Macias et al., 1994). This is an important consideration as the combination of reduced symptoms, better attention to personal health, and a more rested and relaxed family support system provides an excellent foundation for recovery.

It is obvious that more research is needed to assess the overall efficacy of strengths-model case management. However, the overall popularity and dissemination of the model is an indication that program-design specialists and policymakers have confidence in the approach. The strengths model has been adapted in alcohol and drug treatment, child welfare, older adult services, and in public welfare.

UNIQUE CHALLENGES FOR SOCIAL WORKERS

Although still struggling for legitimacy, case management has become a standard service offered in community mental health. In spite of its close connection with the roots of social work practice, many students and professionals eschew this role, preferring instead individual or family therapy positions. As a result, case management can be underappreciated, and case managers often wield little power in the workplace. This issue becomes increasingly complicated when case managers engage in advocacy functions, particularly when they are forced to advocate for consumers' rights within host organizations.

Strengths-model case management requires a professional who is multiskilled and versatile. All aspects of the organization must be structured to support case managers if an effective program is desired. Failure to provide case managers with the authority and power to make and implement decisions, or saddling them with caseloads that make proactive helping impossible, simply affirms the prejudices and predilections of other professionals about the role.

Professional status may well be a reflection of the status on one's clientele. Those facing serious and persistent mental illness are shunned by others. Due to the nature of their challenge, the environments in which they reside, and poverty, they are far from glamorous. Many needlessly fear them. The work that commences is vital but practical. The use of a sophisticated lexicon is usually unnecessary, and thus the work may appear basic and simplistic. With this as a backdrop, case managers must join with consumers and help them begin the arduous and often frustrating road to recovery. At times, case managers may see little progress—but there are glorious times when they do. Consider the following example.

CASE DILEMMA

In her late 30s, Wanda had spent much of the past 10 years in and out of state hospitals. She hallucinated when under stress, which resulted in her making loud and unintelligible sounds at times. Her experience of stress had always been exacerbated by attempts to return to work. It was not unusual for her to secure a job, only to panic and threaten her employers when deeply troubled, which invariably resulted in hospitalization. Due to tardive dyskinesia, brought on by years of heavy medication, she walked rather rigidly, with her head always tilted to one side. She also had an interesting habit that others found either amusing or annoying. Whenever confronting and passing someone Wanda would indiscriminately say, "Hi, how are you?" If she passed you, turned around, and passed you again, she would say it twice. When a case manager became involved, Wanda had just completed her third hospitalization in the past 4 years. Each episode followed the same pattern. Early in the relationship, Wanda expressed a desire to return to work as a maid in a hotel or motel, a job she claimed to enjoy. When the case manager presented her case at a staff meeting, he was greeted by an outburst of laughter, shaking heads, and rolling eyes. The case manager persisted, but was challenged on ethical and professional grounds. According to the team, it was foolish to establish any care plan that included an employment goal. To accent their concerns, the team members liberally used terms like *unethical* and *unprofessional*, and the case manager was implored to reread the chart. Believing in Wanda, the case manager embraced the strengths model, in particular notions of consumer empowerment. How can this dilemma be resolved?

This vignette draws from a real case example, but as an exemplar, it is hardly unique. The strengths perspective has grown in popularity, and you will find few social workers who do not profess to practice in accordance with the values and principles of the model. Practice often falls short of the ideal. Case managers who adhere to the precepts of the model should be prepared for the experience offered in the case example. Rhetoric aside, many professionals strongly feel they know what is best for consumers and feel a personal responsibility to protect them from their own choices. Obviously, intervention is clearly needed at times, but when consumer goals and desires are rejected, opportunities are likely lost.

Practicing from the strengths model is not synonymous with ignoring consumer difficulties or problems. The skillful practitioner works to align individual and environmental assets to provide support, ameliorate deficits, and promote health. People who are successful have discovered and maximized their strengths and compensated for areas where they are less strong; mental health consumers are no different.

The case manager and Wanda began reviewing past employment experiences and the issues that seemed to lead to a downward spiral. Wanda expressed that there were difficulties with co-workers at times, and that her supervisor was perceived to be overbearing. Together, they reviewed what she had learned from her past experiences, in particular, the signs and symptoms that signaled an impending relapse. The case manager also recognized that Wanda found jobs in businesses that always had a high turnover rate, suggesting internal problems and understaffing. Wanda clearly possessed the requisite skills. The trick was to find the right match.

As Wanda and the case manager continued to work, they struck on a novel idea. The issues Wanda had faced in the job seemed endemic to lower-scale establishments. In contrast, upper-scale hotels focus heavily on customer service and are usually well-staffed. There was one additional bonus in these settings: These hotels often hired greeters to meet guests at the door. Here, Wanda found a position that she enjoyed and where her "inappropriate" behavior was valued.

In many ways, case managers work to find the perfect niche, those situations where the requirements and needs of the setting are perfectly matched with the desires, talents, and idiosyncrasies of consumers. In these niches, recovery from serious and persistent mental illness can be realized. The vision of recovery and the voice of consumers beckon social workers that have the desire to help others surmount the challenges of mental illness.

KEY TERMS

Capitation: A method of payment to providers that can take many forms. Most often providers are paid a set amount per individual, upon enrollment, or by diagnostic category of level of functioning. The provider then is obligated to cover the costs of care within these parameters.

Case Management: A creative and collaborative process, involving skills in assessment, counseling, teaching, modeling, and advocacy that aims to enhance the social functioning of consumers.

Civil Commitment: Legal procedures that give authorities the permission to hospitalize an individual against their will. While standards vary by state, generally the person must be deemed a threat to self or others, or gravely disabled.

Community Mental Health Centers: Locally based clinics that provide a range of basic and specialty mental health services. These providers receive federal, state, and local funds and serve many poor and indigent consumers by mission.

Congregate Living: A broad term used to describe domiciles where groups of individual reside together. In mental health, this includes group homes and board-and-care facilities.

Consumer: A term used to describe a person who is now or in the past has been the recipient of mental health services. The individual may not have received such services voluntarily.

Deinstitutionalization: A retrospective label on a series of converging trends that resulted in a shift from inpatient psychiatric hospitals to community-based settings as the primary locus of care.

Managed Care: A broad term used to describe recent efforts to employ fiscal tools and review procedures and treatment protocols to reduce health care costs and/or increase the quality of care offered.

Niche: The place, physically and emotionally, that a person occupies in the social world, as influenced by competencies, resources, and opportunities. As an ecological term, it refers to the contextual fit of a species within a given environment.

Partial Hospitalization: Day services that often feature structured skill-building, information groups, or both. These services are often used to provide structured time for people who are actively struggling with their illness, and are deemed too impaired to engage in competitive work or live independently.

Psychopharmacology: The research and use of specialized medications to treat and ameliorate the causes of mental illnesses.

Psychosocial Rehabilitation: Specialized mental health services that are designed to address the disabilities that result from serious mental illness. These efforts can involve both habilitation and rehabilitation efforts and include skills training, case management, and day programs.

Recovery: The ability to develop individual potential and accomplish personal goals despite the challenges of mental illness.

Schizophrenia: A serious mental disorder that can negatively impact the ability to organize thoughts and behaviors. Delusional thinking and behavior that most would deem bizarre are present at times.

Serious and Persistent Mental Illness: A term used to describe a group of serious mental illness that are for long duration and result in severe social disabilities. Common illness categories include schizophrenia, bipolar disorders, and severe depression.

Tardive Dyskinesia: Often caused by extended use of medication, these conditions result in difficulties in motor control that can be characterized by rigidity, body spasms, and other involuntary body movements.

WEB RESOURCES

National Alliance for the Mentally Ill (NAMI) (http://www.nami.org). The site provides information and resources for families, consumers, and professionals. Family members who have relatives facing serious mental illnesses founded NAMI.

National Institute of Mental Health (NIMH) (http://www.nimh.hih.gov). NIMH is a government agency that supports research and disseminates recent findings about serious mental illness.

National Mental Health Association (http://www.nmha.org). Perhaps the oldest advocacy group for mental health in America, the National Mental Health Association provides support, information, and direct service. Many affiliates are active in policymaking.

National Alliance for Research on Schizophrenia and Depression (http://www. mhsource.com/narsad.html). This Web site is the source for cutting-edge insights and research on serious mental illness, particularly in the biophysical realm.

Schizophrenia and mental wellness (http://www.mentalwellness.com). This online site offers important resources on support and recovery from mental illness.

Recovery from mental illness (http://www.akmhcweb.org/recovery/rec.html). Developed by the Alaska Mental Health Consumer Web, this is an interesting site devoted to recovery.

National Mental Health Consumers Self-help Clearinghouse (http://www. mhselfhelp.org). This Web site provides links to a variety of helpful sites for consumers, families, and professionals.

REFERENCES

Anthony, W. (1993). Recovery from mental illness: The guiding vision of the mental health system in the 1990s. *Psychosocial Rehabilitation Journal, 16*(4), 11–23.

Anthony, W. A., Cohen, M., Farkas, M., & Cohen, B. F. (2000). Clinical care update: The chronically mentally ill: Case management—more than a response to a dysfunctional system. *Community Mental Health Journal, 36*, 97–106.

Austin, C. (1990). Case management: Myths and realities. *Families in Society, 71*(7), 398–405.

Bebout, R. (1993). Contextual case management. In M. Harris & H. Bergman (Eds.), *Case management for mentally ill patients* (pp. 59–82). Langhorne, PA: Harwood Academic Press.

Bentley, K. J., & Belcher, J. R. (1994). Is community-based mental health care destined to fail? In H. J. Karger & J. Midgley (Eds.), *Controversial issues in social policy* (pp. 170–186). Boston: Allyn and Bacon.

Carling, P. (1995). *Return to community.* New York: Guilford Press.

Chamberlain, R., & Rapp, C. A. (1991). A decade of case management: A methodological review of outcome research. *Community Mental Health Journal, 27*(3), 171–188.

Cowger, C. (1997). Assessing client strengths: Assessment for client empowerment. In D. Saleebey (Ed.), *The strengths perspective in social work practice* (2nd ed., pp. 59–73). New York: Longman.

Deegan, P. (1996). Recovery as a journey of the heart. *Psychiatric Rehabilitation Journal, 19*(3), 91–97.

Deitchman, W. (1980). How many case managers does it take to screw in a light bulb? *Hospital and Community Psychiatry, 31*(11), 788–789.

DeJong, P., & Miller, S. (1995). How to interview for client strengths. *Social Work, 40*(6), 729–736.

de Shazer, S. (1988). A requiem for power. *Contemporary Family Therapy, 10,* 69–76.

Dixon, L. (2000). Assertive community treatment: Twenty-five years of gold. *Psychiatric Services, 51*(6), 759–765.

Everett, B., & Nelson, A. (1992). We're not case and you're not managers: An account of a client/professional partnership developed in response to the "borderline" diagnosis. *Psychosocial Rehabilitation Journal, 15*(4), 49–60.

Fallot, R. (1993). The cultures of case management: An exploration of assumptive worlds. In M. Harris & H. Bergman (Eds.), *Case management for mentally ill patients* (pp. 257–278). Langhorne, PA: Harwood Academic Publishers.

Hatfield, A., & Lefley, H. (Eds.). (1987). *Families of the mentally ill.* New York: Guilford Press.

Joint Commission on Mental Illness and Health. (1961). *Action for mental health.* New York: Basic Books.

Kisthardt, W. (1993). The impact of the strengths model of case management from the consumer perspective. In M. Harris & H. Bergman (Eds.), *Case management and social work practice* (pp. 112–125). Washington, DC: American Psychiatric Association.

Kisthardt, W., & Rapp, C. (1992). Bridging the gap between principles and practice: Implementing a strengths perspective in case management. In S. Rose (Ed.), *Case management and social work practice* (pp. 112–125). New York: Longman.

Kretzmann, J., & McKnight, J. (1993). *Building communities from the inside out.* Evanston, IL: The Asset-based Community Development Institute, Northwestern University.

Lamb, R. (1980). Therapist-case managers: More than brokers of service. *Hospital and Community Psychiatry, 31,* 762–764.

Lamb, R., & Weinberger, L. (1998). Persons with severe mental illness in jails and prisons: A review. *Psychiatric Services, 49*(4), 483–492.

Locke, E., Shaw, K., Saari, L., & Latham, G. (1981). Goal setting and task performance: 1969–1980. *Psychological Bulletin, 90*(1), 125–152.

Macias, C., Farley, O. W., Jackson, R., & Kinney, R. (1997). Case management in the context of capitation financing: An evaluation of the strengths model. *Administration and Policy in Mental Health, 24*(6), 535–543.

Macias, C., Kinney, R., Farley, O. W., Jackson, R., & Vos, B. (1994). The role of case management within a community support system: Partnership with psychosocial rehabilitation. *Community Mental Health Journal, 30*(4), 323–339.

McQuaide, S., & Ehrenreich, J. (1997). Assessing client strengths. *Families in Society, 78*(2), 201–212.

Mechanic, D., & Rochefort, D. (1992). A policy of inclusion for the mentally ill. *Health Affairs, 11*(1), 128–150.

Modrcin, M., Rapp, C., & Poertner, J. (1988). The evaluation of case management services with the chronically mentally ill. *Evaluation and Program Planning, 11,* 307–314.

Moore, S. (1992). Case management and the integration of services: How service delivery systems shape case management. *Social Work, 37*(5), 418–422.

Mosher, L, & Burti, L. (1992). Relationships in rehabilitation: When technology fails. *Psychosocial Rehabilitation Journal, 15*(4), 11–17.

Moxley, D. (1997). *Case management by design.* Chicago: Nelson-Hall.

Okin, R., & Pearsall, D. (1993). Patients' perceptions of their quality of life 11 years after discharge from a state hospital. *Hospital and Community Psychiatry, 44*(3), 236–240.

Pescosolido, B., Wright, E., & Sullivan, W. P. (1995). Communities of care: A theoretical perspective on case management models in mental health. *Advances in Medical Sociology, 6,* 37–79.

Raiff, N., & Shore, B. (1993). *Advanced case management.* Newbury Park, CA: Sage.

Rapp, C. A. (1998). *The strengths model.* New York: Oxford University Press.

Rapp, C. A., & Chamberlain, R. (1985). Case management services for the chronically mentally ill. *Social Work, 30*(1), 417–422.

Rapp, C. A., & Wintersteen, R. (1989). The strengths model of case management: Results from twelve demonstrations. *Psychosocial Rehabilitation Journal, 13*(1), 23–32.

Roach, J. (1993). Clinical case management. In M. Harris & H. Bergman (Eds.). *Case management for mentally ill patients* (pp. 17–40). Langhorne, PA: Harwood Academic Publishers.

Rose, S. M. (Ed.). (1992). *Case management and social work practice.* New York: Longman.

Ryan, C. S., Sherman, P. S., & Judd, C. M. (1994). Accounting for case management effects in the evaluation of mental health services. *Journal of Consulting and Clinical Psychology, 62*(5), 965–974.

Segal, S., & VanderVoort, D. (1993). Daily hassles and health among persons with severe mental disabilities. *Psychosocial Rehabilitation Journal, 16*(3), 27–40.

Stannard, R. (1999). The effects of training in a strengths model of case management on client outcomes in a community mental health center. *Community Mental Health Journal, 35*(2), 169–179.

Strauss, J., Hafez, H., Liberman, P., & Harding, C. (1985). The course of psychiatric disorder, III: Longitudinal principles. *American Journal of Psychiatry, 142*(3), 289–296.

Sullivan, W. P. (1994). A long and winding road: The process of recovery from severe mental illness. *Innovations and Research, 3*(3), 19–27.

Sullivan, W. P. (1997). On strengths, niches, and recovery from serious mental illness. In D. Saleebey (Ed.), *The strengths perspective in social work practice* (2nd ed., pp. 183–197). New York: Longman.

Sullivan, W. P. (1998). Recoiling, regrouping, and recovering: First-person accounts of the role of spirituality in the course of serious mental illness. In R. Fallot (Ed.), *Spirituality and religion in recovery from mental illness* (pp. 25–33). San Francisco: Jossey-Bass.

Sullivan, W. P., & Portner, J. (1989). Social support and life stress: A mental health consumers perspective. *Community Mental Health Journal, 25*(1), 21–32.

Sullivan, W. P., & Rapp, C. (1994). Breaking away: The potential and promise of a strengths-based approach to social work practice. In R. Meinhardt, J. Pardeck, & W. P. Sullivan (Eds.), *Issues in social work: A critical analysis* (pp. 83–104). Westport, CT: Auburn House.

Syx, C. (1995). The mental health system: How we've created a make-believe world. *Psychiatric Rehabilitation Journal, 19*(1), 83–85.

Talbott, J. (Ed.). (1981). *The chronic mentally ill.* New York: Human Sciences Press.

Taylor, J. (1997). Niches and practice: Extending the ecological perspective. In D. Saleebey (Ed.), *The strengths perspective in social work practice* (2nd ed., pp. 217–227). New York: Longman.

Timko, C., Nguyen, A., Williford, W., & Moos, R. (1993). Quality of care and outcomes of chronic mentally ill patients in hospitals and nursing home. *Hospital and Community Psychiatry, 44*(3), 241–246.

Weick, A., Rapp, C., Sullivan, W. P., & Kisthardt, W. (1989). A strengths perspective for social work practice. *Social Work, 34*(4), 350–354.

White, R. (1959). Motivation reconsidered: The concept of competence. *Psychological Review, 66*(5), 297–333.

SOCIAL WORKERS AS MEDICATION FACILITATORS

Rosemary Farmer
& Kia J. Bentley

The term *medication manager* has traditionally been used in referring to how social workers, in collaboration with clients, family members, and other providers, address and help to resolve dilemmas and issues pertaining to taking psychotropic medications. For some mental health consumers, however, *manager* may evoke images of a stern, parental figure who rigidly directs them to do what is predetermined by someone else to be good for them (see Chapter 8). Envisioning the role of manager as more benign, less hierarchical, and based on a partnership model of practice (see Chapter 1), we have chosen the term *facilitator* to describe what social workers do to enhance the probability that medication will help alleviate bothersome symptoms, and enhance the quality of clients' lives. In line with using the term *facilitator,* this chapter will argue that we need new ways of thinking about psychotropic medications and their use in the context of contemporary life. This new framework for thinking about medications incorporates the concept of discourse, as will be defined. Chapter 9 argues that the discourse of the medical model is exemplified by the authoritative doctor and the disease model of illness, and the discourse of a client's lived experience is expressed by the client's way of looking at and experiencing the meaning of medication in their lives. Both provide important perspectives, albeit in a tension of ambiguity, and are needed to truly empower clients to make decisions about medication. We argue that, although often thought to be distinct, views of medication from a medical model and from the client's "lived experience" can coexist in a way that is more empowering to clients (Sands & Nuccio, 1992). Specifically, this chapter discusses the major tasks, goals, techniques, strategies, and skills required for a social worker who simultaneously holds the two discourses in a state of creative tension such that the strengths and assets of each model are brought to bear on the consumer of psychotropic medications. We will turn first to a definition of the term *discourse*. We will then discuss each model, the discourse of the medical model, and the discourse of the client's lived experience.

INTELLECTUAL BASE OF MEDICATION FACILITATION

Defining Discourse

Since the 1960s, a variety of philosophers and other thinkers like Jacques Lacan, Roland Barthes, Jacques Derrida, and Michel Foucault (Mills, 1997) have developed the term *discourse* to refer to specific ways of thinking about, looking at, and discussing the world. The discourse about certain topics or phenomena (like the profession of social work, racism in America, or the most recent presidential election) does not merely refer to what is written and spoken, but rather represents a fuller mindset about the phenomena that provide specific ways of constituting and viewing its environmental or cultural context. Thus, discourse goes beyond mere conversation to related images and metaphors. For Foucault, discourse is always shaped by power relations. Importantly, Michel Foucault also said discourse actually "creates the objects" (thoughts, beliefs, and actions) of the world (or a specific phenomenon) as we know it (Foucault, 1972). We do not fully choose the content of our discourses, but rather are born into or join a preexisting discourse. Using the example of the discourse of social work, we would note that those who call themselves social workers have joined the social work discourse, which has been ongoing for a century. Foucault would describe it as involved in a larger cultural discourse of normalizing people for societal purposes (Chambon, Irving, & Epstein, 1999). More optimistically, we see our discourse as, among other things, being concerned with ascribing meaning to the dignity and worth of each human being and voicing themes of social justice.

Discourse of the Medical Model

The profession of social work has been strongly influenced by medicine and the medical model, and although its influence on our practice may be changing, it still provides much that is useful. Stereotypically, a male physician, usually dressed in a white coat (his badge of honor), personifies the medical model. He looks and acts formally and assumes the stance of an authority figure to whom access is often deliberately restricted (see Chapter 15). The medical model is also often associated with a classification system. In mental health, the American Psychiatric Association's *Diagnostic and Statistical Manual of Mental Disorders* (DSM-IV) is such a system, in that it provides specific criteria for each diagnostic category of mental illness and strives to be recognized as reliable and valid.

Similarly, the medical model seems to represent a reliance on scientific inquiry and the quest to find specific, identifiable causes for a particular disease. For example, this is represented in mental health by the disease conceptualization of illness, or seeing mental illness as being caused by some biological phenomena. This suggests we look for the invading virus, germ, or other phenomena that invades or changes the body in some way and causes disease. In the past, the invasive viral agents or toxins were seen as external agents. In more recent years, the medical community is looking for internal agents that cause bodily disruptions, such as genes. However, the point remains the same. The thinking has been in terms of unidirectional causality (A toxin leads to B disease). Once the cause is identified, cure or amelioration (as with medication, or perhaps gene therapy), are the best and perhaps only good treatment options. The unstated implication is that, once the scientist finds the biochemical imbalance or the gene that causes panic (or depression, schizophrenia, or aggression), "everything will be okay." In this model, the physician is seen as having the answers (power), and the patient is basically a passive recipient of intervention. The discourse of the medical model often reflects the idea that a patient's body is an object; and the disease, which has invaded this object, is seen as being separate from the individual. Bordo (1993) describes the medical model as regarding the body as a passive tablet, on which disorder is inscribed. Deciphering the inscription, in her view of the medical model, requires that the cause-seeker be a professional whose expertise alone can unlock the secrets of the disordered body (Bordo, 1993, p. 67). Thus, nonmedical providers, or any provider offering nonmedical services, are often seen as superfluous and are almost, by definition, left out of the medical model.

The parameters of the medical model are slowly changing, especially in regard to emotional and behavioral disorders and mental illnesses. The biological revolution in psychiatry has greatly expanded our knowledge concerning the structure and function of the brain as a possible causative agent in mental illness. However, research conducted over the past 40 years has also found that biological aspects do not tell the whole story. Even the staunchest of biological researchers are now admitting that biology provides a vulnerability or predisposition to certain illnesses, but that environmental influences such as stress and life events are also important. This begins to lead us away from a reductionist paradigm, toward a more interactionist model for viewing health and illness (Aldwin, 1994). For social workers who facilitate medication use, knowledge emerging from the medical model, and the discourse that surrounds it, needs to be utilized in work with people who use psychotropic medications. Yet, we can readily see why social workers, who look at the gestalt of person-in-environment, experience conflict with the mind-set of the medical model, which can be seen as rigidly scientific, reductionist, and viewing the body as merely an object.

What is important for social work medication facilitators, with regard to the intellectual base of knowledge developed by the discourse of the medical model? What do we need to embrace to function effectively with clients who are using psychotropic medications? This base should first include knowledge about the basics of psychopharmacology, which includes the processes of pharmacokinetics, pharmacodynamics, and an understanding of neurotransmission (see also Bentley & Walsh, 2001).

Pharmacokinetics tells us how a person's body responds to the ingestion of a drug and the resulting amount of the drug available for therapeutic action (i.e., bioavailability). Four biological processes are involved in pharmacokinetics. *Absorption* is the process by which a drug moves from the site of administration into the bloodstream. *Distribution* is the process by which a psychotropic medication moves from the bloodstream to its site of action in the brain. *Metabolism* is the process by which the chemical structure of a drug is broken down into inactive metabolites of the original compound, allowing the drug to be eventually eliminated from the body. *Excretion* is the final step in the process of metabolism, referring to the elimination of psychotropic drugs from the body, mainly via the kidneys, through bile, feces, and urine, and also through sweat, saliva, tears, and breast milk. Pharmacokinetics is important to understand, because it determines how much of a drug is concentrated in the blood at any given time (blood level), and how much has already left the system and is therefore unavailable for therapeutic action. Social workers need to know these things to educate clients about what happens to a medication once it enters the body, to understand dosing and the rationale for certain drug choices, and to help clients problem solve dose-related issues, medication reactions, and negative side effects. For example, Ritalin can be taken orally, or via a skin patch. The route of administration will determine when it takes effect and for how long. It is argued that the more knowledge clients have concerning specific drug functions in their bodies, the more likely they will follow prescribed guidelines.

Social workers should also be familiar with the processes of pharmacodynamics, which help in understanding the effects of a drug on the body. For example, a psychotropic medication can stimulate a receptor for a specific neurotransmitter, or it can block action at the receptor site, which results in an increase in neurotransmitter action or results in no effect at all. Therapeutic index reflects a medication's toxicity or safety and is the ratio of the median toxic dose to the median effective dose. With a high therapeutic index, such as in Haldol, the medication is relatively safe in terms of toxicity. With a low therapeutic index, such as exists with Lithium, the drug must be monitored carefully to avoid toxicity. If a client taking Lithium mentions that she is taking less than the prescribed amount because the side effects are unpleasant, the social work practitioner should address the fact that less than a therapeutic dose has no effect at all, while too high a dose could be lethal. Tolerance, dependence, and withdrawal phenomena are also important to understand. Benzodiazepines, like Xanax or Ativan, which are widely prescribed to treat anxiety, can lead to physical and psychological dependence; if abruptly discontinued, these may produce withdrawal phenomena.

Basic information about neurotransmission is a third part of the required knowledge base. Social workers need to understand the rationale for medications themselves and be able to explain this to clients and their families. For example, social work practitioners need to know that neurotransmitters (i.e., serotonin, dopamine) are naturally occurring substances in our body, and that psychotropic medications have their desired effect by either increasing or decreasing the level of neurotransmitters in the system. This bit of knowledge can be most helpful in explaining some of the mystery of how medications work. Social workers must also be knowledgeable about adverse side effects, how these are manifested, and how to manage them. Facilitators can benefit from classes on psychotropic medications and what symptoms they are used to treat. We recommend that social workers take a course in "Psychopharmacology for Social Workers." In addition, have ready access to printed material on medications. Some sources that we have found useful are *The Social*

Worker and Psychotropic Medication, by Kia J. Bentley and Joseph Walsh; *Pocket Handbook of Psychiatric Drug Treatment,* by Harold Kaplan and Benjamin Sadock; *Drug Guide for Psychiatric Nursing,* by Mary Townsend. Social workers may want to keep any one of these books for easy reference and to share information with clients.

Discourse of the Client's Lived Experience

This chapter argues that the medical model is an important discourse for social workers to understand, but only one of the mind-sets or contexts that relate to clients and their treatment situations. The other important discourse is that of the client's lived experience, which refers to the client's deeply personal, but socially influenced, way of looking at, experiencing, and making sense of mental illness and the use of psychiatric medications. By listening to clients' words, ideas, thoughts, and meanings, we can begin to understand the nature of this discourse related to medications and their lives. For instance, for the consumer of psychotropic medication, a biological mind-set may influence their lived experience with medication. Social workers need to be familiar with the biological findings related to various mental illnesses (i.e., the medical model aspects). However, rather than privilege (i.e., make dominant, emphasize) the biological aspects, we also need to hear the voices of those who speak in psychosocial and cultural terms. When a client says, "I can't do anything . . . I have a brain illness . . . it's my brain," we need to help clients pursue the possible meanings of their illnesses that go beyond their brain structure and functioning.

On the other hand, socioenvironmental, cultural, and family attitudes have also influenced discourse around medication. As such, they may or may not be compatible with the discourse of the medical model. Functioning as medication facilitators, social workers are encouraged to recognize the discourse of the client's lived experience, attend to what the client, the client's family, and the client's community are saying with regard to the administered medications. Focus on the meaning and context of medication for a specific person. The discourse framework helps to expand our thinking and seeing, and it allows for a more inclusive biopsychosocial-spiritual view of the person-in-situation. It helps us to be aware of those ideas and beliefs about the use of psychotropic medication that might be marginalized or suppressed. And the discourse of lived experience can encourage us not to privilege our professional knowledge. Instead it encourages us to fully and completely listen to our clients' voices.

People who use psychotropic medications participate in a variety of social and cultural discourses (e.g., those related to race, gender, stage of life, ethnicity) that impact upon them and their medication use. At a minimum, social workers as facilitators should seek to combine what is best and what is useful from various contexts, to the extent that these social or cultural discourses (such as frameworks of meanings) are important to the medication and to the client. To aid in this process, we envision using the discourse of the client's lived experience as the overarching framework, using empowerment strategies and the partnership model of practice. In other words, empowerment strategies and the partnership model of practice will help us to operationalize the concepts of the discourse of lived experience. In their work on empowerment practice, Gutiérrez, Parsons, and Cox (1998) argue for a redefinition of the practitioner's attitude, relationship, and role vis-à-vis people who have a serious mental disability. We believe that this redefinition is required in our practice with *all* clients who are using psychotropic medication. Some of the attitudinal principles described by Gutiérrez et al. can easily be incorporated into the discourse of the client's lived experience. When intervening from a framework that honors the lived experience of the client, medication facilitators will want to be responsible to the whole person, relinquish the role of authoritative expert, and respect the skills and knowledge that consumers bring. Many of the relationship principles of empowerment practice are closely aligned with this discourse perspective. Rather than the clinician having power over the client, empowerment practices focus on deemphasizing the professional role and sharing leadership with the client. Each of these principles emphasizes the idea that each voice is valuable (rather than the voice of the professional being privileged). Within the discourse framework, principles of empowerment practice in social work include the following. Social workers will want to focus on goals and values of the consumer, develop a truly client-centered model of care, build connections through roles, involvement, and community, to replace lost culture, history, and identity, and involve consumers and family members in decision-making roles.

The partnership model of practice, more fully described in Chapter 1, forms the other major component of the operationalized discourse framework. This model of practice emphasizes an alliance between the social worker, client, and family, which respects the viewpoint of the client and family and honors their participation in the helping process. Collaboration and mutuality, between client and social worker, are the key words here. Specific practice principles of the partnership model of practice are as follows: (1) appreciate the participants' strengths and limits, (2) embrace a client-centered practice, (3) reconceptualize the client-clinician relationship, (4) conceptualize the role of the social worker as a resource, and (5) appreciate the family member's perspective.

Combining the Two Discourses

This chapter argues that the social work medication facilitator needs to understand and appreciate both the discourse of the medical model and the discourse of the client's lived experience, to adequately intervene with the person who is using psychotropic medications. In facilitation work, social workers must interpret the results of the medical model to the client. For example, explaining why it is important to take a medication as it is prescribed, *and* helping the client to understand how their view of the world influences their use of medication, helps the facilitator integrate what is desirable from the discourse of the client's lived experience and the discourse of the medical model. In collaboration with the prescribing physician (and the medical staff), facilitators can then assist in monitoring the physical, psychological, and social side effects of medications, and facilitate the client's self-management of his or her medications.

Some specific examples may help to illustrate the importance of using the discourse of the medical model, and also the client's lived experience to mediate between all the social and cultural contexts that are present and that generate meanings for the client. Consider the examples of clients being prescribed, respectively, Ritalin, Prozac, and Risperdal. For example, a child who is prescribed Ritalin may become caught up in the discourse about attention deficit and hyperactivity disorder (ADHD), which often describes children taking Ritalin as being out-of-control and unmanageable. The child may be stigmatized and marginalized by being placed in a category of sick or unwieldy. An adult woman taking Prozac may now be seen (even by her physician in many cases) as "just another complaining, unhappy woman." She too is diminished by the societal discourse about the "worried well" and women suffering from depression. She may be seen as unhappy in love or wanting too much. The young adult male who is prescribed Risperdal may be caught up in the discourse of The Seriously Mentally Ill. The cultural discourse places him at the bottom of the mental illness hierarchy, and it may be assumed he cannot be employed, take care of himself, or contribute to society. He may be so stigmatized that he feels totally powerless to do anything but assume the role of a mental patient. Considering and doing what can be done to bring the best from each of the relevant discourses is reflective of the person-in-situation paradigm that is so integral to the language (discourse) of social work practice.

Another example of the insufficiency of the discourse of the medical model by itself, is the discourse around gender and health. For example, the fact that women account for 70% of the consumption of psychotropic drugs is such a startling statistic that it is natural to seek an interpretation. In western societies, women use psychotropic medication twice as often as men (Ettorre & Riska, 1995). It is appealing to interpret this overrepresentation as a continuation of the corseting and breast binding attitudes toward the female body that now find expression in diet control. Just as Bordo (1993) can see the effects in anorexia nervosa and bulimia, we may be seeing the effects of gender attitudes in the overrepresentation of women who are prescribed antipsychotic medications. The medical model seems inadequate to feminists and others who wish to emphasize the cultural or discursive explanation of such phenomena.

Another example of this discourse is how women and men are usually grouped together when prescribed medication, with the false assumption that both genders respond similarly to medications. Recent studies in pharmacology and psychopharmacology seem to address this problem and point to an initial understanding that gender is a source of variability in pharmacokinetics and pharmacodynamics (Yonkers, Kando, Cole, & Blumenthal, 1992). More than merely the medical model, or merely the discourse of one's lived experience, is needed to understand these phenomena and how they influence the prescribing and taking of psychotropic medications.

The discussion of meaning in social work and in other literature reflects the importance of the concept of discourse in generating and shaping meanings. The meaning of medication is central to one's use of psychotropic medications, and it is closely related to the discourses that exist within society and families. Bentley and Walsh (2001) speak of the importance of understanding the meaning of medication, as an important foundation to forming a helping relationship that can lead to effective interventions related to medication management. For example, medications can mean remedy or cure, poison, or magical charm to clients. Some people hold strong beliefs in medicine or a specific medical practitioner that will color their attitudes about a medication and their expectations of it. The subjective experiences of a consumer of medication are also seen as crucial to the development of meaning (Bentley and Walsh, 2001). As described, the discourses of the medical model and the client's lived experience provide an intellectual foundation for social work roles described in this chapter. We can now move to a discussion of the tasks and goals to be accomplished.

MAJOR TASKS AND GOALS

To fulfill the role of medication facilitator effectively, the social worker's primary goal must be to develop and manage collaborative working relationships among all involved parties. Our partners in this endeavor may vary, but they will always include medical practitioners, mental health and social service practitioners who are involved with the client (e.g., doctors, nurses, clinic staff, residential staff), and the social and cultural influences of the client and significant others in the client's life (e.g., family members, neighbors, friends, co-workers). The partnership model of practice (Bentley and Walsh, 2001) holds the client and their family members in especially high esteem and views the helping process as a mutual endeavor, with all the strengths and limitations that each party brings to the process. To facilitate the action and interaction of the various relevant mind-sets, social workers should aim toward achieving the following four goals: (1) collaborate with the physician (and other medical staff) in their efforts to achieve medical goals; (2) empower the clients to use their own lived experience and ways of looking at the world in order to arrive at their own understanding of the meaning of psychotropic medication; (3) help to monitor the side effects of medications; and (4) facilitate client self-management. Some may wish to link the first and the third of these goals, because there is a strong connection between them. For a parallel reason, they may wish to link the second and the fourth. But these goals are separated in this account to emphasize that both the third and the fourth goals are heavily involved in reconciling use of both the discourse of the medical model and the discourse of the client's lived experience.

Collaborating with Physician and Other Medical Staff

To achieve the goals typical of the medical model, that is to ensure that the client takes medication as prescribed, medication facilitators must closely collaborate with the prescribing physician and other medical staff. This is indeed a major task for social workers who aid clients taking psychotropic medications. This task can usually be accomplished more easily when the prescriber of medication is a psychiatrist, because psychiatrists frequently work with social workers and often understand their role in the psychiatric team. However, when a general or family practitioner prescribes psychotropic medication (as is most often the situation), it may be necessary to educate the physician so they understand the social worker's potential role in facilitating medication use. In these situations, social workers should reach out to the physician to develop a collaborative relationship. Even when the prescribing physician is a psychiatrist, there can be challenges to effective collaboration (see Chapter 11 on Collaboration).

Bentley and Walsh (2001) raise several important issues: Who has the ultimate responsibility for the client's treatment? How can the transference or countertransference of issues be managed? How will the psychosocial treatment and medication treatment influence each other? This is where the tenets of the medical model become most necessary. The social worker must often speak the language of the medical model (participate in the discourse), while concurrently including input from psychosocial and cultural aspects of the client's lived experience.

The following case example helps to explicate such a situation:

> Mr. B. was a 34-year-old Caucasian male referred to a social worker by a psychiatrist who had seen the patient in the hospital, where he was treated for a bipolar disorder. Upon discharge from the hospital, the client was placed on the mood stabilizer, Depakote. He was referred to the social worker for supportive treatment and to work on relationships with his parents, because an altercation with his father (following his discontinuance of medication) had precipitated the hospitalization. When the social worker met with Mr. B., she found that he was a very religious person who considered himself a born-again Christian. Mr. B. wondered what God had in store for him and wanted to work on what he might do with the rest of his life. Using the discourse of the medical model, Mr. B. might be seen as being religiously preoccupied, and the social worker would suggest that they work on managing his chronic illness and affective instability. Using the discourse of the client's lived experience as our lens, we would help Mr. B. to further explore his strong spiritual sense and where medication fits within the context of his life. In our ongoing contacts with the psychiatrist, we would provide a fuller description of Mr. B., including the meaning to him of the medications he was taking. Rather than being marginalized by being seen as religiously preoccupied, he would be empowered to use his religious beliefs to bring meaning to his life and work.

Understanding the Client's Lived Experience and the Meaning of Medication

To manage possible psychological and social side effects of medication use, social workers need to help each client arrive at their own unique understanding of the meaning of psychotropic medication. Participating in the discourse of the medical model with the client would suggest sharing specific information about how the medicine biologically works in the body to alleviate certain symptoms. Participating in the discourse of the client's lived experience, as operationalized by the partnership model of practice, can take us to the next level of meaning.

As an example of using the discourse of the client's lived experience to reach this new level of meaning, consider the case of a 32-year-old married woman seeing a clinical social worker for anxiety and depression. She is taking Paxil and trazodone. The client is intelligent and socially competent (working on a master's degree), but she has very low self-esteem, lacks confidence in her own abilities, and is anxious and worried about all aspects of her life. She reports that she has a handsome husband who has a good job and an adorable 3-year-old daughter, and everyone wonders how she can have everything and still be so unhappy. Initially, she seemed to become psychologically dependent on the medications, relying on them to handle all symptoms, and feeling like she had no control over her anxiety, sleeplessness, and depression. The medication came to mean something she could depend upon without fully taking responsibility for her own actions or thoughts. In discussing what it was like to grow up as a female within her particular family of origin, we learned that women were placed in a dependent, helpless role (her mother also took Paxil). As we consistently deferred to her experiences and prior efforts to cope, she began to see how she might become more assertive and self-confident. Her husband was also invited to join with us as an ally in the helping process, and to contribute his perspective. While we were working with the client and her spouse on these issues, we were also consulting with the psychiatrist, who gradually lowered the doses of the two medications. As we ended our work together, the client was on minimal doses of the medication and feeling much better able to control her anxiety, sleeplessness, and depression.

Monitoring All Types of Side Effects

As a medication facilitator, another task for social workers is to monitor the physical, psychological, and social side effects of medications. Because bothersome side effects adversely affect quality of life and are a major cause of nonadherence, social workers must constantly attend to this issue. While most of the physical side effects occur in the first few days or weeks after beginning a medication, they can occur at any time.

Once a client is stabilized on a specific dose, it is common for the clinician to neglect adherence and side effect issues. But as a client continues to use a psychotropic, there is always the possibility of an unwanted side effect. For example, some antipsychotic medications result in the client feeling sedated. Sedation is usually not a desired effect of the drug, but rather an unpleasant side effect. Social workers need to specifically ask clients if they are feeling drugged-out or sedated, because many people think that sedation is the desired effect of the medication. Good practice assumes that clients routinely be asked about medication administration and any untoward effects. Because of the psychological and social side effects of medications, a person might stop or alter their medication regimen at any time, even in the absence of a physical side effect. For example, a client who initially takes their medication as prescribed, but feels angry about having a chronic condition that requires ongoing medication use, may stop taking medication due to this psychological side effect.

By attending to both the discourse of the medical model and to the discourse of the client's lived experience, social workers can better monitor medication side effects. Social workers must have adequate knowledge concerning how medications work and why, to diminish fear and anxiety around medication issues and increase client and family understanding. For example, we need to know that all antidepressant medications are equally effective in general, but that the SSRIs (selective serotonin reuptake inhibitors) tend to have fewer side effects and are therefore better tolerated by most people. We also need to understand what specific side effects the client has experienced in the past and how these might influence the present. Many psychotropic medications adversely affect sexual functioning, and if this is an especially difficult side effect for a client to tolerate, we need to incorporate this meaning into our work with the client, as well as with the client's prescribing physician. The facilitative task of social workers includes balancing the medical model discourse with the client's way of looking at the world; the facilitative role is to do what can be done to reconcile the seemingly irreconcilable.

Facilitating Client Self-Management Skills

Many mental illnesses are chronic in nature. Learning to manage the illness requires the inclusion of relapse prevention activities. Working with clients on developing self-monitoring skills is especially important. In a true partnership model of practice, all involved parties bear responsibility for the course and outcome of the illness. In the medical model, the patient is diagnosed and prescribed a medication. According to the partnership model, clients participate in the diagnostic process and assume responsibility for taking their own medications. In addition, clients are taught to monitor responses to the medications, considering their own social and cultural dictates. As we bring together the two discourses, we are able to discard the hierarchical structure where the doctor or social worker has all the answers. Instead, we engage in a process that "tries to honor" the beliefs of all involved parties.

To exemplify, consider the case of a 45-year-old man with a schizoaffective disorder who is hospitalized after becoming acutely suicidal. Upon his return home, it is agreed that a residential program separate from his parents' home might provide the structure and independence he desires. Initially, this man's parents are against the thought of him leaving home to live in a supported living apartment. We actively involve the parents in planning for a possible move, encouraging them to discuss the pros and cons, based on their cultural dictates. At the same time, we work closely with the residential staff and client to pave the way for the client's acceptance into this residential program. Once the client moves into the apartment, we develop a relapse plan, in conjunction with the parents, client, and residential staff. A two-column chart is developed that lists "Warning signs of Relapse" in one column and "What to do" in the other column. These are the warning signs of impending suicidal thoughts and ruminations. The client is instructed to record any warning sign that occurs, and then perform the behavior designated to address this sign. All participants are included in this self-monitoring exercise (i.e., residential staff and parents), and each will be encouraged to monitor the others to prevent severe deterioration that warrants hospitalization.

TECHNIQUES, STRATEGIES, AND SKILLS

In this section, we focus on techniques, strategies, and skills used by social work facilitators to achieve the tasks and goals discussed earlier. The overall strategy of the social worker as facilitator is to achieve these goals within the constraints of the particular context. Choice of particular strategies and techniques that social workers should adopt for achieving these goals should be situation-dependent. That is, they should depend on the specific institutional and other circumstances and context within which the social worker and the client encounter one another. Yet, the prospects for success are likely to be increased if social workers adopt a flexible but systematic approach in working toward the goals. A helping relationship and partnership is central to the social worker's mission. An orderly case management process is also facilitative. The latter would include familiar routines for ensuring activities such as listening to the client (and medical personnel), preparing an action plan for the patient, carrying out the plan, and then evaluating the plan and its implementation.

Whatever the desired and possible strategies in the particular context, social workers should seek to develop and use capabilities in four areas. These areas are capabilities (techniques and skills) in empathic uncertainty (or listening), advocacy, negotiating skills, and problem solving. These can be supplemented by other capabilities, such as providing supportive behavior and reflective interpretation. The overarching need in using the four capabilities is to integrate the discourses of the medical model and of the client's lived experience.

Empathic Uncertainty (Listening)

In an effort to simultaneously appreciate the discourses of the medical model and the client's lived experience, it would be best if the clinician (who manages this partnership) were to assume a position of *uncertainty* (Pozatek, 1994) or *tentativeness*, again a contrast to the medical model that conjures images of expertness and certainty. A tentative stance is a client-centered stance. Consider this illustration of the operation of uncertainty. A 48-year-old woman has been seen individually and with her husband concerning long-standing marital problems. She has become increasingly angry about her relationship with her husband and the fact that her three sons do not help her enough at home. She has gained weight, is not sleeping well, and is finding it difficult to concentrate while at her job. The social worker mentions the possibility of depression and wonders if the client would be willing to see a psychiatrist for medication evaluation. The client adamantly refuses, saying she is not depressed and the problem lies in her husband's behavior. If working strictly from a medical model viewpoint, the clinician might try to convince the client to consider medication, bringing to the fore all the scientific knowledge we have concerning the symptoms of depression and how antidepressants often can alleviate these symptoms. However, when the clinician assumes a stance of uncertainty, the scientific data may be suspended, and more focus is placed on what the husband's behavior means for this woman. The clinician truly respects the complexity of this woman's life and relinquishes the suggestion that she consider medication use at this time.

Advocacy

Social workers traditionally serve as advocates for their clients. There are some especially important issues with respect to psychotropic medications. Medications can be used as a means of social control, such as in psychiatric hospitals, nursing homes, and schools. Social workers, who often are employed by institutions, are frequently asked to collude in this social control aspect by helping patients adjust to and accept the medications that are prescribed. For example, an 83-year-old woman resides in a skilled-nursing facility where she is being treated for a hip fracture. She becomes demanding of staff and somewhat aggressive, and is prescribed Haldol as a result. The social worker becomes concerned that the woman is more sedated and less alert as a result of this medication. In an attempt to advocate for this woman, the social worker needs to consider the experience and views of the nursing home staff. Usually caught up in the discourse of the medical model, the limited staff may hold that patients should be docile and well-behaved, so that they can easily care for all the residents. The beliefs of the client and her family, and their lived experiences, also must be considered. The social worker uses his or her relationship-building and empathy skills to elicit thoughts and feelings from the involved parties. If the client and family are opposed to the use of Haldol, the social worker can then intervene with the prescribing physician and present the case for discontinuance of this medication. However, it would also be useful for the social worker to find out why the client is becoming upset and what can be done to ameliorate the problem. If the social worker finds that there is a pattern of prescribing antipsychotics for demanding clients, then advocacy at the systems level may be indicated.

Negotiating Skills

Functioning as an advocate often requires negotiating skills. Also, there are situations in which we will want to teach such skills to clients. The dosage of a medication and negative side effects can frequently raise issues of concern. The medical model discourse usually dictates that symptoms are adequately removed, sometimes with seemingly little regard for ill effects that result from a high dose of a particular medication. After all, the physician's goal is to cure or make well, and if the illness or disease cannot be cured, perhaps at the very least the symptoms can be eliminated. Most people who take medication see the physician as the holder of the power. Therefore, they find it difficult to disagree overtly with what the physician has prescribed. The social worker is usually seen as part of the power system (in this case, the medical model), but when the social worker also uses his or her understanding of the discourse of the client's lived experience, then he or she can hear a client's hesitancy to confront the doctor. Here is where the social worker uses skills in listening and communicating assertively (and her knowledge of power relations), as well as knowledge about the particular medication, its side effects, and alternative medication options.

Consider the case of a 34-year-old man being seen by a social worker for several years for his chronic schizophrenic illness. He was placed on Clozaril, but continued having severe auditory hallucinations. After much discussion of the voices and how to manage them, it became clear that the client had not told his psychiatrist about the voices. We role played with the client, practicing how he might approach the psychiatrist and request a review of his medication, perhaps making some adjustment to address the hallucinations. When this was not effective, we got the client's permission to call the psychiatrist directly concerning the voices. Another antipsychotic was added to the client's medication, and the voices abated.

Problem Solving

Problem solving is a capability or technique necessary for facilitating the effective use of psychotropic medications. This is an important technique to use, because taking psychotropic medication by itself is rarely adequate to resolve the problem for which medication is prescribed. In addition, problems may arise related to medication use. For example, Mrs. D. is being seen by a social worker for generalized anxiety and some depression. She is taking Paxil and trazodone, which has alleviated some of her symptoms. However, she continues to have difficulty remembering to take her medication because she is distracted by her 3-year-old daughter, who is "driving me crazy." We work with Mrs. D. on the problem-solving process, by defining the problem, generating possible solutions, choosing the best solution, and carrying out the solution. In discussing ways to address this problem, we explore child-rearing practices in her own family of origin. We work with her on appreciating the limitations of a 3-year-old and her need for attention and closeness to her mother. In a joint session with Mrs. D. and her husband, we use the steps of problem-solving to address concerns about having the full burden for their daughter and how child care could be shared on weekends and evenings. Mrs. D. learns how to ask her husband for assistance with the child, especially when she is feeling overwhelmed and anxious.

EXEMPLAR PROGRAMS

Some medication-education and intervention models for medication noncompliance found in the literature seem to derive most heavily from a medical model as we have described it, in that they stress what clients ought to be doing and why (see Bentley & Walsh, 2001). One recently published model, however, stands in sharp contrast, in that it seems to emphasize the meaning of medication, which as we have described is related to the client's way of looking at the world, even though that language is not used. It is a unique three-phase semistructured intervention program called "compliance therapy" (Kemp, Kirov, Everitt, Hayward, & David, 1998). It is said to have derived from cognitive theory and motivational interviewing techniques. Over the course of 2 to 3 weeks, each client participates in 4 to 6 sessions lasting 20 to 60 minutes each (approximately 3 1/2 hours total per client). In Phase 1, clinicians review clients' illnesses, their conceptualization of the illness, and their stance toward treatment. Negative experiences are acknowledged, as are the consequences of nonadherence. Phase 2 explores clients' ambivalence toward treatment, the meaning of illness and medication use, including issues of identity. This could be an example of using the discourse of the client's lived experience as we have described. In Phase 3, the clinician introduces analogies of mental illness and treatment with that of physical illness, describes famous people with mental illnesses, and tries to reframe medication use as an "insurance policy." Kemp et al. offer data suggesting that attitudes toward medication can be improved, greater insight into their illness can be achieved, and medication adherence can be improved as well.

UNIQUE CHALLENGES FOR SOCIAL WORKERS

To effectively achieve the role of medication facilitator, at least three major challenges or conflicts must be confronted, especially when the facilitator is simultaneously appreciating both the discourse of the medical model and the discourse of the client's lived experience. First, clinicians must reconcile the medication facilitator role with any antimedication opinions. For example, some medication facilitators favor psychotropic medication use; others hold the view that psychotropic medications are dangerous and unhealthy. Second, facilitators need to reconcile the requirements of the discourse of social work with the discourse of others, like the client. A third challenge is to reconcile the competing demands of the two discourses highlighted in this chapter, that of the medical model and of the client's lived experience.

The first challenge is fairly transparent. Social workers who assume the role of facilitator are presumed to favor appropriate use of psychotropic medication. However, based on their knowledge of and experiences with medications, what if the social worker believes that psychotropic medications are dangerous and unhealthy? If the professional has strong, negative feelings concerning psychotropic medications, might they still be able to function as a medication facilitator for their client? Perhaps, yes, if we can assume that they are aware of their negative feelings and can manage them in a way that does not adversely affect the client or limit their access to differing views. Social workers in this dilemma may be challenged to put aside their own feelings and beliefs to more objectively approach the issue of medication use with a client. They should recognize the possibility of a countertransference reaction.

The second major challenge for social workers who function as medication facilitators is appreciating the influence of the discourse of one's own profession, and the conflicts between that discourse and other relevant ways of viewing the world. As noted earlier in this chapter, one cannot choose the content of one's discourse. Rather, social workers join a profession that has an already-established way of viewing the world. This is a large part of what the master's of social work course of study is all about—becoming socialized to the discourse of social work. In a roundtable discussion on the status of the social work profession, Foucault depicts social workers as the disseminators of society's values (Chambon, Irving, & Epstein, 1999). Think of the kind of work that social workers do, in schools, hospitals, nursing homes, correctional facilities, and child welfare agencies. What readily comes to mind is that social workers are often (if not always) in the position of helping clients to adapt or adjust to the status quo, to fit in with the prescribed values.

Because the values of a society are generally the values held by those in power, social workers are regularly called upon to dictate values, often to those who are less powerful. Recall the earlier example of the child who is placed on Ritalin due to hyperactivity. Our society values children who are able to learn and who behave in certain controlled ways in school. When children are unable to "follow the rules" or behave according to established values, they are often referred for testing and medication. Can the school social worker, in such an instance, argue that the child is just following the dictates of her subculture and learning to freely express herself? We think not, if the social worker wants to keep his or her job. In such a situation, it is presumed that the social worker will function as a medication facilitator if the school psychologist or psychiatrist (people who hold power) determines that the child needs psychostimulant medication.

The third challenge unique to social workers who are functioning as medication facilitators is to simultaneously acknowledge and use the discourse of the medical model and that of the client's lived experience without relinquishing either. There are frequent occasions where the strictures of the medical model are too controlling, and social workers are more interested in empowering their client rather than having them assume a more passive position. The medicalization of certain psychosocial problems often leads to the prescribing of psychotropic medications. For example, when working with couples who are experiencing relationship problems, we may need to heed the referring psychiatrist's diagnosis of one partner's mood disorder, while understanding the two very different family cultures that are making it difficult for the two partners to live together amicably. If the partner with the mood disorder becomes psychologically dependent on the medication prescribed by the powerful physician, and pays little attention to the possible family-of-origin issues that have been transferred onto the relationship, the social worker may have an especially difficult task.

This parallel treatment model, where a psychiatrist has referred a couple to a social worker for psychotherapy (while the physician provides medication treatment), can put the social worker in a difficult position. By holding the discourse of the medical model, the social worker will speak in the language of diagnosis, treatment, and medication management, and she will support the dictates of the prescribing psychiatrist. At times the client may dismiss anything the social worker says concerning the medication or diagnosis issues simply because the social worker is a nonmedical member of the treatment team. Being dismissed by a client can have a tremendous negative effect on the professional self-esteem of the social worker. In addition, when a client dismisses the knowledge and experience of the psychotherapist in one area, it may spill over into other areas. In such a situation, the client may lose faith in the ability of the nonmedical psychotherapist to provide effective therapeutic services. However, we argue that a social worker can alleviate this type of scenario through the concurrent use of the discourse of the client's lived experience. By eliciting information about the client's previous experience with medical practitioners, and family members' experiences that have been transmitted, the social worker can help determine, for this particular client, the meaning behind "making the physician omnipotent," and as a consequence, "making everyone else impotent."

SUMMARY

This chapter has discussed the role of the social worker as a medication facilitator in terms of an intellectual base that makes client empowering use of both the discourse of the medical model and the discourse of the client's lived experience. *Discourse* was defined as a mind-set that provides a specific way of constituting and viewing one's environment. We explained and illustrated the knowledge, goals, capabilities, and unique problems the social worker must acquire or overcome as medication facilitator, in working toward using both the discourse of the medical model and the discourse of the client's lived experience. The knowledge included the understanding of both models, such as basic knowledge (from the medical model) about psychopharmacology and eliciting the meaning of medications for the client (based on family and culture). Four goals were specified for the social worker as medication facilitator. These were collaborating with the physician (and other medical staff) in their efforts to achieve medical goals, empowering clients to use their lived experiences to arrive at their own understanding of the meaning of psychotropic, helping to monitor the side effects of medications, and facilitating client self-management. Techniques, strategies, and skills needed by the facilitator were discussed and illustrated in terms of four capabilities. The capabilities were empathetic uncertainty (listening), advocacy, negotiating skills, and problem solving. We defined and described three challenges. It was argued that the social worker as medication facilitator should make skillful use of relevant material from two discourses, that of the medical model and of the client's lived experience. The basic claim of this chapter is that the social worker can provide useful interventions as a medication facilitator, through the use of specified approaches, holding both the discourse of the medical model and the discourse of the client's lived experience.

KEY TERMS

Client's Lived Experience: The totality of the emotional experience and meaning of mental illness and medication use in the daily lives of clients.

Discourse: The nature of thinking about, looking at, and discussing some topic or phenomena.

Empathic Uncertainty (or Listening): The tentative and flexible nature of the social worker's stance with and recommendations to the client.

Empowering Clients: Helping clients obtain the information and resources (internal and environmental) they need to make decisions and take action to reach their goals.

Medical Model: An approach to the treatment of medical or mental health issues that rests on theories of biological etiology and treatment, authoritative, or paternalistic structures of service delivery.

Medication Facilitator: The role of enhancing the probability that desired medication will help to alleviate bothersome symptoms and, most importantly, enhance the quality of a client's life.

WEB RESOURCES

Yahoo's Psychopharmacology Site (http://dir.yahoo.com/science/biology/pharmacology/psychopharmacology/). This site offers a definition of the medical model.

Foucault Site (http://nakayama.org/polylogos/philosophers/foucault/). This Web site offers print resources on Foucault.

REFERENCES

Aldwin, C. M. (1994). *Stress, coping, and development.* New York: Guilford Press.

Bentley, K. J., & Walsh, J. (1998). Advances in psychopharmacology and psychosocial aspects of medication management: A review for social workers. In J. B. W. Williams & K. Ell (Eds.), *Advances in mental health research* (pp. 309–342). Washington, DC: NASW Press.

Bentley, K. J., & Walsh, J. (2001). *The social worker & psychotropic medication: Toward effective collaboration with mental health clients, families and other providers* (2nd ed.). Belmont, CA: Brooks/Cole–Wadsworth.

Bordo, S. (1993). *Unbearable weight.* Berkeley: University of California Press.

Chambon, A. S., Irving, A., & Epstein, L. (Eds.). (1999). *Reading Foucault for social work.* New York: Columbia University Press.

Ettorre, E., & Riska, E. (1995). *Gendered moods: Psychotropics and society.* London: Routledge.

Foucault, M. (1972). *The archaeology of knowledge* (A. M. Sheridan Smith, Trans.). New York: Pantheon.

Foucault, M. (1977). History of systems of thought: Course description of Foucault's first year at College de France. In D. F. Bouchard (Ed.)., (D. F. Bouchard and S. Simon, Trans.). *Language, countermemory, practice: Selected essays and interviews.* Ithaca, NY: Cornell University Press.

Gutiérrez, L. M., Parsons, R. J., & Cox, E. O. (1998). *Empowerment in social work practice: A sourcebook.* Pacific Grove, CA: Brooks/Cole.

Kaplan, H. I., & Sadock, B. J. (1996). *Pocket handbook of psychiatric drug treatment.* Baltimore, MD: Williams & Wilkins.

Kemp, R., Kirov, G., Everitt, B., Hayward, P., & David, A. (1998). Randomised controlled trial of compliance therapy: 18 month follow-up. *British Journal of Psychiatry, 172,* 413–419.

Mills, S. (1997). *Discourse.* New York: Routledge.

Pozatek, E. (1994). The problem of certainty: Clinical social work in the postmodern era. *Social Work, 39*(4), 396–403.

Sands, R. G., & Nuccio, K. (1992). Postmodern feminist theory and social work. *Social Work, 37*(6), 489–494.

Townsend, M. C. (1995). *Drug guide for psychiatric nursing.* Philadelphia: F. A. Davis.

Yonkers, K. A., Kando, J. C., Cole, J. O., & Blumenthal, S. (1992). Gender differences in pharmacokinetics and pharmacodynamics of psychotropic medication. *The American Journal of Psychiatry, 149*(5), 587–595.

SOCIAL WORKERS AS CONSUMER AND FAMILY CONSULTANTS

CHAPTER

10

Phyllis Solomon, Tina Bogart Marshall, Edie Mannion, & John Farmer

The provision of consultation to consumers of mental health services and their families is a relatively recent phenomenon. Social workers have long been at the forefront of this change, recognizing the value of working together with families in discharge planning and other aspects of the treatment process. While social workers routinely mediate on behalf of clients and families, as consumer and family consultants, social workers join in partnership with consumers and families to achieve mutual goals. Consultation is a process in which a party (the consultee) seeks the advice or opinion of another party (the consultant) for the purpose of clarifying a situation, reaching a decision, solving a problem, or accomplishing an objective (Marsh, 1998). Consultants work collaboratively with the consultee and assume a variety of roles throughout the consultative process, some of which are described in more depth in other chapters, such as that of the educator. Practitioners can provide consultation in a number of positions, including case managers or outpatient clinicians.

Consumer and family consultation has emerged as a result of a shift in attitudes and beliefs about the capabilities of families and mental health consumers. In the past, social work students, similar to trainees in other mental health professions, were taught to expect little from individuals with severe mental illness. When clients were released from a psychiatric hospital to the community, the expectation was that consumers would continue to live highly dependent lives. The pervasive belief regarding people with severe mental illness was that they could not live independent lives, be employed, or be self-sufficient.

Early theories about the family's role in the life of their ill relative hypothesized that families were the causative agent in the onset and exacerbation of their relative's mental illness (Spaniol, Zipple, & Lockwood, 1992). Families were often seen as dysfunctional and in need of family therapy. Consequently, it was considered in the best interest of psychiatric clients to separate them from their families (Terkelsen, 1990).

230

Several factors contributed to the shift away from viewing families as the cause of mental illness and mental health consumers as dependent and helpless. First, tremendous advancements in medications and treatment have allowed consumers to experience recovery or a higher level of functioning than ever before. The increasing amount of research evidence for the biological basis of mental illness has also led to the debunking of the family causation theories (Cook, Pickett, & Cohler, 1997). Second, the growth of consumer and family advocacy groups such as the National Alliance for the Mentally Ill (NAMI) have significantly influenced attitudes and beliefs regarding mental health consumers and their families. Third, the advent of the Community Support Program (CSP) by the National Institute of Mental Health in the late 1970s promoted a new philosophy and ideology with regard to the treatment of those with severe mental illness. The CSP philosophy is oriented toward the creation of opportunities for individuals with major psychiatric disorders, to move toward increased independence rather than "fostering a life of dependency, disability, and 'chronic patienthood'" (Stroul, 1993, p. 47). Currently, mental health consumers are seen as capable individuals who can participate in the development of their own treatment plan, be employed, operate their own businesses, advocate for changes in the mental health system, and become involved in the planning and delivery of mental health services, such as the provision of case management services by consumers (Solomon & Draine, 1995a, b).

As well as the more recent recovery paradigms, the CSP philosophy promotes a new view regarding the role of families in the treatment process. Although remnants of family causation theories still persist among mental health providers and academics (Marsh, 1998), families are now viewed as a resource to practitioners in the care and treatment of their ill relative (Solomon, 1996). Many consumers live with their families, and family members frequently are an integral part of their ill relative's support network (Solomon, 1996). Because the symptoms of severe mental illness may prevent consumers from recognizing when they are becoming ill, families are often the first to recognize signs and symptoms of relapse (Herz, 1985). Practitioners are now cognizant of the knowledge and expertise that family members have gained through their experience of living with and supporting their ill relative. Partnering with families for the treatment of their ill relative has been found to increase the effectiveness of treatment for these clients. Additionally, social workers have found that they share similar goals with family and mental health consumer groups for improving the mental health system, and are working together with these groups as consultants to influence mental health policy and services.

This chapter will define the role of the social worker as a consultant to families and consumers of mental health services, along with the relevant research and theoretical underpinnings of these approaches. Strategies, techniques, and tasks for carrying out these roles will be discussed and exemplar family programs will be presented.

THE INTELLECTUAL BASE OF FAMILY CONSULTATION

Before clarifying the intellectual base of family consultation, it is important for social workers to be clear about the way family consultation has been defined. In the mental illness literature, the term *family consultation* (sometimes called *family systems consultation* or *supportive family counseling*) has come to mean a special type of consultation. It refers to a process, in which family members of an adult with mental illness turn to mental health practitioners with questions or concerns, and that practitioner collaborates with the family to arrive at options for addressing or resolving the family's concerns.

Family consultation is based on a collaborative relationship between families and mental health practitioners (Marsh, 1998; Solomon, 1996). Components of a collaborative relationship include two-way communication between practitioners and families, in which both parties are open, cooperative, and empathic (Budd & Hughes, 1997). Unlike other family interventions, the intensity and frequency of consultation is determined jointly by the practitioner and family. The consultative model focuses on establishing a shared agenda and goals, where problems are identified, assessed, and resolved using the expertise, strengths, knowledge, and skills of both parties, the family and the practitioner.

Family consultation can be provided by a social worker who is treating the ill relative (such as a case manager), on the treatment team of a facility that is treating the ill relative, or separate from the practitioners or agency treating the ill relative. In many cases, families who utilize family consultation have relatives who are refusing treatment, and they are seeking consultation to help their relative agree to try treatment.

Family Consultation

The theoretical basis for this approach is a stress, coping, and adaptation framework for working individually with families of those with severe mental illness (Hatfield, 1990; Hatfield & Lefley, 1987; Marsh, 1992; Solomon, 1996). Families of individuals with severe psychiatric disorders encounter and confront numerous stressful and challenging situations. Families are frequently adjusting to new crises and disruptions in their daily lives, such as suicide threats, delusions, hallucinations, and other sporadic and unpredictable behavior associated with their relative's illness. Families often cope with problem situations through trial and error, or advice and suggestions of friends and families with no knowledge or experience about severe mental illness. The often long and inconsistent course of mental illnesses constantly taxes the family's adaptive resources as they are episodically presented with new crises and problems related to the illness. While some families have received a great deal of help from peer-support groups, many families are not comfortable with group approaches or in discussing their problems with others in a public venue. A consultative approach is often more efficient, as well as offering a sense of security to families confronting problems and crises associated with severe mental illness. Families find that knowing a practitioner is available to answer their questions is very reassuring (Budd & Hughes, 1997). Practitioners who share knowledge, skills, and support resources with families have helped them to reduce their stress, overcome the obstacles they face (Crotty & Kulys, 1986; Potasznik & Nelson, 1994), and make appropriate adaptations for adjusting their lives to living with or supporting a chronically ill family member (Hatfield, 1990; Solomon, Draine, Mannion, & Meisel, 1996b). While practitioners can offer families information to help them better understand the difference between symptoms of the illness, medication side effects, and facets of their relative's personality traits, families can offer practitioners important information regarding their relative's symptoms and behaviors. Sharing information with families has been shown to decrease relapse and recidivism for their ill relative (Anderson, Reiss, & Hogarty, 1986; Falloon, Boyd, & McGill, 1985; Leff, Kuipers, & Berkowitz, 1982).

In contrast to clinical services (such as family therapy), family consultation is a process in which practitioners and families *collaborate* to address the questions or concerns related to their relative with mental illness. Family therapy involves treating the mental and emotional disorders of family members by employing psychological interventions (Marsh, 1998). Family therapy can be loosely defined as the treatment of individual symptoms or relationship problems using relational interventions. There is some overlap, as family therapy can include some aspects of consultation, and consultation can lead to a recommendation for family therapy.

The initial family interventions emanated from a research base that had a deficit orientation. This research found that people with schizophrenia who returned to families with high expressed emotion (EE) upon release from a psychiatric hospitalization, had relapse rates two to three times higher than those returning to low EE families. High EE families are ones that are overly critical, overinvolved, and hostile. Behavioral interventions were developed to reduce the EE of families, as a means to reducing the relapse rates of patients. Consequently, these family interventions were adjunctive to treatment for the patient (Lam, 1991; Mintz, Liberman, Miklowitz, & Mintz, 1987). Generically referred to as family psychoeducation, these family interventions were created in response to this research.

Many families were not very receptive to family psychoeducational interventions (Hatfield, Spaniol, & Zipple, 1987). Some of these interventions required that the ill relative be in treatment and that families commit at least 9 months of their time to these interventions. Furthermore, some of these interventions continue to promote a family-blaming orientation, as families had to be high on EE to enter these programs. Because family consultation uses a strengths perspective, social workers who define their initial role with families as consultants can prevent the mutual alienation that often develops in deficit-based family interventions that promote a family-blaming orientation.

Additionally, helping families within family psychoeducational interventions is a secondary goal. Recognizing the need for education about mental illness and their treatments, families developed family education programs (such as NAMI's Family-to-Family Education Course) that are geared to the specific needs of families. Family education programs are group interventions, in which the ill relative frequently is not a participant (Solomon, Draine, Mannion, & Meisel, 1996a). These are short-term interventions that do not require an enormous commitment of time. Family consultation is an alternative to this group educational approach. Education is a component of the consultation model, but the education is secondary to advise, support, problem solving, and information that is communicated to the family. Additionally, education is based specifically on what the family needs, rather than on general information about severe mental illness (as is the case with the group approach).

Although there has been much research on the efficacy of family psychoeducation interventions (Dixon & Lehman, 1995; Lam, 1991), the research on family consultation has been extremely limited. One study to date has assessed family consultation that was conducted by two social work researchers, Solomon and Draine, in collaboration with a family member and a practitioner (Solomon et al., 1996b; Solomon, Draine, Mannion, & Meisel, 1997). Solomon and her colleagues (1996) conducted a randomized design, which compared family consultation to the group family education and to a wait-list control group. Family consultation significantly increased family members' sense of self-efficacy. The initial effect for self-efficacy at termination of the intervention (which was 3 months after entrance) did not significantly attenuate during the 6-month follow-up period. However, at 6 months, there was no difference between consultation and the control group, due to maturation of the control group over the 9-month study period. (Solomon et al., 1997). It is unclear why the control group improved during follow-up. For ethical reasons, all wait-list control participants were promised either or both services when they completed the protocol. The improvement may have been due to anticipation of entering the educational program at termination of the study (Solomon et al., 1997). These findings indicate that the consultation intervention has promise in speeding up the process of improved self-efficacy, but requires further research and possible refinement. Based on the research, the consultation model that was examined was modified (Mannion, Draine, Solomon, & Meisel, 1997).

Family consultation has been promoted by mental health practitioners who are trained in a variety of disciplines, including psychology, psychiatry, and social work. Joel Kanter, a social worker, has contributed to the knowledge base of this practice intervention. His version of family consultation emerged from 12 years of social work practice in mental health outpatient programs. This approach developed from a need to work with families of ill relatives who refused to participate in treatment (Kanter, 1985). The skills necessary to employ this approach are very consistent with the training and experience of a social worker who has worked with individuals with severe mental illnesses. He acknowledges that this approach is informed by psychoeducational interventions, but requires the creative use of a variety of treatment approaches within a "coherent understanding of mental illness" (Kanter, 1985, p. 22). He believes that, to appreciate the stresses that families encounter, family consultation is most effectively implemented by individuals who have experience with a diversity of mental health settings, such as inpatient units, residential facilities, and partial care programs.

Although practitioners from numerous disciplines may deliver family consultation, the intervention is especially consistent with a social work orientation. The family consultation model focuses on partnership. Compton and Galaway (1994) define social work as a "partnership arrangement [where] clients and social workers function together as partners throughout the problem-solving process" (p. 11). There is no single technique that works with all families. Family consultation is a responsive approach. Unlike other family interventions, such as psychoeducation, which usually consist of highly structured educational sessions, family consultation is an eclectic approach that "uses elements of biological, psychoanalytic, behavioristic, and family systems theories to assist families in coping more effectively" with their ill relative (Kanter, 1985, p. 30). The problem-solving framework from which social workers are trained is integral to the consultation model. This framework guides the client and social workers in thinking through and exploring issues to increase the likelihood of finding an effective response (Compton & Galaway, 1994).

The consultation model incorporates many of the values on which social work is based. Similar to social work practice, the model operates from a strengths perspective rather than a deficit one. Practitioners and families work together as partners sharing their knowledge and skills. Social work also believes in client self-determination and instilling dignity through participation and accountability (Compton & Galaway, 1994). The collaborative relationship requires families and practitioners to reach agreements on their agenda and clearly discuss their expectations. Marsh (1998) notes that "[a] consultative approach fosters collaborative relationships with families, offers an objective and systems-oriented assessment of their concerns, emphasizes family strengths and resources, and facilitates the shift to alternative practitioner roles as appropriate" (p. 138).

For the most part, family consultation has been practiced on the individual level or microlevel. However, given social workers' expertise in agency operations, budgeting, evaluation, and program and system planning, social workers may also provide consultation to family organizations, as well as assist in the development of such organizations. Social workers may also use their research skills to evaluate family consultation programs or programs developed and operated by family organizations. Three of this chapter's authors (Solomon, Mannion, & Marshall) have been involved in consultation to a family organization as an aspect of a larger project, to increase family education activities in a mental health service delivery system in a medium-sized city. The family consultation aspect of this project consisted of working with the local NAMI chapter to expand and enhance their family education efforts. The social work consultants worked together with NAMI-affiliated family members to develop a survey to assess the educational needs of family members. They also faciliate contact between family members and mental health practitioners in the community to develop a basic education series in English and Spanish, and developed a manual summarizing the information necessary to continue the education series on an ongoing basis. The social work consultants utilized their skills in negotiation and mediation to help family members secure funding for the salary of a training coordinator within the NAMI affiliate, and assisted family members in writing grant proposals to cover the costs of educational brochures and presentation materials and equipment. In summary, the consultants utilized their social work skills of community organizing, negotiating, research, and grant writing to meet the goals they shared with NAMI family members.

MAJOR GOALS AND TASKS

The overarching goal of family consultation is to meet the needs of family members and enhance the family's competence and confidence in coping and supporting their ill relative. The first major task of family consultation is to establish trust within the consultative relationship. Consultants may develop trust by recognizing competencies within the family and acknowledging the stresses associated with mental illnesses, such as crises, losses, burdens, and demands.

As in most problem-solving models, the second task is for the consultant to help the family to identify the specific problems on which they wish to work. This is followed by the need to set an agenda, by prioritizing the order in which they desire to work on these problems. Once the agenda has been set, there is a need to begin to work on developing the options for addressing the priority problem. Strategies for addressing each problem in turn are collaboratively developed. The professional role (such as teacher, referral source, mediator, or therapist) assumed by the consultant may change depending on the strategies selected.

TECHNIQUES, STRATEGIES, AND SKILLS

Edie Mannion, third author of this chapter, is the director and co-founder of the Training, Education, and Consultation (TEC) Family Center at the Mental Health Association of Southeastern Pennsylvania. She has identified three major skills integral to providing family consultation, which she refers to as the Three Fs, or feelings, focusing, and finding.

Feelings

As the consultees present their concerns and questions, they often express feelings both verbally and nonverbally. Joining with the family and earning their trust often requires the consultant to responds to these feelings using the techniques of empathizing and normalizing, while gathering information. Empathizing in this intervention means explicitly communicating how anyone, including the consultant, may feel in the situation that the family is describing. For example, if the family is describing how their son walks around their neighborhood behaving in bizarre ways, the consultant might say, "I can imagine it must be very embarrassing." Even when a family member is explicit about their feelings, as when they express how angry they are at their son's psychiatrist for not returning their calls, the consultant can empathize by saying, "I'd be extremely angry and upset if that happened to me." These forms of empathizing validate the family member's experience and help them feel understood. Unfortunately, many practitioners were taught reflective listening such as saying, "You sound angry." These interventions can alienate families and leave them feeling that the practitioner is distant, judgmental, and condescending. For example, during a recent team meeting in which the patient was not able to participate, a well-meaning social worker, who was listening to the patient's mother describe her ex-husband's lack of involvement, said to her, "You sound angry." This single mother sharply replied, "Wouldn't you be angry if you had a sick daughter and nobody to help you?" In this situation, the social worker may have responded empathically, "It must be very scary to feel so alone with this problem. If I had an ill daughter and an ex-husband who wouldn't get involved, I'd also be very angry with him." This form of empathizing incorporates another technique that is particularly important when dealing with families under stress and trauma, that of normalizing natural reactions to difficult or confusing situations. Families who have isolated themselves out of shame, or who have been judged by past practitioners, may question their emotional responses. It means a lot when the consultant identifies their feelings as common and natural by making comments such as, "In my experience, it is almost impossible not to eventually feel anger toward sick people, even if you know they can't help what they're doing." In another example, a consultant comforted a crying sister by saying, "The grief you are feeling is natural. You've lost a lot since your sister became ill."

By empathizing and normalizing throughout consultations, social workers can set the stage, allowing families to feel comfortable and understood, even if the focus of their concerns is not about their feelings. However, it is also important not to make feelings the focus of the consultation, unless they are related to addressing the presenting concerns. For example, discussing guilt may be important if the consultant is trying to help parents with their presenting concerns around feeling tyrannized by their son with bipolar disorder. In teaching limit-setting skills, it may be important to explore how fear, guilt, and pity interfere with implementing these skills.

Focusing

Families coping with mental illness often have an array of pressing questions and concerns. In their urgency, they ask questions or present concerns by lumping a lot of problems together or stating them vaguely, such as, "I want to learn how to cope with my husband." Focusing is the process of helping families clearly define their concerns, and then working on clear, specific problems, one at a time.

The task for the consultant is to start with each consultee's own language or way of stating a problem, and ask questions that will transform the stated problem into one specific problem. The consultant must be clear with how that problem creates difficulties within the family. One technique a consultant can employ in problem definition is to ask the family member to picture in their mind what is happening when the problem is stated. For example, when a consultee expresses that, "My brother refuses treatment," the problem is not defined in specific terms for efficient problem solving. Many possible images could come to mind (the brother getting the prescription filled and then flushing them down the toilet, the brother becoming silent and leaving the room whenever treatment is mentioned, or the brother saying he'll see a doctor, but then missing appointments). Each scenario may lead to a different set of suggestions for problem resolution. Or, there may be several scenarios involved in the brother's refusal of treatment, meaning several specific problems are contained in one vague problem. Trying to solve a complex problem that contains multiple problems as if it is one problem can lead to suggestions that are too simplistic and, therefore, ineffective.

The focusing function of consultation is used in problem definition, as well as throughout the consultation process. Families that are overwhelmed or in crisis may subtly shift to other problems before the first problem is adequately understood or addressed. For this reason, families often need frequent focusing. The consultant may simply acknowledge that the focus has shifted to another problem, and ask the family which problem they want to address first, explaining that it is best to work on one problem at a time. Another technique is to ask the family to bring a written list of concerns, then ask them to prioritize the problem on which they want to focus first. Difficulties can arise in knowing how to prioritize (e.g., should the most life-threatening problem come first, or should they start with easier, less emotionally charged problems?). When consulting with more than one family member, members may have difficulties in agreeing or compromising on the top priority problem and may require interventions. Social workers may suggest mediation or teach families strategies to use when they cannot agree, such as taking turns or making the rule that the person who is the most upset or stressed can pick the initial problem.

Another component of focusing is exploring the underlying issues that make a problem so upsetting for the family. Without this understanding, the consultant's suggestions will probably not address the underlying issues or fears, and lead the family to dismiss the suggestions and lose faith in the consultant's grasp of their situation. If the family is not aware of the issues underlying their concern, they may try the suggestions, only to find that they do not feel any better, despite efforts to solve the problem. Consultants can avoid these false starts by a thorough exploration of the presenting problem. For example, when families are losing patience with the exploration process, Mannion tells them the true story of a wife who expressed that her problem was that her husband ran to the state hospital every time their son called. She was not asked how this was a problem for her. The consultant suggested to the husband that he find other activities, which he did. However, the wife was still angry. Upon further discussion, it became clear that when her husband left the house, she felt neglected and rejected by him. Had the consultant explored the issue more thoroughly, the consultant may have suggested joint activities and helped solve the problem more effectively from the start.

The process of problem definition and staying focused can be tedious and frustrating to families who want immediate answers to many distressing problems at once, without having to dig too deep into themselves to understand the real issues. The consultant may need to explain that, without this part of the process, consultation is likely to be ineffective because the problems are too vague to solve. Furthermore, the problem may contain several problems, each of which requires individual attention. Questions that force families to truly define their stated concerns can steer the consultation process clear of these potential pitfalls.

Finding

Once a problem is well-defined, the consultant can discuss with the family some options for finding relief from or resolution of the problem. This may take the form of the brainstorming phase of problem solving (Falloon et al., 1985). However, in addition to being a problem solver, the consultant can shift to other roles such as teacher, mediator, or therapist. If the consultant cannot or does not want to take on the roles that can address the problem, she can refer the family to other individuals or groups who can. For example, a busy social worker, trying to address a family's concerns about how to set realistic expectations for their daughter with schizophrenia, may start by referring them to a family education course, such as the NAMI Family-to-Family, or asking them to read *Surviving Schizophrenia* (Torrey, 1995), rather than taking on that teaching role.

Sometimes therapy is one of many options for resolving the family's presenting concerns, but other options should be tried before suggesting therapy. When a family consultant's recommendations include therapy, the rationale, cost, benefits, and probability of success of this option should be clarified. Other options may be less time-consuming and expensive, and more appropriate and effective in achieving resolution to the family's concerns. Consultants must decide whether they wish to take on the role of therapist. Shifting from a therapist role back to a consultant role can be difficult. Consultants may, therefore, wish to refer the family to a family therapist who is knowledgeable about mental illness.

There are many roles and activities that a consultant may offer a family to address their top priority problem. The mnemonic device SMARTPRO, which stands for Supporting, Mediating, Advocating, Referring to appropriate resources, Teaching/training, Problem solving, Receiving the family's valuable information, and Offering hope, captures some of the possible roles of family consultants (Mannion, 2000).

Whatever role is taken on or whatever referral is made, a family consultant is wise to explain the potential benefits, and if applicable, the costs and potential risks to families following a suggestion, so that they have the information they need to make an informed decision. For example, when referring a family to a support group, they can be told of the potential benefits, such as practical information, mutual learning, and emotional support from people with similar experiences. They can also be warned that they may get unsolicited and bad advice, or that they may hear stories that can leave them feeling demoralized. The consultant may want to then shift to a teacher/trainer role, and coach them on how to approach support groups so they can get maximum benefit with minimum problems.

Although these components of consultation often overlap and flow into each other, mastering each one can improve the consultant's overall effectiveness. They are also useful for social workers who are new to the role of consultant and want to learn in increments.

EXEMPLAR PROGRAMS AND MODELS IN FAMILY CONSULTATION

One program that has been providing family consultation for many years is the Training, Education, and Consultation (TEC) Family Center at the Mental Health Association of Southeastern Pennsylvania in Philadelphia. At TEC, teams of mental illness practitioners and trained family members provide an array of services to help families cope with mental illness. Families can access family consultants by phone or have face-to-face appointments on an as-needed basis, over many years as they deal with new and repetitive concerns that go with these often chronic conditions. Families can also receive family consultation before, during, or after they participate in specialized family workshops, or without participating in any workshops. Currently, TEC offers multiweek workshops on schizophrenic disorders, mood disorders, borderline personality disorder, and coping with mental illness in a spouse or partner.

Workshop facilitators use a group consultation approach, matching training topics to the needs of each unique group of workshop participants (Mannion et al., 1997). For example, when the majority of participants are relatively new to this illness, the coping topics are likely to include basic information about the disorder, orientation to the behavioral health system, relapse prevention, and promoting hopefulness. For groups in which the majority of participants have been dealing with the disorder for many years, the focus may include planning for the future or re-investing in their own lives. This approach was adapted after a large controlled research study suggested that single family consultation is superior to brief multi-family education using predetermined curriculum in promoting family self-efficacy (Solomon et al., 1996a).

Because TEC is county-funded and does not depend on billing for family therapy, consultations are not limited to a certain number of face-to-face sessions or phone contact, as the service is frequently provided via phone. Because TEC staff are not providing treatment to the ill relative, confidentiality and treatment refusal by the ill relative do not present barriers to providing these family services. In fact, the majority of families who use TEC's services have relatives who have been diagnosed, but refuse treatment. In cases where the ill relative is receiving treatment, family consultants have often been successful in eliciting the ill relative's consent to attend treatment team meetings or allow the consultant to mediate conflicts between providers and the family. Ill relatives are sometimes invited to family consultations when the family and consultant agree that their participation is the best way to address the family's concern. Although TEC offers only nonclinical services and makes referrals for clinical services, the Pacific Clinics Institute in Los Angeles offers both clinical and nonclinical services. Because the Institute is a community mental health center with limited resources and a high demand for their services, a hierarchical approach is used to match families to services (Marsh, 1998).

All family members of clients with schizophrenia, severe mood disorders, or dual diagnoses are initially referred to a 7-week basic education class. About three-fourths who complete the class participate in additional services, such as family consultation or individual family psychoeducation that consists of 6–12 months of supervised practice in applying the coping skills taught in the class. If the family's needs are still not met, or if family issues are a threat to the client's recovery, families are offered clinical services such as individual, marital, or family therapy. The Institute has also developed training seminars, written materials, and videotapes for staff interested in learning these family-focused approaches to schizophrenia, mood disorders, and co-occurring mental illness and substance abuse.

UNIQUE CHALLENGES IN FAMILY CONSULTATION

The family consultant must also decide when it is clinically indicated to include or exclude the client from consultation with family members. Although family consultation can occur outside of the ill relative's treatment, integrating it can offer potential benefits for the ill person, such as improved support from their family, increased awareness of information and resources for their recovery and rehabilitation, fewer and less severe relapses, and fewer hospitalizations. Potential benefits to the treatment team include enhanced understanding of the client, more cooperation from the family in working on treatment goals, enhanced treatment effectiveness, a better understanding of the family experience of severe and persistent mental illness, and reduced burden that comes with sharing decision-making responsibility.

Excluding the client from at least some part of family consultation allows family members the freedom to express strong negative emotions and thoughts that would upset their ill relative if present. Family consultation with the client is also not indicated when the client is in denial of the illness and the family is trying to break through that denial. Rather than trying to manage the often nonproductive and escalating arguments, a consultant seeing the family without the ill relative present could teach them nonprovocative ways to enlist their relative's cooperation in treatment (Anderson et al., 1986). The challenge is maintaining the trust of the client, although they may not be included in meetings with the family.

If the consultant is also involved in the client's treatment process, it is important to preserve the client's control over confidential information. Clients must be asked whom they wish to designate as the people offered family consultation, as well the types of confidential information they are willing to let the consultant provide to the designated family members. Two of this chapter's authors (Marshall and Solomon) have developed model procedures to facilitate the release of confidential information to designated family members (Bogart & Solomon, 1999). See Figure 10.1 for an example of a model release form.

When providing consultation to family members who have had bad experiences with mental health practitioners, social workers are also challenged in earning family members' trust and dealing with their residual anger and skepticism. In these cases, it is important to explicitly clarify your role as a consultant. The skills and strategies discussed in the previous session can also help to diminish anger and build trust.

The major challenge for social workers is being able to provide family consultation within an agency setting, as family consultation is typically not a reimbursable service. Therefore, time may not be available to offer the service, and social workers may have to advocate for the importance of offering such a service.

CASE DILEMMA

Jane Smith, a social worker, is the primary therapist for Andrew Johnson, a 27-year-old man diagnosed with schizoaffective disorder and referred to the partial hospitalization program where she works. The first dilemma she must confront is maintaining her client's trust while being available to his family as a consultant. As part of her routine practice, she assesses Andrew's family situation as she tries to develop a therapeutic alliance. She learns that he lives with his parents and that he acknowledges he has an illness.

After meeting with him a few times, she encourages him to identify a family member who could play a positive role in his recovery if they understood his illness and his needs. She explains that he can choose what kinds of confidential information can be shared with the person or people he designates and whether he wants them invited to his treatment team meetings. She describes the special form her program has developed for releasing information to family members. He designates his parents and gives consent for her to tell them his diagnosis and medications.

Jane then asks if he has any objections to her meeting with his parents by themselves, at least initially, so they have a chance to get to know her and trust her, like he has. She discusses with him that the purpose of the initial meetings with his parents is to reduce their stress and worry, so things can be calmer at home. Upon hearing this, he consents to them meeting without him for one session.

Jane's first phone call to Andrew's parents reveals their sharp anger and mistrust toward practitioners. When Jane asks Mrs. Johnson if she would like to schedule a time when they can talk to her about any questions or concerns they have about Andrew and his illness, Mrs. Johnson's responds, "What, so you can tell us how we've screwed up our son? His first doctor did that, and that's the last thing I need. Just level with me. What's the real reason you want to talk to us?" Jane tries to empathize with Mrs. Johnson by saying, "If that's how you were treated, I can understand why you want to know what I'm up to. All I can tell you is that my purpose for this meeting is to be a resource for you, and for us to help each other to help Andrew get better." Mrs. Johnson interrupts by saying, "I thought you can't talk to us because of confidentiality. That's what I was told the last time I called the hospital." Jane explains that she got Andrew's permission to call and set up a time to talk to her and his father about their concerns. Mrs. Johnson seems to calm down and asks if Andrew will be at the meeting. Jane tells her that Andrew said they could meet without

AUTHORIZATION TO RELEASE CONFIDENTIAL INFORMATION TO FAMILY OR SIGNIFICANT OTHERS

RE: _____ DOB: _____ CLIENT #: _____

I hereby request and authorize {NAME OF AGENCY} to verbally release information regarding myself to the individuals listed below. I understand that the purpose of this release is to provide communication between my provider(s) at {NAME OF AGENCY} and the person(s) listed below. This information exchange is intended to aid and support my treatment.

I hereby request and authorize you to release the information indicated below to the following individuals:

Name: _____   Relationship: _____

Address: _____   Phone: (   ) _____

Name: _____   Relationship: _____

Address: _____   Phone: (   ) _____

You have my permission to *verbally* discuss the following information:

_____ Diagnosis   _____ Scheduled appointments
_____ Medications and side effect(s) _____ Treatment/Service plan
_____ Name of treatment program(s)   _____ Discharge plan
_____ Name of case manager   _____ Progress/obstacles to progress
_____ Name of therapist   _____ Other

_____ You have my permission to invite the above-named individual to participate in treatment team meetings. I understand that this gives my consent for the verbal release of information to the individual(s) listed above. This form will remain in effect for one year. I have been given a copy of this form:

Expiration date: _____   ❑ Accepted   ❑ Declined

Verbal authorization requires two (2) witness signatures.

_____ Verbal authorization given by consumer.

_____
Consumer's Signature   Date

_____
Legal Guardian's Signature   Date   _____
(if applicable)   Witness #1 Signature   Date

_____
Designated Provider   Date   _____
                                                  Witness #2 Signature   Date

THIS CONSENT MAY BE REVOKED AT ANY TIME IN WRITING.

_____ Release of information declined.   _____
                                                   Consumer's Signature
_____ Release of information revoked.   Date: _____

_____ Copy sent to designated family member.   Date: _____

_____ Review with client.   Date: _____

FIGURE 10.1

Sample Release Form Source: Copyright © 1999 Tina Marshall.

him, but asks what she would prefer. Mrs. Johnson explains that she and her husband are having a lot of disagreements, and she wishes they could talk without him present. She asks if everything they say will be shared with Andrew, and Jane explains that she will have to give Andrew a synopsis of the meeting, but not every detail. She also explains that he may wish to be present if they continue to meet. Mrs. Johnson then agrees to come in with her husband. However, when she hears that Jane only works during the day, she adamantly states that neither she nor her husband can take any more time off from work. Jane offers the option of a daytime conference call, which Mrs. Johnson accepts, and they agree on a phone appointment. Jane instructs Mrs. Johnson to talk with her husband and come up with a list of their biggest questions and concerns prior to their phone consultation. She also offers to talk directly to Mr. Johnson if he has any hesitations.

Having successfully met the initial challenges of joining with both Andrew and Mrs. Johnson despite the confidentiality laws, Mrs. Johnson's understandable mistrust of practitioners, and their conflicting schedules, Jane confronts another dilemma. During their phone consultation, Mr. and Mrs. Johnson frequently interrupt each other and make mutually blaming and hostile remarks toward one another as they try to present their questions and concerns, which primarily center on how they can help Andrew. Jane tries to normalize their anger by saying, "Having a child develop a mental illness can put the best of marriages to the test." Here she shifts to a teaching role by stating, "Let me make it clear that neither of you caused this illness. Schizoaffective disorder is a brain disorder. The good news is that you can learn ways to improve the course of this disorder. However, we can only work on one issue at a time, and the two of you may have to make some compromises." Mrs. Johnson laughs and replies, "We haven't been able to compromise since the day we were married. This problem goes back way before Andrew's problems started." Now that it is clear to Jane that this couple might have long-term relationship problems and could benefit from couples therapy, she knows she must be careful not to reinforce any guilt they may be feeling about Andrew's illness, as well as maintain a consultant role. Jane explains that addressing their top priority concern of how they can help Andrew will probably mean compromising on some house rules and avoiding arguments when Andrew is present.

She clarifies that she can try to serve as a mediator in their differences about dealing with Andrew, or she can refer them to an excellent couples therapist she knows who might be able to help them resolve their long-term difficulties in agreeing or compromising. She outlines the potential risks, costs, and benefits of both options. When they ask her what she recommends, she is relieved to hear she is earning their trust and respect. She deflects the decision back to them by saying, "I think both can be helpful to you and to Andrew. It's really a matter of which option you want to pursue right now." This phone consultation ends with the Johnsons thanking Jane for talking to them and telling her they will try to discuss it and come to a decision about what they want to do. She invites them to call her if and when she can be of any further assistance.

THE INTELLECTUAL BASE OF CONSUMER CONSULTATION

As compared to family consultation, consumer consultation is less formalized. Very little has been written describing this model. There is also no research base to determine the effectiveness of consumer consultation. This is due to a combination of factors. One reason is that it is a relatively recent understanding that mental health consumers have the capacity to function in partnership with practitioners. Second, consumer consultation is, by definition, unique to the given situation. Therefore, there is a lack of prescribed model programs. Third, there is limited empirical knowledge related to consumer-delivered services generally, including consumer partnerships (Solomon & Draine, 2000). Finally, due to the difficulty in applying the positivist approach to this type of evaluation, some debate exists as to the appropriate research paradigm with which to evaluate self-help generally, and consumer mental health models specifically (McLean, 1994; Tebes & Kraemer, 1991).

Although consumer consultation is a more recent phenomenon than family consultation, many social workers, especially those who are trained in group work, have been collaborating with consumers for years. These collaborative efforts emerged from the practice of psychosocial rehabilitation and stem from the same stress, coping, and adaptation theory as family consultation. Group workers in the mental health field played a major role in the development of psychosocial rehabilitation, or what today is often referred to as psychiatric rehabilitation, which is the theoretical underpinnings of consumer consultation.

Psychiatric rehabilitation is a "domain [that] fosters supports, skills, and desired environmental qualities that help individuals overcome both disability and handicap, and realize developmental outcomes consumers see as personally relevant and valuable" (Moxley, 1997, p. 620). Psychiatric rehabilitation is directed at not only the individual level of the client, but societal level as well, in terms of combating stigma and changing the environment to enhance the quality of life of mental health consumers (Anthony & Liberman, 1986; Flexer & Solomon, 1993). Thus, psychiatric rehabilitation, similar to clinical social work in the field of mental health generally, is directed at modifying the negative social consequences assigned by society to individuals with a severe psychiatric illness status (Moxley, 1997).

Psychiatric rehabilitation is a philosophy, a set of beliefs, and a process. The basic message of psychiatric rehabilitation is one of hope and positive expectations. It is also a belief that individuals with psychiatric disabilities have strengths that enable them to learn, grow and change, and engage in a process of recovery (Flexer & Solomon, 1993; Pratt, Gill, Barrett, & Robert, 1999). The initial efforts of psychosocial rehabilitation were innovative responses to building support networks and fighting isolation and societal stigma, which included the development of social clubs, clubhouses, and programs developed and run by former patients (Moxley, 1997). These consumer modalities require more collaborative efforts on the part of practitioners who work within these settings. One of the objectives of psychiatric rehabilitation is to empower mental health consumers by helping them to gain the resources and skills necessary to achieve increased independence from the mental health system. In this regard, consumer consultation is merely an extension of the psychiatric rehabilitation model.

Consumer Consultation

Consumer consultation is a process in which social workers and mental health consumers collaborate to address questions and concerns that are related to their illness and arise on an individual or societal level. In contrast to clinical services, such as supportive counseling, consumer consultation is not usually a part of the client's treatment process and does not include a treatment component. While supportive counseling captures the philosophy within the consultation model, this model is applied within a treatment setting. For example, in supportive counseling, practitioners partner with consumers in the development of their treatment plan and support network to help improve the consumer's quality of life by facilitating their increased independence. Additionally, social workers work together with consumers to monitor symptoms and manage medications in supportive counseling.

In consumer consultation, practitioners consult with consumers on an individual basis in a number of ways that are not related to the client's treatment, but are recovery-oriented. For example, mental health practitioners, including social workers, have worked in partnership with consumers to foster leadership within consumer-run groups, such as self-help or advocacy groups. Once leadership has emerged within a group, the practitioners often withdraw. In some instances, due to the instability of the group leadership, the practitioner may continue to facilitate the group. The consultant assists in helping the individuals to function in leadership roles for the maintenance of the group. The consultation is provided at the individual level, as opposed to being a group intervention. The consultant coaches the individual group member to help the member gain leadership skills (Kaufman, Freund, & Wilson, 1989). The degree and nature of the consultant involvement varies by the severity of the disabilities of the group member (Caldwell & White, 1991).

As consumers have increased their roles within the mental health system, supports are needed for consumers who are employed as providers (Mowbray, Moxley, Jasper, & Howell, 1997). Because consumer providers are functioning in a dual role, there is a need for supervision and coaching to negotiate what frequently are difficult situations that may entail role conflicts. A social worker in this role functions as a support person, and not a treating practitioner (Weklar & Parker, 1997). This is an accommodation that is offered outside of the formal supervisory structure, where the mental health practitioner is "someone who assists the consumer to focus on issues created by the job, and is a colleague who is prepared to serve as a sounding board, problem solver, and a front line supporter" (Mowbray et al., 1997). In some cases, where there are a number of consumers working as providers within a given agency, a support group may be formed. These groups are similar to alumni job clubs, which are psychiatric rehabilitation programs that offer mutual support and job adjustment for individuals with severe mental illness, that aim at increasing the chance of maintaining employment (Jacobs, 1988). An experienced mental health practitioner frequently facilitates these support groups. Given that social workers are trained in group processes, social workers are appropriate professionals to facilitate these groups.

On the macrolevel, practitioners may partner with consumer organizations to improve mental health services or raise public awareness regarding mental illness. Consumer consultation involves professionals, such as social workers, working in partnership with consumer organizations who offer their professional expertise for consumers to achieve their goals (e.g., Bentley, 2000). Given this broad definition, consumer consultation encompasses a wide range of professional activities. For example, consumer consultation may entail working with a consumer group to help develop a program, such as facilitating the development of a self-help group, a consumer business, or service. Consumer consultation may offer advice in service planning, strategic planning, or operational aspects of an organization, such as budgeting, staff development, and training. Consumer consultation helps to promote a consumer program to other professionals who may be reticent in accepting these programs and helps to write grant proposals. Finally, consumer consultations can provide or assist in conducting program evaluations. These activities are no different from the provision of services to any organization, group, or individual seeking professional consultation.

Social workers, such as chapter author Phyllis Solomon, have worked with consumer groups to design a consumer case management service and to evaluate the service (Solomon & Draine, 1995a, b). Similarly, Solomon worked with a consumer group to assist in writing a grant in response to a grant announcement from Substance Abuse Mental Health Services Administration and evaluating a consumer service entitled Friends Connection, which is a peer support service for individuals who are diagnosed as having both a mental illness and substance abuse disorder. In this era of managed care and cost containment, consumer groups recognize that conducting evaluations of their services to demonstrate effectiveness is essential to secure future funding for their service. There is a history of consumers and social workers partnering on evaluating agency practice in the psychosocial rehabilitation movement (Prager & Taraka, 1980; Smith, Brown, Gibbs, Sanders, & Cremer, 1984).

Given the skills and expertise of social workers (i.e., knowing community resources, group skills, resource negotiation skills), consumers are attracted to approach them for these collaborative activities. Furthermore, social workers' values of self-determination make them appealing partners to consumers. Social workers have the ability to "demonstrate good advocacy skills, teach strategies for effective communication, and coach clients through the maze of policies and procedures" (Tower, 1994, p. 195).

MAJOR GOALS AND TASKS

The overarching goal of consumer consultation is to meet the needs of consumers as defined by consumers, foster leadership and independence, and enhance consumers' quality of life. Similar to family consultation, the following tasks may be used to work toward this goal.

Task 1: Developing trust.   Consumer groups are often held together by a strong dedication to keeping the group consumer-run. Initially, consumers may be skeptical of practitioners' motives for collaborating. An essential component in developing trust is ensuring consumer partners of your intent to remain true to the group's mission.

Task 2: Defining objectives and setting an agenda.   Although a group may hire a consultant, they may not have clearly specified the issues in a way the consultant may begin to address them. Therefore, the second task for the consultant is to help the consultee identify the specific objectives to be achieved. After defining the objectives, the consultant may assist the client in prioritizing the activities necessary for achieving the objectives and setting an agenda.

Task 3: Clarifying your professional role.   Once an agenda has been set, the consultant may need to clarify the skills and expertise that they have to offer in achieving these objectives. In some cases, it may be appropriate to refer the consultee to other consultants who have the expertise needed to address their objectives.

TECHNIQUES, STRATEGIES, AND SKILLS

Consultation with consumer organizations is predicated on a knowledge base of psychiatric rehabilitation. Therefore, social workers who would like to provide consumer consultation, but do not have this knowledge, will need to acquire it. The skills needed for the role of consumer consultant are similar to those used as a family consultant. Empathic listening, described earlier under "Feelings," is essential in developing the trust needed in a collaborative relationship on the micro- or macrolevel. Depending on the nature of the consultation, it may be necessary to meet one-on-one, in dyads, or with a group or committee in the organization. Listening and showing respect for the consultee's experiences is crucial for developing the partnership that makes the consultative process successful.

In many instances, the consultant may need to speak to several members within an organization as a part of the consultation. Skills in negotiation and mediation are often important to facilitate agreement within the organization or group on the issues to be addressed during the consultative process. Depending on the size of the organization and the initial issues presented, the consultant may begin by conducting a preliminary needs assessment. For example, the consultant may gather information from individuals or small groups within the organization to assess the issues of concern and provide feedback to the group to assist them in defining their objectives and setting an agenda. The social work consultant may take a leadership role in facilitating a group process to define the objectives, or may provide individual consultation to the group leader to assist the group in defining objectives.

Once an agenda has been set, it may be necessary for the consultant to clarify their expertise and skills that may facilitate achieving the objectives. The consultee may hold preconceptions of the types of tasks that social workers perform. The social workers may need to educate the consultee regarding the training and expertise that they have to offer, as well as their limits. It is important to maintain the role as consultant and delineate boundaries before the activities begin. Depending on the activities outlined and the consultant's expertise, the consultant may assist the organization with strategic planning, budgeting, evaluation, grant writing, skills training, or other macrolevel social work activities.

UNIQUE CHALLENGES IN CONSUMER CONSULTATION

One challenge that social workers may face in providing consumer consultation is the challenge to remain within the role of consultant. It is easy for consultants who have the direct practice skills or have provided mental health treatment to fall into the role of a therapist while working one-on-one with consumers. While it is important for consultants to show respect and listen empathically to learn from the consultee's experience, consultants may need to clarify the focus of the consultation and their role for themselves and the consultee. Consultants need to take care so that they do not shift into a role of providing treatment. It is important to maintain a partnership relationship throughout the consultative process. The challenge for social workers is to empower and assist the consultee in acquiring the knowledge and skills needed to fulfill their objectives without the aid of a consultant.

Another challenge of consumer consultation arises when consultants work with consumer organizations or groups in which members hold diverse views or ideologies. Consultants may find fundamental splits within the organization that impede the organization's growth or progress. Consultants often rely heavily on negotiation and mediation skills to assist the group/organization in attaining shared objectives and a working agenda.

Another challenge for social workers in providing consumer consultation is a lack of funding. Consumer consultation is most often made possible by project-related grants. Consumer organizations or groups that have attained a grant to assist them in building an infrastructure or for a particular project often seek social work consultants. For example, a social worker may be brought in to help evaluate a training program or consumer-run service. Consumer consultation may also be incorporated into other community- or grant-supported projects, for which both parties share similar objectives. For example, a social worker may receive a seed grant to start a new program in the community and involve a consumer organization that may continue the program thereafter on an ongoing basis.

SUMMARY

Changes within the field of mental health are opening up many opportunities for consumers and their families to become involved in the treatment process, improve mental health services, and shape mental health policies. By fulfilling the role of family and consumer consultants, social workers may use skills directed on the micro- and macrolevel to support and further the current trend of collaboration.

KEY TERMS

Consultation: The process in which a party (the consultee) seeks the advice or opinion of another party (the consultant) for the purpose of clarifying a situation, reaching a decision, solving a problem, or accomplishing an objective (Marsh, 1998).

Family Education: Programs to educate families about their ill relative's mental illness and treatments for mental illness.

Family Therapy: The treatment of individual symptoms or relationship problems using relational interventions.

Feeling, Focusing, and Finding (3Fs): The major skills integral to providing family consultation.

Psychoeducation: Behavioral interventions for families frequently based on the theory of expressed emotion (EE).

Psychiatric Rehabilitation: A philosophy, a set of beliefs, and a process that fosters supports, skills, and environmental qualities that help individuals overcome both disability and handicap, and realize developmental outcomes that mental health consumers see as personally relevant and valuable (Moxley, 1997).

SMARTPRO: The mnemonic device that captures some of the possible roles of family consultation. SMARTPRO stands for Supporting, Mediating, Advocating, Referring to appropriate resources, Teaching/training, Problem solving, Receiving the family's valuable information, and Offering hope.

Stress, Coping, and Adaptation: The framework on which family and consumer consultation are based.

Supportive Counseling: A model applied within clinical settings in which practitioners partner with mental health consumers in the treatment process.

WEB RESOURCES

National Alliance for the Mentally Ill (http://www.nami.org). This Web site offers resource materials that social workers may use when working with families and consumers. Social workers may access lists of support and education groups for families and consumers nationwide.

National Mental Health Association (http://www.nmha.org). The information center on this Web site contains brochures, facts sheets, and other educational materials that social workers may share with consumers. Lists of support and education groups for consumers by state are also available.

Mental Health Net (http://www.cmhc.com). This Web site offers educational resources, including mental health glossaries and symptom lists by diagnosis. Online advice, such as "Ask the Doctor" and "Ask the Pharmacist," is also available.

Internet Mental Health (http://www.mentalhealth.com). Geared to practitioners, families, and consumers, this Web site offers educational resources with an international perspective on diagnosis, medications, and treatment.

World Schizophrenia Fellowship (http://www.origo.com/wsf). To receive more information about family consultation, social workers may obtain a copy of the World Schizophrenia Fellowship's conference report, "Family Interventions Work: Putting the Research Findings into Practice."

REFERENCES

Anderson, C., Reiss, D., & Hogarty, G. (1986). *Schizophrenia and the family.* New York: Guilford Press.

Anthony, W., & Liberman, R. (1986). The practice of psychiatric rehabilitation: Historical, conceptual, and research base. *Schizophrenia Bulletin, 12*(4), 542–559.

Bentley, K. J. (2000). Empowering our own: Peer leadership training for a drop-in center. *Psychiatric Rehabilitation Journal, 24*(2), 174–178.

Bogart, T., & Solomon, P. (1999). Procedures to share treatment information among mental health providers, consumers, and families. *Psychiatric Services, 50*(10), 1321–1325.

Budd, R., & Hughes, C. (1997). What do relatives of people with schizophrenia find helpful about family interventions? *Schizophrenia Bulletin, 23,* 341–347.

Caldwell, S., & White, K. (1991). Co-creating a self-help recovery movement. *Psychosocial Rehabilitation Journal, 15,* 92–95.

Compton, B., & Galaway, B. (1994). *Social work processes* (5th ed.). Pacific Grove, CA: Brooks/Cole.

Cook, J., Pickett, S., & Cohler, B. (1997). Families of adults with severe mental illness – The next generation of research: Introduction. *American Journal of Orthopsychiatry, 67*(2), 172–176.

Crotty, P., & Kulys, P. (1986). Are schizophrenics a burden to their families? Significant others' views. *Health and Social Work, 11,* 173–188.

Dixon, L., & Lehman, A. (1995). Family interventions for schizophrenia. *Schizophrenia Bulletin, 21*(4), 631–643.

Falloon, I., Boyd, J., & McGill, C. (1985). *Family care of schizophrenia.* New York: Guilford Press.

Flexer, R., & Solomon, P. (1993). *Psychiatric rehabilitation on practice.* Boston, MA: Andover Medical.

Hatfield, A. (1990). *Family education in mental illness.* New York: Guilford Press.

Hatfield, A., & Lefley, H. (1987). *Families of the mentally ill: Coping and adaptation.* New York: Guilford Press.

Hatfield, A., Spaniol, L., & Zipple, A. (1987). Expressed emotion: A family perspective. *Schizophrenia Bulletin, 13,* 221–226.

Herz, M. (1985). Prodromal symptoms and prevention of relapse in schizophrenia. *Journal of Clinical Psychiatry, 46,* 22–25.

Jacobs, H. (1988). Vocational rehabilitation. In R. Liberman (Ed.), *Psychiatric rehabilitation of chronic mental patients.* Washington, DC: American Psychiatric Association.

Kanter, J. (1985). Consulting with families of the chronically mentally ill. In J. Kanter (Ed.), *Clinical issues in treating the chronically mentally ill: New Directions for Mental Health Services,* pp. 21–32 (Vol. 27). San Francisco: Jossey-Bass.

Kaufman, C., Freund, P., & Wilson, J. (1989). Self-help in the mental health system: A model for consumer–provider collaboration. *Psychosocial Rehabilitation Journal, 13,* 5–21.

Lam, D. (1991). Psychosocial family intervention in schizophrenia: A review of empirical studies. *Psychological Medicine, 21,* 423–441.

Leff, J., Kuipers, L., & Berkowitz, R. (1982). Controlled trial of social interventions in the families of schizophrenic patients. *British Journal of Psychiatry, 141,* 121–134.

Mannion, E. (2000). *Training manual for the implementation of family education in the adult mental health system of Berks County, PA.* Philadelphia, PA: University of Pennsylvania Center for Mental Health Policy and Services Research.

Mannion, E., Draine, J., Solomon, P., & Meisel, M. (1997). Applying research on family education about mental illness to development of a relatives' group consultation model. *Community Mental Health Journal, 33*(6), 555–569.

Marsh, D. (1992). *Families and mental illness.* New York: Praeger.

Marsh, D. (1998). *The practitioner's guide for serious mental illness and the family.* New York: Wiley.

McLean, A. (1994). *The role of consumers in mental health services research and evaluation: A report and concept paper.* (Final contract report 92MF03814201D). Washington, DC: Substance Abuse Mental Health Services Administration.

Mintz, L., Liberman, R., Miklowitz, J., & Mintz, J. (1987). Expressed emotion: A call for partnership among relatives, patients, and professionals. *Schizophrenia Bulletin, 13,* 227–235.

Mowbray, C., Moxley, D., Jasper, C., & Howell, L. (1997). *Consumers as providers in psychiatric rehabilitation.* Columbia, MD: International Association of Psychosocial Rehabilitation.

Moxley, D. (1997). Clinical social work in psychiatric rehabilitation. In J. Brandell (Ed.), *Theory and practice in clinical social work.* New York: Free Press.

Potasznik, F., & Nelson, G. (1994). The burden experienced by the family of a mentally ill person. *American Journal of Community Psychology, 12,* 589–607.

Prager, E., & Taraka, H. (1980). Self-assessment: The client's perspective. *Social Work, 25,* 32–34.

Pratt, C., Gill, K., Barrett, M., & Robert, M. (1999). *Psychiatric rehabilitation.* San Diego: Academic Press.

Smith, M., Brown, D., Gibbs, L., Sanders, H., & Cremer, K. (1984). Client involvement in psychosocial rehabilitation. *Psychosocial Rehabilitation Journal, 8,* 35–43.

Solomon, P. (1996). Moving from psychoeducation to family education for families of adults with serious mental illness. *Psychiatric Services, 47*(12), 1364–1370.

Solomon, P., & Draine, J. (1995a). Adaptive coping among family members of persons with serious mental illness. *Psychiatric Services, 46*(11), 1156–1160.

Solomon, P., & Draine, J. (1995b). Subjective burden among family members of mentally ill adults: Relation to stress, coping, and adaptation. *American Journal of Orthopsychiatry, 65*(3), 419–427.

Solomon, P., & Draine, J. (2000). *The state of knowledge of the effectiveness of consumer provided services.* Unpublished report, University of Pennsylvania, School of Social Work.

Solomon, P., Draine, J., Mannion, E., & Meisel, M. (1996a). Impact of brief family psychoeducation on self-efficacy. *Schizophrenia Bulletin, 22*(1), 41–50.

Solomon, P., Draine, J., Mannion, E., & Meisel, M. (1996b). The impact of individualized consultation and group workshop family education interventions on ill relative outcomes. *The Journal of Nervous and Mental Disease, 184*(1), 252–254.

Solomon, P., Draine, J., Mannion, E., & Meisel, M. (1997). Effectiveness of two models of brief family education: Retention of gains by family members of adults with serious mental illness. *American Journal of Orthopsychiatry, 67*(2), 177–186.

Spaniol, L., Zipple, A., & Lockwood, D. (1992). The role of the family in psychiatric rehabilitation. *Schizophrenia Bulletin, 18*(3), 341–347.

Stroul, B. (1993). Rehabilitation in community support systems. In P. Flexer & P. Solomon (Eds.), *Psychiatric rehabilitation in practice.* Boston: Andover Medical.

Tebes, J., & Kraemer, D. (1991). Quantitative and qualitative knowledge in mutual support research: Some lessons from the recent history of scientific psychology. *American Journal of Community Psychology, 19,* 739–756.

Terkelsen, K. (1990). A historical perspective on family-provider relationships. In H. Lefley & D. Johnson (Eds.), *Families as allies in the treatment of the mentally ill.* Washington, DC: American Psychiatric Press.

Torrey, E. F. (1995) *Surviving schizophrenia: A family manual* (3rd ed.). New York: Harper Perennial.

Tower, K. (1994). Consumer-centered social work practice: Restoring client self-determination. *Social Work, 39,* 191–196.

Weklar, E., & Parker, K. (1997). Supporting a consumer employee inside the agency. In C. Mowbray, D. Moxley, C. Jasper, & L. Howell (Eds.), *Consumers as providers in psychiatric rehabilitation* (pp. 387–396). Columbia, MD: International Association of Psychosocial Rehabilitation.

SOCIAL WORKERS AS COLLABORATORS ON INTERAGENCY AND INTERDISCIPLINARY TEAMS

Roberta G. Sands
& Beth Angell

A method that cuts across all fields of practice (Graham & Barter, 1999), collaboration is particularly relevant to social work practice in mental health, where intervention on behalf of a single mental health client often involves numerous professions, agencies, and groups. Social workers, who function in the relational sphere at the intersection between the person and the environment, interact with members of these constituencies in shared activities and partnerships. This chapter describes concepts, theories, tasks, strategies, and models associated with social workers' collaborative roles on interagency and interdisciplinary teams. As the literature that is cited indicates, social workers have made a substantial contribution to the intellectual foundation of this area.

INTELLECTUAL BASIS FOR PRACTICE

Collaboration

Collaboration is a process in which two or more diverse participants work together toward the achievement of common goals (Abramson & Rosenthal, 1995). The parties to this process pool their knowledge, resources, and ideas so that they can realize collectively what they cannot achieve individually (Graham & Barter, 1999). To succeed, those who collaborate need to develop interpersonal relationships characterized by trust (Akhavain, Amaral, Murphy, & Uehlinger, 1999) and a common vision of what is in the best interest of clients (Abramson & Rosenthal, 1995).

Collaboration has become crucial to the provision of quality mental health treatment, with increased fragmentation of the human service delivery system, a lack of coordination and accountability, and a discontinuity in client care (Paulson, 1993). The need for collaboration among providers of care has spawned concepts like *service integration*, comprehensive sites like *multiservice centers*, interagency efforts like *consortia*, and work roles like *case manager*. These approaches, along with interdisciplinary collaboration, are means to offer comprehensive, integrated care across service and professional boundaries.

As suggested, there are various kinds of collaboration. In the field of mental health, collaboration commonly occurs among agencies, members of different professions or disciplines, between professionals and mental health consumers, and between professionals and families. This chapter addresses interagency and interdisciplinary collaboration, but indicates where client consumers and family members participate or might participate in these processes. Chapter 10 ("Social Workers as Consumer and Family Consultants") focuses more on collaboration between professionals and consumers and families.

Collaboration may be informal or formal. Informal collaboration occurs when members of two or more entities confer on an irregular or occasional basis, usually in response to a particular need or in the interest of promoting quality care (Germain, 1984). Formal collaboration occurs when there is a structure and communication "in a planned or regular way" (Germain, 1984, p. 199). Interagency and interdisciplinary teams develop structures, like team meetings, in which groups of professionals and other relevant parties collaborate regarding clients. We turn next to interagency collaboration, which may be formal or informal.

Interagency Collaboration

Interagency collaboration refers to purposeful joint activity among separate human service agencies, usually in a particular geographic area. Agencies serving the same or similar clients have found it useful to discuss common problems, coordinate their efforts, determine which agency can best serve particular clients, and make decisions around service delivery. These activities may occur on administrative and direct service levels.

Interagency collaboration is predicated on the idea that a single agency cannot meet the needs of all clients (Swan & Morgan, 1993), but a cluster of agencies that integrate their services can. For example, agencies can collaborate over how and where they can serve clients who have multiple problems, especially those who are homeless, addicted, severely mentally ill, and in the criminal justice system. Collaboration can help eliminate structural barriers between systems and address differences in treatment philosophies across programs (Ridgely, Lambert, Goodman, Chichester, & Ralph, 1998). The agencies are viewed as complementary rather than as competitors (Graham & Barter, 1999; Swan & Morgan, 1993).

Increased privatization, specialization of services, and decentralization, as well as the emergence of complex social problems, have made collaboration between agencies desirable (Abramson & Rosenthal, 1995). Considering that human problems often span the domains of specific agencies, working collaboratively may be more expedient and cost-effective than working within the confines of a single agency (Graham & Barter, 1999). In mental health, collaboration facilitates responsiveness to consumer needs, which should forestall practitioner burnout (Paulson, 1993).

Interagency activity involves cooperation, coordination, and collaboration. These three processes can be viewed as hierarchical, with interagency cooperation calling for the lowest level, interagency coordination a middle level, and interagency collaboration the highest level of interaction (Swan & Morgan, 1993). *Interagency cooperation* is an informal means of working together, in which autonomous agencies share information about their activities and make referrals to each other (Swan & Morgan, 1993). For example, when a client is admitted to an inpatient psychiatric unit, a social worker on the unit might contact a community mental health center to request the client's case record; subsequently, he or she might refer the client to this same agency upon discharge. The middle level, interagency coordination, is a more formal process, in which agencies interact around the nature of each agency's function and how the various agencies fit together as a whole (Swan & Morgan, 1993). Agencies make adjustments when communication associated with interagency coordination reveals duplication or gaps in services, or a need for procedures that will foster joint planning (Swan & Morgan, 1993). An example on the administrative level is when a children's mental health program arranges to have children participate in partial hospitalization on some days and after-school activities on other days. Interagency collaboration involves a greater commitment of constituent agencies to planning, problem solving, and joint activity than the other two approaches. United around a common goal, the agencies invest more of their resources (including personnel, time, funds, and facilities), work as a team, view their interests as mutual, and integrate their ideas and activities (Swan & Morgan, 1993). For example, agencies may have a formal arrangement in which school social workers, drug and alcohol counselors, juvenile officers, and family therapists collaborate on a common service plan for children with severe emotional disturbances.

An understanding of interagency collaboration requires attention to the constraints and opportunities that agencies face and recognition of the political realities that affect organizational life (Paulson, 1993). Because agencies are interested in preserving themselves and furthering their self-interests, they are motivated by financial and other incentives to collaboration (Paulson, 1993). They need to see that working together will benefit them and clients, and will help them enhance their resources (Beatrice, 1990). Interagency collaboration works best when agencies agree upon and are committed to common goals that fit in with their separate missions (Abramson & Rosenthal, 1995; Beatrice, 1990; Graham & Barter, 1999). Furthermore, it entails a political process in which participants negotiate and bargain among themselves and with funding sources (Graham & Barter, 1999; Paulson, 1993).

Social workers practicing in the field of mental health collaborate, individually or as part of an interagency team, with individuals representing a variety of agencies, organizations, or systems. The particular agency or system is dependent on the client's age and life stage, the services available in the community, and the willingness of these agencies to collaborate. The following is a description of some agencies, programs, and systems with which a mental health social worker might collaborate.

Substance Abuse Treatment Programs

Psychiatric and substance abuse problems frequently co-occur in adolescents and adults. Because mental health and substance abuse programs often operate under different administrative and financial auspices, collaboration is a particular challenge. Moreover, turf battles stemming from differences in philosophy may take place. Intentional development of collaborative working groups may help resolve these tensions and improve continuity of care between these two systems (Ridgely et al., 1998).

Criminal Justice System

Because mental health problems can be associated with criminal behavior, mental health social workers will inevitably come into contact with police, corrections officers, probation and parole officers, and, in work with children and adolescents, the juvenile justice system. At times, interactions with the justice system involve advocating on a client's behalf. On other occasions, the interactions are more fully collaborative, as when case managers and probation and parole officers monitor a mentally ill offender released from jail.

Developmental Disabilities/Mental Retardation System

Interagency teams for children with severe emotional disorders sometimes include providers in the field of developmental disabilities. Also, some adults receiving mental health treatment have developmental disabilities in addition to a psychiatric diagnosis. Because the mental health and developmental disabilities systems are administratively and financially distinct, care for individuals dually diagnosed with mental illness and developmental disabilities is often fragmented, pointing to the need for networking, collaborating, and the development of multisystem services such as specialized residential facilities for this population (Woodward, 1993).

Child Welfare

Another system involved in interagency collaboration is the child welfare (or child protection) system. The county child welfare agency may become involved when children and adolescents with severe emotional disorders need placement in a residential or in-home treatment program. In addition, child welfare agencies sometimes monitor parenting provided by women with serious mental illness who have children. These mothers are at risk of having their children removed to foster care or homes provided by relatives because of neglect, incapacity, unsuitable housing, and/or substance abuse (Sands, 1995; Zemencuk, Rogosch, & Mowbray, 1995). In such cases, collaboration may involve planning for visiting, reunification, or termination of parental rights, in some instances.

Primary Care

Although the majority of individuals with psychiatric disorders receive no mental health services (Kessler et al., 1994), the professionals they are most likely to see are primary care providers (Morlock, 1989). Even when clients receive specialty mental health services, their contacts with primary care serve as a critical entry point. Collaboration between mental health professionals and primary care providers—whether through consultation, a primary care provider's referral to mental health services, or the activities of a formalized interagency team—can improve the quality of mental health services provided to primary care patients. Alternatively, mental health providers may refer clients to primary care physicians for the evaluation and treatment of a physical problem. In working with clients with severe mental illness, social workers may act as "culture brokers" (Schwab, Drake, & Burghardt, 1988), advocates and interpreters for their clients in the primary care setting. For example, a social worker might accompany a woman with a prior history of sexual abuse to a gynecological examination to support her, advocate for sensitive treatment during the examination, and help her understand medical terminology.

Religious Institutions

Like primary care providers, clergy often play a key role in the recognition of mental health problems and subsequent referral to mental health services. Although most clergy are not trained to deal with major mental health problems, they constitute an underutilized resource to social workers because they may know a client well and have an established rapport with the person. Furthermore, churches and other religious organizations offer support and spiritual help to mental health clients and their families. Some religious institutions sponsor or provide space for services to clients.

Schools

Mental health problems in youth are often manifested in school performance or behavior. Thus, social workers and other mental health providers often work closely with teachers, principals, psychologists, social workers, and counselors in the school setting. In some service models, case management teams for a particular child include representatives from the school, ensuring the comprehensiveness and continuity of service (Santarcangelo, Birkett, & McGrath, 1995). In others, school systems actually administer their own mental health programs (Hannah & Nichol, 1996).

A Continuum of Mental Health Care

Clients often move from one mental health program to another, depending on the level of care that they need. Within the field of mental health, they can use a wide range of service modalities and settings, such as inpatient psychiatric units (both long-term and acute); partial hospitalization programs; outpatient mental health clinics offering medication services, individual therapy, and group therapy; case management units and teams; psychosocial rehabilitation programs; supported residential services; and consumer-operated self-help programs. To facilitate this process and avoid duplication, interagency cooperation, coordination, and collaboration are common among practitioners in these specifically mental health settings.

These are some of the agencies with which social workers in mental health agencies are likely to collaborate. Others include legal aid agencies, preschool and afterschool programs, senior citizen programs, and public welfare agencies. These interagency collaborations may also be interdisciplinary and take the form of a team.

We turn next to the related topic of interdisciplinary team collaboration. Much of what is presented below on interdisciplinary team collaboration also applies to inter-agency team collaboration, except that in the latter, the political context and financial incentives loom into prominence (Paulson, 1993).

Interdisciplinary Team Collaboration

The expansion of knowledge and technology, the identification of complex human needs, and an increasing division of labor in health and human service institutions have necessitated the development of specialized professions (Nagi, 1975). Although these professions have carved out their own areas of expertise, they have found it fruitful to work collaboratively with members of other professions (or disciplines).

Interdisciplinary collaboration frequently occurs in structured mental health teams. When they work, their interactions "can have synergistic effects in generating new and creative solutions to clients' needs" (Toseland, Palmer-Ganeles, & Chapman, 1986, p. 46). Teams also contribute to staff satisfaction and learning (Toseland et al., 1986), reduce individual burden and burnout (Diamond, 1996), and break down divisive interprofessional boundaries (Rawson, 1994). As a means of accountability and quality assurance (Fargason & Haddock, 1992), interdisciplinary teams also can benefit organizations and managed care entities (Olsen, Rickles, & Travlik, 1995; Thomas & Hargett, 1999). When they involve clients and families, they make it possible for client systems to become active participants rather than passive recipients of care (Thomas & Hargett, 1999).

Interdisciplinary teams are organized groups of specialists who work interdependently with or on behalf of the same clients. Team members have "a common purpose, separate skills or professional contributions, and some process of communication, coordination, cooperation, or joint thinking" (Kane, 1983, p. 5). Some insight into teams may be gained by examining how they function in the realm of sports. The baseball team, for example, is composed of nine players, each of whom has a specialized role (e.g., pitcher, first base) and a shared role (batter). The team operates as a coordinated unit and is collectively responsible for the outcome of the game. Members are expected to play by the rules and are morally bound not to let the team down. "Team players" are "willing to subordinate personal needs and goals to those of the team" (Yank, Barber, Hargrove, & Whitt, 1992, p. 260). The team has a coach (cf. leader) who promotes cohesion in the team and, if necessary, will discipline players. As with interagency collaboration, interdisciplinary team collaboration varies in the extent to which participants interact as a unit. At the low end is *multidisciplinary* collaboration, which involves cooperation, communication, and conferring on a regular basis, with participants maintaining their discrete roles. Multidisciplinary teams are organized around specialized functions (disciplines) and are hierarchical (Germain, 1984), such as when a psychiatrist is the team leader. In the middle one finds *interdisciplinary* collaboration, in which team members share perspectives and skills, engage in joint problem solving, and are mutually responsible and accountable. Interdisciplinary teams are organized around client needs rather than members' functions and tend to be nonhierarchical (Germain, 1984).

At the highest end is *transdisciplinary* collaboration, in which members move beyond their disciplinary orientations, engage in collective thinking, and integrate their perspectives. When teams are transdisciplinary, professional boundaries become blurred, with members of different disciplines assuming each other's roles or perspectives. In practice, the terms *multidisciplinary* and *interdisciplinary* are often used interchangeably, and *transdisciplinary* is not used much. Ethnographic research on interdisciplinary teams has demonstrated that, rather than three discrete types of team collaboration, these are positions to which the same team may shift from time to time, depending on the interactional context (McClelland & Sands, 2001). Furthermore, some settings are conducive to interdisciplinary or transdisciplinary, whereas others favor multidisciplinary collaboration. Another limitation on the degree of collaboration is licensure, which outlines the boundaries of each profession's domain.

Mental health teams are comprised of members of diverse disciplines or professions, as well as others whose expertise is role-related (e.g., consumers). Members of mental health professions have some common knowledge, for most have had academic exposure to the liberal arts, social sciences, and natural sciences, as well as practice experience in the field of mental health. Different disciplines, however, have different ways of thinking, use different methods of evaluation and intervention, and are socialized differently. Petrie (1976) used the term *cognitive map* to depict such differences:

> By cognitive map here I mean the whole cognitive and perceptual apparatus utilized by any given discipline. This includes, but is not limited to, basic concepts, modes of inquiry, what counts as a problem, observational categories, representation techniques, standards of proof, types of explanation, and general ideals of what constitutes the discipline. Perhaps the most striking of these, and also often the least noted, is the extent to which disciplinary categories of observation are theory and discipline relative. Quite literally, two opposing disciplinarians can look at the same thing and not see the same thing. . . . (p. 35)

Because professionals are socialized to acquire their own cognitive map, they tend to overestimate the contributions of their own discipline (Koeske, Koeske, & Mallinger, 1993), and think that its perception is the perception (Sands, Stafford, & McClelland, 1990).

One is likely to find the following professions represented on mental health teams.

Social Work

Education and training in the field of social work emphasizes ecological and systems perspectives on social problems. Thus, social workers have a unique perspective on the social and familial context of mental health problems, and are uniquely suited to advocate for and link with other systems in which clients are involved, such as child welfare and criminal justice. In many settings on which they serve as a team member, particularly hospitals, social workers may perform the assessment of a client's psychosocial functioning and social supports. On community treatment teams, social workers often serve as generalists, performing assessment, case management, service delivery, and monitoring services. In other mental health settings, they may conduct a range of individual, family, and group interventions.

Psychiatry

In mental health settings, psychiatrists specialize in psychiatric and medical assessment, and the prescription and medical monitoring of psychiatric medications. Some of them also practice psychotherapy. Some psychiatrists' responsibilities on treatment teams are limited to pharmacotherapy, operating in relative isolation from the rest of the team. However, others collaborate in a more interdisciplinary or transdisciplinary manner, participating in psychosocial assessment and service provision and eliciting participation from nonphysicians into pharmacological decision making and monitoring (Diamond, 1996; Knoedler, 1989). In some, but not all, settings, psychiatrists serve as team leaders because of their medical responsibility for clients.

Psychiatric Nursing

Compared to other professional disciplines in the biomedical field, training in nursing is more holistic and less exclusively focused in the biological domain. As members of mental health teams, psychiatric nurses play a key role in the administration and monitoring of medication. Nurses are also especially skilled in acting as a client's liaison to primary medical care, providing an interpretive link between clients and health care providers, and educating clients in the areas of health prevention and maintenance (Allness & Knoedler, 1998). Because of their broad psychosocial orientation, however, nurses also perform many of the same tasks as social workers: assessment, care planning, referral, follow-up, case management, and advocacy (Hawkins, Veeder, & Pearce, 1998), though they may execute them differently from a social worker because of divergent training, cognitive maps, and professional socialization. Consequently, social workers and nurses may be required to pay special attention to their unique strengths in resolving conflicts over the appropriate division of responsibilities in client care (Hawkins, Veeder, & Pearce, 1998).

Clinical Psychology

Training in clinical psychology emphasizes mechanisms within individuals that produce abnormal thinking, feeling, and behavior, including the genetic, biochemical, and sociocultural underpinnings of these abnormalities (Peterson, 1999). The work of clinical psychology focuses on prevention or correction of these abnormalities. Because graduate education in psychology involves rigorous training in psychological, cognitive, and behavioral assessment, psychologists are especially suited to the tasks of assessment and standardized testing when serving on an interdisciplinary team. They are also skilled in the provision of cognitive behavioral interventions. Nonetheless, psychologists also operate in an interdisciplinary manner on treatment teams, sharing responsibility for assessment and cognitive behavioral interventions with other team members, and performing the more generalist roles of coordinator, case manager, and advocate.

Counseling Psychology

In contrast to clinical psychology, counseling psychology draws primarily from a knowledge base of normal development. The work of counseling psychologists in mental health settings focuses on restoring optimal psychosocial functioning through the development of coping skills (Hershenson & Power, 1987). The work of counseling psychologists is often focused in educational settings such as schools and institutions of higher education.

Rehabilitation Counseling and Rehabilitation Psychology

The field of rehabilitation psychology involves the application of principles of psychology to the understanding of the needs of people with physical, mental, and emotional disabilities. In mental health settings, rehabilitation counselors and psychologists act as individual and group counselors, case managers, advocates, and job development and placement specialists to bring about improved functioning in the areas of education, employment, and the social aspects of life. On treatment teams, they may act as generalists, performing many of the same tasks as social workers, but often serve a special role in vocational development (Allness & Knoedler, 1998).

Occupational Therapy

Occupational therapists engage clients with physical, psychosocial, developmental, and cognitive disabilities in purposeful, goal-directed activities (such as working, engaging in recreation, and carrying out daily routines), which are performed for therapeutic purposes (Punwar, 1994). Occupational therapists and occupational therapy assistants understand physical and psychosocial disorders and generalist skills for assessing and treating an array of client populations. These professionals are most frequently members of treatment teams in inpatient and partial hospital settings, but are increasingly present in community settings such as schools and residential care facilities. Typical tasks for occupational therapists in these settings include assessment and treatment planning in the areas of activities of daily living performance, specialized equipment and accommodation, and cognitive/perceptual functioning. For example, an occupational therapist might help a depressed client with concomitant cognitive impairment to develop a personal organizational system (e.g., checklist, color-coded cleaning products) to enable him or her to carry out household tasks independently.

Creative Arts Therapy

Creative arts therapies include art, music, drama, and dance, and are common treatment components in inpatient and partial hospitalization settings. Creative arts therapists receive intensive training in the use of a selected creative art medium in a therapeutic context, and are certified by the appropriate parent association (e.g., the Art Therapy Credentials Board). Creative arts therapists work on treatment teams in inpatient hospitals, outpatient clinics, day treatment programs, alcohol and drug programs, nursing homes, correctional institutions, schools, and residential facilities, using creative media to effect positive changes in psychological and social functioning. For example, painting might provide an opportunity for a client with a history of post-traumatic stress disorder to symbolize and express feelings otherwise nonverbalized regarding experiences of abuse or trauma.

Other Members

Besides the professionals that have been described, representatives of other constituencies often participate in interdisciplinary teams. Their membership is a function of their roles. In recent years, mental health treatment teams have begun to include *consumers* as team members. Because of their own experiences with mental health problems and treatments, consumers possess a unique perspective that can serve to facilitate rapport, empathy with clients, and specialized knowledge regarding management and survival strategies. Similarly, family members may participate in teamwork, especially in systems of care for children, as case managers, collaborators in assessment and care planning, and advocates.

Mental health *paraprofessionals* or technicians may hold a high school degree or have a 2-year associate's degree that may or may not involve specialized training in mental health. Common settings in which paraprofessionals are employed include inpatient settings, community mental health settings, and residential programs. On some teams, paraprofessionals perform a generalist role, which may be limited to the performance of routine tasks (Hershenson & Power, 1987), but on other teams they participate fully in assessment and direct service provision (Allness & Knoedler, 1998). In many settings, paraprofessionals have more face-to-face contact with clients than professionals do.

In community mental health programs, *clerical staff* represent a rarely acknowledged front line of service delivery. Their interactions with clients on the phone and in person serve a triage function between the client and the mental health team members, and may influence decisions to engage in and remain in treatment. In some programs, clerical staff actually provide services themselves, including financial management, distribution of prepackaged medications, assessing and reporting to staff the client's clinical behaviors and information, and communication with the client's family, landlord, guardians, and other informal supports (Allness & Knoedler, 1998; Stein & Santos, 1998).

Although each of the disciplines and roles that have been described has its own area of expertise, when they come together as a team, they become another entity. The next section will describe some theoretical perspectives that illuminate teams as they function in interdisciplinary and interagency collaborative activities.

Theoretical Perspectives on Interdisciplinary and Interagency Teams

A number of theories used to understand the workings of interdisciplinary teams also apply to interagency teams that hold collaborative case conferences. Some of the early writing on interdisciplinary teams within social work (e.g., Kane, 1975, 1983) and other disciplines (Ducanis & Golin, 1979; Sampson & Marthas, 1990) used *small group theory* (group dynamics) to describe teams. These authors discussed group size, roles, power, leadership, and reference groups; examined the development of group norms and the way in which teams made decisions; and considered communication and conflict management by the team. Common themes from this perspective are that teams value cooperation and democratic processes and often make decisions based on consensus (Kane, 1975; Mailick & Ashley, 1981).

Small group theory on interdisciplinary teams describes a series of developmental stages the team passes through over time (Lowe & Herranen, 1981b; Sampson & Marthas, 1990). In the beginning, team members define the purpose of the group and are concerned with their own place in it. Later they develop subgroups and have some conflict between groups. At some point, the group experiences a crisis and conflict is addressed openly. After the crisis is resolved, the team becomes more cohesive, there is wider participation, and decisions are made consensually. These stages are commonly described as forming, storming, norming, performing, and adjourning (Llewelyn & Fielding, 1982; Sampson & Marthas, 1990). In practice it is difficult to identify stages like these because team membership changes over time and new members are at different stages in becoming part of the team. Furthermore, one is not likely to find this kind of development in interagency teams in which participants do not collaborate with each other on a regular basis.

Another theoretical perspective applicable to interdisciplinary and interagency teams is *systems theory* (Akhavain et al., 1999; Ducanis & Golin, 1979). This perspective views the team as a social system that is comprised of subsystems (disciplines or agencies) and is part of a suprasystem (e.g., a mental health center or human service delivery system) that is part of larger suprasystems. Roles within systems are differentiated by function (e.g., member, leader) and specialization (e.g., social work or psychiatry, school or child welfare agency) (cf. Anderson & Carter, 1984). Team members interact with each other in a network in which participants influence and are influenced by each other, client systems (which may include families and consumer groups), the organization, and other external systems. Systems evolve over time, employ control mechanisms, and are hierarchical (Anderson & Carter, 1984). Because the whole (i.e., the team) is considered greater than the sum of its parts, the team has the potential of doing more as a group than they are able to do as separate entities.

Another framework for viewing teams is *constructionist* (McClelland & Sands, 2001). According to this perspective, team members create meaning through a process of social interaction. Team members obtain information from direct interactions with clients and client systems, from using tools of their own discipline or agency, and from their own observations. When the team discusses this information as a group, participants negotiate about what the data mean, consistencies and inconsistencies among reports, and which parts are relevant. Using multiple informants and data sources in such group discussions, teams cooperate "to sustain a particular definition of the situation" (Goffman, 1959, p. 85). The view that the team's decision is a social construction of reality "challenges the rationalist view that patient problems are objective and exist separately from the interpretive actions of the team" (Crepeau, 1994, p. 719).

The language the team uses in this constructionist process derives from the mental health field, specific disciplines, clients and their families, and the larger culture. For example, the team's mental health assessment may incorporate a *DSM-IV* diagnosis, an evaluation of strengths, identification of antecedents, behaviors, and consequences, statements about what the client wants, and a determination of the client's needs. A *DSM-IV* diagnosis is constructed from clusters of behaviors or emotions that are constructed as symptoms of a specific psychiatric disorder. The team uses such constructions of reality when it makes decisions. A constructionist perspective recognizes that social constructions are linked with power within and outside the team. Some teams may, for example, defer to the psychiatrist in what it accepts as its group decision.

Barriers to Team Collaboration

As stated earlier, the presence of a diversely constituted mental health team can create a synergy that produces innovative problem solving. The product of the team's collaboration exceeds the capacity of a single professional to help an individual client. The input of differently trained professionals and agencies with diverse functions can create a holistic picture of a client's functioning from various perspectives and facilitate integrated intervention. Nevertheless, professionals whose values, worldviews, and foci are different can clash with each other.

In mental health settings, where many different types of professionals are called therapists or case managers, conflicts can emerge between different professionals performing a task that one professional believes he or she owns. Even though the ideal situation is one in which the focus is on client needs rather than what the provider is trained to do (Hawkins, Veeder, & Pearce, 1998), professionals are vulnerable to feeling displaced when someone else does what they believe is in their province. Social workers and nurses, who have similar roles on teams, are subject to experiencing such turf conflicts (Lowe & Herranen, 1981a). Social workers may also clash with other professionals on value-related issues. A residential placement decision for a client with serious mental illness can become a contested debate on interdisciplinary teams, for example, if a client living in a group home desires to move to an independent living arrangement. While a social worker might favor the client's choice, viewing the client's right to self-determination as preeminent, other professionals such as psychiatrists might cite concerns about the lack of supervision and the potential for a decline in medication compliance. Although both professionals share a commitment to doing what is best for the client, value conflicts such as these, which are related to professional socialization, can obstruct decision making and must be negotiated within the team.

Interagency teams may conflict with each other because the cultures of their agencies and their constituencies are not compatible. This can result in different visions of what is in the best interest of clients and who can best serve them. A further source of difficulty may be covert. Although it is best that agencies coordinate their services and eliminate overlap, they may be competing with each other for the same funds. Social workers who participate in interagency case conferences may not be aware of such underlying politics until they are played out in the way decisions are made about the care of particular clients.

Because mental health settings are affected by values from the larger society, sexism and racism may operate within teams (Leiba, 1994). The mental health field and many mental health settings are dominated by white male psychiatrists, who have more authority and status than other mental health professionals have. Women and people of color, who are prevalent in nurturing professions like social work and nursing, may feel undervalued and unempowered. Care needs to be taken so that teams do not replicate social inequality and oppression in their interactions with each other and, in particular, their assessments with clients. Sexist and racist constructions of dysfunctioning should not be imposed on women and members of minority racial and cultural groups (Leiba, 1994). Likewise, heterosexist and "ablist" constructions do not have a place in teamwork.

MAJOR TASKS AND GOALS

The tasks and goals of social work participation in interdisciplinary and interagency team collaboration are a function of the purpose of the collaboration and the function of the particular team. In mental health practice settings, teams meet *about* clients and *with* clients. Some teams have formal meetings on a daily basis, while others meet weekly or when there is a need for discharge planning. Although some teams consist only of professionals who work with the same clients directly, others include team members who are only peripherally involved with the client. Interagency teams that confer about clients also differ. Some participating agencies may be local whereas others may be from different parts of the state.

The following description of tasks and goals are generic to a range of teams, settings, and agencies within the mental health field. The goals that will be outlined are common to teams as collectivities. Although diverse team members may engage in common tasks associated with meeting these goals, the focus here will be on goals of the social worker on the team.

Goal 1: Assessment

Social workers usually contribute their own professional assessments to the team. The activities social workers perform to meet this goal are to gather and make sense of information about clients, their psychosocial functioning, and situations, and gather the resources needed to help them enhance their functioning. Their first task, then, is to determine what kind of psychosocial information needs to be collected and from whom. If a face-to-face meeting has not occurred, the social worker can gain some insight into how to proceed by reviewing preliminary information that is in the case record or referral sheet. This data may include the reason for and source of the referral, sociodemographic data, and the living situation. Another influence on how social workers proceed is their role on the particular team. In some mental health settings, focus of social workers is comprehensive; in other settings their assessment is limited to the family or household situation and community resources.

To assess the external situation, the social worker needs to obtain the client's permission to contact individuals or agencies that provide significant support to the client. This includes family members or caregivers, counselors at treatment programs, teachers, or other providers of care. The social worker obtains concise information about the client's functioning from some of these people and asks others (e.g., family members) to participate in an interview. Interviews will be about the client's psychosocial history and functioning, others' interactions with the clients, the kind of support these individuals provide, stressors in the client's situation, and strengths in the client's system of support.

Before sharing this information with the team, the social worker needs to evaluate the extent to which social and environmental conditions promote the client's functioning and/or foster difficulties. These conditions include the client's system of supports and the individual's dependence on others; living environment and economic resources; culture; and spiritual needs and resources. The social worker should also identify coping strategies used by the client and others and their effectiveness in dealing with everyday problems and crises.

Goal 2: Treatment and Discharge Planning

As with the assessment, the social worker contributes to the team's treatment planning. If the setting is a psychiatric hospital or unit, the social worker will be involved in discharge planning, which can begin soon after the client is admitted. Not unusually, the social worker assumes the role of team coordinator or leader in this process. Using assessment information (e.g., the client's needs for services, housing, financial resources, psychiatric care, and emotional support upon discharge), the social worker comes up with a plan that balances needs with available services. In team settings, the social worker's plan must be integrated with the plans of others. Consistencies and inconsistencies across professional assessments are considered. Collaborative treatment planning takes into account information provided by multiple participants and their assessment of the client's ability to benefit from various programs of care. Generally, the team decides to pursue some of the suggestions that are offered and documents its plan. When the team is an interagency one, the participants determine what the client needs, which agency is best able to provide this service, and how relevant agencies will collaborate in their provision of care.

Goal 3: Implementation of an Integrated Treatment Plan

Social workers who occupy the role of case manager assure that the plan the team develops collaboratively is implemented and integrated. There is a need to coordinate this process because there are multiple participants, often from different agencies, whose efforts need to fit with each other's. A task associated with this process is to engage in follow-up conversations, by phone or in person, with the client, the family, and the individuals and agency representatives who agreed to participate in the client's program of care. During follow-up, the social worker gathers specific information about the extent of the client's participation, the staff assigned to work with the client in each setting, and channels of communication among relevant staff. Barriers to the client's participation should be identified and overcome as soon as possible.

In settings in which social workers intervene directly with clients, they will be helping the client deal with the specific issues at hand (e.g., eating disorder). The social worker will be guided by a theoretical approach (e.g., cognitive-behavioral theory) and consider how others in the client's social system affect the problem. Direct intervention may be on the individual, family, or group levels.

Goal 4: Monitoring and Case Review

After interdisciplinary and interagency teams establish initial treatment plans and begin to implement them, some of them monitor the client's progress at established intervals (e.g., every 60 days). At such times, teams review the client's initial plans and elicit information on their functioning since then. If insufficient progress is made, the reasons for this are explored, and the plan is modified. Monitoring is an administrative function performed by the team as a whole, but coordinated by a team leader, who may be a social worker. Social workers in leadership roles elicit input from team members and provide their own observations. The progress report from the social worker, which may be oral or written, describes specific behaviors and events that support his or her evaluation of the client's progress. Social workers also contribute to discussions about the nature of the client's progress by offering their comments and opinions.

Social workers also monitor clients' progress in their interactions with agencies and in the community. When they observe a change in clients' functioning (e.g., development of psychotic symptoms, social withdrawal, acting-out behavior), they make an initial assessment of the seriousness of the client's condition and possible reasons for this (e.g., not taking medication) and address these immediately. Accordingly, the monitoring process involves making rapid assessments and providing crisis intervention. Social workers who are members of community treatment teams may request that the client meet with the rest of the team or with one member (e.g., the psychiatrist). Alternatively, the social worker may explore residential placement in a more protective setting or take the client to a psychiatric hospital. Social workers' expertise lies in their ability to work with community agencies. When agencies are working with the same client, they can keep each other apprised of the client's progress, needs, and impediments to implementing the treatment plan.

As discussed in other chapters, social workers also monitor the client's progress by consulting with family members about the client's functioning. Whether clients live with their families or elsewhere, families that are involved with their relative's treatment should be aware of the client's activities, changes in his or her situation, whether prescribed medication is being taken, and other indicators of client functioning. With the client's consent, family members can be tremendous partners in the monitoring process.

Goal 5: Evaluation and System Change

As a consequence of social workers' involvement in assessment, planning, implementation, and monitoring, they learn the strengths and weaknesses of the team, the participating agencies, and the system of collaboration. Social workers and their teams can systematically evaluate the effectiveness of their collaborative work by assessing outcomes such as client functioning, staff satisfaction, and the extent to which services recommended are used.

Social workers have the professional obligation to use their learning to bring about social change that will enhance the effectiveness of services and promote social justice. Because it usually takes more than one person to effect social change, it is advisable for the social worker to engage the team or others in such an effort.

TECHNIQUES, STRATEGIES, AND SKILLS

Some of the goals and tasks depicted above are consistent with generalist practice across fields of practice and with the role of case manager. Additional generalist skills with which social workers are familiar, and thus not discussed, are resource finding and linkage, problem solving, and advocacy. In the following section, some techniques, strategies, and skills that are particular to working on interdisciplinary and interagency teams will be described. These include presenting a case to the team, negotiating within the team and with external systems, building partnerships, group facilitation and leadership, and reflection on the team's processes.

Case Presentation

Like other team members, social workers present synopses of their assessments to interdisciplinary and interagency teams. Norms specific to each team about the time spent describing the case and the kind of information provided effect the amount of detail social workers will include in their presentation. Accordingly, the following guidelines need to be tailored to the specific setting.

The social worker's oral presentation of her or his assessment will contain the same elements included in a written report, but is more attuned to the purpose and demands of the team meeting. Thus, if this is a new client about whom little is known, the social worker will indicate who referred the client and why; describe the client (age, appearance, marital status) and his or her presenting problem or behavior and mental status at the time of the last interview; report on the history of this problem and other difficulties; describe his or her support system and the quality of support provided; and identify stressors, gaps, and needs. Social workers commonly give special attention to the family system. In some settings, the social worker may offer a *DSM-IV* diagnosis (or at least axes IV and V); elsewhere the psychiatrist or the team as a whole constructs the diagnosis.

In advance of the meeting, social workers should think about and organize their notes on the client, so that they can describe the cases without reading from a written report. Social workers should develop a preliminary intervention plan to address stressors, gaps, and needs to present to the team for its consideration. Practitioners should anticipate the team's questions so that they can respond effectively to their concerns.

Negotiation

From a constructionist perspective, teams make decisions through a process of negotiation, in which team members who present various versions of the case, debate the meaning of these versions, and determine how the pieces fit together as a whole. Once they achieve a consensus on the meaning of the material presented, they discuss various constructions of what the client needs and what interventions and programs can meet these needs. The process of negotiation underlies this entire process. Negotiation is an interactive process in which two or more parties (or stakeholders) work out divergent opinions and interests so that each participant gains something. It is predicated on participants' openness to achieving some, but not all, of what they want in exchange for maintaining the relationship. Negotiation involves expressing needs and wants, recognizing that competing issues exist, bargaining, and compromising. It is mediated through language, which participants use strategically to state their cases and promote their interests.

In interdisciplinary teams, members of different disciplines negotiate over what the data mean, how behavior can be explained, which interventions a client needs, and which team members will provide those interventions. Conflict may arise when professionals from different disciplines construct the problems and solutions differently. Because status and power issues may push some participants to compromise more than others (Mailick & Ashley, 1981), low-status professionals need to learn to hold their own during such negotiations. Interagency negotiations involve discussions about which agency will contribute which services to which client at whose expense. Disagreements may be based on estimated costs, caseload size, and values, as well as prior experience with similar clients. Social workers serving on either of these teams need to develop skill in presenting and arguing for their position, assessing where there is room for a compromise, and offering alternative solutions.

Building Partnerships

On the macrolevel, social workers negotiate with professionals from other agencies when they develop and implement interagency consortia and other collaborative ventures. For these activities, social workers need to develop skills in building partnerships with professionals from other agencies with whom they might interact in interagency teams. Building partnerships involves developing relationships across agency boundaries. Once these relationships are built, they need to be nurtured.

Group Facilitation and Leadership

As a consequence of educational preparation for group work, as well as their increasingly large representation in the mental health workforce (Scheffler, Ivey, & Garrett, 1998), social workers are uniquely positioned to serve as mental health team leaders. Corrigan and colleagues (Corrigan & Garman, 1999; Corrigan, Garman, Lam, & Leary, 1998) note that despite the widespread consensus regarding the importance of teams in mental health treatment, there is little literature on what leadership factors enhance team performance. They adapted and tested a model of team leadership previously developed for research on business and military organizations to the context of mental health teams, and found that when team leaders exhibited certain kinds of leadership characteristics, team members felt lower levels of burnout.

According to their research (Corrigan et al., 1998; Corrigan & Garman, 1999), good team leaders exhibited two kinds of leadership skills: transformational and transactional. *Transformational skills* involve facilitating cohesion and shared vision on the team to help transform programs to meet client needs. This domain of leadership requires the team leader to provide an overarching vision for the team that transcends everyday tasks and inspires team members to persevere despite the lack of immediate gratification germane to working with difficult clients. Moreover, leadership involves creating the perception of a team among the members by encouraging the members to participate in decision making and volunteer for tasks they are interested in rather than arbitrarily assigning duties. It is also critical that team members feel that the goals of the team are congruent with their own personal goals (Yank et al., 1992). This sense of cohesion is further reinforced when team leaders themselves participate fully in the team process, working with clients, attending staff functions outside work, and so forth (Yank et al., 1992).

Transactional skills, on the other hand, are the nuts and bolts of keeping a program running smoothly on a day-to-day level, by delegating and coordinating the distribution of work among team members. A survey of mental health team members conducted by Corrigan et al. (1998) showed that staff burnout was highest when team leaders exhibited several negative transactional leadership characteristics. First, staff disliked leaders who were autocratic, that is, those who communicated with staff only when correcting their behavior, utilized punishment more than praise, and were unreceptive to feedback from the team members. Second, poor team leaders failed to communicate clear roles and goals. Third, staff experienced difficulty when team leaders exhibited a reluctant leadership style, that is, those who were not assertive, were easily manipulated by angry or emotional staff, and shied away from decision making. Thus, effective leaders communicate clear expectations and decisively accept responsibility for decision making, while treating staff with respect, providing praise for positive accomplishments in equal measure to corrective feedback. Other important leadership roles these authors identified included managing diversity issues within the team and facilitating staff development.

Reflection on Team Processes

Conflict among disciplines and agencies is an inevitable development of teams. It is incorporated in descriptions of teams' developmental stages (e.g., Lowe & Herranen, 1981b) as a phenomenon that precedes the development of group cohesion. Although the expression of conflict in teams may be discomfiting, it can also be a stimulus for growth (Sands, Stafford, & McClelland, 1990). When conflict comes to the surface, team members have data that they can examine, think about, and question. Teams that have the courage to do so should find reflection on their own processes a fruitful undertaking.

Schön (1983) has proposed that professions like social work reflect on their processes while they occur, criticize them, develop theory from this process, and modify theory and practice accordingly. Although his *reflective practitioner* operates within specific disciplines, his approach is applicable to interprofessional processes as well. It is proposed here that team members use critical moments in the life of the team as opportunities to explore their team dynamics, including subgroupings, commonalities, and differences in theoretical perspectives, power relations, language usage and interpretation, and values. Teams can, for example, devote time within a meeting to discussing feelings about an event over which they recently clashed, such as whether a client can be responsible for his or her own medication. At the very least, teams can understand their differences and how these differences lead to different conclusions. At most, teams can move toward a shared interdisciplinary framework that unites them as a team (Billups, 1987; Sands, Stafford, & McClelland, 1990).

EXEMPLAR PROGRAMS

Now that major conceptual and practice issues have been addressed, two programs that demonstrate how effective mental health teams work will be described. The first of these collaborative programs is interdisciplinary and is situated within a single agency; the second is interagency.

Program of Assertive Community Treatment in Madison, Wisconsin

Interdisciplinary teams are a centerpiece of the Program of Assertive Community Treatment (PACT) for people with severe mental illness in Madison, Wisconsin. PACT was developed in the late 1960s by the staff of an innovative research unit at the Mendota Mental Health Institute, a state hospital in Madison, Wisconsin. It was led by psychiatrists Arnold Marx and Leonard Stein and psychologist Mary Ann Test (who later became a professor of social work at University of Wisconsin). Discouraged by the tendency of their discharged patients to repeatedly relapse and re-enter the hospital after discharge, Test and Stein became inspired by the success of a social worker on the research unit who acquired the habit of following up her discharged clients after they re-entered the community. To test this practice as an intervention, Test and Stein extracted a treatment team from the inpatient hospital ward and deployed it to the community, where the team provided the necessary supports to help the clients remain there. PACT was thus born and has evolved over time (Dixon, 2000; Greenley, 1995), and its efficacy has been established through extensive research (Mueser, Bond, Drake, & Resnick, 1998). In the three decades to follow, the dissemination of PACT has drastically changed the provision of care to people with severe mental illness in the United States (Stein & Santos, 1998). Replications of PACT are commonly called ACT (assertive community treatment) or CTT (continuous treatment team) programs.

The service needs of consumers with severe and persistent mental illness are extensive. In addition to psychopharmacological interventions to help control the symptoms of the illness, these individuals often need assistance in obtaining and keeping housing, negotiating entitlements, learning social and survival skills, finding work and other purposeful ways of spending time, and coping with everyday life. Equally as important, consumers need a great deal of emotional support in accepting and confronting the daily challenges of living with a mental illness. Working with this population requires providers to be flexible, adapting, and to titrate the level and intensity of support to the client's needs, which fluctuate according to contextual circumstances and the undulating course of illness. Moreover, providers must be prepared to provide this support in an ongoing, continuous manner, as long as the illness and its associated disability persist (Test, 1992).

PACT addresses this array of needs by employing interdisciplinary teams of about eight to ten staff members to provide a comprehensive, seamless web of social support to the client. PACT teams usually consist of a psychiatrist and a mix of other professionals, including social workers, rehabilitation counselors, nurses, occupational therapists, and paraprofessionals. The psychiatrist's role is broader, less focused exclusively on the monitoring of medications, than is typical in mental health settings. For example, PACT psychiatrists are encouraged to see clients in their homes and other natural settings to achieve a more contextualized assessment of functioning (Allness & Knoedler, 1998). Nonphysician team members act primarily as generalists, serving as the primary contact people or case managers for a small caseload of clients (approximately 10), and as a member of the treatment team for other clients in the program. Despite this generalist orientation, staff also assume specialized functions commensurate with their training and expertise. For example, nurses administer indictable medications, and rehabilitation counselors perform a great deal of the vocational assessment for the team. Social workers often play a special role as liaison to other agencies and systems, advocating for income and insurance benefits, and negotiating child custody arrangements and housing accommodations (Stein & Santos, 1998).

Central to the PACT philosophy is the idea that teams form a "fixed point of responsibility," remaining continuously available (24 hours a day) and providing all or nearly all needed services for the client. Clients are seen frequently—the most impaired may receive multiple contacts per day—and the team structure is organized to facilitate frequent communication regarding each client's status and needs. Most teams do this by holding a brief daily meeting in which each client is discussed. In this meeting, the team also divides the service tasks (e.g., medication deliveries, supportive one-to-one contacts before a client's work shift, transportation to a doctor's appointment) for which social workers will be responsible on a given day. Optimally, team membership is stable, allowing for long-term therapeutic and supportive relationships to develop between clients and providers. However, working with multiple team members allows continuity of care to be maintained even when individual staff members leave the program.

Recognizing that it is difficult for an individual with serious mental illness to apply a newly learned skill to novel settings and situations, PACT teams situate the bulk of service provision in vivo, within the client's natural environment. For example, clients learn work skills by obtaining jobs and training on-site, rather than in a prevocational work skills treatment group at the agency. Eschewing a traditional outpatient therapy approach, PACT teams operate using outreach techniques, taking services to the client if the client is unable or unwilling to come into the office. This use of assertive outreach is also used to engage reluctant clients in treatment and discourage dropping out or drifting away from the program.

Vermont's System of Wraparound Services for Children

In 1984, the National Institute of Mental Health initiated the Child and Adolescent Service System Program (CASSP) to provide funds and guidance to states for the development of systems of care for children with severe emotional, behavioral, and mental disorders. One of the guiding principles for a CASSP system of care is that it should contain a comprehensive set of services: mental health (residential and nonresidential, including home-based family preservation), social services, educational services, medical care, substance abuse treatment, vocational services, recreational services, and service coordination (Stroul & Friedman, 1986). It is nearly impossible for a single agency to deliver this array of services alone (Stroul, 1995). Consistent with a systems perspective on service delivery, the conceptual framework of CASSP holds that care for childrens' multifaceted problems is optimal when agencies with specialized functions pool their resources and work collaboratively. Thus, systems of care for children are faced with the challenge of encouraging collaboration between agencies and systems.

One system that has been successful in promoting interagency collaboration is the *wraparound* approach (Burchard & Clarke, 1990). Wraparound services tailor to the unique needs and circumstances of children and their families rather than attempting to serve the family using a "one size fits all" approach. Santarcangelo, Birkett, and McGrath (1995), for example, state that "the underlying elements [of the system of wraparound care used in Vermont] include unconditional care, flexibility, creativity, child- and family-centered services delivery, strengths-based assessment, and interagency collaboration" (p. 301). In the Vermont model, a therapeutic case manager creates an interagency team, which includes the child and his or her family, a representative from each agency with which the child is involved (e.g., child welfare, school, mental health, juvenile justice, developmental disabilities), and other supporters, such as neighbors or clergy whom the family wishes to be included. This interagency team begins work with the client by assessing comprehensively the child's and family's strengths, needs, and goals. As much as possible, this assessment process takes place outside the agencies, in the client's home and recreational arenas. The treatment team may also contract with specialists in a particular area for assessments. Next, the treatment team develops an individualized service plan using both agency services and natural supports in the community. This involves deciding what services will be put in place, and matching appropriate providers to the specific needs and preferences of the child. When a child's individualized need cannot be met using an existing agency, the team works synergistically to develop the service. For all cases, a plan for respite care is created for both the child and the primary caregiver.

Because of the potentially large team size, service coordination is a critical element of the model. The therapeutic case manager acts as the glue for the treatment team, scheduling meetings, monitoring progress and service delivery, facilitating communication among team members, and advocating on the child's behalf. Although the case manager is the leader of the team, the team makes decisions by consensus.

UNIQUE CHALLENGES FOR SOCIAL WORK

Collaborating across disciplines and agencies is a potentially gratifying activity that poses unique opportunities and challenges for social work. Working at critical junctures between clients and professionals, social work is positioned to use its psychosocial perspective and commitment to social justice to promote better practice for mental health clients. A couple of the challenges facing social work concern potential role restriction and new configurations of team.

During the first few decades of the 20th century, when social workers were first employed in psychiatric settings, they were viewed as assistants to the psychiatrist, carrying out medical recommendations "without developing an independent relationship with patients" (Grinker, MacGregor, Selan, Klein, & Kohrman, 1961, p. 118). They performed the functions that were delegated to them, history taking, obtaining information about community resources, and making community visits (Grinker et al., 1961). Although much has changed since that time, in some settings the social work role is limited to discharge planning or is perceived as limited to work-ing with families, addressing social-environmental issues, and making referrals (Cowles & Lefcowitz, 1992), resulting in social workers doing less than they are capa-ble of doing. Some of this has to do with the roles assumed by other professions, leav-ing what remains to social work. Nevertheless, unless social workers are able to use the full repertoire of skills in which they have been educated (e.g., counseling, group intervention), their ability to be who they are and their authority will be limited. One challenge facing social work, then, is to carve out a large enough role for themselves in mental health settings that is consistent with their competencies.

Another challenge social workers face is new configurations of team. With the advances of technology that have been made and are likely to continue to evolve, interdisciplinary and interagency teams may be convening electronically and audio-visually. Sectors of teams may meet with clients and families face-to-face, while other sectors participate through interactive video. How this will affect the quality of care is yet to be determined.

CASE DILEMMA

Martina Lopez, a 32-year-old divorced woman with schizophrenia, is a new client of an assertive community treatment team. Belinda Young, her case manager, is assigned to present the case to the rest of the team following Martina's intake. Martina has been experiencing psychiatric prob-lems since her early 20s, when she was first hospitalized. Martina has two children, aged 8 and 4. Although she experiences periods of time when she feels well and is able to care for her children, at other times, her illness is exacerbated and she essentially withdraws from her children alto-gether, leaving them to care for themselves. This situation is exacerbated by episodic alcohol binges, which occur when Martina gets together with her brother, who is a major source of social support to her. Although Martina's ex-husband lives out of state and does not retain any contact with her or the children, Martina's mother lives in the same town, and often cares for Martina's children when she is having a crisis, which has been happening more and more frequently over the past year. Her mother is thus becoming overwhelmed with her own lack of knowledge about how to help Martina and her worry that her grandchildren will not be adequately cared for and protected. Martina's 8-year-old son, José, has begun to experience severe nightmares, and his teachers report that he has become aggressive with peers at school. Belinda is also concerned that 4-year-old Maria has major developmental delays and will need intensive assistance before start-ing kindergarten next year. When asked about her personal goals, Martina says that she would like to have a job and to get off welfare. She feels that working would provide the structure she needs to control her problems with alcohol abuse.

The following are questions for discussion regarding this case dilemma. What are Martina's major service needs? How can the team address these needs itself? What professionals on the team would be involved? To what extent will interagency collaboration be needed? How might this collaboration be achieved? Do you anticipate potential areas of conflict between these differ-ent agencies and systems? What resources would be available for Martina and her family in your community?

WEB RESOURCES

The following are Web sites for various professional associations that feature information on collaboration and interagency and interdisciplinary teams:

National Association of Social Workers (http://www.naswdc.org).

American Psychiatric Nurses Association (http://www.apna.org/).

American Psychological Association (http://www.apa.org). (See the special divisions for rehabilitation, community, and clinical psychology.)

American Psychiatric Association (http://www.psych.org).

National Coalition of Arts Therapies Association (http://ncata.com).

American Occupational Therapy Association (http://www.aota.org).

The following sites feature collaborative models of service for children:

Center for Effective Collaboration and Practice: Improving Services to Children and Youth with Emotional and Behavioral Problems (http://cecp.air.org/default.htm).

Center for School Mental Health Assistance (http://csmha.umaryland.edu). This center seeks to advance effective interdisciplinary school-based mental health programs through consultation, training, and knowledge development and dissemination.

Children's Mental Health Education Campaign, Center for Mental Health Services (http://www.mentalhealth.org/cmhs/childrenscampaign/index.htm). This site features the Substance Abuse and Mental Health Services Administration (SAMHSA).

Program of Assertive Community Treatment (http://www.nami.org/about/pact.htm). The link will lead you to the Pact Across America Web page, hosted by the National Alliance for the Mentally Ill.

REFERENCES

Abramson, J. S., & Rosenthal, B. B. (1995). Interdisciplinary and interorganizational collaboration. In R. L. Edwards & J. G. Hopps (Eds.), *Encyclopedia of social work* (19th ed., Vol. 2; pp. 1479–1489). Washington, DC: NASW Press.

Akhavain, P., Amaral, D., Murphy, M., & Uehlinger, K. C. (1999). Collaborative practice: A nursing perspective of the psychiatric interdisciplinary treatment team. *Holistic Nursing Practice, 13*(2), 1–11.

Allness, D. J., & Knoedler, W. H. (1998). *The PACT model of community-based treatment for persons with severe and persistent mental illnesses: A manual for PACT start-up.* Arlington, VA: National Alliance for the Mentally Ill.

Anderson, R. E., & Carter, I. (1984). *Human behavior in the social environment: A social systems approach* (3rd ed.). New York: Aldine de Gruyter.

Beatrice, D. F. (1990). Inter-agency coordination: A practitioner's guide to a strategy for effective social policy. *Administration in Social Work, 14,* 45–59.

Billups, J. (1987). Interprofessional team process. *Theory into Practice, 26*(2), 146–152.

Burchard, J. D., & Clarke, R. T. (1990). The role of individualized care in a service delivery system for children and adolescents with severely maladjusted behavior. *Journal of Mental Health Administration, 17,* 48–60.

Corrigan, P. W., & Garman, A. N. (1999). Tranformational and transactional leadership skills for mental health teams. *Community Mental Health Journal, 35,* 301–312.

Corrigan, P. W., Garman, A. N., Lam, C., & Leary, M. (1998). What mental health teams want in their leaders. *Administration and Policy in Mental Health, 26,* 111–123.

Cowles, L. A., & Lefcowitz, M. J. (1992). Interdisciplinary expectations of the medical social worker in the hospital setting. *Health and Social Work, 17,* 57–65.

Crepeau, E. B. (1994). Three images of interdisciplinary team meetings. *American Journal of Occupational Therapy, 4,* 717–722.

Diamond, R. J. (1996). Multidisciplinary teamwork. In J. V. Vaccaro & G. H. Clark (Eds.), *Practicing psychiatry in the community: A manual* (pp. 343–360). Washington, DC: American Psychiatric Press.

Dixon, L. (2000). Assertive community treatment: Twenty-five years of gold. *Psychiatric Services, 51,* 755–758.

Ducanis, A. J., & Golin, A. K. (1979). *The interdisciplinary health care team: A handbook.* Germantown, MD: Aspen Systems Corp.

Fargason, C. A., & Haddock, C. C. (1992). Cross-functional, integrative team decision making: Essential for effective QI in health care. *Quality Review Bulletin, 18,* 157–163.

Germain, C. B. (1984).*Social work practice in health care: An ecological perspective.* New York: Free Press.

Goffman, E. (1959). *The presentation of self in everyday life.* Garden City, NY: Doubleday Anchor.

Graham, J. R., & Barter, K. (1999). Collaboration: A social work practice method. *Families in Society, 80,* 6–13.

Greenley, J. R. (1995). Madison, Wisconsin, United States: Creation and implementation of the Program of Assertive Community Treatment (PACT). In: R. Schulz & J. R. Greenley (Eds.), *Innovating in community mental health: International perspectives* (pp. 83–96). Westport, CT: Praeger/Greenwood.

Grinker, R. R., MacGregor, H., Selan, K., Klein, A., & Kohrman, J. (1961). The early years of psychiatric social work. *Social Service Review, 35,* 111–126.

Hannah, F. P., & Nichol, G. T. (1996). Memphis city schools mental health center. In M. C. Roberts (Ed.), *Model programs in child and family mental health.* Manwah, NJ: Lawrence Erlbaum.

Hawkins, J. W., Veeder, N. W., & Pearce, C. W. (1998). *Nurse–social worker collaboration in managed care: A model of community case management.* New York: Springer.

Hershenson, D. B., & Power, P. W. (1987). *Mental health counseling: Theory and practice.* New York: Pergamon Press.

Kane, R. (1975). The interprofessional team as a small group. *Social Work in Health Care, 1,* 19–32.

Kane, R. (1983). *Interprofessional teamwork.* Manpower monograph number 8. Syracuse, NY: Syracuse University School of Social Work.

Kessler, R. C., McGonagle, K. A., Zhao, S., Nelson, C. B., Hughes, M., Eshleman, S., Wittchen, H.-U., & Kendler, K. S. (1994). Lifetime and 12-month prevalence of *DSM-III-R* psychiatric disorders in the United States: Results from the National Comorbidity Survey. *Archives of General Psychiatry, 51,* 8–19.

Knoedler, W. (1989). The continuous treatment team model: Role of the psychiatrist. *Psychiatric Annals, 19,* 35–40.

Koeske, G. F., Koeske, R. D., & Mallinger, J. (1993). Perceptions of professional competence: Cross-disciplinary ratings of psychologists, social workers, and psychiatrists. *American Journal of Orthopsychiatry, 63,* 45–54.

Leiba, T. (1994). Inter-professional approaches to mental health care. In A. Leathard (Ed.), *Going inter-professional: Working together for health and welfare* (pp. 136–142). London and New York: Routledge.

Llewelyn, S., & Fielding, G. (1982). Group dynamics: Forming, storming, norming, and performing. *Nursing Mirror, 155*(3), 14–16.

Lowe, J. I., & Herranen, M. (1981a). Conflict in teamwork: Understanding roles and relationships. *Social Work in Health Care, 3,* 323–330.

Lowe, J. I., & Herranen, M. (1981b). Understanding teamwork: Another look at the concepts. *Social Work in Health Care, 7,* 1–11.

Mailick, M. D., & Ashley, A. A. (1981). Politics of interprofessional collaboration: Challenge to advocacy. *Social Casework, 62,* 131–137.

McClelland, M., & Sands, R. G. (2001). *Interprofessional discourse: Voices, knowledge, and practice.* Cresskill, NJ: Hampton Press.

Morlock, L. L. (1989). Recognition and treatment of mental health problems in the general health sector. In C. A. Taube, D. Mechanic, & A. A. Hohmann (Eds.), *The future of mental health services research* (DHHS Publication No. ADM 89–1600). Washington, DC: U.S. Government Printing Office.

Mueser, K .T., Bond, G. R., Drake, R. E., & Resnick, S. G. (1998). Models of community care for severe mental illness: A review of research on case management. *Schizophrenia Bulletin, 24,* 37–74.

Nagi, S. Z. (1975). Teamwork in health care in the US: A sociological perspective. *Health and Society, The Millbank Memorial Fund Quarterly, 53,* 75–91.

Olsen, D. P., Rickles, J., & Travlik, K. (1995). A treatment-team model of managed mental health care. *Psychiatric Services, 46,* 252–256.

Paulson, R. I. (1993). Interagency collaboration among rehabilitation, mental health, and other systems. In R. W. Flexer & P. L. Solomon (Eds.), *Psychiatric rehabilitation in practice* (pp. 193–210). Boston, MA: Andover Medical.

Peterson, C. (1999). Psychological approaches to mental illness. In A. V. Horwitz & T. L. Scheid (Eds.), *A handbook for the study of mental health: Social contexts, theories and systems.* Cambridge: Cambridge University Press.

Petrie, H. G. (1976). Do you see what I see? The epistemology of interdisciplinary inquiry. *Journal of Aesthetic Education, 10,* 29–45.

Punwar, A. J. (1994). *Occupational therapy: Principles and practice* (2nd ed.). Philadelphia: Williams and Wilkins.

Rawson, D. (1994). Models of inter-professional work: Likely theories and possibilities. In A. Leathard (Ed.), *Going inter-professional: Working together for health and welfare* (pp. 38–63). London and New York: Routledge.

Ridgely, M. S., Lambert, D., Goodman, A., Chichester, C. S., & Ralph, R. (1998). Interagency collaboration in services for people with co-occurring mental illness and substance use disorder. *Psychiatric Services, 49,* 236–238.

Sampson, E. E., & Marthas, M. (1990). *Group process for health professions* (3rd ed.). New York: John Wiley.

Sands, R. G. (1995). The parenting experience of low-income single women with serious mental disorders. *Families in Society, 76,* 86–96.

Sands, R. G., Stafford, J., & McClelland, M. (1990). "I beg to differ": Conflict in the interdisciplinary team. *Social Work in Health Care, 14,* 55–72.

Santarcangelo, S., Birkett, N., & McGrath, N. (1995). Therapeutic case management: Vermont's system of individualized care. In B. J. Friesen & J. Poertner (Eds.), *From case management to service coordination for children with emotional, behavioral, or mental disorders: Building on family strengths* (pp. 301–315). Baltimore: Paul H. Brookes.

Scheffler, R. M., Ivey, S. L., & Garrett, A. B. (1998). Changing supply and earning patterns of the mental health workforce. *Administration and Policy in Mental Health, 26*(2), 85–99.

Schön, D. (1983). *The reflective practitioner: How professionals think in action.* New York: Basic Books.

Schwab, B., Drake, R. E., & Burghardt, E. M. (1988). Health care of the chronically mentally ill: The culture broker model. *Community Mental Health Journal, 24,* 174–184.

Stein, L. I., & Santos, A. B. (1998). *Assertive community treatment of persons with severe mental illness.* New York: W. W. Norton.

Stroul, B. A. (1995). Case management in a system of care. In B. J. Friesen & J. Poertner (Eds.), *From case management to service coordination for children with emotional, behavioral, or mental disorders: Building on family strengths* (pp. 3–25). Baltimore: Paul H. Brookes.

Stroul, B. A., & Friedman, R. (1986). *A system of care for children and youth with severe emotional disturbances.* Washington, DC: Georgetown University, CASSP Technical Assistance Center.

Swan, W. W., & Morgan, J. L. (1993). *Collaborating for comprehensive services for young children and their families: The local interagency coordinating council.* Baltimore, MD: Paul H. Brookes.

Test, M. A. (1992). Training in Community Living. In R. P. Liberman (Ed.), *Handbook of psychiatric rehabilitation* (pp. 153–170). New York: Macmillan.

Thomas, S. A., & Hargett, T. (1999). Mental health care: A collaborative, holistic approach. *Holistic Nursing Practice, 13,* 78–85.

Toseland, R. W., Palmer-Ganeles, J., & Chapman, D. (1986). Teamwork in psychiatric settings. *Social Work, 31,* 46–52.

Woodward, H. L. (1993). One community's response to the multi-system service needs of individuals with mental illness and developmental disabilities. *Community Mental Health Journal, 29,* 347–359.

Yank, G. R., Barber, J. W., Hargrove, D. S., & Whitt, P. D. (1992). The mental health treatment team as a work group: Team dynamics and the role of the leader. *Psychiatry, 44,* 250–264.

Zemencuk, J., Rogosch, F. A., & Mowbray, C. T. (1995). The seriously mentally ill woman in the role of parent: Characteristics, parenting sensitivity, and needs. *Psychosocial Rehabilitation Journal, 18,* 77–92.

SOCIAL WORKERS AS ADVOCATES AND COMMUNITY ORGANIZERS

Shela Silverman

Each of us comes to a decision about our life's work through independent thought or action. In my case, I decided upon a life of service to others as a small child growing up in New York City. An epiphany occurred when I, a young child of 7 or so, observed people evicted from their housing, living in the streets, surrounded by their furniture and personal belongings. When I saw these people, some old, crying, neighbors came together and went and found the social worker from somewhere. The knowledge that there was someone who could fix things that were seemingly broken appealed to me as a child and continues presently. My life has been a series of fixing broken things, and my goal has always been to be a social worker who can be called upon by those in distress to work this magic.

As a primary mental health consumer[1], diagnosed with chronic depression while still in grade school, I have been personally involved in mental health treatment of sorts for nearly my entire life. When I first became an active participant in the mental health consumer movement nearly 15 years ago, I saw very clearly that what was being discussed and what we were organizing was a civil rights movement. We were an oppressed group, oppressed by both law and public attitudes, deprived of many of our basic civil rights through a process of civil commitment for our illness and also deprived of control over our lives. It was quite obvious to consumers that this coercive system resulted in making us feel powerless over our own lives. Patricia Deegan (1992), a survivor of the psychiatric system who is now a PhD psychologist and director of training at the National Empowerment Center in Lawrence, Massachusetts, said "The more this system takes control of consumer's lives and choices, the more helpless, disempowered, irresponsible, and dependent consumers learn to become . . ." (p. 533).

Ten years ago, I was employed within the same mental health system that acted in such a coercive manner, believing that if I worked diligently, I could effect change

---

[1]The term *consumer* has been chosen by persons who have been treated, are presently being treated, or are considering treatment for mental illness. In addition, the term *consumer/survivor/ex-patient* is used to describe other individuals who see themselves as having survived one's treatment in spite of an oppressive system of care.

from within, and thus, assist my fellow consumers and free them from the stigma and powerlessness of their conditions. When I shared with a supervisor whom I trusted that I too was a consumer, I suddenly became part of the problem, and my actions seemed to be scrutinized in a manner that had not occurred until that time. I realized that I needed to rethink my original thesis of effecting change from within the system, and thus, I began to place most of my energies into developing a true consumer alternative where consumers could be in charge of their lives.

Coincidentally, I was working toward my Master of Social Work at Virginia Commonwealth University. I was quite interested in course work on the history and development of social work, ethics, and practice. I found myself drawn to the original social work model of the settlement house. The settlement houses that were established in major cities became the central place within a community, where individuals came together not only to receive a multitude of services, but where they recognized the need to organize and advocate for political change. In studying these settlement houses, I realized that a critical element was the discussion of community values that directed services. This led me to the recognition that, in order for the consumer-run program "on our own" where I came to work to be a true alternative, we had to develop and articulate our core values and principles. This process took many months, as we had to discuss each concept for long periods of time prior to its acceptance. The result was well worth the effort as we now articulate values that direct all our work. Connecting with each other, or the formation of community, is a universal strategy that people use to overcome the experience of aloneness and powerlessness (Mack, 1994).

It was through this process of developing the consumer community in Virginia, based on many of the core values prevalent in social work, that I embraced the mantle of what I believe is real social work. The following chapter is devoted to explicating what the social worker concept of advocacy and community organization offer us in the consumer movement, a map which, if we follow, can assist us in developing a true alternative system for people with mental illness.

THE INTELLECTUAL BASE OF PRACTICE

One of the most critical services that social workers provide in the mental health system is advocacy. Gerhart (1990) addresses that function of social workers caring for people with mental illness as " . . . [one] who can act to protect their fundamental human rights, with whom they can air complaints, and who will make representations on their behalf" (p. 269).

The profession of social work considers client advocacy an ethical responsibility and one primary function of any social work practice. The National Association of Social Workers (NASW) has taken a clear position on advocacy (Litzelfelner & Petr, 1997). Within the NASW *Code of Ethics,* it states that social workers are bound ethically to take on an advocacy role to fulfill their professional responsibility vis-à-vis clients (Ad Hoc Committee on Advocacy, 1969). Hepworth and Larsen (1990) observed that serving the client as an advocate is a basic role of social work. Few social workers question this role; however, how this role is defined and carried out is far less clear (Litzelfelner & Petr, 1997). According to these authors, much is said in the profession in the name of advocacy, yet there is little attention given to actually defining the concept in social work education, practice, and literature (p. 393). Herbert and Mould (1992) stated, "The concept of advocacy is poorly defined, [and] most have little understanding of the term *advocacy* and therefore can not say if they are doing it or not. It is not service delivery although most look at it this way" (p. 115).

In general, *advocacy* is defined as "the act of directly representing or defending others" (Barker, 1995, p. 11). In the field of social work, Hepworth and Larsen (1990) suggest that there are two basic approaches to client advocacy: social advocacy and case advocacy. *Social advocacy* or class advocacy refers to advocacy on behalf of a group. They define social advocacy as "working to effect changes in policies, practices and laws that affect all people in a specific class or group" (p. 460). Case advocacy, according to Gerhart (1990), usually involves the representation of an individual, family, or a small group. She suggests that advocacy practices involve atypical situations that impact upon the lives of consumers. A case in point would be a denial of Social Security benefits where access is blocked. Similarly, Gerhart and Brooks (1983) described the role of the social worker as advocate. They are the ones who monitor the rights and entitlements of clients and, in keeping with current definitions of social work advocacy, focus on influencing decision makers in favor of an individual or a group of clients. This current definition of advocacy as an activity in which a request is made to a decision-making body, is made specifically with the aim of receiving a decision favorable to the client (Gerhart, 1990). This is not to be confused with the activity of linking clients or consumers to services to which they are already legally entitled. Lourie (1975) has defined advocacy as a "device for increasing pressures against the social structure to achieve social equity and justice" (p. 38). Historically, there has been, and continues to be, an emphasis on issues of human rights for people with mental illness, which clearly impacts on both institutional and community tenure. The social worker as advocate must become knowledgeable on policies, statutes, and laws that impact consumers' lives. In examples of case advocacy, social workers would persuade landlords to rent to disabled people, bring information about unsafe conditions to people in positions of authority to bring about changes, or speak to psychiatrists about unpleasant side effects of psychotropic medications.

Robert Barker, in *The Social Work Dictionary* (1987), defines advocacy as "the act of directly representing or defending others; in social work, championing the rights of individuals or communities through direct intervention or through empowerment." Even though this NASW publication does not delineate the specific techniques of advocacy, the professional *Code of Ethics* (1997) notes that the social worker's primary obligation is "the welfare of the individual or group served, which includes action to improve social conditions. Therefore, a commitment to this code is a commitment to social action." The *Code of Ethics* mandates the championing of the rights of others and also states that "advocacy is a basic obligation of the profession and its members" (p. 4).

In the mid-1960s, during the era of poverty programs directed by the federal government, many social workers began to criticize traditional social work and case-work methods and call for a renewed focus on community organizing. This led to a growing awareness of the limits of traditional, professional methods within social work and an expansion to the role of social worker as expert problem solver (Chandler, 1990). Murray Ross's (1955) *Community Organization* had already intro-duced the idea of community practice to social workers as a "process in which com-munity cooperation and collaboration could be built around problem solving" (p. 39).

Saul Alinsky, a radical social worker from the 1960s, wrote of community organ-izing: "It is the greatest job man [sic] could have—the actual opportunity of creat-ing and building a world of decency, dignity, peace, security, and happiness; a world worthy of man [sic] and worthy of the name of civilization" (Alinsky, 1969, p. XI). In the second edition of *Organizing: A Guide for Grassroots Leaders* (Kahn, 1991), the NASW leaders reaffirmed the commitment of social work to the process of grass-roots organizing (Kahn, 1991, pp. ix–x, 1–4).

There is a strong ideological basis for a commitment of social work to commu-nity organization. Social work is, after all, the profession most concerned about the relationship between environmental and individual well-being, and it also is the pro-fession with client self-determination as a core value (O'Donnell, 1995). The need to organize resources for certain vulnerable groups is clearly a problem that social workers must try to address. Hepworth and Larson (1990) provide five points for a successful model of community organization. These strategies are the sort that strive to empower consumers who are engaged in the entire process rather than being passive recipients who make decisions based on what the professionals believe con-sumers want and need.

1. Active participation by clients results in a greater level of success. Clients who have themselves been personally involved in the issues of resource depletion have a greater understanding of what their needs are.
2. Clients are more likely to utilize resources when they have participated in the planning and development.
3. Resources are more likely to fit when consumers have participated in their development.
4. Clients gain a sense of power when they are involved in improving their own lives. The converse then becomes a truth: powerlessness is then removed from the paradigm.
5. In the operational organization, consumers develop a sense of community, unity and belonging. The action group can then become a support network (pp. 457–458).

MAJOR TASKS AND GOALS

In fulfilling the role of social worker as advocate and community organizer for peo-ple with mental illness, the major tasks and goals continue to be those that initially require a great degree of appreciation and respect for each person's worth. Honoring each consumer's personal history is essential, and as I wrote in a chapter, "Recovery Through Partnership: On Our Own, Charlottesville, Virginia" from

Consumers as Providers in Psychiatric Rehabiliation (Silverman, 1997), the sharing of personal experiences about how mental illness had impacted our lives is empowering. Each person's experience is validated through the process of being part of the supportive community. This process has also been called consciousness raising. During the 1970s, people examined and shared their experiences to learn about the contexts in which their lives were embedded. For example, as used in the feminist movement, consciousness raising helped women to understand that matters of marriage, sexuality, divorce, roles, personal problems, and job discrimination were not individual but were actually indicators of the society's oppression of women (Chamberlin, 1990). Similarly, when consumers share their life stories, it becomes obvious that patterns of oppression exist and that many of the problems and difficulties are not internal and personal, but are systemic.

The tasks that are incumbent upon the social worker as community organizer are to avoid the pitfall of defining the values of the group, but to encourage maximum participation of each member in selecting the values of the community. The values of the social work profession (service; social justice, dignity, and worth of the person; the importance of human relationships, integrity, and competence) are clearly congruent with the values of consumer alternatives (*Code of Ethics*, Preamble), but cannot be imposed upon the community without long and serious discussion.

In the consumer alternative drop-in center discussed in the chapter mentioned earlier, the value of choice was thought to be the primary value. This value recognized that all the services were to be designed and implemented by the membership and would serve to demonstrate respect, enhance individual dignity, and be available whenever, wherever, and for as long as the consumer requests them (Silverman, 1997, p. 129).

The task of the social worker within this framework is also one of facilitating the process of self-determination, consumers deciding their own future community. These tasks are value-driven as well, and by examining them within this context, all of the values listed in the NASW *Code of Ethics* are utilized.

TECHNIQUES, STRATEGIES, AND SKILLS

The original community of consumers in Charlottesville described in the previous sections, people who were dissatisfied with traditional mental health services as provided by professionals, continued to expand. As a new community appeared, people with or without mental illness, some who were homeless, presented new challenges to the founders and to the consumer staff of "on our own." Many had never experienced the status of "helper" and thus felt ill-prepared to assist them. By reaching back to the core values developed during its birthing, the consumer alternative succeeded in recognizing the similarities of their situations and included these people within the community of the drop-in center. The values of social justice, recognizing the oppression of the disenfranchised and the poor, and the value of human relationships, provided the map or guidance needed for the inclusion of this group (Silverman, Taylor, & Blank, 1997).

Advocacy as practiced within the alternative consumer-run program was essential for its continued existence. Utilizing the framework from Gerhart (1990), true advocacy is presenting information to decision-makers with the intention of changing their minds. Gerhart (1990) explicates a hands-on approach to that end, which, when operationalized, is concrete and very effective. Bentley and Walsh (2001) have adapted her approach and present six steps toward advocacy:

1. Reflection and identification of the complaint; a decision whether the issue is worth 'fighting for'
2. Analyzing and identifying the risks inherent in pursuing the complaint; seeking allies
3. Identifying the appropriate decision maker
4. Outlining and preparing arguments and supporting documentation plus considering likely objections
5. Practicing presentation of arguments with allies and/or in front of a mirror; practicing making requests rather than placing demands until presentation is clear and the points are presented in a calm and credible manner
6. Making an appointment (and being on time) with the designated decision maker; presenting the claim as practiced using the skills of negotiation, compromise, clear expression and other communication skills

The obvious need for funding of consumer programs presented an opportunity to challenge the institutions that had historically succeeded in oppressing consumers. This challenge presented the social worker as advocate with a series of questions that required much discussion and consideration. By accessing funds from such an oppressive system (public mental health), did this place the consumer alternative program in jeopardy, and did this co-opt the values of the program? And, if these considerations could be addressed and resolved, how could the mental health system be approached to consider funding an alternative that had little credibility? By utilizing the model offered earlier by Gerhart, many of these questions were addressed in the application of this process. The following is an example of how this was operationalized utilizing the very steps Gerhart laid out in her paradigm.

The latter problem was resolved rather simply, as the leadership in the Department of Mental Health, Mental Retardation, and Substance Abuse in Virginia was held by a social worker. Dr. King Davis, former commissioner and Professor of Social Work at Virginia Commonwealth University, provided a single and unequivocal principle for practice, service delivery, and policy in a 1992 speech (Davis, personal communication): "The quality of life of the person served must be the deciding factor in providing care." There did not have to be much advocacy directed toward this person who clearly understood the dignity and worth of each person. Dr. Davis personified the values of social work through his work as commissioner, so when the consumer group from Charlottesville was in discussion with him regarding funding, there seemed to be a special understanding and respect that did not necessarily exist throughout his large state agency. Thus, during discussions with the rest of the bureaucracy within the Department of Mental Health, there took place lengthy and detailed discussions about accountability and reporting; including requiring items that at that time were not required of even more heavily funded local mental health centers. The expected level of accountability for the small poorly funded consumer program seemed much higher than for any other programs.

The guidance of many of the pioneers within the consumer movement clearly indicated that accepting funding for the program from governmental entities was a source of being co-opted by the very system that had oppressed the consumer for such a long period. A deceased leader of the consumer movement during its organizational phase, Howie the Harp (1988), called this a form of control, because activities that consumers chose to participate in could be limited or even stymied. The specific activities that Howie and other consumer leaders had in mind, advocacy and community organization, tended to be needed by these groups to secure their survival. These two activities are absolute requirements for continued success.

EXEMPLAR PROGRAMS AND MODELS

A program in which a true partnership between the social worker and consumer, survivor, or ex-patient exists is exemplary. The West Virginia Mental Health Consumers' Association is a multifaceted organization that operates seven consumer-run service centers for those consumers wishing to be involved in alternative programs. A major focus of this organization was devoted to developing, administering, and measuring consumer satisfaction about the services received by consumers utilizing the services of the Community Behavioral Health Centers. Staff from the West Virginia Mental Health Consumers' Association conducted the survey because ". . . research shows people tend to answer more honestly when the questions are asked by their peers rather than the employees of the behavioral health centers" (Belcher, 1998, p. 3). Survey results were reported in nine domains: (1) feeling of empowerment; (2) staff's empowerment-enabling attitudes; (3) staff behaviors; (4) overall satisfaction and accessibility; (5) appropriateness/service needs; (6) community integration; (7) consumer involvement; (8) administrative systems; and (9) community supports. The survey ($N = 567$) results showed that consumers generally reported a high level of satisfaction with services provided in their state. Of special interest was that the majority (49%) of consumers surveyed strongly agreed or agreed somewhat with the ability of the centers to strengthen their feelings of empowerment (p. 5).

A project of the West Virginia Mental Health Consumers' Association, Consumer Organization and Networking Technical Assistance Center (CONTAC), a national technical assistance center, serves as a resource center for consumers, survivors, ex-patients, and consumer-run organizations across the country promoting self-help, recovery, and empowerment. CONTAC was developed utilizing research on ideal consumer self-help programs, successful consumer-run programs, community support service philosophy about service delivery, descriptions of mature mental health systems, and management and leadership skills (see the CONTAC Web page, listed in "Web Resources").

The following profile of CONTAC provides an example of advocacy and community organization in the truest sense:

> To provide a forum for exchanging information to end stigma in the field of mental illness; to achieve the best possible community mental health system for all citizens based upon our unique mental health consumer experience and perspective; to provide primacy consumer input into the affairs of all mental health providers; to provide a means to help provide empowering support to all consumers in our search for appropriate health care, employment, housing and other supports; to provide a meaningful voice to consumers so to communicate our needs on issues directly impacting our lives; to ensure that these concerns are heard and not discounted through consumer and public education and advocacy so as to eliminate discrimination and stigma; to provide emotional support to and from consumers; to research consumer empowerment, satisfaction and quality of life issues; and to demand that all consumers are treated with the dignity and humanity due to all human beings (http://www.contac.org, p. 2).

CONTAC is funded through a grant from the Center for Mental Health Services, and thus is required to do extensive evaluations. They received the funding for Alternatives 1999, a national conference for consumers, survivors, or ex-patients. This was the first time they were awarded this grant, and from all accounts, the conference was quite successful. A major effort is devoted toward leadership training. They have provided training in 12 states, and followed up with a "train the trainers" program, so that consumers throughout the country have access to the skills to serve on committees and councils. Consumers also have some understanding of the importance of these skills and the need to speak out clearly as consumers, and not as tokens. They also publish a newspaper that is available on-line (http://www.mhamerica.org), or gratis to any consumer requesting an issue.

Another exemplary program and model is that of the Association of Community Organizations for Reform Now (ACORN). Their statement of purpose, "Who is on the streets, in the neighborhoods, in the workplaces and on the airwaves organizing and building power for low and moderate-income Americans?" (http://www.acorn.org/). This organization is one of the last remnants of the 1960s radical community action groups. The agenda reads like a cry for community organization, unheard of within this country since the demise of local grassroots community action groups. It is really exciting to read the preamble which begins, ". . . We stand for a People's Platform, as old as our country, as young as our dreams. We come before our nation, not to petition with hat in hand, but to rise as one people and demand" (http://www.acorn.org/people's_platform.html). The entire preamble is a cry for action: "We demand our birthright: the chance to be rich, the right to be free." These words are a cry that reverberates and is delivered by this organization as one voice. The language that is used, person-first language, is so different from the language used by those that profess to speak for disenfranchised groups, and is clearly a force to be reckoned with. The particular platforms on which they have taken stands are energy, "put the people before profits at the utilities;" health care, ". . . must be Affordable, Accessible, Of equal quality for all, Controlled by the people of the community, not by doctors, hospitals and insurance companies." There are even action plans included on how to accomplish these goals. Typically these plans are quite radical and the direction is always driven by values that demonstrate the strengths of the people, rather than the institutions that traditionally control people's lives.

The remainder of the platform for ACORN is a selection of issues that is totally congruent with the values of the social work profession. This list includes housing, work and worker's rights, rural issues, community development, taxes, environment, neighborhood security, rape, drugs, civil rights, communications, and education. Issues around resource acquisition often are congruent with the allocation of resources to all impoverished peoples. The majority of consumers receiving Social Security benefits are recipients of Supplemental Security Income (SSI). A program devised for people without substantial, gainful employment prior to their determination of a disability that hampers an individual's ability to work, SSI supports a person at a meager level. The average SSI payment nationwide is $500 per month, far below the U.S. Labor Department's figure of poverty.

ACORN's thrust continues to address issues that directly impact on the quality of life for consumers: housing, hospitals, and health insurance. Consumers are part of the community in which they reside and are not only concerned with mental health practice issues. In fact, consumers become more empowered to effect change for all when they become more involved in recognizing their sameness with others who share the same issues around poverty, control, and the environment.

Historically, consumers living outside of institutions have remained isolated within their own mental health ghettoes, relying on mental health professionals to assume all of their collective issues: housing, shopping, socialization, and employment. This typical scenario, repeated throughout the United States, reduces consumers to the status of mere recipients rather than partners with equal opportunities for decision making regarding choices in their lives. Professionals have bantered about the concept of normalization for consumers released from state institutions since the 1960s. For people with mental illness, it is contended that living within communities is preferable and more normal. The concept is clearly true; however, the reality of how and where consumers are forced to live because of their poverty, as well as the stigma associated with mental illness is well-documented. ACORN and other grassroots organizations are directly involved in improving the quality of life for all poor people. Their operational methods are congruent with those of all consumer empowerment projects. In one project, the ACORN organization selects employees after an extensive training period. Workers are expected to live within the community in which they are working, and are only paid a stipend. Recruitment for these positions is intense, and it is an opportunity for idealistic people to practice their idealism.

These two exemplary practice models are based on macropractice and community organization. The methods utilized are all geared toward system change, where the group or organization effects these changes through active participation of the members, but also through direct involvement at the institutional level. This process is accomplished through attendance at all sorts of public meetings: state, local, and federal. Each attendee is proactive and is able to advocate on behalf of issues that have been decided upon by the group. The goal is frequently increased involvement by the advocacy group, but the long-term goal is generally institutional change. This can be accomplished through legal remedies or by direct changes in the laws.

Consumer groups, developing partnerships with the National Alliance for the Mentally Ill (NAMI), the Mental Health Association, and other professional organizations (i.e., NASW), effectively organized to implement an insurance parity law for mental health treatment. This bill was a major triumph for its constituents, as it united all of these diverse groups into an effective coalition. The unintended consequence of such a bill was also recognition that mental illness is a biologically based illness and consequently must be treated as such. The beneficiaries of this bill are people with private health insurance. Recipients of public mental health treatment are insured through Medicare (a federal program), or Medicaid (a federally funded but state-controlled health insurance program). Consumers who attempt to return to work have, after any absence requiring some form of disability payment, been historically denied insurance in the workplace, based on the concept of a preexisting condition. A positive outcome of the passage of health care legislation was that a mandate was passed for insurance companies to provide insurance without consideration of such conditions when insuring companies with more than 200 employees.

Consumers have also been extremely active in organizing and following legislation that relates to intrusive or forced treatments. Dendron/Support Coalition, a radical consumer voice from Oregon that advocates against electroshock treatment and any form of commitment procedures, is but one example. The director of this group, David Oakes, has been very active in speaking out nationally on many consumer issues. The agenda that his group supports reads like a litany of the issues which organized the initial consumer movement in the 1970s against electroshock treatment, involuntary commitment, forced drugging, and forced treatment. His organization publishes a quarterly newsletter, *The Dendron*. A subscription can be obtained by contacting him through email at dendron@efn.org.

UNIQUE CHALLENGES FOR SOCIAL WORKERS

In this era of Medicaid, Medicaid billing, and health maintenance organizations (HMOs), social workers employed in a public mental health setting must be ever vigilant regarding how services and resources are provided. As stated in the rationale for this text, social workers fill the majority of positions in outpatient and community mental health services for consumers, survivors, or ex-patients. This interesting scenario can be cause for well-trained social workers to impose social work values upon the service delivery system. The key issue is, of course, what does *well-trained* mean in this context? I contend it is for social workers to be well-versed in all areas of public policy and legislation, as it relates to mental health, and to understand the political position of the consumer, survivor, or ex-patient. For example, there are currently states that are considering involuntary outpatient commitment laws that would, if enacted, create a system that could force treatment on consumers. This would create a tension between professionals and consumers that would clearly not be therapeutic and would cause any relationship between them to be severed. In fact, the National Mental Health Association published a paper on this subject and questioned the effectiveness of outpatient commitment. According to the most comprehensive study of outpatient commitment, the Bellevue Study, the outcomes (compliance with treatment, rates of hospitalization, hospital tenure and arrests, or violent acts committed) for consumers involuntarily committed were no different than the outcomes for people voluntarily committed (Ingoglia, 1999).

Thus, the social worker must be aware of popular myths and the stigma regarding people with mental illness. Some of these are perpetrated by those professionals working in the mental health system and the system itself (North, 1993). Consumers report that often professionals speak to them using non-person-first language (i.e., calling a person a "schizophrenic," a "chronic," a "bipolar"), or they expect a person with mental illness to be satisfied with a dishwashing or janitor job. Some professionals have also suggested that mothers with mental illness should not be allowed to raise children. Many still conduct treatment team meetings without inviting the consumer/survivor/ex-patient, or place a consumer/survivor/ex-patient into a residential program because it is "best for her," even though she wants to live with a lover. Professionals have been accused of sitting quietly in a treatment team meeting when the psychiatrist decides to keep the consumer/survivor/ex-patient on Haldol rather than trying one of the newer antipsychotic medications because the consumer/survivor/ex-patient is noncompliant. They have stated unequivocally that it is best for the consumer/survivor/ex-patient not to spend time with her or his family without consulting either, and have refused to allow the consumer/survivor/ex-patient access to her or his medical record. These are but a few of the issues that social workers must be cognizant of. They are not exaggerations but are rather the typical issues that are decided upon by professionals who believe they are operating in the best interests of their customers.

Case management is another area in which social workers must become involved if it is to be the exceptional service it is supposed to be. This service is deemed essential for people with serious mental illness. Clinical case management is often listed first among treatment and service components needed by persons with mental illness. Unfortunately, in Virginia, there is no degree of standards for case management. In fact, there is no certification whatsoever for case managers. The only way to find a definition of what case management is, or what it should do, is by examining the job descriptions for a case manager. Because of the disparity between local mental health centers, a case manager might be a social worker with a master's degree. In another locality, it could be a person with a high school diploma. Now, because social workers are the majority of the workers in public mental health programs, it would behoove the profession if social workers would agree that what most of them do is clinical case management. In that case, they could professionalize this service.

In a letter dated July 11, 2000, the Office of Planning and Regulation of the Virginia Department of Mental Health, Mental Retardation, and Substance Abuse Services requested comments on Regulations for the Certification of Case Management Services (12 VAC 35–170–10 et seq.). This was clearly a new and significant step for the department, one that stands to have serious implications for social workers in this state. The recent demand for regulation and certification for case management services clearly indicates that many consumer, family member, and professional recommendations made during Dr. King Davis's tenure as Commissioner of the Virginia Department of Mental Health, Mental Retardation, and Substance Abuse Services, are finally being followed, albeit more than 8 years after his departure. The most significant challenge for social work practice is the tension between those who define the arena of social work treatment as being one that emphasizes problems, dysfunction, and pathology, rather than the practice of client strengths (Saleebey, 1992). The strengths perspective ". . . seeks to develop abilities and capacities in clients. However it assumes that clients already have a number of competencies and resources that may be used to improve their situation" (p. 15). This approach is clearly indicated for social workers who wish to employ an intervention that is based on utilizing the resources and resourcefulness of the particular individual with whom they are in a therapeutic relationship. By utilizing this approach, practitioners of social work can, and do, base their work with consumers on the ethics, principles, and values of the profession. As a value directly from NASW's *Code of Ethics*, "Social workers understand that relationships between and among people are an important vehicle for change. Social workers engage people as partners in the helping process."

CASE DILEMMA

Because of my work as an advocate for people with mental illness who are also homeless, I have been accepted as a team member by the community mental health team, a full partner, on a new interdisciplinary team for people who have accompanying substance abuse issues. For the first time, our public mental health center has partnered with staff from their substance abuse division, the emergency services staff, the inpatient hospital staff, and our consumer-run drop-in center. The goal for this team is to divert people who have a primary diagnosis of substance abuse from utilizing the state hospital. The reality for people with this problem is that they often receive treatment for their substance abuse from the psychiatric division, as they may come to the emergency room for detoxification or are substantially unable to care for themselves. This can lead to psychiatric hospitalizations at private hospitals where they are detained for a period of days. After the initial detention, they must be committed to the state hospital for additional treatment, as they typically do not have any medical insurance. Policy and practice are two issues that are at cross-purposes during this scenario. Individuals with substantial issues around substance abuse are actually problematic for mental hospitals, and, due to the increased focus on census reduction in these hospitals, the state has issued stringent criteria for admission to these facilities.

Garland is one of the people being served by the diversion treatment team. He is a 50-ish Caucasian male who continues to use alcohol in spite of repeated hospital admissions (more than 20 during the latter part of 1999), and many additional emergency room visits where he is seen, but not admitted. His primary diagnosis has been substance abuse, but he has also been diagnosed with chronic depression and borderline personality disorder. He had several suicide attempts, once placing a loaded pistol in his mouth and asking a drinking buddy to pull the trigger. He did, leaving Garland with some significant damage to his jaw and neck. Another time, Garland swallowed broken glass that required him to have a colostomy.

Garland is a rather attractive person and has a likable personality. His charming manner provides him with an opportunity to relate to others with humor and gentleness that is quite incongruent with his self-abusing behavior. He has been homeless for a number of years, living in one shelter or another, or outdoors, or with friends in a variety of housing options when drinking. The period of time between drinking episodes has decreased from months to days and he is often under the influence for extended periods that can last from weeks to a month. He has been incarcerated for extended periods for activities as diverse as petty theft, forgery, and littering. These activities are directly related to his need for funds for alcohol and drugs. During these periods of incarceration, he has taken his medication as prescribed, remained alcohol- and drug-free, and was emotionally stable.

When he is placed on an antidepressant, he briefly remains sober, but he does not take the prescribed medication while drinking. Because of the Social Security rules for substance-abusing people, he is ineligible for disability, in spite of his physical and emotional problems. While it is recognized by his mental health providers that being declared disabled might not be in his best interest long-term, ongoing discussion suggests that this might aid Garland by providing him with essential resources. Now, providers from the area of substance abuse have declared that they are totally against the application process, as they believe it to be enabling, and that Garland must first hit bottom.

This is the dilemma. As a social worker, it is our responsibility to develop a relationship with people whom we assist. It is also imperative to be an advocate for these people. The staff members from the substance abuse area are generally working from a model that is far more confrontational than any used by social workers. In Garland's case, I continue to be supportive even though he relapses quite often. I typically give him cigarettes, food, clothing, a place to shower, clothing, blankets, and a ride to the hospital or to treatment. There are no restrictions to my support unless his behavior (due to his drinking) causes me discomfort. There have been a succession of unsuccessful plans that Garland and I have developed. We've discussed and developed short-term (only for one day) plans, as well as longer-term and inpatient treatment, employment, housing, and clothing referrals.

As an advocate, and a true partner in any plan with Garland, I cannot do what I believe is in his best interest, apply for disability, until Garland and I both agree on the course of action to pursue. The values I profess do not allow me to pursue any activity without that collaboration. If Garland agrees to this plan, we will submit the application together. The strengths I bring to the partnership are my knowledge of this process and how to utilize language to describe Garland's medical condition in such a way that it will influence those people who will make the determination. During the last 10 years, I have spent considerable time and effort in presenting evidence to people in positions of power, people in offices who make disability determinations. My evidence has been presented in an intentional, factual, critical manner that has persuaded, and in several cases, changed individual people's opinions on their decision. Prior to my intervention, this particular case was decided based solely on evidence supplied by psychiatrists and/or medical records. When I offer my assistance and find supportive documentation, which would not necessarily find its way without my solicitation, the person in the role of decision maker has no recourse other than to make a favorable determination, based on the records that I submit. The evidence I submit is generally about the person's life. When people suffer from mental illnesses, they cannot be competitively employed, often become homeless, and are frequent visitors to emergency rooms, hospital, or jails. These are clearly steps that Gerhart recommends in her advocacy model.

When and if Garland chooses to apply for disability, I will use all of my advocacy-based skills to assist him. In the interim, I continue to be there for him, providing his behavior at the center is acceptable. Consumers and staff do have expectations of safety at the center. If anyone causes another person to feel unsafe due to his/her actions, then she or he is asked to leave. The typical problem occurs when a consumer is intoxicated and becomes argumentative. Garland has done this and left under protest. When he reappears, typically several days later, he is sober and apologizes for his past behavior. This is a significant step for Garland, as he seems to have internalized some of the expectations placed upon him by his peer group. It helps build a foundation for future partnership practice.

KEY TERMS

Consumer Movement: During the early 1970s, former mental patients collectively began to realize that what they had experienced in mental hospitals was unjust and oppressive. These ex-patients began organizing groups to fight for their rights, to stop abuse and oppression of psychiatric hospitals, and to end stigma attached to mental illness. This movement has its roots in the civil rights movement of the 1960s.

Consumer/Survivor/Ex-Patient: This designation is used by various individuals and groups to refer to themselves and others who have been recipients of services of the mental health system.

Empowerment: The process and the outcome associated with individuals (who are disenfranchised) gaining control over their lives and their environments. A measure of this principle is an increased feeling of competence resulting from self-directed activities on the part of the consumer.

Ethics: Norms and ideals that have to do with obligation and responsibility and that guide how we treat others and how we expect to be treated.

Recovery: The lived or real-life experience of people as they accept and overcome the challenge of a disability.

Values: System of meanings that have been developed, based on fundamental, existential, and normative postulates; beliefs and assumptions about what is and what ought to be; the glue that holds a system together and binds it to human conditions, institutions, and practices.

WEB RESOURCES

The Madness Group (http://www.people who.org/Madness/). This site lists pages, with an electronic resources library for people who are consumers of mental health services. Its founder, Sylvia Carras, is wildly outspoken in her attacks on the mental health establishment.

CONTAC (http://www.contac.org). CONTAC is a West Virginia–based advocacy and technical support center for all consumers. Its role is to provide consumers with education and technical support. It is actively engaged in leadership training and offers consumers, family organizations, and the state behavioral health authorities opportunities to come together for training and information sharing.

Disability Rights Education and Defense Fund (http://dredf.org/index.html). This site lists the current legislation and alerts individuals to impending legislative activity on issues of disability rights.

Association for Community Organization and Social Administration (ACOSA) (http://www.acosa.org). This professional organization of social workers publishes research and articles in its journal on macrolevel of practice.

ACORN (http://www.acorn.org/) This association promotes grassroots community organization that operates in several states, cities, and rural areas. It deals with issues of poverty and disenfranchisement for all cultural groups. ACORN is one of the last true grassroots organizations from the 1960s that is still functioning.

REFERENCES

Alinsky, S. (1969). *Reveille for radicals.* New York: Vintage.

Alinsky, S. (1972). *Rules for radicals.* New York: Vintage.

Barker, R. L. (1995). *The social work dictionary* (2nd ed.). Silver Spring, MD: NASW Press.

Belcher, L. (1998). *West Virginia Consumer Satisfaction Survey.* Charleston: West Virginia Mental Health Consumers' Association.

Bentley, K. J., & Walsh, J. (2001). *The social worker & psychotropic medication* (2nd ed.). Pacific Grove, CA: Brooks/Cole.

Chamberlin, J. (1990). The ex-patients' movement: Where we've been and where we're going. *The Journal of Mind and Behavior, 11*(3), 323–336.

Chandler, S. M. (1990). *Competing realities: The contested terrain of mental health advocacy.* New York: Praeger.

Deegan, P. E. (1992). The Independent Living Movement and people with psychiatric disabilities: Taking back control over our own lives. *Psychosocial Rehabilitation Journal, 15*(3), 3–19.

Gerhart, U. C. (1990). *Caring for the chronic mentally ill.* Ithaca, IL: Peacock.

Gerhart, U. C., & Brooks, A. D. (1983). The social work practitioner and antipsychotic medications. *Social Work, 28,* 454–460.

Hepworth, D. H., & Larsen, J. A. (1990). *Direct social work practice.* Belmont, CA: Wadsworth.

Herbert, M. D., & Mould, J. W. (1992). The advocacy role in public child welfare. *Child Welfare, 71,* 114–130.

Howie the Harp. (1988). *Reaching across: Mental health clients helping each other.* Sacramento, CA: California Network of Mental Health Clients.

Ingoglia, C. (1999). State advocacy update: The rise of involuntary outpatient commitment statutes. In *Involuntary outpatient commitment forum: An overview for advocates.* Washington, DC: National Mental Health Association.

Kahn S. (1991). *Organizing: A guide for grassroots leaders* (2nd ed.). Silver Spring, MD: National Association of Social Workers.

Litzelfelner, P., & Petr, C. G. (1997). Case advocacy in child welfare. *Social Work, 42*(4), 392–402.

Lourie, N. (1975). The many faces of advocacy. In I. N. Berlin (Ed.), *Advocacy for Child Mental Health* (pp. 68–91). New York: Brunner/Mazel.

Mack, J. E. (1994). Power, powerlessness, and empowerment in psychotherapy. *Psychiatry, 57,* 178–198.

NASW Ad Hoc Committee on Advocacy. (1969). The social worker as advocate: Champion of social victims. *Social Work, 14,* 16–22.

National Association of Social Workers. (1997). *Code of Ethics.* Washington, DC: Author.

North, C. S. (1993). *Multiple personalities, multiple disorders: Psychiatric classification and media influence.* New York: Oxford University Press.

O'Donnell, S. (1995). Is community organizing "The Greatest Job" one could have? Findings from a survey of Chicago organizers. *Journal of Community Practice, 2*(1), 16.

Rose, S. M. (1992). *Case management & social work practice.* New York: Longman.

Ross, M. (1955). *Community organization.* New York: Harper & Row.

Saleebey, D. (1992). *The strengths perspective in social work practice.* New York: Longman.

Silverman, S. (1997). Recovery through partnership: "On our own," Charlottesville, Virginia. In C. Mowbray, D. Moxley, C. Jasper, & L. Howell (Eds.). *Consumers as providers in psychiatric rehabilitation*, Columbia, MD: International Association of Psychosocial Rehabilitation Services.

Silverman, S. H., Taylor, L., & Blank, M. (1997). On our own: Preliminary findings from a consumer-run service model. *Psychiatric Rehabilitation Journal*, 21(2), 151–159.

Social Workers as Program Evaluators and Researchers

A. Suzanne Boyd &
Wynne S. Korr

Do we need a new program in the community to help homeless people with mental illness? Are our current services to clients with dual diagnoses reducing rehospitalization? How do we develop and test an intervention for people with anxiety disorders? How do we choose a measure to assess the impact of case management services on clients' lives? How do we convince the managed care organization that rape victims need more than four sessions to address post-traumatic stress disorder symptoms?

Mental health social workers raise these and many similar questions daily. Increasingly, social work practitioners, supervisors, and agency directors are designing and conducting studies to address such questions. They may work alone or with the help of consultants. Their findings may be as simple as a one-paragraph report (e.g., "Of 73 clients put on the waiting list in January, February, and March, 65 were offered an assessment within 1 month of their initial call, but only 30 came in"). Or, the report may be a 20-page paper in a professional peer-reviewed journal. To conduct these studies, social workers in mental health settings need to develop skills as evaluators and researchers.

This chapter will describe knowledge and skills that social workers (line staff, supervisors, administrators, and consultants) need to successfully carry out their roles in program evaluation and clinical and services research across a wide range of mental health problems and populations. We include examples of social workers' involvement in these roles.

THE INTELLECTUAL BASE

Social workers are in a unique position to raise important research questions because they provide more mental health services than any other helping profession (Center for Mental Health Services, 1998). They often observe, before anyone else, problems that service systems need to address. By taking an active role in program evaluation and clinical and services research, social workers can shape the development of interventions and mental health programs.

Both the profession and social work education have underscored the commitment to practice evaluation. The 1997 National Association of Social Workers (NASW) *Code of Ethics* makes this commitment an ethical obligation (Sec. 5.02):

- Social workers should monitor and evaluate policies, the implementation of programs, and practice interventions.
- Social workers should promote and facilitate evaluation and research to contribute to the development of knowledge.

Clearly, social workers need the knowledge and skills to fulfill these obligations.

The Council on Social Work Education (CSWE), through its educational policies and accrediting standards, has sought to ensure that all new social workers will get the needed knowledge and skills. The current CSWE Curriculum Policy Statement (CPS) mandates that graduates of Master's of Social Work programs must be able to

- Evaluate relevant research studies and apply findings to practice, and demonstrate skills in quantitative and qualitative research design, data analysis, and knowledge dissemination (M5.7.10).
- Conduct empirical evaluations of their own practice interventions and those of other relevant systems (M5.7.11).

Social work doctoral programs have a special mission in preparing social workers that take on evaluation and research as primary roles. Students in doctoral programs typically take advanced courses in theory, and qualitative and quantitative methods that prepare them for developing the knowledge base of the profession, including its major practice areas, such as mental health.

In 1991, the Task Force on Social Work Research (1991), supported by the National Institute on Mental Health (NIMH), identified a crisis in social work research. The Task Force found insufficient numbers of researchers, insufficient quantity of research to meet the needs of the profession, lack of dissemination of research-based findings to practitioners, and lack of organizational and funding resources to support research development in social work. The Task Force recommendations led NIMH to fund eight social work research-development centers based in universities. Clearly, evaluating interventions, social programs, and social work practice has increasingly gained importance in the social work profession (Kirk & Tripodi, 1994).

The centers and other initiatives have contributed to expanded research training and research dissemination. They have also contributed to research on a variety of mental health topics, including care of the serious mentally ill, organization of mental health services to children and adolescents, poverty risk, and mental health (Austin, 1999). Austin identified the development of intervention research as the continuing challenge. This type of research, described later as services research, requires detailed specification of interventive procedures, so effective interventions can be replicated in other settings. Findings need to be disseminated to practitioners and incorporated into the professional curriculum (p. 705).

Social Work Evaluation and Research—A History

Social work research and evaluation in mental health attempts to respond to the needs of the most vulnerable, and is characterized by collaboration, with clients and their families, and with professionals from all disciplines. Just as the practice of psychiatric social work developed in the Progressive Era to address the needs of people with mental illness in the hospital and community (Vourlekis, Edinburg, & Knee, 1998; Vourlekis, Greene, Knee, & Edinburg, 1994), so did the involvement of social work in mental health research and evaluation. For example, the women of Hull-House studied problems in state hospitals and made recommendations for monitoring quality care (Lathrop, 1905). The period from the 1920s to the 1960s was dominated by Freudian-based casework, and social work drifted from a primary commitment to the public mental health services. With the start of the federally funded community mental health program in 1963 and the burgeoning of deinstitutionalization, social workers were drawn back into publicly supported service delivery and into research on problems faced by people with mental illness in the community. By 1975, the federal legislation (PL 94–63) required that the community mental health centers engage in program evaluation. This requirement stimulated the development of evaluative designs and measurement techniques.

A good example of social workers' contribution to mental health research is seen in the era of deinstitutionalization. By the 1970s, most states had reduced the population in state hospitals and the length of stay for those who were hospitalized. Most former patients were living in the community, but relapse rates were so high that people spoke of the revolving door of discharge and readmission. We knew little about the conditions under which people lived in the community, or what factors predicted adjustment or failure (Segal & Aviram, 1978). Clearly, new interventions needed to be developed to reduce relapse rates and improve adjustment in the community. Traditional outpatient therapy was a failure in clients with severe mental illness.

Social workers were key to the development of two major psychosocial interventions that have become the cornerstone of community-based practice: assertive community treatment and psychoeducation. Mary Ann Test and her colleagues developed programs of assertive community treatment (ACT) to provide comprehensive treatments and supports in the community for adults with severe mental illness (Test, 1998). Research (e.g., Dixon, 2000; Stein & Test, 1980) has consistently shown the effectiveness of this program as discussed elsewhere in this volume.

Although the majority of deinstitutionalized clients returned to live with their families, families knew little about the illnesses of their relative, such as schizophrenia, or about how to manage family situations to reduce relapse. Social workers Carol Anderson and Gerard Hogarty developed and researched psychoeducation to address the needs of families (Anderson, Reiss, & Hogarty, 1986). Social worker Ellen Lukens and others have extended the psychoeducation approach to include multiple family groups (e.g., Lukens & Thorning, 1996; McFarlane et al., 1995).

ACT and psychoeducation approaches are considered necessary components of treatment offered to adults with severe mental illness. The Schizophrenia Patient

Outcomes Research Team (PORT) studies, funded by NIMH and the Agency for Health Care Policy and Research, identified treatments and services known to reduce the symptoms of schizophrenia and promote recovery, including these two approaches (Lehman et al., 1998). The National Alliance for the Mentally Ill (NAMI) also developed a consumer and family guide to treatment that works for schizophrenia (NAMI, n.d., 1998). It also included ACT and family education. In fact, in 1998, NAMI launched a major national initiative to increase access to ACT services for all adults with severe mental illness. NAMI's quarterly publication, *The Advocate*, included a 1-page flier in the Summer 2000 issue on "What Consumers Want to Know about PACT" (p. 28).

Other social work researchers and evaluators have developed and/or studied enhanced interventions and newer programming strategies for clients with mental illness. Rapp (1998) developed a strengths-based approach to case management (see Chapter 8). Rapp and colleagues (1988) also developed the Status Method on client outcome reporting, which helps agencies collect information on client outcomes in four areas for mental health consumers, including independent living status, vocational status, educational status, and hospitalizations (Rapp, 1997). Carol Mowbray and Cheribeth Tan (1993) conducted the first known formative evaluation of the consumer-operated drop-in center model, contributing to the knowledge base about consumer-centered initiatives. Mowbray (1999) is also credited with promoting and developing supported education programs for mental health clients.

Social workers need to be armed with a common research and evaluation knowledge base, though relatively few social workers will devote their entire career to research or program evaluation (Royse, Thyer, Padgett, & Logan, 2001). Although social workers have made significant contributions to social work evaluation and research, we still have a long way to go. For example, a study by Rosen, Proctor, and Staudt (1999) reviewing 1,849 articles, published in 13 social work journals from 1993 to 1997, only identified 863 research articles. Descriptive studies ($n = 314$) and explanatory studies ($n = 423$) accounted for the majority of articles. Only 126 articles involved some type of evaluation or outcome study. Clearly, there are far more descriptive and explanatory studies published in major social work journals compared to evaluation or outcome studies.

Benefits for Social Workers Engaged in Program Evaluation and Research

Social workers are the main provider of mental health services to clients who struggle with problems such as depression, schizophrenia, anxiety, eating disorders, borderline personality disorder, and sexual dysfunction. They are in a unique situation to influence the social service delivery system because of their rich experiences across an array of mental health client problems. As a by-product of conducting research and program evaluation studies, social workers can educate line staff, supervisors, administrators, agency directors, and the larger community on the importance of using evidence-based practice (i.e., knowing mental health programs are achieving positive outcomes for clients). Social workers also possess the skills to translate research and program evaluation findings into meaningful policy changes in the local, state, agency, or national arena, and contribute to the overall knowledge base of the profession. Most importantly, however, social workers fulfill their ethical obligation to evaluate practice as outlined in Section 5.02 of the NASW *Code of Ethics* (1997).

MAJOR TASKS AND GOALS

Social workers are involved in evaluating existing services for mental health clients with specific mental disorders. In this section, we will highlight three types of program evaluation—needs assessment, formative evaluation, and summative evaluation—and the major tasks and goals associated with each.

Program Evaluation

In its simplest view, program evaluation is a collection of methods and skills employed by social workers to determine whether (a) a program or service is needed and the extent to which it will be used, (b) it will meet the need, (c) it is delivered as planned, and (d) it helps mental health clients function effectively (Posavac & Carey, 1992). Ultimately, the relevance of program evaluation is to gather information to improve social service programs.

Needs Assessment

Needs assessments are conducted to determine whether the service needs of mental health clients are being met. Needs assessments specifically determine the nature, scope, and locale of a social problem, and identify useful, relevant, and feasible problem solutions (Gabor, Unrau, & Grinnell, 1998). The term *needs assessment* is used to specify various techniques employed to collect data for program planning purposes (Rubin & Babbie, 2001).

A needs assessment can be used to justify the need for a social service program focusing on social problems or specific client groups like mental health consumers (Gabor et al., 1998). For example, a social worker at a girls' private school notices a large majority of girls visiting the counseling center have lost a significant amount of weight. The social worker may conduct a needs assessment to determine if there is a prevalence of eating disorders among this group of girls.

A needs assessment can also be conducted to determine what barriers, if any, exist preventing mental health clients from accessing services (Royse et al., 2001). A social worker employed at a local community mental health center may notice that the majority of mental health clients using the services complain of the difficulty in accessing local dental services. A needs assessment in this case could be used to ask what barriers are preventing mental health clients from accessing dental services. The possible answers may be transportation, cost, or availability, to name a few.

A needs assessment may also be used to educate people about the magnitude of a social problem (Gabor et al., 1998). A social worker at a family-based agency may conduct a needs assessment to help determine the number of children lacking insurance for mental health services in a small town. This information will help provide evidence of the number of children who need mental health services, and what types of services are needed.

Another reason to conduct a needs assessment may be to document ongoing future needs (Royse et al., 2001). A social worker at a local Salvation Army shelter notices an increase in the number of homeless mental health clients. The social worker may use a needs assessment to demonstrate the ongoing need for a special shelter for them, or project other resulting social problems if the issue of homelessness is not addressed.

A needs assessment can also help plan the budget and planning process within a program, by providing strong indicators about how resources should be allocated (Gabor et al., 1998). For example, a social worker employed at an outpatient program for sexual dysfunction may survey clients' needs on their opinion of the utility of individual treatment. Their responses may indicate group therapy with seven or more members was inadequate to meet their needs. Planning future services may include delegating more funds for additional outpatient groups, thus reducing group membership.

There are a variety of tasks involved in a needs assessment. The first major task is to identify the purpose of the needs assessment (Royse et al., 2001). For example, a social worker notes that mental health clients at the local social service agency lack structured activities during the evening and weekend hours. Mental health clients have indicated their desire to participate in more evening and weekend activities. A needs assessment may be a useful tool to address the lack of available evening and weekend activities. The purpose of such a needs assessment would be to determine the number of mental health clients affected, as well as to identify the types of needed structured activities.

The second task is to define the type of need, "a basic requirement necessary to sustain the human condition, to which people have a right" (Gabor et al., 1998, p. 47). Remember how we define the social problem directly impacts the type of data we gather as well as the data collection methods used (Gabor et al., 1998). We will want to include the viewpoints of all stakeholders, including the mental health clients, social workers, agency administrators, and local community members.

The third task is to determine the resources and amount of money available to conduct the needs assessment (Royse et al., 2001). The social service agency does not have any liquid money to contribute; however, the agency director will provide one staff member and their building to help organize structured evening and weekend social activities. Research at the library uncovers a local foundation that will provide $10,000 to start a new program. Other resource search reveals the local school of social work will place a Bachelor of Social Work student to work in this new program.

The fourth task in a needs assessment is to determine what information is needed for decision making, including whether the information can be obtained with the available resources (Royce et al., 2001). Developing the needs assessment questions is an important part of this step (Gabor et al., 1998). In our example, the social worker needs to determine whether the agency has already tabulated exactly how many clients are affected and the types of activities desired. If not, this information must be collected.

The fifth task is to develop needs assessment questions (Gabor et al., 1998). How many mental health clients are interested in evening and weekend activities? What types of activities should be offered during the evening and weekends? How will clients get to and from the activities? What local resources are already available during the evening and on the weekends?

The sixth task is to identify the target for intervention (the who or what) (Royse et al., 1998). The target for intervention for the previous example would be mental health clients at the local service agency interested in evening and weekend activities.

The seventh task is to develop a data collection plan (Gabor et al., 1998). The social worker also has to decide which methods to use to collect the data. Should the social worker send out a written survey to clients? Or could information on types of activities be collected during a general meeting with clients? Has this type of information been gathered at the agency before? If so, what were client interests?

After the data collection plan has been established, the data need to be analyzed and displayed (Gabor et al., 1998). The social worker could conduct a 1-page survey to identify the hours and types of activities demanded. The results could be displayed in a simple frequency bar chart. The social worker would then write a short report and distribute the findings to the mental health clients and the staff. The findings could be listed on a Web site, distributed in hard copy to everyone, or displayed in a common area of the social service agency.

Formative Evaluation

Formative evaluation (process evaluation) helps social workers obtain useful information in developing a program in its early phases (Weiss, 1972) or improving an already existing program. The goal of formative evaluation is to organize information social workers need for program improvement. Additional goals include program description, program monitoring, and quality assurance (Royse et al., 2001). Program staff and program developers generally use formative evaluations. The term *process evaluation* is used interchangeably with *formative evaluation*.

We will use an example from the literature to illustrate the various steps of a formative evaluation. Mowbray and Tan (1993) conducted the first known formative evaluation of consumer-operated drop-in centers, ". . . focusing on the extent to which the centers met programmatic expectations, collecting retrospective satisfaction and impact assessments from participants, and examining differences in operations across the six centers" (p. 9). Recall that a formative evaluation focuses on either the administrative operations of a program or the mental health, client–service delivery system.

The first major task in a formative evaluation is to make sure the program is well described and can be evaluated with a clearly defined mission, goals, and objectives.

Sometimes this is referred to as an evaluability assessment. Evaluability assessments can help social workers determine whether to conduct a formative or summative evaluation, whether changes may need to be made to the program prior to beginning a formal evaluation, and to decide which program evaluation methods are warranted to measure the performance of a program (Chambers, Wedel, & Rodwell, 1992). (See pp. 119–146 of Chambers et al. for a complete discussion of evaluability assessment.)

The second step of a formative evaluation is to develop clear questions for the evaluation (Gabor et al., 1998). Gabor et al. identify eight questions that may be asked when conducting a formative evaluation: (1) What is the program's background? (2) What is the program's client profile? (3) What is the program's staff profile? (4) What is the amount of service provided to clients? (5) What are the program's interventions and activities? (6) What administrative supports are in place to support the program's client–service delivery system? (7) How satisfied are the program's stakeholders? and (8) How efficient is the program? For example, Mowbray & Tan (1993) answered the following questions in their formative evaluation of a group of consumer-operated drop-in centers: (1) What descriptive information exists on the centers? (2) What are individual consumer's perceptions and evaluations of the center? (3) What are the similarities and differences among the centers? and (4) What is the relationship between those similarities and differences and other factors, including attendance and consumer satisfaction with the drop-in center?

The third task in a formative evaluation is to develop data collection instruments that are easy to use, fit into the daily operation of a program, and include user input in their conceptualization and design (Gabor et al., 1998). It is important to identify and review existing measurement instruments for their relevance to the formative evaluation, so social workers do not "reinvent the wheel." (We will discuss in detail the use of outcome measurement instruments later in this chapter.) It is also important to collect as much data as possible to answer the eight questions posed in the second step. Mowbray & Tan (1993) used a research team to develop the data collection instruments. They developed a face-to-face instrument consisting of six sections: (1) demographic and mental health service utilization information, (2) consumer likes and dislikes about the center, (3) problems regarding center utilization, (4) social environment rating, (5) member assessment of each center's effect on their lives, and (6) member satisfaction (p. 10). They adapted existing instruments for two sections of the interview. First, their social environment section was patterned after Moos's Community Oriented Programs Environment Scale (COPES) (1974) and Moos and Humphrey's Group Environment Scale (GES) (1974). Second, their members' satisfaction section was adapted from Nguyen, Atkisson, and Stegner's Client Satisfaction Questionnaire (CSQ-8) (1983). The remaining interview sections were developed for their study. Social workers can also employ staff, survey research laboratories, and others to develop instruments, in addition to using the help of clients.

The fourth task in a formative evaluation is to develop a data collection monitoring system (Gabor et al., 1998). We need to consider how many cases or units of analysis (i.e., mental health client, staff, program, etc.) to include, when to collect the data, and how to carry out data collection efforts. Mowbray and Tan's (1993) unit of analysis was the mental health client. They decided to collect 20 interviews from each of the six centers for a total of 120 interviews. They collected the data during a 6-week period. Clients who were present at the drop-in center on interview days participated in their study. A research team at each center conducted the data collection efforts.

The fifth task is to code, score, and analyze the data (Gabor et al., 1998). An accurate codebook and data analysis plan help keep the analysis process simple and organized. Mowbray and Tan (1993) wrote a detailed manual on the development of their survey instrument, including coding and statistical analyses used for each scale. The authors also reported accurate use of statistical analysis in their formative evaluation report.

The sixth task is to develop an effective feedback system (Gabor et al., 1998), as such a system will help workers and mental health clients improve how a program works. In Mowbray and Tan's (1993) formative evaluation of drop-in centers, the study results were not only shared with the participating drop-in centers, but also the Michigan Department of Mental Health (MDMH), the Justice in Mental Health Organization (JIMHO), and other nationwide drop-in centers.

The seventh and last task in conducting a formative evaluation is writing the report and disseminating and communicating the results to various audiences (Gabor et al., 1998). Mowbray and Tan (1993) shared their results with the participating drop-in centers and funding sources (i.e., MDMH, JIMHO, and Michigan State University). More importantly, they published their results in a professional journal and also presented the information at national conferences. They have also distributed the interview instrument in a comprehensive report, detailing how it was developed, its use, and statistical analysis. Social workers can also share the results of formative evaluations through conference presentations, in-service trainings, and research monographs, to name a few.

Summative Evaluation

Summative evaluations (outcome evaluations) ascertain the worth of a program once it has been in existence for a period of time (Weiss, 1972). Summative evaluations answer the question, "Did our clients get better (improve)?" (Royse et al., 2001). Summative evaluations are intended to inform decision makers and larger social systems who are thinking about using specific programs in their agency, state, or locality (Weiss, 1972). They are also intended to inform people making decisions on a program's continuation or termination, such as a state legislative body (Weiss, 1972). Summative evaluations rely on specific procedures or methodology. Group evaluation designs are frequently employed to conduct a summative evaluation, from pre-experimental designs to experimental designs at the most rigorous level. Cost-benefit analyses and cost-effectiveness evaluations are also used. The major task is to choose the appropriate methodology or procedures to answer evaluation questions. Successfully carrying out a summative evaluation is a major, complex effort. We will briefly address a few of these techniques in the next section.

The first task in a summative evaluation is to operationalize the program objectives (Gabor et al., 1998). The next task is to decide what instruments to use to measure the objectives (Gabor et al., 1998). Social workers could use a standardized instrument found to be reliable and valid, such as the SCID (discussed later) or a questionnaire, or they can develop a nonstandardized measurement instrument. Social workers could also ask mental health consumers questions directly. For our citywide drop-in center from the needs assessment example, one objective may be to increase the quality of life among consumer members. Will quality of life be defined as a person's overall well-being or something that enhances mood? With our example, social workers may chose to use an already existing quality of life scale or develop their own.

The next task is to develop an evaluation monitoring system (Gabor et al., 1998). A monitoring system should consider the available resources and time demands when social workers are assessing. The system should consider how many mental health consumers to include in the summative evaluation, when to collect the data, and how to collect the summative evaluation data (i.e., in person, via mail, telephone, email, or Internet). The social worker may include all clients or a randomly selected group of clients. The social worker needs to also consider whether the data will be collected when the clients first get to the drop-in center, whether they will develop an interview guide similar to that of Mowbray and Tan (1993), or whether they will interview clients in the home or over the telephone. These are just a few questions to be answered when developing a program monitoring system.

Once a social worker has collected the outcome data for the summative evaluation, it is important to develop a data analysis plan and decide how to visually display the data (Gabor et al., 1998). An accurate data analysis plan includes research questions and hypotheses to be answered. It also specifies what statistical test will be used to examine the research question or hypothesis. An accurate data analysis plan helps to limit social workers from conducting unnecessary statistical tests to merely search for statistical significance. One method social workers can use to assist with data display decisions is to develop a set of "dummy tables" prior to analyzing the data. This also helps us think through other analyses that may be needed. The social worker may have a firm understanding of statistics or may choose to use a consultant to conduct the data analysis according to the data analysis plan.

The next task is to develop some type of a feedback system (Gabor et al., 1998) for social workers and mental health consumers. Regular review of outcome data by stakeholders related to the organization helps them assess program goals. The social worker and mental health consumers may decide to hold biweekly meetings at the center to provide research, evaluate updates, and elicit responses from key stakeholders.

The last step is to write up the report and disseminate the results to relevant stakeholders (Gabor et al., 1998). In our example, a summary of evaluation activities could be posted on the bulletin board in a common area, distributed to clients, staff, and board members, or mailed to other individual stakeholders.

Research

In addition to evaluating existing services, social workers are involved in the development and testing of interventions to help consumers with specific mental disorders and to help their families. We will highlight two types of research on interventions, clinical research and services research, and review the major tasks and goals associated with each phase.

Clinical Research

The goal of this research is to ". . . examine the impact of well-defined treatments under tightly controlled conditions, such as the implementation of interventions by highly skilled clinicians or by use of comprehensive treatment protocols under the close supervision of experts" (Proctor & Stiffman, 1998, p. 260).

Clinical research often begins with concerns about specific treatments for specific mental disorders. The goal is to test these treatments using rigorous research methods so that we can be fairly certain that the treatment works for people who have the disorder. One form of clinical research tests the efficacy of medications. Social workers are more likely to test psychosocial or cognitive treatments.

Major tasks include verifying that people in your study have the disorder you are studying. Clinical researchers typically use a research tool to determine the diagnoses, rather than relying on information in the chart. One such tool is the SCID— the Structured Clinical Interview for *DSM-IV* (First, Gibbon, Spitzer, Williams, & Benjamin, 1997; First, Spitzer, Gibbon, & Williams, 1997). A social worker, Janet Williams, was a key member of the team that developed the SCID.

The next major task is providing the intervention to an experimental group. A team composed of practitioners and researchers has probably spent a long time developing the intervention. Ideally, you have it down to a detailed manual so that all the clinicians that do the intervention do it in a similar way. For example, interpersonal therapy (IPT) is a short-term treatment for depression that is described in a manual (Klerman, Weissman, Rounsaville, & Chevron, 1984). IPT is increasingly used in controlled studies comparing drug treatments to psychosocial treatments. (Myrna Weissman, a social worker, was involved in developing IPT.) IPT, using a person-in-environment approach, focuses on the present situation and how stressful events affect current mood. IPT treatment has three phases: assessment and intervention planning, application of treatment to identified interpersonal problems, and helping the client to extend treatment strategies to future situations.

The final task is to test the outcomes carefully. You will probably be comparing the outcomes both to pretest scores and to posttest scores for both the experimental group and a comparison or control group. The measure used at the pre- and posttest will also be carefully selected for their validity (accuracy and relevance to the problem being studied) and reliability (dependability and consistency). (This is further explained below.) Again, studies of IPT serve as a good example. The effectiveness of IPT has been shown in controlled studies (see reviews by Frank, 1991; Friedlander, 1993; Reynolds, Frank, Houck, & Mazumdar, 1997). Social workers can learn to apply treatments and assess outcomes in clinical experiments. They can also apply known effective treatments in their routine clinical practice and determine effectiveness through the use of single system research (Royse et al., 2001).

Services Research/Effectiveness Studies

The major goal of services research is to ". . . evaluate mental health services interventions in the naturalistic circumstances of care" (Proctor & Stiffman, 1998, p. 260). One common goal here is to test the effectiveness of an intervention developed through clinical research. But services research has other important and broader goals. For example, sometimes we study barriers to access to services. Other goals may be to improve engagement, reduce drop-out rates, and increase adherence to treatment. Services researchers may be interested in clients, providers, organizations, and financing. Often a theoretical or conceptual model guides their research.

The major tasks involve selecting and implementing the best possible design for the research questions. Because services researchers, like evaluators, work in naturalistic settings, the research questions and designs vary widely. For example, we know that many people who need mental health care drop out of treatment, often after the first visit. McKay and her colleagues at an urban mental health facility found that few minority families were staying in treatment (McKay, McCadam, & Gonzales, 1996; McKay, Nudelman, McCadam, & Gonzales, 1996). To address this situation, she developed an engagement intervention working closely with families and providers in the community. She incorporated an ecological perspective in the engagement intervention and trained social work interns to use it, and examined treatment attendance rates. The key elements of the engagement process were: "(a) clarify[ing] the helping process for the client, (b) develop[ing] the foundation for a collaborative working relationship, (c) focus[ing] on immediate, practical concerns, and (d) identify[ing] and problem-solv[ing] around barriers to help seeking" (McKay, McCadam, & Gonzales, 1996, p. 465). She helped the interns learn to balance the need for intake information for the agency with allowing the child and family to tell their story. She then used the strongest research design she could, an experiment involving random assignment to the special engagement strategy versus assignment to routine procedures. More families in the engagement strategy came for a first interview, and they were involved in treatment for more sessions than the control families.

TECHNIQUES, STRATEGIES, AND SKILLS

There are a variety of techniques, skills, and strategies social workers may use for research and program evaluation purposes. We will provide a sampling of such techniques in this section.

Needs Assessment

Recall our previous example of mental health clients' desires for structured social activities during the evening and weekend hours at the local social service agency.

To address this concern, the social worker and a cohort of mental health clients are planning a new citywide drop-in center for people to attend during the evening and weekend hours. How many people with mental health needs live in the city? What are the immediate needs of this group? How many people are employed, during the day or in the evening? How many mental health clients participate in recreational services at the local community mental health center? What local resources are already available during the evening and on the weekends? How many clients will you need to plan for? What types of activities are they interested in? These are just a few questions to be answered.

Rubin and Babbie (2001) identified five techniques that can be employed in a needs assessment to answer such questions: (1) the key informants approach, (2) the community forum approach, (3) the rates under treatment approach, (4) the social indicators approach, and (5) the community survey approach.

The first technique, the key informants approach, obtains opinions from experts in the field who have specific information about the needs and problems of the target population at hand. Key informants can also identify service delivery gaps to the population in question. Key informants assessing the need for a new citywide drop-in center for mental health clients include consumers and family members, social workers who work with them, agency directors, leaders of other consumer-operated organizations, the director of the community mental health center, and community members.

The second technique that can be employed in conducting a needs assessment is called the community forum approach. Using this approach, a meeting is held to provide a forum for concerned community members to discuss their opinions and needs. With the previous example, a community forum for community members to share their concerns about opening a drop-in center in their neighborhood or near their businesses may be held.

The third technique, the rates under treatment approach, is also referred to as the patterns of use or client utilization data (Royse et al., 2001). By examining the number and characteristics of people using an existing service, it helps estimate the number of underserved clients and services. The social worker may want to find out how many people currently participate in evening and weekend activities planned by the local mental health center, or participate in evening and weekend activities on their own.

The social indicators approach, like the rates under treatment approach, also uses existing data. This technique "examines aggregated statistics that reflect conditions of an entire population" (Rubin & Babbie, 2001, p. 588). For example, the rates of people using mental health services in a community is important information for the drop-in center.

The fifth technique that can be used to conduct a needs assessment is to survey the community or target group in question. This involves applying various sampling and survey research techniques. For example, the social worker and other mental health clients may interview current mental health clients about what evening and weekend activities would be important to them as part of a drop-in center. They could be interviewed face-to-face, over the telephone, sent a survey in the mail, or even post the survey on a Web page. The social worker and research team may survey the entire population of mental health clients at the social service agency or a random sample of every third client on the agency list.

The most important thing to remember, however, is to conduct a careful assessment of the advantages and disadvantages of each of the techniques listed above. Though a thorough discussion of the advantages and disadvantages of the five principal approaches to conduct a needs assessment is beyond the scope of this chapter, the reader should consult Rubin and Babbie (2001) for a complete discussion.

Single-Subject Designs

Single-system designs (or single-subject designs) can also be a useful technique in research or program evaluation. Such designs, however, are usually associated with social workers that evaluate their own practice with individual clients. Single-system designs have the potential to be used with different units of analysis. The unit of analysis in clinical social work practice can be an individual client, a dyad such as a family or couple, or a group. The unit of analysis in program evaluation can be defined as one program, one organization, an agency, or a city (Royse et al., 2001). In single-system designs, a social worker first identifies the target problem and goals of treatment. Then, they must be defined in operational terms. The problem is measured over a certain period of time and the results are graphed. The social worker must then make a determination whether the data reflect client improvement over time.

Recall our previous example of mental health clients' desires for structured social activities during the evening and weekend hours at the local social service agency. Let's assume the new citywide drop-in center has been established and open for about 6 months. The social worker at the local social service agency decides to employ a single-system design to assess whether consumers' quality of life has improved over the course of a 6-month period. The unit of analysis for this single-system experiment is a group of 20 consumers who have attended the drop-in center regularly over the 6-month period. The social worker uses Lehman's Quality of Life Interview-Brief Version (Lehman, Kernan, & Postrado, 1995) to operationalize quality of life. Each consumer is interviewed face-to-face once a month over the 6-month period. The social worker graphs the average and median scores for the group over a 6-month period on each QOL-B, subjective and objective domain. Based on the data, the social worker would visually inspect the graphed data and then determine if the data reflect client improvement. (See Rubin & Babbie, 2001, Chapter 10, and Royse et al., 1998, Chapter 6, for a thorough review of the advantages and disadvantages of single-system design, and a discussion of the various types of single-system designs, from simple to complex.)

Formative and Summative Evaluations

Just as with single-system designs, a variety of group research designs can be employed to help social workers carry out formative and summative evaluations.

Group designs are arranged in a hierarchy of complexity, including pre-experimental, quasi-experimental, and experimental designs. Consult Rubin and Babbie (2001, Chapter 9) and Royse et al. (1998, Chapter 9) for a comprehensive review of these designs, because a discussion of each type of design is beyond the scope of this chapter.

Recall that Mowbray and Tan (1993) conducted the first known formative evaluation of the consumer-operated drop-in center model. They used a pre-experimental design called a one-shot case study. In a one-shot case study, the group participates in an intervention, and the dependent variable is measured after the intervention (Rubin & Babbie, 2001). A group of 120 drop-in participants were interviewed around various dependent variables after they participated in the drop-in center services, the intervention or stimulus in the study.

If a social worker wants to conduct a summative evaluation of the citywide drop-in center, a quasi-experimental design called a nonequivalent control group design could be used to assess the implementation of the drop-in center services with mental health consumers at the local social service agency. A group of consumers who attend the drop-in center are the group who receives the intervention of the drop-in center services. In our example, a group of consumers sharing similar characteristics to the first consumer group, but who do *not* attend the drop-in center, serves as the control group. In the nonequivalent control group design, both groups are pretested on a measure of quality of life before the intervention. After the intervention (with first group), *both* groups are posttested, and the data is compared.

OUTCOME MEASURES USED BY SOCIAL WORKERS IN PROGRAM EVALUATION AND RESEARCH

Outcome measurement has been emphasized by funders, advocates, and professional organizations. Whether funding sources are public (federal, state, county) or private (insurers and managed care organizations), funders want to know if services are effective and efficient. To assess effectiveness, we need outcome measures. Whether choosing measures for evaluations or clinical or services research, the social worker confronts the same concerns (Mullen & Magnabosco, 1997). The social worker must grapple with *what* to measure and *how* to measure it. We will consider both issues.

Since the 1970s when evaluations of federally funded community mental health centers were mandated by federal legislation (PL 94–63), researchers have suggested frameworks for considering what to measure (Schainblatt & Hatry, 1979; Speer, 1998). Speer, drawing on the early work of Strupp and Hadley (1977) in psychotherapy research, suggests we should begin by identifying the stakeholders and their views about outcomes. Key stakeholders include consumers, community groups, and mental health professionals. The mental health consumer is the primary stakeholder. Even if the consumer has not sought services voluntarily, but participates because of an inpatient or outpatient commitment, he or she has views about whether mental health services are effective. The client has goals, and the services may or not help achieve those goals.

Community groups are stakeholders in outcome assessment because mental health services are supported by tax dollars and because consumers live in the community. Broadly conceived, the community includes a variety of stakeholders, not all with the same interests. The community encompasses family, neighbors, employers, police, funders, and society itself. For example, neighbors and families of persons with mental illness may have different concerns about how a group home should be evaluated. Neighbors may be primarily concerned with property values, any additional traffic on the street, or fears for safety. Family members may be more concerned with whether consumers are enhancing their living skills to survive and thrive independently in the community.

Finally, social workers and other mental health professionals are also stakeholders with views about client adjustment and change. For example, psychiatrists may focus more on reducing symptoms, while social workers may focus on enhancing consumer strengths and moving toward greater independence. The views of all groups of stakeholders should be considered in deciding what to measure, although one may not always be able to take into account all the differing views.

Although not all researchers and evaluators agree about a specific set of measures, consensus has developed on what domains we should examine. They include distress level, symptom severity, and social/role functioning (Speer, 1998). People receiving mental health services often seek treatment because of distress—pain, anguish, discomfort, grief, and loneliness—rather than because of symptoms—hallucinations, emotional dysregulation, inappropriate affect. While measures of distress and of symptoms overlap, it is helpful to distinguish the two domains conceptually, especially because distress implies more of a client-oriented perspective, focusing on how clients feel, not only about the illness, but about their experiences and environment.

Functioning covers our multiple role domains. For example, are we functioning appropriately in student roles, work roles, and family roles? Can we support ourselves financially? Can we shop, cook, and do laundry? Can we behave appropriately with family, friends, and others in the community? Sometimes research looks at global indicators that reflect a major failure in role functioning, such as hospitalization or incarceration.

Examining quality of life is an important approach to looking at outcomes. This approach is attractive because it emphasizes clients' whole life situations over a focus on pathologies. Emphasis on clients' views of quality is also consonant with consumer involvement in evaluating services. Measures of quality of life include many domains, such as social support, safety in the community, and opportunities for recreation. In addition, researchers are now recognizing domains that were often ignored. Spirituality and sexuality, for example, also contribute to quality of life.

Speer (1998) suggests that in choosing measures, we can use a framework that puts together the *who* and the *what*. We can consider the source for information (clients, significant others, public gatekeepers, independent observers, and therapists or providers) and the domain to be measured (distress, symptoms, and functioning). For example, in assessing the outcome of a particular program, we might use client ratings of distress and ratings of client functioning from independent observers. Clearly, no one study will have measures of all domains from all sources.

In choosing specific measures, we have two additional concerns, the psychometric properties of the measures and their utility. The major psychometric properties we consider are reliability and validity. (For example, see Rubin & Babbie, 2001, Chapter 6 on "Measurement," for a review.) One frequently cited measure of reliability on certain types of scales is Cronbach's alpha, a measure of internal consistency, how items correlate with each other. A useful heuristic is that alphas should be greater than 0.70. Validity, however, is more complicated to assess. Validity refers broadly to the accuracy of our measure as an indicator of an underlying concept. We want to ensure that our measure correlates with related concepts, but does not correlate so highly that we could conclude that the measures really deal with the same concept (e.g., a measure of depression and one of self-esteem should have a negative correlation, but one that is not too high). Another validity concern might relate to dimensions of our concept. For example, if we are concerned about measuring the burden of care-giving, we might theorize that there are subjective and objective components. A researcher could do factor analysis to determine if the instrument actually had those dimensions. We are also concerned about whether the instrument has been used with populations that resemble the ones we are studying. Has it been used with the same age group? Has it been used with members of the same minority groups, or with people who have schizophrenia?

Finally, utility also needs to be considered. How long are scales that clients and clinicians fill out? Will your stakeholders have the time to fill them out? Also, if any instruments are copyrighted, you must purchase copies or receive permission from their owners to use them.

Locating Instruments

Finding instruments that are relevant for mental health research and program evaluation has become much easier in recent years. One can turn to books that summarize a variety of measures, including information on their reliability and validity, and on populations that have been previously studied. An example of such books is *Measures for Clinical Practice* (Fischer & Corcoran, 1994).

Electronic databases that review instruments are also available. One such database, Health and Psychosocial Instruments (HAPI), provides access to information on a variety of measurement instruments in mental health and other fields. Some libraries have this database on CD-ROM or on networks. It can also be found at the following Web site: http://ovid.med.yale.edu/fldguide/hapidb.htm. If you want a particular instrument, you can then purchase it from Behavioral Database Services (see the address on the Web site).

We can also search databases such as Social Work Abstracts for articles discussing instruments. If we wanted to find a multidimensional measure that clients with severe mental illness could complete, we know that quality of life instruments often are multidimensional. A search of Social Work Abstracts for "quality of life and measures" for articles published since 1995 yields one that sounds promising, a 24-item measure developed by Greenley, Greenberg, & Brown (1997). (Greenberg is a social worker.) It assesses subjective quality of life in seven areas: (1) living situation, (2) finances, (3) leisure, (4) family, (5) social life, (6) health, and (7) access to medical care. The development of the scale was based on testing of more than 900 clients at community support programs in Wisconsin. Items for each of these areas formed a scale with good reliability (0.72 to 0.89). Validity was good as well. For example, clients who were rated by their case managers as less symptomatic, reported higher quality of life that those who were more symptomatic (p. 252). (Readers interested in how an instrument is developed and tested should read this article. It provides an excellent model.)

EXEMPLAR STUDY: EMPOWERMENT EVALUATION

Mental health consumers are usually the focus of research and evaluation inquiry and clinical intervention. However, there are a variety of other roles consumers can play in the research or evaluation process. Empowerment evaluation represents one example of an innovative evaluation approach involving consumers in other roles. The proliferation of consumer-operated programs and consumerism in the mental health field presents social work with a unique opportunity to teach program stakeholders how to evaluate their own programs. Consumers' personal experiences with a mental illness and knowledge of the mental health system are a benefit to involving them in evaluation (Morrell-Bellai & Boydell, 1994). Other positive benefits of involving consumers in the research process include financial reward, education, development of vocational skills, and increased self-esteem (Smith, 1998; Morrell-Bellai & Boydell, 1994).

Empowerment evaluation has emerged as an innovative evaluation approach involving program stakeholders. David Fetterman (1994a), the founder of empowerment evaluation, describes it as follows: "Empowerment evaluation is the use of evaluation concepts and techniques to foster self-determination. The focus is on helping people help themselves. This evaluation approach focuses on improvement, is collaborative, and requires both qualitative and quantitative methodologies. . . . It is a multifaceted approach with many forms, including training, facilitation, advocacy, illumination, and liberation" (p. 1).

Using a form of self-evaluation and reflection, empowerment evaluation is designed to help participants help themselves and improve particular programs. In empowerment evaluation, evaluators train individuals not only to conduct their own evaluations, but to also be more self-sufficient in doing so. Evaluators also facilitate the evaluation process in conducting self-evaluations and often conduct an evaluation after the goals and design have been mutually agreed upon. According to

Fetterman (1996), empowerment evaluation can be an enlightening experience, and can also free an evaluator and participants from preexisting goals.

The role of the evaluator varies from helping consumers facilitate their own evaluation to working with them to set goals and the program design, or teaching them to conduct their own evaluation. Taking stock and determining the rating as a program, focusing on strengths and weaknesses, is the first step in empowerment evaluation. The second step involves setting program goals, specifically where the program sees itself in the future and focusing on program improvement. Developing strategies to establish the goals and objectives of the programs follows as the third step. Then, program participants are assisted to identify evidence needed to document the program's legitimate progress toward goals (Fetterman, 1994b). (See Fetterman, 1996, for further exemplars on empowerment evaluation.)

Recently, Mary Secret, a social worker, and her colleagues reported on the application of empowerment evaluation to a community-based HIV intervention program (Secret, Jordan, & Ford, 1999). A statewide community planning committee on HIV prevention was convened in Kentucky. The selected HIV prevention outreach program selected targeted African-American women who were not only low income, but also at risk of drug use. The overall goal was the development of an evaluation design for statewide HIV prevention programs. Empowerment evaluation was chosen as the evaluation model, because it could sustain its role once researchers were not part of the evaluation process. The first step for Secret et al. was to critically review and evaluate the program's strengths and weaknesses. The team determined the current "shotgun" approach to HIV prevention to be ineffective. Through the process of identifying the strengths and weaknesses, a new outreach strategy was adopted. Their second step was to help the stakeholders, through a series of meetings, set new program outcome objectives. Then, the team helped the HIV program identify measurement instruments to help them demonstrate the program's effectiveness. Their case study illustrates that empowerment evaluation can be a useful approach where program stakeholders have the interest, time, and resources to get involved.

UNIQUE CHALLENGES FOR SOCIAL WORKERS

We conclude this chapter with a brief discussion of the unique challenges for social workers involved in evaluating existing services, and the development and testing of interventions to help mental health consumers with specific disorders.

Major Issues

One major issue confronting social workers involved in evaluation and research activities is the influence of politics on the evaluation and research process. Remember our example of the formative evaluation of consumer-operated drop-in centers (Mowbray & Tan, 1993). What should a social worker do, for example, if the data indicated the consumer-operated drop-in center model is not effective? Most commonly, social workers may feel pressure, when involved in the evaluation and research process, from the funding source to employ a research design or to put the program in a positive light. Social workers may also feel pressure to manipulate data or interpret findings so that a program is also viewed favorably. Should the social worker report the findings as is? Or should the social worker subtly manipulate the data to pacify the funding source (foundation, state agency, grant)? These are just a few questions social workers may grapple with as part of the evaluation and research process.

Another major issue confronting social workers, with respect to evaluation and research studies, is finding the time in their professional schedules to participate in such activities. Budget cutbacks are a reality facing many mental health agencies in which social workers are employed. It is a challenge for agencies to stretch limited professional staff, just as it is a challenge for social workers to fulfill their professional obligations to evaluation and research as stated in the NASW *Code of Ethics* (1997). How can social workers and agencies streamline the paperwork process, for example, to collect data for evaluation and research studies as part of the natural agency processes? This is an important question yet to be addressed.

Social workers employed in the mental health arena also need access to continuing education opportunities on research and evaluation. Activities that may fulfill this goal include attending a professional development workshop on clinical research practice or grand rounds at a research hospital, or completing college courses on research and evaluation.

Special Challenges/Obstacles

One special challenge social workers involved in research and program evaluation activities face are the ethical dilemmas raised throughout the research process. Ethical challenges present themselves in many forms. Many times social workers are left to use the NASW *Code of Ethics* (1997) as a guide for those situations. The NASW *Code of Ethics* (1997), Subsection 5.02, lists the 16 ethical guidelines of evaluation and research. Suppose a social worker at a mental health agency discovers, through face-to-face client interviews, false contact reports are recorded in agency charts. Does the social worker immediately raise the reliability of this information in the middle of a program evaluation, or wait until the evaluation is complete? What if a social worker discovers client information is being used in a manner not consistent with the informed consent guidelines? What does the worker do? What if a social worker discovers agency funding is being used inappropriately? The NASW *Code of Ethics* is one tool social workers engaged in research and program evaluation can use to guide their decision-making process in such dilemmas. They may also consider using additional codes to solve ethical dilemmas (e.g., the Evaluation Research Society's Standards for Program Evaluation or the American Evaluation Association's Guiding Principles for Evaluation). Using a framework for making ethical decisions, such as that of Newman and Brown (1996), may also help guide ethical decision making (see p. 102 of their text).

Another challenge social workers frequently face in the research process is the dilemma of what to do with negative or "no difference" findings. These findings still inform the mental health knowledge base, and may be just as important as favorable findings. Social workers have the responsibility to report study findings, good or bad, in professional journals such as *Social Work, Research on Social Work Practice, Social Service Review, Psychiatric Rehabilitation Journal, Community Mental Health Journal, Journal of Mental Health Administration,* and *Psychiatric Services.* A case dilemma follows and discusses what to do when the data suggest an intervention is not effective.

CASE DILEMMA: HOMELESSNESS STUDY

In both evaluation and services research, we hypothesize that programs and interventions will work. What happens when they do not? What can researchers do when they encounter negative findings? One of the authors of this chapter confronted that dilemma (Korr & Joseph, 1996). We had studied the effectiveness of an ACT-type program for people with severe mental illness who were also homeless (Korr & Joseph, 1995). The program was highly successful. The experimental group was twice as likely to be housed as the control group at the 3-month follow-up.

Then the program was implemented at a second location. As we monitored client progress, we found that clients in the experimental group were dropping out or not doing well. We had not seen this happen at the first site. We felt we had an ethical obligation to try to give early feedback so the program could be adjusted if necessary. We tried unsuccessfully to discuss the situation with program supervisors and administrators. Finally, when it became apparent that something was radically wrong, the funders terminated the program. We then had to determine why the program succeeded at one site and failed at the other. We drew on a theoretical framework (Chen, 1990) that helped us identify factors operating at different systemic levels that could have influenced the different outcomes at the two sites. We examined client characteristics, the immediate environment of the clients, organizational characteristics such as management style, and factors on the macrocontext (social, economic, and political). The macrocontext was ruled out because it was the same for both sites. While client characteristics were similar, a significant feature of the client environment differed. At the first site, clients were successfully placed in single room occupancy hotels (SROs), a form of housing familiar to and acceptable to the clients. Clients rejected similar placements at the second site because they had traditionally used board and care homes in their communities. While organizational structure appeared to be the same at the two sites, our own observations were that the management style of the two program directors differed. The first was positive, working toward overcoming any obstacle. The second was passive, almost avoidant of any problems.

We were able to help administrators and funders understand the situation, as well as to publish the explanation along with the negative findings, which are otherwise often difficult to publish. This is just one example of balancing various issues faced by social workers.

KEY TERMS

Clinical Research: A type of research concerned with specific treatments for specific mental disorders; the goal is to test these treatments using rigorous research methods to be fairly certain that the treatment works for people who have the disorder.

Empowerment Evaluation: "The use of evaluation concepts and techniques to foster self-determination. The focus is on helping people help themselves. This evaluation approach focuses on improvement, is collaborative, and requires both qualitative and quantitative methodologies. . . . It is a multifaceted approach with many forms, including training, facilitation, advocacy, illumination, and liberation" (Fetterman, 1994a, p. 1).

Formative Evaluation (Process Evaluation): A type of program evaluation that focuses on obtaining useful information in developing a program in its early phases or improving an already existing program, and is concerned with the administrative operations of a program or the mental health client service delivery system.

Needs Assessment: A type of program evaluation conducted to determine whether the service needs of mental health clients are being met.

Program Evaluation: A collection of methods and skills to determine whether a program or service is needed and the extent to which it will be used, it will meet the need, it is delivered as planned, and it helps mental health clients effectively (Posavac & Carey, 1992).

Reliability: Dependability and consistency of a measure.

Services Research/Effectiveness Studies: A type of research that evaluates the worthiness of mental health service interventions in their natural environment.

Summative Evaluation: A type of program evaluation used to ascertain the worth of a program once it has been in existence for a period of time (Weiss, 1972).

Validity: The accuracy of a measure as an indicator of an underlying concept.

WEB RESOURCES

American Evaluation Association (AEA) (http://www.eval.org/). The AEA is an international professional association comprised of members from various disciplines interested in evaluation. More than 30 Topical Interest Groups (TIGs) on specific areas provide members with an opportunity to communicate with other professionals in one area. In addition to an annual conference, links to many relevant sites are offered.

Center for Mental Health Services (CMHS) (http://www.mentalhealth.org/cmhs/index.htm). Created in 1992, the CMHS, as part of Substance Abuse and Mental Health Services Administration, leads efforts at the federal level to treat mental illness. This Web page offers links to the offices of community support, HIV/AIDS, employment services, homelessness, managed care, mental health statistics, protection and advocacy, specific populations, and state planning. The Knowledge Exchange Network (KEN) also provides a plethora of mental health information and links to other important mental health home pages.

FedStats (http://www.fedstats.gov). This site provides social workers access to statistics from more than 70 U.S. federal government agencies.

Health and Psychosocial Instruments (HAPI) (http://ovid.med.yale.edu/fldguide/hapidb.htm). This site offers social workers and other professionals information on measurement instruments across fields. It helps social workers to easily identify measurement instruments needed for clinical practice, grant proposals, evaluation studies, and research projects.

Institute for the Advancement of Social Work Research (http://www.cosw.sc.edu/iaswr/). This site promotes the scientific knowledge base of social work practice and provides information on research training opportunities, linking practitioners with researchers, and funding and technical assistance.

National Institute of Mental Health (NIMH) (http://www.nimh.nih.gov). The NIMH generates information to understand, treat, and prevent mental illness. The Web site offers links to news and events, clinical trials, funding opportunities, information for the public, practitioner, and researcher, and other resources.

National Mental Health Association (NMHA) (http://www.nmha.org). The NMHA, comprised of more than 340 affiliates, is dedicated to improving the mental health of individuals. This Web site provides resources, discussion boards, news of upcoming events, and links to other mental health Web sites.

National Mental Health Consumers' Self-Help Clearinghouse (http://www.mhselfhelp.org). This site offers social workers and consumers advocacy resources and technical assistance information about self-help groups and peer-operated programs.

REFERENCES

Anderson, C., Reiss, D., & Hogarty, G. (1986). *Schizophrenia and the family: A practitioner's guide to psychoeducation and management.* New York: Guilford Press.

Austin, D. M. (1999). A report on progress in the development of research resources in social work. *Research on Social Work Practice, 9*(6), 673–707.

Center for Mental Health Services. (1998). *Mental health, United States, 1998.* (DHHS Publication No. SMA 99–32385). Washington DC: U.S. Government Printing Office.

Chambers, D. E., Wedel, K. R., & Rodwell, M. K. (1992). *Evaluating social programs.* Boston: Allyn & Bacon.

Chen, H. (1990). *Theory-driven evaluations.* Newbury Park, CA: Sage.

Council on Social Work Education. (1991). *Curriculum Policy Statement* (4th Ed.). Alexandria, VA: Author.

Dixon, L. (2000). Assertive community treatment: Twenty five years of gold. *Psychiatric Services, 51,* 755–758.

Fetterman, D. (1994a). Empowerment evaluation. *Evaluation Practice, 15,* 229–238.

Fetterman, D. (1994b). Steps of empowerment evaluation: From California to Cape Town. *Evaluation and Program Planning, 17*(3), 305–313.

Fetterman, D. (1996). Empowerment evaluation: Introduction to theory and practice. In D. M. Fetterman, S. J. Kaftarian, & A. Wandersman (Eds.), *Empowerment evaluation: Knowledge and tools for self-assessment and accountability* (pp. 3–46). Thousand Oaks, CA: Sage.

First, M. B., Gibbon, M., Spitzer, R. L., Williams, J. B. W., & Benjamin, L. S. (1997). *Structured Clinical Interview for DSM-IV Axis II personality disorders (SCID-II).* Washington, DC: American Psychiatric Press.

First, M. B., Spitzer, R. L., Gibbon, M., & Williams, J. B. W. (1997). *Structured Clinical Interview for DSM-IV Axis I Disorders (SCID).* New York: New York State Psychiatric Institute, Biometrics Research Department.

Fischer, J., & Corcoran, K. (1994). *Measures for clinical practice: A sourcebook* (Vols. 1–2). New York: Free Press.

Frank, E. (1991). Interpersonal psychotherapy as a maintenance treatment for patients with recurrent depression. *Psychotherapy, 28,* 259–266.

Friedlander, M. L. (1993). Does complimentarity promote or hinder client change in brief therapy: A review of the evidence from two theoretical perspectives. *Counseling Psychologist, 21,* 457–486.

Gabor, P. A., Unrau, Y. A., & Grinnell, R. M. (1998). *Evaluation for social workers: A quality improvement approach for the social services* (2nd ed.). Boston: Allyn & Bacon.

Greenley, J. R., Greenberg, J. S., & Brown, R. (1997). Measuring quality of life: A new and practical survey instrument. *Social Work, 42,* 244–254.

Kirk, S. A., & Tripodi, T. (1994). Evaluation research in social work. *Social Work Research, 18*(4), 195–196.

Klerman, G. L., Weissman, M. M., Rounsaville, B. J., & Chevron, E. S. (1984). *Interpersonal psychotherapy for depression.* New York: Basic Books.

Korr, W. S., & Joseph, A. (1995). Housing the homeless mentally ill: Findings from Chicago. *Journal of Social Service Research, 21,* 53–68.

Korr, W. S., & Joseph, A. (1996). Effects of local conditions on program outcomes: Analysis of contradictory findings from two programs for homeless mentally ill. *Journal of Health & Social Policy, 8,* 41–53.

Lathrop, J. C. (1905). *Suggestions for visitors to county poorhouses and to other public charitable institutions.* Public Charities Committee of the Illinois Federation of Women's Clubs.

Lehman, A. F., Kernan, E., & Postrado, L. (1995). *Evaluating the quality of life for persons with severe mental illness.* Baltimore: Center for Mental Health Services Research.

Lehman, A. F., Steinwachs, D. M., and the Survey Co-Investigators of the PORT Project (1998). Patterns of care for schizophrenia: Initial results from the schizophrenia Patient Outcomes Research Team (PORT) client survey. *Schizophrenia Bulletin, 24,* 11–20.

Lukens, E., & Thorning, H. (1996). Schizophrenia and the family. In C. Kaufman & J. Gorman (Eds.), *Schizophrenia: New directions for clinical research and treatment* (pp. 197–206). New York: M. A. Liebert.

McFarlane, W., Lukens, E., Link, B., Dushay, R., Deakins, S., Newmark, M., Dunne, E., Horen, B., & Toran, J. (1995). Multiple family groups and psychoeducation in the treatment of schizophrenia. *Archives of General Psychiatry, 52,* 679–687.

McKay, M. K., McCadam, K., & Gonzales, J. J. (1996). Addressing the barriers to mental health services for inner city children and their caretakers. *Community Mental Health Journal, 32,* 353–361.

McKay, M. K., Nudelman, R., McCadam, K., & Gonzales, J. (1996). Evaluating a social work engagement approach to involving inner-city children and their families in mental health care. *Research on Social Work Practice, 6,* 462–472.

Moos, R. H. (1974). *Evaluating treatment environments: A social ecological approach.* New York: John Wiley.

Moos, R. H., & Humphrey, B. (1974). *Group environment scale form.* Palo Alto, CA: Consulting Psychologists Press.

Morrell-Bellai, T. L., & Boydell, K. M. (1994). The experience of mental health consumers as researchers. *Canadian Journal of Community Mental Health, 13*(1), 97–111.

Mowbray, C. T. (1999). The benefits and challenges of supported education: A personal perspective. *Psychiatric Rehabilitation Journal, 22*(3), 248–254.

Mowbray, C. T., & Tan, C. (1993). Consumer-operated drop-in centers: Evaluation of operations and impact. *The Journal of Mental Health Administration, 20*(1), 8–19.

Mullen, E. J., & Magnabosco, J. L. (Eds.). (1997). *Outcome measurement in the human services: Cross-cutting issues and methods.* Washington, DC: NASW Press.

NAMI. (n.d.). *NAMI consumer and family guide to schizophrenia treatment: Treatment works.* Arlington, VA: Author.

NAMI. (1998). Schizophrenia PORT: Call to consumers and families to take charge of system that fails to provide effective treatments and supports. *NAMI Advocate, 19*(6), 1,8.

NASW. (1997). *Code of ethics.* Washington DC: Author.

Newman, D. L., & Brown, R. D. (1996). *Applied ethics for program evaluation.* Thousand Oaks, CA: Sage.

Nguyen, T. D., Atkisson, C. C., & Stegner, B. L. (1983). Assessment of patient satisfaction: Development and refinement of a service evaluation questionnaire. *Evaluation and Program Planning, 6,* 299–314.

Posavac, E. J., & Carey, R. G. (1992). *Program evaluation: Methods and case studies* (4th ed.). Englewood Cliffs, NJ: Prentice-Hall.

Proctor, E. K., & Stiffman, A. R. (1998). Background of services and treatment research. In J. B. W. Williams & K. Ell (Eds.), *Advances in mental health research: Implications for practice* (pp. 259–286). Washington, DC: NASW Press.

Rapp, C. A. (1997). *The Kansas consumer status reporting system.* Lawrence, KS: The University of Kansas, School of Social Welfare.

Rapp, C. A. (1998). *The strengths model: Case management with people suffering from severe and persistent mental illness.* New York: Oxford University Press.

Rapp, C. A., Gowdy, E., Sullivan, W. P., & Wintersteen, R. (1988). Client outcome reporting: The Status Method. *Community Mental Health Journal, 24*(2), 118–133.

Reynolds, C. F., Frank, E., Houck, P. R., & Mazumdar, S. (1997). Which elderly patients with remitted depression will remain with continued interpersonal psychotherapy after discontinuation of antidepressant medication? *American Journal of Psychiatry, 154,* 958–962.

Rosen, A., Proctor, E. K., & Staudt, M. M. (1999). Social work research and the quest for effective practice. *Social Work Research, 23*(1), 4–14.

Royse, D., Thyer, B. A., Padgett, D. K., & Logan, T. K. (2001). *Program evaluation: An introduction* (3rd ed.). Belmont, CA: Wadsworth.

Rubin, A., & Babbie, E. (2001). *Research methods in social work* (4th ed.). Pacific Grove, CA: Brooks/Cole.

Schainblatt, A. H., & Hatry, P. (1979). *Mental health services: What happens to the clients?* Washington, DC: Urban Institute.

Secret, M., Jordan, A., & Ford, J. (1999). Empowerment evaluation as a social work strategy. *Health and Social Work, 24*(2), 120–127.

Segal, S. P., & Aviram, U. (1978). *The mentally ill in community-based sheltered care: A study of community care and social integration.* New York: Wiley.

Smith, M. K. (1998). Empowerment evaluation: Theoretical and methodological considerations. *Evaluation and Program Planning, 21,* 255–261.

Speer, D. C. (1998). *Mental health outcome evaluation.* San Diego, CA: Academic Press.

Stein, L. I., & Test, M. A. (1980). Alternative to mental hospital treatment. I. Conceptual model, treatment program, and clinical evaluation. *Archives of General Psychiatry, 37,* 392–397.

Strupp, H. H., & Hadley, S. M. (1977). A tripartite model of mental health and therapeutic outcomes. *American Psychologist, 32,* 187–196.

Task Force on Social Work Research. (1991). *Building social work knowledge for effective services and policies—A plan for development.* Austin: University of Texas, School of Social Work.

Test, M. A. (1998). Community-based treatment models for adults with severe and persistent mental illness. In J. B. W. Williams & K. Ell (Eds.), *Advances in mental health research: Implications for practice* (pp. 420–436). Washington, DC: NASW Press.

Vourlekis, B. S., Edinburg, G. M., & Knee, R. R. (1998). The rise of social work in public mental health through aftercare of people with serious mental illness. *Social Work, 43,* 567–575.

Vourlekis, B. S., Greene, R. R., Knee, R. I., & Edinburg, G. M. (1994). Collaboration between social work and psychiatry in aftercare in the early 1900s. *Hospital and Community Psychiatry, 45,* 749–751, 764.

Weiss, C. (1972). *Evaluating action programs: Readings in social action and education.* Boston: Allyn & Bacon.

SOCIAL WORKERS AS ADMINISTRATORS AND POLICY ANALYSTS IN MENTAL HEALTH SETTINGS: LIVING WITH UNCERTAINTY

Robert Paulson

Today's world is characterized by rapid change. This change has become a fact of life for social work administrators who must therefore live with and try to manage considerable uncertainty. The reality of ongoing change and uncertainty is reflected in the content of this chapter, as it shapes what administrators and policy analysts do and how they approach their jobs.

Although there are a number of common tasks shared by both disciplines, it is important to recognize that administration and policy analysis are very different jobs with different academic and credentialing traditions. Policy analysts usually work for federal, state, or local governments. They are charged with recommending or analyzing legislation or administrative rules from the perspective of the public good, and explicating the advantages and disadvantages of competing policy alternatives and how these alternatives will differentially affect various stakeholders or constituencies. As one of their many functions, administrators need to analyze policy in terms of its impact on their particular organizations, which is a fundamentally different point of view from that of the policy analyst.

Policy analysts tend either to train in schools of public policy (under the auspices of political science) or they come from a variety of disciplines and focus their policy-analysis activities on their specialty (e.g., economists on economic policy). In contrast, administration is taught in a wide variety of disciplines, such as public administration, health administration, social work, business administration, education, and urban affairs (Crow, 1995; Einbinder, 1995). However, most of the issues discussed in this chapter apply equally well to both administrators and policy analysts working in mental health.

THE INTELLECTUAL BASE OF PRACTICE

One's approach to administration (the terms *management* and *administration* are used synonymously) depends on the assumptions one has about organizations and how they operate. Social workers usually come into the field with strong values and an ideology of how the world ought to be. While it is important to keep these values and vision of a just society in mind, it is also essential to adopt the point of view of the world as it is, rather than how it could or should be. Unless we appreciate the political realities of organizational life, how public policy shapes organizational behavior in often contradictory ways, and learn to design policies and structures that are based on these realities, we will be ineffective as administrators and policy analysts.

Mental health organizations, like other human service organizations, are extremely vulnerable to their task environment (Hasenfeld, 1983; Thompson, 1967), those entities they depend on to achieve their goals. They are frequently faced with serving different constituencies (e.g., multiple client populations, funders, state and local regulators, professional groups, advocate organizations, complementary service organizations) who may have different ideas about what the agency should be doing, whom they should be serving, and how their services should be evaluated. Also they are often given broad mandates that lead to unclear operational goals (e.g., reduce poverty, improve mental health), as there can be multiple interpretations of how agencies should approach the mandate, as well as how they should go about achieving this goal (Au, 1996; Hasenfeld, 1996; Patti, 1983).

This is complicated further by the fact that we have imperfect technologies in many instances, that is, there is no agreed upon and/or recognized cure for many social problems. In mental health, for example, most experts agree that there is a biological component for major mental illness and that medication helps many people. There are also those who believe the side effects of medication are worse than the cure, and still others emphasize that, while medication reduces symptoms, recovery can only be achieved through rehabilitative strategies (including self-help programs).

In short, for human service organizations, nothing is a given and nothing can be taken for granted. There is no one best way to achieve vague and perhaps conflicting or contradictory expectations (e.g., mental health organizations are expected to serve people in the least restrictive environment and promote consumer rights, but are held accountable for ensuring public safety).

It used to be taught that organizational decision making (e.g., goal setting and budgeting) was a rational process. In a seminal article, Lindblom (1959) first asserted that, at best, we muddle through or "satisfice." That is, we settle for a satisfactory, rather than an optimal, course of action (Cyert & March, 1963; March & Simon, 1958; Simon, 1997). Lindblom pointed out that even 40 years ago, the world's complexity resulted in more information than could be rationally and systematically processed. It is now well-recognized that decision making in organizations is a political process where decisions are made by fluid decision making coalitions, which do not necessarily represent official lines of authority or power (Au, 1996; Cyert & March, 1963). Participants in these coalitions bring with them their own values and agendas that may or may not coincide with the goals of the organization. Organizational leaders also seek to reduce uncertainty. In this context, the control of information, access to important resources, or uncertainty, are all important sources of informal power (Gummer, 1998).

This means that mental health administrators must complete their functions and tasks within a political context, where people and organizations in their environments control many of the resources. They too can only be influenced through a political process.

Social work has several essential perspectives that make a unique contribution to mental health administration. Social work as a profession subscribes to the ecological model, that is, that behavior is shaped by biological, social, psychological, and environmental factors taken together, and must be understood from this holistic perspective. Administrators must use a similar approach in understanding their organization and its environment. The open systems approach (Hasenfeld, 1983; Perrow, 1979; Thompson, 1967), which recognizes the interplay between an organization and its environment, and the political and rational elements involved in organizational behavior, is an expression of this holistic approach.

Secondly, creating change within individuals, groups, communities, or organizations is the essential task of social work practitioners (Brager & Halloway, 1978). Furthermore, social work understands change in terms of the ecological perspective. As will be shown in the next section, an essential function of mental health administration is creating organizational change, with respect to both community and organizational policy, and the behavior of individual workers, such that these theories of change are an important tool for administrators. Together, the holistic approach and the importance of change form an important intellectual base of practice.

MAJOR TASKS AND GOALS

There is widespread agreement about the basic functions of administrators that has changed little over the years, although the activities and methods for accomplishing these tasks have been modified in response to changes in the environment. In addition, there is recognition of the fact that, because human service organizations differ from for-profit organizations in fundamental ways, the tasks of their managers are, of necessity, different (Menefee, 1998). There are essentially seven major administrative functions: (1) planning and program development, (2) financial management and resource development, (3) designing organizational structures and processes, (4) staffing, (5) evaluating, (6) managing organization–environment relations, and (7) changing the organization (Menefee & Thompson, 1994). While all of these essential functions are common to all organizations, the specific activities and the importance of each differs for human service organizations and their specific environmental context. A brief description of each of these functions follows.

Planning and Program Development

One of the most important tasks of mental health administrators is to understand the threats and opportunities for the organization, and prepare the organization to maximize the opportunities and minimize the threats. At the same time, they must be sure that the agency's mission is not compromised, that there is a clear vision the staff and community can respect, while still responding to these environmental challenges. To meet the changing conditions and demands of the organization's environment and its major stakeholders, administrators must develop a strategy for positioning the organization to meet the new expectations. For example, to prepare for a completely different method of operation, many community mental health centers (CMHCs) anticipated the advent of managed care and developed detailed plans for such things as training staff, changing management information systems, and developing new fiscal management techniques.

Program development is a more specialized type of planning. In response to a request from funders or an identified need, a plan is developed for implementing a new program. The plan includes such tasks as developing resources, specifying activities, designing staffing patterns, and identifying and securing the physical location for the program.

Financial Management and Resource Development

For an organization to survive and prosper, managers must develop and manage sufficient resources for the organization to achieve its goals. A major part of this function is to develop realistic goal-oriented budgets so that resources are directed at the activities most essential to achieve the agency's objectives. A second major function is maintaining adequate accounting and management information systems to track expenditures and provide the leadership with information to evaluate the cost-effectiveness of programs, calculate the costs of delivering services, and project future revenue. Careful monitoring of budgets allows managers to make adjustments in their budgets to prevent cash flow problems or operating deficits. The third major function is developing resources, preferably from diverse sources, to keep the program on a strong financial footing.

Organizing and Developing Effective Structures and Processes

One of the most complex and important tasks for social work managers is to structure the organization so that communication and authority flows in the appropriately focused ways, so that information and decision making reside closest to the service delivery. Similarly, processes must be efficient, effective, and provide for quality control and standardization while allowing for flexibility and innovation. In a well-structured organization, staff are clear about what they should be doing, have the information they need to make informed decisions, and understand the limits of their discretion and authority. Of paramount importance is ensuring that these organizational processes are truly client-centered and reinforce the responsiveness of the organization to the people it serves.

Staffing

For effective performance, an organization must have a sufficient number of people with the knowledge, values, skills, and credentials necessary for goal attainment. The tasks associated with staffing are recruitment and retention, salary and benefit administration, staff development, affirmative action, and maintaining appeal, grievance, and disciplinary processes. Effective performance of these tasks maximizes the likelihood that staff will be motivated and productive.

Evaluating

The main purpose of the evaluation function is to measure the progress of the organization in achieving its goals and to assess whether its services are both effective and efficient. To accomplish this, clear goals and objectives must be set for each service element, and a measurement and performance evaluation system that accurately reflects the breadth and depth of the work must be established. These measures should include outcomes as well as process information, and be analyzed and presented in a useful way, so that the results are fed back to employees to self-correct their behavior.

Managing Organization-Environment Relations

Because most mental health organizations are highly dependant on their environment, the agency's leadership needs to establish and maintain good relationships with citizen groups, policy makers, and other organizations. Through such relationships, the manager learns about threats and opportunities, and uses this information to help shape the policies that affect the organization's future.

Changing the Organization

As noted, human service organizations must constantly change to stay abreast of the changes in the environment, such as changes in funding, client populations, consumer needs, and regulations. These changes often mean the organization must change how it does business. For example, mental health centers used to be involved in long-term therapy for people who had family problems. Managed care has led to the use of short-term, solution-focused therapy, or group therapy for many problems. Increased diversity of the workforce and client population is another example. Frequently, therefore, the organization must change its culture as well as its behavior. It is important, therefore, that managers ensure that the policies, procedures, expectations, and incentives change as well, to reinforce the new behaviors and attitudes. Otherwise, workers will be caught in double binds or conflicting expectations.

Changing Patterns of Management

Recent surveys of social work administrators have compared the relative importance of each of these functions and associated activities, and have shown remarkable stability over time (Menefee, 1998; Menefee & Thompson, 1994; Patti, 1977, 1983). In general, administrators' jobs have become much more complex as they can no longer only focus on the internal operations of the agency, but must interact strategically with their environment (Menafee & Thompson, 1994), spend considerable time anticipating the future, and position their agency to be prepared for anticipated changes. For instance, they can no longer simply monitor their agency budget, but must actively develop new resources and sophisticated techniques for managing budgets under changing circumstances. In the past, social work administrators were also involved in direct practice; the increasing complexity and size of today's organizations preclude this in most instances (Menefee & Thompson, 1994)

For the internal policy analyst, it is necessary to understand the repercussions of a proposed policy on each of the administrative functions. In contrast, a government policy analyst is likely to be concerned with the second, third, and sixth functions only, the organization and financing of services and the coordination or interactions of agencies in the service system. Policy analysts will be concerned with looking at a system as a whole and not just the needs of an individual organization. Hence, the issues discussed are equally relevant for the policy analyst, although from a different perspective. This next section will focus primarily on the administrator, but will also highlight the unique issues for the policy analyst.

TECHNIQUES, STRATEGIES, AND SKILLS

A detailed discussion of each of these major functions, and all of the activities associated with them, is beyond the scope of this chapter, but is widely available in many administrative texts. Instead, we will focus on the impact the major issues facing mental health organizations have on each of these functions and the adaptations necessary to successfully meet the challenges. In many instances, there are no ready solutions, and one can only be aware of the major dilemmas and attempt to craft the best possible compromise. It must also be remembered that many of these tasks are interrelated, such that what happens in one function may greatly impact another. The task environment can also have an impact on several of the functions at the same time, not always in the same way.

Planning and Program Development

The factor that most affects this function is the turbulence and uncertainty in a mental health organization's environment. It is critical for organizational leaders to have a clear vision reflected in a statement of mission and core principles that are communicated and understood throughout the organization. At the very least, the mission statement should identify the target population served, the need areas to be addressed, and the services to be provided. Administrators must be explicit about shared values (e.g., services will be easily accessible, affordable, client-centered, culturally competent, etc.) in this statement to shape the activities of the organization.

Without such a vision, an organization is truly like a ship without a rudder, and there is no context for conducting planning.

Traditional Planning

Planning is important as a vehicle for keeping the organization's eye on the future. Otherwise, as Peter Drucker (1974) has noted, "All service institutions are threatened by the tendencies to cling to yesterday rather than slough it off, and to put their best and ablest people on defending what no longer makes sense or serves a purpose." This is particularly apt in the current situation where conditions are always changing. Given the uncertain future, the survival of traditional strategic planning is somewhat curious, particularly as many such plans are for 3- to 5-year periods, and may lag behind the rapidity of change.

There are a number of long-standing problems with traditional planning, however. Traditional planning assumes that there is sufficient stability to reasonably predict the future, and only allows for one "official future." Once the plan is made, the organization can be locked into that vision of the future. If the assumptions prove false, the plan is no longer viable. Consequently, the plan ends up on a shelf, and all effort was wasted. Even worse, the organization now has no plan unless it undergoes the expensive and time-consuming process all over again. Finally, traditional planning promotes more narrowly based linear vision (McGrath & Paulson, 1996) than other planning alternatives.

Scenario Planning

Fortunately, a viable alternative called scenario planning (Schwartz, 1992; 1991) was developed almost a decade ago. While it has been widely adopted by Fortune 500 companies, it is almost unknown among human service administrators. Scenario planning is designed for today's highly volatile and turbulent environment. It challenges mental maps to allow for more flexible and creative thinking. It creates a series of widely varied, but plausible, future scenarios based on current driving forces and trends, and provides a mechanism for monitoring trends to track the future. The use of alternative scenarios facilitates changing direction midstream as events warrant. This approach provides guidance for preparing an organization to survive in a rapidly changing environment under differing conditions. It changes the organization's way of operating from a reactive to a proactive mode and allows it to help create the future. Scenario planning makes you aware of your assumptions and helps you test them against plausible alternatives. Further, it helps expand your way of thinking and seeing to enable you to consider opportunities that were once outside your field of view.

The initial preplanning steps in scenario planning are similar to that of strategic planning, in that a SWOT (strengths/weaknesses of the organization, opportunities/threats in the environment) analysis is conducted through a survey of key informants in a wide variety of fields (both inside and outside the organization) and research in the relevant literature. A participant list is then developed, which is likely to differ significantly from the participants in strategic planning. In the latter case, the participants are usually limited to board members and key staff, which

limits the effort to an internal planning process (which is often considered proprietary and secret). At least for the initial steps of scenario planning, the participant
representation should be very broad. In addition to board members and key staff,
participants should include state and county government representatives, providers
of essential complementary services, contractors (including managed care organizations), and consumer and family advocates. Background material on scenario planning is then developed for and provided to the participants.

In the actual planning process that takes place over a number of sessions, participants brainstorm the key factors and driving forces in the environment that are
likely to shape the organization's future, based on the background information provided to the participants. The next step is to identify which factors are uncertainties
(e.g., governmental funding levels), and which are predetermined factors (e.g.,
existing legislation). A focal question or decision that faces the organization is then
developed (some examples may have been prepared in advance). For example, in
one scenario planning process for a community mental health center (CMHC), the
focal question was whether the CMHC should comprehensively serve all people or
focus on niche markets, such as people with serious mental illness or people with
mental illness in the corrections system. The driving forces and key elements affecting the focal question are then ranked through a voting process (each participant
had 10 votes) to establish the top five factors. Following discussion of these five factors, two axes are developed to create four quadrants, after considering several
competing axes to determine which are the best fit. In the CMHC process, the two
axes were (1) the structure of the cash flow and (2) the public perception of mental
illness. On the first axis, the continuum was from a "lower risk noncapitated controlled process" to a "flexible, higher risk, capitated process." On the perception axis,
at the positive end, mental health was valued and people with mental illness were
integrated into the community. On the negative side of the continuum, the medical
model was dominant, people with mental illness were out of view, and mental health
care was not valued.

Once the axes have been developed, stories and a name for each of the four scenarios are developed (each may be done by a separate small group and presented to
the larger group for refinement). In the case just cited, the following four scenarios
were developed. The first scenario, *Californiacation*, refers to where the medical
model reigns supreme. The outcomes are focused on record keeping and process
control, there are fewer resources, narrow spectrum approach to treatment, partnerships are not empowered, and mental health is not in the driver's seat. The second
scenario, *An Ideal World*, is characterized by a mental health model (in contrast to a
medical model), with more available resources, importance placed on outcome tracking, a wide spectrum approach to treatment, empowered partnerships, value placed
on mental health services, and consumers in the driver's seat. The third scenario, *A
Lot Like Now*, was distinguished by high regulation, a carved-out (from the capitated
health plan) fee-for-service payment scheme, with many services and niches. The
final scenario, *The Big Shrink*, consisted of an institutionally led environment with the
market limited to high-need patients, with fewer niches such as prisons and hospitals.

Once the scenarios are fleshed out, strategic options for each of the four scenarios are generated. Key indicators that would signal which of the scenarios is unfolding are then identified, and strategies for monitoring the indicators developed. For example, people might volunteer to read a specific journal or visit a specific Web site on a regular basis to look for specific indicators and clip out relevant material, in exchange for a subscription to the journal or Web site. The group then "wind tunnels" strategic options, that is, the group discusses how realistic the options are given the predicted trends. Out of this process, strategic priorities for success in each scenario are determined. These strategic options are then reviewed for overlap, and the core competencies are identified, which would be essential for success in any and all of the four environments. The organization then needs to create a plan to develop and/or maintain the core competencies so it can flexibly adjust its operations, if indicators signal a change in the scenario. For each of the four scenarios, the strategic options form a game plan that guides the operations and program development of the agency as long as that particular scenario still holds.

In the case of CMHC, the scenario planning was triggered by the "imminent" passage of comprehensive health and mental health care reform legislation in the state. All of the other mental health centers in the state assumed its passage as fact, and conducted all of their planning and program development based on that scenario. CMHC was the only one that was able to anticipate that the tide had suddenly turned against the legislation. It had a plan for succeeding in an environment without health care reform, and was able to change its operations to accommodate a new scenario that would have been considered impossible only six months prior.

Planning Pitfalls

The scenario planning provides the template for more detailed program development and planning. Without describing in detail the program development process, it is worth noting a few common pitfalls (Simpson, 1992). One common mistake is to confuse need with demand. In other words, professional staff may determine that there is a need for a particular service, or potential users may be asked in an informal or formal needs assessment whether they would like to see such a service. This is quite different from asking whether they would use the service if it were developed in a particular way (demand). Most people will always answer in the affirmative if they are asked if they would like such a service (Why not? It's not costing them anything), but accessibility, availability, price, and relevance of the way the service is delivered will all determine whether there is actually a demand. Many mental health programs have been started with great anticipation because they were "needed," and were discontinued because no one utilized them. For example, a number of CMHCs opened special outpatient clinics to capture the private-pay market, but either because of the stigma associated with a mental health center, insurance coverage, location, or hours, they failed to pay for themselves. The other aspect to this is, of course, to be sure that any barriers to service utilization (e.g., transportation) have been lowered or removed in the program planning process.

A second major pitfall is to fail to involve key stakeholders in the early phases of the process, where unanticipated consequences of the program and its implementation can be identified. Having a broad range of participants in the scenario planning is likely to mitigate such a situation and establish the necessary buy-in and sense of ownership of the new program. All too often, a small group of managers have planned programs in isolation without adequately consulting the staff who are expected to implement it, the consumers, and family members who will participate in the program, or other complementary services or referral sources (either within or outside the agency) that might be impacted by the new program. This will not only lead to a lack of felt ownership, but frequently will result in a faulty design, because the front-line staff and consumers will most likely know what will or will not work. Finally, the greater the complexity of the program and the larger number of actors involved, the greater the probability that there will be implementation problems (Pressman & Wildavsky, 1979). There is a lot of evidence still supporting the common cliché "KISS" (keep it simple, stupid), as the key principle of program design and implementation.

This discussion is also relevant for the policy analyst. Scenario planning is a useful tool for the policy analyst, as well as the administrator, both in understanding what policy developments might occur and to test the impact of a policy under a variety of scenarios. What might have started out as a sound policy under the scenario in which it was originally developed, might exact opposite consequences of the legislative or administrative intent under a different scenario. The conflict between government regulators, advocates for increased regulation, and those who are regulated (e.g., nursing homes) is testimony to the fact that interpretations of what is needed or wanted is not clear cut in the policy sphere either. Keeping things simple and the including major stakeholders are applicable to the policy analysis process as well.

Financial Management and Resource Development

Environmental uncertainty probably has the biggest impact on today's financial management and resource development tasks. In a bid to hedge against uncertainty, agencies have tried to diversify their funding sources. The advent of managed care has created a proliferation of provider panels for different health care plans so that a relatively simple budgeting task has become increasingly complex, with multiple billing and reporting formats, and different fiscal years for various sources of funds, and so on. Developing the technical capacity to process all of this information and meet the different requirements has become an expensive challenge. In addition, with the advent of competition with the private-for-profit sector, pricing services, technology, and facing mental health administrators have become new tasks. Price setting is a complicated task that many not-for-profit agencies are ill-equipped to handle because of a lack of prior experience with grants and reimbursement systems. This is also an inherent part of competitive bidding in response to request for proposals, which are now an integral part of purchasing service contracts in many mental health systems.

An even greater impact of recent trends has been on the resource development issues. Until recently, mental health agencies dealt with government agencies regarding funding. Even with the normal tensions affecting funder-fundee relationships, there was usually a shared set of values and responsibilities for ensuring that high-quality care was provided to a target population. With the increasing influx of for-profit organizations, and managing or contracting for service systems, mental health administrators have to deal with corporations who may not share the same values, and for whom profit is the major goal. This can present a whole set of value and ethical dilemmas where tough compromises must be made to secure adequate funding to keep the agency viable. For example, social work holds individualization and a holistic approach as major values. Increasingly, under managed care or federal regulations, a specific diagnosis may require that a particular treatment protocol be followed, indicating not only how many visits will be authorized, but also the type of interventions allowed, leaving little flexibility for individual variations.

Managed Care

Managed care evolved in the health care system, and in most instances, managed mental health care has followed the medical model as well. This philosophical approach plus cost considerations frequently lead to an over reliance on medication as the strategy of choice, and in some instances, a reliance on older, less effective, but cheaper, medications. Thus, an agency and its practitioners may have to trade off significant autonomy for sufficient resources. This is an example of the general rise of fiscal management and the decline of professionalism in key decision making (Hasenfeld, 1996). As will be discussed later, treatment protocols are not necessarily negative, because all too often the latest research findings and best practices are not being followed. To the extent that protocols improve practice, they are helpful. The key is whether they are treated as flexible guidelines or rigid requirements.

With or without managed care, cost containment has become an expectation that severely affects program decision making. This has several potential negative impacts. It is important for the long-term effectiveness and survival of an organization that it understands its business (Drucker, 1974) and keeps its focus. The pursuit of diversified resources can lead financial managers to pursue money simply for the sake of organizational growth and survival, despite the relevance to the mission. In such situations, the tail can end up wagging the dog. At an extreme point, rather than concentrating its energies on financing its core services, an agency can pursue multiple funding sources, which result in a conglomeration of services without a concentrated focus. This would make it impossible to provide effective services to a particular target group, and the agency would risk doing nothing well, once it overstepped its area of core competence.

A good illustration of the fiscal vulnerability of mental health organizations to policy decisions in the environment has been the experience with Medicaid-managed mental health care. In the last two decades, states focused their funding on services to people with major mental illness, and CMHCs reconfigured themselves to provide comprehensive services to this publically funded target population. However, as Medicaid is an entitlement, CMHCs in some states have been confronted with an influx of people with serious problems, but who do not have major mental illness. They were not previously required to see this group, but now they must serve them. However, in such cases, the state did not provide funding to increase service capacity, essentially resulting in an unfunded mandate. Ultimately, the people with major mental illness receive less service and become more vulnerable to psychiatric decompensation (Mechanic & McAlpine, 1999). This phenomenon has led to crisis proportions in some systems, leading to soaring caseloads of 80 to 90 people or more. Supports for housing and jobs obviously cannot be provided with such unmanageable caseload sizes. This is an example where scenario planning might have predicted an otherwise unanticipated consequence, and where policy advocacy might have provided a solution.

With respect to resource development, major advocacy organizations such as consumer groups, the National Alliance for the Mentally Ill, the Federation of Families for Children with Serious Emotional Disturbances, and the Mental Health Association, have become the best advocates for funds with legislators. They are not seen as self-serving the same way providers are, and their personal stories show the impact of insufficient funding on actual people. Building coalitions, therefore, has become one of the most important skills mental health administrators need. In other words, the extent to which an agency can mobilize its constituencies to advocate for it, the better off it will be.

Developing Constituencies

As an example of developing constituencies, a CMHC assertively sought the support of local businesses, a constituency that is usually ignored. The agency realized that local retailers' main concerns were that the bizarre behavior of a person with major mental illness would scare away or harass their customers or staff. They also realized that efforts to educate or lecture retailers to be sensitive to people with mental illness was not likely to succeed as a first strategy. Therefore, they asked retailers to call them whenever there was a perceived problem. They recognized the unfortunate reality that, if retailers did not call the CMHC, they would probably call the police, rather than a mental health specialist who could better serve a person with mental illness. While there are certainly complex civil rights and stigma issues in these cases, the CMHC pragmatically decided that these problems could not be resolved overnight. With time and sensitive handling of situations, they were able to educate retailers about mental illness. The mental health provider showed them how to interact with people with mental illness and not escalate a situation. The merchants also learned to respect the civil rights of people with mental illness, which reduced stigma and gained the support of the business community. The year following the introduction of this program, the local chamber of commerce lobbied city council for more funds for the CMHC.

To sum up, the major challenges with respect to financial management and resource acquisition are (1) developing the technology to manage the increasing complexity of multiple funding sources and the need for real-time utilization review; (2) negotiating for as much program and professional control as possible, while simultaneously providing systems and resources to ensure that clinicians use accepted standards of research based practice; (3) pursuing diversified funding without losing focus on the central mission of the mental health agency and, particularly, not diluting the core competencies; (4) keeping abreast of new funding schemes and conducting quick but thorough policy analysis to provide data on the potential impact on the agency, both to help shape policy and to position the agency to manage the new fiscal realities; and (5) building coalitions to support the activities of the agency.

As the previous discussion makes clear, the way fiscal incentives are designed shapes the way programs can operate, as well as the outcomes that can be achieved. Likewise, regulations that stipulate qualifications for personnel and service standards have similar impacts in terms of both the cost of providing a service and the flexibility of the agency's operations. It is essential, therefore, that the policy analyst understands how proposed policies affect these areas. For the administrator, the task is to manage the resources within the constraints placed on the agency. The policy analyst creates these constraints to shape the desired organizational behavior, which it is believed will accomplish the government's goals. The policy analyst's task is more complicated, however, as she or he must develop a financing system that benefits the community as a whole and not just one agency and also promotes cooperative behavior and system goals.

Organizing and Developing Effective Structures and Processes

For organizations to be effective, administrators must figure out how to structure the organization and its processes to maximize the efficiency and effectiveness of its staff. For this to happen, ideally all of the incentives should reinforce the desired staff behaviors. One way of analyzing whether or not incentives support the desired behavior, or whether there are conflicting expectations and rewards, is to use a multiple-incentive system framework based on learning theory and contingency management practices. An incentive system is defined as the rewards and punishments dispensed, the mechanisms by which they are distributed, and the assessment criteria used to evaluate performance to determine what the appropriate consequences of the performance should be.

Multiple Incentive System Framework

The theoretical basis of incentive and contingency analysis is that behavior is determined by its consequences. Some approaches have recognized the need to analyze the interrelationships between individuals, groups, and subunits in an organization because the behavior of individuals in a given unit is, in part, a response to consequences resulting from the other units in its environment (Brethower, 1972; Kunkel,

1970; Luthans & Kreitner, 1974, Mager & Pipe, 1970). Nonetheless, none have fully integrated these interrelationships into a single framework. Regardless of the inter-relationships, the underlying behavioral principles are the same.

The conceptual underpinning of the behavioral analysis framework is that there are four major sources of reinforcement and punishment (i.e., incentive systems) in an organization. They are the external, official, unofficial, and intrinsic task characteristics. It is the structure and interaction of these various contingencies that shape and maintain organizational behavior, and must be taken into account when analyzing organizational processes. The following briefly describes these four sources.

The external incentive system is made up of the external task environment elements, which regulate an organization, or control important resources (reinforcers). These external elements structure the contingencies (rewards and punishments) for the organization. For example, key external elements for a CMHC might be the local mental health authority, the state mental health department, the state hospital, state licensing departments, and advocacy groups. The more an administrator's organization is dependent on an external entity for critical resources, the more power the external entity has over the organization, and the more the administrator will try to meet that entity's expectations (Gummer, 1994; Thompson, 1967). Hence, the assessment criteria used by key task environment elements to measure the organization's performance, and determine whether it will be rewarded, is crucial in determining the nature of the internal (official) contingencies established by the organization. For instance, the local mental health authority that funds an agency might insist that the agency in developing a program to deal with the homeless mentally ill population or risk losing its funding.

The official incentive system consists of the important incentives (e.g., promotions, assignments, job discretion, and training opportunities) distributed by an agency through its official mechanism according to agency-set criteria. To illustrate, mental health administrators might reward people based on their productivity and billable hours, or, in contrast, on functional improvements of people on their caseloads and consumer satisfaction. Similarly, it might punish workers whose style of service delivery was inappropriate to the needs of the minority clientele being served. Whether an agency reinforces or discourages active participation of consumers and family members in treatment, for example, could have an important impact on staff behavior.

Informal groups that form around work units, common jobs (e.g., secretarial or supervisory, case managers, employment specialists, or therapists), union shops, and professional affiliations (e.g., psychiatrists, psychologists, social workers, psychiatric nurses) can be considered as alternative, unofficial incentive systems operating in the organization, over which agency administrators have little control. These groups can play an important socialization function, and can become an informal base of power in the organization as well (Gummer, 1994). Such groups, for instance, can reinforce either positive or negative expectations of the recovery potential of people with major mental illness.

Finally, there are aspects of a particular job that a worker finds to be either intrinsically rewarding or aversive. These make up the intrinsic reinforcement characteristics of the task. For example, a worker might find community outreach to seriously mentally ill people challenging and stimulating, which would be experienced as intrinsically rewarding. In contrast, individual therapy with a person with borderline personality disorder might be exhausting and complicated, and thus highly aversive.

For implementation of a program to be successful, these various incentive systems must interact in such a way that the desired behavior of the workers occurs. Thus, the interaction between the systems varies with each unique situation. In a given situation, some of the contingencies might favor a particular type of behavior while others discourage it. The outcome would depend on which systems had a greater impact on the worker at a given point in time.

Environmental Intrusions

Today, agencies are having to adopt new structures and forms. There are two critical ways in which the environment has intruded on internal organizational structure. The first is the pressure to include consumers and family members in many aspects of the organization's operations, and second, the reality that mental health programs and service delivery for people with multiple problems is interorganizational. In the former case, consumers and family members expect to be involved in policy making, treatment planning, and interventions as collaborative partners. While there has been much talk about client-centered services (Rapp & Poertner, 1992; Rose & Black, 1985), most mental health agencies have a long way to go in actually achieving this goal. The multiple incentive system framework is a useful way to analyze the ways in which the organization encourages or discourages such involvement. Administrators need to recognize that actively including consumers introduces uncertainty into a worker's life, may make their work more difficult from their perspective, and involves the sharing of power. It is important to recognize that these are powerful disincentives. Unless the organization actively builds in incentives for workers and helps them see the advantages of such practices for improving organizational effectiveness, they are unlikely to actively pursue consumer involvement.

Implementation Structures

With respect to the latter issue, we need to seriously rethink our conceptualization of organizational programs. In the implementation, service integration, and organizational literature, most of the emphasis has been on a focal organization (Paulson, 1996). These approaches inherently assume a certain degree of administrative control, internal communications, and coordination over program implementation. According to two researchers, we have tended to look at the implementation of social programs from a "lonely organization view," failing to appreciate the involvement of other organizations. In other words, "when a new program is enacted, it is assigned to a single organization, and everyone walks away secure in the belief that somehow (perhaps by magic) it will be implemented" (Hjern & Porter, 1981).

A pioneer study on manpower training systems has challenged the accuracy of this organizational focus in explaining both the implementation and ongoing operations of social programs. This research indicated that the number of actors, the extent of interorganizational relationships, and the patterns of interaction were much more complex than was apparent from formal and official descriptions. Reports from agency executives consistently underestimated these interactions (Hjern & Porter, 1981). As a case in point, most mental health programs depend on the ongoing actions of individuals in a variety of organizations. Suppose a county-wide mental health center/probate court project for outpatient commitment was assigned to the mental health center. It could not function without both the court and mental health agency personnel engaging in activities that go well beyond coordination and cooperation. The program has an administrative (program) rationale of its own, which goes beyond the rationales of each of the organizations for which the employees work. However, the mental health agency, to which the program is technically assigned, has limited control over the court personnel who are so essential to the program. Therefore, the mental health agency must rely on persuasion to obtain the desired results. As a consequence, the director of the mental health center may direct workers to institute certain program changes, which they cannot implement because the workers in the other agencies (in this case, the court), are prohibited by their own organization's policies. Supported employment and housing programs as well as services to dual diagnoses clients (mental illness/substance abuse or mental illness/mental retardation) are other clear examples where such organizational interdependencies are especially important for program success.

Hjern and Porter (1981) concluded that focusing on single organizations and their interaction with other organizations was inadequate to describe, analyze, and manage the degree of interdependence they observed. They propose that there are implementation structures for programs, which are legitimate units of administrative analysis. According to this perspective, it becomes clear that social service programs are, in fact, parts of organizations, while organizations can be seen as pieces of programs (Hjern & Porter, 1981). In other words, implementation structures can be viewed as informal interorganization networks, which evolve for the purposes of a specific program. A single agency is a part of many of these informal interorganizational networks that others have called service networks (Provan & Milward, 1995). This is consistent with the image of a "Service Mosaic," as described in the Cleveland Federation of Planning Study of aftercare services to patients discharged from a state mental hospital (Solomon, Gordon, & Davis, 1984).

To the extent that this model is accurate, our theories for the management of mental health agencies are anachronistic. Policy, planning, program, and resource allocations decisions are based on the assumptions inherent in these theories, that agencies have a degree of control over programs that they implement, when, in fact, the necessary degree of control may not exist. The decisions fail to take into account the existence of the real, albeit, not legally or officially recognized program implementation structures that have evolved. This, in fact, represents the reality in many localities where the community support system is a concept operationalized through interorganizational activities, but without any entity having the overall authority or administrative responsibility for the coordination of the system. No one is in control and there is no fixed point of responsibility.

The Community Support Program (CSP) and Children and Adolescent Service System Program (CASSP) were developed in recognition of the fact that the needs of both children and adults with major mental illness could not be met by a single organization alone. Even though mental health organizations have assumed many of the responsibilities (e.g., housing, supported employment) that other agencies were supposed to carry out, they still must rely on complementary services from other organizations if their interventions are to be successful. A case example will be used to illustrate how the multiple incentive system framework can be applied to how an agency facilitates or inhibits such coordination. It should be clear from this discussion that the development and management of well-integrated systems of care for people with major mental illness are fraught with potential difficulties. This concrete example provides a basis for discussing practical recommendations regarding strategies to facilitate a well-coordinated interorganizational system of care. A study funded by the Ohio Department of Mental Health of an urban Ohio county is the basis of the case example.

A CASE STUDY

In general, the County "X" Mental Health service delivery system could be described as a loosely coupled system (Weick, 1979) with a low degree of formalization, medium intensity, and a high degree of reciprocity. Interorganizational exchanges occurred principally for the purposes of exchanging clients and information. Once those exchanges took place, each organization tended to go its own way, with little integration or ongoing treatment collaboration between organizations serving the same clients. There were three clearly identifiable subsystems, the community mental health agencies, the psychiatric hospitals, and the nonmental health agencies. The relationships between these subsystems contained a degree of friction, particularly between the mental health and nonmental health subsystems, which reduced the overall effectiveness of their collaboration and prevented their relationships from reaching full potential.

The lack of formalization meant that, in most instances, the mechanisms for controlling exchanges, which is one of three prerequisites for interorganizational coordination cited in the literature, was absent or occurred informally (Reid, 1964). Coordination was almost exclusively ad hoc case coordination, rather than a better mix of case, program, and system coordination.

More importantly, few of the incentive systems supported interorganizational service delivery. The productivity rates and reimbursement system of the external incentives did not lend themselves to reinforcing the kind of service delivery that is most effective for severely mentally disabled people or seriously emotionally disturbed children. The official incentives did not explicitly monitor, reinforce, or sufficiently recognize these interorganizational services in job expectations or in calculating workloads. Nor were official incentives used to positively encourage the development and maintenance of the informal service delivery networks.

The major conclusion of the study was that formal arrangements are necessary, but not sufficient, to guarantee effective interorganizational cooperation and coordination in service delivery efforts. It was also concluded that the quality and intensity of the formal relationships between two organizations are not a good indicator of the quality of the informal networking at the service delivery level. These informal networks were analogous to implementation structures because they were composed of workers in many different programs and agencies (i.e., pieces of organizations), and a particular organization's activities were made possible by many of these different interorganizational networks.

It was found that these informal networks that workers developed were either on a case-by-case basis over time, or as a result of collegial friendships that were maintained as workers changed jobs throughout the system. Very little structuring of worker interaction occurred with other agencies. The identification of systems problems and handling of conflicts were almost always negotiated on an informal basis, with only the most serious and prolonged issues shifted to more formal channels for resolution.

Barriers to Coordination

Despite the complexity of the interorganizational systems, many of the factors that were identified as important in the smooth working of the formal and informal networks were rather obvious, if not mundane. Workers found problems in establishing relationships, exchanging information; accepting referrals and collaborating treatments, and gaining consensus on roles and responsibilities. The ability to establish relationships was one of the most important variables in explaining effective working relationships. Yet, this proved to be surprisingly difficult to accomplish. The sizes and structures of the interacting agencies seemed to be important. In large agencies such as the Department of Human Services (welfare), where functions and geography are not differentiated and where the turnover rate in cases and workers is frequently high, it is very difficult for workers from other agencies to establish informal relationships.

The exchange of information was a primary reason for interorganizational interaction. The ease with which information flowed back and forth, in a timely manner and in usable form, was critical in forming the workers' opinions of the interorganizational relationships. Workers encountered problems when misunderstandings arose regarding (1) the need for certain client information within specified, limited time frames (e.g., acute care facilities, the courts); (2) the specific, technical way certain information needed to be presented (e.g., social security disability claims); (3) periodic feedback on client progress or the disposition of a referral; (4) difficulties in sending and receiving messages ("telephone tag"); and, (5) the absence of standardized policies and procedures around confidentiality and the release of information. In short, when feedback and information exchanges were scarce and difficult, workers were considerably more reluctant to refer or collaborate with other agencies on either an informal or formal basis.

Referral acceptance was another factor that dramatically affected the informal referral system and overall cooperative relationships. It did not take many rejections before a worker became reluctant to contact an agency as a collaborative resource. Reasons for rejections included confusion over eligibility, severe delays caused by waiting lists, and the lack of an information system on service capacity and availability

In addition, collaborative treatment and case consultation are important issues when concurrent or follow-up treatment is involved. While all agencies publicly and officially supported the concept, ongoing treatment collaboration between workers in different agencies only occurred infrequently. Workloads, agency incentives, differences in treatment philosophy, and scheduling conflicts all contributed to this situation. If workers were not included in case conferences or did not feel that their information and advice was valued, they were much less likely to rely on the collaborating agency in the future.

Disagreements or confusion over the respective roles and responsibilities of agencies and the predominate treatment philosophy was another element that proved to be problematic in maintaining working relationships, and shaped the pattern of interagency referrals in the system. The informal nature of the system only contributed to the considerable role confusion. Therefore, not surprisingly, one of the most important predictors of interorganizational coordination and perceived effectiveness was the presence of a conflict resolution mechanism.

The importance of this information is for both administrators and practitioners to remember that more pragmatic, technical and logistical details can sometimes be as problematic as the larger systems and policy issues, and that issues and problems in both areas need to be addressed.

Removing the Barriers

Removing barriers does not necessarily involve complex solutions. As a result of research, a series of logical steps was recommended which, taken together, could result in improvements in system functioning with applicability to other community support systems as well. Many of these were suggested by respondents or were observed to be successful in isolated instances. The thrust of these recommendations involves improving the quality of communications; developing more regularized mechanisms that will both increase mutual knowledge and understanding (hence, prevent disputes), and resolve problems and disagreements when they occur; and encouraging and shaping the formation of informal networks.

The absence of regular, joint training or information exchanges between organizations, or the failure to reach all of the people who needed it made it difficult for workers to meet face-to-face, even if they had been communicating by telephone for a number of years. Given the tremendous difference in trust and rapport that can occur, even as the result of a single meeting, creating such opportunities would seem to be important. At a minimum, there should be regular meetings between key agencies at least once or twice a year, for the purposes of orienting new workers (a major problem with high turnover rates) and updating people on changes in services, policies, and procedures. Specialized joint training around technical issues that present continuing problems between organizations or systems can also greatly facilitate working relationships. One example is training between Social Security and mental health workers, to train the latter in the proper completion of the social security forms to meet the legal and medical criteria used in disability determinations.

An additional option is the use of joint meetings to establish consensus on how mutual case interactions should be handled. This is similar to the reliability training conducted with research assistants or quality assurance committees that perform content analyses (Newmann & Sorenson, 1985). That is, cases are presented that represent typical problems and misunderstandings between the two groups. Representatives of each group discuss how they would have handled their respective part and the rationale for their actions. This helps both sides understand each other's concerns and issues. Combining these more formal meetings with informal gatherings, such as open houses, provides staff with a real opportunity to mix and exchange ideas and to meet the face behind the telephone. With personal contacts established, it greatly facilitates the development of working relationships and trust, with both parties becoming more willing to be responsive and flexible regarding each other's needs than they would be with strangers.

These three types of events should help enhance the quality of communications, referral acceptance, collaborative treatment, feedback, evaluations (or actual improvements) of a counterpart unit's performance and competence, and diminish difficulties in communicating ideas and gaps in expectations and philosophy. All of these factors were found to be critical in producing effective interorganizational relationships.

Another obvious recommendation is to make greater use of liaisons that could further encourage improvements in all of the areas mentioned above. The liaison role should be one of a problem solver and troubleshooter whose use is voluntary. The obligatory use of one person as a gatekeeper renders the system much too dependent on an individual personality, and ineffective liaisons are certainly worse than no liaisons.

Liaisons could also serve another important systems function as specialist/liaison case managers for programmatic functions that are particularly critical in community support systems. In most entitlement programs, for example, the rules and regulations are extremely complex and change on a regular basis. It would be both unreasonable and inefficient to expect that every case manager be able to develop sufficient expertise and keep current in these areas.

Greater use of formalized protocols and interagency or systemwide agreements also facilitates the coordination between the different sectors. While these arrangements are not answers to problems in and of themselves, they do provide a basic framework within which the more informal adaptations can take place. Further, they also make mutual expectations clearer and the terms of the relationship more explicit (Paulson, 1993).

Other Issues in Organizational Design

There is a caveat to be learned from the recent interorganizational research that highlights the importance of managers ensuring that the best practices are followed. In an evaluation of the large scale systems change effort of the Robert Wood Johnson Foundation Program on Severe and Persistent Mental Illness, which supported the development of local mental health authorities as vehicles for creating integrated systems of care, it was concluded that systems change was necessary, but not sufficient (Lehman, Postrado, Roth, McNary, & Goldman, 1994). In this case, there was no attempt to evaluate or improve the actual interventions, and in fact, partially as a way of saving costs, an almost exclusive emphasis on case management diminished other important psychiatric interventions. In other words, if you integrate or coordinate ineffective or inappropriate services, you cannot expect improvements on outcomes. This focus on effective services should be the goal that guides how the organization is structured and the processes employed.

However, it is often overlooked that providing effective services does not occur in a vacuum and that fiscal and policy constraints can prevent this from happening. For example, managed care in particular is presenting several major dilemmas in this regard. In most instances, an extra layer of decision making has been added so that agencies must obtain approval provide services. While this makes more sense with an insurance population and with acute episodes, it is very problematic with populations who have major (and therefore chronic) mental illness. As already noted, decisions about what treatments to provide may also be severely constrained. Perhaps the greatest concern is the imposition of a medical model, where recovery clearly requires rehabilitative models as well.

The CSP and CASSP evolved when it was clear that other systems were not providing the necessary services to people with mental illness, such that the mental health agencies assumed many of these responsibilities, as well as a brokering and advocacy role in leveraging other services. However, in many instances, the imposition of strict definitions of medical necessity and restrictive benefit packages has provided no fiscal resources to support social services, such as housing, skills training, and vocational services. Nor are they often mandated as services the managed care organization must provide. This makes it especially important for administrators to make careful decisions regarding what services and programs to provide and how to finance them. If services are subcapitated, where the providers are passed on a portion of the total capitation payment, then they have much greater flexibility and incentives to provide these other services, because they have been shown to reduce hospitalization and other high-cost services.

Fiscal restraints can have another important consequence on organizational design. A mantra of cost cutting is the reduction of redundancy. Agencies may be forced, as a condition of accepting funding, to cut back on certain services that are seen to be duplicative or to create a centralized service for a jurisdiction, such as a single-access point or emergency service. This perpetuates the fallacy that all redundancy is bad, when in fact the issue should be about planned versus unplanned redundancy. In an innovative paper, Martin Landau pointed out that when one is concerned about reliability, then planned redundancy is the preferred strategy (Landau, 1969). This is epitomized in the manned space program, where multiple levels of redundancy are built in to assure the crew's safety. Would we want to give up the dual braking systems in our cars to save a few hundred dollars? The issue is to identify those areas where reliability is critical and where to build in redundancy.

For example, if you believe that both intake and crisis services are crucial and need reliability, then completely centralizing the system means that, if assistance can not be obtained from one specific place, it cannot be obtained anywhere. In contrast, the community mental health centers traditionally have had multiple satellite clinics located close to where people lived to maximize accessibility. Crisis services were provided in the clinic and also as a function of mobile outreach teams. However, if services could not be obtained from that center, they could be obtained from the emergency room or another center. On the other hand, if all crises services are only provided in the emergency room, but the person is turned away, as all too frequently happens, there exists a tragedy in the making. In England, the access problem has been solved by creating special access agencies (citizen advisory bureaus) where anyone can walk in off the street with a problem and be linked up with the service (Kahn, 1969).

The major task of the administrator is to figure out how to align all of the incentive systems to obtain the desired results within the organizational constraints. Increasingly, this means interacting with other organizations and groups in the environment whose actions must be coordinated to achieve good outcomes. For the internal policy analyst, the task is to assess how a policy might change the various incentive structures, and what accommodations may need to be made so there is not a disruption of successful operations. As with the resource management tasks, an external policy analyst is concerned with how a whole service system is organized for a particular jurisdiction. An external policy analyst is also concerned with the types of incentives and regulations necessary for ensuring that the needs of the whole, and not just that of the organization, are taken into account. These policies and evaluative standards, of course, make up much of the external environment for the individual organization.

Staffing

The staffing or human resource function in mental health agencies has also become more complex over the years. Like other human service organizations, mental health organizations were initially often administered rather loosely. The nature of social work and mental health tended to rely on interpersonal processing to manage personnel issues. However, mental health organizations have rapidly developed highly organized professional staffing functions. Increases in regulations and litigation in such areas as affirmative action, due process, and sexual harassment have made this a necessity. In this increasingly litiginous society, it is almost expected that a court suit will result from staff who have been fired. Therefore, good personnel practices and documentation have become very important. The increase in unionization in community mental health settings has also changed the nature of personnel management.

Two key trends will be highlighted here. The most obvious is that mental health organizations are increasingly multicultural organizations with more diverse work forces and client populations. There is an expectation that an organization be culturally competent with respect to both its internal operations and the services it provides (U.S. Department of Health and Human Services, 1999). Unfortunately, while everyone pays lip service to these ideas and ideals, they only become a reality with considerable effort and persistence. Diversity and cultural competence are all too often viewed as a moral issue only, without full recognition that the changes usually involve not only differences in fundamental values, but issues of power differentials, and major changes in how business is conducted.

A crucial administrative task is to ensure that these efforts do not become divisive, and to create a culture in which differences can be discussed and used in creative ways. This means that the incentives must be carefully structured to reinforce a no-tolerance policy for discrimination, stigma, and prejudice. For example, the employment of consumers and family members as providers is a growing trend. Yet, a recent study showed that the stigma within mental health organizations, with respect to employing people with mental illness, was greater than in other social service organizations (Paulson, Herinckx, Demmler, Clarke, Cutler, & Birecree, 1999).

A further challenge is how to accommodate cultural differences while maintaining standards and practices that are seen to be equitable by all groups. Furthermore, how is a balance obtained between keeping costs down and developing the capacity to serve different populations? Are specialized programs designed for each target population? Are specialists available on more generalist teams? Is there a greater reliance on extensive training and interpreters? These are the kinds of questions to ask and choices to be made.

A second major trend, which is relevant to culturally competent organizations, is the increasing pressure under managed care to credential and privilege staff. This presents another staffing challenge. Balancing credentials with diversity is extremely difficult, because in many cases, the pool of ethnic minority or consumer professionals is considerably smaller than their representation in the larger population, and they can command higher salaries because of the increased demand. In addition, there is a long and distinguished history of employing paraprofessionals because their life experiences can provide skills that are important complements to those of professionals. The greater empathy of paraprofessionals with consumers is also important in providing effective services. The emphasis on credentialing can be even more constraining to the extent that it places restrictions on those who can provide and be reimbursed for those services.

While staffing per se is not a function of the policy analyst, affirmative action and personnel standards are two major areas of governmental policy that have a direct effect on this administrative function.

Evaluating

In a rapidly changing environment, evaluation is essential for success. Unfortunately, evaluation is an activity that is difficult to fund as a purely administrative cost, and can be expensive. Also, evaluations are frequently not utilized. The literature on utilization-focused evaluation (Patton, 1997) is consistent in emphasizing the inclusion of all major stakeholders in the planning of evaluations, and the necessity to answer some of the questions that key stakeholders view as important, in addition to those of the evaluator. With the demands for accountability and outcome measures, evaluation is all the more important (see Chapter 13). Given the current trend of the information revolution, mental health administrators now have the potential for using service utilization, outcome, and consumer satisfaction data to evaluate programs in ways that were not previously possible, and to anticipate when innovative service technologies need to be developed. However, management information systems are all too often geared more to process measures or fiscal data and are good at collecting data, but lack the capacity to provide feedback as useful information. It is a real challenge, therefore, for administrators to make sure that the management information systems (MIS) developers consider the ways in which the information can be used for evaluative purposes. The new computer capacity provides impressive new opportunities for internal monitoring and control. This can be seen in well-developed managed care organizations that have utilization, cost, and outcome profiles for every provider, which are fed back to them in addition to comparisons with the averages of all other providers. While this can have important positive effects, it is important to remember that there are special dangers as well.

It is critical that evaluation measures for either individuals and programs are multifaceted and well-balanced, and not based on a simplistic set of statistics (Rosenheck & Cicchetti, 1998). Statistical evaluation measures have powerful effects on behavior, and can create serious distortions in what happens in organizations. To the extent the statistics measure only one aspect of performance, that is what will be emphasized, as people strive to score well on the recognized criteria. Equally important, unmeasured activity is less likely to be noted (Rosenblatt, Wyman, Kingdon, & Ichinose, 1998). It is common knowledge that in the absence of multiple measures and more sophisticated ways of evaluating performance, all kinds of gaming and manipulation can occur to place a positive spin on the statistics. Finally, to keep a motivated workforce, it is important that workers not view an MIS as a vehicle for spying and for punishment. Rather, the entire process should be structured for workers to receive feedback in advance of formal evaluations, so that they can self-correct their own behavior. This information should also be useful for identifying organizational issues, as well as employee issues. That is, the information should identify areas where there are barriers or insufficient supports for effective performance.

Perhaps the greatest task of the administrator as evaluator is to create a culture that supports a continuous learning organization. In many organizations, evaluation focuses on conformance to rules and regulations. Deviation from rules is seen as reason for punishment, even if the worker has had good reasons for the deviation. Similarly, workers are punished for mistakes rather than the organization viewing mistakes as opportunities for learning. This is exactly the opposite of how science progresses (Landau, 1973). If a researcher was punished every time a cancer experiment failed, there would be little scientific progress. Instead, the results of a failed experiment are analyzed for what light they shed on the problem. Therefore, one possible explanation or solution to a problem is eliminated.

In a learning organization, the fear of failure is abolished. Despite all of the advances in mental health interventions, we still have much to learn regarding the reintegration of people with mental illness into society as fully functioning citizens. Yet many agencies have perpetuated programs (such as day treatment), despite research that has shown such programs to be of limited value because rigorous evaluation is not conducted. In contrast, the work of Thresholds, a psychosocial rehabilitation program in Chicago, shows how an organization can systematically innovate with new programs, while rigorously evaluating them (Bond et al., 1989; Bond & Dincin, 1986). Essentially, when a new program was implemented, consumers were randomly assigned to the new program, to an alternative program, or to the agency's traditional program. The results were then analyzed, and if the innovation was successful, it was expanded and replicated. If not, a different type of program was designed. The important point is that staff did not feel that their jobs were jeopardized if the newly implemented program was not successful. They knew they would be utilized in a more effective program or in a new innovation. In this way, program decisions were based on results, and the staff, who valued effectiveness, learned to respect and value the evaluative process as an opportunity to learn and grow.

Evaluations are important sources of information for policy analysts as they determine whether current policies are effective and what policy changes might be needed. By requiring formal evaluation reports, or in requesting systematic submission of data for evaluation purposes, governmental policy analysts can have a big impact on both the evaluation processes of the agency and in shaping the behavior of the organization itself. All of the caveats discussed earlier, with respect to having multidimensional measures of evaluation, apply here as well.

Interacting with the Environment

Much of the information in the previous sections considered various aspects of interaction with the environment, because so many of an organization's internal tasks are impacted by external forces. In fact, one of the biggest tasks of administrators is deciding how to manage their time to sufficiently attend to both spheres. It is easy for a CEO to become so involved in representing the agency in external tasks, that insufficient time is spent on internal matters. A common solution is to establish a second in command (e.g., chief operating officer, associate director, deputy director) to be mainly responsible for internal affairs, while the CEO functions as the chief boundary spanner or person interacting with the external environment.

Given the competitive nature of the external environment, mental health administrators have, for the first time, been forced to pay attention to marketing their agencies and to public relations. Hospitals have spent major dollars on advertising for psychiatric units, while mental health centers have usually had to content themselves with public service announcements or press releases. Establishing good relationships with the media has become critical, because it is not uncommon for a sensational incident involving a former client of the mental health organization, to be viewed by the public as the responsibility of the mental health organization. Good relationships with the media maximize the chances that such unfortunate incidents are handled sensitively and that balanced reporting will occur.

The growing litigious nature of our society was discussed earlier in conjunction with personnel practices, but raises other issues for mental health administrators as well. Questions of civil rights used to be played out in somewhat simple terms, with a right side and a wrong side. With today's complexity, as often as not, there are conflicting equal rights that are extremely difficult to mediate and balance. For example, the rights of consumers to privacy, the right for family members to be informed regarding their loved one's illness, the right to understand course of treatment and prognosis, the agency's responsibility to protect confidentiality, and the proprietary nature of the agency's records, all must constantly be worked out.

Similarly, there is the consumer's right to refuse treatment and society's right to protect its citizens. Inject a managed care organization into the mix, and the problems become even more complicated. The main message is that none of these issues have simple solutions, and they all involve both legal and ethical concerns. The reality is that, in many instances, such as in the first example, carefully respecting and involving all parties will frequently prevent conflicts from occurring. It is important, however, for administrators not to allow concerns for legal suits to become barriers to providing effective services. Otherwise, an agency can become paralyzed into ineffectiveness and inaction. While legal council is increasingly important, common sense has become no less so in these situations.

To recapitulate some of the key issues mentioned earlier, mental health agencies are faced with a greater intrusion of their external task environment into the organization. Consumers and family members expect to be included on boards and involved in the treatment process in ways unheard of in years past. Local mental health authorities, state government, and managed care organizations are all increasing their oversight and imposing rules and standards to which agencies must adhere.

The recognition by mental health agencies of the interorganizational nature of their services and programs is another aspect of interacting with the environment, which has already been discussed. Increasingly, the demands of managing the external environment are outstripping the resources of mental health agencies that must seriously consider whether they need to affiliate or merge with other agencies for survival. For instance, the costs have become extremely expensive to upgrade MIS, campaign to increase or hold on to market share, and advocate with governmental organizations for services and support. Furthermore, employers and public funders place greater demands to provide more comprehensive coverage in terms of geographic areas, client populations (e.g., "cradle to grave"), and range of treatment alternatives that can be beyond the means of most smaller organizations. In many states, community mental health centers have affiliated with hospitals to obtain a source of capital, or have banded together into large statewide or regional networks with centralized access and joint MIS to stay in business. As noted before, many mental health services are provided in primary care settings, and the ultimate policy goal of both the state and federal government is to create an integration of the health and behavioral health systems. An important future task of mental health administrators will be to establish close relationships with the primary care sector, to either provide specialty mental health assessment or treatment in primary care settings, or to educate physicians in the identification of the mental health needs of their patients and to facilitate quick and easy referrals to the mental health agency.

A final way today's mental health administrator must interact with the environment is coalition building. Managers have recognized the importance of collaborating with other agencies in organized ways to influence the policy making process, and the need to spend considerable time forming coalitions with other groups on behalf of mental health services. With the increasing impact of regulations and legislation and extreme competition for funding from both the public and private sectors, organizing constituencies to shape these policies has become essential for survival. Private-for-profit organizations can devote considerable resources to these efforts. The public and not-for-profit sectors do not have such funds and must replace it with collaborative efforts. Coalitions with advocacy groups and complementary service organizations become particularly critical during the legislative budget process, so that a united front can be presented in creating a demand for adequate funding and favorable policies.

Increasingly, therefore, administrators need to look outside their organizations to be effective. Managing the external environment, and marshaling external resources to accomplish organizational goals has become one of their most important tasks.

This is also a function that is of great import to the policy analyst. By its very nature, policy analysis in mental health will concern itself with interorganizational systems of care. The policy making process itself must involve numerous stakeholders if it is to be effective, so the policy analyst must be extremely skilled in interacting with the external environment. Again, understanding the issues discussed from the perspective of how the policy will impact on individual agencies, as well as the system as a whole, is essential in creating good social policy.

Changing the Organization

If the environment of mental health organizations is constantly changing, then it makes sense that the individual organization itself must constantly change to keep pace with the changing environment. The advent of managed care, for instance, has required agencies to change the practices of its practitioners (Beinecke, Goodman, & Lockhart, 1997). New developments in psychopharmacology and the promising results of research with new psychosocial rehabilitation models make change essential. The emergence of new population groups with ever greater needs and for which current treatment interventions are ineffective, requires agencies to develop new interventions that are appropriate and effective for them. A major problem for administrators, however, is motivating workers to change the way they practice to conform to the latest and best practices. The recent Schizophrenia Patient Outcomes Research Treatment (PORT) project, for example, showed that for all but one of the project's recommendations, less than 50 percent of the clients interviewed ($N = 700$) were receiving the recommended treatment. Conformance with recommendations for psychosocial treatments was generally less than for psychopharmacological recommendations (Lehman, 1999; Lehman & Steinwachs, 1998).

Creating the culture of a learning organization is one step needed in the change process. As with evaluation, involving all groups who will be impacted by the change is critical. Of greatest importance, however, is to be sure that the expectations of desired changed behaviors be followed by changes in the way workers are evaluated and rewarded, and that any existing standard operating procedures that conflict with the new expectations are revised or eliminated. Potential organizational barriers to the new behaviors must be identified and minimized or eliminated. It is not uncommon for organizations to place new expectations on workers in addition to their existing duties, without adjusting the workload. A caveat to administrators, however, is that, in this case, to keep workloads at manageable levels, workers may sabotage the change or make their own decisions about what duties will no longer be performed, if the necessary incentives are not in place.

Some organizations have created special programs or structures to facilitate change. One agency received money to set up a new idea fund (Cohen, 1999). Staff submitted proposals for new ideas or programs that they wanted to implement. These ideas were then reviewed by a steering committee composed of representatives from all aspects of the organization. The ideas that were judged to be feasible and met other criteria such as replicability, and impact on quality of staff and clients' lives, were then funded and implemented (Cohen, 1999). In another instance, an agency undergoing major change established a staff-management council, which met on a monthly basis, consisting of elected representatives from each program area and level (e.g., clerical, professional, supervisory, middle management), the agency head, and top staff. Staff was to contact their elected representative with any questions or issues. The ground rules were that any issue or question could be raised, and that the person who raised the issue would not be identified. The group was then expected to problem solve the issue. If the group made no decision, such as when insufficient information was available, the CEO made the commitment to obtain the information, or make a decision within a set time frame. Over time, the established trust led to a climate that was far more receptive to organizational change (Paulson, 1977).

Other more traditional practices, such as providing funds for training and conferences and for subscriptions to key journals, are also important incentives in facilitating changes. It is critical, however, that new ideas are followed up with literature searches to explore the empirical evidence of the effectiveness of the proposed intervention, and what other alternatives exist. It is not that infrequent that a staff member will hear a charismatic person present an approach at a conference, and lobby to adopt the approach without any formal exploration of its effectiveness. To avoid dampening the enthusiasm of the worker, it is important to involve the worker in the analysis. Fortunately, the Internet has made such searches easier and affordable.

Another strategy for encouraging change is to involve the agency board of directors in program evaluation efforts. It is interesting that many not-for-profit boards will have a finance committee that examines every detail of the budget, but may not have an organized way of examining the effectiveness of the programs that the money is spent on. A program evaluation committee of the board can agree with program staff on key outcome indicators, and receive outcome reports on a regular basis. Choosing one or two areas a year for more systematic evaluation comprises a manageable workload, and assists both board and staff to think seriously about the way the services are being delivered, and to explore better ways to accomplish program goals.

The policy analyst sits in a similar position to an agency administrator. The former must figure out how to change the actions of multiple organizations in a coordinated way, while the latter must try and facilitate internal changes. Nevertheless, the trends and issues creating the need for such change, and the problems in securing it are similar for both.

EXEMPLAR PROGRAMS AND MODELS

Since deinstitutionalization, attempts to organize the community care of people with serious and persistent mental illness has been plagued by the difficulties in integrating an array of human service systems to meet multiple client needs, such as housing, vocational training, and income supports. The exemplary program briefly described here was designed to overcome interorganizational issues, such as categorical funding, service fragmentation, and discontinuity of care. They recognized that it was unreasonable to expect people who might have cognitive and functional difficulties to negotiate multiple service systems. Instead, the mental health system needed to take responsibility for assuring that all of the needed services were provided in an integrated manner.

The Program for Assertive Community Treatment (PACT) uses a multidisciplinary team to provide the majority of services needed by its clients. Consumers are assigned to the team as a whole (not to individual case managers). This promotes continuity of care (i.e., a case manager can be ill, on vacation, or leave, and the rest of the team has the relationship to competently serve the client) and provides services on a 24-hours-a-day, 7-days-a-week basis. The team serves consumers in their natural environment and does not expect them to report to an office to receive services. Supports are provided wherever the consumer requires them, such as on the job, in the home, and at the intensity needed at that moment. The team takes ultimate responsibility to assure that all service needs are met. If consumers must leave a community setting, for a more restrictive environment (e.g., hospital, jail), the team follows them, and begins immediately working with the facility staff to prepare for community reintegration. If clients need to be referred elsewhere for a specialized service, the team ensures that they are assisted in obtaining the needed service, and that needs are met. In this way, a self-contained unit (e.g., PACT) can provide integrated services to a core group of consumers.

UNIQUE CHALLENGES FOR SOCIAL WORKERS

Given the vulnerability of human service organizations to their environments, there are several trends affecting them that have a particularly important impact on mental health administrators and policy analysts, and may constrain and shape the way they seek to fulfill their organizations' missions (Hasenfeld, 1996; Menefee, 1997; Paulson, 1996).

The Growing Inequality Gap
There has been a growing gap between the most affluent and the poor, with a redistribution of wealth to the most affluent group. Globalization, technology, and downsizing have resulted in a decline in income for many groups who previously had well-paying industrial jobs, who are now working in lower paying, service sector jobs (Hasenfeld, 1996). This has been accompanied by a general decline in the provision of social welfare and safety net services, which has led to an increase in inequality in the United States. Unlike most western industrialized countries, there is less political pressure to provide adequate public services in the United States, because we do not have universal social services. This has negatively impacted on the poor and disabled populations who depend on social workers and the public sector for needed support.

The income gap has meant that two systems of mental health care have developed; the public sector for the poor, and the private sector for the middle class and wealthy. This has been exacerbated by the lack of parity between health and mental health care. This reality has had a particularly hard impact on people with serious and persistent mental illness who, because of their disability, are dependant on public income support, and therefore are almost always very poor.

The Merging of Public and Private Sector Care
One of the most important trends is a rapid collapsing of the boundaries between public, not-for-profit, and for-profit care. For years, social work, more than any other profession, has worked in either the public or private not-for-profit sectors

with publically funded clients. These vulnerable populations are frequently stigmatized and seen as less deserving and less desirable to work with. Now, however, many private businesses are finding that under the right fiscal circumstances, there is profit to be made with these populations. Hence, social work agencies that previously had a monopoly in a publicly funded service area, are now facing increasing competition from all sectors (Boehm, 1996). Entire new industries have grown up around these new markets (e.g., for-profit correctional facilities), and few, if any, social service areas are exempt from these competitive pressures. A corollary has been the rapid move to purchase of service contracting for social services to these private sectors. Agencies that previously relied on grant mechanisms must now learn to manage contracting arrangements involving a whole set of new skills, such as price setting, demand limits, sophisticated budgeting and accounting standards, performance standards, reporting requirements, service utilization tracking, and quality assurance. The future portends that privatization will occur on a widespread basis and that few distinctions will remain between the public and private sectors. The contracting of the public Medicaid mental health sector to private-for-profit managed care companies or to national provider networks (e.g., Byodine) are two examples of this trend in mental health.

The Dominance of Managed Care in Both the Public and Private Sectors

The initial rapid growth in managed care was restricted to private insurers. This is no longer the case. Public payers are swiftly adopting managed care strategies as a method of holding down costs, and are increasingly willing to contract with for-profit managed care companies to manage public Medicaid programs (U.S. Department of Health and Human Services, 1999). As of now, close to 80 percent of private or publicly insured people are covered by managed behavioral health plans (Findlay, 1999).

There is a tendency to see managed care as either good or bad (Paulson,1996), when, in fact, there are so many different variations as to make generalizations useless. Medicaid-managed care has varied state by state, and in many states, it even varies on the county or local level. There are, however, several major issues of great import to the delivery of mental health services. Much of the promised savings of managed care has already been obtained through reductions in hospitalization and other high cost services. Yet, pressure to reduce costs further still exists, as does the danger that this will be accomplished through denying appropriate services. The traditional cost-cutting strategies, which include authorization procedures, utilization review, and quality control mechanisms, were developed for an employed insurance population and do not necessarily fit people with major mental illness. In many instances, capitation or case rates have been developed without setting a separate rate for people with severe and chronic mental illnesses. Even more importantly, the array of complementary social services that is essential for maintaining both adults and children in the community, in addition to the core mental health services, do not meet strict definitions of medical necessity and may not be included in either the benefit package or capitation rates (Mechanic & McAlpine, 1999). This places such services in jeopardy and threatens successful community integration.

Merger, Acquisition and Alliance "Fever," and Blending Insurers: Managed Care Entities and Providers

The capital and information demands of managed care and the growing need for large provider networks has led to an explosion of mergers, acquisitions and alliances as organizations seek vertical and horizontal integration to better position themselves in a highly competitive market. Consequently, traditional organizational configurations no longer exist. For example, insurance companies are developing or acquiring managed care companies, and HMOs and for-profit hospitals are buying not-for-profit hospitals. The result is a blending of these traditionally separate roles and functions.

Continued Development of Integrated Provider Networks and Mixed Large Volume Purchasers

Solo private practice is expected to be considerably diminished, if not extinct, within a very short period of time. The wave of the future is large, integrated networks that provide a full array of services and continuum of care. Similarly on the purchasing side, there is an increasing recognition of the need for mechanisms that join individuals and small employers in the purchase of insurance, and it is likely that large purchasing cooperatives will either be formed voluntarily or mandated by legislation. This will result in purchasers obtaining increasing leverage over insurers and providers.

Increased Governmental and Nongovernmental Regulation of Practice

One of the new utilization management technologies of managed care is the regulation of practice patterns through staff privileging, staff profiling, and treatment protocols. These have added new constraints to social work practice and a greater degree of accountability. Privileging is the process by which a practitioner's training and experience is evaluated to determine which treatment interventions will be allowed with which specific target populations. In the past, for example, a clinician could be shifted from serving an older adult population to a children's population to meet staffing needs, based solely on the credential of a MSW degree, rather than specialized training. Similarly, a practitioner could utilize a new treatment modality in the absence of adequate training. Staff profiling is the creation of profiles for each clinician using process and outcome information, and comparing the practitioners' performance to others either in the same organization, network, or with a national database, and feeding back this information to the practitioner. Treatment protocols are packages of interventions considered to be best practices for a particular diagnosis based on research evidence.

At this juncture, however, treatment protocols have been developed for most of the discrete mental health diagnoses that detail the recommended treatment intervention and expected length of treatment. Managed care organizations regularly develop staff profiles that illustrate an individual clinician's productivity, use of treatment modalities, average length of treatment time, and adherence to treatment protocols, in comparison to colleagues within the organization and/or region as a whole. Recently, the government has been paying attention to such protocols and audits in agencies billing for Medicaid or Medicare payments, and are now beginning to disallow payment for services provided that are not in accord with accepted treatment protocols. These practices represent radical departures from previous social work practice, and, unless carefully and skillfully implemented, could inappropriately impinge on practitioner autonomy and professional judgement. Practice regulations such as these are becoming standard throughout the industry, whether or not social work practitioners and administrators willingly accept them.

Greater Risk Sharing Among All Parties
Another clear pattern that is developing is the growth of risk sharing (Mechanic & McAlpine, 1999). Many managed care contracts are capitated, that is, a set fee is paid per member per month to agencies for providing services within the defined benefit level. This financial risk may be passed on to individual or organizational providers through the use of subcapitation, and to individuals by co-payment schemes.

Pressure to Integrate Behavioral and Physical Healthcare and Increased Access to Primary Care
The integration of physical and mental healthcare is the ultimate goal of most policy makers. Short-run concerns that mental health will receive short shrift in the larger healthcare system have led to mental health carve outs. This separation, however, is likely to be only an interim step. At the same time, the public support for the goal of universal healthcare means that demands for increased access to primary healthcare will grow. Furthermore, in many instances, much of the mental health care is provided in the primary care setting. Considering these trends, mental health practitioners and organizations must form much closer relationships with primary healthcare providers who will increasingly become the major referral sources and access points for mental healthcare.

Price, Outcomes, Service, and Quality as Key Buying Factors for Purchasers of Healthcare
As mental health providers move into a competitive marketplace, they will need to compete and perform in areas that are new to public and private not-for-profit providers. One of the greatest challenges will be for organizations and their staffs to be held accountable for outcomes rather than process measures, such as the number of hours of service. Competing in the arena of price, outcomes, service, and quality will demand that practice patterns and information systems be radically altered in the future.

Continued Advances in Neuroscience, Psychopharmacology, Genetics, and Biotechnology
Current progress in the understanding of the brain, the etiology of serious and persistent mental illnesses, the biological components of these illnesses, including genetic markers and genetic predispositions, can only accelerate. Ongoing breakthroughs in discovering new classes of drugs, such as Respirdal, can be expected

with increased knowledge of brain chemistry (Norquist & Hyman, 1999; U.S. Department of Health and Human Services, 1999). While it is highly unlikely that a magical treatment will be discovered that will cure or completely control all symptoms of mental illness, advances in drug therapies should make an increasing number of people amenable to psychosocial rehabilitative interventions. There will remain a strong need for rehabilitative interventions in conjunction with medications. This is particularly true of certain subgroups (e.g., young adults) with frequent co-morbidity between primary psychiatric diagnoses and substance abuse and/or personality disorders, unless medical advances take place that better control these problems.

In a number of situations, it is also likely that genetic markers will be discovered that will identify people who are predisposed to these illnesses so that careful monitoring and preventive measures can be established. Further, it is possible that genetic defects that affect brain chemistry may be identified and therapeutic techniques developed that will lead to less intrusive and more effective management of these illnesses. Medical advances have already raised a host of ethical issues. One example is the recently initiated clinical trial in which people deemed at risk for schizophrenia were treated with psychotropic drugs to determine if the onset of the illness would be prevented. At the same time, opponents believe that considerable dangers from the side effects of the drugs themselves were not adequately considered.

Necessity for the Development of Community-based Innovations

The shift to capitated forms of financing and outcome measurement will produce a constant impetus for ongoing innovations in community-based services. There will be a shift in emphasis from facility based, "medically necessary" services to wraparound, flexible, support services that can be adjusted to the immediate needs of the consumer at a particular point in time.

Increasing Roles for Consumers and Family Members (Secondary Consumers)

The growth of the family movement (National Alliance for the Mentally Ill and the Federation of Families for Children with Serious Emotional Disorders) and the consumer movement is profoundly impacting the mental health system (U.S. Department of Health and Human Services, 1999). As a matter of federal law (and, in many instances, state law), the participation of consumers in policy making has been mandated, and their participation in treatment planning encouraged and protected. The involvement of consumers as providers in their own right, as participants in their own treatment, and as watchdogs and advocates, will continue to expand.

Expansion of Need and Demand Populations

Current demographic and epidemiological trends all point to the rapid growth in high demand populations that will stress current and future resources beyond their limits. The growth in the elderly population, HIV-infected people, people with chemical dependency, and cultural and ethnic minority groups are a few of the obvious examples. The needs of the populations to be cared for will be more difficult to meet and will require innovations in services that are responsive to special needs. This resource demand will further focus concerns on efficiency and cost containment.

Given these trends, it is certain that social workers in the mental health field will be working exclusively in integrated consumer-sensitive networks of health care, as providers in some form of a managed care system.

Technological Advances in Computers, Communications, and Management Information Systems

Managed care, especially in capitated systems, requires extremely sophisticated online computer information systems. The emphasis on outcomes, service, consumer responsiveness, and quality, which are critical in a competitive environment, require a rapid response to consumer needs, especially in crisis situations that necessitate quick transfers of information. Social workers will be utilizing computers, fax machines, cellular telephones, palm pilots, and the next generation of communications innovations among the tools of their normal work. New concerns will arise regarding the balance between the needs for quick information sharing and the protection of confidentiality.

It is also likely that computers and interactive video will be routinely used for testing and evaluation purposes, conducting intakes and assessments and providing psychoeducation and counseling services. Video conferencing will be utilized to reach rural areas or to connect satellite offices of an urban agency to reduce travel costs and better utilize scarce, highly trained, expensive personnel. These technologies also hold great promise for a more flexible use of group interventions, including self-help groups. Where transportation is an issue, or people cannot or will not leave their own homes, wider video conferencing innovations are likely to play an active role.

CASE DILEMMA

A mental health agency director has operated successfully for years in a fee-for-service environment with a relatively steady funding flow through the county. Most of the agency's services are directed at people with serious mental illness or children with serious emotional disturbances, also utilizing a small outpatient program that serves the general community. The agency is located in the inner city and is the largest serving the minority population, although 50 percent of its caseload is Caucasian.

Suddenly, however, the environment has changed rapidly. The state has phased in the mental health portion of the state Medicaid plan. Mental health dollars are now being contracted through two managed care organizations. One is county operated, and the other is a large national for-profit company. Both entities insist on contracting with a network rather than an individual provider organization, based on a discounted fee-for-service structure. The addition of the two administrative layers (managed care organization and network) and the discounted payments has resulted in a reduction of income of between 25–35 percent. Secondly, any person who qualifies for Medicaid is entitled to mental health services, therefore greatly expanding the prior mandate of serving children and adults who had major mental illness, but with significantly reduced resources.

What strategies should you follow as the administrator to adapt to this new environment? Discuss the pros and cons of each of the alternate strategies. As administrator, would your organization benefit more by (1) seeking alternative funding sources, by developing programs that have more systems resources (e.g., corrections, substance abuse); (2) laying off workers to adjust to the new revenue constraints; (3) initiating an across-the-board salary cut and reducing operations expenses through aggressive cost-saving measures; (4) reorganizing the agency to become more efficient; or (5) pursuing a merger or strategic alliance with another agency (hopefully with more resources) to strengthen your position and achieve economies of scale?

SUMMARY

As we have seen, the task of the mental health administrator has become increasingly complex and sophisticated. Agencies that were operated as mom and pop operations in the past, now face a competitive market and greater demands for outcomes and accountability. While the tasks of the administrator have remained stable, the nature of the tasks has changed in response to an ever-more turbulent external environment. The days of the clinician–administrator are essentially numbered, and the direct practice component replaced with the activities of boundary spanning and anticipating the future. Increasingly, administrators are faced with the dilemma of using scarce resources to address both the internal and external needs of the organization. Most of all, mental health administrators face the challenge of managing uncertainty and constant change.

KEY TERMS

Administration: Setting an organization's overall direction and structuring the activities and processes to accomplish its goals.

Cultural Competence: Having the knowledge, skills, and understanding necessary to plan and deliver services to a particular group that respects and is relevant to their culture.

Evaluation: The process for measuring the progress of the organization or program in achieving its goals and to assess whether its services are both effective and efficient.

Financial Management: The function of developing and managing sufficient financial resources for the organization to achieve its goals including the maintenance of adequate accounting and management information systems to track expenditures and provide management, with information to evaluate the cost-effectiveness of programs, calculate the costs of delivering services, and project future revenue.

Incentive Systems: An incentive system is defined as the rewards and punishments dispensed, the mechanisms by which they are distributed, and the assessment criteria used to evaluate performance to determine what the appropriate consequences of the performance should be.

Management Information Systems (MIS): An electronic system to collect, organize, and report information essential to the operation of an agency.

Planning: Planning is the process of setting organization goals and developing the steps needed to align the agency's resources, structure, and processes to accomplish those goals.

Program Development: A more specialized type of planning in response to a request from funders or an identified need. A plan is developed for implementing a new program and includes such tasks as developing resources, specifying activities, designing staffing patterns, and identifying and securing the physical location for the program.

Service Integration: Structuring a variety of services from multiple agencies or programs in a way that produces coordination, continuity of care, and reduces the effort needed by the consumer to receive these services.

Staffing: The process for obtaining a sufficient number of people with the knowledge, values, skills, and credentials necessary for goal attainment. The tasks associated with staffing are recruitment, salary and benefit administration, staff development, affirmative action, and maintaining appeal, grievance, and disciplinary processes.

Task Environment: Those organizational entities in an agency's environment relevant for its goal attainment.

WEB RESOURCES

Academy of Management Online (http://www.aom.pace.edu/). This organizational Web site lists activities, publications, and major links.

American Society for Public Administration (http://www.aspanet.org/). This Web site of the national organization for public administration includes activities, conferences, publications, and relevant links.

Association for Community Organization and Social Administration (ACOSA) (http://www.acosa.org). The ACOSA Web page provides organizational information, national activities, major organizational links, and journal abstracts.

Internet Resources-Mental Health Administration (http://www.hsls.pitt.edu/intres/mental/admin.html). This site offers a host of links to major sites related to mental health administration.

Internet Nonprofit Center (http://nonprofits.org/). The Internet Nonprofit Center offer online information for and about nonprofit agencies.

National Council for Community Behavioral Health Care (http://www.nccbh.org/). This is the Web site of the national organization for community mental health centers and other community behavioral healthcare agencies.

National Academy of Public Administration (http://www.napawash.org/napa/index.html). This site offers information from the nonpartisan organization chartered by Congress to assist federal, state, and local government agencies.

National Network for Social Work Managers (http://www.socialworkmanager.org/). This is an organizational Web site with listings of activities and links to other relevant sites.

Peter F. Drucker Foundation on Nonprofit Management (http://www.pfdf.org/). This site provides articles and tools for nonprofit managers.

San Francisco State University's Public Administration Online (http://bss.sfsu.edu/~mpa/paonline/paonline.htm). This Web page offers links to major sites in all major content areas of public administration.

REFERENCES

Au, C. (1996). Rethinking organizational effectiveness: Theoretical and methodological issues in the study of organizational effectiveness for social welfare organizations. *Administration in Social Work, 20*(4), 1–21.

Beinecke, R., Goodman, M., & Lockhart, A. (1997). The impact of managed care on Massachusetts mental health and substance abuse providers. *Administration in Social Work, 2*(2), 41–53.

Boehm, A. (1996). Forces driving competition in human service organizations and positional competitive responses. *Administration in Social Work, 20*(4), 61–78.

Bond, G., & Dincin, J. (1986). Accelerating entry into transitional employment in a psychosocial rehabilitation agency. *Rehabilitation Psychology, 31*, 143–155.

Bond, G., Witheridge,T., Wasmer, D., Dincin, J., McRae, S., Mayes, J., & Ward, R. (1989). A comparison of two crisis housing alternatives to psychiatric rehabilitation. *Hospital and Community Psychiatry, 40*(2), 177–183.

Brager, G., & Holloway, S. (1978). *Changing human service organizations: Politics and practice.* New York: Free Press

Brethower, D. (1972). *Behavioral analysis in business and industry: A total performance system.* Kalamazoo, MI: Behavioradelia.

Cohen, B. J. (1999). Fostering innovation in a large human services bureaucracy. *Administration in Social Work, 23*(2), 47–59.

Crow, R. T. (1995). Planning and management professions. *Encyclopedia of social work.* Washington, DC:NASW Press.

Cyert, R., & March J. (1963). *A behavioral theory of the firm.* Englewood Cliffs, NJ: Prentice-Hall.

Drucker, P. (1974). *Management.* New York: Harper & Row.

Einbinder, S. (1995). Policy analysis. *Encyclopedia of social work.* Washington, DC: NASW Press.

Findlay, S. (1999). Managed behavioral health care in 1999. *Health Affairs Quarterly, 18*(5) 116–124.

Gummer, B. (1994). Getting in, and staying in, "the loop": Networking and organizational power. *Administration in Social Work, 18*(1), 107–124.

Gummer, B. (1998). Social relations in an organizational context: Social capital, real work and structural holes. *Administration in Social Work, 22*(3), 87–105.

Hasenfeld, Y. (1983). *Human service organizations.* Englewood Cliffs, NJ: Prentice-Hall.

Hasenfeld, Y. (1996). The administration of human service: What lies ahead. In P. Raffoul & C. McNeece (Eds.). *Future issues for social work practice* (pp. 191–202). Boston: Allyn & Bacon.

Hjern, B., & Porter, D. O. (1981.) Implementation structures: A new unit of administrative analysis. *Organization Studies, 2,* 211–227.

Kahn, A. (1969). *Theory and practice of social planning.* New York: Russell Sage Foundation.

Kunkel, J. (1970). *Society and economic growth.* New York: Oxford University Press.

Landau, M. (1969). Redundancy, rationality, duplication, and overlap. *Public Administration Review, 29* (4), 346–358.

Landau, M. (1973). On the concept of self-correcting organizations. *Public Administration Review, 33*(6), 533–542.

Lehman, A. (1999). Quality of care in mental health: The case of schizophrenia. *Health Affairs, 18*(5), 52–65.

Lehman, A., & Steinwachs, D. (1998). Translating research into practice: The patient outcomes research team (PORT) treatment recommendations. *Schizophrenia Bulletin, 24*(1), 1–10.

Lehman, A., Postrado, L., Roth, D., McNary, S., & Goldman H. (1994). An evaluation of continuity of care, case management and client outcomes in the Robert Wood Johnson program on chronic mental illness. *Milbank Quarterly, 72,* 105–122.

Lindblom, C. (1959). The science of "muddling through." *Public Administration Review,* Spring. 59–74.

Luthans, F., & Kreitner, R. (1974). *Organizational behavior modification.* Glenview, IL: Scott, Foresman.

Mager, R., & Pipe, P. (1970). *Analyzing performance problems or "You really oughta wanna."* Belmont, CA: Fearon.

March, J .G., & Simon, H. (1958). *Organizations.* New York: Wiley.

McGrath, M., & Paulson, R. (1996). *Scenario planning.* Washington Community Mental Health Council Workshop, Seattle, Washington.

Mechanic, D., & McAlpine, D. (1999). Mission unfulfilled: Potholes on the road to mental health parity. *Health Affairs, 18*(5), 7–21.

Menefee, D. (1997). Strategic administration of nonprofit human service organizations: A model for executive success in turbulent times. *Administration in Social Work, 21*(2) 1–19.

Menefee, D. (1998). Identifying and comparing competencies for social work management II. *Administration in Social Work, 22*(2), 53–61.

Menefee, D., & Thompson, J. (1994). Identifying and comparing competencies for social work managers: A practice driven approach. *Administration in Social Work, 18*(3),1–25.

Newman, F. L., & Sorensen, J. E. (1985). *Integrated clinical and fiscal management in mental health.* Norwood, NJ: Ablex.

Norquist, G., & Hyman, S. (1999). Advances in understanding and treating mental illness: Implications for policy. *Health Affairs, 18*(5), 32–47.

Patti, R. (1977). Patterns of management activity in social welfare agencies. *Administration in Social Work, 1*(1), 5–18.

Patti, R. (1983). *Social welfare administration.* Englewood Cliffs, NJ: Prentice-Hall.

Patton, M. (1997). *Utilization focused evaluation* (3rd ed.). Beverly Hills, CA: Sage.

Paulson, R. (1977). *A behavioral view of goal displacement in a social welfare agency.* Unpublished doctoral dissertation, University of California at Berkeley.

Paulson, R. (1993). Interagency collaboration among rehabilitation, mental health and other systems. In R. W. Flexer & P. Solomon (Eds.), *Psychiatric rehabilitation in practice* (pp. 193–210). Andover, MA: Andover Medical.

Paulson, R. (1996). Swimming with the sharks or walking in the Garden of Eden: Two visions of managed care and mental health practice. In P. Raffoul & C. McNeece (Eds.), *Future issues for social work practice* (pp. 85–96). Boston: Allyn & Bacon.

Paulson, R. I., Herinckx, H., Demmler, J., Clarke, G., Cutler, D., Birecree, E. (1999). Comparing practice patterns of consumer and non-consumer mental health service providers. *Community Mental Health Journal, 35*(3), 251–269.

Perrow, C. (1979). *Complex organizations: A critical essay,* (2nd ed.). Glennview, IL: Scott, Foresman.

Pressman, J., & Wildavsky, A. (1973). *Implementation.* Berkeley, CA: University of California Press.

Provan, K., & Milward, H. B. (1995). A preliminary theory of interorganizational effectiveness: A comparative study of four community mental health systems. *Administrative Science Quarterly, 40*(1), 1–33.

Rapp, C. A., & Poertner, J. (1992). *Social administration: A client-centered approach.* New York: Longman.

Reid, W. (1964). Interagency co-ordination in delinquency prevention and control. *Social Service Review, 38*(4), 418–428.

Rose, S., & Black, B. L. (1985). *Advocacy and empowerment: Mental health care in the community.* Boston: Routledge & Kegan Paul.

Rosenblatt, A., Wyman, N., Kingdon, D., & Ichinose, C. (1998). Managing what you measure: Creating outcome-driven systems of care for youth with serious emotional disturbances. *Journal of Behavioral Health Services Research, 25*(2), 177–193.

Rosenheck, R., & Cicchetti, D. (1998). A mental health program report card: A multidimensional approach to performance monitoring in public sector programs. *Community Mental Health Journal, 34*(1), 85–106.

Schwartz, P. (1991). *The art of the long view.* New York: Doubleday Currency.

Schwartz, P. (1992). Composing a plot for your scenario. *Planning Forum, 20*(3), 4–9.

Simpson, D. G. (1992). Key lessons for adopting scenario planning in diversified companies. *Planning Forum, 20*(3),10–17.

Solomon, P., Gordon, B., & Davis, J. (1984). *Community services to discharged mental patients.* Springfield, IL: Charles C. Thomas, 1984.

Thompson, J. D. (1967). *Organizations in action.* New York: McGraw-Hill.

U. S. Department of Health and Human Services. (1999). *Mental health: A report of the surgeon general.* Rockville, MD: National Institute of Mental Health.

Weick, K. (1969). *The sociology psychology of organizing.* Reading, MA: Addison-Wesley.

EMERGING KNOWLEDGE AND FUTURE TRENDS IN MENTAL HEALTH: IMPLICATIONS FOR SOCIAL WORK

Harriette C. Johnson

What lies ahead? The 21st century has arrived at a time of unprecedented change in the mental health field. The book's author and editor, Kia J. Bentley, intended for this concluding chapter to summarize emerging knowledge and future trends in mental health, and to consider the implications of this knowledge and these trends for social work. Her first goal has already been met by a mammoth work on the state of the art in mental health, published by the U.S. Department of Health and Human Services, under the imprimatur of the Surgeon General of the United States (1999). *Mental Health: A Report of the Surgeon General* (referred to hereafter as the *Report*) has been widely disseminated and has received accolades from readers around the country, including a front-page article in *NASW News* (O'Neill, 2000). This extraordinary document compiled information from 3,000 references and was a collaborative undertaking of about 200 contributors nationwide in leadership roles in the mental health field.

To address the editor's second goal, implications of emerging knowledge and trends for social work, major themes and findings in the *Report*, will be summarized briefly here. However, I urge everyone with an interest in mental health, whether professional, personal, or scholarly, to read as much of the document as possible. There is surely no better way to become conversant with state-of-the-art knowledge.

Several trends in mental health, begun in the 1980s and 1990s, have converged to usher in the new millennium. These trends are the subject of this chapter. We will emphasize practice issues, in accordance with the practice focus of the book. However, readers should not interpret this focus as any indication that macroforces are less important. In fact, the directions of mental health practice are almost entirely dependent on national and international economics and politics. More will be said about these connections in the conclusion of the chapter.

Among the most noteworthy trends at the beginning of the 21st century are advances in neuroscience; epidemiological and interventions outcome research; efforts to develop cultural competence in service delivery; erosion of societal support for people with mental disabilities, offset to some degree by beginning successes in efforts to achieve parity; new definitions of recovery and heightened awareness of prevention; special developmental issues in children and adolescents; special developmental issues regarding the elderly and aging; issues pertaining to diagnostic conventions; attention to co-occurring disorders, also referred to as dual diagnosis; onslaught of the managed care juggernaut in the organization and funding of mental health services; and the ascendance of consumer and family organizations as political forces.

ADVANCES IN NEUROSCIENCE RESEARCH

Advances in neuroscience research have unearthed critical knowledge about relationships between psychological phenomena, brain functions, and structures, opening windows to the brain for the first time in human history. Neuroscience has revolutionized our understanding of human behavior in the social environment, mental health and mental illness, and addiction during the past two decades. The principle that formerly ran counter to prevailing wisdom has now become axiomatic, that is, that mental illnesses are biological illnesses in the brain, not disembodied psychological characteristics or dynamics. Neuroscience's central premises are (1) all psychological functions are manifestations of molecular processes, mediated by cells and larger structures in the brain and nervous system; (2) mental illnesses are disorders of an organ, the brain, similar to diseases in other body organs such as the lungs or the kidney; and (3) inputs from the environment continually influence these molecular processes, and behavioral outputs of the organism continually influence the environment. All psychological phenomena (emotions, behavior, thought, addiction) reflect biological processes. The mind–body separation is an intellectual construct not borne by scientific evidence (*Report*, pp. 32–62). As it processes human experience, the brain continually undergoes changes in its cellular functions. Its cellular structures may also change.

Just as stresses of environmental origin can precipitate or exacerbate episodes of other illnesses (e.g., diabetic coma, heart attack), they can influence the onset or severity of mental disorders. Parenting styles and practices, short of egregious abuse or neglect, do not cause illnesses in the brain any more than they cause diabetes or heart disease. In addition to triggering the onset of mental distress, the environment is critical in influencing outcomes, how severe the condition will be, how quickly it will remit, and how long the person will remain in a state of remission.

Mental disorders are defined by signs, symptoms, and functional impairment, using criteria as reliable as those for general medical conditions (*Report*, pp. 43–44). The precise causes of most mental disorders are not known, but the broad forces that shape them *are* known. Mental health and mental disease are products of interactions between biological, psychological, and sociocultural factors. Inborn (constitutional) vulnerabilities and resiliencies interact with environmental inputs (including biological, environmental inputs such as viruses, head injury, maternal illness during gestation), to create psychological phenomena at any moment in time (*Report* p. 49).

Theories of normal development form the basis for popular approaches to understanding and treating mental disorders, but these theories have not succeeded in explaining how children grow into mentally healthy adults (*Report*, pp. 124–5). The two approaches that have replaced theories as a basis for understanding the origins of mental disorders, as well as normal mental functioning, are *empirical advances in neuroscience* and *behavioral research* (*Report* p. 129).

Major obstacles still exist in accepting and incorporating this knowledge. Although many social workers have embraced and applaud the emerging findings, others have shown reluctance to accept the new knowledge. For many years, some social workers had resisted applying the so-called medical model to psychological problems (Miller, 1980; Pilsecker, 1983; Weick, 1983).

This antipathy to the medical metaphor arose as a reaction to the widespread acceptance of the diagnostic approach of ego psychology and other psychoanalytic derivatives, in an era in which all mental illness was believed to arise from pathogenic forces in the individual's early environment—forces equated with deficient or toxic parenting, usually by the mother (Caplan & Hall-McCorquodale, 1985). Practitioners using this theoretical frame cast themselves in the role of head doctors who diagnosed and treated psychological disorders assumed to be nonbiological in nature. Thus, the medical model was truly a metaphor, because it was applied to problems assumed to be unambiguously nonmedical.

The gender bias of psychoanalytic approaches associated with the medical metaphor, pertaining to the presumed roles of mothers in making their children mentally ill, offended many. In addition, growing awareness of the multifactorial determinants of psychological problems during the 1960s and 1970s, including macroforces such as poverty, racism, and unemployment, led many to equate a medical model with victim blaming. Some writers argued that dark skin color was associated with inferior intelligence (Albee, 1982; Hirsch, 1997; Jensen, 1976; Rushton, 1992, 1996; Simon, 1997). Not only the medical metaphor applied to nonbiological phenomena, but also biology itself, acquired a bad name. Feminists and human rights activists called for the repudiation by the social work profession of the medical model and the notion that inborn biological factors could cause or contribute to mental problems (Johnson et al., 1990).

Several questions are still at issue. What is the role of the medical model in contemporary mental health practice? (See also Chapter 9.) Are mental disorders really diseases? Are conditions that meet criteria for *DSM-IV* diagnoses really even disorders (Wakefield, 1999)? Judgments about intensity and duration of signs and symptoms necessary to qualify for diagnoses such as major depression and attention deficit and hyperactivity disorder are arbitrary, not scientific. Thresholds for mental illnesses or disorders have been set by professional convention. Yet the same is true for other areas of medicine (*Report*, p. 39). For example, 10 years ago, a serum cholesterol of 200 was considered normal, whereas today the same number alarms medical practitioners.

Implications for Social Work

Social workers whose thinking was molded in the era of the 1960s and 1970s, and the younger practitioners whom they have mentored, may carry with them distrust of or even antipathy to the messages of neuroscience for social work practice. Thus the historical antecedents that deter receptiveness to state-of-the-art knowledge must be made explicit, so that we can identify the real ethical and intellectual dilemmas faced today. Other forces that contribute to antipathy to a biological understanding of psychological functioning are suggested by Saleebey (1985), such as suspicion that the biological knowledge base conceals a conservative political agenda, a long history of preference for focus on interpersonal relationships, prevalence of theoretical models conceived before knowledge about biological foundations of behavior, perceived lack of expertise, and turf issues.

On the organizational level, dynamics within institutions may militate against curriculum change. Examples include the need to deploy people on the full-time faculty rather than adjuncts who may have the specialized knowledge required, competing claims for space in the curriculum, or the belief that biological content is not congruent with the program's articulated mission or unarticulated ideology. At the macrolevel, at least two conditions impede the adoption of biological content: lack of specific requirements for inclusion of biological content by the Council on Social Work Education (CSWE) and lack of continuing education requirements for biological content for licensure on either national or state levels (Johnson et al., 1990).

Despite the thorny scientific and philosophical issues inherent in a disease model for constellations of psychological characteristics, knowledge about mechanisms by which these conditions occur is usually important in developing effective interventions. Learning about these mechanisms requires knowledge about the fundamentals of neuroscience. New knowledge generated by neuroscience has supported discoveries of many psychotropic medications that offer greater effectiveness and safety, combined with more benign side effect profiles, than their predecessors.

Unfortunately, offensiveness of the medical model to many practitioners has often resulted in dismissal of science and repudiation of interventions that have been demonstrated to offer the most effective help for a given condition (Breggin & Breggin, 1994; Eberle, 1996). Issues surrounding the medical model are related to the theoretical frameworks social workers and other professionals draw on in their choice of interventions (Johnson et al., 2000).

A long-standing assumption of the Council on Social Work Education's (CSWE) Curriculum Policy statements, with which we concur, has been that social work practice theory is importantly related to knowledge about human behavior in the social environment and human development through the lifespan (CSWE, 1999). Even if not a direct outgrowth of this knowledge, practice theory should at least be consistent with such knowledge.

Yet the surgeon general's *Report* asserts that all existing *theories* of human behavior and human psychological development have failed to explain how children grow into mentally healthy adults (or, by implication, mentally disordered adults) (*Report*, pp. 124–5). The findings of the meta-analysis of existing prospective longitudinal research on human development by Kagan and Zentner (1996) support this conclusion. These findings imply that existing human behavior theories cannot effectively guide assessment and intervention planning.

The *Report* states that theory should be replaced with a combination of neuroscience and behavioral research (p. 129). The behavioral research to which it refers is not limited to individuals or even families. It also comprises macrosystem factors (economic, political) and mesosystems (organizations, social groups) (Bronfenbrenner, 1979), variables often studied by disciplines such as epidemiology, sociology, economics, political science, and social psychology. The work of Henggeler and colleagues (1998) and Elder (1974) provide examples of mental health-related research that address some of these variables. The *Report* adds that perhaps a new theory can be developed that will in fact be consistent with research. What does the history of social work practice theory tell us about the *Report*'s challenge?

In the late 1960s and early 1970s, social work became excited about general systems theory as a conceptual framework for understanding human behavior that could weave together macrodimensions (so emphasized in the 1960s), with microdimensions of psychological functioning. However, general systems theory fell into disrepute because, although it offered a comprehensive biopsychosocial perspective, it was criticized for lacking specific tools for translating that perspective into real work with real people.

The ecological or life model (Germain & Gitterman, 1980) attempted to address this criticism by emphasizing a person's life situations (ecology) and developmental challenges (transitions). The life model was successful at humanizing general systems theory, as well as correcting for one of ego psychology's deficiencies, by depathologizing the assessment of emotional and interpersonal distress. However, it was criticized for perceived naive optimism, failure to address or incorporate conflict, and lack of the macroforce analysis necessary to understand the person-in-environment transactions that it emphasized (Gould, 1987; Johnson, 1980). In other words, a person-in-environment transaction itself must be seen as an entity embedded in much larger environments, and those larger environments themselves must be assessed and targeted for intervention when possible.

EPIDEMIOLOGICAL RESEARCH
AND INTERVENTION OUTCOMES RESEARCH

These two research practices have supplied knowledge that is also critical to competent social work practice. Epidemiological research, organized around the model of risk factor/protective factor assessment, has obtained information about associations between populations, environments, and mental conditions. Interventions outcomes research has supplied answers to some questions pertaining to effectiveness of specific interventions in enhancing psychological well-being. For what populations, with what specific problems, under what environmental conditions, has intervention X, or a combination of interventions X+Y+Z, been shown to be effective?

Epidemiologic Surveys

Epidemiologic surveys indicate that in any given year, one in five Americans experiences symptoms that meet the *DSM-IV* diagnostic criteria for a mental disorder. In addition, many people that *do* receive mental health services do not meet *DSM* criteria for a diagnosis, but suffer from a psychological or emotional problem (as distinguished from an illness) that causes them pain and/or functional disablement. The numbers of people with these kinds of problems, but without mental disorders, cannot be reliably estimated, but it is certainly a very large population (*Report*, pp. 4–5), and probably includes almost everyone at points in their lives marked by extreme stress.

The conceptual model developed in the field of epidemiology—based on the understanding that all mental difficulties arise from ongoing interactions through time of biological and environmental risk and protective factors—has advanced the biopsychosocial or person-in-environment approach so long advocated by social work. The epidemiological model plugs in empirical data to identify risk and protective factors, specifies a range of possible biological and environmental risk and protective factors, and captures the notion of change through time. This is done by emphasizing that the configuration of risk and protective factors is continuously subject to alteration by the introduction, removal, or modification of a risk or protective factor. The point at which the delicate balance between risk and protective factors is upset by adding or strengthening a risk factor, or losing or weakening a protective factor, is the point at which the person's manifestations of stress are recognized as indicators of a mental illness, disorder, or problem. This event has been recorded for many decades in case records as the precipitating factor for the onset of a mental condition.

Implications for Social Work

The roles of the social worker, expressed in epidemiological terms, are to help diminish risk factors or lessen their effects, while developing protective factors or enhancing their effects. The various ways that social workers do this are the subjects of the chapters in this book. Is it possible that the epidemiological model, as simple as it appears, could be the core of the elusive theory that the authors of the *Report* have yet to identify? It is science-based; no other theory except behavioral can claim a substantial empirical base. It takes cognizance of developmental factors, because new demands, maturing capabilities, new roles with their related new responsibilities, or other challenges over the life span, may be either risk factors or protective factors, and may be activated at any point in the lifespan.

As a core practice theory, the epidemiological model converges with so-called strengths and empowerment perspectives. It calls for social workers and other mental health practitioners to help clients identify and maximize protective factors and is congruent with all the social work roles elaborated in this book. In the roles of therapist, case manager, or administrator, the same principles apply. The posture of collaboration and consultation, rather than a professional expert ministering to service users, fits well with a risk factor/protective factor understanding of etiology. Social workers offer their expertise for clients to consider. Clients offer their own expertise for social workers to consider. Together they develop understanding of the client's problems, strengths, and needs, and the environment's capacities to meet those needs. They brainstorm together about how to make best use of the client's own capabilities and to exploit the capacities of the environment. No one is expected to have all the answers. The participants work together to formulate questions and to experiment with possible answers. (See Chapter 10.)

The epidemiological model is also egalitarian and universalistic. It assumes that all human beings have strengths and weaknesses and that good fortune is not equitably distributed. Everyone is subjected to risk factors and [almost] everyone is blessed with protective factors. The theory does not categorize individuals with a high preponderance of risk factors as having severe pathology, but rather looks at biology and environment interactions through time, recognizing that the person's illness is realistically attributable to a bad roll of the dice. The epidemiological model as a unifying mental health practice theory is congruent with our knowledge base at the beginning of the 21st century.

Interventions Outcome Research

Interventions outcome research has made it possible to document efficacy for a range of interventions addressing mental disorders and problems. These include psychopharmacology, psychotherapy or counseling, behavioral skills training, and interventions targeted on aspects of the environment (Henggeler et al., 1998; *Report*, p. 15). First-line interventions should be those that are evidence-based (validated by the American Psychiatric Association's (APA) standards for "well-established" or "probably efficacious" treatments), when available. When evidence-based treatments either have not been identified for a given mental problem, or are known but not accessible in a consumer's geographical location, promising interventions (those shown to be useful in clinical trials but not yet validated by the APA's criteria) are the second choice (Chambless et al., 1996). Other interventions should be used only if first- and second-line treatments are not available and the proposed intervention has not been demonstrated to be harmful. Gaps often exist between optimally effective interventions and what service facilities actually offer (*Report*, p. 72). As of August 2000, no conclusions about the safety and effectiveness of alternative treatments (also referred to as natural remedies) can be drawn. Controlled clinical trials are underway for Saint-John's-wort (as a treatment for depression) and omega-3 fatty acids (as a mood stabilizer).

Interventions typically work better in clinical research trials than in real-world clinical practice settings (a fact referred to as the efficacy-effectiveness gap).

Efficacy is the term for what works in a clinical trial, *effectiveness* for what works in typical practice settings. This gap exists both for psychotherapy and for pharmacotherapy, and can be surprisingly high. For example, one review article reported that relapse rates for traditional antipsychotic medications to treat schizophrenia were about 23 percent in clinical research trials, as contrasted with a relapse rate of about 50 percent in clinical practice (Dixon, Lehman, & Levine, 1995; *Report*, p. 72).

Interventions most supported by research are sometimes referred to as "best practices." Examples of well-supported interventions are Multisystemic Therapy (Henggeler et al., 1998) for youths in the juvenile justice system with serious emotional disorders, and Assertive Community Treatment (ACT) for people with serious mental illnesses (Lehman & Steinwachs, 1998; Scott & Dixon, 1995). It is noteworthy that many of the best-supported intervention approaches involve multimodal combinations of strategies, targeting the environment as well as the individual with the mental disability and the family members (*Report*, pp. 175–176, 286–287). Multimodal interventions often include medication, client and family education about possible etiologies and intervention alternatives, skills training, emotional support, family support groups, and environmental supports.

Placebo response is found in up to 50 percent of consumers in any study of a medical treatment. For example, placebo effect in trials of antidepressants averages about 30 percent, and even higher for anxiolytics (antianxiety drugs). To establish a drug's efficacy, it must be statistically superior to placebo (*Report*, p. 71). Possible explanations for placebo effects are spontaneous remission, personality variables (e.g., social acquiescence), client expectations, attitudes of compassion by the clinician, and receiving treatment in a specialized setting (Schweizer & Rickels, 1997).

Implications for Social Work

To comply with the National Association of Social Workers (NASW) *Code of Ethics* (1997), practitioners must develop the habit of looking at relevant research findings pertinent to the populations, problems, and environmental contexts that relate to their practice. Engaging in interventions without first ascertaining what knowledge already exists for the efficacy and effectiveness of these interventions is tantamount to violation of the NASW *Code of Ethics*. Benefit–risk ratios for proposed treatments should be considered by the service provider *and the client* (informed consent) before deciding on a course of action for mental disorders.

These admonitions apply equally to medications and nonsomatic therapies. Most medications or other somatic therapies have side effects, but a likelihood of significant clinical benefit often overrides side effects in support of a treatment recommendation (*Report*, pp. 71–72). Nonsomatic therapies are not risk-free either, and require as much scrutiny as somatic therapies with regard to potential benefits and possible adverse side effects. For example, people treated with talk therapy have later been diagnosed with serious physical conditions that caused or contributed to their psychological symptoms, leading to failure to diagnose underlying conditions (DeLeo et al., 1999; Hall et al., 1981; Odell et al., 1997).

Yet social workers have had difficulty spanning the gap between research and practice. In a study of 1,416 respondents randomly selected from national registers of NASW, subdivisions of the American Psychological Association (APA), and the American Academy of Child and Adolescent Psychiatry, NASW members were the least likely to agree that research knowledge is important for practice. In addition, they were least likely to endorse cognitive-behavioral and neuropsychological orientations, two theoretical orientations strongly supported by research. Theoretical preferences of NASW members were for ego psychology and family systems theory, orientations generally considered to have less research support than cognitive-behavioral and neuropsychological. A national random sample of clinical social workers agreed even less than NASW general members that research knowledge is important (Johnson, 2001).

CULTURAL COMPETENCE

Cultural competence practice that is responsive to the diverse beliefs, values, and norms of different racial, ethnic, and national groups, is becoming a centerpiece of mental health practice. In the wake of publication of data demonstrating clearly that people of color and people of different national origins encounter barriers to access, quality care, and culturally sensitive practitioners and policies, the federal government has condemned this discrimination and called for changes in the way services are offered and delivered.

The *Report* documents widespread failures in the U.S. mental health system. Manifold barriers deter ethnic and racial minority groups from seeking treatment, and even when individuals do succeed in accessing services, the treatments offered may be inappropriate to their needs. "[The system] is not well equipped to meet the needs of racial and ethnic minority populations . . . generally considered to be underserved" (*Report,* p. 80). Culturally appropriate services have been designed but are not widely available (*Report,* pp. 90–91).

Stereotyping by lumping everyone in a certain racial or ethnic group together is a major deterrent to providing help. Not only do racial and ethnic minority populations differ from each other, but within each group, many differences exist, just as they do within the mainstream culture. In fact, what is now considered mainstream (white upper-middle, middle, and working class) is expected to become minority during this century. People of color and Hispanic ethnicity are projected to comprise 47 percent of the U.S. population by mid-century (U.S. Bureau of the Census, 1996).

Implications for Social Work
Service providers must understand culturally shaped coping styles and ties to family and community if they are to succeed in reaching and helping people with diverse cultural backgrounds. Culture denotes a common heritage and set of beliefs, norms, and values. Yet people have multiple ethnic or cultural identities that may include language, country of origin, degree of acculturation into North American society,

gender, age, sexual orientation, social class, economic class, religious/spiritual beliefs, and physical disabilities (Lu, Lim, & Mezzich, 1995).

Not only do social workers and other providers need to become familiar with multiple cultural characteristics, but they also must gain awareness of the multiple cultural identities that guide their own thoughts and judgments. Not the least among these are the professional cultures in which they have been socialized. For example, Western mental health professional culture typically views psychotherapy as a first-line intervention for emotional distress, and professional expertise as a necessary condition for successful treatment. Other cultures may see religious practices as a first-line intervention, spiritual healers as divinely inspired rather than the product of specialized training, and Western psychiatry as irrelevant at best, intrusive or otherwise oppressive at worst.

Moreover, even among clients of Anglo and European heritage, beliefs about treating emotional distress may differ widely. Some perceive psychotropic medication as a welcome tool to relieve suffering. Others see its use as a sign of weakness or capitulation to temptation. Successful practice with clients of any persuasion requires respect for their beliefs and their right to act in accordance with their beliefs, no matter how incorrect or self-defeating the worker judges these beliefs to be. As a general approach to work effectively with issues of diversity, social workers need humility, willingness and even eagerness to learn from clients, and awareness of their own biases and agendas.

Language has long been recognized as a major vehicle through which cultures express respect or disrespect for difference (Bentley, Harrison, & Hudson, 1993; Gambrill, 1999). The struggle for racial equality in the early and mid-20th century, followed by the women's movement, brought into public consciousness the view of language as an instrument for communicating oppressive beliefs. During the past two decades, use of language has figured prominently in the battles of diverse groups to be spoken about with respect.

For people with mental problems and for members of their families, professional culture has acquired a verbal repertoire that many find offensive. Professionals have tried to remedy this by using various expressions and changes in language. "Person-first" expressions are now considered respectful. For example, rather than saying, "he's a schizophrenic," it is considered more respectful to say, "he is a person with schizophrenia." The rationale behind "person-first" language is that the illness or disability does not comprise the whole person, just a facet of that person. A person with schizophrenia is like a person with a broken leg, or with influenza. Imagine referring to the latter as a "broken legic" or an "influenzian." As ludicrous as these examples sound, the logic is valid. Global designations that equate people with their disabilities, relegate them to a separate, different, and implicitly inferior status from the rest of us.

Judgments about behaviors of people, such as "she's manipulative" (or "she's resisting" or "she's acting out"), serve the emotional function for people using these words of validating their importance as professionals or psychological experts. Again, however, the person being referred to is relegated to an implied inferior position, while the speaker is propping up his or her sense of importance, expertise, or professional status. More respectful language involves describing an actual behavior ("She elicits concerned responses from the staff by slashing her wrists," or "She hasn't kept her last two appointments.").

Social workers and other mental health providers have long talked about dysfunctional, enmeshed, or rigid families in situations where a family member has a mental problem, frequently conveying an inference of causality by the use of these words. How often have we said that the mother of a person with a mental disorder is controlling, hostile, or rejecting? These global (and denigrating) words may accurately describe the family member's behavior at some moment in time, under specific conditions, but in many other situations and at other times, that person's behavior is in no way controlling, hostile, or rejecting. Behaviors, emotions, and thoughts are situation-specific (Kagan, 1994), not global omnipresent characteristics. Furthermore, the oft implied etiological significance of the attribute seldom is based on any knowledge about why the person with the mental disability behaves as he or she does. There simply is no factual justification for inferring causality based on some attribute. This kind of use of language is to be deplored, because it denigrates the person or family being spoken about without conveying any useful information.

Were the tables to be turned, and the minutiae of our daily lives subject to scrutiny and judgment, how would we stack up? The family movement of the past two decades has called for professionals to stop blaming and judging (Hatfield, 1983; Johnson, Cournoyer, & Bond, 1995). Yet recent research suggests that these practices continue (Johnson et al., 2000).

Finally, the Surgeon General's *Report,* as comprehensive as it is, has neglected a major sector of mental health practice in the United States, a sector loosely denoted by the phrase *pop psychology.* This sector of popular practice derives from beliefs, not scientific knowledge or validated practice methods. Its practitioners and proponents may or may not possess recognized professional credentials. This sector has attracted large numbers of adherents and has become a multibillion dollar industry (Dawes, 1994). Family members, especially parents of adults and youth with mental disabilities, have suffered disapproval and even vilification at the hands of practitioners of pop psychology. Its historical roots are traceable to the hegemony of Freudian psychology dating from the 1920s, joined by the family therapy movement from the 1960s, to the present. Typical are popular culture's recovery movement (not to be confused with the new mental health establishment's concepts of recovery, to be discussed later), and *codependence,* a purported psychological dysfunction that encompasses almost everyone.

The recovery movement in popular culture has extended far afield from its origins in substance abuse. Most recently, it has burgeoned around the theme of recovered memories of early sexual abuse, memories often found to be false (Loftus & Polage, 1999). Numerous court actions have elicited testimony pertaining to false memories elicited by zealous therapists, and then firmly believed by vulnerable clients, leading to criminal prosecution of innocent family members (Dawes, 1994), not to mention heartbreaking rifts in family bonds. Feminists such as Tavris (1992,

1998) have attributed the popularity of sexual abuse explanations for almost any unexplained misery to women (who have been victimized in other more subtle ways by society), to find a cause for their unhappiness. That is, sexual victimization has become a metaphor for feelings of powerlessness among women.

Similarly, almost anyone with a family member who has any kind of psychological problem is suspected of being codependent and deemed to need treatment. Yet empirical evidence that an entity, codependency, exists is lacking. In a study of young adult children of alcoholics, Gotham and Sher (1996) failed to find any independent characteristic that could be identified as codependency, other than negative affectivity, a global descriptor that could encompass almost any kind of unhappiness or dissatisfaction.

The villains of these stories most often are parents (in the past or present). One of many possible etiological factors—trauma—is believed to be the most important if not the only cause of psychological dysfunction and emotional pain. The underlying assumptions are appealingly simple. They help unhappy people explain and find a culprit responsible for their suffering. In addition, purveyors of these therapies *assume* that some standard of normality or functionality exists, both for individual psychological life and for family relationships. They also appear to assume that they know what that standard is and how the individual client or family is falling short of that standard (Dawes, 1994; Fancher, 1995; Walsh, 1993).

Flaws in these approaches are legion. They fail to take cognizance of the complexity of biopsychosocial determinants of emotional pain, and they have a dismal history of magnifying family hostilities, sometimes irreparably (see for example *Divided Memories,* a 4-hour documentary originally aired on *Frontline,* 1995). Neuroscience is challenging these assumptions, with some success. However, vast domains of a therapy empire, in which scientific advances of the past decade have had little or no influence, still exist in popular culture and sometimes even among credentialed professionals. This therapy empire stands in contrast to interventions, including psychotherapies, that have been validated by outcomes research and have met the APA's standards for "well-established" or "probably efficacious" treatments (Chambless et al., 1996; Chambless et al., 1998).

Major advances in service providers' knowledge and cultural awareness are needed if the mental health establishment is to become truly culturally competent. Cultural differences exacerbate problems of access to appropriate mental health services (See the discussion on "The Managed Care Juggernaut: Organization and Funding of Mental Health Services" later in this chapter).

EROSION OF SOCIETAL SUPPORT

Erosion of societal support and services leads to homelessness and criminalization. Mental health care continues to require contributions not only from services designated as mental health, but also from a host of related supports and services in areas such as income assistance, housing, employment, general health care, legal advocacy, and socialization. In many areas of the country, devastating trends have developed in response to retrenchment of federal and state welfare, housing subsidies, and other benefits needed by people with mental illness. These trends include increases in the population of homeless mentally ill, and the criminalization of the mentally ill, who now often are incarcerated in jails rather than treated in medical and residential facilities.

A Medline database search in August 2000 yielded 373 publications with key words *mental illness and homelessness,* 84 publications with key words *mental illness and incarceration.* In recent years, we have seen the expansion of research documenting these phenomena and the consequences of ignoring them, and conversely the encouraging results obtained in the quality of life of people with chronic mental illness in several other countries (such as Finland, England, and Norway) that do provide more adequate supports for people with disabilities (Honkonen, Saarinen, & Salokangas, 1999; Melle et al., 2000; Trieman, Leff, & Glover, 1999). Yet Republican Congresses, with the support of some Democrats, have continued to relentlessly pursue cutbacks in social spending that further undermine the progress made by years of political action on behalf of the mentally ill.

Implications for Social Work

Political action is required to effect any meaningful change in the larger environment for more funding for housing, health care, and employment support for clients, or to ameliorate the way services are organized and delivered. Because very few paying social work jobs include these activities as part of a job description, we may have engage in political advocacy activities on our own time, with no monetary compensation (see Chapter 12, "Social Workers as Advocates and Community Organizers," and Chapter 14, "Social Workers as Administrators and Policy Analysts in Mental Health Settings").

RECOVERY AND PREVENTION

The concept of recovery is expanding the mental health landscape. Recovery from mental health illnesses and problems is now regarded as a legitimate goal, reflecting not necessarily the removal of biological, emotional, and behavioral problems, but rather the possibility of a productive and satisfying life even with these problems. There is no single, agreed upon definition of *recovery.* It is alternatively called a process, an outlook, a vision, and a guiding principle. New views of recovery, inspired by mental health consumers themselves and reinforced by longitudinal research, convey a message of hope to people with mental problems and their families. The contemporary notion of recovery involves restoration of self-esteem and identity (see Chapters 1 and 8). It also targets attaining meaningful roles in society, even in the presence of chronic disability or deficits (*Report,* p. 97), in contrast to the notion of return to psychological normality. The popular psychology connotation of recovery is somewhat different, emphasizing the unearthing and "working through" of long-repressed feelings pertaining to childhood trauma (whether due to having drug-abusing parents or to being sexually abused). This is seen as the sine qua non of achieving normal adulthood.

Implications for Social Work

The word *recovery* has traditionally denoted the return to a healthy state. Although most of us are aware that people with some kinds of psychiatric disabilities do not usually metamorphose into people without disability, it is important to explicitly embrace the new concept of recovery for several reasons. First, workers whose aspirations for their clients involve improvement to typical or normal behavior or emotional state, will be disappointed or frustrated in most cases. The concept of recovery that can best serve clients and their workers is measurable improvement in behavioral, emotional, or cognitive spheres. Recognition of improvement is a powerful motivator for continued effort toward more improvement. In working with people with mental illnesses or mental problems, no matter what the level of functioning at the onset of treatment or interventions, very small—incremental—*achievable* goals should be set by collaboration between the client and the worker. These goals will be mostly behavioral, but measures of subjective states (that involve emotions or cognitions) can also be specified and progress measured. At the outset of treatment, clients should be identified as "in recovery," that is, involved in a plan that will help them move toward improved quality of life. Each increment of improvement in the specific areas designated in the treatment plan should be measured, recorded, and reinforced. Success in small tasks motivates clients to continue and helps workers avoid burnout (Miltenberger, 1997).

Recovery usually requires an environment that provides prosocial supports. Discharge of a hospitalized person with a mental illness into a community poor in supports such as housing, health care, and family, peer, and professional contacts, is often a ticket to rehospitalization and compounded feelings of failure and hopelessness. The social worker acting as case manager and/or therapist must work energetically to set up a support network prior to discharge, as well as a mechanism to coordinate the efforts of providers in different specialties (such as income maintenance, health care, employment support). Recovery is truly a person-in-environment status. The efforts of social workers must be as energetic in developing community supports as in giving the client individual counseling. In instances where the client has a family, support and education of family members is critical (see Chapter 10, "Social Workers as Consumer and Family Consultants").

Prevention is another concept and legitimate goal that is changing the mental health field. Historically, little money has been spent on prevention. Development of preventive interventions has been slow in mental health, sometimes because there is insufficient knowledge about etiology, and often because there is inability to alter risk factors that contribute to etiologies even when these contributors are known (*Report*, pp. 62–64). Nevertheless, rigorous scientific trials have documented some successful prevention programs for dysthymia, major depressive disorder, conduct problems, risky behaviors leading to HIV infection, lead poisoning, and other conditions (*Report*, p. 62).

Implications for Social Work

Preventive interventions have been shown to improve social and emotional development by providing services, such as educational programs for young children, parent education programs, and nurse home visits. Preventive efforts are similar to the tasks of promoting recovery, and impact a client either before a severe episode has occurred, or after the episode, in which case the goal is reducing instances of relapse. Workers should learn to accept relapse as a part of the recovery process, and should convey to clients that relapse does occur and does not indicate treatment failure. Life continues on a trajectory that involves improvements as well as setbacks.

SPECIAL DEVELOPMENTAL ISSUES IN CHILDREN AND ADOLESCENTS

In mental health care, children and adolescents have been recognized, and field trials of programs targeted on the needs of these populations have had some success. However, political obstacles to these newer approaches have limited the degree to which various states have adopted them.

Development is characterized by periods of transition and reorganization, making it critical to assess the mental health of children and adolescents in the context of familial, social, and cultural expectations about age-appropriate thoughts, emotions, and behavior. The range of what is considered normal is wide; still, children and adolescents do have developmental disorders that are more severe than the ups and downs in the usual course of development. Approximately one in five children and adolescents experiences the signs and symptoms of a *DSM-IV* disorder during the course of a year, but only about 5 percent of all children experience what professionals term *extreme functional impairment*.

Mental disorders and mental health problems appear in families of all social classes and of all backgrounds. No one is immune. Yet there are children who are at greatest risk by virtue of a broad array of factors. These include genetic propensities; physical problems; intellectual disabilities (retardation); low birth weight; family history of mental and addictive disorders; multigenerational poverty; and separation, abuse, or neglect from a caregiver.

A range of efficacious psychosocial and pharmacologic treatments exists for many mental disorders in children, including depression, attention deficit and hyperactive disorder, and other disruptive disorders. Research is under way to ascertain the effectiveness of most treatments for children in actual practice settings.

Schools are the most utilized venue for the recognition of mental disorders and delivery of mental health services to children and adolescents, yet trained staff are limited, as are options for referral to specialty care. The multiple problems associated with serious emotional disturbance in children and adolescents are best addressed with a systems approach, in which multiple service sectors work in an organized, collaborative way.

Implications for Social Work

Contemporary child and adolescent mental health practice emphasizes a concept called *systems of care* (SOC). The SOC concept represents several changes in theoretical perspectives, from traditional child and adolescent mental health services, and from psychological models focusing mostly on intra- and interpersonal phenomena, to more complex biopsychosocial and ecological models. Contemporary practice has evolved from a focus on pathology and deficits to a focus on strengths and empowerment, from a focus on "child saving" to a focus on preserving and supporting families, and from a primary view of families as objects of intervention (client, patients) to families as partners in the design, delivery, and evaluation of services (Friesen, 1993).

These changes in perspective are expressed in the following expanded concepts of service delivery and practice roles:

- From program-centered services, emphasizing eligibility and appropriateness of referrals, to child- and family-centered services that are individualized and flexible, where the emphasis is placed on the needs, values, and preferences of families, including culturally competent practice
- From a solely therapeutic focus on the child's behavior, emotional life, and family dynamics to comprehensive services that address the full range of the child's needs (e.g., health, mental health, education, recreation)
- From an exclusive focus on formal services to recognition that informal supports such as extended family, friends, neighbors, churches, and social clubs are important resources and constitute potentially valuable family strengths
- From agency-based expert professional roles to professionals who work collaboratively with the family, in settings of the family's choice, sharing information, responsibility, and power
- From interdisciplinary team functioning that is experienced by the family only as a sequence of interactions with different professionals, to true interprofessional collaboration that involves coordinated planning, with family members as full members of the team
- From a specialized, fragmented set of services to an emphasis on coordination at the interagency and case level
- From limited service options, consisting mostly of outpatient, inpatient, or residential to a wide array of services, including day treatment, in-home intervention, family support, respite, therapeutic foster care, supported education, recreation, and afterschool activities, among others. This means moving from a system that sinks most of its financial resources into out-of-home care to a system that puts most resources into flexible, community-based alternatives and flexible funds (Friesen, 1993).

Some states have begun to implement these principles, embodied in "wraparound" and multisystemic models of practice, some of which have already qualified as best practices, (Henggeler et al., 1998) and others that are being evaluated to determine the level of empirical support for their effectiveness (Burchard et al., 1999). Social workers need exposure to SOCs and to innovative strategies for delivering services to devise ways to advance these approaches in their own communities. The recently enacted Child Health Insurance Program (CHIP) could significantly increase funding for youth in the states that opt to include mental health coverage in their CHIP benefits.

SPECIAL DEVELOPMENTAL ISSUES IN THE ELDERLY AND AGING

This population also faces some special developmental issues in mental health. Important life tasks remain for individuals as they age. Older individuals continue to learn and contribute to society, in spite of physiologic changes due to aging and increasing health problems. Continued intellectual, social, and physical activity throughout the life cycle are important for the maintenance of mental health in late life. Stressful life events, such as declining health and loss of mates, family members, or friends often increase with age. However, persistent bereavement or serious depression is not normal and should be treated.

Normal aging is not characterized by mental or cognitive disorders. Mental or substance use disorders that present alone or co-occur should be recognized and treated. Disability due to mental illness in individuals over 65 years old is expected to become a major public health concern in the near future because of demographic changes. In particular, dementia, depression, and schizophrenia, among other conditions, present special problems in this age group. Dementia produces significant dependency and is a leading contributor to the need for costly long-term care in the last years of life. Depression contributes to high rates of suicide among males in this population. Schizophrenia continues to be disabling in spite of recovery of function by some individuals in mid- to late life.

Implications for Social Work

There are effective interventions for most mental disorders experienced by older people (for example, depression and anxiety), and for many mental health problems, such as bereavement. Older individuals can benefit from advances in psychotherapy, medication, support groups, paid and volunteer work, social and recreational groups, and other activities. Treating older adults with mental disorders confers other benefits to overall health by improving the interest and ability of individuals to care for themselves and follow their primary care provider's directions and advice, particularly about taking medications.

Front-line social workers are critical links in identifying and addressing mental disorders in older adults. Opportunities are missed to improve mental health and general medical outcomes when mental illness is underrecognized and undertreated in primary care settings. Barriers to access of services for aging citizens are often encountered with Medicare, Medicaid, nursing homes, and managed care (see the *Report* for further discussion).

DIAGNOSTIC CONVENTIONS

Distinctions between mental illnesses (conditions that meet criteria for *DSM-IV* diagnoses) and mental problems (emotional, behavioral, and cognitive states of people whose characteristics fall short of criteria for a psychiatric diagnosis) are now being recognized. Some psychiatrists and other mental health professionals have been calling for the replacement of categorical diagnosis, embodied in successive editions of the *DSMs* and *ICDs* (World Health Organization, 1992), with a dimensional approach (Kaplan & Sadock, 1998; Shekim et al., 1986). (See also Chapter 3.)

Implications for Social Work
Although there is undoubtedly some validity to these critiques, our view is that the real villains are the funding systems themselves, not the use of diagnostic labels. Health care for profit, not surprisingly, distorts priorities in the direction of profitability, not helping people. The alternative to categorical methods, dimensional diagnosis (describing an individual's characteristics and problem areas, then devising interventions targeted on these) is sensible on the face of it. However, if instituted on a large scale, dimensional diagnosis would also be subject to manipulation by managed care companies interested in maximizing profit rather than providing the best possible services. Social workers must continue to use the required diagnoses with caution, using the least stigmatizing diagnoses and finding ways to maximize benefit to clients, because the repudiation of *DSM* classification by psychiatry does not appear likely in the imminent future, and because no alternative scheme has been successful at displacing it (Karls & Wandrei, 1992). Social workers have had some input into the latest versions of *DSMs*, and apparently have had some influence in the decision of *DSM-IV* writers to omit diagnoses stigmatizing to women, such as "masochistic personality."

DUAL DIAGNOSIS: CO-OCCURRING MENTAL ILLNESS AND SUBSTANCE ABUSE

As many as half of people with serious mental illness develop alcohol or other drug abuse problems at some time (Regier et al., 1993). The causes of widespread co-occurrence are unknown, because evidence to support any of the proposed explanations is inconclusive (Mueser, Drake, & Wallach, 1998). It is well-known, however, that substance abuse by people with mental illness is associated with symptom exacerbation, treatment noncompliance, more frequent hospitalizations, greater depression, greater likelihood of suicide, greater risk of violence, incarceration, family friction, HIV infection, greater service use, and higher costs (Bartels, Drake, & Wallace, 1995; Bellack & Gearon, 1998; Havassy & Arns, 1998; Institute of Medicine, 1995; Mueser, Drake, & Miles, 1997).

Implications for Social Work
Given the high prevalence of co-occurrence and the serious risks it entails for people with mental illness, development of effective treatments for the dually diagnosed merits top priority. During the past decade, increasing recognition of the importance of co-occurring conditions is illustrated in the number of listings that appear in the Medline Web site. The key words *dual diagnosis* and *mental disorder*

and substance abuse increased by a factor of 35 in the past decade, from 22 in 1989 to 710 listings as of August 2000.

Historically, people with mental illness and with substance abuse or addiction have been treated in separate facilities, with diverging etiological beliefs. Treatment methods have sometimes been incompatible. For example, confrontation, often used with substance abuse, is frequently contraindicated for people with mental disorders (Mueser, Drake, & Miles, 1997), and some members of Alcoholics Anonymous (AA) have shown disapproval toward people with mental illness taking psychotropic medication. Growing awareness of the frequency of co-occurring mental illnesses or mental problems with substance abuse and addiction has led to calls for integration of services in these two areas.

Research supports a change to combined treatment for mental disorders and substance abuse by the same providers (Kosten & Ziedonis, 1997). However, currently, there are few combined service programs relative to the need. Components of successful combined treatment include case management, group interventions such as social skills training, and assertive outreach to bring people with co-occurring diagnoses into treatment (Mueser, Drake, & Miles, 1997). An important aspect of successful combined programs is the understanding that mentally ill people tend to have cognitive and motivational deficits. Some investigators have found interventions using motivational approaches to substance abuse treatment to be superior to traditional 12-step programs (such as AA) for people with mental illnesses (Drake et al., 1998). This is possibly because these structured behavioral methods are more congruent with the cognitive disabilities often accompanying mental illlness. Other researchers have found self-help groups modified for clients with co-occurring diagnoses to be helpful (Vogel et al., 1998).

To avail themselves of this new information, practitioners can search on Medline and other databases that are available without charge on the Web, and can form peer supervision groups to share information and support each others' work. The more challenging parts of the task are to put together all these disparate fragments of information into meaningful guides to practice. Agencies serving substance abusing and dually diagnosed clients would do well to offer ongoing in-service trainings using these research findings. A practical way to convert fragments of information into meaningful treatment guides might be to present the information in in-service workshops or as assigned reading prior to meeting, and then to use the meeting time to work together drawing up practice guidelines.

THE MANAGED CARE JUGGERNAUT: ORGANIZATION AND FUNDING OF MENTAL HEALTH SERVICES

In 1999, 177 million Americans were enrolled in managed care behavioral health organizations (*Report,* p. 422). Managed care has commandeered the organization and funding of mental health and other health care services during the 1990s and early 2000s. Although managed care companies were initially private for-profit, public and not-for-profit health care systems have increasingly turned to managed care to help them achieve efficiency and lower costs. For example, in some states, not-for-profit Blues (Blue Cross, Blue Shield) are now operated by managed care companies, and Medicaid has also turned to managed care in some states.

Managing care emphasizes supply-side controls on spending (incentives to providers, changes in organizational structures, and administrative mechanisms) to control costs, supplanting the almost sole reliance on demand-side measures (deductibles and co-payments) intended to discourage overuse of services. Many of the administrative techniques used in managed care (such as case management, utilization review, and implementation of standardized criteria) have the potential to improve quality of care by enhancing adherence to professional consensus guidelines (Berndt et al., 1998) and possibly improving patient outcomes (Katon et al., 1997). However, when these measures are combined with cost sharing (as is often the case for nonparity mental health benefits), impossible cost burdens on individual consumers seriously inhibit the provision of full and necessary treatment and lower the quality of care.

Many different managed care plans have proliferated, each with a different model for matching treatment need with insurance. Behavioral health plans differ considerably in their access and quality of care offered. Current practices often offer little incentive to improve quality (*Report*, p. 426). In some extreme cases, annual limits have been only $5,000 for inpatient and $2,000 for outpatient care (Buck et al., 1999). Maximum lifetime limits for both inpatient and outpatient services have typically been $25,000.

Many practitioners who cannot deliver services without authorization for reimbursement experience the nightmare of attempting to negotiate for services with a plethora of companies. They are so burdened with having to negotiate and advocate to receive reimbursement that their time and energy to actually provide services to their clients is severely curtailed.

The U.S. mental health service system is complex and connects many sectors (public and private, specialty and general health, income support, housing, criminal justice, and education). It is widely acknowledged that the system is really a collection of systems, organizationally fragmented, financed from many funding streams, and rife with barriers to access. Services are provided in diverse facilities in both public and private sectors, and are referred to collectively as the de facto mental health service system (Regier et al., 1993). Approximately 15 percent of adults and 21 percent of children in the United States obtain mental health services in the de facto system (health or mental health care providers, the clergy, social service agencies, and schools) in a given year (Regier et al., 1993, p. 405). Each sector of the de facto mental health service system has different patterns and types of care and different patterns of funding. Issues of cost shifting between federal, state, and local governments often drive treatment and placement decisions.

The de facto mental health system has four major sectors (*Report*, pp. 405–408): (1) the *specialty mental health* sector (mental health professionals such as psychiatrists, psychologists, social workers, and nurses specializing in work with people with mental disorders); (2) the *general medical/primary care* sector, which consists of health care professionals such as general internists, pediatricians, and nurse practitioners in office-based practices, clinics, acute medical and surgical hospitals, and nursing homes; (3) the *human services* sector (social services, school-based services, activity centers such as the YMCA or YWCA, residential rehabilitation services, vocational rehabilitation, criminal justice and prison-based services, religious counselors, and others); and (4) the *voluntary support network* sector (self-help groups and peer counselors). For children, school mental health services are a major source of care (used by 16 percent out of a total of 21 percent of all children and adolescents using any kind of mental health service).

Despite apparently high use of help, critical gaps exist between those who need service and those who receive it. Recent epidemiological surveys have shown that about half of the 15 percent of the adult population that use mental health services have a specific mental or addictive disorder (8 percent). (Most of the remainder of service users have a mental health problem but do not qualify for a *DSM* diagnosis). These surveys estimated that during a 1-year period, about one in five Americans— 44 million people—have diagnosable disorders. In one year, 19 percent of adults have a mental disorder alone, 3 percent have both mental and addictive disorders, and 6 percent have addictive disorders alone. Thus 28 percent of the adult population has either a mental or an addictive disorder (Kessler et al., 1994; Regier et al., 1993). Because only 8 percent with diagnosable disorders use mental health services, the *Report* (p. 408) concludes that a substantial majority of those with specific mental disorders do not receive treatment.

Inequities in insurance coverage for mental health—the product of decades of stigma and discrimination—have prompted corrective efforts through legislation designed to create *parity* (equality of coverage) between mental health and other health coverage. The magnitude of the inequity is illustrated by data from one economic study that found that, for a family with mental health treatment expenses of $35,000 a year, the average out-of-pocket burden was $12,000. For those with $60,000 in mental health expenses in a year, the average out-of-pocket share was $27,000, as contrasted with only $1,500 and $1,800 respectively for medical/surgical treatment (Zuvekas, Banthin, & Seldon, 1998). During the past decade, a growing number of states have implemented parity, with marked variation between the stipulations in different states (*Report*, p. 428). Although partial parity legislation has been enacted, the gap in insurance coverage between mental health and other health services has been getting wider (Buck et al., 1999; HayGroup, 1998). Despite cries of profligacy from (mostly) conservative members of Congress, implementing parity has resulted in negligible cost increases where the care has been managed.

At least two major types of financial concerns have driven mental health policy during the 1990s. The first is the so-called *moral hazard* (unnecessary utilization of services by consumers because they are not required to bear much of the costs). The second is *adverse selection,* (plans that provide the most generous coverage attract individuals with the greatest need for care, leading to elevated service use and costs for those insurers independent of their efficiency in service provision). To control moral hazard, insurers incorporate cost sharing and care management into their policies. To control adverse selection, insurers try to restrict mental health coverage to avoid enrolling people with higher mental health needs (*Report*, p. 420).

Among the fastest-rising expenses for mental health services from 1986 to 1996 were outpatient prescription drugs, accounting for 9 percent per year of direct mental health care costs, with an average annual growth rate of about 10 percent. This growth reflects in part the increasing availability and demonstrable efficacy of medications in treating mental disorders. Psychiatrists prescribe only one-third of psychotropic medications, while physicians and other medical specialists prescribe the remaining two-thirds. Medicaid pays for most available medications in some states but not others. For example, some states refuse newer drugs because of their much higher costs than second- and third-generation medications. Medicare does not cover prescription drugs at all. Thus the most effective medications are not accessible to millions of Americans who do not have the financial means to pay out-of-pocket or buy supplemental insurance. These funding mechanisms represent de facto discrimination against the poor, moderate-income workers and their families, and Social Security recipients.

Although most social workers who deal with managed care have experienced harmful and sometimes egregious disregard for the needs of clients by managed care companies, there do appear to be some positive effects. Prior to managed care, services were often reimbursed with almost no demands for evidence that they really helped suffering people. There were many anecdotal accounts of people receiving psychotherapy for years with no appreciable improvement in their conditions (Dawes, 1994). Others people had long periods of hospitalization that did not appear to help them. In fact, this hospitalization may have harmed them by isolating them from their communities, not helping them develop real-world survival skills, and not constructing networks of support in their communities that could give people suffering from mental illnesses the best chances to have satisfying and productive lives (Carling, 1993).

By most accounts, managed care has substantially reduced the amount of these ineffective treatments. However, it has amplified other kinds of harm by refusals to pay for needed services. Managed care has no credibility as an institution dedicated to the welfare of service consumers. It is widely perceived as an ill-disguised tool to cut expenditures no matter what the human costs (Silberman & James, 2000). Social workers providing mental health services in any of the service sectors report feeling embattled and overtaxed by the need to fight for services that should be entitlements, not crumbs from the health industry's table (Schamess & Lightburn, 1999).

Implications for Social Work

Relatively few mental illnesses have an unremitting course marked by the most acute manifestations of illness. Rather, for reasons that are not yet clearly understood, the symptoms associated with mental illness tend to wax and wane. These patterns pose special challenges for social workers implementing treatment plans, and for the design of service systems that can be optimally responsive to an individual's needs during every phase of illness. Managed care allocations of a few visits, combined with annual caps on funded visits, are ill-suited to respond to the intermittent and long-term needs of people with mental illnesses and mental problems.

Social workers need to understand the structures and functions of federal, state, and local institutions to fight effectively for benefit increases and equalization of opportunity for mental health care. An array of quality-monitoring and quality-improvement mechanisms has been developed (*Report*, pp. 423–426). There is increasing concern about consumer satisfaction and consumers' rights. A Patients' Bill of Rights has been developed and implemented in Federal Employee Health Benefit Plans, with broader legislation defeated this year in the Congress. To help consumers hold providers accountable, social workers can volunteer their efforts to support future versions of the Patients' Bill of Rights legislation by phoning, writing, or better yet visiting, their congresspersons.

Technological advances have brought privacy issues to the fore in all health care, and are especially felt in the mental health field because of stigma, fear of job discrimination, and fear of subsequent denial of health insurance or higher premiums related to history of mental health issues. An assurance of confidentiality is understandably critical in individual decisions to seek mental health treatment, yet the fact that a person has received treatment and sought insurance reimbursement for that treatment becomes a matter of record. Although an extensive legal framework governs confidentiality of consumer–provider interactions, the possibility of information leaks is a realistic concern, which social workers should validate (*Report*, pp. 438–450).

CONSUMER AND FAMILY ORGANIZATIONS

Consumer and family organizations have burgeoned since their formation, starting in the late 1970s, into formidable political forces as well as critical sources of support for people with mental disorders and members of their families. Although the term *consumer* was first used to destigmatize people with mental disabilities, some service users objected because the term erroneously implied that service users have the power to choose services suited to their needs. Some service users prefer to call themselves survivors or ex-patients, denoting that they have survived oppression by mental health systems (Chamberlin & Rogers, 1990). Views differ among service users. Some oppose all forms of involuntary treatment, support the prohibition of electroconvulsive therapy, and reject psychotropic medications and hospitalization. Others advocate improving mental health systems rather than dispensing with them (Frese, 1998; Lefley, 1996).

Self-help groups assume three different postures toward mental health professionals: separatist, supportive (professionals are allowed to help in auxiliary roles), and partnership models. Programs run entirely by consumers include drop-in centers, case management programs, outreach programs, businesses, employment and housing programs, and crisis services (*Report*, p. 94). Consumers are also involved in more conventional mental health services as job coaches, case manager extenders, and other roles. Increasingly, mental health agencies are employing consumers, not only because of the self-efficacy and skills training benefits to those employed. Also consumers can relate to and support other consumers in ways that professionals cannot. Twenty-seven state mental health authorities now have paid positions for consumers in central offices (Geller, Brown, Fisher, Grudzinskas, & Manning, 1998). Consumers are now being hired at all levels in mental health systems, ranging from case manager aides to management positions in state and national advocacy organizations (*Report*, p. 95; see also Chapter 12).

The family movement has paralleled the consumer movement in its rapid expansion of membership and domains. However, it differs with consumers of the separatist persuasion in that it strongly endorses a partnership model of work with professionals. In particular, family members, who have watched helplessly as their loved one deteriorated and suffered great pain, have welcomed psychotropic medication for the relief and improvement it brings.

Major national family organizations have played a decisive role in public education and legislative lobbying. In addition to dozens of regional and local independent groups, at least four major family organizations are currently active nationally and in most states: National Alliance for the Mentally Ill (NAMI), Federation of Families for Children's Mental Health (FFCMH), National Mental Health Association (NMHA), and Children with Attention Deficit Disorder (CHADD). Information about these organizations is available on the Internet.

Stigma associated with mental disorders is being actively combatted by family and consumer organizations, in collaboration with the federal government agencies charged with mental health research and services (National Institute of Mental Health, Substance Abuse and Mental Health Services Administration, and Center for Mental Health Services). NAMI recently launched a Campaign to End Discrimination. The campaign has been supported by top professionals in the mental health establishment through appearances on national television news and talk shows.

Implications for Social Work

Principles of the new paradigm of practice with families have been enunciated by various writers (see Chapter 1, "A Context and Vision for Excellence in Social Work Practice," and Chapter 10, "Social Workers as Consumer and Family Consultants"). The following are some of the principles of the new paradigm:

1. The organic/functional dichotomy has been replaced by a systemic view of etiology of mental problems as well as diagnosable mental disorders. Mutually influencing forces of genetics, other biological factors, culture, behaviors of significant others, organizational processes, economics, and politics impinge on families and shape their levels of well-being.

2. The notion of toxic, pathogenic families is replaced by the notion of risk-factor-heavy systems (e.g., income support, employment, health care).

3. Parents are calling for approaches that emphasize empowerment rather than therapy, because many psychotherapies and family therapies have been associated with a philosophical position that defines families as disturbed, pathological, pathogenic, or dysfunctional.

4. The language of therapy is associated with repairing or remediating disturbance, pathology, pathogenesis, or dysfunction in individuals and families. It is offensive to parents in the same way that gender-biased or ethnic-biased language is found offensive. Therapy terminology expresses a long-standing tradition of attributing virtually every emotional or behavioral problem to parental pathogenesis.

5. In the language of empowerment, recipients of service are seen as people with problems to be addressed. In this way, they are no different from the professionals who serve them.

6. Services offered by professionals are intended to empower families and children by helping them gain accurate information; facilitating access to resources such as financial assistance, respite care, transportation, and home help; helping to develop coping skills for managing difficult behaviors or participating in meetings with people in the community who affect their lives; and connecting family members with social supports such as parent and sibling groups and parent-to-parent individual support.

Professionals have expertise in these areas that they place at the service of families. Their roles are better defined as *consultants* and *partners* than as treaters, therapists, or healers, even though their efforts should have therapeutic and healing effects.

In support of the Campaign to End Discrimination, a documentary video on mental health issues through the eyes of family members has recently been produced. The video was produced to educate mental health professionals about the needs and insights of parents, to raise consciousness about the stereotypes and prejudices many practitioners hold with respect to families of people with mental and emotional disabilities, and to supply research-based information about mental disorders (Johnson & Trivella, 1999).

THE MACROECONOMIC CONTEXT

As immersed as we all are in the health care financing and delivery system that we have in the United States, it is easy to lose sight of the underlying economic forces that converge to dampen hopes of accessible quality health and mental health care for all Americans (see Chapter 14). The patchwork mental health services and funding in place prior to managed care was also rife with violations of equity and humane practice. Under managed care-dominated mental health services, human casualties are hard to estimate, but our experience tells us they are legion. Who among us [mostly middle-class, educated] with medical needs in recent years has not had the experience of being denied reimbursement, or had visits curtailed, or medication reimbursement refused, or emergency room visits disallowed?

Why in the richest country in the world do we have a system so irrational, inequitable, expensive, and inefficient? A system that can offer some of us, some of the time, outstanding state-of-the-art medical care, and at other times poor care, too little or too late, or no care when it is urgently needed? The answers undoubtedly can be found from the interplay of cultural, economic, and political forces. Few industrialized countries today still endorse free market health care (or mental health care), having learned from their own or others' experiences. We have learned that a model of competitive enterprise is incompatible with any criteria of fairness, quality, accessibility, or societal burden sharing in what social work and other helping professions consider a basic human right.

In the United States, however, misapplication of so-called free market capitalism to design, delivery, and funding of health and mental health care is congruent with the rhetoric of the national and multinational corporate giants that control our economy and wield powerful influence on our legislative and executive branches of government. Attempts by reformers in any of the areas of social benefits and costs are routinely derailed by the power of corporate interests that control the media and much of the political process (Greider, 1990, 1997). As long as the American people continue to accept the ideologies purveyed by corporate interests, the irrationality, fragmentation, and unfairness of our health and mental health care may be doomed to remain in place.

Implications for Social Work

Does this mean we should stop fighting? No, because small gains are better than no gains, and vocal protest and opposition at least keep alive the notion that other ways of doing it are still possible. The current political and economic context stymies practitioners in their attempts to get more funding for housing, health care, and employment support for their clients. Although many of us entered the profession because of interest in working directly with individuals and families (not in engaging in political action), the social work mission now requires political action by all of us as part of our commitment to further the quality of life for those we serve.

KEY TERMS

Epidemiology: Pertains to the study of the health and mental health of populations. Research in the field of epidemiology forms the basis, together with neuroscience and outcome studies, for knowledge about mental health and mental illness.

Neuroscience: Knowledge and research about brain structures and functions that is central to understanding mental health, mental illness, and addiction.

Surgeon General: The government office that released the major report on the state of mental health at the turn of the century.

WEB RESOURCES

Surgeon General's Office (http://www.surgeongeneral.gov). This site contains the entire text of *Mental Health: A Report of the Surgeon General*, (December, 1999), as well as a call to action documenting the state of our knowledge about suicide in the *U.S. Mental Health*.

This report can be downloaded chapter by chapter. Some chapters are long (100+ pages) and require a lot of memory.

Medline (http://www.ncbi.nlm.nih.gov/PubMed/). Medline offers a premier database for articles from all disciplines related to mental health.

National Institute for Drug Abuse (http://www.nida.nih.gov/). This site provides information about publications and other offerings.

REFERENCES

Albee G. W. (1982). The politics of nature and nurture. *American Journal of Community Psychology, 10*(1), 4–30.

Bartels, S. J., Drake, R. E., & Wallach, M. A. (1995). Long-term course of substance use disorders among patients with severe mental illness. *Psychiatric Services, 46,* 258–251.

Bellack, A. S., & Gearon, J. S. (1998). Substance abuse treatment for people with schizophrenia. *Addictive Behaviors, 23,* 749–766.

Bentley, K. J., Harrison, D. F., & Hudson, W. W. (1993). The impending demise of "designer diagnoses": Implications for the use of concepts in practice. *Research on Social Work Practice, 3*(4), 462–470.

Berndt, J., Hu, T., Wallace, N., Cuffel, B., Hausman, J., & Schaffer, R. (1998). Mental health costs and outcomes under alternative capitation in systems in Colorado: Early results. *Journal of Mental Health Policy and Economics, 1,* 3–13.

Breggin, P. R., & Breggin, G. R. (1994). *The war against children: How the drugs, programs, and theories of the psychiatric establishment are threatening America's children with a medical "cure" for violence.* New York: St Martin's Press.

Bronfenbrenner, U. (1979). *The ecology of human development: Experiments by nature and design.* Cambridge, MA: Harvard University Press.

Buck, J. A., Teich, J. L., Umland, B., & Stein, M. (1999). Behavioral health benefits in employer-sponsored health plans. *Health Affairs, 18,* 67–78.

Caplan, P. J., & Hall-McCorquodale, I. (1985). Mother-blaming in major clinical journals. *American Journal of Orthopsychiatry, 55*(3), 345–353.

Carling, P. J. (1993). Housing and supports for persons with mental illness: Emerging approaches to research and practice. *Hospital and Community Psychiatry, 44*(5), 439–49.

Chamberlin, J., & Rogers, J. A. (1990). Planning a community-based mental health system: Perspective of service recipients. *American Psychologist, 45,* 1241–1244.

Chambless, D. L., Baker, M. J., Baucom, D. H., Beutler, L. E., Calhoun, K. S., Crits-Christoph, P., Daiuto, A., Sanderson, W. C., Shoham, V., Stickle, T., Williams, D. A., & Woody, S. R. (1998). Update on empirically validated therapies II. *Clinical Psychologist 51,* 3–16.

Chambless, D.L., Sanderson, W.C., Shohman, V., Bennett, J.S., Pope, K.S., Crits-Cristoph, P., Baker, M., Johnson, B., Woody, S.R., Sue, S., Beutler, L., Williams, D.A., & McMurry, S. (1996). An update on empirically validated therapies. *Clinical Psychologist, 49,* 5–18.

Council on Social Work Education. (1999). *Curriculum policy statement.* Alexandria, VA: Author.

Dawes, R. (1994). *House of cards: Psychology and psychotherapy built on myth.* New York: Free Press.

DeLeo , D., Scocco, P., Schmidtke, A., Billie-Brahe, U., Kerkhof, A. J., Lonnqvist, J., Crepet, P., Salander-Renberg, E., Wasserman, D., Michel, K., & , Bjerke, T. (1999). Physical illness and parasuicide: Evidence from the European Parasuicide Study Interview Schedule (EPSIS/WHO-EURO). *International Journal of Psychiatry 29*(2), 149–63.

Dixon, L. B., Lehman, A. F., & Levine, J. (1995). Conventional antipsychotic medications for schizophrenia. *Schizophrenia Bulletin, 21*, 567–577.

Drake, R. E., Mercer-McFadden, C., Mueser, K. T., McHugo, G. J., & Bond, G. R. (1998). Review of integrated mental health and substance abuse treatment for patients with dual disorders. *Schizophrenia Bulletin, 24*, 589–608.

Eberle, A. (1996) Perspectives: War on children. *Claiming Children*, June, 12–13.

Elder, G. H. (1974). *Children of the great depression.* Chicago: University of Chicago Press.

Fancher, R. T. (1995). *Cultures of healing.* New York: W. H. Freeman.

Friesen, B. J. (1993). Overview. In H. C. Johnson (Ed.), *Child Mental Health in the 1990s: Curricula for Graduate and Undergraduate Professional Education* (pp. 11–13). Washington, DC: U. S. Department of Health and Human Services, Public Health Service, National Institute of Mental Health.

Frese, F. J. (1998). Advocacy, recovery, and the challenges of consumerism for schizophrenia. *Psychiatric Clinics of North America, 21*, 233–249.

Gambrill, E. (1999). Evidence-based practice: An alternative to authority-based practice. *Families in Society, 80*, 341–350.

Geller, J. L., Brown, J. M., Fisher, W. H., Grudzinskas, A. J., Jr, & Manning, T. D. (1998). A national survey of "consumer empowerment" at the state level. *Psychiatric Services, 49*, 498–503.

Germain, C. B., & Gitterman, A. (1980). *The life model of social work practice.* New York: Columbia University Press.

Gotham, H. J., & Sher, K. J. (1996). Do codependent traits involve more than basic dimensions of personality and psychopathology? *Journal of Studies in Alcoholism, 57*(1), 34–39.

Gould, K. (1987). Life model vs., conflict model: A feminist perspective. *Social Work, 32*, 345–352.

Greider, W. (1990). *Who will tell the people? The betrayal of American democracy.* New York: Simon & Schuster.

Greider, W. (1997). *One world, ready or not.* New York: Touchstone.

Hall, R. C., Gardner, E. R., Popkin, M. K., Lecann, A. F., & Stickney, S. K. (1981). Unrecognized physical illness prompting psychiatric admission: A prospective study. *American Journal of Psychiatry, 138*(5), 629–635.

Hatfield, A. (1983). What families want from family therapy. In W. MacFarlane (Ed.), *Schizophrenia and the Family* (pp. 41–65). New York: Guilford.

Havassy, B. E., & Arns, P. G. (1998). Relationship of cocaine and other substance dependence to well-being of high-risk psychiatric patients. *Psychiatric Services, 49*, 935–940.

HayGroup. (1998). *Health care plan design and cost trends—1988–1997.* Arlington, VA: Author.

Henggeler, S. W., Schoenwald, S. K., Borduin, C. M., Rowland, M. D., & Cunningham, P. B. (1998). *Multisystemic treatment of antisocial behavior in children and adolescents.* New York: Guilford.

Hirsch, J. (1997). Some history of heredity-vs-environment, genetic inferiority at Harvard, and the (incredible) Bell Curve. *Genetica, 99*(2–3), 207–24.

Honkonen, T., Saarinen, S., & Salokangas, R. K. (1999). Deinstitutionalization and schizophrenia in Finland II: Discharged patients and their psychosocial functioning. *Schizophrenia Bulletin, 25*, 534–551.

Institute of Medicine. (1995). *Development of medications for the treatment of opiate and cocaine addictions: Issues for the government and private sector.* Washington DC: National Academy Press.

Jensen, A. R. (1976). Twins' IQs: A reply to Schwartz and Schwartz. *Behavioral Genetics, 6*(3), 369–71.

Johnson, H. C. (1980). *Behavior, psychopathology, and the brain.* New York: Curriculum Concepts.

Johnson, H. C. (2001). Unpublished data. West Hartford, CT: University of Connecticut School of Social Work.

Johnson, H. C., & Renaud, E. F. (1997). Professional beliefs about parents of children with mental and emotional disabilities: A cross-discipline comparison. *Journal of Emotional and Behavioral Disorders , 5*(3):149–161.

Johnson, H.C., & Trivella, M. (1999). *Our fight: Parents tell it like it is* (Documentary). Greenfield, MA: Deerfield Valley.

Johnson, H. C., Cournoyer, D. E., & Bond, B. M. (1995). Professional ethics and parents as consumers: How well are we doing? *Families in Society, 76*(7), 408–420.

Johnson, H. C., Atkins, S. P., Battle, S. F., Hernandez-Arata, L., Hesselbrock, M., Libassi, M. F., & Parish, M. S. (1990). Strengthening the "bio" in the biopsychosocial paradigm. *Journal of Social Work Education, 26*(2), 109–123.

Johnson, H. C., Cournoyer, D. E., Fisher, G. A., McQuillan, B. E., Moriarty, S., Richert, A., Stanek, E. J., & Yirigian, B. (2000). Children's emotional and behavioral disorders: Attributions of parental responsibility by professionals. *American Journal of Orthopsychiatry, 70*(3), 327–339.

Kagan, J. (1994). *The nature of the child* (10th ed.). New York: Basic Books.

Kagan, J., & Zentner, M. (1996). Early childhood predictors of adult psychopathology. *Harvard Review of Psychiatry, 3*(6), 341–350.

Kaplan, H. I., & Sadock, B. J. (1998). *Synopsis of psychiatry: Behavioral sciences/clinical psychiatry,* (8th ed.). Baltimore: Williams & Wilkins.

Karls, J., & Wandrei, K. E. (1992). The Person-in-Environment System for classifying client problems: A new tool for more effective case management. *Journal of Case Management, 1*(3), 90–95.

Katon, W., VonLorff, M., Lin, E., Unutzer, J., Simon, G., Walker, E., Ludman, E., & Bush, T. (1997). Population-based care of depression: Effective disease management strategies to decrease prevalence. *General Hospital Psychiatry, 19,* 169–178.

Kessler, R. C., McGonagle, K. A., Zhao, S., Nelson, C. B., Eshleman, S., Wittchen, H. U., & Kendler, K. S. (1994). Lifetime and 120 month prevalence of *DSM-III-R* psychiatric disorders n the United States: Results from National Comorbidity Survey. *Archives of General Psychiatry, 51,* 8–19.

Kosten, T. R., & Ziedonis, D. M. (1997). Substance abuse and schizophrenia: Editors' introduction. *Schizophrenia Bulletin, 23,* 181–186.

Lefley, H. P. (1996). Impact of consumer and family advocacy movement on mental health services. In B. L. Levin & J. Petrila, (Eds.), *Mental health servcices: A public health perspective* (pp. 81–96). New York: Oxford University Press.

Lehman, A. F., & Steinwachs, D. M. (1998). Patterns of usual care for schizophrenia: Initial results from the Schizophrenia Patient Outcomes Research Team (PORT) Client Survey. *Schizophrenia Bulletin, 24,* 11–20.

Loftus, E. F., & Polage D. C. (1999). Repressed memories: When are they real? How are they false? *Psychiatric Clinics of North America, 22*(1), 61–70.

Lu, F. G., Lim, R. F., & Mezzich, J. E. (1995). Issues in the assessment and diagnosis of culturally diverse individuals. In J. Oldham & M. Riba (Eds.), *Review of psychiatry* (Vol. 14, pp. 477–510). Washington DC: American Psychiatric Press.

Melle, I., Friis, S., Hauff, E., & Vaglum, P. (2000). Social functioning of patients with schizophrenia in high-income welfare societies. *Psychiatric Services, 51*(2), 223–228.

Miller, W. L. (1980). Casework and the medical metaphor. *Social Work, 25*(4), 281–5.

Miltenberger, R. G. (1997). *Behavior modification, principles and procedures.* Pacific Grove, CA: Brooks/Cole.

Mueser, K. T., Drake, R. D., & Miles, K. M. (1997). The course and treatment of substance use disorders in persons with severe mental illness. *NIDA Research Monograph, 172,* 86–109.

Mueser, K. T., Drake, R. D., & Wallach, M. A. (1998). Dual diagnosis: A review of etiological theories. *Addictive Behaviors, 23,* 717–734.

National Association of Social Workers (1997). *Code of ethics.* Washington, DC: Author.

Odell, S. M., Surtees, P. G., Wainright, N. W., Commander, M. J., & Sashidharan, S. P. (1997). Determinants of general practitioner recognition of psychological problems in a multiethnic inner-city health district. *British Journal of Psychiatry, 171,* 537–541.

O'Neill, J. V. (2000). Surgeon General's report lauded. *NAWS News, 45*(2), 1, 6.

Pilsecker, C. (1983). The mischievous medical model. *Social Work, 28,* 70–85

Regier, D. A., Narrow, W., Rae, D. S., Manderscheid, R. W., Locke, B. Z., & Goodwin, F. K. (1993). The de facto U.S. mental health and addictive disorders service system: Epidemiologic catchment Area Prospective 1-year prevalence rates of disorders and services. *Archives of General Psychiatry 50,* 85–94.

Rushton, J. P. (1992). Contributions to the history of psychology: XC. Evolutionary biology and heritable traits (with reference to oriental-white-black differences): The 1989 AAAS paper. *Psychological Report 71*(3, Pt. 1), 811–821.

Rushton, J. P. (1996). Race, genetics, and human reproductive strategies. *Genetics and Social Genetics Psychology Monograph, 122*(1), 21–53.

Saleebey, D. (1985). Is clinical social work is the body politic? *Social Service Review, 59,* 578–592.

Schamess, G., & Lightburn, A. (1999). *Humane managed care?* Washington, DC: NASW.

Schweizer, E., & Rickels, K. (1997). Placebo response in generalized anxiety: Its effects on the outcome of clinical trials. *Journal of Clinical Psychiatry, 58* (Suppl. 11), 30–38.

Scott, J. E., & Dixon, L. B. (1995). Assertive Community Treatment and case management for schizophrenia. *Schizophrenia Bulletin, 21,* 657–668.

Shekim, W.O., Cantwell D.P., Kashani J., Beck N., Martin J., & Rosenberg J. (1986). Dimensional and categorical approaches to the diagnosis of attention deficit disorder in children. *Journal of the American Academy of Child Psychiatry, 25*(5), 653–658.

Silberman, P., and James, K. (2000). Managed care regulations: Impact on quality? *Quality Managed Health Care 8*(2), 21–39.

Simon, J. L. (1997). Four comments on The Bell Curve. *Genetica. 99*(2–3), 199–205.

Tavris, C. (1992). *The mismeasure of woman.* New York: Simon & Schuster.

Tavris, C. (1998). The science and politics of gender research: The meanings of difference. *Nebraska Symposium on Motivation, 45,* 1–23.

Trieman, N., Leff, J., & Glover, G. (1999). Outcome of long stay psychiatric patients resettled in the community: Prospective cohort study. *British Medical Journal 319*(7201), 13–16.

U. S. Bureau of the Census, Economics and Statistics Administration (1996). *Current population reports: Population projections of the U.S. by age, sex, race, and Hispanic origins: 1995–2050.* Washington, DC: Author.

U. S. Department of Health and Human Services (1999). *Mental health: A report of the Surgeon General.* Rockville, MD: U.S. Department of Human Health and Services, Substance Abuse and Mental Health Services Administration, Center for Mental Health Services, National Institutes of Health, National Institute of Mental Health.

Vogel, H. S., Knight, E., Laudet, A., & Magura, S. (1998). Double trouble in recovery: Self-help for people with dual diagnosis. *Psychiatric Rehabilitation Journal, 21,* 356–364.

Wakefield, J. C. (1999). The concept of disorder as a foundation for the *DSM's* theory-neutral nosology: Response to Follette & Houts, Part 2. *Behavior Research and Therapy, 37*(10), 1001–1027.

Walsh, F. (1993). *Normal family processes* (2nd ed.). New York: Guilford.

Weick, A. (1983). Issues in overturning a medical model of social work practice. *Social Work, 28*(6), 467–471.

World Health Organization. (1992). *International classification of diseases and related health problems* (10th ed.). Geneva, Switzerland: Author.

Zuvekas, S. H., Banthin, J. S., & Selden, T. M. (1998). Mental health parity: What are the gaps in coverage? *Journal of Mental Health Policy and Economics, 1,* 135–146.

Index

D

CPSIA information can be obtained
at www.ICGtesting.com
Printed in the USA
FFOW02n0628161015
17793FF

9 780534 549206